USING
WORD 5
FOR THE
M A C

Using Word 5 for the Mac®

Special Edition

Bryan Pfaffenberger

Library of Congress Catalog No.: 91-68373

ISBN: 0-88022-850-4

94 93 92   5 4 3 2 1

Interpretation of the printing code: the rightmost double-digit number is the year of the book's printing; the rightmost single-digit number, the number of the book's printing. For example, a printing code of 92-1 shows that the first printing of the book occurred in 1992.

Screen reproductions in this book were created using Collage Plus from Inner Media, Inc., Hollis, NH.

Clip art images used in certain screen shots in this book are from the ClickArt Series of Image Portfolios provided by T/Maker Company.

Using Word 5 for the Mac, Special Edition, is based on Microsoft Word for the Macintosh, Version 5.0.

Publisher: Lloyd J. Short

Acquisitions Manager: Rick Ranucci

Product Development Manager: Thomas H. Bennett

Managing Editor: Paul Boger

Book Designers: Scott Cook and Michele Laseau

Production Team: Claudia Bell, Scott Boucher, Paula Carroll, Brad Chinn, Michelle Cleary, Mark Enochs, Brook Farling, Denny Hager, Audra Hershman, Betty Kish, Bob LaRoche, Laurie Lee, Anne Owen, Juli Pavey, Cindy Phipps, Caroline Roop, Louise Shinault, John Sleeva, Kevin Spear, Bruce Steed, Lisa Wilson, Allan Wimmer, Phil Worthington, Christine Young

Product Directors

Shelley O'Hara
Karen A. Bluestein

Production Editor

Lori A. Lyons

Editors

Fran Huber
Diana R. Moore
Anne P. Root
Colleen Totz

Technical Editor

Doug White

*Composed in ITC Garamond and
MCPdigital by Que Corporation.*

Dedication

To Suzanne

About the Author

Bryan Pfaffenberger

A professional writer on computer-related subjects, Bryan Pfaffenberger, Ph.D., teaches technology studies and technical writing at the University of Virginia (School of Engineering and Applied Science), where he is Associate Professor of Humanities. A Word user since the not-so-glorious Version 1.0 of 1984 (!), Bryan has used Microsoft Word to write the lion's share of his more than 30 books on computer-related subjects, including Que's *Computerizing Your Small Business* and *Que's Computer User's Dictionary*. Very happily married to his wife of 15 years, Suzanne, he is the father of two Macintosh-using children (Michael and Julia). His hobbies and interests include space and New Age music, folk guitar, model aeronautics, hiking, and restoring his Charlottesville, Virginia home.

Trademark Acknowledgments

ue Corporation has made every effort to supply trademark information about company names, products, and services mentioned in this book. Trademarks indicated below were derived from various sources. Que Corporation cannot attest to the accuracy of this information.

Adobe, Adobe Illustrator, and PostScript are registered trademarks and Adobe Type Manager is a trademark of Adobe Systems, Inc.

Apple, AppleTalk, ImageWriter, LaserWriter, Mac, Macintosh, MultiFinder, QuickDraw, StyleWriter, and TrueType are registered trademarks and Finder and SuperDrive are trademarks of Apple Computer, Inc.

dBASE III Plus and dBASE IV are trademarks of Ashton-Tate.

HP is a registered trademark of Hewlett-Packard Company.

IBM and IBM PS/2 are registered trademarks of International Business Machines Corporation.

Lotus and 1-2-3 are registered trademarks of Lotus Development Corporation.

MacDraw and MacWrite are registered trademarks of Claris Corporation.

Microsoft, Microsoft Excel, Microsoft Windows, Microsoft Works, and Microsoft Word are registered trademarks of Microsoft Corporation.

PageMaker is a registered trademark of Aldus Corporation.

SuperLaserSpool is a trademark of Silicon Beach Software, Inc.

WordPerfect is a registered trademark of WordPerfect Corporation.

Zapf Dingbats is a registered trademark of International Typeface Corporation.

Trademarks of other products mentioned in this book are held by the companies producing them.

Acknowledgments

A project like this one requires help from many people: I would like to thank Lloyd Short, publisher; Shelley O'Hara, product director; Lori Lyons, production editor; Doug White, technical editor; and the other editors and production personnel.

Conventions Used in This Book

The conventions used in this book have been established to help you learn to use the program quickly and easily. As much as possible, the conventions correspond with those used in the Microsoft Word 5 documentation.

- Material the user types is in *italic* type or on a line by itself.

- Screen messages appear in a `special typeface`.

- Menu options, dialog box names, and commands are in uppercase and lowercase (the Custom Tabs dialog box).

- Icons are used in the margins to indicate various points. The Word 5 icon indicates features new to Version 5. The System 7 icon indicates features that take advantage of Apple's new System 7 capabilities. The Speed Key icon indicates keyboard shortcuts you can use to issue commands. Caution icons indicate operations that can cause undesired effects. Tips and notes give additional information to help you get the most out of Word 5.

Contents at a Glance

Part III: Document Recipes

Table of Contents

7   Formatting Pages 235

8 Formatting with Styles 267

9 Checking Spelling and Grammar 301

Part II: Creating More Complex Documents

12 Outlining 367

16 Dividing a Document into Sections 463

18 Using Math and Typing Equations 511

19 Numbering and Sorting Lines and Paragraphs 535

20 Creating and Importing Graphics 557

21 Positioning Text and Graphics 583

26 Working with Long Documents 691

27 Customizing Word 5 705

Part III: Document Recipes

Introduction

Already well established as the premier word processing program in the Macintosh environment, Word has earned a well-deserved reputation as the first program to blend word processing and page design capabilities in one, seamless package. The new version of Word, Version 5, improves this enviable achievement and brings it in line with Apple's new System 7 software—with all that System 7 compatibility implies for improved performance and advanced features.

The previous version of Word, Version 4, was the first program to blend text editing and page design features so successfully, making it the program of choice for many professional writers. They found that Word offers unbeatable features for both writing and page design:

- To create text effectively, writers need features that help them organize, expand, edit, restructure, and proofread the text they have written. That's the purpose of a good text editor.

- To express the text on paper with a design that's appropriate to its content, writers also need page design software—software that presents an on-screen simulation of page design elements, such as fonts, font sizes, headers, footers, page numbers, graphics, borders, columns, and footnotes.

Until Word, getting a good text editor and good page design features meant buying two expensive programs (such as Word and a desktop publishing program like PageMaker) or settling for a memory-hungry,

sluggish behemoth of a program that tried to do everything (and wound up doing little of it well). In Word, text editing and page design come together in a package that's truly astonishing for its speed and elegance.

Outlining permits you to construct (and edit) a view of your document that shows its overall structure. Style sheets, a unique Word feature, give you a way to enter several formats at once (instead of choosing them one by one). Version 5 enhancements enable you to create, organize, and apply styles more easily.

These features complement an impressive armada of word processing features that rival any of the popular MS-DOS packages. Some of these features include automatic footnote numbering and placement, automatic generation of form letters, automatic generation of tables of contents and indexes, spell checking, and much more.

Word's page design features would do credit to a world-class desktop publishing program. Table commands set up a spreadsheet-like matrix of rows and columns, simplifying the tasks of creating and editing text in tables—and all without setting tabs! You can add lines and borders so that, in minutes, you've created a form that would cost big bucks were it designed by a professional layout artist.

Positioned text and graphics stay where you've anchored them on the page so that text flows around them. With this feature you can easily create professional-looking newsletters, brochures, and fliers.

With Page Layout view, you can view and edit your document precisely as it will appear on the page, including footnotes, headers and footers, fonts, font sizes, and more.

There's much more to Word's capabilities. This program has always offered an unbeatable combination of writing and page design capabilities. So what's so special about the new version of Word?

Exploring Version 5's New Features

There are two kinds of program upgrades. With the first kind, the new version is pretty nice; many users will upgrade, but many other users are quite content to stick with the previous version. In the second kind of program upgrade, the new version is so superior that just about everyone upgrades!

Version 5 of Word falls into the second category—a "must upgrade"— and for three reasons: Microsoft has gone through the program and corrected a huge number of program shortcomings. They've also added some very nifty new features. And finally, they've taken full advantage of System 7 (and in a very impressive way).

As you explore the new version of Word, it becomes obvious that Microsoft has listened carefully to user complaints about previous versions of Word. If you've used any of these previous versions, you'll find that the menus have been reorganized in a much more logical way. For example, Version 5 no longer has any Document menu to be confused with the Document command. As you work with the program, you find dozens of thoughtful improvements.

New features extend and broaden Word's legendary list of capabilities:

- *Drag-and-drop editing.* To move text, just select it and drag the pointer to the place you want the text to appear.

- *Stationery documents.* You can store a template of a well-formatted document and make sure it doesn't get ruined, by storing it as a stationery document. Word opens stationery documents as Untitled documents, preserving the template on disk.

- *Ribbon.* Quickly choose fonts, font sizes, character emphases, character position (superscript and subscript), and even multiple-column formats. Just display the ribbon, and click a button.

- *Draw-format graphics.* You can create a quick illustration just by clicking the Picture button on the ruler to display a Picture window, complete with drawing tools such as lines, rectangles, shading, and arrows.

- *Grammar.* If you are unsure of your punctuation, word choices, and sentence structure, choose Grammar and let Word analyze your document for a huge variety of writing flaws.

- *Equation Editor.* Need to insert an equation in your document? Don't fuss with mathematical typesetting—although you can still use it, if you've already learned it. Activate Equation Editor, a program packaged with Word, and create your equation right on the screen, just as it will appear when printed.

- *Find File.* If you can't find a file, choose Find File and let Word search your entire hard disk to find just the file you want—even if the only way you can locate it is to ask Word to search every document on your disk to find a word or phrase embedded somewhere in the text.

Introduction

■ *Print Merge Helper.* Maybe you struggled with form letters and mailing lists in previous versions of Word. Print Merge Helper guides you through the building of data document and a form letter, using easy-to-use dialog boxes at every step of the way.

Probably the most impressive capabilities of Word 5, however, stem from its thorough exploitation of System 7 capabilities:

■ *Dynamic linking.* When you paste an Excel spreadsheet into Word, you can do so in such a way that changes you make to the spreadsheet are automatically reflected in your Word document. (In previous versions of Word, you had to update the link manually.)

■ *Publish and subscribe.* If you have documents you'd like to make available to other users, whether of your machine or others on a Macintosh network, you can publish the document in such a way that others can subscribe to it. Subscribers import the document into theirs—and what's more, if you make changes to the source documents, the changes are automatically reflected in the copies.

■ *Object linking and embedding.* Perhaps the most impressive System 7 capability, OLE enables you to embed another application's data (such as a chart or spreadsheet) right in your Word file. If you need to update the data, you just double-click the data. Word starts the native application (the one that created the data), and you get all the native application's tools in an on-screen window—and all without leaving Word! It's as if Word were suddenly capable of doing charts, spreadsheets, presentation graphics, database management, and more.

The many needed program revisions, the wonderful new features, and the System 7 compatibility make a strong argument for upgrading. If you're just learning Word, you've come on the scene at a particularly timely moment. Many experts on computerized word processing believe that Version 5 of Microsoft Word is the finest word processing program available for any computing environment.

Why a Book about Word?

he Macintosh was designed to be easy to use, and it is. For this reason, you can use Word at an elementary level, ignoring the complexity that lies beneath the surface of this program.

Introduction

But business and professional writers aren't interested just in ease of use. They're busy people, and their organizations depend on their productivity. Unfortunately, that's where the trouble starts. Even with a Macintosh program, a computer's manuals don't always make obvious how you can apply the program to get those big gains in productivity—gains that people frequently assume are all but automatic. They aren't. Experience in applying word processing technology in business and professional environments is necessary in order to realize the promise of higher productivity—just learning which button to press when is not enough.

This book was written to show you how to apply word processing in business and professional environments, which is also why this book is not like the manuals that come with Word. This book does teach you how to use Word—you will find step-by-step tutorials, which assume that you're a beginner with the program. But this book moves far beyond that level, revealing the techniques professional writers have developed to realize big gains in the productivity and the quality of their work. You will find ample guidance in the form of tips and keyboard shortcuts, both of which are highlighted by icons in the margins, and summary sections outlining the high-productivity techniques introduced in each chapter.

How This Book Is Organized

Part I, "Getting Started," builds a solid foundation of Word knowledge. Included among the fundamentals, along with the usual features such as character and paragraph formatting, is Word's powerful style sheet formatting feature, which some people still consider to be an "advanced" feature. As you will see, however, style sheet formatting really is fundamental to the use of Word at high levels of productivity. To master Microsoft Word, you should read all these chapters in sequence.

Chapter 1, "Quick Start: Creating a Business Letter," walks you through the fundamentals of using Word. You follow a keystroke-by-keystroke tutorial that emphasizes high-productivity tricks and techniques from the start.

Chapter 2, "Understanding Word's Workplace," fully introduces the basics of using Word, including understanding the screen display, moving the insertion point, scrolling the screen, and choosing commands.

Chapter 3, "Creating and Saving Text," explores every aspect of the text-creation process, including controlling line breaks, using special characters, using hyphenation, and saving your work safely.

Chapter 4, "Editing Text," comprehensively surveys all of the Word 5 text editing techniques. You fully explore the many keyboard and menu options you have for editing your document.

Chapter 5, "Formatting Characters," builds a solid foundation of character formatting expertise. You learn how to choose emphases, position, fonts, font sizes, and more.

Chapter 6, "Formatting Paragraphs," continues building the foundations of your formatting knowledge, with the emphasis placed on paragraph formatting. You learn how to align, indent, and shape paragraphs as you please.

Chapter 7, "Formatting Pages," concludes the foundations of your formatting knowledge by covering the basics of page design with Word.

Chapter 8, "Formatting with Styles," introduces this important, high-productivity formatting technique, which every Word user can employ. You learn how to save the effort involved in choosing dozens or even hundreds of commands just by developing a few styles using these simple techniques.

Chapter 9, "Checking Spelling and Grammar," thoroughly surveys Word's extensive proofing tools, including the important new Grammar feature.

Chapter 10, "Printing Documents," shows you how to get the most out of your printer.

Chapter 11, "Managing Documents," introduces Find File and all the other Word features that help you organize your documents on disk.

Part II, "Creating More Complex Documents," delves into intermediate and advanced areas of the program—the ones professional writers will use to produce newsletters, journal articles, dissertations, business reports and analyses, and book-length manuscripts. You needn't read all these chapters, nor do you need to read them in sequence.

Chapter 12, "Outlining," thoroughly surveys this important Word feature, which can help you keep your document well organized and help you plan it before writing. This chapter is for anyone who writes long complex documents, such as proposals, business reports, technical documentation, or dissertations. You learn how you can develop an outline structure that parallels the headings in your document, and how

Introduction

Word dynamically updates this outline as you restructure your document. You even learn how you can restructure your entire document just by making a few quick changes on the outline. If you have ever struggled with the organization of a lengthy, complex document, Word has a better way, which is explained in this chapter.

Chapter 13, "Using Glossaries," reveals the mysteries of Word's glossaries, which you can use to store standard passages of text (called boilerplate). As you will quickly discover, you don't need to type the same passage of text twice when you can store and retrieve often-used passages in glossaries. You learn how you can use Word's glossaries to create a comprehensive system for responding rapidly and consistently to business inquiry letters. The glossary feature is one of the biggest productivity boosters revealed in this book.

Chapter 14, "Linking Data Dynamically," fully explores the use of Word's new System 7 capabilities, including dynamic data linking, object linking and embedding, and Publish and Subscribe. If you're still using System 6, this chapter is still worth reading because you can link documents with manual updating.

Chapter 15, "Adding Headers, Footers, and Footnotes," comprehensively surveys these features, which you will need for business reports, proposals, and academic manuscripts.

Chapter 16, "Dividing a Document into Sections," explores the uses of Word's Section command, which enables you to break up your document into divisions that have their own headers, footers, footnotes, and page number formats.

Chapter 17, "Creating Tables," explores Word's remarkable Table commands, which create a spreadsheet-like matrix of rows and columns (without the old hassle of setting tabs). You still can set all the tabs you want, but you surely will agree after trying the Table commands that this feature is a blessing for anyone who types tables or lists. As you master the Table commands, you will cut significantly—by as much as 50 percent in typical cases—the time you need to spend fussing with table formatting.

Chapter 18, "Using Math and Typing Equations," surveys Word 5's new Equation Editor, which enables you to create mathematical formulas without using mathematical typesetting. It's so easy, you will know how to use it moments after you see the Equation Editor window on-screen! This chapter also covers Word's on-screen math, which enables you to quickly sum columns and rows of numbers.

Chapter 19, "Numbering and Sorting Lines and Paragraphs," explores Word's Renumber and Sort commands. You learn how you can number and sort items automatically. Don't alphabetize anything in your document manually, when you can let Word do the job almost instantly.

Chapter 20, "Creating and Importing Graphics," explores Word 5's new Picture capabilities, which gives you a scaled-down version of MacDraw within Word. You also learn how to import, size, and scale the many graphics files that Word can read directly, including PICT, PICT2, EPS, and TIFF graphics.

Chapter 21, "Positioning Text and Graphics," shows you how to use Word 5's Frame command, which enables you to position text and graphics absolutely on the page so that text flows around them. You learn many useful techniques for quick and impressive document designs.

Chapter 22, "Using Borders and Shading," explores Word 5's improved Borders command, which now enables you to add shading as well as lines and boxes.

Chapter 23, "Adding an Index and Table of Contents," is for anyone who prepares reports, proposals, or technical documents that will be reproduced directly from Word printouts. You learn all about Word's outstanding indexing features, which you can use to code terms in your document so that Word will automatically compile them into a professional-looking index. And if you have created an outline for your document, you learn how Word can generate a table of contents for your document after you give just one command.

Chapter 24, "Creating Form Letters," details the use of Word 5's new Print Merge Helper, a much-improved feature that makes form letter applications much easier. You learn how to create a mailing list and send form letters, taking full advantage of advanced features such as conditional merging.

Chapter 25, "Printing Mailing Labels," shows you how to print mailing labels successfully on a variety of printers.

Chapter 26, "Working with Long Documents," details Word 5's new File Series command, which makes it much easier to link many separate files together for printing with continuous pagination.

Chapter 27, "Customizing Word 5," details the many ways you can customize Word's menus and keyboard.

Part III, "Document Recipes," provides three in-depth, keystroke-by-keystroke tutorials that summarize and complete your mastery of

Word 5. You learn how to put all of your Word knowledge together in a very impressive package of document design skills.

Chapter 28, "Designing Résumés," shows you how to use Word's Frame capabilities to advantage in designing an attractive, attention-getting resume.

Chapter 29, "Tackling Business Correspondence," presents a nifty way to automate a tedious task—recording the name and address of a new correspondent. You learn how to harness Word's Print Merge capabilities so that you type a name and address just once: Word takes care of placing the name and address in the response letter you write.

Chapter 30, "Creating Business Forms," shows you how you can unite Word's Border and Table capabilities to produce professional-looking business forms. You also learn how you can use Print Merge instructions to fill out a form on-screen, and have Word calculate totals automatically.

Two appendixes round out this book's treatment of Microsoft Word 5.

Appendix A, "Installing Word 5," helps you get started with Microsoft Word. If you haven't installed Word, begin this book by reading this appendix.

Appendix B, "Word 5 Keyboard Shortcuts," provides a handy reference guide to Word's keyboard commands.

A Word of Encouragement

If you're just getting started with Word 5, you may feel daunted by the program's complexity. But you will be surprised at how far you can get if you take just one step at a time. You're not a failure at personal computing if you don't understand some features right away. And remember, too, that you don't need to memorize long lists of commands and procedures. In this book, you will find that any procedure requiring more than a step or two is explained in a handy step-by-step format. Make your own index (or just dog-ear the pages) to highlight the procedures you think you will need to look up again, and keep this book by your computer.

Before you know it, Word 5 will come naturally to you, even when you're exploiting the program at its intermediate and advanced levels. As your knowledge of the program grows, you will learn how to customize it so that it's truly an extension of your preferences and ways of doing things. All in all, it's a journey well worth making.

PART

I

Getting Started

Includes

USING
WORD 5
FOR THE
MAC

Quick Start: Creating a Business Letter

Microsoft Word is well known as one of the most powerful word processing programs available for the Macintosh. The program is also easy to use at an elementary level. With the Macintosh's intuitive user interface, you don't need much instruction to start producing simple letters, memos, and reports right away.

If you are familiar with the Macintosh and Word, you still should pay special attention to the tutorials in this chapter. The tutorials introduce you to high-productivity Word techniques—the same ones developed by business and professional writers to maximize this marvelous program's efficiency. If you already have created simple letters with Word, this chapter still can prove valuable. At the most elementary level, tricks and strategies can help you improve the quality and quantity of the work you produce with Microsoft Word. This chapter starts right in with tips, keyboard shortcuts, and other high-productivity techniques.

This chapter assumes that you have installed Word (see Appendix A if you haven't). The text also assumes that you have basic Macintosh skills, such as opening and sizing windows, clicking and dragging, and using pull-down menus. For an introduction to these skills, see the lessons in the manual that came with your Macintosh.

USING
WORD 5
FOR THE
MAC

Exploring Word's Screen

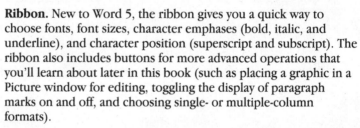

Start Word by double-clicking the Word icon. (If you're using System 7, you can start Word by choosing the Word alias from the Apple menu. For information on creating an Apple menu alias for Word, see Appendix A.)

After Word starts, the program displays a blank, untitled document (see fig. 1.1). On-screen you see the features in the following list:

Menu bar. At the top of the screen are Word's pull-down menus. These menus contain the commands you use to open, save, print, edit, format, and display documents. If you're running MultiFinder (System 6) or System 7, you see the application icon at the extreme right of the menu bar. In System 6, you click this icon to switch to the next application (or to the Finder, if no other application is running). In System 7, clicking this icon drops down the Application menu, from which you can choose additional applications or the finder.

Ribbon. New to Word 5, the ribbon gives you a quick way to choose fonts, font sizes, character emphases (bold, italic, and underline), and character position (superscript and subscript). The ribbon also includes buttons for more advanced operations that you'll learn about later in this book (such as placing a graphic in a Picture window for editing, toggling the display of paragraph marks on and off, and choosing single- or multiple-column formats).

Ruler. The ruler measures your document with the 0 mark set at the left margin in Word's default (Normal) view of your document. You can set indents from the margin by dragging the indent marks (the black triangles). You also can set the margins for your whole document by clicking the Margin button (the button with the two brackets) and dragging the brackets. Additionally, you can choose paragraph alignments (flush left, centered, flush right, and justified), line spacing (single, one and one-half line spacing, and double spacing), blank lines before paragraphs, and tabs.

Document window. Below the ruler is the document window, where you write and edit your documents. You can open more than one window at a time—23, in fact—although you seldom will open more than two or three at a time. You can display a different document in each opened window. You can display two or more parts of the same document in two or more different windows. You can even split one window into two panes, revealing two parts of the same document.

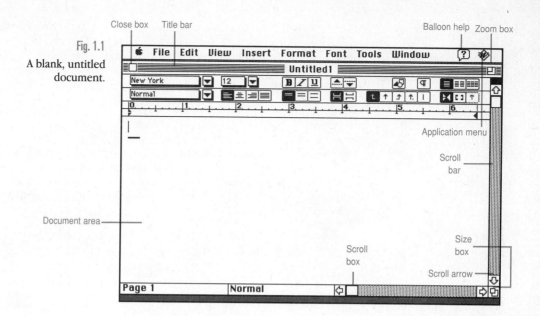

Fig. 1.1
A blank, untitled document.

You learn more about the individual features of the document window in Chapter 2. For now, just note that the insertion point shows you where text will appear when printed. The end mark shows the end of your document; you can push the end mark down by typing text or pressing Return. The I-beam pointer is a special mouse pointer shape that enables you to position the mouse pointer *between* characters for precise editing. Table 1.1 gives a quick review of basic Macintosh window-manipulation skills.

Table 1.1
Review of Macintosh Window Skills

Task	Technique
Reduce size of window	Drag size box up or left
Zoom window to full size	Click zoom box
Unzoom window to reduced size	Click zoom box again
Move window	Drag title bar
Make a window active	Click anywhere in the document area
Close a window	Click close box
Scroll line-by-line	Click scroll arrows
Scroll screen-by-screen	Click scroll bar above or below scroll box
Scroll longer distances	Drag scroll box

Chapter 1

Quick Start: Creating a Business Letter

If you're running Word under System 7, you see the Help icon on the menu bar (refer to fig. 1.1). If you click this icon and choose Balloon Help from the drop-down menu, Word displays Help balloons as you move the mouse pointer around the screen. Choose Balloon Help now to aid you in understanding Word's on-screen features.

If you're working with System 7, choose Hide Others from the Application menu so that only Word is visible on-screen. If the Finder's windows, or some other application's windows, are visible beneath the Word window, you might click one of them accidentally while editing. The Finder then will switch to the application you've clicked, forcing you to use the Application menu to return to Word. By choosing Hide Others, you prevent this minor but annoying accident from happening.

Now take a closer look at the features of the document window. If you're using System 7, move the pointer to each item you're reading about so that you can see what Balloon Help says about the item.

Writing the First Draft of a Business Letter

Professional and business people write letters every day. Every time you send a first-class letter, you put yourself and your organization on the line. You have the opportunity to create a favorable impression of your organization, but you also can leave a negative impression, one that may have damaging consequences. For this reason, preparing letters with a fine word processing program like Word is an excellent idea; you can experiment with the wording of the letter until you get it just right.

This chapter presents a single quick start tutorial that walks you through a "real-world" writing experience. You start with a poorly written letter and alter it until it meets the professional standards of today's business environment.

Imagine yourself in this situation: You're the director of a small training firm that specializes in training corporate employees in security techniques. You frequently make use of videos to show potential security problems. Last week, you spent a day training some employees at Atlantic Electronic Enterprises, Inc. Everything went fine, except that the video projector bulb blew in the final moments of the presentation. You had a backup, however, and before long you were back in action.

This week, you received a letter from Mr. Nelson T. Jones, your contact at Atlantic Electronic Enterprises, Inc. In the letter, Mr. Jones thanked you for the presentation but complained about the equipment break-down. The ball's in your court now; you have to answer the letter. You have a problem, however; you're annoyed at Mr. Jones and your annoyance probably will show in your first draft of the letter.

Getting Started

To begin the tutorial, make sure that a blank, untitled document is on your screen (refer back to fig. 1.1). If you have another document displayed, pull down the File menu and choose the New option.

To write and revise effectively, you should see as much text as possible on the screen. The more text you can see, the more easily you can keep track of what has been written and where you're going with the text. On a small, 9-inch Classic screen, the ruler takes up a lot of space (as does the ribbon). So that you can see more lines on-screen when necessary, learn to turn the ribbon and ruler on and off. To toggle the ruler on and off, choose Ruler from the View menu, or use the ⌘-R keyboard short-cut. To toggle the ribbon on and off, choose Ribbon from the View menu, or use the ⌘-Option-R keyboard shortcut.

When you're writing and editing with Word, you may want to display the paragraph marks. The paragraph marks show where you have pressed Return. Seeing paragraph marks is helpful for two reasons. First, you join paragraphs by deleting the marks. Second, you might accidentally delete one of the marks if they're hidden.

To display the paragraph marks, click the paragraph mark button on the ribbon, choose Show ¶ from the View menu, or use the ⌘-J shortcut.

Centering the Return Address

The first step in entering the letter to Mr. Jones is to type your company's return address, centered at the top of the window.

To type the return address, follow these steps:

1. On the ruler, click the Centered Alignment button or press ⌘-Shift-C.

   The insertion point moves to the center of the screen.

2. Type *Albemarle Valley Associates* and press Return.

   If you make a typing mistake, press the Delete key (also called Backspace on some keyboards). Then type the correct characters.

The text you type is centered. When you press Return, Word inserts a paragraph mark. Notice that Word copies the centered format to the next line.

3. Type the rest of the return address as shown in figure 1.2, pressing Return where you see paragraph marks.

Fig. 1.2

Typing the return address.

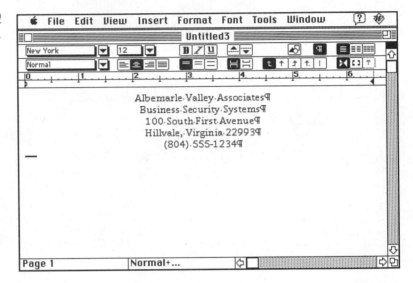

```
 🍎  File  Edit  View  Insert  Format  Font  Tools  Window        ?  🐝
                              Untitled3
New York       ▼  12  ▼      B Z U  ▲▼           🔊  ¶   ▤ ▦ ▤  ⬆
Normal         ▼  ▤ ▤ ▤ ▤   ▤ ▤ ▤   ⊟ ⊟  ⌊ ↑ ↑ ↑↓ ↓  ⋈ ⫶ ↑
0        1        2        3        4        5        6


                    Albemarle·Valley·Associates¶
                    Business·Security·Systems¶
                    100·South·First·Avenue¶
                    Hillvale,·Virginia·22993¶
                        (804)·555-1234¶

           —



Page 1                     Normal+...          ◁ ▯                  ▷ ▯
```

4. Press Return three times after you type the telephone number to leave two blank lines under the return address.

5. Click the Left Alignment button on the ruler, or press ⌘-Shift-P.

   The insertion point jumps to the left margin, but the lines already centered stay centered.

SPEED KEY

Keep this document on-screen. The tutorial continues in this chapter.

If you want to take a break at any point in this chapter, choose Save As from the File menu and type *Letter* in the Save Current Document As box. Then choose Quit from the File menu. You will see the Finder on-screen after you quit Word. To resume work, find this document's icon and double-click it. Word starts up and opens the Letter document automatically so that you can resume the tutorial.

Boldfacing the Firm's Name

TIP

The Bold button on the ribbon shows the character emphasis currently assigned to the selected characters. If you're not sure whether text is boldfaced or not, you can tell right away by selecting the text and looking at the ribbon.

You have already learned how to enter one kind of Word format—paragraph alignment (specifically, centered and flush-left alignment). Now you learn how to format character emphasis by adding boldface to your document. To attach emphasis to characters already typed, you select the characters to highlight them on the screen. You then choose the desired emphasis from the Format menu (or use one of the keyboard shortcuts).

To boldface the name of the firm in the quick start document, do the following:

1. Move the pointer toward the left window border so that its shape changes to an arrow pointing up and to the right. When the pointer takes on this shape, you have moved the pointer to the selection bar, a special area of the screen that selects lines and paragraphs quickly.

2. Click to select the whole line.

3. Do one of the following:

   Click the Bold button on the ribbon.

   Choose Bold from the Format menu.

   Use the ⌘-B or ⌘-Shift-B keyboard shortcuts.

SPEED KEY

Word boldfaces the firm's name (see fig. 1.3).

Fig. 1.3
Boldfacing the firm's name.

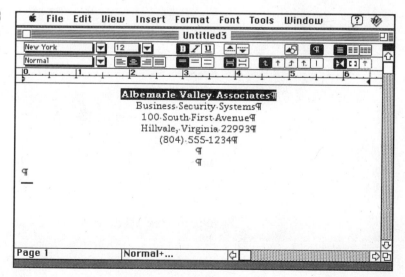

Chapter 1

Quick Start: Creating a Business Letter

With Word you can format text in two ways: after it is typed (as you did with the company name in the preceding steps), and before you type it (as shown in the steps that follow). You should understand how to use both methods. You also learn to use Undo:

1. Highlight *Albemarle Valley Associates,* but don't highlight the paragraph mark, as shown in figure 1.4.

Fig. 1.4
Highlighting text, but not
the paragraph mark.

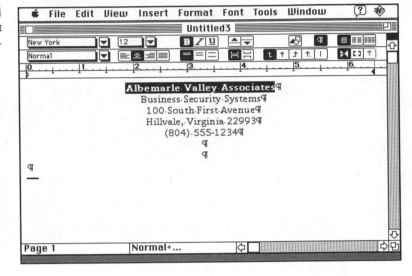

TIP

To highlight the three words quickly, double-click the first word *Albemarle*, but hold down the mouse button after the second click. Drag right to extend the selection word by word, but without selecting the paragraph mark.

SPEED KEY

2. Choose Cut from the Edit menu, or press ⌘-X.

   All the text disappears.

   If you ever delete text accidentally, you can restore it easily by following the next step.

3. Choose Undo Cut from the Edit menu, or press ⌘-Z.

   Word instantly restores the deletion.

4. Choose Redo Cut from the Edit menu, or press ⌘-Z again.

   Word removes the text again.

5. Choose Bold from the ribbon or from the Format menu, or press ⌘-B.

6. Type *Albemarle Valley Associates* again. The text you type appears in bold.

Part I

Getting Started

As you can see, Word uses the formats currently in effect when you type. Had you pressed Return, the program would have copied these formats down to the new next line, enabling you to continue typing with these formats (centered and bold).

Inserting the Date Automatically

You can type the current date manually, if you want, but a nifty command can do it for you automatically. To insert the date automatically, use the following steps:

1. Place the insertion point on the flush-left paragraph mark below the return address.

2. Choose Date from the Insert menu.

Word enters today's date surrounded by dotted lines (see fig. 1.5). The lines won't print. They tell you that the date isn't made up of ordinary text; it's generated by the Date command. If you try to select the date, you'll find that it's just one character.

Fig. 1.5
Inserting the date
automatically.

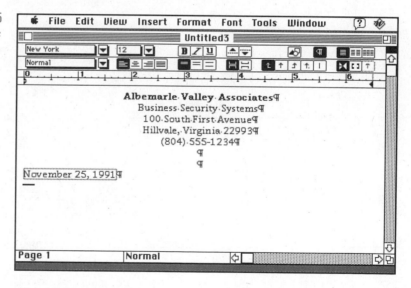

Typing the Body of the Letter

When you finish typing the return address and the date, do the following:

1. Place the insertion point after the colon in *Dear Mr. Jones:* (but before the paragraph mark), and press Return to start a new line.

2. Click the Blank Spacing button on the ruler.

   The Blank Spacing button is just right of the line spacing buttons—the one that shows space between the two horizontal brackets.

   After you click this button, the paragraph mark moves down one line. The Blank Spacing button automatically enters 12 points (one line) of blank space *before* each paragraph.

3. Type the correspondent's address and the salutation as shown in figure 1.6.

Fig. 1.6
Typing the address and salutation.

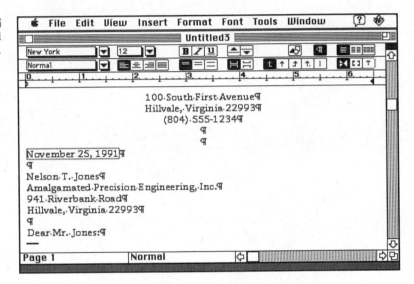

4. Type the text of the letter, dreadful as it is (you're going to revise it later). Don't press Return until you come to the end of the paragraph, and let Word enter the blank lines automatically:

   Thank you for your letter of November 12. I'm disappointed you weren't happy with the equipment failure that occurred during our recent training session.

   I'm sure you understand, however, that machines do sometimes fail! Really, an engineer ought to know that! We had a substitute machine and got it up and running immediately.

Part I

Getting Started

We have replaced the unreliable projection display system that failed during our final presentation. Now that the new computer-based overhead display systems are available, we—and our customers—won't have to rely on those unreliable projection devices.

This letter is a *flame*, an ill-considered and highly emotional response. It's totally focused on the writer's feelings about the situation. To write effectively in business, a writer must learn to revise so that the focus shifts to client and customer needs. (Actually, a letter this bad probably should go straight to the trash can so that you can start with a clean slate—but that's why it's great for this tutorial. It's going to need a lot of work!)

As you type, don't press Return until you start a new paragraph. Words that go past the right margin are automatically "wrapped" to the next line.

When you finish typing, your letter should look like the one in figure 1.7.

Fig. 1.7
First draft of a
business letter.

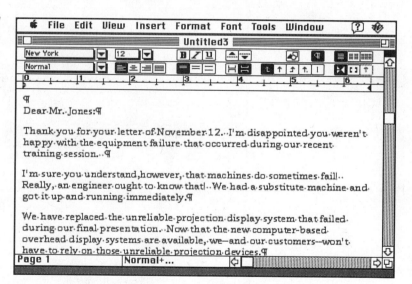

Revising the Letter

his letter needs to be reworked. In the sections to follow, you revise this letter substantially (and, along the way, learn many fundamental Word techniques).

Chapter 1

Quick Start: Creating a Business Letter

Joining Paragraphs

Your first revision involves joining the first two paragraphs together to see whether doing so improves the letter. To join two paragraphs, follow these steps:

1. At the end of the first paragraph (the one ending with *training session*), select the paragraph mark that divides the two paragraphs. If you don't see the paragraph marks, choose Show ¶ from the View menu or click the ¶ button on the ribbon.

2. Press Backspace or Delete.

The paragraphs are joined as shown in figure 1.8. You may need to enter a space or two to separate the sentences you just joined.

Fig. 1.8
Joined paragraphs.

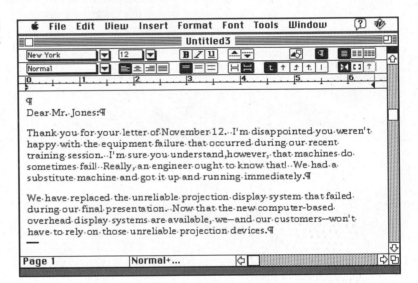

Splitting Paragraphs

Now that you know how to join paragraphs, take a moment to learn how to split them again. You will have many occasions to do so. A real paragraph—the grammatical paragraph, not the artificial paragraphs defined by Word—is unified: it expresses and develops a single idea. If more than one idea is in a paragraph, you may want to split the paragraph. To split paragraphs, use the following steps. Experiment on the first paragraph of your letter—you will undo the change later.

1. Place the insertion point where you want the split to occur. Normally, place the insertion point on the first character of what is to become the second paragraph.

2. Press Return. Word splits the paragraphs. Press Return again to leave a blank space between the paragraphs.

3. Because you're just experimenting, join the paragraphs again by deleting the paragraph marks you just inserted.

Deleting a Paragraph

As you inspect your letter after joining the two paragraphs, you see that the whole first paragraph must go. The paragraph is too negative, and besides, it violates the first principle of excellence in business communication: focus on the customer, not your own feelings and preoccupations.

To get rid of the first paragraph, follow these steps:

1. Move the pointer to the selection bar next to the letter's first paragraph.

2. When the pointer changes shape to an arrow pointing up and to the right, double-click the mouse button. Alternatively, triple-click in the paragraph. This action selects the whole paragraph.

3. To delete the paragraph, choose Cut from the Edit menu or press ⌘-X.

When you choose Cut or press ⌘-X, Word removes the highlighted text from your document and places it on the clipboard—a special, temporary storage area. To see what's on the clipboard, choose Show Clipboard from the Windows menu. Figure 1.9 shows the Clipboard window on-screen. To close the clipboard, click the Clipboard window's Close box.

Adding More Text to the Letter

When you look over the remaining text of the letter, you realize that you goofed when you deleted the whole first paragraph. You could have left the sentence, *Thank you for your letter of January 22.* You can bring the deleted paragraph back by choosing Undo or Paste, if you haven't cut or copied anything else to the clipboard. First, however, you should learn how to insert additional text in text you already have typed. To do this, use the following steps:

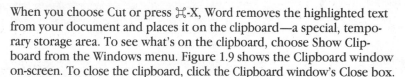

1. Place the insertion point before the *W* in *We have replaced...* (the first line of the letter's body).

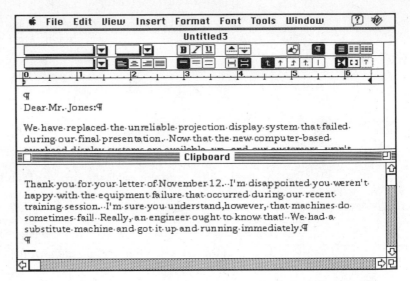

2. Type the following text:

   Thank you for your letter of January 22. Mr. Jones, it was a pleasure serving you and your staff! Won't you consider firming up your plans for training your staff in the security techniques we detailed in our presentation? If you will give me a call or drop me a note, I'll have a proposal for you right away.

3. Press Return when you finish typing this paragraph. Your letter should look like the one in figure 1.10.

Moving Text

The letter is looking better, but in examining what you have written, you realize that what you just typed belongs at the end of the letter, not at the beginning. (You remember your business communication teacher again: "End with a call for action! End on a personal note and invite a response!") You decide to move part of the first paragraph to the end of the letter.

Fig. 1.10
Adding new text to the
letter.

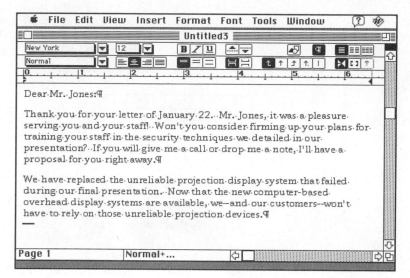

You can move text in several different ways with Word. See Chapter 4 for a complete survey of your options. Here, you sample a nifty new Word 5 feature: *drag-and-drop editing*. With drag-and-drop editing, you can move text just by dragging a selection on-screen.

To turn on drag-and-drop editing, follow these steps:

1. Choose Preferences from the Tools menu.

2. Activate the Drag-and-Drop Text Editing check box.

3. Click the Close box.

To move text, follow these steps:

1. Place the insertion point at the end of the last paragraph, and press Return.

   You've entered a paragraph mark at the end of your document. You need this paragraph mark so that you can move the text there.

2. In the first paragraph, double-click the word *Mr.* and continue holding down the mouse button. Drag right and down to select the rest of the text shown highlighted in figure 1.11. ***Do not select the trailing paragraph mark!***

3. Release the mouse button, leaving the selection on-screen.

4. Click anywhere in the selection, and drag down.

Chapter 1

The mouse pointer gains a gray bracket underneath the arrow, indicating that you're moving text. A gray insertion point appears, showing you where the text will appear when you release the mouse button.

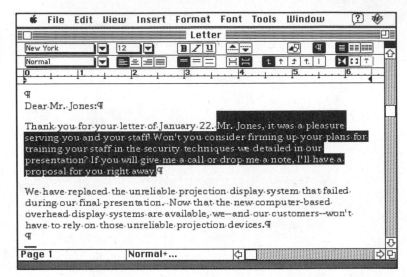

5. Place the gray insertion point before the last paragraph mark, the one at the end of the document, and release the mouse button.

   You have moved the text successfully (see fig. 1.12).

Finishing the Letter

Now you are ready to add the complimentary closing, by following these steps:

1. Place the insertion point just before the last paragraph mark and press Return.

   When Word enters the new line, the program copies the paragraph formats from the last paragraph. The new paragraph mark is preceded by 12 points of blank space.

2. With the insertion point next to the last paragraph mark on the screen, point to the lower of the two left indent marks, and drag right to the 3.5-inch mark on the ruler.

Part I

Getting Started

Word moves both indent markers. You've indented the paragraph 3.5 inches.

Fig. 1.12
Paragraph moved with drag-and-drop editing.

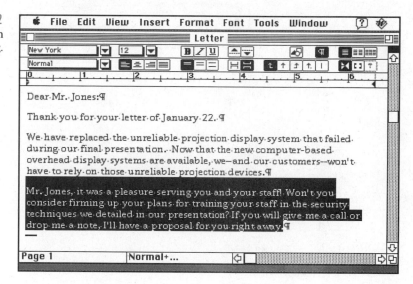

3. Type *Sincerely,* and press Return twice.

   Because Word is still copying the current paragraph format of 12 points blank space, you enter four lines of blank space by pressing Return twice.

4. Type *Diane B. Smith* and press Return.

   Word enters another blank line—but this time, you don't want it.

5. With the insertion point positioned just before the paragraph mark you just entered, click the No Blank Line Spacing button on the ruler. (The No Blank Line Spacing button has two horizontal brackets, with no space between them.)

   Word moves the paragraph mark up one line.

6. Type *Corporate Training*.

You're finished. The closing of your letter should look like that shown in figure 1.13.

Fig. 1.13
The finished closing.

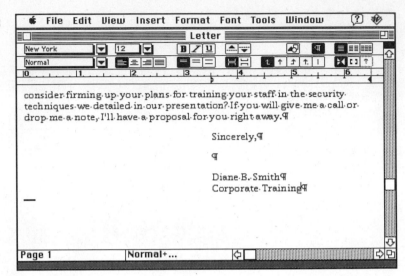

consider firming up your plans for training your staff in the security techniques we detailed in our presentation? If you will give me a call or drop me a note, I'll have a proposal for you right away.¶

Sincerely,¶

¶

Diane B. Smith¶
Corporate Training¶

Previewing and Printing

In this section, you learn how to preview your letter's appearance so that you can adjust the formatting before printing. With Word 5, you can look at your document in four ways: Normal view, Outline view, Page Layout view, and Print Preview. You learn more about all these viewing modes in Chapter 2.

So far, you have been working in Normal view because your concern has been with the text of the letter, not with its appearance when printed. Now you are ready to use the Print Preview option to preview the formats you selected. To do this, follow these steps:

1. Choose Print Preview from the File menu, or press ⌘-Option-I.

   If you've used previous versions of Word, note a significant keyboard change. ⌘-I, which formerly started Print Preview, is now used for italic.

2. When the Print Preview window appears as shown in figure 1.14, notice how the text is laid out relative to the page as a whole.

As you can see, the text is too high—it's jammed up against the return address. To cure the problem, follow these steps:

1. Click the Close button to exit the Print Preview window.

Fig. 1.14
Print Preview of the letter.

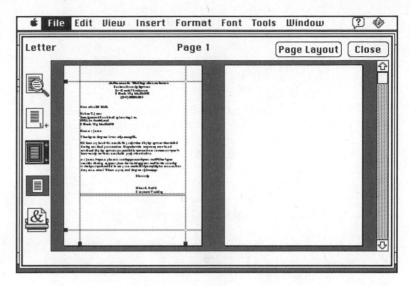

2. Click the insertion point just to the left of the date, and press Return three or four times.

   Choose the Print Preview option from the File menu again; as you can see in figure 1.15, the letter now is balanced on the page.

Fig. 1.15
The letter after balancing
on the page.

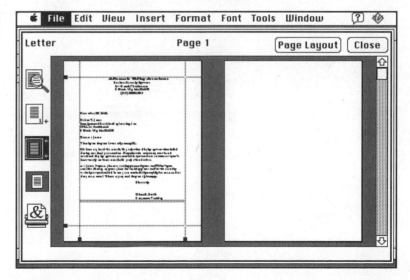

3. To print the letter from within Print Preview, just click the Printer button.

If you were working in Normal or Page Layout view, you would print by choosing Print from the File menu, or by using the ⌘-P keyboard shortcut.

What you see next depends on which printer you're using. Each printer has its own Print dialog box, which enables you to control its unique capabilities. Some features, however, are present in all Print dialog boxes. You can choose the number of copies you want to print, the page range, and automatic or manual feeding. You can usually choose many other options as well, depending on the printer's capabilities. You learn more about these options in Chapter 10. Figure 1.16 shows the Print dialog box for StyleWriter printers.

Fig. 1.16
Print dialog box for
StyleWriter printer.

```
🍎  File  Edit  View  Insert  Format  Font  Tools  Window        ⑦ ◈

    StyleWriter                                    7.0      Print

    Copies:      1         Quality:   ⦿ Best    ○ Faster   Cancel

    Pages:     ⦿ All    ○ From:        To:

    Paper:     ⦿ Sheet Feeder    ○ Manual

    Section Range: From:  1      To:  1      ☐ Print Selection Only
    ☐ Print Hidden Text    ☐ Print Next File
```

                                                ¶
                                                ¶
                                                ¶

November 25, 1991¶
¶
Nelson·T.·Jones¶
Amalgamated·Precision·Engineering,·Inc.¶

Page 1   Normal+...

4. Choose Print to print your letter. Figure 1.17 shows the result.

Quitting Word

SPEED KEY

Now that you have printed the letter, you are ready to quit Word. To do this, choose Quit from the File menu or press ⌘-Q.

If you haven't saved your letter, you see an alert box. This box asks you whether you want to save the document you created. Click No if you want to abandon the letter. To save the letter, click Yes. (If you have not already saved the document in a previous session, Word displays the Save As dialog box so that you can name the document.) If you have changed your mind about quitting Word, click Cancel or press Esc.

Fig. 1.17
Printed version of letter.

Albemarle Valley Associates
Business Security Systems
100 South First Avenue
Hillvale, Virginia 22993
(804) 555-1234

January 7, 1992

Nelson T. Jones
Amalgamated Precision Engineering, Inc.
941 Riverbank Road
Hillvale, Virginia 22993

Dear Mr. Jones:

Thank you for your letter of January 22.

We have replaced the unreliable projection display system that failed during our final presentation. Now that the new computer-based overhead display systems are available, we--and our customers--won't have to rely on those unreliable projection devices.

Mr. Jones, it was a pleasure serving you and your staff! Won't you consider firming up your plans for training your staff in the security techniques we detailed in our presentation? If you will give me a call or drop me a note, I'll have a proposal for you right away.

Sincerely,

Diana B. Smith
Corporate Training

Quick Review

The section "Productivity Tips" gives a review of high-productivity tips and tricks.

Chapter 1

Quick Start: Creating a Business Letter

Productivity Tips

- You can choose many formats from the ribbon and ruler just by clicking the appropriate button. Use Balloon Help to explore the ribbon and ruler, and learn what each button does.

- If you're using a Classic or some other Mac with a small screen, learn how to toggle the ribbon and ruler on and off. You'll need more space on the screen for composing your text.

- Display the paragraph marks so that you can see what you're doing while editing. If you find them distracting, you can turn them off when you're not editing.

- Use drag-and-drop editing for moving text. It's much easier than using the Mac's normal clipboard technique.

- Preview your document's overall page balance before printing using Print Preview. If it looks fine, save a few mouse motions by starting printing directly from Print Preview.

Understanding Word's Workplace

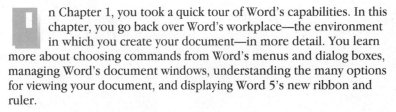n Chapter 1, you took a quick tour of Word's capabilities. In this chapter, you go back over Word's workplace—the environment in which you create your document—in more detail. You learn more about choosing commands from Word's menus and dialog boxes, managing Word's document windows, understanding the many options for viewing your document, and displaying Word 5's new ribbon and ruler.

In this chapter you learn about the following:

■ *Choosing Commands*. You learn all the Word techniques for choosing commands and navigating dialog boxes with the mouse or the keyboard. This section includes many shortcuts that will help you work with Word more productively.

■ *Managing Windows*. In this section, you learn all the fundamental window-manipulation skills. With Word, you can open up to 23 windows at a time, including some dialog boxes—such as the Find dialog box—that behave as if they are windows. You also can split a document window so that you can view two portions of a document at a time.

■ *Viewing Your Document*. In Chapter 1 you learned two ways to view your document: Normal view for fast text entry and editing and Print Preview to see how your document will look when printed. In this section, you learn all the ways you can control your view of your documents with Word.

■ *Displaying the Ribbon and Ruler*. The ribbon and ruler appear optionally at the top of each document window, giving you easy-to-use tools for many common formatting commands. With the ribbon and ruler displayed, you seldom may need to use Word's formatting dialog boxes or keyboard formatting commands. Because the ribbon and ruler take up a lot of room on the screen, this chapter teaches you how to toggle each on and off. You learn how to format your documents with the ribbon and ruler in future chapters.

Choosing Commands

Word fully conforms to Apple's standards for menus, dialog boxes, and keyboard command assignments, and chances are you're already familiar with the basics of choosing commands. This section provides many shortcuts that can help you work more productively with Word.

This section begins with an exploration of Word's pull-down menus and dialog boxes and concludes with an examination of Word's keyboard shortcuts for writers who prefer to keep their hands on the keys.

Using Word's Pull-Down Menus

In Chapter 1, you learned how to choose a command from the menu bar by using the mouse. When you pull down a menu, a list of command options appears (see fig. 2.1).

You see the following symbols on Word's pull-down menus:

Checked Options (✓). These options are currently in effect. If you choose one of them or another option that cancels the currently checked option, Word removes the check mark. In the View menu, a check mark appears beside the Normal option, indicating that you're looking at your document in the Normal view. If you choose one of the other View options, Word removes the check mark.

Group Separators. Three lines divide the View menu into four groups. At the top of the menu you find three options for viewing your document: Normal, Outline, and Page Layout. Next you find three options for displaying command information at the top of the active document window: Ribbon, Ruler, and Print Merge Helper. You will learn more about these and other command groupings elsewhere in this book. For now, notice that group lines show you which commands have similar functions.

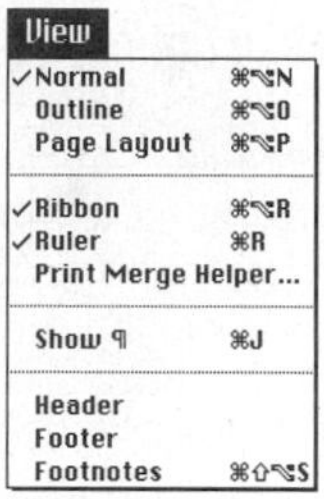

Fig. 2.1
Command options in the
View menu.

View	
✓Normal	⌘⌥N
Outline	⌘⌥O
Page Layout	⌘⌥P
✓Ribbon	⌘⌥R
✓Ruler	⌘R
Print Merge Helper...	
Show ¶	⌘J
Header	
Footer	
Footnotes	⌘⇧⌥S

Three Dots (Ellipsis ...). Three dots indicate that you will see a dialog box or window if you choose this option.

Keyboard Shortcuts (⌘ ⇧ ⌥ S). Many command options have keyboard shortcuts, which you can use if you would rather not take your hands away from the keyboard. The symbols indicate the keys you press to choose this option. See table 2.1 for a guide to these symbols. You learn more about keyboard shortcuts and how to use them later in this chapter.

Table 2.1
Keyboard Shortcut Symbols

Symbol	Key
⌘	Command
⌥	Option
⇧	Shift
↵	Return
⌤	Enter
␣	Space bar
⇥	Tab
⌫	Delete or Backspace
▦	Key on numeric keypad
⌧	Esc
↑	Up arrow
↓	Down arrow
←	Left arrow
→	Right arrow

Choosing Menu Options with the Keyboard

TIP

If you find the keyboard shortcut symbols distracting, you can hide them. Choose Preferences from the Tools menu and choose the View option. When the View options appear, activate the Show Function Keys on Menus option. Then click the close box on the title bar to close the Preferences dialog box.

Although the Mac's pull-down menus are easy to use, many writers dislike removing their hands from the keyboard to choose commands from the menus. This section provides techniques for accessing pull-down menus by using the keyboard.

To access a pull-down menu with the keyboard, follow these steps:

1. Press ⌘-Tab. If you prefer, you can press the period key on the numeric keypad instead.

   Word highlights the menu bar, as shown in figure 2.2. The menu bar will remain highlighted for a few seconds, long enough for you to choose a command name.

2. With the menu bar highlighted, choose the name of the menu you want to pull down. You can do so in several ways:

   To choose the menu name using the arrow keys, press the right-arrow key to move the highlight right. (If you go past the last command name, the highlight reappears on the left.) Press the left-arrow key to move the highlight to the left.

   To choose the menu name using the keyboard, just type the menu name's first letter. To choose Insert, for example, just press I. (It doesn't matter whether you type uppercase or lowercase.) If you want to choose the Format or Font options, hold down the Shift key before pressing F, and keep pressing Shift-F until you have highlighted the command name you want.

   To choose the menu name by number, press a number from 1 through 7. File is menu name 1, Edit is menu name 2, and so on.

3. To close a menu without choosing an option, just press Esc, ⌘-period, or Backspace.

Fig. 2.2
Highlighted menu bar.

   ⌘ File Edit View Insert Format Font Tools Window Work

You can use the keyboard to choose options from a pull-down menu by following these steps:

1. To pull down a menu, press ⌘-Tab, followed by the first letter of the command name.

Part I

Getting Started

2. With the menu pulled down, highlight the option you want. You can do so in several ways:

   To choose the menu name using the arrow keys, press the down-arrow key to move the highlight down. (If you go past the last command name, the highlight reappears on the top.) Press the up-arrow key to move the highlight in the opposite direction.

   To choose an option using the keyboard, just press the option's first letter. To choose Page Layout from the View menu, for example, just press P (uppercase or lowercase). If two options have the same first letter and you want to choose the second one, just press the letter again.

3. Press Return to choose the option you have highlighted.

Understanding Word's Dialog Boxes

Word's dialog boxes appear when the program needs more information to carry out a command. Figure 2.3 shows the Character dialog box, which appears after you choose Character in the Format menu. Figure 2.4 shows the System 6 version of the Save As box, which appears when you choose Save As in the File menu. These two figures illustrate all the features you will find in Word's dialog boxes. (The System 7 version is slightly different, as explained in Chapter 4.) Don't worry right now about what all the options in these dialog boxes do or how to choose options with the keyboard.

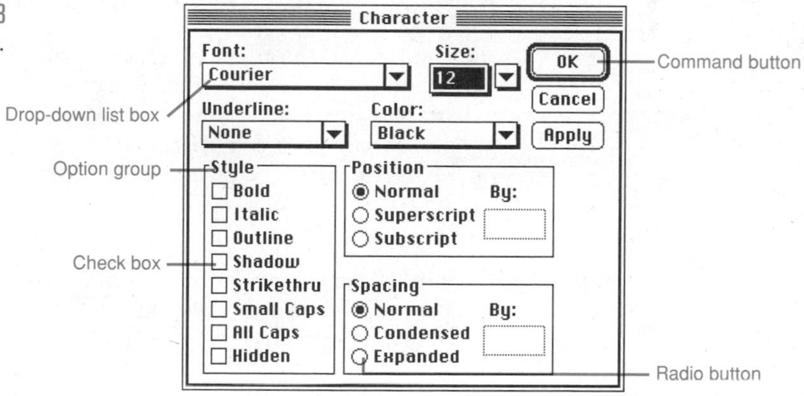

> **TIP**
>
> If you pull down a menu and realize you really wanted an option on another menu, you can quickly access the correct menu using the keyboard. Just hold down the Shift key and press the menu name's first letter. To open the Insert menu while the Format menu is open, press Shift-I.

Fig. 2.3
The Character dialog box.

Drop-down list box

Option group

Check box

Command button

Radio button

Character

Font: Courier
Size: 12
OK
Cancel
Apply

Underline: None
Color: Black

Style
☐ Bold
☐ Italic
☐ Outline
☐ Shadow
☐ Strikethru
☐ Small Caps
☐ All Caps
☐ Hidden

Position
● Normal   By:
○ Superscript
○ Subscript

Spacing
● Normal   By:
○ Condensed
○ Expanded

Chapter 2
Understanding Word's Workplace

Fig. 2.4
The Save As dialog box.

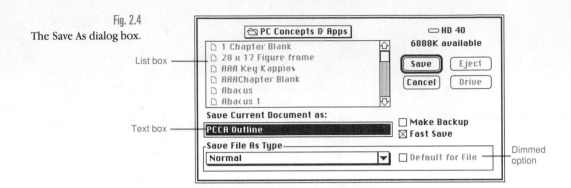

List box

Text box

Dimmed
option

The following list describes some of the features you find in Word's dialog boxes:

Option Group. Related options are grouped and boxed in most dialog boxes. In the Character dialog box, for example, all the emphasis options—such as Bold and Italic—are grouped in the Style area.

Check Box. Click a check box to activate the option; after you do, an X appears in the box. If you click an activated check box, the X disappears. In an option group containing several check boxes, you can choose more than one option.

Radio Button. When you see a radio button (a small circle), you can click the button to turn the option on (a dot appears in the circle) or off (the dot disappears). These buttons are called radio buttons after the push buttons found in old car radios.

Unlike check boxes, however, only one option button in a group can be on at any time. When you choose one option, Word turns off the other ones in the group. Note that in the Position area you can choose just one option at a time. This makes sense because a character cannot be printed superscript and subscript at the same time.

List Box. A list box, such as the one shown in figure 2.4, shows a list of items from which you can choose. You can use the scroll bar to scroll up and down the list. To choose an item, just double-click it.

Drop-down List Box. To reduce clutter in dialog boxes, Word uses drop-down list boxes, such as the Save Files As Type list box in figure 2.5. To use a drop-down list box, you click the arrow, and the list appears. A check mark indicates the currently selected option. To choose an item from the list, just pull the highlight

TIP

To restore the default settings in an option group, click the option group name. To restore the default character emphasis style (plain) in the Character dialog box, for example, click the word Style at the top of the emphasis option group.

Part I

Getting Started

down the list until you highlight the item you want, and then release the mouse button. Your choice then appears in the box, and the list disappears.

Fig. 2.5
Drop-down list box.

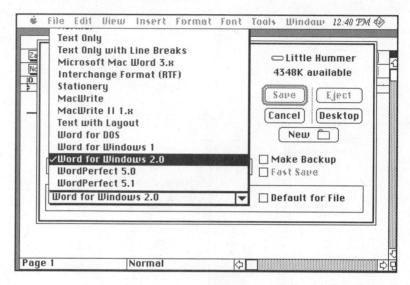

Text Box. In a text box, you type information that Word needs, such as a file's new name. Word requires that you type information only when it can obtain the needed information in no other way.

Within a text box, standard Macintosh editing techniques apply. To delete the text, highlight the text and press Delete. If no text is highlighted, pressing Delete erases the character left of the insertion point.

Drop-down Text Box. Some drop-down list boxes also are text boxes, meaning that you can type in your own option instead of choosing one from the list. An example is the Size drop-down list box in the Character format menu. You can choose a size from the list or type the size you want. If you prefer, you can treat the drop-down text box as if it were an ordinary text box and choose the option you want from the drop-down list.

Dimmed Options. If you see dimmed or grayed options, such as the Default for File option in the Save As dialog box, you cannot choose this option at present. Some dimmed options become active when you choose other options in the dialog box. If you choose an option other than Normal in the Save File As Type list box, for example, the Default for File option becomes active; you

TIP

When a text box is highlighted, just start typing. Word will erase the text currently in the text box, saving you the trouble of selecting it and deleting it.

Chapter 2
Understanding Word's Workplace

then can choose this option to make the non-Normal option the default setting for the current file.

Command Button. A command button, such as the OK and Cancel buttons in the Document dialog box, carries out the choices you have made in the dialog box (see fig. 2.6). In some menus, command buttons have ellipses (three dots), indicating that they open up a second-level dialog box (a dialog box within a dialog box). The File Series button in the Document dialog box, for example, opens the File Series dialog box, which is accessible only through the Document dialog box. When you exit the File Series dialog box, you return to the Document dialog box.

> **TIP**
>
> When you see a highlighted command button—such as OK in the Document dialog box—pressing Return or Enter chooses this button immediately. You can press Esc or ⌘-period to choose the Cancel button quickly.

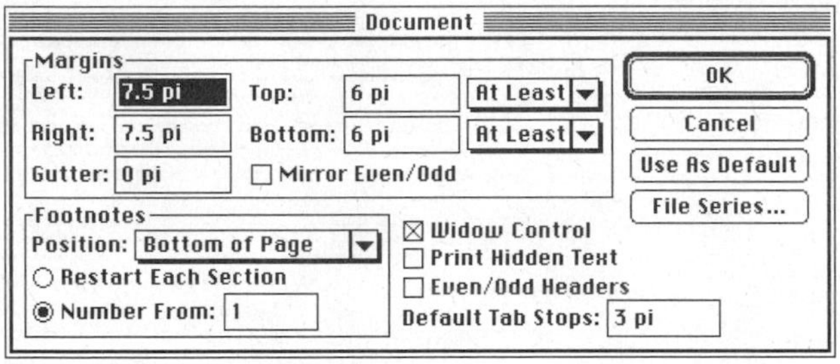

Fig. 2.6
File Series command button in Document dialog box.

Choosing Dialog Box Options with the Keyboard

If you like to use the keyboard, you can use the following keys to select options within dialog boxes:

Tab/Shift-Tab. In dialog boxes that have more than one text box or drop-down text box, press Tab to move the highlight from one text box to the next. (When you reach the last text box, pressing Tab activates the first one again.) You can press Shift-Tab to reverse the cursor's movement from one dialog box to the next.

⌘-Tab/⌘-Shift-Tab. When you press ⌘-Tab, Word moves a blinking gray underline to the next option, list, text area, or button in the dialog box, as shown in figure 2.7. The blinking gray underline indicates that the option is selected; you must press Keypad-0 (zero) or ⌘-space bar key to activate the option. ⌘-Shift-Tab moves the underline to the previous option, list, text area, or button.

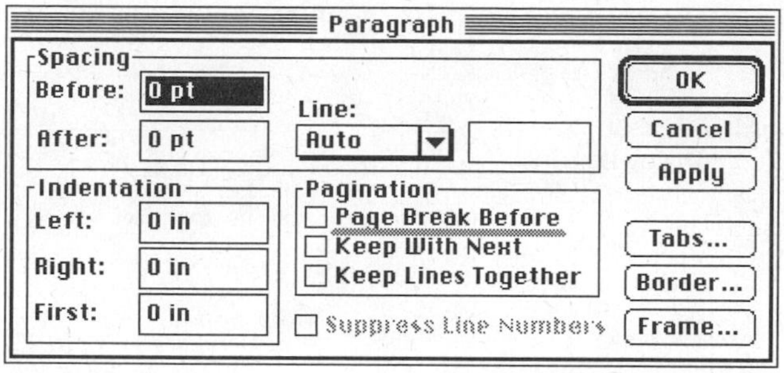

⌘-space bar or Keypad-0 (zero). Press Keypad-0 or ⌘-space bar to activate the selected option (the one with the blinking gray underline). If you select a drop-down list box, pressing Keypad-0 or ⌘-space bar drops down the list. If no blinking gray underline is visible, press ⌘-Tab to see which option is currently selected.

Down Arrow/Up Arrow. Within a list box, you use these keys to move the highlight to the item you want. When you have selected the item, press ⌘-Tab if you want to make any additional selections within the dialog box, or just press Return or Enter to select your choice immediately.

⌘-Down Arrow/⌘-Up Arrow. These keys apply when you're working in a list of files that contain folders, such as the list box you see in the System 6 version of the Open dialog box (see fig. 2.8). (The System 7 version is slightly different, as explained in Chapter 5.) Next to the file names, you see icons indicating whether the item is a document (indicated by the page icon) or a folder (indicated by the folder icon). When you highlight a folder, such as the folder called PCCA in figure 2.8, you can open the folder and display its files by pressing ⌘-Down arrow. When you open a folder, you can close it and return to the next folder up by pressing ⌘-Up arrow.

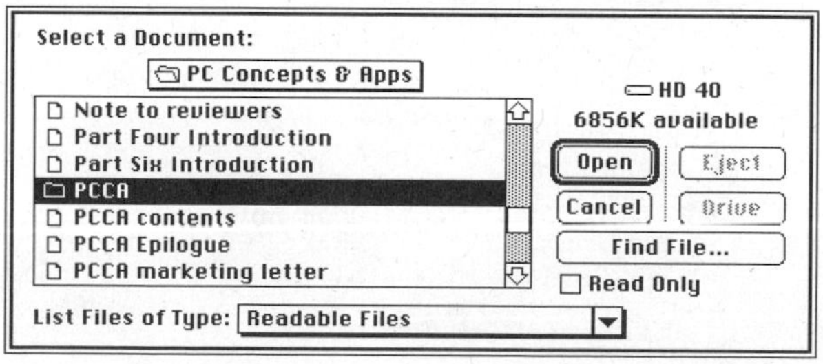

Fig. 2.8
The Open dialog box.

Chapter 2

Understanding Word's Workplace

Table 2.2 summarizes all the keys you can use within dialog boxes.

Table 2.2
Keyboard Techniques for
Dialog Boxes

To	Press
Move to the next text box down	Tab
Move to the previous text box	Shift-Tab
Select the next option	⌘-Tab or Keypad-period
Select the previous option	⌘-Shift-Tab or Shift-Keypad-period
Choose underlined option	⌘-Space bar or Keypad-0 (zero)
Highlight item within list	Up or down arrow
Choose option or button and activate	⌘-*first letter*
Open folder in a files list box	⌘-Down arrow
Open next folder up in a files list box	⌘-Up arrow
Cancel choices and close dialog box	Esc
Confirm choices and close dialog box	Return or Enter

Choosing Commands with Keyboard Shortcuts

NOTE

In Word's default shortcut key assignment, you can redefine Word's keyboard just as you want. You will find more information on customizing Word's keyboard in Chapter 27.

Because Word is designed for keyboard users as well as mouse users, most mouse techniques are duplicated by one or more keyboard commands. You needn't learn both methods in order to use Word effectively. If you're planning to use the mouse, however, exploring the keyboard techniques still makes sense. When you use the keyboard techniques, you don't remove your hand from the keyboard, which is somewhat faster than the mouse techniques.

Table 2.3 lists keyboard shortcuts to frequently used dialog boxes. For a complete list, see Appendix B.

Command	Keyboard shortcut
New (File menu)	⌘-N
Open (File menu)	⌘-O
Close (File menu)	⌘-W

Command	Keyboard shortcut
Save (File menu)	⌘-S
Print Preview	⌘-Option-I
Print (File menu)	⌘-P
Quit (File menu)	⌘-Q
Undo (Edit menu)	⌘-Z
Repeat (Edit menu)	⌘-Y
Copy (Edit menu)	⌘-C
Cut (Edit menu)	⌘-X
Paste (Edit menu)	⌘-V
Find (Edit menu)	⌘-F
Replace (Edit menu)	⌘-H
Go to (Edit menu)	⌘-G
Select All (Edit menu)	⌘-A
Normal (View menu)	⌘-Option-N
Outline (View menu)	⌘-Option-O
Page Layout (View menu)	⌘-Option-P
Ribbon	⌘-Option-R
Ruler	⌘-R
Character (Format menu)	⌘-D
Paragraph (Format menu)	⌘-M
Bold (Format menu)	⌘-Shift-B
Italic (Format menu)	⌘-Shift-I
Underline (Format menu)	⌘-Shift-U
Plain Text (Format menu)	⌘-Shift-Z
Spelling (Tools menu)	⌘-L

TIP

The keyboard shortcut icons in the margin alert you to additional keyboard shortcuts you can use, and to details about using the shortcuts mentioned in tables 2.3 and 2.4.

If your Macintosh is equipped with an extended keyboard, you can use the function keys (numbered F1 through F15) to access frequently used dialog boxes and commands. Table 2.4 lists the function keys available to users of these keyboards. (If you have an extended keyboard, you still can use the keyboard shortcuts listed in table 2.3.) In tandem with the Option and Shift keys, more function key shortcuts are available than the ones listed in table 2.3; for a complete list, see Appendix B.

Chapter 2

Understanding Word's Workplace

Table 2.4
Keyboard Shortcuts for
Extended Keyboards

Command	Function key shortcut
Undo (Edit)	F1
Cut (Edit)	F2
Copy (Edit)	F3
Paste (Edit)	F4
New (File)	F5
Open (File)	F6
Save (File)	F7
Print (File)	F8
Revert to Style (Format)	F9
Bold (Format)	F10
Italic (Format)	F11
Underlining (Format)	F12
Page Layout (View)	F13
Character (Format)	F14
Spelling	F15

Users of previous versions of Word should note the following keyboard changes:

Command	Previous keyboard shortcut	Word 5 shortcut
Bold	⌘-Shift-B	⌘-B
Find Formats	⌘-Options-R	None—choose Find (Edit menu)
Italic	⌘-Shift-I	⌘-I
Normal view	None	⌘-Option-N
Outline view	⌘-U	⌘-Options-O
Page layout	⌘-B	⌘-Option-P
Repeat Action	⌘-A	⌘-Y
Select Whole Document	⌘-Option-M	⌘-A
Show Paragraph Marks	⌘-Y	⌘-J
Underline	⌘-Shift-U	⌘-U

Choosing Commands with Hotspots

Too few Word users explore the program's hotspots. A *hotspot* is an area of the screen that, when double-clicked, calls forth a dialog box. For example, you can display the Paragraph dialog box just by double-clicking any of the alignment or spacing buttons on the ruler. Table 2.5 lists the hotspots.

Table 2.5
Hotspots

To open	Double-click
Character dialog box	Ribbon background
Document dialog box	Margin indicators on ruler or corners of page outside the margins (Page Layout view only)
Footnote window	Footnote reference mark
Go To dialog box	Page number in page number area
Paragraph dialog box	Alignment or spacing buttons on ruler
Section dialog box	Section mark
Styles dialog box	Style name in style name area
Tabs dialog box	Tab stop or tab icon on ruler

Undoing Commands

When a command goes awry, you can choose Undo from the Edit menu to cancel its effects. Alternatively, use the ⌘-Z or F1 shortcuts. You can undo the effects of most editing, formatting, and text-processing commands, including sorts and automatic numbering.

Just what Undo undoes is shown by the Edit menu. If you have been typing text, the Undo command reads `Undo Typing`, as shown in figure 2.9. Choosing Undo Typing removes all the text you have entered since the last time you chose a command, which may be quite a lot of text. If you have just cut some text, however, Undo Typing changes to `Undo Cut`, as shown in the same figure. And if you have just performed a paste, Undo Cut changes to `Undo Paste`.

You cannot undo all commands. If the Undo option is grayed and says, `Can't undo`, you're stuck with the consequences of the command you have just given.

Fig. 2.9
The Undo command shows
what can be undone.

After you choose Undo, you have a chance to change your mind yet another time. To restore the effects of the command you have just undone, choose Undo again. You will find that the name of the command has changed to Redo followed by the name of the command or action that can be redone.

Because Undo can erase the only consequences of the last action you undertook, be sure to use Undo immediately should a command go awry.

Repeating the Last Action

The Repeat command (⌘-Y) in the Edit menu shares one trait in common with Undo: The command's name changes, depending on what actions Word can repeat. When you're typing, you will find that the Repeat option reads Repeat Typing, and if you choose it, Word will insert, at the cursor's location, a copy of all the text you have typed since the last time you chose a command. Users of previous versions of Word, note: This command was formerly called Again.

You can repeat the action as many times as you want, so long as you don't type any additional text or choose another command.

Learning when to use the Repeat command takes some practice. The following suggestions should help you.

Suppose that you used the word *utilize* several times in a paragraph, and you want to replace this word with the simpler *use*. Highlight the first instance of *utilize* and type *use*. Now the Repeat command reads Repeat Typing. Without choosing any other commands or typing any additional text, highlight the next instance of *utilize* and choose Repeat Typing from the Edit menu (or press the ⌘-Y keyboard shortcut). Word replaces the selection with the repeated text, *use*.

Suppose that you have just chosen several options from one of the Format dialog boxes and you want to apply them to a second unit of text. After choosing the formats, select the second unit of text that you want to format the same way and choose Repeat.

Using Windows

Word uses standard Macintosh window features, adding to them some special features germane to Word's document-processing functions. In this section, you explore the features of Word's document windows. You also learn how to open windows—as many as 23, if your system is equipped with enough memory. As you will learn, you can open two or more documents at a time, each in its own window. You even can open two or more windows on the same document, with each window showing a separate portion of the document. You can split any document window into two panes.

With all these windows on-screen at once, you will be glad to know that you can easily activate other windows, even when you cannot see them, and you can size, move, and close windows as you please.

Understanding Document Windows

This section includes a complete description of the document window in which you create your documents with Word.

Title Bar. With Word, only one window can be active at a time, even if more than one window is visible on-screen. When a window is active, you see highlight lines in the title bar and scroll bars (see fig. 2.10). When a window is inactive, the highlight disappears from the title bar and scroll bars, as do many other features (see fig. 2.11).

Close Box. In an active window, a Close box is placed on the left of the title bar. To close the window, click the Close box. If your work hasn't been saved, Word will alert you and give you the opportunity to do so.

Zoom Box. Click the Zoom box to switch the window between its original size (the window's size at the beginning of the operating session) and its alternative size/location. If you have never moved or sized the window, Word automatically sets the alternative size/location to approximately 50 percent of the original size. To expand the window to its original size, click the Zoom box again.

Fig. 2.10
Active document window.

Title bar

Close box

Insertion point

End mark

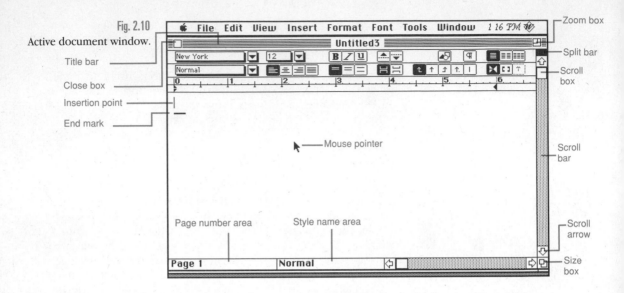

Zoom box

Split bar

Scroll box

Mouse pointer

Scroll bar

Page number area   Style name area

Scroll arrow

Size box

Fig. 2.11
Inactive document
window.

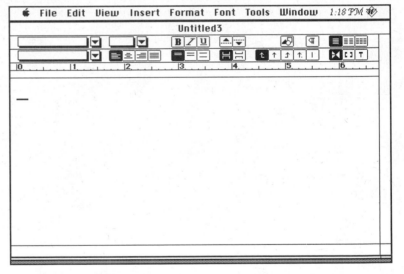

Insertion Point. This blinking vertical line shows where your text will appear when you start typing. If you have ever used an MS-DOS computer, note that the insertion point isn't quite the same as a cursor: an MS-DOS cursor is always *on* a character, while the Mac's insertion point is always *between* two characters.

Part I

Getting Started

Mouse Pointer. This pointer shows you where the mouse is currently located on-screen. In a document, clicking the mouse moves the cursor to the mouse pointer's location. Within a document window, the mouse pointer resembles a capital letter I; this shape enables you to reposition the cursor precisely between characters of text, even if you're using a small font (such as 9 points or 10 points). Note that the mouse pointer changes shape when you move the pointer out of the document window. You will learn more about what these shape changes mean in the next chapter.

End Mark. The end mark shows the end of the document. You cannot move the cursor or type text past the end mark.

Split Bar. A black rectangle at the top of the vertical scroll bar, the split bar enables you to split the window into two panes. You do this by dragging the split bar down the scroll bar.

Scroll Boxes. Drag the scroll boxes to view additional parts of your document.

Scroll Bars. Clicking in the vertical or horizontal scroll bar displays other parts of your document if you have created one that's more than one screen in length. To scroll your document down one screen, for example, you click below the vertical scroll box. To scroll your document right one screenful, click to the right of the horizontal scroll box.

Scroll Arrows. Clicking the vertical scroll arrows scrolls your document line-by-line. If you click the horizontal scroll arrows, Word scrolls your document right or left in half-inch jumps.

Size Box. To size the window, you drag on the size box.

Style Name Area. This area shows the name of the style that's applied to the current paragraph. Until you create your own styles or apply Word's styles, you will see the default style, Normal, in this area. You learn more about styles in Chapter 8.

Page Number Area. In this area, you see the number of the page currently displayed. Some commands display other information in this area while they're active. In previous versions of Word, this area was sometimes called the Status Area, which made some sense because many commands present messages in this area.

Opening Additional Documents

Even though a document is open and displayed on-screen, you can open additional documents without closing the open document or losing your work. To open an existing document, choose Open from the File menu or use the ⌘-O keyboard shortcut. To open a new document, choose New from the File menu or use ⌘-N.

When you open a new document, the new document's window is placed on top of the first one, filling the screen. For this reason, you cannot see the first document, and you may worry that you have lost your unsaved work. Don't worry! It's still there. You can display the first document by making it active again, as explained later in the section "Activating Windows."

Opening Two Windows on the Same Document

A window gives you a picture frame through which you can view a document that's in Word's memory. With Word you can open more than one window on the same document. Suppose that you open a document. You can open another window on the same document by choosing New Window from the Window menu or by using the F5 shortcut. Doing so is useful, for example, when you want to keep one part of a document in view while you write in another.

Word calls the second window Untitled3:2, as shown in figure 2.12. Note that the Window menu shows all of the open windows, including the two windows on Untitled3.

Fig. 2.12
Second window on an
open document.

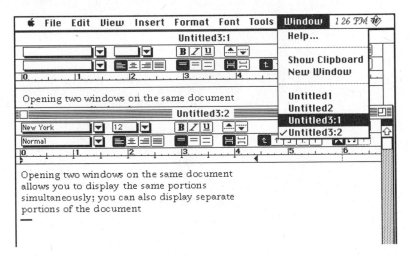

Note that this window gives you a second "picture frame" through which you can view the same document. If you make changes to this document in the window titled Untitled3:2, for example, these changes will appear in the original window, which is now titled Untitled3:1.

When two or more windows are open on a document, you can display different parts of the document, and scrolling one window doesn't affect what's displayed in the other.

Activating Windows

Only one window can be active at a time. To activate a window, just click anywhere within it; this automatically closes the window which was open. If you cannot see the window you want to activate, use the Window menu, as explained in the following procedure:

1. Pull down the Window menu (see fig. 2.13).

    Note that a check mark appears beside the window that's currently active.

Fig 2.13
Window menu showing open windows.

2. Choose the window you want to activate.

You also can activate windows you cannot see by pressing ⌘-Option-W. Word activates and displays the next active window, using the *reverse* of the sequence of windows as they're listed in the Window menu. If the Windows menu lists Example:1, Example:2, and Example:3, pressing ⌘-Option-W will cycle through the open windows in the sequence Example:3, Example:2, and Example:1. If you press ⌘-Option-W again, Word displays Example:3.

Splitting a Window

As you just learned, you can open two windows on the same document. You can achieve much the same effect—viewing two parts of the same document—by splitting a window into two panes, as shown in figure 2.14. After you split a window, each pane has its own vertical scroll bar.

You can view different parts of the document: scrolling one pane doesn't affect the other. However, you cannot display two different documents in the same window. To display two different documents, you must open two separate windows.

If you want to view two portions of the same document, splitting a window is more convenient than opening two windows on the same document. You don't need to size or move the windows to get them aligned correctly, and only one title bar takes up room on the screen.

Fig. 2.14
Window split into two
panes.

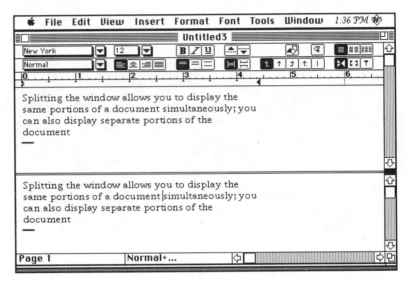

When you split the window, you can choose where you want the split to occur, or you can split the window into two equal-sized panes.

To split a window and choose where you want the split to occur, follow these steps:

1. Move the mouse pointer to the split bar until the shape changes (you will see a horizontal bar with up and down arrows).

2. Drag the split bar down the vertical scroll bar until you have positioned the split where you want it.

3. Release the mouse button.

Use this nifty shortcut to split the window into two equal-sized panes:

1. Move the mouse pointer to the split bar until the shape changes (you will see a white bar with up and down arrows).

2. Double-click the mouse. Alternatively, use the ⌘-Option-S keyboard shortcut.

After you split the window, you can easily adjust the location of the split in the document. Just move the pointer to the split bar until the mouse pointer changes shape, and then drag up or down.

To remove the split, just double-click the split bar or press ⌘-Option-S. If you are displaying different parts of the document, the part displayed in the bottom pane will remain on-screen.

TIP

If you want to keep the top pane on-screen after you remove the window split, just drag the split bar off the bottom of the vertical scroll bar.

Sizing a Window

To quickly reduce the window to a smaller size—called the alternative size/location—you can click the Zoom box or double-click the title bar. Just which size Word chooses for the alternative size/location depends on how many documents are currently open, how large a screen you are using, and other factors. Generally, Word shrinks the document by approximately 50 percent.

After you reduce a window's size, you can zoom it back to its original size by clicking the Zoom box again or by double-clicking the title bar.

Another way to change a window's size is to use the size box in the window's lower right corner. Just drag the size box in any direction to change the window's size.

After you size a window using the size box, the size you have chosen becomes the window's alternative size/location for the current Word session. When you click the Zoom box (or double-click the title bar), Word restores the window's original size. If you click the Zoom box (or double-click the title bar) again, Word restores the size you chose when you manually resized the window.

If you want to work with two documents on-screen at once, this technique automatically sizes them so that the screen area is split between them:

1. Open the first document.

2. Click the Zoom box.

   Word shrinks the document to its alternative size/position, which fills the top half of the screen.

3. Open the second document.

4. Click the second document's zoom box.

   Word shrinks the document to its alternative size/position, filling the bottom half of the screen.

Chapter 2

Understanding Word's Workplace

Moving Windows

You can move a window's position on the desktop by dragging the title bar. After moving the window, you can restore its original location by clicking the Zoom box.

When you move a window, the new location you choose becomes the window's alternate position. Suppose that you move a window and then click the Zoom box to restore its original location. Then you click the Zoom box again: Word moves the window back to the location you chose.

Closing Windows

Before closing a window, save your work by choosing Save or Save As from the File menu (or use the ⌘-S keyboard shortcut). Then click the Close box, choose Close from the File menu, or use the ⌘-W keyboard shortcut.

Exploring Word's Views

ord's View menu includes commands that toggle three of the program's four view options on and off (see fig. 2.15). You will find the fourth View option, Print Preview, in the Print menu.

Users of previous versions of Word will find many changes here. The menus have been reorganized so that these View options are grouped together, and the former Page View has been named Page Layout view. In addition, the keyboard shortcuts for these views have changed.

Writing and Editing in Normal View

Word's Normal view, shown in figure 2.16, offers the fastest screen updating and is the best choice for day-to-day writing. Normal view is the default view. You can change the default view by choosing Preferences from the Tools menu, as explained in Chapter 27. You can see most character and paragraph formats on-screen, and you can even see graphics. Some formats, however, do not appear in Normal view the same way they will appear when printed.

Fig. 2.15
The View menu.

View	
✓Normal	⌘⌥N
Outline	⌘⌥O
Page Layout	⌘⌥P
✓Ribbon	⌘⌥R
✓Ruler	⌘R
Print Merge Helper...	
Show ¶	⌘J
Header	
Footer	
Footnotes	⌘⇧⌥S

In Page Layout view, you see most formats on-screen the way they will print, including the formats you don't see in Normal view. These formats include newspaper columns, headers and footers, footnotes, page numbers, and frames that you anchor to an absolute position on the page.

You still create text in these formats in Normal view. The Normal view displays text in one continuous stream of text, with page breaks shown by a dotted line across the screen. When you type newspaper columns (multiple columns), you don't see the multiple-column layout on-screen; the text appears in a single, narrow column.

If you fix text or graphics to an absolute position on the page, using the Frame option in the Format menu (as discussed in Chapter 21), the position isn't shown on-screen. Instead, you see the text or graphics in line with the rest of the text. In figure 2.16, for example, the headings are shown in line with the rest of the text. Page Layout view, shown later in figure 2.18, shows you how the headings will appear when printed.

SPEED KEY

To display a document in Normal view, choose Normal from the View menu or use the ⌘-Option-N shortcut.

Working in Outline View

In Outline view, you see your document shown as an outline, with the text hidden from view (see fig. 2.17). You must code your headings with Word's built-in heading styles (such as Heading 1 and Heading 2) if you want to view your headings and subheadings as outline headings. In Outline view, you can see the logical structure of your document, and more importantly, you can restructure your document quickly by rearranging headings on the outline. You learn more about Word's Outline view in Chapter 3.

Fig. 2.16
Normal view of a
document.

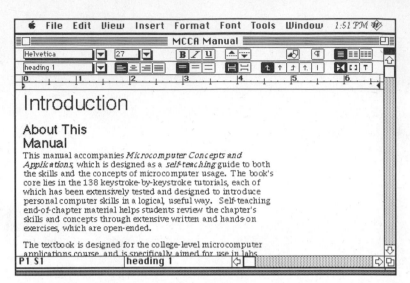

To view your document in Outline view, choose Outline from the View menu or use the ⌘-Option-O keyboard shortcut. If you have an extended keyboard, you also can use the Shift-F13 keyboard shortcut.

Fig. 2.17
Outline view of a
document.

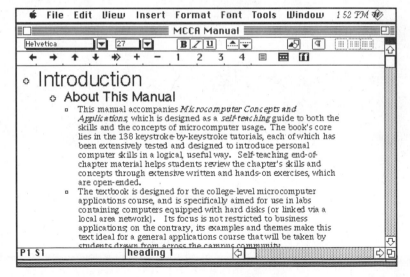

Part I
Getting Started

Viewing the Page Layout

In Word's Page Layout view, shown in figure 2.18, you see and edit your document on-screen almost as it will appear when printed. The program displays the page, using the text's actual size. Visible on-screen are headers, footers, page numbers, newspaper columns, footnotes, and frames that you have absolutely positioned on the page.

Fig. 2.18
Page Layout View.

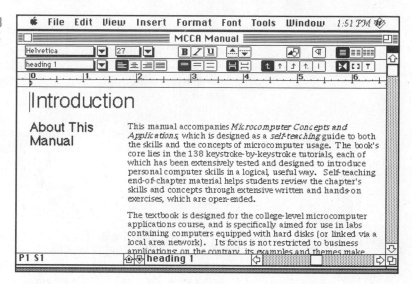

Word runs sluggishly on standard Mac systems, so you may want to switch to Page Layout for only a final preview and cosmetic edit before printing. If you have a Mac based on the 68030 microprocessor, however, you can make Page Layout the default view for writing and editing. For information on changing the default view, see Chapter 27.

SPEED KEY

To display your document in Page Layout view, choose Page Layout from the View menu or use the ⌘-Option-P shortcut.

You will want to remember these important points about Page Layout view:

■ When you add headers, footers, and footnotes in Page Layout view, Word doesn't display a separate window, like it does in Normal view. Instead, the program moves the insertion point to the text area where the text will actually appear when printed.

■ Unlike Normal view, you can directly edit headers, footers, page numbers, multiple-column text, and text that you have fixed to a position on the page. To edit any of these areas, just move the insertion point to these areas and use Word's normal text entry and editing features.

■ You can page through your document by clicking the down and up paging buttons, which appear within the style area when you switch to Page Layout view. Just remember that scrolling the screen doesn't move the insertion point; if you want to type or edit in a page to which you have just scrolled, click the insertion point on this page.

■ In Normal view, the Ruler always places the zero (0) at the left margin you have established for the document. In Page Layout view, the zero is positioned at the left boundary for the current text area.

■ If you choose Show ¶ in the View menu, you see gray lines that demarcate the boundaries of text areas, such as columns, headings, headers, footers, footnotes, and frames (paragraphs that have been fixed to an absolute position on the page).

■ If you create mathematical formulas using Word's built-in mathematical typesetting language, Page Layout view displays the formulas as they will appear when printed.

■ If you prefer to move the cursor with the keyboard, note that special cursor-movement keys become available in Page Layout view. These keys enable you to move the cursor quickly from one text area to the next. For more information on these keys, see Chapter 4.

Use this nifty trick to view and edit your document in Page Layout view without sacrificing the Normal view's speed. Divide the window into two panes. Place the insertion point in the top pane and choose Page Layout from the View menu. Leave the bottom pane in Normal view. You can work as fast as you want in the bottom pane and view the results in the top pane, where Word's beautiful Page Layout view shows you just how it will appear when printed.

Previewing the Printed Page

Print Preview closely resembles Page Layout view in that it displays all formats as they will appear when printed (see fig. 2.19). Print Preview, however, isn't editable: you cannot make changes to the text.

Fig. 2.19
Print Preview.

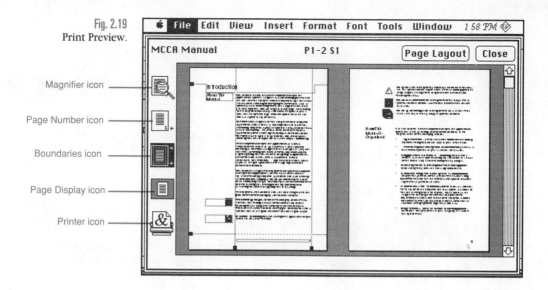

Magnifier icon

Page Number icon

Boundaries icon

Page Display icon

Printer icon

Why use Print Preview, when Page Layout view is available? Page Layout view always shows your text full size, but not all Mac users have a full-page display. Print Preview automatically reduces the size of the page so that one or two pages fit in whatever screen you happen to be using. Although the text becomes difficult or impossible to read on small screens, you still can see the overall page layout.

Another good reason for using Print Preview is that you can adjust many formats interactively by dragging them around on the screen. The following quick overview briefly describes the formats you can adjust in Print Preview:

Page and Column Breaks. You can adjust a bad page or column break by dragging the page break symbol. For more information, see Chapter 7.

Margins. Does the text appear unbalanced on the screen? You can reposition the margins for your document by dragging the handles (the small black squares) that appear on the margins' boundary lines. For more information, see Chapter 8.

Frames. You can format a paragraph or graphic so that it is fixed in an absolute position on the page: It won't budge if you insert or delete text above it, and if its width is less than the column width, text will flow around it. The space set aside for this absolute position is called a *frame*. In Print Preview, you can move frames by dragging them with the mouse. For more information, see Chapter 21.

Chapter 2
Understanding Word's Workplace

Headers and Footers. A *header* is text that repeats on all the pages of your document (or a section of your document), and is positioned within the top margin. A *footer* appears within the bottom margin. After you create headers and/or footers for your document, you can adjust the position of headers and footers just by dragging them around. For more information, see Chapter 15.

Page Numbers. You can adjust the position of page numbers, which are inserted with either Print Preview's Page Number icon or with the Section dialog box. For more information, see Chapter 15.

To view your document in Print Preview, follow these steps:

1. In Normal or Page Layout view, display the page you want to preview.

2. Choose Print Preview from the File menu or use the ⌘-Option-I keyboard shortcut. If you have an extended keyboard, you can press Option-F13.

   When you choose Print Preview from the File menu, Word automatically sizes the document so that you can see two full pages in the display that you're using. The program also paginates the document and displays the page you were viewing when you chose the command.

While viewing your document in Print Preview, you can take advantage of the icons along the left side of the screen (refer to fig. 2.19).

For a quick guide to the Print Preview icons and what they do, see the following list:

Magnifier Icon. Click this icon to turn the pointer into a magnifying glass. To magnify a portion of the page, move the magnifying glass to the place you want magnified and click again. You see a magnified view of your text (see fig. 2.20). After you switch to magnified view, you can scroll the screen just as you would in the reduced view. To switch back to the reduced view, click the Magnifier icon again. As a shortcut, you must double-click the mouse where you want to magnify.

Page Number Icon. To quickly add page numbers to a document, click on the Page Number icon and drag the page number to the place you want the page numbers to print. Then click outside the page to update the screen. To insert page numbers 0.5 inch from the top and right of the page, double-click the Page Number icon. If you want to remove page numbers you have added this way, click the Boundaries icon to display the boundaries around the page number you have inserted. Then drag the page number off the page, and click outside the page to update the screen.

Fig. 2.20
Using the Magnifier icon to magnify text.

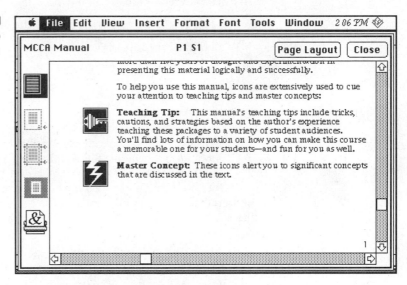

Boundaries Icon. When you click the Boundaries icon, Word displays the boundaries of text areas, such as columns, headers, and footnotes. The boundaries you can adjust are shown with handles (black squares). Note the handles on the left page in figure 2.19. By dragging these handles, you can adjust the boundaries of the text area for your document. Note that the change affects all the pages, not just the one shown.

Page Display Icon. You can display either two facing pages (with the even-numbered page on the left and odd-numbered page on the right) or a single page. To toggle between these two options, click the Page Display icon.

Printer Icon. Click this icon to print your document. You will see the Print dialog box, just as you would if you chose Print from the File menu.

Within Print Preview, special keys and procedures come into play for scrolling your document.

To display the next or previous page or pages, do one of the following:

- Click the bottom or top scroll arrows.

Chapter 2

Understanding Word's Workplace

- Click below or above the scroll box.
- Press the down- or up-arrow key.

To exit Print Preview, do one of the following:

- Click the Cancel button to return to the previous view.
- Click the Page Layout View button to return to the Page Layout view for the current page.

Displaying the Ribbon and Ruler

icrosoft's programmers are responsible for many user interface innovations, including the Tool Bar that appears in Microsoft Excel, and now in Version 5 of Microsoft Word. The Tool Bar makes the most commonly used operations available through the use of buttons that are constantly displayed in a bar running across the top of the document. Word has two such bars: the *ribbon* and the *ruler* (see fig. 2.21).

New to Word 5 is the *ribbon*, which you use to format characters, display and edit graphics, show or hide the paragraph marks, and even choose multiple-column formats. (The term "ribbon" suggests an analogy to a typewriter; these are the options that affect how your text will appear when printed.) Using the ribbon, you can choose fonts, font sizes, emphases (bold, italic, and underline), add superscripts or subscripts, show or hide the paragraph marks, and choose multiple-column layouts.

You use the *ruler* to format paragraphs. With the ruler, you can choose styles, alignments (such as flush left, centered, or justified), line spacing, blank lines before a paragraph, tabs, and indents.

Fig. 2.21
The ribbon and ruler.

Ribbon
Ruler

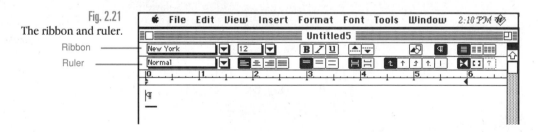

TIP

If you want Word to open documents without the ribbon and ruler, you can change Word's defaults. For information, see Chapter 27.

Formatting with the ribbon and ruler will be discussed later in this book. For now you will just learn how to toggle them off and on. By default, the ribbon and ruler both appear at the top of every new document window. If you're using a 9-inch or 12-inch screen, the ribbon and ruler take up a lot of room, so you may want to toggle them off until needed.

To hide or display the ribbon, choose Ribbon from the View menu, or use the ⌘-Option-R keyboard shortcut.

To hide or display the ruler, choose Ruler from the View menu, or use the ⌘-R keyboard shortcut.

Quitting Word

Don't quit Word by just shutting off the power—it's bad for Word, and it's bad for your Mac. Always quit Word by choosing Quit from the File menu; then turn off your Mac by choosing Shut Down from the Special menu in the Finder. As the following paragraphs explain, your files and computer are protected only when you properly quit Word and shut down your Mac.

When you quit Word by choosing Quit from the File menu or by using the ⌘-Q shortcut, the program checks to see whether you have saved all your work—including work in documents that may be hidden under the windows you have opened on the screen. In addition, the program saves any configuration and default choices that you have made during the operating session and deletes the many temporary files the program created while you were working. In short: Quitting Word properly safeguards you from lost work, preserves your choices, and keeps unnecessary files from filling up your disk.

When you shut down your Macintosh by choosing Shut Down from the Special menu before turning the power off, the Finder saves your choices and places your hard disk's read/write heads in a location where they're less likely to harmed by accidental jostling. In short: Shutting down your Mac properly saves your configuration choices and may protect your hard disk from fatal damage.

Quick Review

This section concisely summarizes the most useful information in this chapter. Check "Productivity Tips" for a review of high-productivity tips and tricks, and review "Techniques" when you forget how to perform a specific procedure.

Chapter 2

Understanding Word's Workplace

Productivity Tips

■ If you're a good typist and prefer to keep your hands on the keyboard, learn how to access menus and dialog box options with the keyboard.

■ Don't bother deleting text from text boxes if you want to replace this text completely. When a text box is highlighted, just start typing to delete all the existing text.

■ In a dialog box, pressing Return or Enter is the same as choosing OK, just as pressing Esc is the same as choosing Cancel.

■ In a list box that contains folder names, remember that you can quickly open a folder and display its files by highlighting the folder and pressing ⌘-down arrow. Press ⌘-up arrow to move back up through the folder hierarchy.

■ If a command has unwanted effects, choose Undo immediately, before doing any additional typing or choosing any additional commands.

■ Learn to use the hotspots! They bring up dialog boxes immediately, without a lot of fussing with the menus or keyboard.

■ Familiarize yourself with the Repeat command. Use it to enter a word or phrase repeatedly and to copy paragraph formats from one paragraph to several others.

■ To work with two documents, learn the procedure that automatically splits the screen area between them.

■ On most systems, write and edit in Normal view, then switch to Page Layout view for a final preview before printing. If you're using a Mac with a small (9-inch) screen, preview your document with Print Preview instead.

■ If you're working with the 9-inch or 12-inch screen, you may prefer to hide the ribbon or ruler until needed.

■ Use the Preferences command (Tools menu) to enable Fast Saves if you plan to work with lengthy documents. Be sure to activate the Save Reminder option to remind you to save your documents frequently. Wise users save at 10- to 15-minute intervals.

■ Back up your work frequently. A file isn't safe if the only copy is on your hard disk! Use the Finder to copy the file to a floppy disk.

■ Quit Word properly. Choose Quit from the File menu. Don't just shut off the power while Word's still on-screen.

Techniques

This section provides concise, quick-reference summaries of all the procedures introduced in this chapter.

Choosing Commands

To access a pull-down menu:

1. Press ⌘-Tab or Keypad-period.

2. Use the arrow keys to choose the menu you want. Alternatively, type the menu name's first letter or a number from 1 (File) to 7 (Tools).

To choose an option from a menu:

1. Press the down-arrow key until you highlight the menu option you want. Alternatively, press the option's first letter.

2. Press Return or Enter.

To open a menu other than the one you have just displayed:

Hold down the Shift key and press the menu's first letter.

To move the highlight to the next text box in a dialog box:

Press Tab.

To move the highlight to the previous text box in a dialog box:

Press Shift-Tab.

To select the next option, list, text area, or button in a dialog box:

Press ⌘-Tab.

To select the previous option, list, text area, or button in a dialog box:

Press Shift-⌘-Tab.

To activate a check box, radio button, or drop-down list box in a dialog box:

Press ⌘-space bar or Keypad-0 (zero).

To choose an item in a list box:

Use the down or up arrow keys to select the item.

To open a folder listed in a list box:

Press ⌘-down arrow.

Chapter 2
Understanding Word's Workplace

To close the current folder in a list box and display the files in the folder immediately above the current folder:

Press ⌘-up arrow.

To cancel your choices in a dialog box:

Press Esc or click the Close box.

To confirm your choices and close the dialog box:

Press Return.

To repeat typing or the last command:

Choose Repeat from the Edit menu (⌘-Y).

To undo typing or the last command:

Choose Undo from the Edit menu (⌘-Z or F1).

Displaying the Ribbon and Ruler

To hide or display the ribbon:

Choose Ribbon from the View menu, or press ⌘-Option-R.

To hide or display the ruler:

Choose Ruler from the View menu, or press ⌘-R.

Quitting Word

To quit Word and shut off your Macintosh:

1. Choose Quit from the File menu.

2. Choose Shut Down from the Special menu.

3. If necessary, switch off the power.

Working with Windows

To open a new window:

Choose Open from the File menu (⌘-O) to open an existing document.

or

Choose New from the File menu (⌘-N) to create a new document.

Part I

Getting Started

To open an additional window on a document:

>   Choose New Window from the Window menu.

To activate a window:

>   Click within the window.
>
>   or
>
>   Choose the window's name from the Window menu.
>
>   or
>
>   Press ⌘-Option-W until you have activated the window.

To split a document window:

>   Drag the split bar down the vertical scroll bar, until you have positioned the split where you want it, then release the mouse button.
>
>   or
>
>   Double-click the split bar (⌘-Option-S) to split the window into two equal-sized panes.

To adjust the split:

>   Drag the split bar up or down.

To remove the split and keep the bottom pane on-screen:

>   Double-click the split bar.
>
>   or
>
>   Use the ⌘-Option-S shortcut.
>
>   or
>
>   Drag the split bar down the vertical scroll bar until it disappears off the bottom of the window.

To size a window:

>   Drag the size box in any direction.

To toggle between the original and a smaller size or different location:

>   Click the Zoom box.
>
>   or
>
>   Double-click the title bar.

To move a window:

Drag on the title bar.

To close a window:

Click the Close box.

or

Choose Close from the File menu (⌘-W).

Creating and Saving Text

Word is the consummate writer's tool. Even if you seldom use the program's advanced formatting capabilities, Word is well worth the money (and the time spent learning the program) for its unique combination of text-creation tools. To safeguard the text you have created, you should master saving techniques, which also are discussed in this chapter. The following is an overview of the chapter's treatment of creating and saving text:

■ *Creating Text with Word*. This chapter shows you how to change the default font to one that takes full advantage of your printer's capabilities. You learn how to include special characters and symbols while you write and how to control line breaks. You learn about Word's spaces, hyphens, and the en- and em-dashes you need for desktop publishing applications. This chapter also shows you how to control Word's page breaks.

■ *Finding the Right Word with Thesaurus*. Word's Thesaurus command helps you find the words you need to express the right meaning for your documents.

■ *Saving Documents*. You learn several ways to save documents with Word, including saving your document in ASCII (plain text) format for telecommunications and other purposes.

Typing Text

Typing a document with Word is simpler than working with a typewriter. You can type the text without worrying about typing past the right margin, and you can make corrections with Delete (Backspace) as you go. The text is not printed until you revise and proof it.

When you type your document, you can use many special features of Word. In this section, you learn when to use the Return, Tab, and Shift-Return (new line) keys. You also learn how to choose a new default font for your document. You investigate the use of the Macintosh's many special characters, and you learn how to control line and page breaks with precision.

Moving from a Typewriter to a Word Processor

Typing a document with Word is much easier than using a typewriter, but you need to keep the following points in mind:

■ Don't press the Return or Enter keys at the end of a line; Word wraps text at the right margin down to the next line. Press Return only to start a new paragraph or to end a line before it reaches the right margin.

■ Always align text with tabs instead of pressing the space bar. Most of the fonts you use with Word are proportionally spaced fonts; the letters vary in width (the *m* and *w* are wider than the *i* and *l*). Word doesn't show these width differences on-screen. If you use spaces to align text, the result may look aligned on-screen, but not when printed. To indent text to start a new paragraph, for example, press Tab instead of entering five spaces.

> **TIP**
>
> For desktop publishing applications, you needn't press the space bar twice at the end of each sentence. Typeset-quality text lacks the typescript's two spaces after each period.

Inserting the Date

If you're typing a letter or report, you don't have to type today's date: Word can insert the current date for you. To insert the current date at the insertion point's location, choose Date from the Insert menu. Word inserts a date in the following format: December 21, 1991.

> **TIP**
>
> If you frequently type the current time in your documents, follow the procedure detailed in Chapter 27 to add the Time command to the Insert menu.

Part I

Getting Started

Working with Paragraphs

In Word, a *paragraph* is any unit of text that ends with a paragraph mark. By this definition, a one-word, centered heading that ends with a paragraph mark is a paragraph. The following examples are paragraphs:

A Heading¶

¶

P1X14-J   (Stock No. 14-0119)   Quantity: 112¶

¶

This paragraph is more like a traditional paragraph—a unit of meaning that develops and expresses a concept. All its sentences are unified and pertain to the concept it's discussing. Word cannot distinguish, however, between the two preceding "paragraphs" and a real paragraph such as this one. The program only detects a series of characters followed by a paragraph mark.

Actually, five paragraphs are in the preceding examples. Even a solitary paragraph mark is a paragraph.

Keep this definition in mind when you work with Word, because it has many implications for formatting and other purposes. Many of Word's formatting commands act on a whole paragraph of text. The Centered Alignment button in the ruler, for example, acts on the paragraph where the insertion point is positioned.

In this book, the word paragraph refers to paragraphs in Word's sense. You explore methods to split and join paragraphs and to start new lines without starting a new paragraph.

Splitting Paragraphs

To split a paragraph, follow these steps:

1. Place the insertion point where you want the paragraph break to occur.

2. Press Return.

Word splits the paragraph, leaving the insertion point at the beginning of the new paragraph.

TIP

When you work with paragraphs, be sure to display the paragraph marks (choose Show ¶ from the View menu, or use the ⌘-J shortcut). If the paragraph marks are displayed, you can see what you're doing when you join, split, and edit paragraphs.

Chapter 3
Creating and Saving Text

You usually split paragraphs because you want to add some text to the end of the first part of the original paragraph. You can use a command to split the paragraph and leave the cursor at the end of the first part of the original paragraph, as in the following steps:

1. Place the insertion point where you want the paragraph break to occur.

2. Press ⌘-Option-Return.

Joining Paragraphs

To join two paragraphs, follow these steps:

1. Select the paragraph mark at the end of the first paragraph.

2. Press Delete (Backspace).

3. If necessary, add one or two spaces between the joined sentences.

When you join two paragraphs that have different formats, you lose the first paragraph's formats, and the joined paragraph takes on the format of the former second paragraph. If you want the joined paragraph to have the first paragraph's format, you must choose the paragraph formats again.

Inserting a Line Break

You can start a new line before the text reaches the right margin without starting a new paragraph by using the New Line command (Shift-Enter). When you press Shift-Enter, Word moves the insertion point to the beginning of the next line but does not place a paragraph mark in your document. Instead, the program places a new line mark in your document, as shown in figure 3.1.

The New Line command keeps lines together that you want to treat as a unit for formatting or sorting purposes. Suppose that you type a mailing list with the names listed last name first. If you type each name and address as a unit with the lines separated by New Line marks except for the last line, you can use Word's Sort command (Tools menu) to alphabetize all the names and addresses.

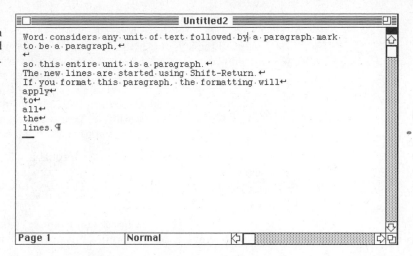

Fig. 3.1
New lines started with
New Line command
(Shift-Enter).

Inserting a Blank Line

Don't space your paragraphs by pressing Return twice. This method creates problems when you use formatting options, such as Keep with Next option in the Paragraph dialog box. See Chapter 7 for more information on formatting paragraphs.

To add a blank line before a paragraph, follow these steps:

1. Place the insertion point in the paragraph.

2. Click the Blank Line button on the ruler (see fig. 3.2).

Fig. 3.2
The Blank Line button
on the ruler.

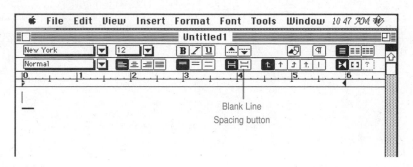

Chapter 3
Creating and Saving Text

Choosing a New Default Font

TIP

If you're not sure which font gives you the best performance on your Macintosh system, be sure to read the sections on fonts in Chapter 5.

One of the joys of the Macintosh is its fluency with fonts, but Word's default font—New York—isn't everyone's favorite. Although New York is easy to read on-screen, the ImageWriter printout of this font is far from ideal, even when you choose the best print quality. If you print with a LaserWriter or another laser printer, your Macintosh tries to translate New York to its laser substitute, Times. You may find that proportional spacing and justification are not handled well by this translation.

For these reasons and others, you probably will decide to choose another font for your documents. You can choose one of the other default Macintosh fonts, such as Helvetica, or a font you added to your Macintosh's system files.

You can choose the font you want from the Font menu when you start a new document, but performing this procedure for every document is bothersome. The solution is to create a new default font for all documents. In previous versions of Word, this procedure was tedious. With Word 5, however, creating a new default font is easy.

To define a default font for all the new Word documents you create, follow these steps:

1. Choose Default Font from the Font menu.

   Word opens the Preferences window and displays the Default Font and Default Size list boxes.

NOTE

Your Default Font list may differ from the one shown in figure 3.3, depending on which fonts you installed in your Mac's system files. For more information on fonts, see Chapter 5.

2. Drop down the Default Font list box and choose the font you want to use as the default font for all your documents. The check mark shows the current font (see fig. 3.3).

3. To choose a new default size, choose the size you want from the Default Size list box. If the size is not on the list, type it in the box.

4. After you choose the font and font size you want, click the close box to confirm your choices and close the Preferences window.

   You can change the default font again by repeating these steps.

Using Special Characters

For anyone who uses foreign-language or technical characters when writing, the Macintosh is truly a pleasure to use. Depending on the font you use, you can access many special characters by holding down Option or Shift-Option when you press a key. To see the characters available, you have three options: you can use the Key Caps desk accessory; you can use Word 5's new Symbol command (Insert menu) to find and enter special characters; or you can use Word's zero-width characters to enter accent marks.

Fig. 3.3
The Default Font list box in the Preferences window.

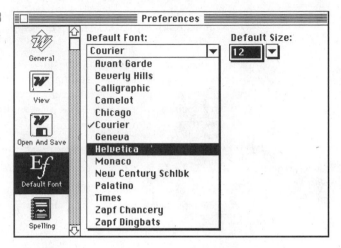

If you plan to use a character extensively and need to memorize its keyboard location, use Key Caps to help locate the key. If you need to insert a character and don't care where it's located on the keyboard, the Symbols command is easier to use than Key Caps. To enter an accented character, use the zero-width characters. The sections to follow detail each procedure.

Using the Key Caps Desk Accessory

The Key Caps desk accessory displays a keyboard map on-screen. By displaying this map, you can see which characters are available with a given font. If you installed the Key Caps desk accessory when you installed your Macintosh system software, you will find Key Caps in the Apple (🍎) menu at the left of the menu bar.

To use Key Caps, pull down the Apple menu and choose Key Caps. Choose a font from the Key Caps menu, and then press Option to see the characters available.

If you press a key on the keyboard while using Key Caps, the character you type appears in the text box. You can select the character, choose Copy or Cut from the Edit menu, and paste it in your Word document by choosing Paste from the Edit menu in Word. If you prefer, you can type the character directly in your Word document by holding down the Option key and pressing a key on the keyboard. To enter a bullet (a dot), for example, hold down the Option key and press 8 (on the keyboard, not the keypad).

Plenty of resources for desktop publishing and dressing up your Word documents are available among your Macintosh's many characters. Table 3.1 shows some useful characters and symbols found in most standard Macintosh fonts, such as Helvetica, Times-Roman, Palatino, and New York.

Table 3.1
Useful Characters and Symbols for Desktop Publishing

To enter	Press
• (bullet)	Option-8
¶ (paragraph mark)	Option-7
™ (trademark)	Option-2
° (degree)	Shift-Option-8
® (registered trademark)	Option-R
© (copyright)	Option-G
« (European quote mark)	Option-\
» (European quote mark)	Shift-Option-\
. . . (ellipsis)	Option-;

Using the Symbol Command

New to Word 5, the Symbol command displays a dialog box listing all the characters available for the current font (see fig. 3.4). You can quickly enter a whole series of special characters by clicking them in the Symbol dialog box. Each character you click appears in your document at the insertion point's location.

Fig. 3.4
The Symbol dialog box.

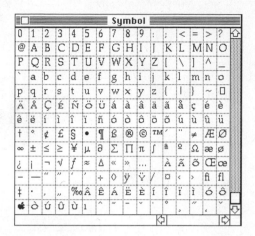

To use the Symbol dialog box to enter special characters, follow these steps:

1. Place the insertion point where you want the special character to appear.

2. Choose the font you want to use from the Font menu.

3. Choose Symbol from the Insert menu, or press ⌘-Option-Q.

   The Symbol dialog box appears.

4. Click one or more characters you want to use.

   When you click each character, Word enters the character in your document. At the bottom of the dialog box, Word displays the decimal code (and key or key combination) for this character.

5. Click the Close box when you finish choosing characters.

Your System file probably includes fonts that have many more special characters. Figure 3.5 shows some of the special characters available with the Symbol font. Figure 3.6 shows a portion of the Zapf Dingbats characters. The Cairo font has even more graphic images and symbols.

SPEED KEY

NOTE

If you forgot to choose the font before choosing the Symbol command, you still can access the Font menu.

Chapter 3
Creating and Saving Text

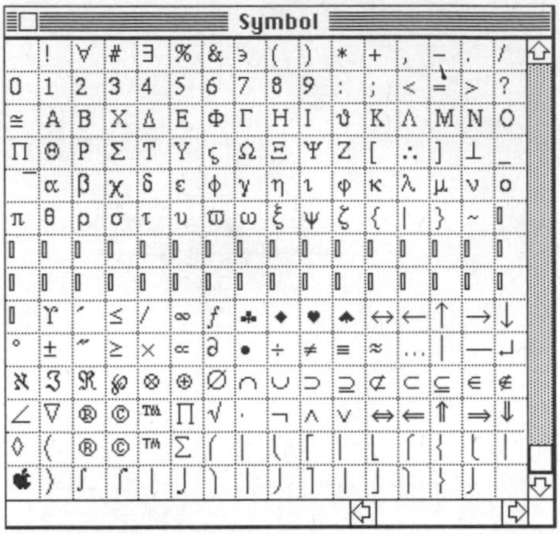

Fig. 3.5
Special characters
(Symbol font).

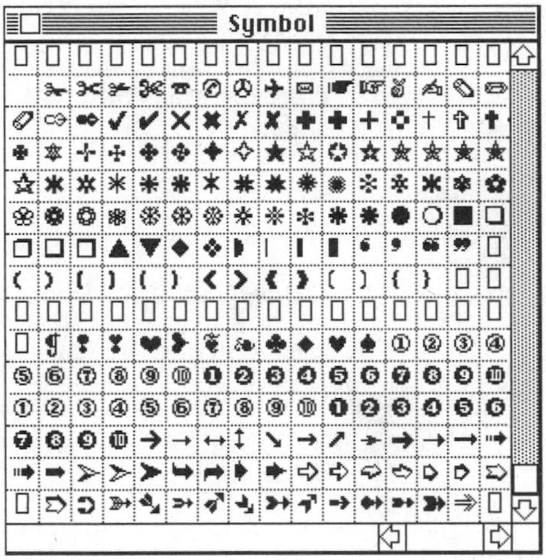

Fig. 3.6
Special characters (Zapf
Dingbats font).

Entering Accent Marks

Use the zero-width characters listed in table 3.2 to enter diacritical marks
such as accents or umlauts. A zero-width character is a character that,
when entered, does not advance the insertion point to the next space.
To use these characters, press the keys for the character (the insertion
point doesn't advance), and then press a letter key. Word enters the
mark and the letter together. To enter the zero-width character by itself,
press the Option key combination twice.

Table 3.2 Zero-Width Characters	*Press*	*To enter*
	Option-`	Grave accent (à)
	Option-e	Acute accent (à)
	Option-i	Circumflex (^)
	Option-n	Tilde (~)
	Option-u	Umlaut (ä)

Using Smart Quotes

When you press the quote key on the keyboard, an application normally enters the ASCII code 34 character ("); the apostrophe key produces an ASCII code 39 character (').

    ASCII code 34 (quote):   "Example"
    ASCII code 39 (apostrophe): 'Example'

With Word's Smart Quotes, however, the program enters quotes and apostrophes that slant in the appropriate direction (toward the character they precede or follow):

    Smart Quote (quote):   "Example"
    Smart Quote (inverted commas)   'Example'

Word automatically uses the character that slants in the correct direction. Smart Quotes aren't confused by punctuation.

Smart Quotes is turned on by default. To turn Smart Quotes off, deactivate the Smart Quotes option in the General section of the Preferences dialog box.

You can save your document to ASCII text so that you can give your file to colleagues or coworkers who don't use Word. If you do, turn off Smart Quotes before creating such a document. When you use Smart Quotes, Word doesn't enter the ASCII code 34 or 39 characters; it uses characters assigned the decimal codes 210, 211, 212, and 213 in most Macintosh fonts. These characters aren't part of the standard ASCII character set and display as garbage characters on the other end of the transfer.

Using Hyphens and Nonbreaking Spaces

Word offers a variety of hyphens you can use to improve your document's appearance and gain control over how Word breaks lines. You can even use Word's Hyphenation command (Tools menu) to look up correct hyphen locations for a selected word. The sections to follow detail the uses of hyphens and the Hyphenation command.

Adding Hyphens and Dashes

The following list gives a quick overview of the hyphens and dashes available:

- *Normal Hyphen* (-). To enter a normal hyphen, press the hyphen key (-). Word breaks a line after the hyphen but not before it. The name Erskine-Brown, for example, might be broken as follows:

    Erskine-

    Brown

    But never like this:

    Erskine

    -Brown

- *Em Dash* (Shift-Option-hyphen). In typesetting, an em dash is a long dash used to indicate a break in the flow of a sentence—like this one—that's less pronounced than parentheses. With typewriters, people usually type two hyphens to indicate an em dash. Using two hyphens in Word can cause problems. If Word needs to break the line within the dash, it will do so. Using the em dash prevents bad line breaks; the program treats the em dash as if it were an ordinary hyphen.

- *En Dash* (Option-hyphen). The en dash is shorter than an em dash but longer than a normal hyphen. Some style handbooks require that the en dash be used in place of all normal hyphens. Others restrict the usage of the en dash to specialized contexts, such as compound words (audio–visual). If you're preparing a document for publication in a professional context, consult the style handbook relevant to the field in which you're working to determine when to use en dashes.

- *Nonbreaking Hyphen* (⌘-~). In the preceding example, Word placed a line break within a proper, hyphenated noun—a no-no in most style handbooks. To prevent Word from breaking up a hyphenated proper noun, you can use a nonbreaking hyphen.

To enter a nonbreaking hyphen, press ⌘-~ (tilde). The tilde is to the right of the space bar on most keyboards. (You don't have to press Shift to type the tilde because ⌘-` works too.)

■ *Optional Hyphen* (⌘-hyphen). If you type an especially long word, such as *anticonstructivism*, Word might leave large gaps between words when it aligns the right margin of your document. This problem becomes acute when you're working with short line lengths (less than 3 inches) or with right-justified text. You can solve this problem by using optional hyphens in long words. The hyphen is used only when Word needs it to align the right margin.

When you choose Show ¶ from the View menu, Word displays optional hyphens and inserts special symbols indicating which hyphens you chose. These symbols, normal hyphens, em dashes, and en dashes are shown in figure 3.7.

Fig. 3.7
Word's hyphens and
dashes.

```
normal·hyphen·◆            -¶
em·dash◆                   —¶
en·dash◆                   –¶
nonbreaking·hyphen◆        ≈¶
optional·hyphen◆           ¬¶
```

If you choose Hide ¶, the optional hyphens disappear (except where they are needed to align the right margin).

Looking Up Hyphen Breaks

Word's Hyphenation command (Tools menu) inserts optional hyphens where needed throughout your document. Word inserts hyphens only in those words that need hyphens so that the right margin appears more even. You shouldn't use this feature when you write, except to hyphenate an occasional lengthy word (as explained momentarily). If you later insert or delete text to your document, most of the optional hyphens Word inserts will not be needed, and the words that need optional hyphens will not have them.

Run automatic hyphenation as part of the proofing process, just before you print your document. Automatic hyphenation is discussed in Chapter 9.

If you're not sure where to place optional hyphens in a lengthy word, the Hyphenation command can come in handy.

To look up hyphen breaks, follow these steps:

1. Type the word you want to look up. For example, type *dysfunctional*.

2. Highlight the word.

3. Choose Hyphenation from the Tools menu.

   The Hyphenation dialog box appears (see fig. 3.8). Note that Word shows where *dysfunctional* can be hyphenated, and the program proposes to place an optional hyphen as follows: `dys-functional`.

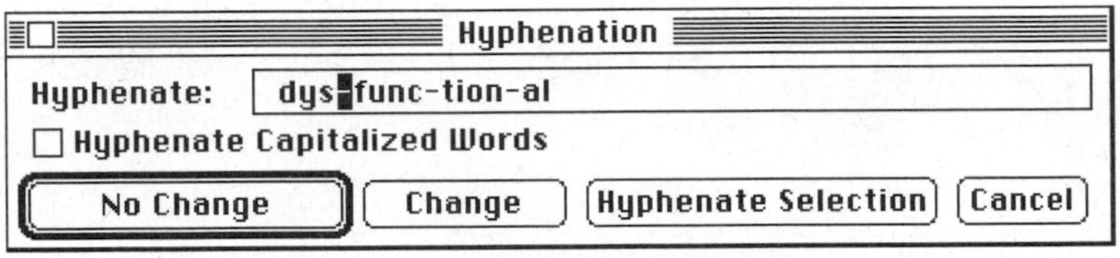

Fig. 3.8
The Hyphenation
dialog box.

☐	═══════════ Hyphenation ═══════════
Hyphenate:	dys█func-tion-al
☐ **Hyphenate Capitalized Words**	
	[No Change] (Change) (Hyphenate Selection) (Cancel)

4. To insert a hyphen at one of the other locations Word identifies, click the hyphen at that location. To insert the optional hyphen, choose Change. Word inserts the optional hyphen and closes the dialog box.

Word's Hyphenation utility relies on a sophisticated hyphenation program that can hyphenate almost any English word. This program, however, is not infallible. Occasionally it inserts a hyphen in the wrong place. If you're publishing your document directly from Word printouts, be sure to proofread all of Word's hyphen breaks carefully.

Using Nonbreaking Spaces

Some style handbooks consider breaking a line between two parts of a proper noun (such as El Capitan or Sri Lanka) bad form. You can prevent line breaks between words that aren't hyphenated by entering a nonbreaking space between them (Option-space bar or ⌘-space bar).

If you chose the Show ¶ option in the Edit menu, Word displays nonbreaking spaces as a tilde over the tiny dot that usually appears when you press the space bar.

Inserting a Page Break

By default, Word inserts page breaks as you type. This feature is called *background pagination*. (You can turn background pagination off by using the Preferences dialog box, but you should have no reason to do so unless you're working with a lengthy document.)

The page breaks Word inserts are called *soft page breaks*. They're indicated in Normal view by a row of dots across the screen. The position of a soft page break isn't fixed; the program adjusts the soft page break's location as you insert or delete text. In Page Layout view, you see the effects of soft pages breaks when Word paginates and displays your document.

Sometimes you may want to break a page before it's filled with text (to set off a title page from the body of a document, for example). A page break you enter manually is called a *hard page break*. To enter a hard page break, choose the Insert Page Break option from the Insert menu or use the Shift-Enter keyboard shortcut. You can distinguish between soft and hard page breaks on-screen because the line marking a hard page break has twice as many dots (see fig. 3.9).

Fig. 3.9
Soft and hard page breaks.

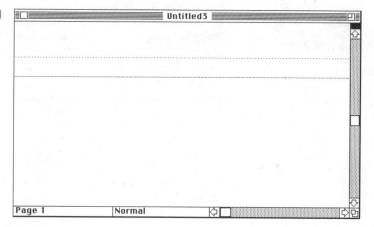

To remove a hard page break, move the mouse pointer to the selection bar (the column to the extreme left on-screen). When the mouse pointer becomes an arrow pointing up and to the right, click the mouse to select the page break and then press Delete or Backspace. You cannot delete a soft page break this way.

Create hard page breaks only when necessary (to separate one chapter from another, for example). Don't use hard page breaks to keep text together on a page or to prevent a widowed heading (a heading that appears with no text underneath it at the bottom of a page). If you add or delete text later, the hard page break may produce an unattractive result, such as a page only half-filled with text. Choose paragraph formats, such as Keep With Next and Keep Lines Together, that prevent bad page breaks from occurring. For more information on these options, see Chapter 6.

Finding the Right Word with Thesaurus

Word 5's Thesaurus, an add-on program in previous versions, is now fully integrated with Word. You can look up synonyms of one or more words while working in a document. You also can view antonyms (words with opposite meanings).

NOTE

Unlike most other computers, the Mac assigns different functions to the Return and Enter keys. If you press Shift-Return, for example, Word inserts a line break; Word inserts a page break only if you press Shift-Enter.

To look up a word in Thesaurus, follow these steps:

1. Double-click the word you want to look up.

   Word highlights the word. If you forget to highlight the word before choosing Thesaurus, Word looks up the word in which the insertion point is positioned, or the word nearest the insertion point.

2. Choose Thesaurus from the Tools menu.

   You see the Thesaurus dialog box (see fig. 3.10). In the Meanings For list box, the various shades of meaning for the highlighted word (*great* is used here) are shown. The first meaning, *big*, is highlighted by default, and the Synonyms list box displays the synonyms of *big*.

3. To choose one of the displayed synonyms, highlight the synonym in the Synonym list box.

   To see synonyms of other meanings of the word *great*, highlight the meaning in the Meanings For list box.

   To see synonyms of words in the Synonyms list box, highlight the synonym and choose Look Up.

   To redisplay the meanings and synonyms for a word you've viewed previously, drop down the With list box and choose the word from the list.

To redisplay the word you originally looked up, choose Original.

To view antonyms of the word currently listed in the With box, choose Antonyms in the Meanings For list box. (Not all words have antonyms.)

4. After you display the right word in the With box, choose Replace. If you cannot find a better word, choose Cancel.

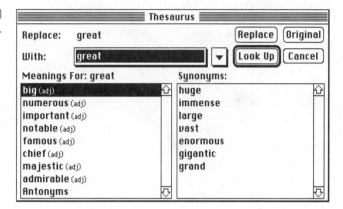

Fig. 3.10
The Thesaurus dialog box.

Saving Documents

In this section, you learn all about saving files with Word 5. Even though you already have learned how to save documents, you should still read this section carefully. Your work with the computer is highly vulnerable to accidental data loss due to careless file management.

This section begins with a discussion of your options for changing Word's file-saving defaults. You explore the Save As dialog box, both in its System 6 and System 7 guises. You learn why you should fill out those summary info dialog boxes that appear when you save a document for the first time. You also learn how to save to file formats other than Word's default, including ASCII (text) files. (A *file format* is the technique a given program uses to preserve your formatting choices. Generally, one program's file format isn't compatible with another's.)

Choosing Preferences for Saving Files

Take some time now to investigate the Open And Save options in the Preferences dialog box. To display the dialog box, choose Preferences from the Tools menu, then choose the Open and Save icon. The Open And Save preferences are shown in figure 3.11 and described in the list that follows.

Fig. 3.11
Open And Save
preferences.

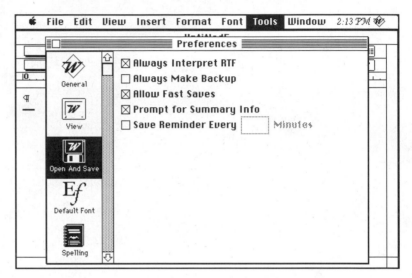

Always Interpret RTF (On). RTF stands for Rich Text Format, a Microsoft standard that enables users of different word processing programs to exchange formatted documents, even when the files are exchanged via telecommunications or mainframe computers. With this option activated, Word automatically interprets RTF documents that you open. If you have deactivated the option, you will see a dialog box when you open such a file, asking whether you want to interpret the RTF codes.

Always Make Backup (Off). If you activate this option, Word automatically makes a backup copy of your document every time you save it. An important point for you to understand and remember, however, is that this copy is made of the previous version of your document, not the one you're saving. Don't confuse this command with a well-conceived backup strategy for your

NOTE

If you activate the Always Make Backup option, Word always uses normal saves (the Fast Save option won't have any effect).

documents! (You learn more about how to back up your work later in this section.) This option also consumes a lot of disk space because it automatically keeps the previous copy of every file you save. If you really want to keep a copy of the previous version of a file, you can do so for only one file by choosing the Make Backup option in the Save As dialog box, as explained later in this section.

Allow Fast Saves (On). When Word performs a normal save, the program rewrites the whole file on disk, taking into account all your changes during an editing session. For a lengthy document, a normal save can take some time—as much as a minute or more. In a fast save, Word doesn't rewrite the whole document; it just creates a table that shows where the changes should be made. Both types of saves are safe, but fast saves consume more disk and memory space.

Prompt for Summary Info (On). With this option activated, Word displays a summary info dialog box every time you save a new document. By all means leave this feature activated and fill out those summary boxes! In Chapter 11, you will see why filling out the summary boxes makes good sense; doing so gives Word more ways to find an elusive document stored somewhere on your disk.

Save Reminder (Off). You should activate this option. When Save Reminder is activated, Word displays a dialog box that reminds you to save your work at an interval you specify (see fig. 3.12). When this dialog box appears, you just choose OK to save your work. If you don't want to save, you can postpone the reminder for 10 minutes or for an interval you specify, or you can choose Cancel. Try activating the Save Reminder option and typing 10 or 15 in the Minutes text box.

Fig. 3.12
The Save Now? dialog box.

When you finish choosing options, just click the Close box to return to your document. The changes you have made will affect all your documents, not just the one in the active window.

Chapter 3
Creating and Saving Text

Exploring the Save As Dialog Box

Word displays the Save As dialog box when you save a document for the first time. Figure 3.13 shows the Save As dialog box that appears with System 6, while figure 3.14 shows the System 7 version.

Fig. 3.13
Save As dialog box
(System 6).

Fig. 3.14
Save As dialog box
(System 7).

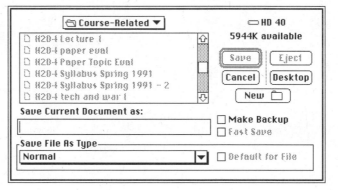

The Desktop button, which gives you a new way to change drives, is new with System 7. (To change drives with System 6, click the Drive button until you see the drive you want.) With System 7, you click the Desktop button to see a list of all the disks mounted currently on your Macintosh. To open one of the disks, just click the disk icon in the list box. Another new feature enables you to create and name a folder using the New Folder button.

Why is the System 7 Desktop button an advantage? With System 6, you can view the contents of a disk only if it is physically inserted in the disk drive. But as you may have already noticed, you can *mount* more than one disk at a time. (To *mount* a disk means to place its icon on the desktop. A disk can remain mounted even if it's no longer physically inserted in the disk drive.) For this reason, System 7's Save As dialog box enables you to choose any disk you have mounted during the current operating session.

A quick overview of the Save As dialog box's areas and features follows:

Current Folder Title. A drop-down list box at the top of the dialog box shows the current folder (the System 6 version has no drop-down arrow). To drop down the list, just point to the folder list and hold down the mouse button. You will see a list of all the folders *above* the current folder in your disk's folder hierarchy.

Document List Box. By default, this list box shows all the documents present in the current folder that Word can read. These files are displayed so that you can see what's in the current folder. In addition, the display of file names reminds you of patterns or conventions you're using to name files.

Current Drive Indicator. This feature indicates the current drive and the amount of free space remaining.

Save Current Document As. Type a name for your document here, not exceeding 31 characters, including spaces. You can use any character, including special characters, with one exception: the colon (:).

Command Buttons. Choose Open to open the document currently highlighted in the Document List Box. To switch drives with System 6, choose the Drive button; to eject a disk in a disk drive, choose Eject. To take advantage of Word 5's new Find File command (discussed in Chapter 11), choose Find File. In System 7, choose Desktop to view all the disks mounted currently on your system, or choose New Folder to create and name a new folder for your document. To exit the dialog box without opening a file, choose Cancel.

Make Backup. Activate this check box to preserve the version of the file currently on disk—the one that *doesn't* have the changes you have just made. Please note that this file is *not* a true backup copy: It isn't even a copy of the most recent version of your file.

TIP

For a good shortcut, press ⌘-Up arrow to display the documents in the directory immediately above Word's.

TIP

If you want a document's name to appear at the top of the file list box in the Open dialog box, press the space bar before typing the document's name. Use this trick for frequently accessed files. They will appear at the top of the list box, saving you the trouble of scrolling down to find their names in the list.

Chapter 3
Creating and Saving Text

You should activate this check box only if you want to preserve previous versions of your files—but as you will learn momentarily, it's much better simply to save new versions of your document with a new document name.

Fast Save. Fast Save enables you to choose Word's fast save technique for storing your file on disk. Fast saves are safe and save time if you're working with a lengthy document, but files saved with Fast Save take up more room on your disk. Word also requires more memory to perform fast saves.

Save File As Type. This drop-down list box controls the file format Word uses to save your file. The term *file format* refers to the method a program uses to store your file on disk so that your formatting choices are preserved. Few standards exist; each program uses a unique method. Word 5 saves its documents using the Normal file format by default. Note that this format is not compatible with earlier versions of Word.

If you want to exchange your files with colleagues who are using other computers, or if you want to send your file via telecommunications linkages, you need to choose a file format other than Normal. You will find a discussion of file formats elsewhere in this section.

Default for File. If you choose a file format other than Normal, you can use the Default for File check box to establish the format as the default format for the file. If you are planning to transmit your file via modem, for example, choose the Text Only with Line Breaks option in the Save File as Type list box. This option saves your document as an ASCII file, which contains nothing but the standard ASCII characters.

When you open a file that has been saved as an ASCII file, make a few changes, and save it again, Word reverts to the Normal file format, which is the default format for all Word files. To avoid this problem, you should activate the Default for File check box when you're saving to a file format other than Normal.

With this overview of the Save As dialog box completed, a comprehensive summary of the file-saving procedures follows.

SPEED KEY

To save a document for the first time, do the following:

1. Choose Save from the File menu, or press ⌘-S or Shift F7.

   The Save As dialog box appears, with the insertion point positioned in the Save Current Document As box (refer to figs. 3.13 and 3.14).

2. If you want to save the file to a different disk, use the Drive button (System 6) or the Desktop button (System 7) to activate the drive.

3. If you want to save the file to a different folder, use the current folder box to activate the folder you want. If you're using System 7, you can create and name a new folder, and make it the current folder, by choosing the New Folder button.

4. To instruct Word to preserve the existing disk file the next time you save this document, activate the Make Backup button.

5. Type the document name in the Save Current Document As box.

   You can use up to 31 characters, using any character except the colon (:).

6. Choose Save.

   If you type the name of a document that already exists, you see a dialog box asking you whether you want to replace the file. Choose No to return to the Save As dialog box, where you may choose another document name, or choose Yes to overwrite the existing document.

7. The Summary Info dialog box appears.

   If you want, fill out the Summary Info dialog box and choose OK. Alternatively, leave the box blank and choose OK, or choose Cancel to force Word to redisplay the Summary Info dialog box the next time you save. (For more information on the Summary Info dialog box, see the section "Filling Out Summary Info," later in this chapter.)

After you save the document, Word displays the number of characters saved in the page number area.

Resaving a File with the Save As Command

When you save your document for the first time, Word displays the Save As dialog box, and you name your document. The next time you save your file using the Save command or by pressing ⌘-S, you don't see this dialog box—Word just saves the document, using the exact settings you chose in the Save As dialog box (with the exception of the file format type, which reverts to Normal unless you activate the Default for File check box). You won't see the Save As dialog box again unless you choose the Save As command from the File menu.

Chapter 3
Creating and Saving Text

Resave the file using the Save As command in the following situations:

■ *You want to rename the document.* Choose Save As and type a new file name in the Save Current Document As text box. The changes you made in this editing session will not affect the version of the file named with the previous name. Word shows the new name in the title bar, and when you next choose Save, Word resaves the file using the new name.

■ *You want to save each version of an important document.* Suppose that you're writing an important contract or proposal, and because you're not sure your revisions are carrying the document in the right direction, you want to keep each version on disk. Each time you save, choose Save As and specify a new document name. This procedure is much better than using the Make Backup option which, as already noted, loses its usefulness when you save at periodic intervals (such as every 10 or 15 minutes).

■ *You want to save the document to a new location.* Choose Save As and choose a new folder or disk for the file. The changes you made in this editing session will not affect the version of the file stored in the original location. The next time you choose Save, Word resaves the file using the new location.

■ *You want to enable the Make Backup option.* You can turn on the Make Backup option for any file. If you do, Word will keep the existing copy of the document on disk, renaming it `Backup of filename`. Some writers like to keep the previous version of their document—the version that they last saved—in case they decide they don't like the changes made in the current editing session. This consumes a lot of disk space, however, and if you save regularly (every 10 or 15 minutes is the suggested rule), the current version of the file will not be that much different from its backup version. Don't confuse this option with a true backup copy of your current file.

For valuable files, use the Finder to copy them to floppy disks or—better yet—purchase a backup utility program such as DiskFit, which automatically detects all new or altered files and backs them up speedily to floppy disks.

■ *You want to disable the Fast Save option.* If you activate the Allow Fast Saves option in the Preferences dialog box, this option is grayed the first time you save a file, but is available afterwards. It's on by default. To choose a normal save, deactivate this option.

■ *You want to save the file to a file format other than Word's default file format.* A file format is the method used to store the document on disk so that your formatting choices are preserved. Word's default format, Normal, saves all these choices. If you want to exchange your file with other computer users or send it to others via telecommunications links, you may want to choose a format other than Normal to save your file. The alternative formats are discussed in the next section.

TIP

When using Save As, you should always save the file by using a new name.

If you choose Save As to save an existing file but don't change its name or location, you see an alert box asking you to confirm overwriting the previous version of the file. To be on the safe side, you should *always* save the file using a new name. Many of the options you can choose in this dialog box will wipe out document formats that took hours to enter. Deleting an unneeded copy of a document is a lot easier than reconstructing hours of work!

Saving to Other File Formats

Word normally saves your document using its Normal format, which preserves all your formatting choices. If you want, you can save to other formats by using the Save File As Type list box. When you pull down this list box, the options that appear depend on which file conversion options you chose when you installed Microsoft Word.

File format options you can choose include the following:

Text Only. Choose this option to transfer a Word document to another word processing program that cannot read Word's files. This option saves only the text of the file without any formatting or graphics. New line, section, and hard page breaks are converted to paragraph marks.

Text Only with Line Breaks. Choose this option to transfer a Word document via your modem and telecommunications links; it creates an "ASCII" or "plain text" file. Like the Text Only option, this option saves only the text of the file without any formatting or graphics. Every line ends in a paragraph mark (hard return).

Text with Layout. This option closely resembles Text Only, except that it preserves indents, tables, line spacing, paragraph spacing, and tab positions by inserting spaces in the file.

Interchange Format (RTF). This format saves your document using nothing but the standard ASCII characters; at the same time, however, it adds codes that preserve your formatting choices. You can transmit the file via telecommunications or give a disk to someone using another program, and as long as this program can read RTF files, the formatting can be recovered.

Stationery. This option, used with System 7, enables you to save a file as a *template*, which remains unmodified on disk. Suppose that you create a letterhead for your business; it contains your return address and logo, but nothing else. If you save this document as stationery, you make sure that you will never overwrite this document accidentally. Every time you open a stationery document, Word displays a copy of the document, not the original. For more information on creating and using stationery, see Chapters 13 and 29.

After you choose one of these options, you can make that option the default format for the file by activating the Default for File option. If you don't choose this option, Word will revert to the Normal format if you make changes to the document and save them. For this reason, you should activate this option if you have chosen any of the nonstandard formats and think you might do a little more editing in the document.

Resaving the Document

To resave a file with Save As, follow these steps:

1. Choose Save As from the File menu, or press ⌘-S or Shift-F7.

   The Save As dialog box appears, with the current document name highlighted.

2. To delete the current document name, just start typing the new name. To edit the name, click the insertion point within the name to cancel the highlight.

3. To disable the Fast Save option, click Fast Save until the X disappears.

   If the box is dimmed, you need to activate Allow Fast Saves in the Preferences dialog box.

4. If you want to save the file to another disk, choose Drive (System 6) or Desktop (System 7), and choose the drive you want.

5. If you want to save the file to a folder other than the current folder, use the current folder box to highlight the folder you want. System 7 users can create, name, and activate a new folder by choosing New Folder.

6. If you want to save the file to a format other than Word's default Normal format, choose the format in the Save File As Type box. To make this format the default for future save, activate the Default for File check box.

7. Choose Save.

   If you have chosen the name of an existing document, you see a dialog box asking you to confirm replacing the existing file. Choose No to return to the Save As dialog box without overwriting the existing file, or choose Yes to replace the file.

Filling Out Summary Info

New to Word 5 is Find File, a file-retrieval command that can scan a huge disk in search of an elusive file. This command can locate an elusive file in seconds! If you have ever spent precious time hunting for a file you inadvertently saved to the wrong folder, you will agree that Find File is a boon. You can find a complete discussion of Find File in Chapter 11.

To get the most out of Find File, you need to diligently fill out the Summary Info dialog box that appears when you save a document for the first time (see fig. 3.15). If you always fill out Summary Info, you will be able to use Find File to retrieve files by title, subject, author, version, and keywords, in addition to the information that Finder automatically records when you save the file (the document's name, the date the document was created, and the date the document was last saved).

Fig. 3.15
Summary info dialog box.

```
══════════════ Summary Info ══════════════
Title:     [                        ]   ( OK )
Subject:   [                        ]   (Cancel)
Author:    [                        ]
Version:   [                        ]
Keywords:  [                        ]
```

This next section provides a quick overview of the Summary Info dialog box's areas, together with suggestions on using them productively:

Chapter 3
Creating and Saving Text

Title. Type the document's full title, not the abbreviated, 31-word-maximum title that you type in the Save As dialog box. Although the Title text box doesn't look big, it scrolls right as you type text. You can enter up to 255 characters in all of the Summary Info dialog boxes.

Subject. In this text box, type one or more descriptors for your document. A *descriptor* is a key word that categorizes your document so that it can be grouped with others. You may want to categorize documents using these descriptors: Letter, Report, Memo, Proposal, and so on. Or you may want to use descriptors relevant to your profession, such as Contract, Will, Deposition (for a legal practice), and so on.

Author. Word automatically inserts the name you typed in the Your Name area of the Preferences dialog box, so you can just let Word do the typing for you. Sometimes, however, more than one person uses a computer. In this case, the user can type his or her own name here.

Version. If you like to keep each version of a document intact on disk, save all changes using the Save As dialog box and, every time you save the file, specify a new document name—such as Report, New Report, Yet Another Report. If you type the same Title in Summary Info every time you save the file, however, Find File can group all the versions of the file together. Use the Version text box to record the number of the version you're now saving.

Keywords. Use the Keywords text box to type one or more *identifiers*—words or phrases that uniquely identify the document you're saving. In contrast to descriptors, which group this document with others, identifiers provide a way to differentiate documents and enable pin-point searches. For example, an attorney may want to type the name of a client here, together with a descriptor (such as *Edward B. Smith, trust*).

TIP

If you don't want to fill out Summary Info, just choose OK when the dialog box appears. If you choose Cancel, the Summary Info box will appear again the next time you save the document.

If you didn't fill out a Summary Info sheet and want to, choose the Summary Info option in the File menu. Word will display the Summary Info dialog box for the current document.

If you don't want Word to display Summary Info sheets automatically when you save a document for the first time, you can change Word's default Preferences. You still can access a document's Summary Info by choosing Summary Info from the File menu when the document is active.

To prevent Word from displaying Summary Info automatically the first time you save a document, follow these steps:

1. Choose Preferences from the Tools menu.

2. Choose Open and Save.

3. Turn off the Prompt for Summary Info option.

4. Click the Close box.

Quick Review

This section concisely summarizes the most useful information in this chapter. Check "Productivity Tips" for a review of high-productivity tips and tricks, and review "Techniques" when you forget how to perform a specific procedure.

Productivity Tips

- Press Return only at the end of a paragraph. Align text only with tabs, not spaces. Enter blank lines with the Blank Line button on the ruler instead of pressing Return twice.

- To sort items (such as names and addresses in a mailing list or bibliographic references), use the new line command (Shift-Enter) when you type them and press Return only at the end of the item. Word will treat the item as a paragraph for sorting purposes.

- Choose a default font for all your documents. You always can override this choice for a particular document, and your choice probably will be better than Word's (New York).

- If you want to add special characters, use Key Caps to find and memorize the key to press. Use Symbols (Insert menu) to quickly insert a character with the mouse. Use zero-width characters to enter accent marks.

- Use em dashes (Shift-Option-hyphen) rather than two hyphens to keep Word from breaking a line within a dash. Use nonbreaking hyphens (⌘-~) to keep Word from breaking a line within hyphenated proper nouns and insert optional hyphens within lengthy words to help Word align the right margin. If you're not sure where to put the optional hyphens, highlight the word and choose Hyphenation from the Tools menu.

Chapter 3
Creating and Saving Text

■ Avoid hard page breaks. They might lose their purpose and cause new page break problems if you add or delete text to your document above the page break. To prevent bad page breaks, format paragraphs with the Keep With Next and Keep Lines Together options, as explained in Chapter 7.

■ To resave documents quickly, activate Allow Fast Saves in the Preferences dialog box (Tools menu).

Techniques

This section provides concise, quick-reference summaries of all the procedures introduced in this chapter.

Inserting the Date

To insert the current date at the insertion point:

Choose Date from the Insert menu.

Choosing the Default Font

To change the default font for all new documents:

1. Choose Default Font from the Font menu.

2. Drop down the Default Font list box and choose the font you want to use as the default font for all your documents.

3. To choose a new default size, choose the size you want from the Default Size list box, or type the size if it's not on the list.

4. After you choose the font and font size you want, click the close box to confirm your choices and close the Preferences window.

Joining and Splitting Paragraphs

To join two paragraphs:

1. Select the paragraph mark that divides the two paragraphs.

2. Press Delete (Backspace).

3. If necessary, add a space or two between the joined sentences.

To split a paragraph:

1. Place the insertion point where you want the paragraph break to occur.

2. Press Return.

To split a paragraph and leave the cursor at the end of the first part of the original paragraph:

1. Place the insertion point where you want the paragraph break to occur.

2. Press ⌘-Option-Return.

To start a new line without starting a new paragraph:

Press Shift-Enter.

To add a blank line before a paragraph:

1. Place the insertion point in the paragraph.

2. Click the Blank Line button on the ruler.

Using Page Breaks, Hyphens, Dashes, and Nonbreaking Spaces

To enter	Press
Hard page break	Shift-Enter
Em dash	Shift-Option-Hyphen
En dash	Option-Hyphen
Nonbreaking hyphen	⌘-~ (tilde) or ⌘-'
Optional hyphen	⌘-hyphen
Nonbreaking space	Option-space bar

To look up hyphen breaks and insert an optional hyphen in a word:

1. Highlight the word you want to hyphenate.

2. Choose Hyphenation from the Tools menu.

3. If you want, click a hyphen break other than the one Word selected.

4. Choose Change.

Saving Your Work

To save your document the first time:

1. Choose Save from the File menu, or press ⌘-S or Shift F7.

2. Type the document name in the Save Current Document As box.

3. Choose Save.

To resave your document:

Choose Save from the File menu, or press ⌘-S.

To resave your document to a different file name:

1. Choose Save As from the File menu, or press ⌘-S or Shift-F7.

   The Save As dialog box appears, with the current document name highlighted.

2. To delete the current document name, just start typing the new name. To edit the name, click the insertion point within the name to cancel the highlight.

3. Choose Save.

To enable fast saves for all documents:

1. Choose Preferences from the Tools menu.

2. Choose the Open and Save icon.

3. Activate the Allow Fast Saves option.

4. Click the close box.

To disable fast saves for an existing document:

1. Choose Save As from the File menu.

2. Deactivate the Fast Save option.

3. Choose Save.

4. Choose Yes.

To display a save reminder at an interval you specify:

1. Choose Preferences from the Tools menu.

2. Choose the Open and Save icon.

3. Activate the Save Reminder option.

4. Type an interval in the Every text box (suggested interval: 10 or 15 minutes).

5. Click the close box.

To save your document to ASCII format so that you can send it via telecommunications:

1. Choose Save As from the File menu.

2. Drop down the Save File As Type list box.

3. Choose Text Only with Line Breaks.

4. If you want to make this option the default format for the file, activate the Default for File check box.

5. Type a new name for the document in the Save Current Document As text box.

6. Choose the folder where you want to store the document or, if you're using System 7, choose the New Folder button to create a new folder for your document.

7. Choose Save.

To save your document to RTF format so that you can exchange a disk with a colleague:

1. Choose Save As from the File menu.

2. Drop down the Save File As Type list box.

3. Choose Interchange Format (RTF).

4. Activate the Default for File check box.

5. Type a new name for the document in the Save Current Document As text box.

6. Choose the folder where you want to store the document or, if you're using System 7, choose the New Folder button to create a new folder for your document.

7. Choose Save.

To save your document as stationery:

1. Choose Save As from the File menu.

2. Drop down the Save File As Type list box.

3. Choose Stationery.

Chapter 3
Creating and Saving Text

4. Activate the Default for File check box.

5. Choose Save.

6. Choose the folder where you want to store the document or, if you're using System 7, choose the New Folder button to create a new folder for your document.

7. Choose Save.

To skip Summary Info:

Choose OK in the Summary Info dialog box without filling out any of the fields.

To skip Summary Info for now, so you can fill it out the next time you save the document:

Choose OK in the Summary Info dialog box without filling out any of the fields.

To prevent Word from displaying Summary Info automatically the first time you save a document:

1. Choose Preferences from the Tools menu.

2. Choose Open and Save.

3. Turn off the Prompt for Summary Info option.

Special Characters

To find out which key to press to enter a special character:

1. Choose the font you want to use.

2. Choose Key Caps from the Apple menu.

   If necessary, press Option to see additional characters.

3. Click the close box to return to your document.

To enter special characters with the Symbols command:

1. Choose the font you want to use.

2. Choose Symbols from the Insert menu or press ⌘-Option-Q.

3. Click the character or characters you want to insert.

4. Click the close box to return to your document.

To enter accented characters:

1. Press one of the zero-width character keys:

Press	To enter
Option-à	Grave accent (à)
Option-e	Acute accent (à)
Option-i	Circumflex (ˆ)
Option-n	Tilde (~)
Option-u	Umlaut (ä)

2. Type the letter you want accented.

To turn Smart Quotes on or off:

1. Choose Preferences from the Tools menu.

2. Activate (or deactivate) the Smart Quotes check box.

3. Click the close box.

Thesaurus

To look up a word in Thesaurus:

1. Double-click the word you want to look up.

2. Choose Thesaurus from the Tools menu.

3. To choose one of the displayed synonyms, highlight the synonym in the Synonym list box.

   To see synonyms of other meanings of the word, highlight the meaning in the Meanings For list box.

   To see synonyms of words in the Synonyms list box, highlight the synonym and choose Look Up.

   To redisplay the meanings and synonyms for a word you previously viewed, drop down the With list box and choose the word from the list.

   To redisplay the word you originally looked up, choose Original.

Chapter 3
Creating and Saving Text

To view antonyms of the word currently listed in the With box, choose Antonyms in the Meanings For list box. (Not all words have antonyms.)

4. After you display the right word in the With box, choose Replace. If you cannot find a better word, choose Cancel.

CHAPTER

Editing Text

B ecause good writing involves revision, Word 5's many options for reshaping words until they are just right are a writer's tool *par excellence*. This chapter explores the following editing capabilities:

■ *Opening Documents*. The first step in editing is to retrieve existing documents. In this chapter, you explore all the ways you can retrieve documents, including documents created by other programs.

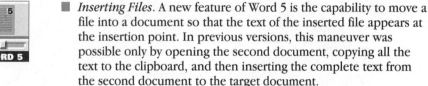

■ *Inserting Files*. A new feature of Word 5 is the capability to move a file into a document so that the text of the inserted file appears at the insertion point. In previous versions, this maneuver was possible only by opening the second document, copying all the text to the clipboard, and then inserting the complete text from the second document to the target document.

■ *Moving the Insertion Point and Scrolling*. As you edit your document, you need to move around quickly and efficiently—especially in long documents. This chapter includes an extensive discussion of the Word 5 techniques for moving the insertion point and scrolling the screen, including Version 5's improved Go Back command.

USING
WORD 5
FOR THE
MAC

■ *Finding Text*. The Find command in the Edit menu enables you to locate a word or phrase in your document quickly. Version 5's new features give you the capability to search for specific occurrences of a word, phrase, character, or paragraph format. If you want, you can find in your document all text with a specific format. You also can search for styles, special characters, graphics, and footnotes. In this chapter, you learn how to use Find to search for text. Other Find functions are discussed extensively in subsequent chapters.

■ *Replacing Text*. The Replace command in the Edit menu enables you to substitute one word or phrase for another word or phrase throughout your document. In addition, Word 5 gives you the capability to replace formats as well as text—a welcome improvement. Using the Replace command, you can change a word from boldface to italic format throughout your document. In this chapter, you also learn how to use Replace to search and replace text. Replace's many uses for finding and replacing formats are discussed extensively in subsequent chapters on character, paragraph, and style formatting.

■ *Selecting Text*. Text selection is basic to editing and formatting, but few Word users fully explore the options for quickly selecting fixed units of text—words, lines, sentences, and paragraphs.

■ *Deleting Text*. The better your understanding of what happens when you delete text, the less likely you are to delete text accidentally. In the section on deleting text, you learn deletion techniques that make the recovery of accidentally deleted text more possible.

■ *Copying and Moving Text*. This section broadens your knowledge of copying and moving techniques. You learn why moving text without copying to the clipboard is sometimes preferable. You also learn how to use Word 5's new Paste Link capability, which enables you to create a "live" link between one Word document and text pasted into another Word document. With this link, Word automatically updates the target document whenever the source document is updated.

Opening Documents

When you start Word, you see a blank document, called Untitled1, in a document window. You can create a new document simply by typing in this window and, as you have already learned, you can create a new document at any time by choosing New from the File menu (or by using ⌘-N). Each new document has an Untitled number

(Untitled2, Untitled3, for example). In this section, you learn how to retrieve for revision documents that you have already created and saved.

Starting Word and Opening a Document at the Same Time

When you want to work with an existing document, you can save time by opening Word at the same time you open the document. Follow these steps:

1. In the Finder, open the folder or disk that contains the Word document you want to open.

2. Double-click the document's icon. Word starts and displays the document. You have no Untitled1 document to close.

Opening a Document within Word

TIP

To move the insertion point to where you stopped editing in a previous session, use the Go Back command (⌘-Option-Z).

After starting Word, you use the Open dialog box (File menu) to find and open existing documents. This section comprehensively covers all the options available in the Open dialog box except Word 5's new Find File option, which is covered in Chapter 11.

What you see when you choose Open depends on which version of the Mac's system software you're using. System 6 users see the dialog box shown in figure 4.1; System 7 users see the dialog box shown in figure 4.2.

Fig. 4.1
The Open dialog box (System 6).

Current folder title

Current drive indicator

Document list box

Command buttons

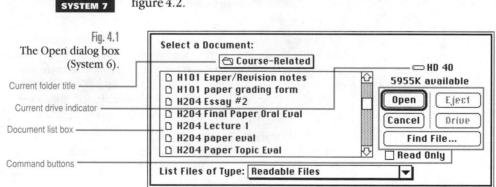

The Open dialog box has the following areas and features:

> **Current folder title.** At the top of the dialog box is what amounts to a drop-down list box (although with no drop-down arrow)

showing the current folder. To drop down the list, point to the folder list and hold down the mouse button. You see a list of folders *above* the current folder in your disk's folder hierarchy. (As a shortcut, press ⌘-Up arrow to display the documents in the directory immediately above the Word directory.)

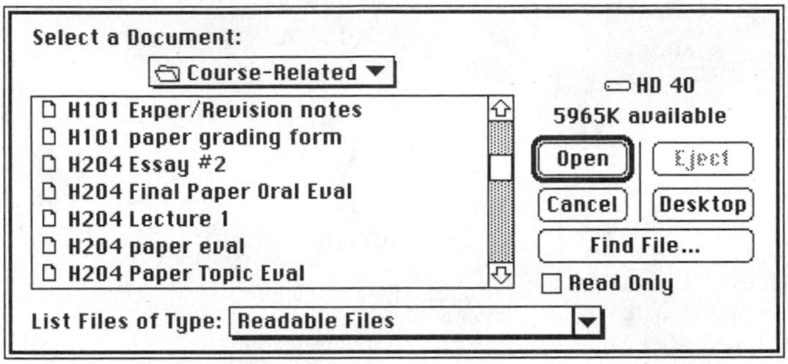

Fig. 4.2
The Open dialog box
(System 7).

Document list box. By default, this list box shows all the documents that Word can read in the current folder. Because the Readable Files category includes many files that would not be useful if Word opened them, you may want to use the List Files of Type option to restrict the display of files to Word documents, as explained in the next section.

Current drive indicator. Indicates the current drive and the amount of free space.

Command buttons. Choose Open to open the document currently highlighted in the Document List Box. To switch drives, choose the Drive button. To eject a disk from a disk drive, choose Eject. To take advantage of Word 5's new Find File command (discussed in Chapter 11), choose Find File. To exit the dialog box without opening a file, choose Exit.

Read Only option. To open a document so that you cannot overwrite the file currently on disk, activate the Read Only option. You can alter a read-only document, but to save the alterations, you must specify a new file name.

List Files of Type box. This drop-down list box controls what is included in the Document List Box display. If you choose the Word Documents option, the Document List Box lists only Word documents. Which options you see in the List Files of Type list box depends on choices you make when you install Word 5.

Opening Word Documents

Now that you know your way around the Open dialog box, follow these steps to open existing Word files:

SPEED KEY

1. Choose Open from the File menu, or press ⌘-O. You see the Open dialog box.

2. To reduce the number of files displayed in the Document List Box, choose List Files of Type. Then choose the Word Documents option.

3. Use the Document List Box and Current Folder List to locate the document you want to open.

TIP

Take advantage of the Finder's capability to search the Document List Box. Type the first letter of the file you want to find. The Finder will move the highlight to the next file that begins with the letter you typed. If you type *Q*, for instance, the Finder moves the highlight to the next file that begins with *q*.

   If the document you want to open is not in the current folder, do one of the following:

   To open a folder above the current folder, click the folder title box and choose from the list the name of the folder you want (or use the ⌘-Up arrow keyboard shortcut).

   To open a folder below the current folder, find the folder in the Document List Box and double-click the folder icon; or highlight the folder name and use the ⌘-Down arrow keyboard shortcut.

   If you cannot find the file in the Document List Box, choose Find File. Chapter 11 explains this new Word 5 feature.

   If the document you want to open is not in the current drive, insert the disk that contains the document, and do one of the following:

   System 6 users: Choose the Drive button to switch to the drive that contains the disk.

   System 7 users: Choose the Desktop button, and double-click the drive that contains the disk.

4. When the Document List displays the document you want to open, double-click the document's name. Alternatively, use the arrow keys to highlight the document's name and press Enter.

Opening Recently Edited Documents

WORD 5

In Word 5, you can reopen any recently edited document quickly by choosing the document's name from the File menu. Word stores up to four of the last documents you edited—even if you have left the program.

Opening Stationery Documents

In Chapter 3, you learn that you can save files as *stationery*. A file saved as stationery becomes a read-only file by default; you can open a stationery file, but Word opens the file as an untitled document, leaving the original file intact. You can save this file, but doing so will not affect the Stationery document. For this reason, you can use Stationery documents to store ready-to-use templates of frequently used documents such as letters, memos, and quarterly reports.

To open a Stationery document, follow these steps:

1. Choose Open from the File menu or press ⌘-O. You see the Open dialog box.

2. Choose List Files of Type.

3. Choose Stationery.

4. Use the document list box and Current Folder list to locate the Stationery document you want to open.

5. Double-click the name of the document you want to open. Alternatively, use the arrow keys to highlight the document's name, and press Enter.

Opening Documents Created by Other Programs

When you install Word, you have the option of installing file-conversion utilities that enable Word to read a wide variety of documents created by other Mac and IBM-PC programs, including WordPerfect, MacWrite, Microsoft Works, and Microsoft Word for Windows. In addition, Word can open text files (ASCII), files saved with RTF (Rich Text Format) formatting instructions, files saved using the Apple File Exchange Binary format, and even graphics files. This section explains how to open a document that has been saved to a format other than Word's.

To open a non-Word document, follow these steps:

1. Choose Open from the File menu or press ⌘-O. You see the Open dialog box.

2. Choose List Files of Type. Then choose the format of the document you want to open. If you're not sure which format to use, choose All Files.

3. Use the Document List Box and Current Folder List to locate the document you want to open.

4. Double-click on the Document List the name of the document you want to open. Alternatively, use the arrow keys to highlight the document's name, and press Enter.

Inserting Files

Word 5 includes two much-needed new commands: the File and Picture commands (Insert menu), which insert documents and graphics at the insertion point. This section gives an explanation of the Insert File command. Chapter 20 gives a detailed description of the Insert Picture command.

You can use the Insert File command in several different ways:

■ To put together a long document, you can create the chapters in separate Word documents, and then use Insert File to merge the chapters into a single document for printing.

■ You can append a copy of a mailing list, price list, or bibliography to a letter or report you're writing.

■ You can incorporate a copy of a previous report as a chapter of a report you currently are writing.

To insert a file in your document, follow these steps:

1. Place the insertion point where you want the file to appear.

2. Choose File from the Insert menu.

   You see the Select a File to Insert dialog box, which closely resembles the Open dialog box (see figs. 4.3 and 4.4).

3. Highlight the file you want to open. If necessary, use the Current Folder list to open other folders.

4. Choose Open, or press Enter.

Fig. 4.3
The System 6 Select a File to Insert dialog box.

Select a File to Insert:

📁 Course-Related

| ▢ H101 Exper/Revision notes |
| ▢ H101 paper grading form |
| ▢ H204 Essay #2 |
| ▢ H204 Final Paper Oral Eval |
| ▢ H204 Lecture 1 |
| ▢ H204 paper eval |
| ▢ H204 Paper Topic Eval |

💾 HD 40
5932K available

Open   Eject
Cancel   Drive
Find File...
☐ Read Only

List Files of Type: | All Files | ▼ |

Chapter 4
Editing Text

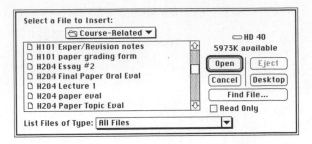

Choose Save immediately after you insert a file into your document. Word copies on disk the file that you inserted into your document. In other words, you have preserved the original file by inserting a copy rather than the actual file.

Moving around the Document

You have learned how to scroll, and you have used the arrow keys to move the insertion point. The following sections give you complete information about how to move the insertion point and scroll the screen with Word 5. These sections cover mouse and keyboard techniques, as well as the Go To and Go Back commands.

As you type, Word moves the insertion point to show where the program is placing the characters you are typing. In Normal view, Word automatically scrolls the screen when you reach the end of the window.

Understanding Scrolling

The simplest way to move the insertion point is to move the pointer to a new location in the window and click the mouse button. If you want to move the insertion point to a location not visible in the window, scroll the screen.

To understand what happens when you scroll the screen, you need to distinguish between moving the insertion point and scrolling. When you *move* the insertion point, you change the place where Word places your characters when you type. When you *scroll* by using the scroll bars, scroll boxes, or scroll arrows, you change the position of the window on the document, as though you were moving a picture frame over a long strip of paper. The insertion point stays put, however.

The keyboard commands do two things: move the insertion point *and* scroll the screen. For example, if you press the Page Down key on a Macintosh extended keyboard, Word scrolls down one screen and positions the insertion point at the top of the screen.

Mouse scrolling techniques, however, do *not* move the insertion point as they scroll. This fact can cause problems if you don't know what's happening. Suppose that you are writing on page 19 and you realize that you want to edit something on page 11. You scroll to page 11, click the insertion point there, and do some editing. Then you scroll back to page 19 and start typing, only to discover that, because you left the insertion point on page 11, Word has scrolled back to page 11 and is entering the characters you are typing there. To resume working on page 19, you must first click the insertion point on that page.

TIP

After you use the mouse to scroll the screen with the scroll bars, boxes, or arrows, remember to click the insertion point in the new location.

The scroll boxes show graphically where the current window is positioned within the document as a whole. (The top of the scroll bar is the beginning of the document and the bottom is the end.) To move to another position within your document, you can drag the scroll box. Just how far you scroll with a one-inch drag depends on the length of your document. In a one-page document, a one-inch drag will scroll the screen only a few lines. In a 500-page document, a one-inch drag could take you 100 pages!

You can use the vertical scroll box to move to a specific page. As you drag the scroll box up or down, keep your eye on the page number area at the lower left corner of the window. Even if Word is slow to update the screen, the program updates the page number quickly, so you can tell at a glance where you have positioned the scroll box. To scroll to page 15 of a long document, for example, drag the scroll box until you see Page 15 in the page number area, then release the mouse button. (This technique doesn't work if you have disabled the Background Repagination option in the Preferences dialog box.)

Moving with the Mouse and Keyboard

Table 4.1 lists all the mouse techniques for scrolling, and Table 4.2 lists the keyboard techniques you can use to move the insertion point. Even if you prefer to use the mouse, investigate the keyboard techniques. You may find several particularly useful keyboard techniques. If your Macintosh keyboard has a numeric keypad, Word's usage of the keypad is identical to the mapping of cursor-movement keys on IBM-PC keyboards. The cursor movement keys form a cross (8 = up, 2 = down, 4 = left, and 6 = right), and as table 4.1 shows, the keypad offers several ways to move the insertion point that are not available on the keyboard.

Chapter 4
Editing Text

To Scroll	Technique
Up line-by-line	Click the up scroll arrow
Down line-by-line	Click the down scroll arrow
Left one-half inch	Click the left scroll arrow
Right one-half inch	Click the right scroll arrow
Up one screen	Click the scroll bar above the scroll box
Down one screen	Click the scroll bar below the scroll box
Left one screen	Click the scroll bar left of the scroll box
Right one screen	Click the scroll bar right of the scroll box
Beginning of document	Drag scroll box to top of scroll bar
End of document	Drag scroll box to bottom of scroll bar

Table 4.1
Mouse Scrolling
Techniques

In Page Layout view, you can scroll with the Page Up and Page Down icons at the bottom of the window (see fig. 4.5).

Fig. 4.5
Page Up and Page Down
icons in Page Layout view.

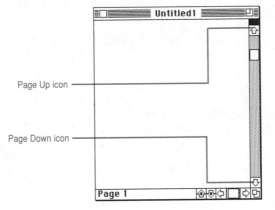

Be careful not to wipe out your selection when you use the numeric keypad for insertion-point movement. Such a disaster can happen if you select some text for formatting purposes, then decide to scroll up to look at a previous passage before completing the action, and you do not realize that you have pressed the Clear key, thus toggling the keypad to its number-entry mode. When you begin to scroll up, using Keypad-9, Word enters a 9 instead. You now have typed over a selection, so the selection disappears. You can correct this problem by immediately

Part I

Getting Started

choosing Undo from the Edit menu, but if you type additional text or choose a different command, the selection is irretrievably lost.

Table 4.2
Keyboard Techniques for
Moving the Insertion Point

To Move	On keyboard	On keypad
Up one line	Up arrow	Keypad-8
Down one line	Down arrow	Keypad-2
Left one character	Left arrow	Keypad-4
Right one character	Right arrow	Keypad-6
Left one word	⌘-Left arrow	⌘-Keypad-4
Right one word	⌘-Right arrow	⌘-Keypad-6
To start of line		Keypad-7
To end of line		Keypad-1
To preceding sentence		⌘-Keypad-7
To next sentence		⌘-Keypad-1
To preceding paragraph	⌘-Up arrow	⌘-Keypad-8
To next paragraph	⌘-Down arrow	⌘-Keypad-2
To top of window	Home*	⌘-Keypad-5
To bottom of window	End*	
One screen up	Page Up*	Keypad-9
One screen down	Page Down*	Keypad-3
Next page	⌘-Page Down*	
Previous page	⌘-Page Up*	
Beginning of document	⌘-Home*	⌘-keypad- 9
End of document	⌘-End*	⌘-keypad -3

*Extended keyboard only.

TIP

If Word enters a number into your document when you use the numeric keypad for moving the insertion point, look for the Num Lock message in the page number area. To use the keypad for insertion point movement, press Clear again.

Word users have discovered ways around this hazard. One favorite method is to reprogram the keyboard, as explained in Chapter 27, so that the Clear key deletes the character right—an intelligent mapping, since the adjacent Delete key rubs out the character left. You then can program ⌘-Clear to toggle the Num Lock mode on and off. Reprogramming the keys in this way reduces the chances of accidentally toggling on the number-entry mode. If reprogramming the keyboard sounds scary, take heart—it's easy. Chapter 27 details the whole procedure, keystroke by keystroke.

Chapter 4
Editing Text

If you use a Classic keyboard (numeric keypad, but no function keys), table 4.2 suggests another excellent reason for reprogramming the keyboard: a Classic keyboard has no keypad equivalent for ⌘-Page Up (scroll to top of previous page) and ⌘-Page Down (scroll to top of next page), both of which require the Extended keyboard. You can reprogram Keypad-9 and Keypad-3 so that they duplicate the functions of ⌘-Page Up and ⌘-Page Down. You still can scroll up or down one screen quickly by clicking above or below the scroll box. Keypad-9 and Keypad-3 work the way they used to in Normal view. Page scrolling is available only in Page Layout view, where it's most handy.

Scrolling to a Specific Page

As long as the Background Repagination option is turned on, Word paginates your document as you type and edit. (Background Repagination, which is in the Preferences dialog box, is activated by default, and you should leave it that way.) Because pagination occurs automatically, the page numbers Word displays in the status line are accurate (although the program may need a few seconds to update the page numbers as you scroll through your document). You can use the Go To command in the Utilities menu to move rapidly to a page number you specify.

To move the insertion point to the top of a specific page, follow these steps:

1. Choose Go To from the Edit menu or press ⌘-G.

2. When the Go To dialog box appears (see fig. 4.6), type the number of the page to which you want to move the insertion point.

3. Choose OK.

Fig. 4.6
The Go To dialog box.

Going Back to the Location of Previous Edits

As you type and edit, Word stores the last three locations where you inserted or deleted text and keeps this list of locations, even if you exit Word. To move the insertion point to these locations quickly, press the Go Back command (⌘-Option-Z). The first time you use this key, you

NOTE

If you have turned off the Background Repagination option in the Preferences dialog box, choose Repaginate Now from the Tools menu before choosing the Go To command.

return to the most recent location. If you use the command again, Word moves the insertion point to the second recorded location, and so on. On the fourth Go Back command, Word returns the insertion point to the starting location.

The Go Back command's name isn't quite accurate. For example, if the insertion point's preceding location was farther along in the file, the insertion point moves forward. If the last location of text editing or deletion was off the screen, Word scrolls the screen automatically.

The following list shows you ways to use Go Back to increase your writing and editing productivity:

- Suppose that you type a sentence on page 9, and as you do, you realize that you need to fix something you said on page 6. You scroll to page 6 and edit the text there. To return to the exact place where you stopped typing on page 9, press ⌘-Option-Z.

- You quit writing for the day and switch off your Macintosh. At the beginning of the next session, you open your document. To move the insertion point to the exact place you stopped yesterday, press ⌘-Option-Z.

Searching for Text

If you're looking for a specific passage of text, don't strain your eyes scrolling through your document: use the Find command to locate text quickly. You see the Find dialog box, as shown in figure 4.7.

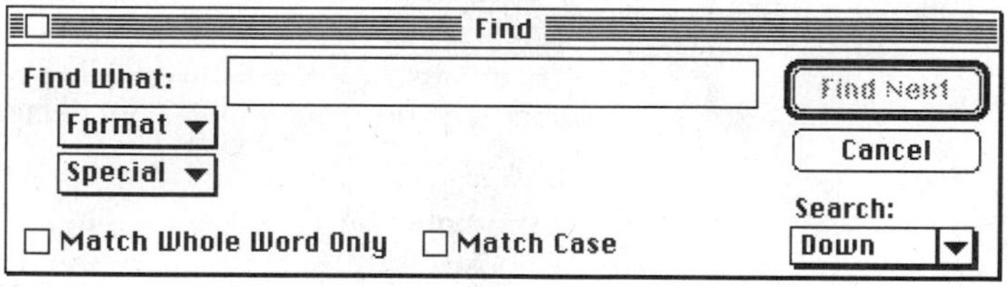

Fig. 4.7
The Find dialog box.

The Find dialog box contains the following items:

Find What. In the Find What text box, you type the character, word, or phrase you want to match. You can type up to 255 characters (including spaces and any Mac or Word special characters). As explained later in this section, you also can use wild cards.

Format. Use the Format list box when you want Word to search for text that has a certain format. Word limits the search to the characters in the Find What text box that have the formats you have chosen. For example, if you choose Bold in the Format list box and type *Yosemite* in the Find What text box, Word finds only those instances of the search word that are formatted in boldface. (The use of this important new Word 5 capability is explained in detail in Chapters 5, 6, and 8).

Special. To search for any of Word's special characters, such as paragraph marks or end of line marks, you can use the Special list box to enter the characters rather than typing their codes, as you had to do with previous versions of Word. In this list box, you can choose a wide variety of special characters and features for which Word can search. These characters include tab marks, end of line marks, paragraph marks, hard page breaks, nonbreaking spaces, optional hyphens, footnotes, graphics, white space, and formula characters. (If you know the codes, you can type them in the Find What text box; the use of the Special list box is optional.)

Match Whole Word Only (default: off). To restrict the search to whole words, activate the Whole Word box. If you type *report* in the Find What box, Word finds *report* but not *reporting*, *reports*, or *reported*.

Match Case (default: off). By default, Word's searches are not case-sensitive. The search program ignores uppercase and lowercase. For example, if you type *WORD* in the Find What text box, the program matches *Word*, *word*, *WORD*, or any other combination of upper- and lowercase letters.

Search (default: Down). From the Search list box, you choose the direction of the search (up or down). You can also choose All (search the whole document). If you select text before choosing Find, the program replaces the default direction (Down) with Selection.

Command Buttons. Choose Find Next to start the search. Choose Cancel at any time to stop the search and return to your document.

Word's new Find command can locate character and paragraph formats as well as styles. With the Replace command, you can replace one style with another throughout your document. This welcome change is explained in Chapters 5, 6, and 8. In addition, with Word 5's Find you can search for Word's special symbols (such as paragraph marks and new-line symbols) by choosing them from the Special list box. You no longer have to type a code to search for these characters. Find can even search for footnotes, graphics, and formula characters.

Performing a Search

The best way to understand Find is to use the command. Open a document that contains at least a few paragraphs of text and position the insertion point at the beginning of the document.

To find text in your document, follow these steps:

1. Choose Find from the Utilities menu or press ⌘-F.

2. When the Find dialog box appears, type in the Find What box the text you want to find.

3. To perform a case-sensitive search, activate the Match Case option.

4. To perform a whole-word search, activate the Match Whole Word Only option.

TIP

You can type a maximum of 255 characters in Find What. The search for a long entry takes longer but is more accurate. If you type *report*, for example, Word finds the next occurrence of the characters you typed, even if they're embedded in a word (such as *reporting* or *reported*). If you type *Quarterly Report 1 of 1992*, however, Word matches precisely—and only—what you specify.

5. If necessary, choose the correct search direction in the Search list box. By default, Word searches Down, unless you have selected text before choosing Find, in which case Word searches the selection.

6. Choose Find Next. If Word finds a match, the Find dialog box stays on-screen and highlights the match in your document. Choose Cancel to close the box or choose Find Next again to repeat the search.

You can repeat the search as many times as you want. If Word doesn't find a match, an alert box appears, asking whether you want to continue the search from the beginning of the document (or the end, if you're searching up). Choose OK or Cancel. If you choose OK and Word finds no match, another alert box informs you that Find did not find the text you specified in the document.

If Word cannot find the text you're searching for, take the following steps:

- Check the text you typed in the Find What box for a spelling mistake or a typographical error. Correct any errors you find and then click the Start Search button again.

- If you typed a long phrase, perhaps some word in the phrase does not match what's in the document. Type a shorter version of the phrase, using only words that you know are correct.

- Deactivate the Match Whole Word Only and Match Case options.

- Make sure that you have cleared any formats you searched for in a previous Find operation. If you choose formats, you see the formats you have chosen (such as Times Roman Bold) under the Find What text box. To clear your format choices from a previous Find operation, drop down the Format list box and choose Clear.

Finding Text with Wild Cards

In a card game, a wild card—such as the Joker—can stand for any other card. In a computer search, a *wild-card character* stands for any character in a search. You can use a wild-card character when you search with the Find command (or with the Replace command, which is discussed later in this chapter).

Word 5 has an expanded repertoire of wild-card codes, as shown in table 4.3. You can search for any character, as in previous versions, using the question-mark wild card. In Version 5, you can search for any number (0 through 9), any letter (A-Z or a-z), or any mathematical typesetting formula.

Table 4.3
Word 5's Wild-Card
Characters

Wild-card character	Matches
?	Any character
^ #	Any number
^ *	Any letter (A-Z or a-z)
^ \	Any formula character

Suppose that you want to search for all the passages that mention the date of a letter you wrote sometime toward the end of May, but you don't remember exactly which day. If you type *May* ^ # ^ # in the Find What text box, Word matches any day in May from May 1 through May 31.

Because the question mark and caret characters are used for wild cards, you must take a special step to search for these characters in your document. You type a caret (^) before the question mark or caret character. Suppose that you want to find every sentence in your document that ends in a question mark; type ^ ? in the Find What text box. Instead of typing this code (or the ^ ^ code, which searches for a caret), you can simply choose Question Mark or Caret from the Special list box.

To search with wild cards in Word 5, you don't have to type the complicated wild-card characters, complete with carets. You simply choose them from the Special list box. Table 4.4 lists the choices in the Special list box that you can use to search with wild-card characters.

To search with this wild card	Choose this option
? (Any character)	Any character
^ # (Any number)	Unspecified digit
^ * (Any letter)	Unspecified letter
^ \ (Formula character)	Any formula character

Using Advanced Search Capabilities

Word enters special characters in your document when you press any of the following keys: Return or Enter (paragraph mark), Shift-Return (end-of-line mark), Shift-Enter (hard page break), ⌘-Enter (section break), space bar (space mark), Tab (tab mark), ⌘-tilde (nonbreaking hyphen), ⌘-hyphen (optional hyphen), or Option-space bar (nonbreaking space). You can use the Find command to search for most of these characters in your document. Searching for these characters would be useful in the following situations:

- You want to find the places where you pressed the space bar two times rather than once at the end of a sentence and to close up the extra space.

- You want to find the places where you pressed Tab at the beginning of a paragraph and replace the Tab keystrokes with automatic first-line indentation.

- You want to find the beginning of the next section. (A section is a division of your document that you create for formatting purposes. Sections are discussed in Chapter 7.)

Searching for Word's special characters closely resembles searching with wild cards. You enter a code that begins with a caret symbol (^) in the Find What dialog box. Table 4.5 lists the codes. You can type these codes directly or choose them from the Special list box.

You can use Find to search for special characters, but these commands are most useful when you use the Replace command (discussed elsewhere in this chapter) to substitute one character for another throughout your document. For example, suppose that you pressed Return twice at the end of each paragraph and you later decide to add space between paragraphs by using the Blank Line Spacing button in the ribbon. Instead of removing the blank lines from your document manually, you can use Replace to search for two paragraph marks ($^p^p$) and replace them with one (^{p}).

Table 4.5
Searching for Word's
Special Characters

To find	Type
Tab mark	^{t}
End-of-line mark	^{n}
Paragraph mark	^{p}
Section mark	^{d}
Hard page break	^{d}
Nonbreaking space	^{s}
Optional hyphen	$^-$

Word 5 has another useful feature: you can use number codes to search for document features such as footnotes and graphics. The codes are the ASCII codes of the characters Word uses to indicate these document elements. As long as you precede the code with a caret, you can search for any ASCII character by using its decimal code. Table 4.6 lists the document elements you can search for using these codes. You can type the codes or you can use the Special list box to enter the Footnote and Graphics codes. (These two options are listed in the Special list box.)

Table 4.6
Searching for Document
Elements with ASCII codes

To search for	Use this code
Footnote	^{5}
Graphic	^{1}
Section Mark	^{12}
Nonbreaking hyphen	^{30}
Space (ordinary)	^{32}

TIP

You can search for more than one special character at a time. For example, to search for places in your document where you pressed the Tab key followed by a space, type $^t^{32}$ in the Find What text box.

You also can search for white space with Word. In a Word search, the term *white space* refers to any special character that produces white space on-screen, including spaces, nonbreaking spaces, paragraph marks, tab marks, end of line marks, section marks, and hard page breaks. When you search for white space, Word finds and highlights the

Part I

Getting Started

next white space of any kind. If more than one special character produces the white space (for example, a paragraph mark followed by a tab mark), Word selects all the characters.

Selecting Text

You have selected text for editing purposes, and you're aware that editing and formatting commands act upon the text you have selected. You probably have been selecting text by dragging over the text you want to highlight. In this section, you expand your knowledge of Word's text-selection commands by exploring all possible ways to highlight text on-screen. By learning the commands that, in just one operation, select a word, line, sentence, paragraph, or even the whole document, you can save time and increase your Word productivity.

You can select text in the following three ways:

- *Fixed units of text*. You can select fixed units of text: words, lines, sentences, paragraphs, and even the whole document. The commands, which are useful for performing editing and formatting operations on one unit of text at a time (such as a word or paragraph), are easy to learn and to use. Fixed Units of Text enables Word to detect the beginning and the end of a unit.

- *Variable units of text*. When you select variable amounts of text, you show Word where the selection begins and ends. Such a selection could include part of a word, two sentences and part of a third, or any other unit of text that you want to highlight.

- *Columns*. You also can select any rectangular area on the screen. For example, if you were looking at this document on a Word screen, you could select the three bullets (dots) in the left margin of this and the preceding two paragraphs, without selecting any text. You then could change the font or size or delete the bullets.

The following sections explain these three selection techniques in detail. Before you go farther, note that some of the selection techniques you are about to explore use the selection bar. The selection bar (see fig. 4.8) is a narrow column of white space running down the left side of every document window, between the text and the left window border. (In Page Layout view, the selection bar runs just to the left of the text boundary.) When you move the mouse pointer over the selection bar, the I-beam pointer changes shape, becoming an arrow pointing up, tilted slightly to the right.

Chapter 4
Editing Text

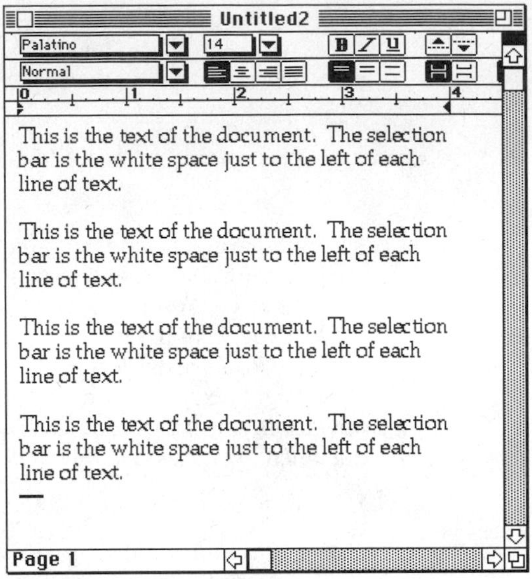

Fig. 4.8
The selection bar.

Fig. 4.8
The selection bar.

> **TIP**
>
> You can easily extend a fixed-unit selection. Simply hold down the Shift key and drag. If you initially selected a word, the selection expands word-by-word. If you initially selected a sentence, the selection expands sentence-by-sentence.

Remember that you can cancel any selection simply by clicking the insertion point outside the selection or by pressing an arrow key.

Selecting Fixed Units of Text

Table 4.7 lists the techniques you use to select fixed units of text.

Table 4.7
Selecting Fixed Units of
Text with the Mouse

To select	Do this
A word	Double-click the word to select the word and its trailing space.
A line	Move the pointer to the selection bar and click.
A sentence	⌘-click the sentence to select the sentence and its trailing space.
A paragraph	Move the pointer to the selection bar and double-click, or triple-click anywhere in the paragraph.
A graphic	Click within the graphic.
Entire document	Move the pointer to the selection bar, hold down the ⌘ key, and click.

Selecting Variable Units of Text

You can choose from mouse and keyboard techniques to select variable amounts of text. To select variable units of text with the mouse, follow these steps:

1. Click at the beginning of the block of text you want to select.

2. Hold the mouse button and move the mouse away from the first character you selected. If you move the mouse to the top or bottom window borders, Word scrolls the screen, line-by-line, until you move the pointer away from the border or release the button.

3. When you finish expanding the highlight, release the mouse button.

TIP

If you're selecting several pages or more of text, the Shift-click technique is easier and faster than the dragging technique.

To select a block of text with a mouse using the Shift-click method, follow these steps:

1. Click where you want the selection to start.

2. If necessary, scroll the screen using the scroll bars, scroll boxes, or scroll arrows.

3. Hold down the Shift key and click the last character you want to select.

To select a block of text using the keyboard, follow these steps:

1. Hold the Shift key and use the arrow keys or their keypad equivalents to expand the highlight.

2. When you finish expanding the highlight, release the Shift and arrow keys.

NOTE

This technique is limited in use because you can type only one character, and Word selects up to the next occurrence of the character, which may not be very far if the character is a common one (such as *a* or *e*). You can extend the selection farther, however, by holding down the Shift key and pressing an arrow key to expand the highlight.

To select a block of text ending with a character you specify, follow these steps:

1. Place the insertion point where you want the selection to begin.

2. Press Option-⌘-H or press the minus key on the keypad. The message Extend to appears on the status line. To cancel the command, press Esc.

3. Type the character to which you want to expand the selection.

After you have selected text, you can extend or contract the selection if you want to. To extend the selection, follow these steps:

1. Hold down the Shift key.

2. Drag the mouse or press an arrow key to expand or contract the selection if necessary.

Selecting Columns (Rectangular Areas)

To select a column of text, hold down the Option key and drag the mouse to highlight a rectangular area on-screen, beginning at the insertion point's location and extending down without highlighting the whole line (see fig. 4.9). This selection technique is used most frequently to select columns of text or numbers in a tabbed table. For this reason, it's called *column selection*. Chapter 17 covers uses for column selection.

Fig. 4.9
Column selection.

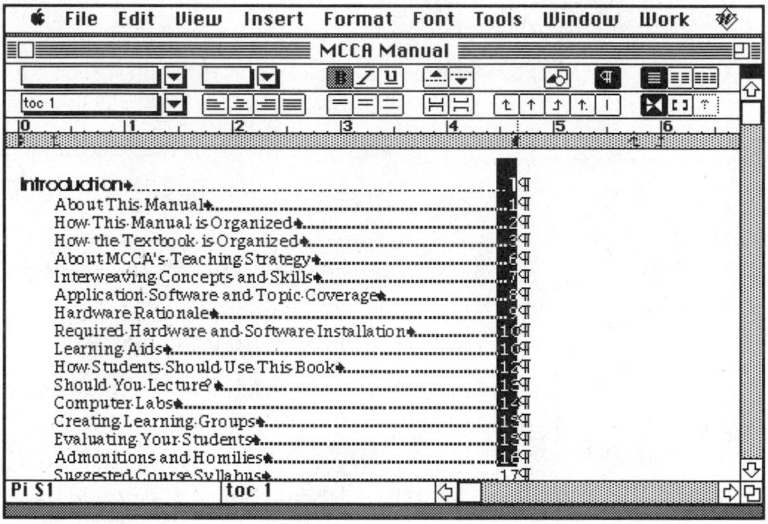

🍎 File Edit View Insert Format Font Tools Window Work
MCCA Manual

Introduction◆..1¶
   About·This·Manual◆.............................1¶
   How·This·Manual·is·Organized◆.........2¶
   How·the·Textbook·is·Organized◆........3¶
   About·MCCA's·Teaching·Strategy◆.......6¶
   Interweaving·Concepts·and·Skills◆......7¶
   Application·Software·and·Topic·Coverage◆....8¶
   Hardware·Rationale◆............................9¶
   Required·Hardware·and·Software·Installation◆.....10¶
   Learning·Aids◆.................................10¶
   How·Students·Should·Use·This·Book◆.....12¶
   Should·You·Lecture?◆..........................13¶
   Computer·Labs◆...............................14¶
   Creating·Learning·Groups◆..................15¶
   Evaluating·Your·Students◆...................15¶
   Admonitions·and·Homilies◆.................16¶
   Suggested·Course·Syllabus◆.................17¶

Pi S1   toc 1

TIP

If the column selection didn't work out right the first time, and you have let go of the mouse button, you can still make adjustments. Simply press the Shift key and move the mouse to adjust the selection.

Deleting Text

The simplest—and probably the most frequently used—deletion technique is to press Delete (called Backspace on some keyboards). If no text is selected, Delete erases the character left of the insertion point. If you have selected text, Delete removes the selection.

Delete removes text permanently—unless you immediately choose Undo from the Edit menu. Equally permanent is typing over a selection, which deletes the text as if you had pressed Delete. Similarly permanent is an Edit menu option, Clear.

If you're editing an important document, think about how to recover an ill-considered deletion. None of the permanent deletion techniques—pressing Delete, typing over a selection, or choosing Clear from the Edit menu—routes the text to the clipboard. Although you can recover text by choosing Undo from the Edit menu or by pressing ⌘-Z, you must do so immediately after you perform the deletion. As soon as you type additional text or choose another command, the deleted text is wiped out forever.

Undo and Paste restore deletions differently. When you restore a deletion with Undo, Word puts the text back from where it came, and always preserves the original formats. When you restore a deletion with Paste, Word places the text at the insertion point. You may lose the original format of the cut text unless you included a trailing paragraph mark in the cut.

Using the Cut command (⌘-X in the Edit menu) to delete text to the clipboard gives you a better chance of recovering deleted text. If you cut the text to the clipboard, you can return the text to the same place by pressing Undo (⌘-Z) immediately. When you cannot use Undo, you still can recover the text (provided you haven't cut or copied anything else to the clipboard in the meantime) by choosing Paste from the Edit menu.

Table 4.8 lists several keyboard commands for deleting text, in addition to Delete or Backspace.

Table 4.8
Keyboard Commands for Deleting Text

To delete	Press
Preceding character	Delete or Backspace
Next character	⌘-Option-F or Del
Preceding word	⌘-Option-Delete or ⌘-Option-Backspace
Next word	⌘-Option-G

Deleting the next character right with the mouse and keyboard wastes time, because you must move your hand to the mouse, move the I-beam pointer to the right of the character, and press Delete. If you have an extended keyboard, learn how to use the Del key. If you have a classic keyboard, learn ⌘-Option-F. Better yet, redefine the Clear key to delete the character forward, and assign the Num Lock function to ⌘-Clear. You learn how to redefine keys in Chapter 27.

Chapter 4
Editing Text

Copying and Moving Text

lmost all Macintosh applications, including Word, enable you to copy and move text using the clipboard (as you did in Chapter 1). Follow these steps:

1. Select the text.

2. Choose Copy or Cut from the Edit menu.

3. Move the insertion point to the text's new location.

4. Choose Paste from the Edit menu.

TIP

If you cut or copy a large block of text to the clipboard and exit Word, a dialog box asks whether you want to save the clipboard. If you don't need the clipboard anymore, choose No. If you are transferring the text to another application, press Return or choose Yes. To return to Word to reconsider, choose Cancel.

Copying through Macintosh's built-in clipboard has many advantages. One advantage is that all applications can use the clipboard. Text you have copied or cut to the clipboard can be inserted into other documents, and even into documents created by applications other than Word. If you cut text to the clipboard and exit Word, the text remains in the clipboard, ready to be pasted anywhere you choose.

Despite its advantages, the clipboard does not provide the easiest or safest way to copy or move text within a Word document. The clipboard holds only one unit of text at a time. If you copy or cut additional text to the clipboard, the new text wipes out the old text without any warning. Losing work is all too easy when you move text with the clipboard.

Suppose that in a major reorganization of your document, you cut a big block of text to the clipboard so that you can move the copy elsewhere. As you scroll to the new location, however, you notice—and stop to fix—something wrong in another area of text, perhaps a word or two. By fixing a small error, you cut more text to the clipboard and wipe out the huge chunk you're moving. When you arrive at the new location and use the Paste command, you are in for a surprise.

You can avoid this pitfall in the following two ways:

■ Use Outline view to rearrange large blocks of text. Restructure large units of text by rearranging headings in the Outline view as explained in Chapter 12.

■ Use keyboard copying and moving techniques that bypass the clipboard. These techniques, which are explained in the following sections, only work within a single Word document, however. To copy or move text from one document to another, you have to use the clipboard techniques.

Copying Text without Using the Clipboard

The following technique works only for copying text from one location to another within a document. To copy text from one document to another, you need the clipboard.

To copy text without using the clipboard, follow these steps:

1. Select the text you want to copy.

2. Press ⌘-Option-C. The message Copy to appears on the status line and the insertion point becomes a dotted vertical line.

3. Click the insertion point where you want the copied text to appear. Because the command is incomplete until you press Return, you can adjust the location of the insertion point as often as you want. To cancel the command, press Esc.

4. Press Return to copy the text.

Copying Text with Drag-and-Drop Editing

New to Word 5 is drag-and-drop editing, which was introduced in Chapter 1. When you try drag-and-drop editing, it probably will become your favorite technique.

To enable drag-and-drop editing, choose Preferences from the Tools menu, and activate the Enable Drag-and-Drop Editing check box.

To copy text with drag-and-drop editing, follow these steps:

1. Select the text, and point to the selection.

2. Hold down the ⌘ key and the mouse button.

    You see a dotted box under the pointer, indicating that Word is prepared to copy the text.

3. Move the pointer where you want the text to appear, and release the mouse button.

Moving Text without Using the Clipboard

The following technique works only for moving text from one location to another within a document. To move text from one document to another, you need the clipboard.

To move text without using the clipboard, follow these steps:

1. Select the text you want to move.

2. Press ⌘-Option-X. The message Move to appears on the status line. The insertion point becomes a dotted vertical line.

3. Click the insertion point where you want the text you are moving to appear.

4. Press Return.

Moving Text with Drag-and-Drop Editing

The easiest way to move text is to use drag-and-drop editing. If necessary, activate the Enable Drag-and-Drop Editing Check box in the Preferences dialog box (Tools menu).

To move text with drag-and-drop editing, follow these steps:

1. Select the text and point to the selection.

2. Hold down the mouse button. You see a small dotted box under the pointer.

3. Move the insertion point where you want the text to be moved, and release the mouse button.

Replacing Text

So far in this chapter, you have reviewed foundational Word skills for scrolling, finding specific locations in your document, selecting text, and editing. With Word's Replace command, you can automate certain editing tasks, such as replacing one word with another throughout your document. The Replace command on Word 5's Edit menu is a relocated, renamed, and much-improved version of the Change command of Version 4. Replace is much like Find, in that the command locates text, special characters, or formats in your document. If you use Replace rather than Find, however, you can specify a replacement for text, characters, or formats.

Using the Replace Command

The following list shows you some of the ways that you can use Replace:

■ *Replace one word or phrase with another throughout your document.* Suppose that your company, Small-Scale Enterprises, is acquired by Big Conglomerate, Inc., and you get a memo informing you that the name "Small-Scale Enterprises" is never to be used again. In all your documents, you replace "Small-Scale Enterprises" with "Big Conglomerate, Inc."

- *Replace an extraneous word or phrase with nothing.* If you suspect that you have overused a word, such as *really*, *very*, or *significant*, you can perform a Replace operation that removes the word from your document without replacement and closes up the space.

- *Substitute one special character for another.* Suppose that you need to transmit by modem a document in which you have used tabs extensively, and tabs give the receiving system fits. With the Replace command, you can replace each tab with five spaces.

- *Search for and replace a format or style.* This is one of the most useful new features of Word 5. With Word 5's Replace command, you can search for italic throughout your document and change it to underlining, or you can search for flush-left paragraph formating and change it to justified. You learn more about this use of the Replace command in Chapters 5, 6, and 8.

- *Search for a particular word or phrase you typed in a particular format, and replace the format.* Suppose that you typed your company name in boldface in some places but not in others. For consistency, you decide to remove the boldface from all occurrences of your company's name. You can search for the boldfaced name and replace the name with standard text.

When you choose Replace from the Edit menu, you see the Replace dialog box (see fig. 4.10). The Replace dialog box has the following features:

Fig. 4.10
The Replace dialog box.

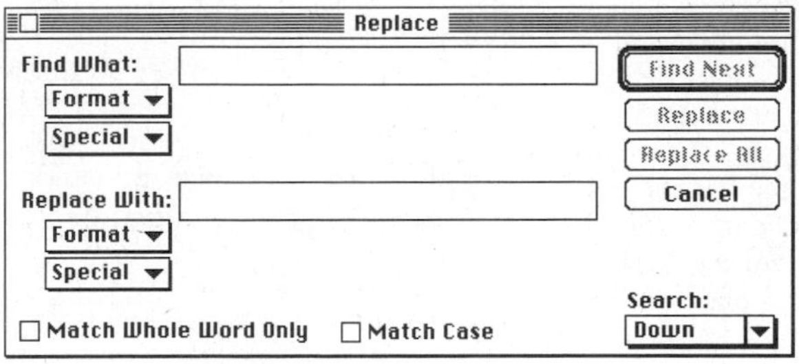

Find What. In this text box, you type the character, word, or phrase you want Word to find. You can type up to 255 characters, including spaces and any of the Mac's or Word's special characters, and you can use wild cards.

Chapter 4
Editing Text

Replace With. In this text box, you type the character, word, or phrase you want Word to substitute for the text in the Find What text box. You can replace the search text with the following special characters: tab mark (^t), end of line mark (^n), paragraph mark (^p), hard page break (^d), nonbreaking space (^s), and optional hyphen (^-). This field does not accept wild cards.

Format. New to Word 5 is the capability to search and replace formats (character formats, paragraph formats, and styles). You use the Format list box under Find What to specify the format for which you want to search, and you use the Format list box under Replace With to choose the format you want to substitute. For example, you can search for bold text and replace the boldface with italic. You do not need to use the Find What and Replace With boxes for a format search; Word searches for and replaces any text with the format you specify. This important feature is discussed in more detail in the chapters on character and paragraph formatting and in Chapter 8.

Special. Use the Special list boxes to place special characters (such as tab marks or end of line marks) in the Find What and Replace With text boxes. If you place a tab mark code (^t) in the Find What box and a paragraph mark code (^p) in the Replace With box, Word will replace tab marks with paragraph marks.

Match Whole Word Only (default: off). To restrict the search to whole words, click the Whole Word box. If you type *report* in the Find What box with Whole Word turned on, Word then finds *report* but not *reporting, reports,* or *reported*.

Match Case (default: off). By default, Word's searches aren't case-sensitive—the program ignores uppercase and lowercase as it searches. For example, if you type *WORD* in the Find What text box, the program will match *Word, word, WORD,* or any other combination of upper- and lowercase letters.

Search (default: Down). From this list box, you choose the direction of the search (up or down). You also can choose All (search the whole document). If you selected text before choosing Replace, Selection replaces the default direction (Down).

Command Buttons. Choose Find Next to find the next occurrence of the search text or choose Replace All to replace all occurrences without confirmation. If you have chosen Find Next, you can choose Replace to make one substitution or choose Find Next to skip to the next occurrence. Choose Cancel at any time to stop replacing.

TIP

To replace the search text with more than 255 characters of replacement text or with a graphic, copy the text or graphic to the clipboard before choosing Replace. Type ^c in the Replace With text box or choose Clipboard Contents from the Special list box in the Replace With area.

Performing a Replace

In this section, you learn how to replace a word, phrase, or special character throughout your document. In subsequent chapters, you can learn more about replacing formats.

Before you choose Replace, think carefully about whether you want to replace with or without confirmation. The Replace All command button tells Word to perform all the replacements without asking you to confirm each of them. Confirming each replacement of a word or a special character that appears dozens or hundreds of times in your document can be tedious. Replacing without confirmation can be hazardous, however. If you're not careful, Word may perform the replacement in inappropriate places.

Suppose that you have decided to remove the word *very* from your document. You set up Replace to find *very* and replace it with nothing. Then you choose Replace All. Word dutifully removes *very* from all instances of the word *every*, as well as removing the whole-word instances of the search text. So instead of reading "Every so often," your document reads, "E so often." Word's spelling checker will not catch this mistake, because the spelling checker ignores single letters. To avoid this and other unwanted replacement problems, follow these suggestions:

- Use the Match Whole Word Only option if you're changing a word. The use of this option would have prevented Word from removing *very* from *every*, in the example just given.

- Always try the replacement with confirmation first. After you see how Word is performing the replacement and you are convinced that there's no problem with the Replace dialog box settings, you can safely choose Replace All to perform the rest of the replacements without confirmation.

With these cautions in mind, you're ready to replace text in a document you don't need or by copying an existing document to a new file to create a practice document.

Like the Find dialog box, the Replace dialog box retains the settings from the preceding Find or Replace operation within the current operating session. Clear the old settings before you perform a new Replace operation. When you start typing, Word deletes the old text, but does not automatically remove previous format-search information from the Format list box. You must clear the format before proceeding. To clear the format, drop down the Format list box (under Find What) and choose Clear.

To replace a word or phrase with confirmation, follow these steps:

1. Choose Replace from the Edit menu or press ⌘-H. You see the Replace dialog box.

2. In the Find What box, type the word or phrase you want Word to match. You can type up to 255 characters. (When the typed characters fill the text box, the box scrolls to make more room.)

3. In the Replace With box, type the word or phrase you want Word to substitute. You can type up to 255 characters in this box, too.

4. To perform a case-sensitive search, activate the Match Case option.

5. To perform a whole-word search, activate the Match Whole Word Only option.

6. If necessary, choose the correct search direction in the Search list box. By default, Word searches Down, unless you have selected text before choosing Replace (if so, Word searches the selection).

7. Choose Find Next to initiate the search.

   If Word finds a match, the match is highlighted in your document. Choose Replace to make the substitution and move on to the next occurrence of the search text or choose Cancel to stop the replacement operation. Word continues to find matches until no more matches are found or until you choose Cancel.

   If Word or cannot find a match or more matches, an alert box appears asking whether you want to continue the search from the beginning of the document (or the end, if you're searching up). Choose OK or Cancel. If you choose OK and Word still doesn't find a match, another alert box appears to inform you that the end of the document has been reached without finding the text you specified.

Quick Review

This section concisely summarizes the most useful information in this chapter. Check "Productivity Tips" for a review of high-productivity tips and tricks, and review "Techniques" when you forget how to perform a specific procedure.

Productivity Tips

- To work with an existing document in your Word session, start the program by double-clicking the document icon.

- To move the insertion point quickly to the place you last edited a document, press ⌘-Option-Z immediately after you open the document.

- Within Word, open a recently edited document by choosing the document's name from the File menu.

- System 7 users: search a long list of files in the Open dialog box by typing the document's first letter.

- To reduce the number of documents Word displays in the Open dialog box, choose Word documents in the List Files of Type list box.

- If you see numbers when you use the keypad to move the insertion point, press Clear to toggle the Num Lock mode off.

- Don't scroll line-by-line or screen-by-screen through a long document when you try to locate text. If you know the page number, use Go To; otherwise, use Find.

- Practice using Go Back to return to the location of previous edits.

- Master the techniques for selecting fixed units of text: words, lines, sentences, and paragraphs. You save time by letting Word locate the beginning and end of the selection. To extend the selection by the unit you originally selected (for example, sentence-by-sentence or paragraph-by-paragraph), hold down the Shift key and move the mouse.

- To highlight a large block with the mouse, don't drag the selection for more than a page or two. Click the insertion point at the beginning of the text you want to select, and then use the scroll bar, boxes, or arrows to scroll to the end of the selection. Hold down the Shift key and click where you want the selection to end.

- To delete a selection and insert something else, type over the selection.

- Your best chance of recovering an accidental deletion is to delete a selection with Cut (Edit menu). Text deleted this way can be restored by using Undo or Paste.

- Don't try to reorganize a long document by cutting and pasting. Use the Outline view.

Chapter 4
Editing Text

■ For maximum protection against accidental data loss while moving text, learn how to bypass the clipboard.

■ Use Replace with caution. Before carrying out a replacement without confirmation, try the replacement settings with confirmation a few times.

Techniques

This section provides concise, quick-reference summaries of all the procedures introduced in this chapter.

Copying Text

To copy text through the clipboard:

1. Select the text.

2. Choose Copy from the Edit menu or press ⌘-C.

3. Click the insertion point where you want the copied text to appear.

4. Choose Paste from the Edit menu or press ⌘-V.

To copy text within a Word document (bypassing the clipboard):

1. Select the text you want to copy.

2. Press ⌘-Option-C.

3. Click the insertion point where you want to place the copied text.

4. Press Return.

To copy text with drag-and drop editing:

1. Select the text, and point to the selection.

2. Hold down the command key and the mouse button.

3. Drag the pointer to the place you want the text to be copied.

4. Release the mouse button.

Deleting Text

To delete the selection, choose one of the following techniques:

Press Delete, or choose Clear from the Edit menu, or type over the selection to remove the text without cutting to the clipboard.

Choose Cut from the Edit menu or press ⌘-X to store the deletion in the clipboard.

Finding Text

To search for a word or phrase, choose one of the following techniques:

1. To search only the text you select, select the text or position the insertion point where you want the search to begin.

2. Choose Find from the Utilities menu or press ⌘-F.

3. When the Find dialog box appears, type the text you want to find in the Find What box.

4. To perform a case-sensitive search, activate the Match Case option.

5. To perform a whole-word search, activate the Match Whole Word Only option.

6. If necessary, choose the correct search direction in the Search list box.

7. Choose Find Next.

To find and replace special characters, use the following codes:

To search for	Use this code
Any character	?
Caret	^ ^
End-of-line mark	^n
Footnote	^1
Graphic	^5
Hard page break	^d
Formula character	^\
Nonbreaking space	^s
Optional hyphen	^-
Nonbreaking hyphen	^32
Paragraph mark	^p

To search for	Use this code
Question mark	$^?$
Section mark	^{d} or ^{32}
Space	^{32}
Tab mark	^{t}
Unspecified digit.	$^\#$
Unspecified letter	*

Using Go To

To move the insertion point to the beginning of a specific page:

1. Choose Go To from the Edit menu or press ⌘-G.

2. When the Go To dialog box appears, type the number of the page to which you want to move the insertion point.

3. Choose OK.

Inserting a File

To insert a Word file into the active document:

1. Choose File from the Insert menu.

2. To reduce the number of files displayed in the Document List Box, choose List Files of Type. Then choose the Word Documents option.

3. Use the Document List Box and Current Folder List to locate the document you want to open.

4. When the Document List displays the document you want to open, double-click the document's name or use the arrow keys to highlight the document's name, and press Enter.

Opening Documents

To start Word and open an existing document at the same time:

1. In the Finder, open the folder or disk that contains the Word document you want to open.

2. Double-click the document's icon.

To open an existing Word document within Word:

1. Choose Open from the File menu or press ⌘-O.

2. To reduce the number of files displayed in the Document List Box, choose List Files of Type. Then choose the Word Documents option.

3. Use the Document List Box and Current Folder List to locate the document you want to open.

4. When the Document List displays the document you want to open, double-click the document's name. Alternatively, use the arrow keys to highlight the document's name and then press Enter.

To open a recently edited document:

Choose the document's name from the File menu.

To open a stationery document:

1. Choose Open from the File menu or press ⌘-O.

2. Choose List Files of Type.

3. Choose the Word Documents option.

4. Use the Document List Box and Current Folder List to locate the document you want to open.

5. When the Document List displays the document you want to open, double-click the document's name. Alternatively, use the arrow keys to highlight the document's name, and press Enter.

To open a non-Word document:

1. Choose Open from the File menu, or press ⌘-O.

2. Choose List Files of Type.

3. Choose the format of the document you want to open.

4. Use the Document List Box and Current Folder List to locate the document you want to open.

5. When the Document List displays the document you want to open, double-click the document's name. Alternatively, use the arrow keys to highlight the document's name and then press Enter.

Moving Text

To move text through the clipboard:

1. Select the text.

2. Choose Cut from the Edit menu or press ⌘-X.

3. Move the insertion point to where you want the text to appear.

4. Choose Paste from the Edit menu or press ⌘-V.

To move text without the clipboard:

1. Select the text you want to move.

2. Press ⌘-Option-X.

3. Click the insertion point where you want the text to appear.

4. Press Return.

To move text with drag-and-drop editing:

1. Select the text.

2. Point to the selection, and hold down the mouse button.

3. Move the points to the place you want the text to be moved.

4. Release the mouse button.

Replacing Text

To replace a word or phrase throughout your document:

1. Choose Replace from the Edit menu.

2. In the Find What text box, type the word or phrase you want Word to match.

3. In the Replace with box, type the word or phrase you want Word to substitute.

4. If necessary, choose the correct search direction in the Search list box.

5. Choose Find Next to initiate the Search.

6. Choose Replace to perform the replacement, Replace All to replace all additional instances without confirmation, Find Next to skip this instance and confirm the next replacement, or Candel to return to your document.

Selecting Text

To select a word and its trailing space:

> Double-click the word.

To select a line:

> Move the pointer to the selection bar and click.

To select a sentence:

> ⌘-click the sentence to select the sentence and its trailing space.

To select a paragraph:

> Move the pointer to the selection bar and double-click, or triple-click anywhere in the paragraph.

To select a graphic:

> Click within the graphic.

To select the entire document:

> Move the pointer to the selection bar, hold down the ⌘ key, and click.

To select a block by dragging:

1. Click at the beginning of the block of text you want to select.

2. Hold the mouse button and move the mouse away from the first character you selected.

3. After you expand the highlight, release the mouse button.

To select a block with the keyboard:

1. Hold the Shift key and use the arrow keys or their keypad equivalents to expand the highlight.

2. After you expand the highlight, release the Shift and arrow keys.

To select a block by Shift-clicking:

1. Click where you want the selection to start.

2. If necessary, scroll the screen, using the scroll bars, boxes, or arrow.

3. Hold down the Shift key and click the last character you want to select.

To select a block ending in a specific character:

1. Place the insertion point where you want the selection to begin.

2. Press Option-⌘-H or press the minus key on the keypad. The message Extend to appears on the status line. To cancel the command, press Esc.

3. Type the character to which you want to expand the selection.

To extend the selection:

1. Hold down the Shift key.

2. Drag the mouse or press an arrow key to expand or contract the selection.

To select a column (rectangular area):

Hold down the Option key and select by dragging.

Formatting Characters

With Word, formatting falls into four broad categories or *domains*: character, paragraph, section, and document formats. Character formats, the subject of this chapter, affect the appearance of the characters you type in Word documents.

By default, Word enters characters in the New York font, using a 12-point font size. (A *point* is a printer's measurement. There are 72 points per inch, so Word's standard font size is one-sixth inch high.) You can alter characters as often as you like, choosing other fonts and other font sizes, character styles (such as bold, italic, shadow characters, and outline characters), position (superscript or subscript), spacing (condensed or expanded), and case (all uppercase, all lowercase, first letter in each word capitalized, or first letter in each sentence capitalized).

After you have chosen character formats, you can repeat and copy them elsewhere in your document. Important new Word 5 features enable you to search and replace character formats throughout your document.

Focusing on character formats, this chapter nevertheless provides a comprehensive, in-depth treatment of character formatting with Word and introduces the distinctive Word way of formatting documents. This chapter discusses the following topics:

- *Designing Effective Documents.* The first step in formatting effectively is to learn some fundamentals of document design.

- *Formatting with Word: an Overview.* You learn how Word distinguishes among character, paragraph, section, and document formats.

- *Understanding Formatting Options and Strategies.* You learn what options are available and the ways to access each option.

- *Choosing Fonts and Font Sizes.* This section explains how to choose fonts and font sizes for your document.

- *Choosing Character Styles.* You learn how to choose character styles, such as boldface and italic.

- *Choosing Position.* You find complete guidance for using technical or mathematical superscript or subscript characters.

- *Choosing Spacing (Kerning).* For attractive effects, you can add additional space between characters—and as this section explains, you also can squeeze a word into a narrow space by taking some space away.

- *Choosing Case.* New to Word 5 is a Change Case command that you can use to change the case (capitalization) of a selection without retyping.

- *Finding and Replacing Character Formats.* New to Word 5 are important new capabilities in Word's Find and Replace commands.

- *Repeating and Copying Character Formats.* In this section, you learn important shortcut techniques for repeating character formatting commands and copying them elsewhere in your document.

Understanding Document Design

n *The Psychology of Everyday Things* (New York: Basic Books, 1988), Donald A. Norman lists two basic attributes of a good design. A design should be *visible*. Design elements should be obvious; the eye shouldn't have to hunt for them. A design also should be *intuitive*. The relationship of one design element to the next should be natural and logical so that the viewer can grasp the relationship without thinking about it.

All the major principles of good design follow from Norman's two points. Consider the following principles:

- Use display type to call attention to headings. In typography, the term *display type* refers to the *typeface* (the distinctive design, such as Helvetica or Avant-Garde) chosen for headings and titles.

  Many designers prefer to use *sans serif* typefaces such as Helvetica for display type. (A sans serif typeface lacks the little finishing lines at the end of the strokes in a letter.) The use of a sans serif typeface for display type helps the reader distinguish the headings from the *body type* (the document's text), which is usually smaller and printed in a serif font (such as Times Roman or New York). (A serif font *does* have the little finishing strokes on each letter.)

- Use font sizes and emphases logically to show the relationship among headings. First-level headings, for instance, should be centered, boldfaced, or printed in a larger font to make them obvious and to indicate their importance. Second-level and third-level headings, in contrast, should be smaller and less conspicuous.

- Use white space effectively. Break up text on the page by using lists with bullets or numbers. Scientific studies of document readability show that people remember details better if they are listed and set apart from the text.

- Strive for simplicity and consistency to keep your design visible and intuitively logical. Your design choices should guide your readers through your document. The simpler and more consistent your design choices and usage, the easier the reader's task. Try to restrict your design to two typefaces, one for display type and one for body type. Use emphases, such as boldface or italic, sparingly.

Good design involves more than choosing beautiful typefaces and arranging text elements pleasingly. Above all else, good design is a matter of choosing design elements that communicate effectively and naturally with your readers. Remember that you can break any design rule if doing so improves the document's capability to communicate.

Microsoft Word for the Macintosh is a superb environment for interactive document design. The Mac's treasure trove of typefaces, which you can expand to your heart's content, is at your fingertips. Equipped with even a modest laser printer, Word can produce output that the untrained eye cannot distinguish from the output of professional typesetting machines. You can use paragraph formats, such as indentations, alignments, and blank lines, to break up text on the page so that logical relations are clear. Because you see your formatting choices on-screen before you print, judging the effectiveness of the design is easy.

Before creating an elaborate design for a document, remember that many publishers, government and private funding agencies, professional associations, and colleges impose strict style guidelines—so strict that your document may be rejected on the basis of style alone. Before you submit your document for publication or review, contact the organization to which you plan to submit the document and ask for a copy of their style guidelines.

Formatting with Word: An Overview

To design an effective document with Word 5, you should understand the Word approach to formatting. You learn in the following sections that Word divides formats into four domains and that you can format while you type or after you type. You also find a brief explanation of your font and font size options and an overview of your character formatting options with Word 5.

Understanding the Four Formatting Domains

You format documents by applying four different kinds of formatting commands: *character*, *paragraph, section*, and *document* formats. The following sections give a brief overview of the four formatting domains.

Character Formats

The smallest unit of formatting in Word is character formatting. Character formats include *font* (typeface design), *font size* (in printer's points), *style* (emphases such as boldface, outlining, italic, or underlining), *position* (superscript or subscript) and *spacing* (compressed or expanded), *case* (uppercase, lowercase, first letter of word capitalized, or first letter of sentence capitalized), and *hidden text* (text that does not display or print). You can format as many characters as you choose, from one character to all the characters in the document.

Paragraph Formats

In Word, a paragraph is any block of text between two paragraph marks (or between the beginning of a document and the first paragraph mark). A paragraph can be a single word or a single character. Paragraph formats, such as indents, line spacing, tabs, and borders, apply to the entire paragraph or paragraphs, if more than one is selected. Chapter 6 discusses paragraph formats.

Section Formats

Section formats are page style formats that can vary within a document. These formats include page numbers, columns, line numbers, headers, and footers. For single-section documents, section formats apply to the whole document. If you divide your document into sections by pressing ⌘-Enter, however, you can change the section formats. Section breaks are useful for creating documents with separate chapters.

Document Formats

Document formats are page style formats that apply to the whole document. These formats include margins, footnote position, and default tab width. Chapter 7 examines section and document formatting.

Formatting Strategies

You can format your document in two different ways. You can choose formats before you start typing. As you type, Word enters the formats and text simultaneously. To stop formats, choose commands that cancel character formatting (the Plain Text option on the Font menu or ⌘-Shift-Z) or paragraph formatting (⌘-Shift-P). You also can choose formats after you type. When you format this way, you select text and apply a formatting command to the text in the selection.

One advantage of formatting before you type is that you don't have to select the text before formatting. The disadvantage is that you must think about formatting ("What command do I want?") at the same time you are thinking about other writing concerns ("What tense am I using? Is that modifier dangling or not? What the heck am I trying to say?"). If you have trouble writing, you may want to format later.

Writing may be easier for you, however, when you can see on-screen how your printed text will look. In technical writing, for instance, many document elements, such as instructions, are easier to write (and edit) when you set them off from the rest of the text.

Unless you're a beginning writer, document processing theory suggests a good reason to format as you type rather than formatting later. Character and paragraph formats aren't simply variations of the way ink is stamped, sprayed, or fused onto the page—formats have meaning. Font choices, list formats, fixed-width characters, and other formats signal something to the reader about the nature and significance of the document. Is the document formal or informal? Personal or impersonal? Conservative or trendy? Solemn or serendipitous? As you become more conscious of the meaning of formats, you see that with Word you have two ways to express what you want to say. The first is the meaning of the text you type; the second is the signals you send by the formatting choices you make.

Understanding Your Font and Font Size Choices

Your font and font size options with Word depend on which fonts you have installed in your Mac's System file. With System 6 and previous Mac Systems, you install fonts by using Font/DA Mover, a utility program that comes with your Mac's system software. With System 7, you install fonts simply by dragging them to the System Folder, and you can see which fonts you have installed by double-clicking the System file.

To use your Mac's fonts effectively with Word, you need to understand some terminology. In the Macintosh world, the term *font* refers to the distinctive design of a set of characters. Each design has its own name, such as Helvetica, Times Roman, or Palatino. The term *font size* refers to the height of the tallest characters, measured from the base line. Font size is measured in *printer's points* (72 per inch). By default, Word prints a standard six lines of 12-point type per vertical inch on the page.

In the following sections, you explore additional, important information about your Mac's fonts and how Word uses them. You learn the distinction between bit-mapped and scalable fonts and how this distinction affects the appearance of fonts on-screen and in your printed documents. You also learn the difference between proportionally spaced and monospace fonts.

Bit-Mapped and Scalable Fonts

Your Macintosh can use two kinds of fonts: *bit-mapped* fonts and *scalable* fonts. A bit-mapped font (also called a *fixed-size font*) forms characters with hundreds of tiny dots. Bit-mapped fonts reside in a disk file, which contains a complete set of characters for a given size (such as

New York 12). For most fonts, a variety of frequently used sizes (such as 10, 12, 14, 18, and 24) is available. Your Macintosh can display a bit-mapped font quickly, but the font may not look good on-screen in a size other than the ones installed in your System file. If you choose a font size other than the ones available on disk, your Macintosh must try to scale the font. In figure 5.1, for example, the bit-mapped Venice font is supported by a disk file for only one font size (14 points); if you choose another size, the font looks inferior on-screen and not much better on paper.

Scalable fonts (also called *outline* fonts) generate characters of any size (within the Mac's range of 4 to 16,238 points), using a mathematical formula. For this reason, you can choose font size and the scalable font will produce a good looking screen image. In figure 5.1, for example, the scalable New York font looks good no matter which size you choose. Scalable fonts have a disadvantage, however; because your Macintosh must calculate the appearance of each character, scalable fonts display more slowly on-screen.

Fig. 5.1
Bit-mapped versus
scalable fonts.

Bit-mapped
font

Scalable
font

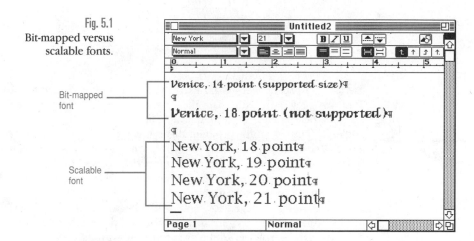

You can tell at a glance which bit-mapped font sizes will display well on your screen. The Font menu shows the 14-point font size with outline characters (see fig. 5.2). This font size is fully supported by a bit-mapped font in your Mac's System file, so it looks good on-screen. If you choose a font size that is not outlined on the font menu, the font will look jagged or even illegible on your Mac's screen.

Chapter 5

Formatting Characters

Fig. 5.2
An outlined font size
(Venice 14) on the
Font menu.

Font

9 Point
10 Point
12 Point
✓14 Point
18 Point
24 Point

Up   ⌘]
Down   ⌘[
Other...
Default Font...

Athens
Avant Garde
Bookman
Cairo
Chicago
Courier
Geneva
Helvetica
London
Los Angeles
Monaco
N Helvetica Narrow
New Century Schlbk
New York
Palatino
San Francisco
Symbol
Times
✓Venice
Zapf Chancery
Zapf Dingbats

Two kinds of scalable fonts are used commonly in the Mac world: Adobe Type Manager (ATM) and, with the arrival of System 7, TrueType fonts. Adobe Type Manager, a program available from Adobe Systems, is an add-on Macintosh utility program that manages Adobe's PostScript fonts and enables you to print these fonts even on a non-PostScript printer. When your Mac runs ATM, the ATM-compatible PostScript fonts installed in your System file look good on-screen, no matter what font size you choose. In addition, these fonts and font sizes also look good when printed, even if you have a low-end printer such as an ImageWriter or StyleWriter. Adobe Type Manager, however, does not affect fonts other than those sold by Adobe or compatible with its Type 1 font specifications.

The TrueType software, developed by Apple, is built into System 7. You do not have to run an add-on utility program to take advantage of TrueType fonts. Like ATM fonts, TrueType fonts look good on-screen and on paper no matter which font size you choose. When you installed System 7, you installed the following TrueType fonts in your System file: Chicago, Courier, Geneva, Helvetica, Monaco, New York, Symbol, and Times. Additional TrueType fonts are available from font design firms such as Letraset (800-343-TYPE). If a TrueType font is installed in your

System folder, the Font menu uses outline characters to display all the font size options for that font, an indication that you can expect good results when you print your document.

You can tell at a glance which fonts are installed in your System file. In the Finder, double-click the System file in the System folder. A window opens, listing the fonts. You also can tell which fonts are TrueType fonts and which are bit-mapped fonts because TrueType fonts are listed without any font size. Double-click the font's icon to see on-screen what a font looks like displayed in three font sizes.

If all these options confuse you, find out whether your Macintosh is equipped with a PostScript-compatible laser printer such as the Laser-Writer NT. If so, buy a copy of Adobe Type Manager (ATM). ATM comes with scalable screen fonts corresponding to the PostScript fonts built into your laser printer. If you don't have a PostScript printer, you are better off with TrueType fonts, which don't require you to purchase ATM.

Fixed Width Versus Proportionally Spaced Fonts

The characters in a fixed-width font (such as Monaco or Courier) always occupy the same width, whether the character is narrow (like *l*) or wide (like *w*). Fixed-width fonts look like typewritten characters—not surprising, considering that typewriters produce fixed-width type. Sometimes Courier is chosen for business correspondence and memos because the "typewriter-like" appearance suggests that a document has been typed especially for the recipient.

In proportionally spaced fonts (such as Chicago, Geneva, or New York), the wide characters take up more space than the narrow characters. The result looks professional, but also has an impersonal typeset appearance. People often react to such type the way they react to a printed book; they assume that the text has been scrutinized, edited, and proofread. As a result, proportionally spaced type (especially when printed with a laser printer) carries all the authority—and the responsibility for accurate reporting and good judgment—of a printed document.

Figure 5.3 shows the difference between a fixed-width and a proportionally spaced font.

Fig. 5.3
Fixed-width versus
proportionally spaced
fonts.

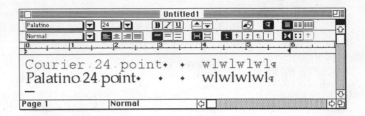

Understanding Character Formatting Options

Now that you know the fundamentals of Word's formatting capabilities and have mastered some basic terminological distinctions, you are ready to survey the range of character formatting options. With Word, you can vary the following format attributes of any character you can display on-screen:

Font (default: New York). The font is the type design of the characters you enter. Word uses all the fonts currently available in your System folder. To add more fonts, see Appendix A.

Font Size (default: 12 points). Size is the height of a font, measured in printer's points.

Color (default: black). If you have a color monitor, you can display characters in six colors (blue, cyan, green, magenta, red, and yellow).

Style (default: plain text). Choose emphases such as boldface, italic, outline characters, shadow characters, and strikethrough characters. Style choices include *hidden text*, which doesn't show on-screen or in print, and *small caps*, a format in which lowercase letters are displayed in print using small uppercase letters.

Underlining (default: single underline). You can choose from four kinds of underlines: single underline, word-only underline, double underline, and dotted underline.

Position (default: Normal). You can position superscript or subscript characters above or below the line (at a height you specify). By default, Word superscripts or subscripts by three points.

Spacing (default: Normal). You can adjust the space between the characters. The Expanded option widens the space, and the Condensed option narrows the space. The Expanded and Condensed options are in the Spacing options group of the Character dialog box.

Case. You can choose from the following case options: all uppercase, all lowercase, first letter capitalized in each word (Title Case), and first word capitalized in each sentence (Sentence case).

Figure 5.4 illustrates Word 5 character formatting options.

Fig. 5.4
Examples of character
formatting options.

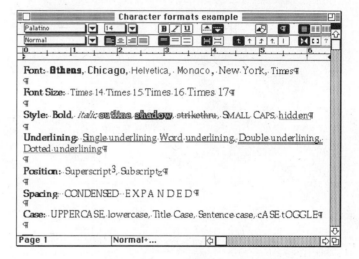

Font: **Athens**, Chicago, Helvetica, Monaco, New York, Times¶
¶
Font Size: Times 14 Times 15 Times 16 Times 17¶
¶
Style: **Bold**, *italic*, outline, shadow, strikethru, SMALL CAPS, hidden¶
Underlining: Single underlining Word underlining, Double underlining, Dotted underlining¶
¶
Position: Superscript^{3}, Subscript$_{2}$¶
¶
Spacing: CONDENSED EXPANDED¶
¶
Case: UPPERCASE, lowercase, Title Case, Sentence case, cASE tOGGLE¶
¶

Understanding Character Formatting Strategies

Y ou can apply many character formats in six ways (or more, when you consider that you can apply formats *before* or *after* you type). Word always gives you many options, but you may be confused by all the different character formatting options. The following overview discusses the six ways you can choose character formats and gives you tips on when to use them.

Ribbon. From Word 5's new ribbon, you can choose fonts, font sizes, the most commonly used emphases (bold, italic, and underlining), and superscript or subscript (see fig. 5.5). To choose a format, click the appropriate icon on the ribbon menu. The ribbon is a great way to choose character formats—*unless* you have a Classic or SE with a nine-inch display, in which case you may find that the ribbon takes up too much of your screen space.

Fig. 5.5
The ribbon.

SPEED KEY

Format menu. From the Format menu shown in figure 5.6, you can choose commonly used emphases (bold, italic, and underline). You also can use the Plain Text option to cancel emphasis choices. The Format menu gives mouse users a quick way to choose emphases, but the keyboard shortcuts are quicker. If you don't see the ribbon on-screen, choose Ribbon from the View menu or use the ⌘-Option-R keyboard shortcut.

Fig. 5.6
The Format menu.

WORD 5

Font menu. From the Font menu, you can choose common font sizes (such as 9, 10, 12, 14, 18, and 24 points), and you can raise or lower the font size a point at a time by choosing the Up or Down options (new to Word 5). The Font menu also displays all the fonts that you have installed in your Mac's System file. If you are not using the ribbon, the Font menu provides a good way to choose fonts.

TIP

To display the Character dialog box quickly, use the ⌘-D keyboard shortcut, or double-click the ribbon background.

Character dialog box. The Character dialog box is the slowest of all the character formatting options. You can use it, however, to choose Color and Spacing formats, which aren't available elsewhere (see fig. 5.7). The Character dialog box also has a unique capability: you can use the Apply button to see what a format looks like (if your screen is large enough to see the formatted text behind the dialog box, which remains on-screen). If you don't like what you see, you can choose Cancel without permanently affecting the text.

Fig. 5.7
The Character dialog box.

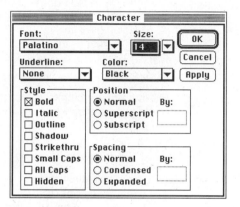

Shortcut keys. If you prefer to use the keyboard rather than the mouse, you can use keyboard shortcuts to enter many character formats. These shortcuts are listed and discussed in this chapter and summarized in the Quick Review at the end of this chapter. Most of Word's formatting shortcut keys all employ the ⌘-Shift key combination; ⌘-Shift-H, for example, applies the small caps format. An exception is made for the most frequently used formats: bold, italic, and underline. You need not press the Shift key (⌘-B, ⌘-I, and ⌘-U).

The ribbon and the Character dialog box always show the formats in effect at the insertion point. To see the current formats, position the insertion point where you want to start typing and glance at the ribbon or display the Character dialog box. The ribbon and Character dialog box's options are blank or grayed if you select text that has two or more conflicting formats.

You now know all the ways you can choose character formats. The rest of this chapter discusses the individual formats, starting with fonts and font sizes.

Choosing Fonts and Font Sizes

In this section, you learn how to change the default font and font size for all your documents and how to change fonts within a specific document.

Changing the Default Font and Font Size

By default, Word uses the 12-point New York font in all new documents. Furthermore, the program returns to this font when you cancel fonts or font sizes you have chosen. For example, suppose that you choose Helvetica 14 for a heading. You then type the heading and press ⌘-Shift-space bar or choose Revert to Style from the Format menu to cancel your font choice. Word reinstates the 12-point New York default.

Choosing the correct default font for your documents is important. If you use your Macintosh primarily for business correspondence and memos, you may want to choose Helvetica 12 to give your letters a clean, modern look. If you write business reports or articles, you may prefer to choose Times instead.

Figure 5.8 shows the fonts that probably are installed in your System file if you use a PostScript laser printer. Some of these fonts (specifically, Avant Garde, Bookman, Helvetica Narrow, Palatino, and Zapf Chancery) are not available if you use an ImageWriter, StyleWriter, or Hewlett-Packard DeskWriter, unless someone has installed the fonts.

Fig. 5.8
Typical font options for a PostScript laser printer.

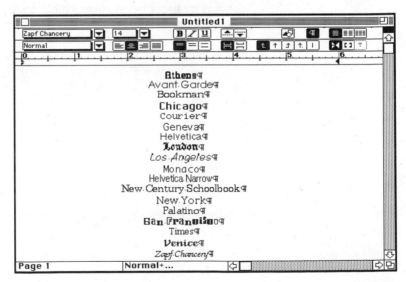

To change the default font, follow these steps:

1. Choose Default Font from the Font menu. The Default Font Preferences dialog box appears.

2. Choose the font you want from the Default Font list box.

3. Choose the font size you want from the Default Size list box.

4. Click the Close box to confirm your choice and return to the document.

After you learn how to define and apply styles, as explained in Chapter 11, you can establish default fonts for stationery documents (introduced in Chapter 2).

A *stationery document* is a generic version of a document, such as a letter that includes your letterhead, return address, today's date, and your signature, but no text or salutation. You can create and save stationery documents so that they include everything you need to develop a document quickly, including a redefined default font and font size. For example, you can create stationery for a business letter that defines Helvetica 12 as the default font and stationery for reports that defines Times Roman 10 as the default font.

Changing Fonts

Changing fonts and font sizes within your document is simple—either before you type or after you type. You can choose fonts and font sizes in many different ways. Try them all so that you can choose the technique that you find most convenient.

Changing Fonts before You Type

TIP

With Word, your font and font size choices are independent of each other. Suppose that you choose Helvetica 14, type a heading, choose Times from the Font menu, and keep typing. Word enters the text in Times 14. To change the size as well as the font, you must make two choices: font and font size.

When you change a font or font size before you type, you "reprogram" the insertion point so that Word enters characters with the font you have chosen.

The ribbon's font and font size boxes always show the font and font size that Word will enter when you start typing. If you glance at the ribbon before typing text, you can see which font and size Word will use.

To change the font before you type, follow these steps:

1. Click the insertion point where you want the font to start.

2. Use one of the following techniques to choose a font:

Choose the font from the drop-down list box on the ribbon.

Choose the font from the Font menu.

Choose Character from the Format menu or press ⌘-D, and when the Character dialog box appears, choose the font from the Font list box in the Character dialog box. Choose OK to confirm your choice.

Use the ⌘-Shift-E keyboard shortcut. When the message Font appears on the status line, type the name of the font you want to use.

3. Type the text.

4. After you finish typing with the font you have chosen, choose a new font or font size, using any of the listed techniques; or restore the previous font or font size.

Your font or font size choice remains in effect until you choose a new font or font size, press ⌘-Shift-space bar, choose Revert to Style from the Format menu to restore the formats in effect for the current style, or click the insertion point within text that has a different font or font size.

Until you create and define your own styles, you will be using the default Normal style. When you choose Revert to Style, Word enters the formats that Microsoft assigned to this style in Word's default style sheet. You learn more about styles, style sheets, and style sheet formatting in Chapter 8.

TIP

For now, remember that choosing Revert to Style is powerful; the Revert to Style command cancels all your formatting choices and restores Word's basic defaults (New York 12 text, flush left paragraph alignment, and single-line spacing).

You can use the Revert to Style command in the Format menu or the ⌘-Shift-space bar shortcut to switch off your font or font size choices. Remember, however, that this command restores all the default formats in Word's Normal style: plain (nonemphasized) text, flush-left paragraph alignment, single-line spacing, and New York 12 font. This command is powerful. Use it only when you want to restore all the formats that are in effect when you open a new Word document.

To change the font size before you type, follow these steps:

1. Click the insertion point where you want to start typing.

2. Use one of the following techniques to choose the font size:

Drop down the point size list box on the ribbon and choose the point size you want or type in the point size list box the point size you want to use.

Choose a point size from the Font menu.

To increase the point size by one point, choose Up from the Font menu or press ⌘-]. After you increase the point size, a message appears in the page number area, confirming the point size you have chosen.

To increase the point size to the next larger point size shown on the Font menu, use the ⌘-Shift-> keyboard shortcut.

To decrease the point size by one point, choose Down from the Font menu or press ⌘-[. After you increase the point size, a message appears in the page number area, confirming the point size you have chosen.

To decrease the point size by the next-smaller point size shown on the Font menu, use the ⌘-Shift-< keyboard shortcut.

Choose Character or Other from the Format menu (or press ⌘-D), and when the Character dialog box appears, choose the point size from the Size box. Choose OK to confirm your choice.

3. When you finish typing with the font size you have chosen, use any of the preceding techniques to choose a new font size or to restore the previous font size.

If you're using nonscalable (bit-mapped) fonts, choose point sizes from the Font menu. Only the Font menu displays installed point sizes in outline characters. When you choose point sizes in other ways, you cannot tell whether a font of the size you have chosen has been installed in the System file. If you are using Adobe Type Manager or TrueType fonts, however, the Font menu offers no advantages over other methods of choosing point sizes; all the point sizes will be shown in outline characters.

Changing Fonts after You Type

Some writers prefer to choose fonts and font sizes after typing the text of the document. To format this way with Word, you select the text you want to format and choose the font or font size.

To change the font or font size after you type, follow these steps:

1. Select the text.

2. Choose a font or font size from the ribbon, the Font menu, or the Character dialog box. Alternatively, use the ⌘-Shift-E keyboard shortcut, type the name of the font, and press Enter.

To change the font or font size for the whole document, follow these steps:

1. Select the entire document in one of the following ways:

   Move the mouse pointer to the selection bar, hold down the ⌘ key, and click.

   Choose Select All from the Edit menu.

   Use the ⌘-A keyboard shortcut.

2. Change the font size by choosing a font or font size from the ribbon, the Font menu, or the Character dialog box. Alternatively, use the ⌘-Shift-E keyboard shortcut, type the name of the font, and press Enter.

Restoring the Default Font and Font Size

To change font or font size choices you have made, select the text and choose the font or size you prefer. Then press ⌘-Shift-space bar, choose Revert to Style from the Format menu, or choose Revert to Style from the Format menu to restore the default font and font size.

To restore the default font and font size throughout your document, select the entire document by ⌘-clicking in the selection bar, by choosing Select All from the Edit menu, or by pressing ⌘-A. Then press ⌘-Shift-space bar or choose Revert to Style from the Format menu to revert to the default font and font size.

Choosing Colors

I f you have a color printer, you can assign colors to selected characters, and Word will print the colors you have chosen. The colors appear on-screen if you're using a color monitor. If you have a black-and-white monitor, Word displays all colors as black on-screen, but the colors will print on a color printer.

To assign color to characters, follow these steps:

1. Place the insertion point where you want the colored text to begin, or select the text.

2. Choose Character from the Format menu or press ⌘-D. The Character dialog box appears.

TIP

With some black-and-white printers, you can choose colors to produce a dimmed effect. Figure 5.9 shows the effect of color choices on characters printed with an Apple Laserwriter NT.

3. Choose a color from the Color list box.

4. Choose OK.

To remove color formatting, follow these steps:

1. Select the colored text.

2. Choose Character from the Format menu or press ⌘-D. The Character dialog box appears.

3. Choose Black from the Color list box.

4. Choose OK.

Fig. 5.9

Effect of color choices on characters printed with a black-and-white printer.

This document was printed on an Apple LaserWriter NT (black)
This document was printed on an Apple LaserWriter NT (blue)
This document was printed on an Apple LaserWriter NT (cyan)
This document was printed on an Apple LaserWriter NT (green)
This document was printed on an Apple LaserWriter NT (yellow)
This document was printed on an Apple LaserWriter NT (magenta)
This document was printed on an Apple LaserWriter NT (red)

Using Character Styles

ord uses the term *style* to refer to character emphasis such as boldface or italic, as well as other character formats (small caps, hidden text). Microsoft also uses the term *style* to refer to the named formats you create and save using the Style option in the Format menu. You learn about the Style option in Chapter 8. To avoid confusion, this book uses the term *character style* to refer to the styles discussed in this section: bold, italic, outline characters, shadow characters, strikethrough, small caps, all caps, hidden characters, and the four underlining styles (single, word, double, and dotted).

TIP

You can add options for choosing formats other than bold, italic, and single underlining to the Format menu. For more information, see Chapter 27.

As with fonts and font sizes, you can apply character styles in many ways. Only bold, italic, or single underline are available through the ribbon or the Format menu, however. To choose other character styles (outline characters, shadow characters, strikethrough characters, small caps, all caps, hidden characters, word underlining, double underlining, or dotted underlining), you have to use the Character dialog box or the shortcut keys.

Applying Character Styles before You Type

When you choose a character style before you type, you "reprogram" the insertion point so that Word enters characters with the character style you have chosen. You can choose more than one character style at a time. For example, if you choose bold and italic before you type, Word enters characters in bold italic characters. If you choose small caps and underlining, Word enters the characters in underlined, small capital letters.

To choose character styles before you type, follow these steps:

1. Click the insertion point where you want to start typing.

2. Choose the character style you want, using one of the following techniques:

   Choose the style from the ribbon. You can choose boldface, underlining, superscript, or subscript by clicking the appropriate icon.

   Choose the style from the Format menu. You can choose bold, italic, and single underlining from this menu or you can restore nonemphasized text by choosing the Plain Text option.

   Choose any character style from the Character dialog box.

   Choose any character style by pressing the keyboard shortcuts (listed in table 5.1).

3. Type the text.

4. To stop using the character style you have chosen, choose the command again to toggle it off. If you are typing in boldface, for example, stop using boldface by clicking the bold icon on the ribbon (or use any other technique you used to choose boldface).

NOTE

Not all character formatting keys work as toggles. The keys for changing fonts and font sizes and for entering subscript and super-script do not work as toggles.

If you have chosen more than one character style, you can cancel them all by choosing Plain Text from the Format menu or by pressing ⌘-Shift-Z. Word cancels all the character styles you have chosen, but not the font or font size.

Table 5.1
Keyboard Shortcuts for Character Emphasis

Emphasis	Keyboard shortcut	Keyboard shortcut with function keys
All Caps	⌘-Shift-K	Shift-F10
Bold	⌘-B or ⌘-Shift-B	F10

TIP

If you have an extended keyboard with function keys, note the useful mapping of bold (F10), italic (F11), and underline (F12).

Emphasis	Keyboard shortcut	Keyboard shortcut with function keys
Dotted underline	⌘-Shift-\	Option-F12
Double underline	⌘-Shift-[	Shift-F12
Hidden	⌘-Shift-X	Option-F9
Italic	⌘-I or ⌘-Shift-I	F11
Outline	⌘-Shift-D	Shift-F11
Shadow	⌘-Shift-W	Option-F11
Small Caps	⌘-Shift-H	Option-F10
Strikethrough	⌘-Shift-/	--
Underline	⌘-U or ⌘-Shift-U	F12
Word Underline	⌘-Shift-]	⌘-F12

Choosing Character Styles after You Type

If you have typed the text already, you can apply character styles by selecting text and then choosing the style.

To assign character styles after you type, follow these steps:

1. Select the text you want to format.

2. Choose the character style you want by using the ribbon, the Format menu, the Character dialog box, or the keyboard shortcuts listed in Table 5.1.

Cancelling Character Styles

NOTE

Word's character styles are additive, which means that you can add a new character style on top of one you have already chosen. If you have already formatted a heading with bold, for example, you can select the heading and add underlining or italic.

To remove a character format you have already applied, follow these steps:

1. Select the text.

2. Use the same character style command again. To remove boldface, for example, click the Bold button in the ribbon, choose Bold from the Format menu, activate the Bold check box in the Character

dialog box, or press ⌘-Shift-B. To cancel all the character styles you have applied to the text, choose Plain Text from the Format menu or press ⌘-Shift-Z.

Using Hidden Text

When you format characters with Hidden style, which is grouped with the character emphasis options in the Style area of the Character dialog box, the hidden text does not appear on the screen (or in print) unless you want them to appear. Hidden style has many uses in Word, including the following:

- Entering notes to a colleague in collaborative writing situations.

- Hiding special Word commands, such as the commands that mark table-of-contents and index entries (see Chapter 23).

- Hiding PostScript commands (for owners of LaserWriter or other PostScript-compatible printers who want to include PostScript programming commands in Word documents).

To format text as hidden text, click the Hidden box in the Character dialog box or press ⌘-Shift-X. Word displays hidden text on-screen with a dotted underline.

By default, Word displays hidden text. To hide or to redisplay hidden text, follow these steps:

1. Choose Preferences from the Tools menu.

2. Choose View. The View options appear (see fig. 5.10). If you see an X in the Hidden Text check box, Word is set to display hidden text.

Fig. 5.10
View options in
Preferences.

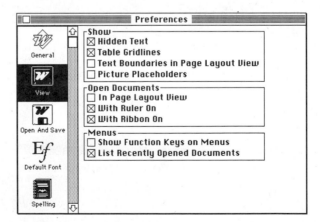

3. Click the Hidden Text check box in the Show area.

4. Click the Close box to confirm your choice and return to your document.

To transform hidden text into normal text, follow these steps:

1. Select the hidden text. If the text is not visible on-screen, activate the Hidden Text check box in View Preferences.

2. Choose Plain Text from the Format menu or press ⌘-Shift-Z.

Whether or not you display hidden text, you control the printing of hidden text by clicking the Print Hidden Text box in the Document dialog box. By default, Word is set to skip hidden text during printing. To print the hidden text, display the Document dialog box and choose Document from the Format menu. (Users of previous versions of Word should note that this check box was formerly in the Print dialog box.) Even if hidden text is not visible on-screen, you can print the text by clicking the Print Hidden Text box.

Using Underlining Options

You can choose from four underline formats:

- *Single Underline* (⌘-Shift-U). All characters are underlined, including spaces.

- *Word Underline* (⌘-Shift-]). Complete words and punctuation marks are underlined, but not white space (tabs and spaces).

- *Double Underline* (⌘-Shift-[). A double underline appears below all words and spaces.

- *Dotted Underline* (⌘-Shift-\). A dotted underline appears below all words and spaces.

To add single underlining, follow these steps:

1. Place the insertion point where you want underlining to begin when you start typing; or select the text you want underlined.

2. Use one of the following techniques:

   Click the Underline button on the ribbon.

   Choose Underline from the Format menu.

   Use the Shift-⌘-U keyboard shortcut.

Choose Character from the Format menu. When the Character dialog box appears, choose Single from the Underline list box. Then choose OK.

To add word underlining, double underlining, or dotted underlining, follow these steps:

1. Place the insertion point where you want underlining to begin when you start typing, or select the text you want underlined.

2. Choose Character from the Format menu. When the Character dialog box appears, choose the underlining option you want from the Underline list box. Then choose OK. Alternatively, use one of the keyboard shortcuts.

To remove underlining, follow these steps:

1. Select the underlined text.

2. Do one of the following:

Choose again the command you used to apply the formatting.

Choose Plain Text.

Press Shift-⌘-Z to cancel underlining and all other character formats (but not fonts or font sizes).

Using Subscript and Superscript

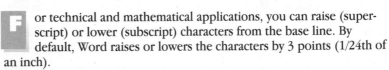

For technical and mathematical applications, you can raise (superscript) or lower (subscript) characters from the base line. By default, Word raises or lowers the characters by 3 points (1/24th of an inch).

To superscript or subscript characters, follow these steps:

1. Position the insertion point where you want the subscript or superscript characters to appear. If you have typed the characters already, select them.

2. Do one of the following:

Click the Superscript or Subscript buttons on the ribbon.

Press ⌘-Shift-equals (superscript) or ⌘-Shift-hyphen (subscript).

Choose Character from the Format menu. When the Character dialog box appears, activate the Superscript or Subscript options.

Part I

Getting Started

If you want, you can type a measurement other than 3 points in the By box. Then choose OK.

To cancel superscript or subscript formatting, select the characters and choose the format again from the ribbon; or choose Normal in the Character dialog box's Position area.

Using Spacing Options (Condensed and Expanded)

The Spacing options in the Character dialog box give you a way to condense or expand letters by decreasing or increasing the space after each letter. In figure 5.11, for example, Word has added 12 points to the normal space between the characters.

Fig. 5.11
Text expanded by
12 points.

Expanded text has many uses for document design. Condensed text, in contrast, is useful when you cannot quite squeeze a word into a narrow space, as shown in figure 5.12. Note that the word *Exploration* does not fit into the narrow (1.25-inch) paragraph. In figure 5.13, the condensed word fits.

Fig. 5.12
Condensed text needed.

Fig. 5.13
A long word condensed
by 1.5 pts.

Expanding and Condensing Text

In this section, you learn how to expand and condense text in your document. You can use these techniques for special effects or to solve problems when a word or phrase does not fit within narrow margins.

To expand text, follow these steps:

1. Select the text.

2. Choose Character from the Format menu or use the ⌘-D shortcut. The Character dialog box appears.

3. In the Spacing area, choose Expanded. You see 1.5 pts. in the By box. Word proposes to expand the characters by inserting an additional 1.5 points between each character.

4. To adjust the spacing, type a measurement in the By box. You can type any number from 1.0 to 14 in .25-point increments (for example, 3.0, 3.25, 3.5, 3.75, and so on).

5. Choose OK.

To condense text, follow these steps:

1. Select the text.

2. Choose Character from the Format menu or press ⌘-D. The Character dialog box appears.

3. In the Spacing area, choose Condensed. You see 1.5 pts. in the By box. Word proposes to condense the characters by taking away 1.5 points of space between each character.

4. To adjust the spacing, type a measurement in the By box. You can type any number from 0.25 to 1.75, in 0.25-inch increments.

5. Choose OK.

To restore normal spacing, follow these steps:

1. Select the condensed or expanded text.

2. Choose Character from the Format menu.

3. Choose Normal in the Position area.

4. Choose OK.

Kerning Characters

Word's capability to control the spacing between characters makes it possible to *kern* a pair of characters. *Kerning* is the adjustment of spacing between specific pairs of characters for the best possible aesthetic appearance. Kerning manually is a tedious job, and you are well advised to avoid kerning body text. You can improve the appearance of headings and titles, however, especially if you have chosen a large font size, by condensing certain pairs of characters that seem to have too much space between them. In figure 5.14, for instance, too much space seems to follow the capital letters (T and W) in the title *Technical Writing*. In figure 5.15, the pairs *Te* and *Wr* have been kerned. The difference, though subtle on the Mac's display, is more noticeable in the printed document.

Fig. 5.14
A title before kerning.

To kern pairs of characters, select the pair, choose Character from the Format menu, and then choose the Condensed option.

Fig. 5.15
A title after kerning 1.75
points (note selected pair
of characters).

Changing Case

As you have learned, you can choose an All Caps character style in the Character dialog box. When applied to selected characters, this style changes the appearance of the characters on-screen without changing the characters themselves. If you save your document using the Text Only or Text Only with Line Breaks options in the Save As dialog box—as you might do if you were planning to send your file by modem—you would lose the uppercase formatting. For this reason, using Word 5's new Change Case option in the Format menu to change case is preferable. The Change Case option gives you more ways to change case than does the Character dialog box (see fig. 5.16).

Fig. 5.16
Change Case dialog box.

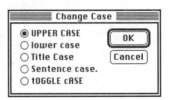

You can choose from the following case options:

> **UPPER CASE.** The UPPER CASE option changes all the characters to uppercase letters, as though you had typed them holding down the Shift key.

lower case. The lower case option changes all characters to lowercase letters, as though you had typed them in lowercase.

Title Case. The Title Case option capitalizes the first letter of each word.

Sentence case. The Sentence case option capitalizes the first letter of each sentence.

tOGGLE cASE. The tOGGLE cASE option reverses the case pattern of the selection: uppercase characters become lowercase and lowercase characters become uppercase. In a combination of uppercase and lowercase characters, this option reverses the case letter-by-letter.

To change case, follow these steps:

1. Select the text.

2. Choose Change Case from the Edit menu.

3. Choose a case option.

4. Choose OK.

Because Change Case actually changes the characters, as though you had typed them with or without using the Shift key, you cannot remove your case choices the way you remove character style choices (for example, by choosing ⌘-Shift-Z). You can undo a case choice, however, by choosing Undo from the Edit menu, so long as you haven't performed any other editing or command actions. You also can choose Change Case again, and choose another case formatting option.

Searching for Character Formats

Word 5 has an enhanced Find command that can help you locate text to which you have applied one or more character formats. (As you learn in the next chapter, you can search for paragraph formats, too.) You can search for any text that has one or more formats, including fonts and font sizes, or you can search for any word or phrase to which you have given a distinctive format.

The following sample of searches that you can perform with the Find dialog box illustrate this improved capability:

■ Find the next occurrence of the phrase *Albemarle Valley Associates* formatted in 18-point Palatino and skip all occurrences of the phrase in other fonts and font sizes.

■ Find any text formatted with small caps.

■ Find any text—regardless of font—formatted in nine-point font size.

■ Find any text formatted with bold as well as italic.

To search for a character format, follow these steps:

1. Choose Find from the Edit menu or press ⌘-F. The Find dialog box appears (see fig. 5.17).

Fig. 5.17
The Find dialog box.

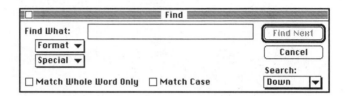

2. Choose a character format.

   Choose Character from the Format list box, which brings up the Character dialog box. Alternatively, you can use any of the techniques you've already learned to choose character formats (such as keyboard shortcuts, the ribbon, the character formatting options on the Format and Font menus, or the Character command on the Format menu). You also can search for more than one format. For example, you can search for text formatted with bold, New Century Schoolbook, and 3.0 pts of expansion.

   After you choose the formats, the Find dialog box appears again. The format you have chosen is shown below the Find What text box, as shown in figure 5.18.

Fig. 5.18
The Find dialog box after you choose Bold.

3. To search for specific text that has the formats you specified under the Find What text box, type the text in the Find What dialog box. To search for any text with this format or formats, leave the Find What box blank.

4. To change the direction of the search, use the Search dialog box.

   By default, Word searches Down (from the insertion point to the end of the document), but you can choose Up (from the insertion point to the beginning of the document) or All (begin at the insertion point, but search the entire document).

5. Choose Find Next. Word highlights any text with the format you have specified. Choose Find Next again to find the next occurrence of the format, or choose Cancel to return to your document.

   If Word cannot find any text with the format you have specified, a dialog box appears asking you whether you want to extend the search from the beginning of the document (or the end, if you're searching up). Choose Yes to extend the search or No to cancel.

After you use the Find dialog box to search for a format, Word retains for the duration of the current operating session that format setting—as well as any text you may have typed in the Find What text box, below the Find What text box. If you again choose Find, you must clear these settings to perform a different search. To clear the text from the Find What text box, select the text and press Delete. To clear the format, pull down the Format list box and choose Clear.

Replacing Character Formats

Word 5 provides an important new capability: you can replace one format with another throughout your document. You even can replace a group of formats (such as bold, italic, Palatino, and 14 point) with another group (such as underlined, Courier, and 12 point) throughout your document. These significant new capabilities are made possible by the addition of the Format drop-down list box to the Replace dialog box.

The following examples show you how this capability can save you hours of manual formatting:

■ You find out that you were supposed to underline the titles of books in a huge bibliography, instead of using italic. You need to replace the italic with underlining.

Chapter 5
Formatting Characters

■ When you inspect a printout of your document, you find that your headings look terrible in 18-point Chicago. You decide to replace the Chicago font with 14-point Helvetica.

■ You use boldface here and there throughout your document to emphasize important ideas, but when you see the printed document, you realize the effect is overbearing. You decide to replace the boldface with plain text.

NOTE

If you frequently find yourself replacing formats, consider using style formatting. With style formatting, you can update all occurrences of text formatted with the style, just by making one simple change to the document style sheet. See Chapter 7 for information on styles.

Word 5's Replace command (Edit) menu can perform all these tasks and more, thanks to the Format drop-down list boxes. With Replace, you can replace paragraph formats and styles as well as character formats. In the following steps, you learn how to replace character formats; subsequent chapters detail the procedures you use to replace paragraph formats and styles.

To replace one character format with another throughout your document, follow these steps:

1. Choose Replace from the Edit menu or press ⌘-F. The Replace dialog box appears (see fig. 5.19).

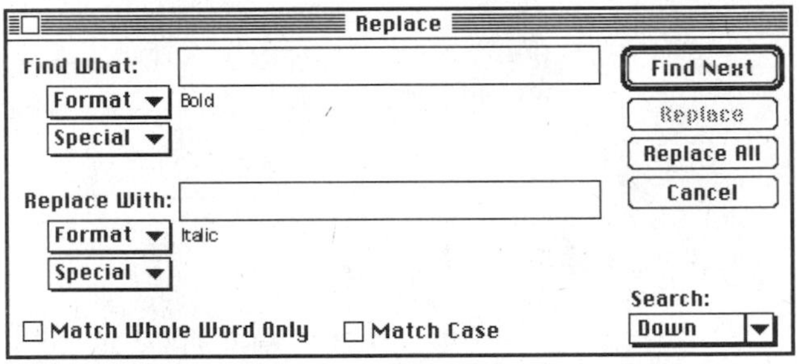

Fig. 5.19

The Replace dialog box.

2. With the insertion point in the Find What text box, choose a character format:

   Choose Character from the Format list box, which brings up the Character dialog box. Alternatively, you can use any of the techniques you've already learned to choose character formats (such as keyboard shortcuts, the ribbon, the character formatting options on the Format and Font menus, or the Character command on the Format menu). You also can search for more than one format. For example, you can search for text formatted with bold, New Century Schoolbook, and 3.0 pts of expansion.

After you choose a format, the Find dialog box appears again. The format you have chosen is shown below the Find What text box (refer to fig. 5.18). The format or formats you have chosen appear below the Find What text box.

3. With the insertion point in the Replace With area, use any of the techniques described in step 2 to select the format(s) you want Word to substitute for the format you want to replace. You see the format you have chosen below the Replace With text box, as shown in figure 5.19.

4. To search for specific text having the formats you have specified below the Find What text box, type the text in the Find What text box. To search for all text having the formats you specified, leave the text box blank.

5. To replace specific text having the formats you have entered below the Replace With text box, type the text in the Replace With text box. To search for all text having the formats you specified, leave the text box blank.

6. To change the direction of the search, use the Search dialog box.

7. Choose Find Next, if you want to confirm each replacement before it is made; or, if you're sure you want to perform the replacement throughout your document, choose Replace All.

If you choose Find Next, Word finds and highlights the next occurrence of the text that has the format you specified. To find further occurrences of the format, continue to choose Find Next. To return to your document, choose Cancel.

If Word finds no text with the format you specified, a dialog box appears asking you whether you want to extend the search from the beginning of the document (or the end, if you're searching up). Choose Yes to extend the search or No to cancel.

After you use the Replace dialog box to search for a format, Word retains the format setting below the Find What text box and any text you have typed in this text box, for the duration of the current operating session. Moreover, the format and text will appear in the Find dialog box, too. If you choose Replace or Find again, you must clear these settings before you can begin a different search. To clear the text from the Find What text box, select the text and press Delete. To clear the format, pull down the Format list box and choose Clear.

Repeating and Copying Character Formats

You can repeat elsewhere in your document a complex format you have created—providing that you do so immediately. Even if you have done something else since you applied the format, you can copy the format, using procedures described in the following sections.

Repeating Character Formats

You can repeat a character format immediately after you have applied the formatting by following these steps:

1. Apply a character format using any technique discussed in this chapter.

2. Select the text to which you want to apply the same format.

3. Choose Repeat from the Edit menu or use the ⌘-Y keyboard shortcut.

Copying Character Formats

If you type some text or choose another command after you apply the character format, you cannot repeat the format using the technique introduced in the preceding section. You can copy the format, however, by using the following technique.

To copy character formats, follow these steps:

1. Select a word that has the formats you want.

2. Press ⌘-Option-V.

3. Select the text to which you want the format copied. A dotted underline appears below the selection.

4. Press Return.

To cancel, press ⌘-period before pressing Return.

TIP

To repeat multiple formats (such as Palatino 18, Bold, and Outline), choose the formats from the Character dialog box during step 1. If you choose the formats from the ribbon, the menus, or the keyboard shortcuts, Word will repeat only the last format you choose.

TIP

If you find yourself copying formats frequently, learn how to create and apply styles. Styles are named and saved formats you can choose quickly anytime they're needed (see Chapter 7).

Quick Review

This section concisely summarizes the most useful information in this chapter. Check "Productivity Tips" for a review of high-productivity tips and tricks, and review "Techniques" when you forget how to perform a specific procedure.

Productivity Tips

- If you format before you type, you don't have to select the text, but you add another level of complexity—choosing formats—to the writing process. If writing gives you trouble, format after you type.

- To maximize Word's screen updating, be sure to install in your System file bit-mapped fonts that correspond to the fonts and font sizes you commonly use.

- You can save money and get good results with TrueType fonts. You need Adobe Type Manager and PostScript fonts only if you have a PostScript printer.

- Unless you use a nine-inch Classic monitor, display the ribbon and use it to choose fonts, font sizes, common emphases, and position.

- If your system isn't equipped with TrueType or PostScript fonts, you get the best printing results by choosing font sizes that appear in outline characters on the Format menu.

- Redefine the default font to one appropriate for most of your documents and that prints well on your printer.

- Glance at the ribbon or display the Character dialog box to see which character formats are currently in effect at the insertion point.

- When you format by choosing character formats before you type, switch the format off by repeating the command you used to apply the format.

- If you cannot fit a long word into narrow margins, try condensing the word using Word's default condense setting (1.5 points).

- Rather than retype words to change case, use Word 5's new Change Case command.

- Use the Replace dialog box to replace formats throughout your document.

Chapter 5
Formatting Characters

■ Immediately after you apply a character format, you can repeat the format elsewhere—as long as you have not typed any characters or chosen any commands.

■ To repeat a format after you have typed additional text or chosen another command, copy the format using the ⌘-Option-V shortcut.

Techniques

This section provides concise, quick-reference summaries of all the procedures introduced in this chapter.

Choosing Bold

To choose the bold character style before you start typing:

1. Click the insertion point where you want to start typing.

2. Choose the bold character style using one of the following techniques:

   Click the Bold button on the ribbon.

   Choose Bold from the Format menu.

   Choose Character from the Format menu and activate the Bold option in the Character dialog box. Then choose OK.

   Press ⌘-Option-B.

3. Type the text.

4. To stop using the character style you have chosen, toggle off the character style by repeating the command.

To assign bold after you type:

1. Select the text you want to format.

2. Use one of the following techniques to choose the bold character style:

   Click the Bold button on the ribbon.

   Choose Bold from the Format menu.

   Choose Character from the Format menu and activate the Bold option in the Character dialog box. Then choose OK.

   Press ⌘-Option-B.

Changing Case

To change the case of a selection to all uppercase letters:

1. Select the text.
2. Choose Change Case from the Format menu.
3. Choose UPPER CASE.
4. Choose OK.

To change all the letters in a selection to lowercase:

1. Select the text.
2. Choose Change Case from the Format menu.
3. Choose lower case.
4. Choose OK.

To capitalize the first letter of each sentence in a selection:

1. Select the text.
2. Choose Change Case from the Format menu.
3. Choose Sentence case.
4. Choose OK.

To capitalize the first letter of each word in a selection:

1. Select the text.
2. Choose Change Case from the Format menu.
3. Choose Title Case.
4. Choose OK.

To reverse the uppercase and lowercase pattern in a selection:

1. Select the text.
2. Choose Change Case from the Format menu.
3. Choose tOGGLE cASE.
4. Choose OK.

Choosing Colors

To choose colors:

1. Select the text.

2. Choose Character on the Format menu, or press ⌘-D.

3. Choose a color from the Color box.

4. Choose OK.

Copying Character Formats

To copy character formats:

1. Select a word that has the formats you want.

2. Press ⌘-Option-V.

3. Select the text to which you want the format copied. A dotted underline appears below the selection.

4. Press Return.

Changing Fonts

To change the default font for all new documents:

1. Choose Default Font from the Font menu.

2. Choose the font you want in the Default Font list box.

3. Click the Close box to confirm your choice and return to the document.

To change the font before you type:

1. Click the insertion point where you want the font to start.

2. Choose the font you want, using one of the following techniques:

   Choose the font you want from the drop-down list box on the ribbon.

   Choose the font you want from the Font menu.

   Choose Character from the Format menu or use the ⌘-D keyboard shortcut. Then choose the font you want from the Font list box in the Character dialog box. Choose OK to confirm your choice.

Use the ⌘-Shift-E keyboard shortcut. When the message Font appears on the status line, type the name of the font you want to use.

3. Type the text.

4. When you finish typing with the font you have chosen, choose a new font or font size by using any of the preceding techniques; or restore the previous font or font size.

To change the font or font size after you type:

1. Select the text.

2. Choose a font from the ribbon, the Font menu, or the Character dialog box; or, use the ⌘-Shift-E keyboard shortcut, type the name of the font, and press Enter.

To change the font throughout the document:

1. Use one of the following techniques to select the document:

   Move the mouse pointer to the selection bar, hold down the ⌘ key, and click.

   Choose Select All from the Edit menu.

   Use the ⌘-A keyboard shortcut.

2. Choose a font from the ribbon, the Font menu, or the Character dialog box. Alternatively, use the ⌘-Shift-E keyboard shortcut, type the name of the font, and press Enter.

Changing Font Size

To change the font size before you type:

1. Click the insertion point where you want to start typing.

2. Use one of the following techniques to choose the font size:

   Drop down the point size list box on the ribbon and choose the point size you want or type in the point size list box the point size you want to use.

   Choose a point size from the Font menu.

   Increase the point size one point by choosing Up from the Font menu or by using the ⌘-] keyboard shortcut. After you increase the point size, a message appears in the page number area to confirm the point size you have chosen.

Chapter 5

Formatting Characters

Increase the point size to the next larger point size shown on the Font menu by using the ⌘-Shift-> keyboard shortcut.

Decrease the point size by one point by choosing Down from the Font menu or by using the ⌘-[keyboard shortcut. After you decrease the point size, a message appears in the Page Number area to confirm the point size you have chosen.

Decrease the point size to the next smaller point size shown on the Font menu by using the ⌘-Shift-< keyboard shortcut.

Choose Character or Other from the Format menu or use the ⌘-D keyboard shortcut. When the Character dialog box appears, choose the point size from the Size box. Choose OK to confirm your choice.

3. When you finish typing with the font size you have chosen, use any of the preceding techniques to choose a new font size or to restore the preceding font size.

To change the font size after you type:

1. Select the text.

2. Use one of the following techniques to choose the font size:

Drop down the point size list box on the ribbon and choose the point size you want. Alternatively, type in the point size list box the point size you want to use.

Choose a point size from the Font menu.

Increase the point size one point by choosing Up from the Font menu or by using the ⌘-] keyboard shortcut. After you increase the point size, a message appears in the page number area to confirm the point size you have chosen.

Increase the point size to the next larger point size shown on the Font menu by using the ⌘-Shift-> keyboard shortcut.

Decrease the point size by one point by choosing Down from the Font menu or by using the ⌘-[keyboard shortcut. After you decrease the point size, a message appears in the page number area to confirm the point size you have chosen.

Decrease the point size to the next-smaller point size shown on the Font menu by using the ⌘-Shift-< keyboard shortcut.

Choose Character or Other from the Format menu or use the ⌘-D keyboard shortcut. When the Character dialog box appears, choose the point size from the Size box. Choose OK to confirm your choice.

Choosing Hidden Text

To turn on hidden text formatting before you start typing:

1. Click the insertion point where you want to start typing.

2. Choose the hidden text character style by choosing Character from the Format menu, activating the Hidden Text option in the Character dialog box, and then choosing OK. Alternatively, press ⌘-Shift-X.

3. Type the text.

4. To stop using hidden text, toggle off the character style by repeating the command.

To assign hidden text character style after you type:

1. Select the text you want to hide.

2. Choose Hidden Text character style by using one of the following techniques:

   Choose Character from the Format menu and activate the Hidden Text option in the Character dialog box. Then choose OK.

   Press ⌘-Shift-X.

To prevent hidden text from being displayed on the screen or to redisplay hidden text:

1. Choose Preferences from the Tools menu.

2. Choose View.

3. Click the Hidden Text check box in the Show area.

4. Click the Close box to confirm your choice and return to your document.

To transform hidden text into normal text:

1. Select Hidden Text. (If the text is not visible on-screen, activate the Hidden Text check box in the View Preferences dialog box.)

2. Choose Plain Text from the Format menu or press ⌘-Shift-Z.

To print hidden text:

1. Choose Document from the Format menu.

2. Activate the Print Hidden Text box in the Document dialog box.

3. Choose OK.

Choosing Italic

To choose the italic character style before you start typing:

1. Click the insertion point where you want to start typing.

2. Choose italic character style using one of the following techniques:

   Click the Italic button on the ribbon.

   Choose Italic from the Format menu.

   Choose Character from the Format menu, activate the Italic option in the Character dialog box, and then choose OK.

   Press ⌘-I.

3. Type the text.

4. To stop using the character style you have chosen, toggle off by repeating the command you used to activate the character style.

To assign italic character style after you type:

1. Select the text you want to format.

2. Choose Italic character style, using one of the following techniques:

   Click the Italic button on the ribbon.

   Choose Italic from the Format menu.

   Choose Character from the Format menu, activate the Italic option in the Character dialog box, and then choose OK.

   Press ⌘-I.

Choosing Outline Characters

To choose the outline character style before you start typing:

1. Click the insertion point where you want to start typing.

2. Choose outline character style, using one of the following techniques:

   Choose Character from the Format menu, activate the Outline option in the Character dialog box, and then choose OK.

   Press ⌘-Shift-D.

3. Type the text.

4. To stop using the character style you have chosen, toggle off by repeating the command you used to activate the character style.

To assign outline character style after you type:

1. Select the text you want to format.

2. Choose outline character style using one of the following techniques:

   Choose Character from the Format menu, activate Outline option in the Character dialog box, and then choose OK.

   Press ⌘-Shift-D.

Replacing Character Formats

To replace one character format with another throughout your document:

1. Choose Replace from the Edit menu or press ⌘-H.

2. With the insertion point in the Find What text box, choose Character from the Format box, and choose one or more character formats from the Character dialog box. Alternatively, choose one or more character formats using the ribbon, the menus, or keyboard shortcuts.

3. With the insertion point in the Replace With area, choose a character format using one of the methods explained in step 2.

4. To search for specific text having the formats you specified below the Find What text box, type the text in the Find What text box. To search for all text having the formats you specified, leave the Find What text box blank.

5. To replace specific text having the formats you specified below the Replace With text box, type the text in the Replace With text box. To search for all text having the formats you specified, leave the Replace With text box blank.

6. To change the direction of the search, use the Search dialog box.

7. Choose Find Next or, if you're sure that you want to perform the replacement throughout your document, choose Replace All.

Searching for Character Formats

To search for a character format:

1. Choose Find from the Edit menu or press ⌘-F .

2. With the insertion point in the Find What text box, choose Character from the Format box, and choose one or more character formats from the Character dialog box. Alternatively, choose one or more character formats using the ribbon, the menus, or keyboard shortcuts.

3. Search for specific text having the formats you specified under the Find What text box by typing the text in the Find What dialog box. To search for all text with this format or formats, leave the Find What box blank.

4. To change the direction of the search, use the Search dialog box.

5. Choose Find Next.

Repeating Character Formats

To repeat a character format:

1. Apply a character format using any technique discussed in this chapter.

2. Select the next text to which you want to apply the same format.

3. Choose Repeat from the Edit menu or press ⌘-Y .

Choosing Shadow Characters

To choose the shadow character style before you start typing:

1. Click the insertion point where you want to start typing.

2. Choose the shadow character style, using one of the following techniques:

   Choose Character from the Format menu and activate the Shadow option in the Character dialog box. Then choose OK.

   Press ⌘-Shift-W.

3. Type the text.

4. To stop using the character style you have chosen, toggle off by repeating the command you used to activate the character style.

To assign shadow character style after you type:

1. Select the text you want to format.

2. Choose Shadow character style, using one of the following techniques:

   Choose Character from the Format menu, activate the Shadow option in the Character dialog box, and then choose OK.

   Press ⌘-Shift-W.

Choosing Small Caps

To choose the small caps character style before you start typing:

1. Click the insertion point where you want to start typing.

2. Choose the small caps character style, using one of the following techniques:

   Choose Character from the Format menu and activate the Small Caps option in the Character dialog box. Then choose OK.

   Press ⌘-Shift-H.

3. Type the text.

4. To stop using the character style you have chosen, toggle off by repeating the command you used to activate the character style.

To assign the small caps character style after you type:

1. Select the text you want to format.

2. Choose the Small Caps character style using one of the following techniques:

   Choose Character from the Format menu and activate the Small Caps option in the Character dialog box. Then choose OK.

   Press ⌘-Shift-H.

Controlling Spacing and Kerning

To expand text:

1. Select the text.

2. Choose Character from the Format menu or press ⌘D.

3. In the Spacing area, choose Expanded.

4. To adjust the spacing, type a measurement in the By box.

5. Choose OK.

To condense text:

1. Select the text.

2. Choose Character from the Format menu or press ⌘D.

3. In the Spacing area, choose Condensed.

4. To adjust the spacing, type a measurement in the By box.

5. Choose OK.

To restore normal spacing:

1. Select the condensed or expanded text

2. Choose Character from the Format menu.

3. Choose Normal in the Position area.

4. Choose OK.

Choosing Superscript/Subscript

To superscript or subscript characters:

1. Position the insertion point where you want the subscript or superscript characters to appear. If you already have typed the characters, select them.

2. Use one of the following techniques to superscript or subscript the characters:

   Click the Superscript or Subscript button on the ribbon.

   Press ⌘-Shift-equals (superscript) or ⌘-Shift-hyphen (subscript).

   Choose Character from the Format menu. When the Character dialog box appears, activate the Superscript or Subscript options. If you want, type a measurement other than three points in the By box. Then choose OK.

Choosing Strikethrough

To format existing text to display and print with strikethrough characters:

1. Select the text you want to format.

2. Choose the strikethrough character style, using one of the following techniques:

   Choose Character from the Format menu, activate the Strikethrough option in the Character dialog box, and then choose OK.

   Press ⌘-Shift-/.

Choosing Underline

To choose single underlining before you type:

1. Click the insertion point where you want to start typing.

2. Choose the underline character style, using one of the following techniques:

   Click the Underline button on the ribbon.

   Choose Underline from the Format menu.

   Choose Character from the Format menu. In the Character dialog box, choose Single Underline from the Underline list box. Then choose OK.

   Press ⌘-Shift-I.

3. Type the text.

4. To stop using the character style you have chosen, toggle off by repeating the command you used to activate the character style.

To assign underlining after you type:

1. Select the text you want to format.

2. Choose the underline character style, using one of the following techniques:

   Click the Underline button on the ribbon.

   Choose Underline from the Format menu.

   Choose Character from the Format menu. In the Character dialog box, choose Single Underline from the Underline list box. Then choose OK.

   Press ⌘-Shift-U.

Chapter 5
Formatting Characters

To choose word, double, or dotted underlining before you type:

1. Click the insertion point where you want to start typing.

2. Choose the underlining style you want, using one of the following methods:

   Choose Character from the Format menu or use the ⌘-D shortcut. Choose Word Underline, Double Underline, or Dotted Underline from the Underline list box. Choose OK.

   Press ⌘-Shift-] to choose Word underline, ⌘-Shift-[to choose double underline, or ⌘-Shift-\ to choose dotted underline.

5. Type the text.

6. To stop using the character style you have chosen, toggle off by repeating the command you used to activate the character style.

To assign word, double, or dotted underlining after you type:

1. Select the text you want to format.

2. Choose the underlining style you want, using one of the following methods:

   Choose Character from the Format menu or use the ⌘-D shortcut, choose Word Underline, Double Underline, or Dotted Underline from the Underline list box, and then choose OK.

   Press ⌘-Shift-] to choose word underline, ⌘-Shift-[to choose double underline, or ⌘-Shift-\ to choose dotted underline.

Formatting Paragraphs

Paragraph formats, the second of Word's three formatting domains discussed in Part I, control the way Word indents and aligns text. Word defines many other formats as paragraph formats: line spacing, blank space before and after a paragraph, custom tabs, lines, borders, and more. These formats can vary for each new paragraph you create; therefore, there are few page-layout challenges that Word cannot meet.

This chapter surveys the paragraph formats you are most likely to use in day-to-day formatting. These topics are covered:

- ■ *Understanding Paragraph Formats*. Defines the formats Word 5 considers to be paragraph formats.

- ■ *Reviewing Paragraph Formatting Basics*. Briefly reviews what you already have learned about creating and formatting paragraphs.

- ■ *Choosing Paragraph Formats*. Discusses the three different ways you can format paragraphs and mentions the strengths and limitations of each one.

- ■ *Controlling Paragraph Alignment*. Comprehensively surveys your options for aligning text.

- ■ *Indenting Paragraphs*. Presents the many ways you can indent text from the left or right margin, including instructions for creating nested paragraphs and hanging indentations.

USING
WORD 5
FOR THE
MAC

■ *Controlling Line and Paragraph Spacing*. Discusses line spacing and commands that automatically add blank space before and after a paragraph.

■ *Using Tabs*. Covers all aspects of tabs, including changing the default tab width and creating custom tabs.

■ *Searching for Paragraph Formats*. Details the use of Word 5's new Find command, which enables you to search your document for paragraphs that have a specific format or combination of formats.

■ *Replacing Paragraph Formats*. Covers Word 5's new Replace command, which enables you to replace one paragraph format (or a combination of formats) for another throughout your document.

■ *Repeating and Copying Paragraph Formats*. Details the procedures you can use to repeat or copy paragraph formats so that you don't have to enter a complex format in the document more than once.

Understanding Paragraph Formats

f you have used other word processing programs, you may think it odd that blank lines, borders, and tabs are paragraph formats in Word. A paragraph format in Word, however, is simply any format that applies to a single paragraph as a unit—and that includes borders, blank lines, thick lines, shading, custom tab formats, and much more.

Because these formats can be varied from paragraph to paragraph, you have the opportunity to set up complex new formats every time you press Return to start typing a new paragraph. The format can include the usual ingredients of paragraph formatting (indents, alignment, and line spacing), as well as the "extras": lines, boxes, a unique pattern of tabs, automatically entered blank lines, and page-break controls.

This chapter tells you how to assign the following formats to any paragraph in a Word document:

Alignment (default: flush left). Choose from flush-left, flush-right, right-justified, or centered formats for a paragraph.

Indents (default: none). You can indent the right margin, the left margin, and the paragraph's first line. Using negative values, you can create hanging indents and other effects.

Line spacing (default: auto). You can format paragraph spacing with auto (single spacing with automatic adjustment of line height to accommodate the largest font), 1 1/2 space (18 point), and double-space (24 point). You can set other line spacings using measurements specified in lines or points.

Blank space (default: none). You can format a paragraph so that Word automatically enters blank space before or after the paragraph.

Tabs (default: every half inch). Choose from flush-left, flush-right, centered, and decimal tabs. You can set a vertical tab, which inserts a vertical line at the position you specify.

The following additional paragraph formats are covered in other chapters of this book:

Page-break control (default: none). Choose from options that force a page break before a paragraph or prevent one from following a paragraph. You also can keep all the lines in a paragraph together on one page. You learn more about page-break control in Chapter 7.

Absolute position on the page (default: none). You can anchor a paragraph of text or a graphic—also a "paragraph," as far as Word is concerned—so that its position is fixed on the page. The special space you establish when you anchor text or graphics in this way is called a *frame*. You can choose the size of the frame, both horizontally and vertically. If the horizontal size of the frame is narrower than the text column, text flows around the frame automatically. You learn more about positioning text and graphics in frames in Chapter 21.

Borders (default: none). Choose from lines, boxes, and shading options. You learn more about borders in Chapter 22.

NOTE

For information on creating tables with Word's Table command, as well as creating list formats, see Chapter 17. Chapter 19 details Word's automatic line-numbering, paragraph-numbering, and sorting capabilities.

Because you can add so many formats to a paragraph, it makes sense to save all the work you have done in adding these formats so that you can reuse them later. This reuse is the rationale underlying Word's styles. A *style* is a collection of formats you have named and saved so that you can apply them all with just one command. You can create and save a format called Text ¶, for example, which includes all the formats you typically use to create body text paragraphs: Times Roman 12, justified alignment, 0.5" first-line indentation, and double-line spacing. Styles belong in your repertoire of basic Word formatting skills; therefore, Chapter 8, "Formatting with Styles," is included in Part I, "Getting Started."

Reviewing Paragraph-Formatting Basics

T his section reviews the paragraph-formatting basics introduced in preceding chapters. A *paragraph* is a series of characters of any length followed by a paragraph mark (¶). By this definition, a paragraph can be a one-line heading, an ordinary paragraph of body text, or a 55-line table where each line ends with an Insert Line Break command (Shift-Return).

Every time you press Return (or Enter), Word starts a new paragraph. Each paragraph is a unit for paragraph-formatting purposes. For this reason, don't press Return at the end of every line as you do when you use a typewriter. Let Word start new lines automatically by wrapping text. Press Return only when you want to start a new paragraph of text.

When you press Return (or Enter) to start a new paragraph, Word copies to the new paragraph the formats that are in effect. If you want to change the formats, do so immediately after you start the new paragraph. Alternatively, you can come back later, select the paragraph, and choose new formats.

If you are applying a paragraph format to a single paragraph, you don't need to highlight the whole paragraph to select it for formatting purposes. Just place the insertion point anywhere within the paragraph, and choose the format.

To highlight an entire paragraph, which is necessary only if you want to add a character format as well as a paragraph format, move the pointer to the selection bar (an invisible line running along the left side of the screen) until the pointer changes to an arrow, and then double-click.

If you see a small black box in the selection bar, you have applied *invisible properties* to the paragraph, such as Keep With Next ¶. Double-click the black box to see the formats you have assigned or to change or cancel them.

A paragraph mark stores the paragraph formats you have chosen for the paragraph. If you delete the mark, you lose the formats. When you are moving a paragraph, be sure to select and move the paragraph mark too; if you move the text without the mark, you lose the paragraph formats you have chosen.

If you accidentally delete a paragraph mark, the text before the paragraph mark becomes part of the next paragraph and takes on that paragraph's formatting. (This loss of formatting isn't a bug in the program: it's a direct consequence of Word storing your paragraph formatting choices in the paragraph mark.) If you delete the mark, you lose the formats. If you delete a mark accidentally and lose a lot of formatting, you can recover it by immediately choosing Undo from the Edit menu. To prevent accidental deletions of paragraph marks, edit with the paragraph marks displayed.

To display paragraph marks, choose Show ¶ from the Edit menu or click the ¶ button on the Ribbon.

Choosing Paragraph Formats

You can choose paragraph formats in three ways:

- *Ruler*. With the ruler displayed, you quickly can choose alignments, line spacing, blank lines before paragraphs, tabs, indents, and even left and right margins. The ruler always shows the formats in effect for the paragraph in which the insertion point is positioned. When you choose formatting options on the ruler, Word alters only the selected paragraph or paragraphs with the exception that changing the margins affects the whole document.

  Remember that the ruler doesn't make all paragraph formatting options available; it offers only the most frequently accessed options—single-, 1 1/2-, and double-line spacing. Paragraph formats not available on the ruler include pagination options, line-spacing options, and blanks lines after paragraphs.

- *Paragraph Dialog Box*. Unlike the ruler, which offers only the most frequently accessed paragraph formats, the paragraph-format dialog box makes most of the paragraph-formatting options available (one exception: alignment options). This dialog box is more time-consuming to use than the ruler because you must type measurements for spacing and indentation formats. Unless you dislike manipulating the ruler's buttons, you should use the Paragraph dialog box only when you want to choose a format not available on the ruler.

- *Keyboard Shortcuts*. Most paragraph formats can be applied by using keyboard shortcuts that, like character-formatting shortcuts, use the ⌘-Shift key combination. Most keyboard shortcuts work the same way as their ruler or dialog box counterparts, but some of the keyboard commands are additive in their effects. For example, if you press ⌘-Shift-N, Word indents the paragraph a half-inch. If you press the command again, Word adds another half-inch to the indentation.

Chapter 6

Formatting Paragraphs

Using the Ruler

Word's ruler has two purposes: It displays the formats in the selected paragraph or paragraphs, and it also provides a way to change these formats. Like all of Word's formatting commands, the choices you make in the ruler affect the paragraph or paragraphs you have selected in your document.

SPEED KEY

To display the ruler, choose Ruler from the View menu or press ⌘-R. Figure 6.1 shows the following features on Word 5's ruler:

Fig. 6.1
The Word 5 ruler.

Style selection box   Alignment buttons   Line Spacing buttons   Tab buttons   Margin Marker button

| Normal | ▼ |

Left indent   First line indent   Blank Line between paragraphs   Indent Marker button   Table Boundary button

Style selection box. This list box provides a handy way to choose styles. For more information on styles, see Chapter 8.

Alignment buttons (default: flush-left alignment). Choose these buttons to select flush-left, centered, flush-right, or justified alignment.

Line Spacing buttons (default: single-line spacing). Choose these buttons to select single-spacing, 1 1/2-line spacing (18 points), or double-spacing (24 points). To choose other line-spacing options, you should use the Paragraph dialog box.

Blank Line Space buttons (default: no blank line before paragraph). Choose to select no blank line before the paragraph (closed paragraph) or 12 points (1/6 inch) of blank space before the paragraph (open paragraph). To select other blank-spacing options, such as adding blank lines automatically after a paragraph or changing the amount of blank space added, you should use the Paragraph dialog box.

Tab buttons (default: flush-left tabs). To set a tab, choose and hold one of these buttons. A tab button emerges; drag it to the location you want. You can choose from flush-left, centered, flush-right, and decimal tab stops. The vertical tab isn't actually a tab; it enters a vertical line at the position you specify. The line is the same height as the line spacing you specify in the Paragraph dialog box. If you prefer to type the tab's location or to add leaders to tabs, you need to choose the Tabs button in the Paragraph dialog box.

Indent Marker button (default: Indent markers displayed). This button activates the display of indent markers on the ruler. When the indent markers are visible, you can change indents by dragging the markers. (If they are not visible, choose the Indent button to display them.) If you prefer to set indents by typing measurements, go to the Paragraph dialog box.

Margins Marker button (default: Margin markers not displayed). This button hides the indent markers and displays the left and right margin markers. When the margin markers are visible, you can change the left and right margins for the whole document. You also can set margins (including top and bottom margins) by choosing the Document option in the Format menu.

Table Boundary button (default: Grayed). This button becomes available when you position the insertion point within a table created by the Table command in the Insert menu. When you activate this button, Word displays T-shaped markers to mark the cell boundaries. You can change cell widths by dragging these markers. For more information on tables, see Chapter 17.

Indent markers. You should see two solid triangles on the left side of the ruler. The top left triangle is the first-line indent marker; drag this icon to control automatic first-line indents. The bottom left triangle is the left-indent marker for all succeeding lines of the paragraph. The larger triangle at the right side of the ruler is the right-indent marker.

What you see on the ruler depends on how many paragraphs you have selected. If you have one paragraph selected, the highlighted buttons show the formats in effect for the selected paragraph. If you choose a button or move a marker, the change you make applies to the selected paragraph.

If you have two or more paragraphs selected with the same formatting, the highlighted buttons show the formats in effect for both paragraphs. If you choose a button or move a marker, the change you make applies to all the selected paragraphs. Word changes only the format you specify, and leaves the other formats alone.

If you have two or more paragraphs with different formatting selected, the ruler fills with gray, and no buttons are highlighted. The ruler displays the indents for the first selected paragraph. You still can choose formats. If you choose a button or move a marker, the change you make applies to all the selected paragraphs. Word changes only the format you specify, and leaves the other formats alone.

Using the Paragraph Dialog Box

SPEED KEY

Choosing paragraph formats with the ruler is easy, but not all formats can be chosen that way. To control page breaks and specify indents and line spacing with precision, you must use the Paragraph dialog box (see fig. 6.2). Choose Paragraph from the Format menu or press ⌘-M to use the Paragraph dialog box.

Fig. 6.2
The paragraph
dialog box.

Paragraph		
Spacing Before: 0 pt		OK
After: 0 pt	Line: Auto ▼	Cancel
		Apply
Indentation Left: 0.5 in	**Pagination** ☐ Page Break Before ☐ Keep With Next	
Right: 0 in	☐ Keep Lines Together	Tabs...
First: -0.5 in	☐ Suppress Line Numbers	Border...
		Frame...

If you work with the ruler in view, use this method to quickly access the Paragraph dialog box: Double-click the right-indent marker (the big triangle on the right side of the ruler). You also can double-click the paragraph-properties mark to bring up the Paragraph dialog box. The paragraph-properties mark appears as a small, black box in the selection bar if you have chosen *invisible* formats for a paragraph, such as the Keep With Next option.

To choose indents and spacing in the Paragraph dialog box, enter the measurements in one of the measurement formats Word recognizes. The following list summarizes these formats.

Inches (in or "). An inch is Word's default measurement format for horizontal formats, such as indents.

Point (pt). In addition to being Word's default measurement format for line and paragraph spacing, points are the default measurement for character spacing and position. Each inch contains 72 points.

Centimeters (cm). One centimeter equals 0.39 inches, or 28.35 points.

Pica (pi). One pica equals 1/6 inch, 0.42 centimeters, or 12 points.

Lines (li). Use this format for vertical measurements only. One line equals 1/6 inch, 0.42 centimeters, or 12 points.

NOTE

If you type a measurement without specifying one of the recognized abbreviations (in, ", pt, cm, pi, or li), Word assumes that you are using the default measurement format for that option: inches for indents, and points for spacing.

Keep this information about measurements in mind when you type measurements in the Spacing boxes. If you enter *2* in the Line Spacing box, for instance, assuming that you will see double-line spacing, you're in for a surprise. You have entered line spacing of 2 points (1/36 of an inch). To enter double-line spacing, type *24 pt*, *2 li*, or *2 pi*.

If you select two or more paragraphs whose paragraph formatting is not homogeneous, the Paragraph dialog box shows settings for the formats shared by the paragraphs. No other format settings are shown. You can choose additional formats for the selected paragraphs without affecting the formats already chosen. You also can override the current settings. Any changes you make in the Paragraph dialog box are applied to both paragraphs.

Using Keyboard Shortcuts

The third way to create paragraph formats—and arguably the best way for adept typists—is with keyboard shortcuts. Table 6.1 lists the keyboard shortcuts for paragraph formatting.

Table 6.1
Keyboard Shortcuts for
Paragraph Formatting

Format	Keyboard shortcut
Flush-left alignment	⌘-Shift-L
Flush-right alignment	⌘-Shift-R
Centered alignment	⌘-Shift-C
Automatic first-line indent	⌘-Shift-F
Indent paragraph one tab stop	⌘-Shift-N
Outdent paragraph one tab stop	⌘-Shift-M
Hanging indentation	⌘-Shift-T
Double-line spacing	⌘-Shift-Y
Blank line before paragraph	⌘-Shift-O
Restore normal paragraph formats	⌘-Shift-P

TIP

Avoid the shortcut that restores normal paragraph formats, ⌘-Shift-P, if you are working with a font or font size other than the defaults. This command restores all the default character and paragraph formats: flush-left alignment, single-line (auto) spacing, and the current default font and font size.

To cancel a paragraph format you have just assigned with a key without losing your font and font-size choices, just use another command. Suppose that you choose centered alignment by pressing ⌘-Shift-C, for example, and want to restore flush-left alignment. Just press ⌘-Shift-L.

Most of these keyboard shortcuts work the same way as their ruler and Paragraph dialog box counterparts do, but the following list shows additive keys also:

- *⌘-Shift-N.* Every time you press this key, Word adds a 1/2 inch to the current paragraph's left indent. To indent a paragraph 1 1/2 inches, use this command three times.

- *⌘-Shift-M.* Every time you press this key, Word subtracts 1/2 inch from the current paragraph's left indent. If a paragraph is indented 1 1/2 inches and you press this command twice, the indent becomes 1/2 inch.

- *⌘-Shift-T.* This command creates a hanging indentation, a format in which the first line is flush with the left margin, and the second line is indented 1/2 inch. Every time you use this command, Word adds 1/2 inch to the indent. If you use the command twice, you create a hanging indent with a 1/2-inch first-line indentation and a 1-inch indentation for the second and subsequent lines.

Now that you have learned the fundamentals of choosing paragraph formats, the following sections of this chapter explain each format in detail.

Controlling Paragraph Alignment

B y default, Word aligns paragraphs flush left, with a ragged-right margin. To make your documents look more like a printed book or magazine, you may be tempted to use right-margin justification. Use it with caution because right-margin justification makes text more difficult to read. Moreover, Word may introduce unsightly spaces between words in an attempt to even the right margin. Although you can resolve some of these spacing problems by running Word's automatic-hyphenation utility, as explained in Chapter 3, flush-left justification is the best choice for most documents.

To change paragraph alignment before you type, follow these steps:

1. Press Return to start a new paragraph (unless you want to format the current paragraph).

2. Choose an alignment option on the ruler or use one of the keyboard shortcuts listed in table 6.1. (If the ruler is not visible, choose Show Ruler from the Edit menu or press ⌘-R.)

   By default, Word formats your text flush left. You can choose centered, flush-right, or justified alignments.

3. Type the text of the new paragraph.

To change paragraph alignment after you type, follow these steps:

1. Select the text.

   To select one paragraph, choose the insertion point anywhere in the paragraph. (You do not have to highlight the whole paragraph; just placing the insertion point in the paragraph is sufficient to select it.)

   To select more than one paragraph, double-click in the selection bar next to the first paragraph, and drag down or up until the screen scrolls and the desired paragraphs are highlighted.

2. Choose an alignment option in the ruler or use one of the keyboard shortcuts listed in table 6.1.

To cancel the alignment options assigned to the text and return to flush-left formatting, follow these steps:

1. Select the text.

2. Choose the flush-left button on the ruler or press ⌘-Shift-L.

Indenting Paragraphs

NOTE

Indenting lines from the left or right does not change the margins for the page. The margins stay the same; you are just setting up a temporary indentation format. To change the margins in your document, choose Document from the Format menu and type new measurements in the Left and Right Margins boxes.

ord has three ways to indent paragraphs: indenting only the first line, indenting all lines from the left, and indenting all lines from the right. Using these three types of indents, you can create a variety of paragraph formats (see fig. 6.3).

You also can indent paragraphs from the left, from the right, or both. To indent paragraphs from the left, you can choose from keyboard shortcuts (⌘-Shift-N and ⌘-Shift-M), the ruler, or the Paragraph dialog box. To indent text from the right, you must use the ruler or the Paragraph dialog box; there are no keyboard shortcuts.

Fig. 6.3
Various indented
paragraphs.

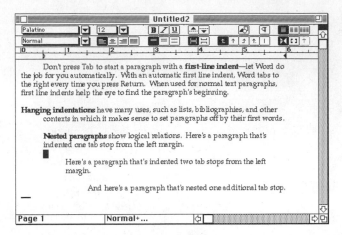

To use keyboard shortcuts to indent text from the left margin, follow these steps:

1. Select the paragraph or paragraphs you want to format. Alternatively, press Return to start a new paragraph.

2. Press ⌘-Shift-T. Word positions the left-indent and first-line markers at 0.5 inch on the ruler scale.

3. To increase the indentation an additional 1/2 inch, use the command again. To decrease the indentation by one tab stop, press ⌘-Shift-M.

To use the ruler to create a left or right indentation, follow these steps:

1. Select the paragraph or paragraphs you want to format. Alternatively, press Return to start a new paragraph.

2. On the ruler, drag the left-indent marker (the bottom left triangle on the left side of the ruler) to the position in which you want the paragraph to be indented. (The first-line indent marker moves also.) Drag the right-margin marker (the larger triangle on the right side of the ruler scale) to create an indentation from the right margin.

To create an indentation using the Paragraph dialog box method, follow these steps:

1. Select the paragraph or paragraphs you want to format. Alternatively, press Return to start a new paragraph.

2. Choose Paragraph from the Format menu or press ⌘-M.

3. When the Paragraph dialog box appears, type a measurement in the Left and Right boxes in the indentation area.

4. Choose OK.

Creating Automatic First-Line Indentations

Don't press Tab to enter a first-line indentation. Word can do it for you automatically. To create an automatic first-line indentation, follow these steps:

1. Select the paragraph or paragraphs you want to format. Alternatively, press Return to start a new paragraph.

2. On the ruler, drag the first-line indent marker to create the indentation. The first-line indent marker is the top left triangle on the left side of the ruler.

   Alternatively, type a measurement in the First text box in the Paragraph dialog box or press ⌘-Shift-F.

   Pressing ⌘-Shift-F indents the paragraph by one default tab stop (1/2 inch) unless you have changed the default tab-width setting in the Document dialog box.

Creating Hanging Indentations

Hanging indentations are useful whenever you want to emphasize the first few words in a paragraph. Figure 6.4 shows two uses for hanging indentations: bibliographic citations and word-definition lists. Hanging indentations also are useful for numbered lists (with the number flush to the margin).

Word gives you a choice of three techniques to create a hanging indentation: using keyboard shortcuts, the ruler, or the Paragraph dialog box. The keyboard technique is by far the easiest of the three methods.

To create a hanging indentation using keyboard shortcuts, follow these steps:

1. Select the paragraph or paragraphs you want to affect.

2. Press ⌘-Shift-T. Word positions the first-line indent marker at 0 inches; the right-indent marker is positioned at 0.5 inches.

TIP

When you set indents with the ruler, keep your eye on the page-number area. As you drag the indent markers, Word indicates the marker's current location in the page-number area. As you can see, Word moves the indent marker in 1/16-inch increments. You can set a more precise measurement by typing this measurement in the Paragraph dialog box.

SPEED KEY

Chapter 6
Formatting Paragraphs

The paragraph has a hanging indent with the first line flush left. Turnover lines (the second and subsequent lines) are indented one default tab stop (1/2 inch).

3. To increase the indentation an additional 1/2 inch, use the command again.

Fig. 6.4
Applications for hanging
indentations.

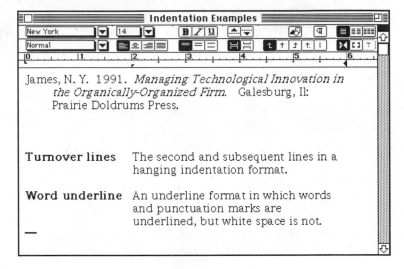

This command is additive: If you press it again, Word indents the whole paragraph another default tab stop so that (with default tabs) the first line is positioned at 0.5 inch and turnover lines begin at 1.0 inch.

To create a hanging indentation using the ruler, follow these steps:

1. Select the paragraph or paragraphs you want to affect.

2. On the ruler, hold down the Shift key and drag the left-indent marker (the bottom left triangle on the left side of the ruler) to the place where you want the paragraph's second and subsequent lines (the turnover lines) to be positioned.

   If you hold down the Shift key while you drag the markers, you can move them independently.

To create a hanging indentation using the Paragraph dialog box method, follow these steps:

1. Select the paragraph or paragraphs you want to affect.

TIP

If you want the turnover lines indented more than one default tab stop, create the hanging indentation with the ruler. Pressing ⌘-Shift-T always sets up a hanging indentation with turnover lines indented one tab stop. With the ruler, you can set the turnover lines' indentation anywhere you want.

2. Choose Paragraph from the Format menu.

3. When the Paragraph dialog box appears, type a negative measurement (such as *-0.5*) in the First box. Type a positive measurement (such as *1.0*) in the Left box.

   When you type a negative number in the First box, you tell Word, "Start the first line to the left of the left indentation." If the left indentation is 1.0 inch and you type -0.5 inch in the First box, Word starts the first line 1/2 inch from the left margin, and the turnover lines 1.0 inch from the left margin.

4. Choose OK.

Controlling Line and Paragraph Spacing

B y default, Word automatically uses automatic single-line spacing. In this format, the program automatically adjusts line spacing to make room for the largest font size you have chosen on a line. The program also automatically adjusts for superscript and subscript characters.

You can choose other line-spacing options or set up a paragraph format that automatically adds blank space before or after a paragraph. These options are discussed in the following sections.

Understanding Line-Spacing Options

Word 5 gives you more ways to control line spacing than did previous versions of the program. In previous versions you could choose between an Auto option—which created a single-space format that automatically made room for superscripts, subscripts, or characters typed in a larger font size—and fixed-size line-spacing formats—such as 18 points or 24 points—which also adjusted automatically. You had no easy way to lock the program into a fixed line spacing. Word 5 gives you two more choices: the At Least option—which automatically accommodates superscript, subscript, and larger font sizes—and Exactly, which doesn't adjust automatically. The following list explains the line-spacing options in the Line list box of the Paragraph dialog box (see fig. 6.5) and indicates when you would need them.

NOTE

Word uses printer's points as the default measurement format for line-spacing in the Paragraph dialog box (72 points per inch). In a 12-point font, Word prints 6 lines per inch (12 times 6 equals 72), unless you change to a larger font or use superscript or subscript.

Fig. 6.5
Line-spacing options in the
Line list box.

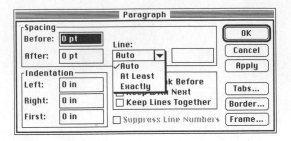

Auto. Single-spaces lines, but adjusts the line spacing to accommodate the largest font you use, as well as superscript, subscript, and graphics. This option is the best one for single-spaced documents. Word uses this option when you choose the Single Line Spacing button on the ruler.

At Least. Spaces lines using, at the minimum, the figure shown in the text box to the right of the Line list box. If you type *18* in the text box and choose At Least, Word uses 18-point line spacing. The program, however, increases the line spacing if necessary, to accommodate larger fonts, superscript, subscript, or graphics. This option is the best one for double-spaced documents.

Exactly. Spaces lines using the line-spacing measurement you type in the text box. Word's automatic line-spacing adjustments may give some lines more space than others, and produce an uneven effect. When you choose Exactly, Word does not adjust the line spacing to accommodate larger fonts, subscript, or superscript. The Exactly option assures you, therefore, that every line is given the same space. Just be sure not to choose a font size larger than the line spacing you have allowed!

Choose this option only if you want absolute control over line spacing. Such control may be required for desktop publishing, in which the smooth, even appearance of the page—layout artists call it *color*—is important.

The easiest way to choose line-spacing and blank-line options is to choose buttons on the ruler, but you should understand the limitations of choosing line spacing this way. The following list explains each button.

Single Line Spacing Button. When you choose this button, Word always uses Auto line spacing, regardless of the font size selected. The program adjusts the line spacing, if necessary, to accommodate larger fonts, graphics, superscript, or subscript.

1.5-Line Spacing Button. When you choose this button, Word always creates an 18-point line spacing. It also selects the At Least option. The 18-point line spacing creates the appearance of 1 1/2-line spacing as long as you are using 12-point type. Used with 10-point type, this option looks more like double spacing.

Double Line Spacing Button. When you choose this button, Word always creates 24-point line spacing. It also selects the At Least option. The 24-point line spacing creates the appearance of double spacing with 12-point type. The effect is more like triple-spacing with a smaller font and resembles 1 1/2-line spacing if you are using an 18-point font.

Adjusting Line Spacing

Now that you know what the line-spacing options and ruler buttons do, you can choose the correct line-spacing option for your document. Like all other paragraph-formatting commands, the line-spacing options affect the selected paragraph or paragraphs. If you choose a line-spacing option and start typing, Word creates the text with the formats chosen.

If you have chosen other line spacing and want to change back to single spacing, choose the Single Line Spacing button on the ruler. Alternatively, choose Paragraph from the Format menu, Auto from the Line list box, and OK to confirm your choice.

To double-space your document, follow these steps:

1. Place the insertion point where you want the line-spacing option to begin. Alternatively, select the paragraph or paragraphs you want to format.

2. To double-space your document if you are using 12-point type, choose the Double Line Spacing button on the ruler. If you are using another font size, choose Paragraph from the Format menu and choose At Least from the Line list box. Then multiply the font size by 2, and type the answer in the Line text box. Choose OK to confirm your choice.

To use fixed line spacing that Word doesn't adjust automatically, follow these steps:

1. Place the insertion point where you want the line-spacing option to begin. Alternatively, select the paragraph or paragraphs you want to format.

2. Choose Paragraph from the Format menu, and choose Exactly from the Line list box. Then type the line spacing you want in the Line text box, and choose OK to confirm your choice.

Adding Blank Spacing before and after Paragraphs

You may think it odd that blank lines before or after a paragraph are paragraph formats, but Word defines them that way. One of the many formats you can assign to a paragraph is blank spacing before or after a paragraph. If you have set up a paragraph format that includes blank spacing, Word enters the blank spacing automatically when you press Return. You also can apply blank spacing to paragraphs you already have typed.

When should you add blank space before or after a paragraph? The following list suggests some ways you can use this format.

- *Headings*. Style handbooks and guidelines typically specify precisely how much blank space should precede and follow a heading. A second-level heading, for instance, may require two blank lines before, and one blank line after. Use the Paragraph dialog box to specify with precision a heading's blank spacing.

- *Single-spaced paragraphs*. Choose the Blank Line Spacing button to add 12 points of blank space automatically every time you press Return.

- *Footnotes*. Add a blank line before every footnote paragraph to keep them separated whenever you have more than one footnote on a page. For more information on footnotes, see Chapter 15.

Don't press Return to create blank space in your document. If you do, you cannot control page breaks with the Keep With Next option because the next paragraph is an *empty* paragraph: one that contains nothing but a paragraph mark.

To add blank lines to your paragraph formats, use the Blank Line Spacing button in the ruler or the Spacing Before and After boxes in the Paragraph dialog box. Then Word disregards the blank lines when it carries out the Keep With Next option. If you use the Spacing After box and the Keep With Next option in the Paragraph dialog box to add 24 points of blank space under a heading, Word does not break a page between the heading and the next text paragraph that follows.

Like all other paragraph formats, blank-spacing options affect the selected paragraph or paragraphs. If you have selected more than one paragraph, the line-spacing options you choose affect all the paragraphs selected. If you choose a blank-spacing option and start typing, Word creates the text with the formats you have chosen.

Like line spacing, blank lines can be added using the ruler or the Paragraph dialog box. Also like line spacing, the ruler option limits your choices. If you choose the Blank Line Spacing button on the ruler, for example, Word inserts 12 points of blank space before the selected paragraph or paragraphs. To add more or less than 12 points before the paragraph or to add any blank space after the paragraph, you must use the Paragraph dialog box.

To add 12 points of blank space before a paragraph (or before all the paragraphs you select), follow these steps:

1. Place the insertion point where you want the line-spacing option to begin. Alternatively, select the paragraph or paragraphs you want to format.

2. Choose the Blank Line Spacing button on the ruler.

To choose other blank-spacing options, follow these steps:

1. Place the insertion point where you want the line-spacing option to begin. Alternatively, select the paragraph or paragraphs you want to format.

2. Choose Paragraph from the Format menu.

3. Type a measurement (in printer's points) in the Before text box to add blank space before the paragraphs.

4. Type a measurement (in printer's points) in the After text box to add blank space after the paragraphs.

5. Choose OK.

TIP

To find out how much blank space is allotted to a paragraph, select the paragraph by moving the pointer to the selection bar and double-clicking. The resulting highlight includes any blank line added before or after the paragraph.

Using Tabs

ord employs two kinds of tabs: default and custom. By default, every paragraph has flush-left tabs every 1/2 inch across the screen. To change the default tabs, you have two options:

TIP

Most people set tabs to type tables. Before typing a complex table, however, you should investigate Word's Table command, which inserts a spreadsheet-like matrix of rows and columns within your paragraph. Typing your table within a Table matrix is much easier than fussing with tabs. For more information on the Table command, see Chapter 17.

■ You can change the default tab width for the entire document. The new tab width you choose applies automatically to all the paragraphs in your document, unless you choose custom tabs for selected paragraphs.

■ You can set custom tabs for any paragraph you want, even if you reset the default tabs.

The following sections detail these topics.

When you press Tab, Word doesn't enter spaces in your document. The program enters a tab character instead, as shown in figure 6.6. Tab characters are much like paragraph marks: you view both in the same way. To view tab characters, choose Show ¶ from the View menu, or choose the ¶ button on the ribbon.

Just as you can accidentally join two paragraphs by deleting a paragraph marker, you also can cause text to shift to the left by deleting a tab character. When you delete a tab character, the text after the tab character rejoins the previous text, as though you never had pressed Tab.

Don't use spaces to indent; use Tab instead. When you press Tab, Word enters a tab character that tells the program to advance the next text to the next tab stop (which is by default the next half-inch or inch mark on the ruler). Word always positions the text correctly if you indent the text with the Tab key. If you try to indent with spaces, Word may fail to align the text correctly, even when it appears aligned on-screen.

Fig. 6.6
Tab characters.

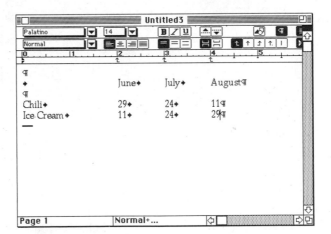

Most of the Mac's fonts are proportionally spaced fonts—wide characters (such as *m* or *w*) occupy more space than narrow ones (*i* or *l*). If you try to align text with spaces, the character-width differences, which may not be obvious on-screen, can cause alignment problems when you print.

Changing the Default Tabs

By default, Word places flush-left tabs every 1/2 inch across the screen. (A flush-left tab aligns the left edge of text at the tab stop. As you learn in the next section, you can set other kinds of tabs also, such as centered tabs.) If you would rather Word used a different default tab width, such as 0.4", you can change the default tab width for the current document or for all the documents you create. Some style guidelines call for tab spacings other than Word's default, so the option to change the default width may come in handy for you.

To change the default tab width for the current document, follow these steps:

1. Choose Document from the Format menu.

   The Document dialog box appears (see fig. 6.7).

Fig. 6.7
The Document dialog box.

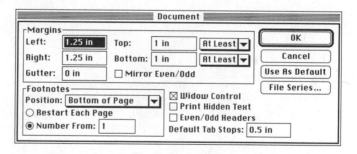

2. Type the new tab width in the Default Tab Stops text box.

3. Choose OK.

To change the default tab width for all documents, follow these steps:

1. Choose Document from the Format menu.

2. Type the new tab width in the Default Tab Stops text box.

3. Choose the Use As Default button.

4. Choose OK.

Chapter 6
Formatting Paragraphs

Understanding Custom Tabs

In Word, custom tabs are paragraph formats. When you create custom tabs, the tabs you choose apply to the selected paragraph or paragraphs. If you press Return after choosing custom tabs, the tabs you have set remain in effect as you type the new paragraph.

When you set a custom tab, Word automatically cancels the default tabs that precede the custom tab on the ruler. For example, if you set a tab at the 3" mark on the ruler, Word cancels the default tabs that would have been positioned at 0.5", 1.0", 1.5", 2.0", and 2.5". Word does not delete the default tabs to the right of the custom tabs.

Why set custom tabs, when Word already has set up tabs every 1/2 inch across the screen? The following examples provide some reasons.

Suppose that you want to align text at 3.0" and 4.5". With custom tabs set at these locations, you must press Tab only once to move the insertion point to the 3.0" mark, and just twice to move the insertion point to the 4.5" mark. Without custom tabs, you would have to press Tab nine times to move the insertion point to the 4.5" mark.

After typing a table, suppose that you want to select a larger or smaller font size. If you have used the default tabs, changing the font size might push one of the tab characters past the next tab stop. The result may be misaligned text on the printout. With custom tabs set, there are fewer tab characters and less chance that one of them will get pushed past a tab stop.

When you set custom tabs, you can choose from four alignment options, and you can even enter a vertical line. You can have Word automatically enter leaders also, such as dots or dashes. Commonly used in tables of contents, *leaders* are repeated characters that lead up to the tab stop, and fill in the blank space and guide your eyes across the page.

All four kinds of custom tabs are illustrated in figure 6.8:

Flush left. The text or numbers you type after pressing Tab appear to the right of the tab stop. The flush-left tab is set at 1.0".

Flush right. The text or numbers you type after pressing Tab appear to the left of the tab stop. The flush-right tab is set at 5.5".

Centered. The text or numbers you type after pressing Tab are centered at the tab stop. The centered tab is set at 3.0".

Decimal. The numbers you type after pressing Tab are aligned by decimal points; text is aligned flush right. A decimal tab is set at 4.5". Note how the numbers align at the decimal point.

In addition to these four tabs, you can set a *vertical* tab stop, which places a vertical line at the position at which you insert the tab (see the two vertical lines in fig. 6.8). These vertical lines aren't characters you can wipe out or misalign by typing over them; they stay where they are unless you remove them by removing the vertical tab stop.

Fig. 6.8
Custom tabs.

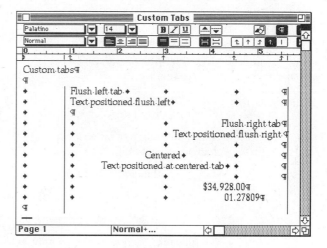

Setting Custom Tabs

To set custom tabs, you have two choices: You can set tabs with the ruler or you can use the Tabs dialog box, accessed by choosing the Tabs button in the Paragraph dialog box.

Setting Tabs with the Ruler

By far the easiest way to set, move, and cancel custom tabs is to use the ruler. To set custom tabs with the ruler, follow these steps:

1. Select the paragraph or paragraphs that will contain the tabs. Alternatively, press Return to start a new paragraph that will have the custom tabs.

2. Choose the button for the kind of tab you want to set. From left to right on the ruler, the buttons are Flush-Left, Centered, Flush-Right, Decimal, and Vertical Bar.

3. On the ruler scale, choose the position or positions at which you want to set tabs with the selected alignment.

To move tabs using the ruler, follow these steps:

1. Select the paragraph or paragraphs that contain the tabs you want to move.

2. Drag the tab stop to its new position.

To remove a tab stop using the ruler, follow these steps:

1. Select the paragraph or paragraphs that contain the tabs you want to remove.

2. Choose the tab stop you want to remove, and drag it down and away from the ruler scale.

To use the ruler to change a tab stop from one kind to another—such as changing a centered tab to a decimal tab—follow these steps:

1. Clear the tab by dragging it down and off the ruler.

2. Choose the button for the kind of tab you want to set.

3. Choose the position or positions at which you want to set the tab.

The following section teaches you how to access the Tabs dialog box to clear all the tabs you set or to choose leaders.

Using the Tabs Dialog Box

The ruler provides the easiest way to set tabs, but in three specific circumstances, you may prefer to use the Tabs dialog box. First, you can type more precise measurements in the Tabs dialog box.

Second, you use the Tabs dialog box to set leaders—characters that Word enters automatically before a tab stop. You can choose from dot, dash, and underline leaders (see fig. 6.9). Word enters the leaders when you press Tab to move to the stop that includes the leaders. Word automatically adjusts the leader to provide room for text you type.

Third, to clear tabs from the ruler, you drag them one at a time off the ruler scale. With the Tabs dialog box, you can clear all the tabs at once.

To display the Tabs dialog box, follow these steps:

1. Choose Paragraph from the Format menu.

   The Paragraph dialog box appears.

TIP

As you drag the tab, keep your eye on the page-number area, which shows the tab's location as you move it.

TIP

To set a tab and then quickly display the Tabs dialog box, set a tab on the ruler and then double-click the tab you have just set. The Tabs dialog box pops up, and its buttons and boxes show the characteristics of the tab you just set. If you make changes in the Tabs dialog box, these changes affect the tab on which you double-clicked.

2. Choose the Tabs button.

    The Tabs dialog box appears (see fig 6.10). To return to your document without choosing any options, just choose Cancel; when the Paragraph dialog box appears, choose Cancel again.

Fig. 6.9
Leaders.

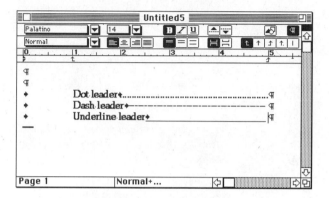

Fig. 6.10
The Tabs dialog box.

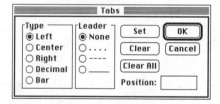

To set a tab using a precise measurement, follow these steps:

1. Choose Paragraph from the Format menu.

2. Choose the Tabs button.

3. To set a tab other than a flush-left tab, choose an option in the Type area.

4. Type a measurement in the Position text box.

5. Choose OK.

6. Choose OK in the Paragraph dialog box.

To create leaders, follow these steps:

1. Set a tab on the ruler; this tab receives the leader formatting. For a table of contents, set a flush-right tab at the right margin.

2. Double-click the tab arrow you just placed in the ruler scale.

3. When the Tabs dialog box appears, choose the tab stop on the ruler you created in step 1.

4. Choose the leader format you want from the Tabs dialog box. Choose from dot, dash, or underline leader formats.

5. Choose Set.

6. Choose OK.

To enter the leader, type some text and press Tab. The insertion point jumps to the tab stop you set and leaves the leader characters in its wake.

To clear all the custom tabs in the selected paragraph or paragraphs and restore the default tabs, follow these steps:

1. Choose Paragraph from the Format menu or press ⌘-M.

2. Choose the Tabs button in the Paragraph dialog box.

3. When the Tabs dialog box appears, choose Clear All.

4. Choose OK.

5. Choose OK in the Paragraph dialog box.

Searching for Paragraph Formats

n the preceding chapter, you learned about Word 5's enhanced Find command, which can help you locate text to which you have applied one or more paragraph formats. You can search for any text that has one or more paragraph formats of any kind, blank spacing, line spacing, Keep With Next options, indentations, alignment options, tabs, lines, borders, or Frame options.

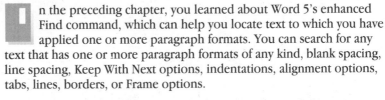

This sampling of searches you can conduct with the Find dialog box illustrates how this much-improved capability can be used.

- Find in your document every location at which you typed an extended quotation with a 1" indentation on both sides.

- Find in your document the heading after which you added three blank lines, not two, as in all other headings.

Part I

Getting Started

- Find the paragraph that has a decimal tab at 4 1/2 inches as well as a flush-right tab at 6 inches.

- Find the next paragraph that has an automatic, 0.5" first-line indentation.

The Find dialog box, in short, can come in handy when you have made formatting mistakes in a lengthy document and want to correct the error quickly—without missing any paragraphs that have the faulty format.

The best way to avoid formatting inconsistencies is to create and define styles for a document. When you define a style, all the paragraphs to which you apply the style have exactly the same format. If you later find that you want to change the formatting, you just make the change to the style, and all the paragraphs to which you have applied the style are updated automatically. Changing the style is much easier than making all the corrections manually, page by page, throughout your document— even if you have the help of Word 5's enhanced Find command. For more information on styles, see Chapter 8.

To search for a paragraph format, follow these steps:

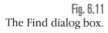

1. Choose Find from the Edit menu or press ⌘-F.

    The Find dialog box appears (see fig. 6.11).

Fig. 6.11
The Find dialog box.

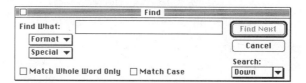

2. Use one of the following techniques to choose a paragraph format while the Find dialog box is on-screen. You can choose more than one format.

    Use the ruler, the Paragraph dialog box, or the keyboard shortcuts to choose formats. To display the Paragraph dialog box, choose Paragraph from the Format menu or Paragraph from the Format list box (under Find What, in the Find dialog box).

    To search for text to which you have applied one blank line before the paragraph as well as double-line spacing, for example, choose the Blank Line Spacing and Double Line Spacing buttons on the ruler.

Chapter 6
Formatting Paragraphs

You can search for character formats, such as the double-spaced text you typed in Palatino 12. To locate character formats, use any character-formatting technique to identify the formats, or choose Character in the Format list box to display the Character dialog box.

After you have chosen the formats, the Find dialog box reappears. The format you have chosen is shown beneath the Find What text box (see fig. 6.12). Note that this search finds a paragraph with centered alignment, a flush-right tab stop at 4.5 inches, line spacing of at least 24 points, and 12 points of blank space before the paragraph.

Fig. 6.12
The Find dialog box after choosing several paragraph formats.

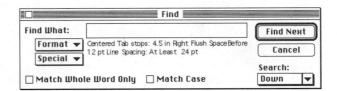

3. If you want to search for specific text that has the formats you specified under the Find What text box, type the text in the Find What dialog box. Leave the Find What text box blank to search for any text with this format or formats.

4. If you want to change the direction of the search, use the Search dialog box.

5. Choose Find Next.

If Word finds text with the format you have specified, Word highlights the text. Choose Find Next to find the next occurrence of the format, or choose Cancel to return to your document.

If Word cannot find any text with the format you have specified, a dialog box asks whether you want to extend the search from the beginning of the document (or the end, if you are searching up). Choose Yes to extend the search, or No to cancel.

After you use the Find dialog box to search for a format, Word retains the format setting beneath the Find What text box—as well as any text you may have typed in the Find What text box—for the duration of the current operating session. If you choose Find again, you must clear these settings to perform a different search. To clear the text from the Find What text box, select the text and press Delete. To clear the format, pull down the Format list box and choose Clear.

Replacing Paragraph Formats

WORD 5

As you learned in the preceding chapter, Word 5 has an important new capability: You can replace one format with another throughout your document. You can even replace a group of formats (such as double-spaced, justified paragraphs) with another group (such as single-spaced, flush-left paragraphs with one blank line between them) throughout your document. These significant new capabilities are made possible by the addition of the Format drop-down list box to the Replace dialog box.

Here are some examples of situations in which this capability can save you as much as several hours of manual formatting:

- You have added two blank lines under some of the headings in your document, but you discover that you were supposed to insert only one line of blank space.

- The bulleted lists you added to your document with a 0.19" indentation don't look right; you want to increase the indentation to 0.25".

- You use double-line spacing throughout your document with a blank line before each paragraph, but the spacing is unattractive. You want to close up the blank space.

Word 5's Replace command (on the Edit menu) can perform all these tasks and more, thanks to the Format drop-down list boxes. You already have learned how to replace character formats that you will find in the Replace dialog box. The following sections show you how to replace paragraph formats.

To replace one paragraph format with another throughout your document, follow these steps:

1. Choose Replace from the Edit menu or press ⌘-F.

    The Replace dialog box appears (see fig. 6.13).

Fig. 6.13
The Replace dialog box.

```
┌──────────────────────── Replace ════════════════════════┐
│ □▦                                                       │
│ Find What: ┌──────────────────────────┐  ┌───────────┐  │
│            └──────────────────────────┘  │ Find Next │  │
│   ┌ Format ▼ ┐                           └───────────┘  │
│   ┌ Special ▼ ┐                          ┌───────────┐  │
│                                          │  Replace  │  │
│                                          └───────────┘  │
│ Replace With: ┌───────────────────────┐ ┌───────────┐  │
│               └───────────────────────┘ │Replace All│  │
│   ┌ Format ▼ ┐                          └───────────┘  │
│   ┌ Special ▼ ┐                          ┌───────────┐  │
│                                          │  Cancel   │  │
│                                          └───────────┘  │
│                                          Search:         │
│ □ Match Whole Word Only  □ Match Case   ┌ Down   ▼┐    │
└─────────────────────────────────────────────────────────┘
```

Chapter 6

Formatting Paragraphs

2. With the insertion point in the Find What text box, use one of the following techniques to choose a paragraph format.

   Use the ruler, the Paragraph dialog box, or the keyboard shortcuts to choose formats. To display the Paragraph dialog box, choose Paragraph from the Format menu or Paragraph from the Format list box (under Find What in the Find dialog box).

   You can choose more than one format. To search for text to which you have applied one blank line before the paragraph as well as double-line spacing, for example, choose the Blank Line Spacing and Double Line Spacing buttons on the ruler. You also can search for character formats. For example, you can search for the double-spaced text you typed in Palatino 12. To add character formats, use any character-formatting technique to identify the formats, or choose Character in the Format list box to display the Character dialog box.

   After you have chosen the formats, the Find dialog box appears again. The format selected is shown beneath the Find What text box.

3. With the insertion point in the Replace With area, use any of the preceding techniques to choose the format you want Word to insert in place of the format you chose previously.

   In figure 6.14, the format just selected is shown beneath the Replace With text box. The settings in this box tell Word to find all paragraphs preceded by 12 points of blank space and then to remove the blank space.

Fig. 6.14
The Replace dialog box.

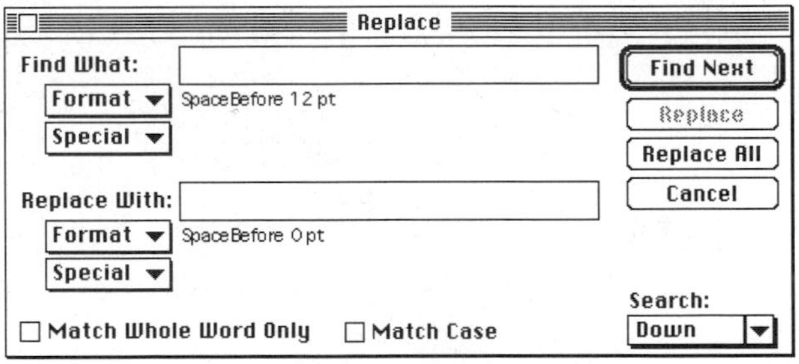

4. To search for specific text that has the formats you specified under the Find What text box, type the text in the Find What text box. Leave the text box blank to search for text with the formats you specified.

Part I

Getting Started

5. To replace specific text that has the formats you specified under the Replace With text box, just type the text in the Replace With text box. Leave the text box blank to search for text with the formats you specified.

6. To change the direction of the search, use the Search dialog box.

7. Choose Find Next, or if you are sure you want to perform the replacement throughout your document, choose Replace All.

Unless you chose Replace All, which performs all the replacements without asking for confirmation, you see a dialog box asking you to confirm replacement. When Word finds the first occurrence of the Search text, Word highlights the search text in context, scrolling the window so that you can see the text beyond the dialog box. Choose Find Next to find and confirm the next occurrence of the format, or choose Cancel to return to your document.

If Word cannot find any text with the format you have specified, you see a dialog box asking you whether you want to extend the search from the beginning of the document (or the end, if you are searching up). Choose Yes to extend the search, or No to cancel.

After you use the Replace dialog box to search for a format, Word retains the format setting beneath the Find What text box, as well as any text you have typed in the text box, for the duration of the current operating session. Moreover, the format and text appear in the Find dialog box too. If you choose Replace or Find again, you must clear these settings to perform a different search. To clear the text from the Find What text box, you just select the text and press Delete. To clear the format, pull down the Format list box and choose Clear.

Repeating and Copying Paragraph Formats

If you have entered a complex paragraph format and want to use it elsewhere in your document, you don't have to choose the commands again. You can repeat the format if you have just used it. If you have done something else since you applied the format, you can copy it. The following sections detail the procedures.

Chapter 6
Formatting Paragraphs

Repeating Paragraph Formats

To repeat the formatting of a paragraph format you have just applied, follow these steps:

1. Apply paragraph formats using any technique discussed in this chapter.

2. Select the next text you want to format in the same way.

3. Choose Repeat from the Edit menu or press ⌘-Y.

Copying Paragraph Formats

If you have typed some text or chosen another command since you applied the paragraph format, you cannot repeat the format using the technique just introduced. You can copy the format, however, using the ⌘-Option-V technique described here. (As you learned in Chapter 5, you can copy character formats with this command, but the procedure for copying paragraph formats differs slightly.)

To copy paragraph formats, follow these steps:

1. Select the paragraph from which you want to copy the formats. You must highlight the whole paragraph.

   To select the whole paragraph, move the pointer to the selection bar until the arrow changes direction. Then double-click.

2. Press ⌘-Option-V.

3. Choose the insertion point in the paragraph to which you want the formats applied.

   You see an insertion point made up of dots.

4. Press Return to confirm copying the formats.

To cancel, press ⌘-period before pressing Return.

Quick Review

This section concisely summarizes the most useful information in this chapter. Check "Productivity Tips" for a review of high-productivity tips and tricks, and review "Techniques" when you forget how to perform a specific procedure.

Part I
Getting Started

Productivity Tips

- Remember that Word defines paragraphs in a mechanical way. Every time you press Return, you start a new paragraph. By Word's definition, a paragraph can be a blank line (because it has a paragraph mark!), a one-word heading, or a paragraph of body text.

- The fastest way to choose paragraph formats is with the ruler. Use the Paragraph dialog box only for formats you cannot enter on the ruler. Keep in mind that the ruler limits your line-spacing and blank-spacing options.

- To access the Paragraph dialog box quickly, double-click the right indent mark on the ruler.

- Don't create blank lines by pressing Return. If you do, you cannot control page breaks using the Keep With Next option because the next paragraph is an *empty* paragraph—one that contains nothing but a paragraph mark. Add blank lines by using the Blank Line Spacing button on the ruler or by typing measurements in the Before and After boxes in the Paragraph dialog box. For more information on the Keep With Next option, see Chapter 7.

- Use the ruler to set, move, and cancel custom tabs. You use the Tabs dialog box only when you choose leaders. To add leaders quickly, set the tab and double-click the tab arrow on the ruler scale; the Tabs dialog box appears. This dialog box, accessible through the Paragraph dialog box also, is useful when you want to clear all tabs with just one command rather than drag them all off the ruler, one by one.

- If you plan to create a table, use Word's Table command (on the Insert menu) rather than set tabs. For more information on the Table command, see Chapter 17.

- Always use tabs to align text. Don't press the space bar to add blank spaces to your document because Word may not align the text properly when you print your document.

- You can search and replace formats using Word 5's new Find and Replace commands, but formatting with styles enables you to avoid formatting inconsistencies. For more information on styles, see Chapter 8.

Chapter 6
Formatting Paragraphs

Techniques

This section provides concise, quick-reference summaries of all the procedures introduced in this chapter.

Aligning Text

To center a paragraph:

1. Place the insertion point in the paragraph you want to format, or select two or more paragraphs.

2. Use one of these techniques:

   Choose the Centered button on the ruler.

   Press ⌘-Shift-C.

To align a paragraph flush left:

1. Place the insertion point in the paragraph or paragraphs you want to format.

2. Use one of these techniques:

   Choose the Flush-Left button on the ruler.

   Press ⌘-Shift-L.

To align a paragraph flush right:

1. Place the insertion point in the paragraph or paragraphs you want to format.

2. Use one of these techniques:

   Choose the Flush-Right button on the ruler.

   Press ⌘-Shift-R.

To right-justify a paragraph:

1. Place the insertion point in the paragraph or paragraphs you want to format.

2. Use one of the following techniques:

   Choose the Flush-Right button on the ruler.

   Press ⌘-Shift-J.

Automatic First-Line Indentation

To create an automatic first-line indentation:

1. Select the paragraph or paragraphs you want to format.

2. On the ruler, drag the first-line indent marker to create the indentation. The first-line indent marker is the top left triangle on the left side of the ruler. Alternatively, type a measurement in the First text box in the Paragraph dialog box or press ⌘-Shift-F.

Blank Space

To add 12 points of blank space before a paragraph (or before all the paragraphs you select):

1. Place the insertion point where you want the line-spacing option to begin. Alternatively, select the paragraph or paragraphs you want to format.

2. Choose the Blank Line Spacing button on the ruler.

To choose other blank-spacing options:

1. Place the insertion point where you want the line-spacing option to begin. Alternatively, select the paragraph or paragraphs you want to format.

2. Choose Paragraph from the Format menu.

3. To add blank space before the paragraphs, type a measurement (in printer's points) in the Before text box.

4. To add blank space after the paragraphs, type a measurement (in printer's points) in the After text box.

5. Choose OK.

Copying Paragraph Formats

To copy paragraph formats:

1. Select the paragraph from which you want to copy the formats. You must highlight the whole paragraph.

   To select the whole paragraph, move the pointer to the selection bar until the arrow changes direction. Then double-click.

2. Press ⌘-Option-V.

3. Place the insertion point in the paragraph to which you want the formats applied.

4. Press Return to confirm copying the formats.

Hanging Indentation

To use keyboard shortcuts to create a hanging indentation:

1. Select the paragraph or paragraphs you want to affect.

2. Press ⌘-Shift-T. Word positions the first-line indent marker at 0 inches; the right-indent marker is positioned at 0.5 inches.

3. To increase the indentation 1/2 inch, use the command again.

To use the ruler to create a hanging indentation:

1. Select the paragraph or paragraphs you want to affect.

2. On the ruler, drag the left-indent marker (the bottom left triangle on the left side of the ruler) to the position at which you want to place the paragraph's second and subsequent lines (the turnover lines). (The first-line indent marker moves also.)

3. Drag the first-line indent marker back to the position at which you want the first line to begin.

To use the Paragraph dialog box method to create a hanging indentation:

1. Select the paragraph or paragraphs you want to affect.

2. Choose Paragraph from the Format menu.

3. When the Paragraph dialog box appears, type a negative measurement (such as −0.5) in the First box. Type a positive measurement (such as 1.0) in the Left box.

4. Choose OK.

Indenting Text

To use keyboard shortcuts to indent text from the left margin:

1. Select the paragraph or paragraphs you want to format.

2. Press ⌘-Shift-T. Word positions the left indent and first-line markers at 0.5 inches on the ruler scale.

3. To increase the indentation 1/2 inch, use the command again. To decrease the indentation by one tab stop, press ⌘-Shift-M.

To use the ruler to create a left or right indentation:

1. Select the paragraph or paragraphs you want to format.

2. On the ruler, drag the left-indent marker (the bottom left triangle on the left side of the ruler) to the position at which you want the paragraph to be indented. (The first-line indent marker moves also.) To create an indentation from the right margin, drag the right-margin marker (the larger triangle on the right of the ruler scale).

To use the Paragraph dialog box method to create an indentation:

1. Select the paragraph or paragraphs you want to format.

2. Choose Paragraph from the Format menu, or press ⌘-M.

3. When the Paragraph dialog box appears, type a measurement in the Left and Right boxes.

4. Choose OK.

Line Spacing

To double-space your document:

1. Select the paragraph or paragraphs you want to format.

2. To double-space your document if you are using 12-point type, choose the Double Line Spacing button on the ruler. If you are using another font size, choose Paragraph from the Format menu, and then choose At Least from the Line list box. Multiply by two the font size you are using, and type the answer in the Line text box. Choose OK to confirm your choice.

To use a fixed line spacing that Word doesn't adjust automatically:

1. Select the paragraph or paragraphs you want to format.

2. Choose Paragraph from the Format menu, and choose Exactly from the Line list box. Then type the line spacing you want in the Line text box; choose OK to confirm your choice.

Replacing Paragraph Formats

To replace one paragraph format with another throughout your document:

1. Choose Replace from the Edit menu or press ⌘-F.

2. With the insertion point in the Find What text box, use any paragraph-formatting technique to choose the format for which to search. Alternatively, choose Paragraph from the Format list box to display the Paragraph dialog box, and choose the format option.

3. With the insertion point in the Replace With area, use any paragraph-formatting technique (or the Format list box) to choose the format you want Word to insert in place of the format you just chose.

4. If you want to search for specific text that has the formats you have indicated beneath the Find What text box, type the text in the Find What text box. Leave the text box blank to search for any text with the formats you indicated.

5. If you want to replace specific text that has the formats you have indicated beneath the Replace With text box, just type the text in the Replace With text box. Leave the text box blank to search for any text with the formats you indicated.

6. If you want to change the direction of the search, use the Search dialog box.

7. Choose Find Next, or if you are sure you want to perform the replacement throughout your document, choose Replace All.

Repeating Paragraph Formats

To repeat a paragraph format:

1. Apply paragraph formats using any of the techniques discussed in this chapter.

2. Select the next text you want to format in the same way.

3. Choose Repeat from the Edit menu or press ⌘-Y.

Searching for Paragraph Formats

To search for a paragraph format:

1. Choose Find from the Edit menu or press ⌘-F.

2. Use any paragraph-formatting technique to choose a paragraph format while the Find dialog box is on-screen. Alternatively, choose Paragraph from the Format list box to disay the Paragraph dialog box.

3. If you want to search for specific text that has the formats you indicated under the Find What text box, type the text in the Find What dialog box. To search for any text with this format or formats, just leave the Find What box blank.

4. If you want to change the direction of the search, use the Search dialog box.

5. Choose Find Next.

Tabs

To change the default tab width for the current document:

1. Choose document from the Format menu.

2. Type the new tab width in the Default Tab Stops text box.

3. Choose OK.

To change the default tab width for all documents:

1. Choose Document from the Format menu.

2. Type the new tab width in the Default Tab Stops text box.

3. Choose the Use As Default button.

4. Choose OK.

To use the ruler to set custom tabs:

1. Select the paragraph or paragraphs that will contain the tabs. Alternatively, press Return to start a new paragraph that will have the custom tabs.

2. Choose the button for the kind of tab you want to set. From left to right on the ruler, the buttons are Flush-Left, Centered, Flush-Right, Decimal, and Vertical Bar.

3. On the ruler scale, choose the position or positions at which you want to set tabs with the selected alignment.

To use the ruler to move tabs:

1. Select the paragraph or paragraphs that contain the tabs you want to move.

2. Drag the tab stop to its new position.

To use the ruler to remove a tab stop:

1. Select the paragraph or paragraphs that contain the tabs you want to remove.

2. Choose the tab stop you want to remove and drag it down and away from the ruler scale.

To use the ruler to change a tab stop from one kind to another—for example, to change a centered tab to a decimal tab:

1. Clear the tab by dragging it down and off the ruler.

2. Choose the button for the kind of tab you want to set.

3. Choose the position or positions at which you want to set the tab.

To clear all the custom tabs in the selected paragraph or paragraphs and restore the default tabs:

1. Choose Paragraph from the Format menu or press ⌘-M.

2. Choose the Tabs button on the Paragraph dialog box.

3. Choose Clear All.

4. Choose OK.

5. Choose OK in the Paragraph dialog box.

To set a tab with a precise measurement:

1. Choose Paragraph from the Format menu.

2. Choose the Tabs button.

3. To set a tab other than a flush-left tab, choose an option in the Type area.

4. Type a measurement in the Position text box.

5. Choose OK.

6. Choose OK in the Paragraph dialog box.

To create leaders:

1. Set a tab on the ruler.

2. Double-click the tab arrow you just placed in the ruler scale.

3. When the Tabs dialog box appears, choose the tab stop on the ruler that you created in step 1.

4. Choose the leader format you want from the Tabs dialog box. Choose from dot, dash, or underline leader formats.

5. Choose Set.

6. Choose OK.

Chapter 6
Formatting Paragraphs

Formatting Pages

T he last of Word's three formatting domains, page formats,
controls the apportionment of your text to the printed page. By
default, Word determines page breaks automatically and prints
your document with standard margins (1 inch top and bottom, and 1 1/4
inch left and right) on standard U.S. letter paper (8 1/2- by 11-inch). For
all but the simplest documents, you probably will change the page
design. The following is an overview of the page design choices covered
in this chapter:

- *Adding Page Numbers*. By default, Word doesn't print page
  numbers. In this chapter, you learn a simple technique for placing
  page numbers in your document. In Chapter 15, you learn how to
  add page numbers to headers and footers (text repeated within
  the top or bottom margins of all pages).

- *Changing the Margins*. You can easily change Word's default
  margins by using the ruler or the Document dialog box. You even
  can adjust margins dynamically and visually in Print Preview.

- *Controlling Page Breaks*. When you fill up a page with text, Word
  automatically starts a new one, but you can begin a new page
  manually. You also can format paragraphs so that Word inserts a
  page break before a paragraph, keeps a paragraph with the next
  one, or keeps all the lines of a paragraph together on one page.

■ *Choosing Paper Sizes and Page Orientation.* Depending on your printer's capabilities, you may be able to choose paper sizes other than 8 1/2 by 11 inches. You also may be able to change the page orientation so that lines of text run across the longer dimension of the page (landscape orientation). You also can change the paper size and page orientation defaults.

This chapter covers the fundamentals of page formatting, but other chapters contain additional information to guide the design of your document's pages. Chapter 16 covers techniques for creating more than one page design in your document. Chapter 15 treats headers, footers, and footnotes. Chapter 21 covers Word 5's Frame command and how it positions paragraphs in absolute positions on the page. Chapter 25 covers paper size and page formatting procedures for printing mailing labels and envelopes. Finally, in Chapter 26 you learn how to link several documents for printing, with continuous page numbering.

With the Section and Document dialog boxes (discussed extensively in this chapter), you can save page-formatting choices as new defaults. Word formats the current document and all new documents you create with the settings you have chosen. You can modify Word, for example, so that it always prints page numbers (unless you turn page numbers off). Such changes can be useful, but you should wait until you fully understand the consequences of such changes before making them permanent. For more information on changing the defaults, see Chapter 27.

Adding Page Numbers

 s you probably have already learned, Word doesn't print page numbers on your document unless you instruct the program to do so. You can turn on page numbers in three ways.

The easiest way is to use the Page Number icon in Print Preview. With the mouse, you can position page numbers anywhere on the page. Use this technique to add page numbers quickly.

You also can add page numbers by using the Margin Page Numbers option in the Page Number area of the Section dialog box (Format menu). You can suppress page numbers on the first page and specify that the second page be numbered 2 (or 1 if the first page is a title page or an abstract). You can change the number format (options include the default Arabic numerals, Roman numerals, and uppercase or lowercase letters) and specify an exact location on the page for your page numbers. Use this option when you want to specify how Word handles the first page.

Word prints your page numbers using the default font and font size. To format page numbers differently, you have two options: You can add page numbers in headers or footers, which gives you the option of formatting them directly. Or, as explained in Chapter 8, you can change Word's default page number style for the current document or for all new documents.

SPEED KEY

Fig. 7.1

Previewing the page design with Print Preview.

A third way to add page numbers is to include them in a header or footer. Use this technique when you want page numbers to appear in the same area as a header or footer.

The following sections detail the first two of these techniques; see Chapter 16 for information on adding page numbers to headers or footers.

Managing Page Numbers with Print Preview

With Print Preview, you can add page numbers, reposition them, and remove them. This section discusses each procedure in detail.

Print Preview's Page Number icon provides the easiest way to add page numbers to your document. Double-click the Page Number icon to add page numbers at the default location (the upper right corner), or drag the page number to another location.

To add page numbers with Print Preview, follow these steps:

1. Choose Print Preview from the File menu or press ⌘-Option-I.

   Word displays a Print Preview of your document (see fig. 7.1).

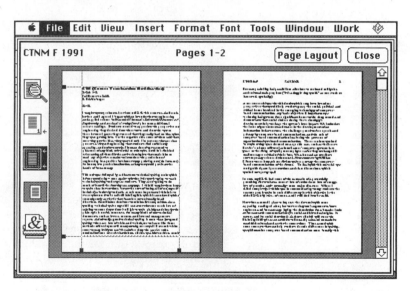

2. Add the page numbers by using the Page Number icon.

To quickly add page numbers in the upper right corner of the page (one-half inch from the top and one-half inch from the right), double-click the Page Number icon.

To position page numbers elsewhere, choose the Page Number icon and hold down the mouse button. Position the page number and release the mouse button to confirm adding page numbers to your document.

3. Choose Close to return to your document, or choose the Printer icon to print your document.

After you add page numbers to your document, you can reposition or remove them by using Print Preview.

To reposition or remove page numbers with Print Preview, follow these steps:

1. Choose Print Preview from the File menu or press ⌘-Option-I.

2. Place the mouse pointer on the page number in your document. When the pointer is positioned over the page number, it changes to a cross hair.

3. Drag the page number to its new location. (Watch the page number area to know the exact position of the pointer when you drag it.) To remove the page number, drag it off the page.

4. Choose Close to return to your document.

Adding Page Numbers with the Section Dialog Box

The Section dialog box provides a second way to add page numbers to your document. With this dialog box, you can suppress page numbers on the first page, specify the starting number, and choose formats other than Arabic.

By dividing your documents into sections, you can change page formats within your document. These formats include newspaper columns, headers and footers, and page numbers. If you are creating a complex document, such as a newsletter or Ph.D. dissertation, you may want to change formats several times within a document. You divide sections using ⌘-Enter to create a section break, and then you format each section using the Section dialog box. (For a detailed explanation of the Section dialog box, see Chapter 15.)

TIP

When you drag the page number with the mouse, keep your eye on the page number area in the bottom left corner of the screen. Word shows the mouse pointer's current location.

NOTE

Changing the page number position or removing the page number affects the page numbers on all the pages, not just the one on which you make the change. If you divide your document into sections (see Chapter 16), the change affects the current section only.

If you haven't pressed ⌘-Enter to divide your document into sections, the entire document is a section. You can use the Section dialog box to choose newspaper column, header/footer, and page number formats for your whole document.

To add page numbers with the Section dialog box, follow these steps:

1. Choose Section from the Format menu. The Section dialog box appears (see fig. 7.2).

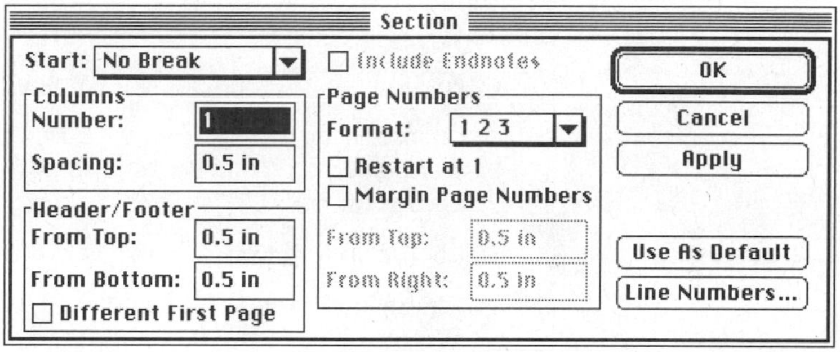

Fig. 7.2
The Section dialog box.

2. Activate the Margin Page Numbers option to turn page numbers on. By default, Word places page numbers in the upper right corner of the page, as you can see in the From Top and From Right boxes. These boxes become active when you activate Margin Page Numbers.

3. If you want to change the page number position, type the new position in the From Top and From Right boxes.

4. Choose OK to confirm your page number choices.

Suppressing Page Numbering

In many documents, you will want to suppress page numbers on the first page. A lengthy letter, for example, should begin with your letterhead, on which no page number is printed, but second and subsequent pages should be numbered. An article or report should begin with an unnumbered title page or abstract; unlike a letter, though, the first text page should be numbered page 1. With the section dialog box, you can handle both of these common page-numbering configurations.

To suppress page numbering on the first page and number the second page *Page 2*, activate the Different First Page option in the Section dialog box. This option suppresses the printing of page numbers on the first page of your document. Choose OK to confirm your page number choices.

To number the second page *Page 1*, you must enter a section break. The following steps detail this procedure, which you cannot perform until you create at least one full page of text.

To suppress page numbering on the first page and number the second page *Page 1*, follow these steps:

1. Position the insertion point at the beginning of the second page.

2. Choose Section Break from the Format menu, or press ⌘-Enter. Word enters a section break (a double row of little dots) in your document.

3. Choose Section from the Format menu.

4. Activate the Margin Page Numbers option to turn page numbers on.

5. If you want to change the page number position, type the new position in the From Top and From Right boxes.

6. Activate the Restart at 1 option.

7. Choose OK to confirm your page number choices.

Changing the Numbering Format

You also can use the Section dialog box to change the page numbering format. The Format list box (see fig. 7.3) lists your page number format options: Arabic (1, 2, 3), uppercase Roman (I, II, III), lowercase Roman (i, ii, iii), uppercase letters (A, B, C), and lowercase letters (a, b, c). Non-Arabic page number formats are frequently used for appendixes, introductions, and prefaces.

To change the page number format, follow these steps:

1. Choose Section from the Format menu.

2. Activate the Margin Page Numbers option to turn page numbers on.

3. If you want to change the page number position, type the new position in the From Top and From Right boxes.

4. Drop down the Format list box by choosing the drop-down arrow.

5. Choose the page number format you want from the list.

6. Choose OK to confirm your page number choices.

Fig. 7.3
The Format list box
dropped down (Section
dialog box).

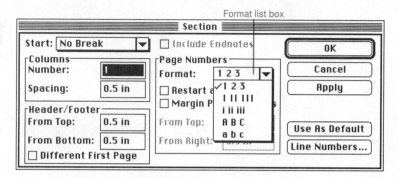

Repositioning Page Numbers with the Section Dialog Box

After you add page numbers with the Section dialog box, you can reposition or remove them. With this procedure, you can reposition or remove page numbers added with Print Preview and with the Section dialog box because Print Preview's Page Number icon is directly linked to the Section dialog box. When you make a page number change in Print Preview, Word updates the Section dialog box. (Changes you make in the Section dialog box also are reflected in Print Preview's display of page numbers.)

To reposition page numbers with the Section dialog box, follow these steps:

1. Choose Section from the Format menu.

2. Type the new position in the From Top and From Right boxes. To position page numbers centered at the bottom of the page, for example, type *10.5"* in the From Top box and *4.5"* in the From Right box.

3. Choose OK to confirm your page number choices.

Removing Page Numbers

To remove page numbers with the Section dialog box, follow these steps:

1. Choose Section from the Format menu.

2. Deactivate the Margin Page Numbers option.

3. Choose OK to confirm your page number choices.

If you add page numbers with Print Preview or with the Section dialog box but later decide to add page numbers to headers or footers, be sure to remove the original page numbers. Otherwise, Word might print page numbers in two places.

Starting Page Numbering with a Number Other than 1

If you're writing a long document, you may want to place each chapter or section in a separate file. Doing so improves Word's performance—the program scrolls small files more quickly—and lessens the chance that you will lose all your document if one file becomes corrupt. In Chapter 26, you learn how to link separate files so that they print with continuous pagination. If you prefer, you can set the starting page number of each document manually, as described in the following steps:

1. Choose Document from the Format menu.

   The Document dialog box appears.

2. Choose the File Series button.

   The File Series dialog box appears (see fig. 7.4).

3. Type the starting page number in the Number From box.

4. Choose OK in the File Series dialog box, and choose OK again in the Document dialog box.

   Word numbers the first page of your document beginning with the number you typed.

Changing Margins

The difference between indents (which are paragraph formats) and margins (which are document formats) is important in Word. You can choose indents for each paragraph, including single-line *paragraphs*, like headings. You can vary indents as you please, creating in your document complex patterns to highlight important text.

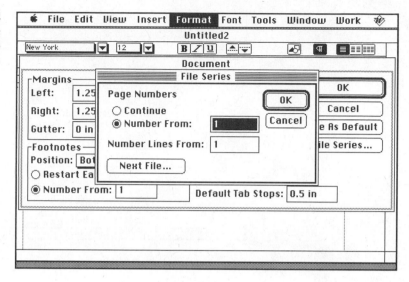

Fig. 7.4
Typing a new starting page
number in the File Series
dialog box.

In contrast to indents, you choose margins for the whole document. The margin setting doesn't vary, even if you break your document into sections (see Chapter 21 for more information on sections).

Figure 7.5 illustrates one of the design possibilities that stem from the difference between indents and margins. In this document, the left margin is set at 3 inches from the left edge of the page. (In this Page view of the document, the left margin is displayed as a vertical dotted line positioned at the 0 mark on the ruler. The 0 mark always shows the position of the document's left margin.) The paragraphs containing the headings, however, are formatted with a negative indent of –1 1/2 inches, so that they are positioned in the left margin. A thick line under each heading, added with the Border command, creates a visually pleasing effect. (For more information on the Border command, see Chapter 22.) To sum up this example, you set *margins* for the whole document. You can set *indents* separately for individual paragraphs, including *outdents* (negative indents).

By default, Word uses 1-inch margins top and bottom, and 1 1/4-inch margins left and right. These margins are good for business letters, but the left and right settings may not be appropriate for reports or articles. You also may want to add extra space on the page (called a *gutter*) to make room for binding your document. The following sections detail the procedures you use to change the margins and add a gutter.

Fig. 7.5
Document with wide (3")
left margin and outdented
headings.

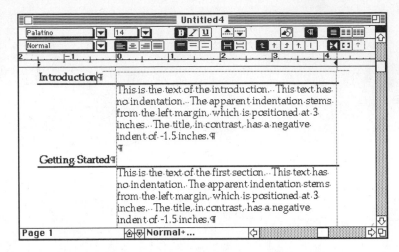

Understanding Your Margin-Changing Options

You can change margins in more than one way. In Print Preview, you can change any margin—top, bottom, left, or right—by dragging the margin boundary.

The ruler provides a second way to change margins. When you activate the margin button on the ruler, Word displays brackets showing the current locations of the left and right margins. By dragging these brackets, you can change the left and right margins. The change affects the whole document, not just the current paragraph.

The Document dialog box provides the greatest degree of flexibility for changing the margins in your document. With this dialog box, you can change all the margins. You also can create gutters, define mirror margins for documents that will be duplicated on both sides of the page, and control the way Word adjusts the top and bottom margins to make room for headers, footers, and footnotes.

NOTE

When you view two pages at once, only one page shows the boundary markers at a time. To see the boundary markers on the other page, click that page. Because margin changes affect the whole document, it does not matter which page is current when you drag the handles.

Changing Margins in Print Preview

In Print Preview, boundary markers indicate your margin settings. Dotted lines, each with a black square at one end, show all four margin settings (see fig. 7.6). These black squares are called *handles* because you can use them to manipulate the margins. To change the margins, drag the icons.

Fig. 7.6
Boundary markers and
handles (Print Preview).

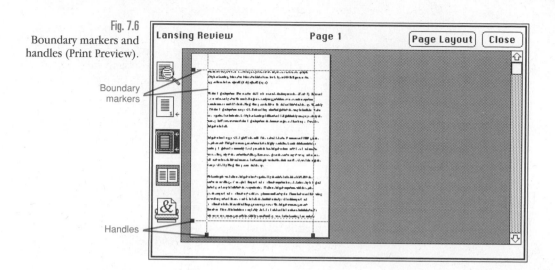

Boundary
markers

Handles

To change margins in Print Preview, follow these steps:

1. Choose Print Preview from the Print menu, or press ⌘-Option-I.

2. If you do not see the boundary markers, activate the boundary marker button.

3. Move the pointer to one of the black squares until the pointer changes to a cross hair.

4. Drag the handle. While you drag it, keep your eye on the area that normally displays the page number. Word informs you where the pointer currently is positioned.

5. When the margin is where you want it, release the mouse button.

6. Choose Close to exit Print Preview, or choose the Print button to print your document.

After you set the margins with Print Preview, you can adjust them at any time by using the same technique.

Changing Margins with the Ruler

The ruler (when displayed) provides a fast and convenient way to change the right or left margins. You cannot change the top and bottom margins with the ruler; use Print Preview or the Document dialog box instead.

To change the left or right margin with the ruler, follow these steps:

1. Activate the Margin button, the next-to-last button (with the brackets) on the right of the ruler. After you activate the Margin button, brackets replace the indent markers on the ruler (see fig. 7.7).

Fig. 7.7
Brackets on the ruler show
current margin settings.

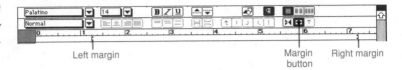

Left margin   Margin   Right margin
button

2. To change the left margin, drag the left bracket. To change the right margin, drag the right bracket. When you drag the bracket, watch the page number area in the lower left corner of the screen to see the pointer's current location.

3. When the bracket is at the desired location, release the mouse button.

4. Choose the Indent button to restore the indent markers on the ruler.

Changing Margins with the Document Dialog Box

The techniques you just learned—changing margins with Print Preview and the ruler—have some limitations. When you drag the boundary marker or the margin bracket, you can make changes only in 1/16-inch increments. You also cannot use these techniques to create gutters or mirror margins. To specify margin measurements with greater than 1/16-inch precision and to create gutters or mirror margins, use the Document command (Format menu).

SPEED KEY

To set margins with the Document dialog box, follow these steps:

1. Choose Document from the Format menu, or press ⌘-F14. The Document dialog box appears (see fig. 7.8).

2. Type measurements in the Top, Bottom, Left, and Right boxes. If you do not type a measurement abbreviation, Word assumes that you are expressing the measurements in inches.

3. Choose OK.

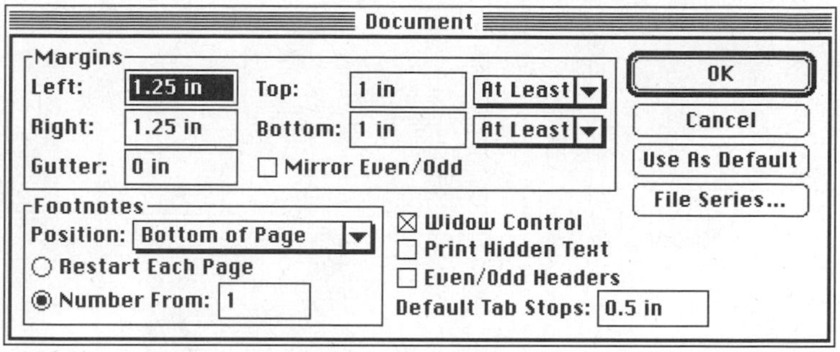

Fig. 7.8
The Document dialog box.

When you choose top and bottom margins with the Document dialog box, you can specify whether Word will adjust these margins to make room for lengthy headers or footers. In the list boxes to the right of the Top and Bottom boxes, you can choose from two options—At Least (the default) and Exactly. With At Least, Word makes room, if necessary, to accommodate headers or footers with multiple lines.

With the Exactly option, Word always prints your chosen margins. In desktop publishing applications such as newsletters, your document might not look good if Word adjusts the margins; it looks much better to have them all placed in the same location.

Accommodating Bindings

If you are planning to bind your document after printing it, you may want to add extra space to make room for the binding. You can add extra space in three ways:

- *Increase the Left Margin*. Use this option if you plan to duplicate your document using one side of the paper. Try adding 1/2 inch to the left margin setting, but leave the right margin setting as it is.

- *Add a Gutter*. Use this option if you plan to duplicate your document using both sides of the page (facing pages). Word adds the binding gutter to the left side of odd-numbered pages and to the right side of even-numbered pages. To add the gutter, type a measurement in the Gutter box of the Document dialog box. Figure 7.9 shows a binding gutter.

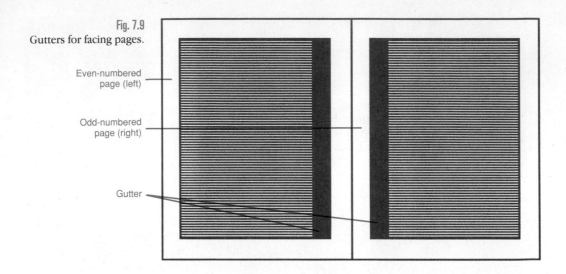

Fig. 7.9
Gutters for facing pages.

Even-numbered
page (left)

Odd-numbered
page (right)

Gutter

■ *Use Mirror Margins*. Use this option if you plan to duplicate your document using both sides of the page, and you want to create different running heads for the odd and even pages. Add extra space to the left margin. When Word prints your document, it reverses the left and right margin settings on even-numbered pages, producing the effect shown in figure 7.10. To print your document using mirror margins, type a larger left margin measurement in the Left box of the Document dialog box, and activate the Mirror Margins option.

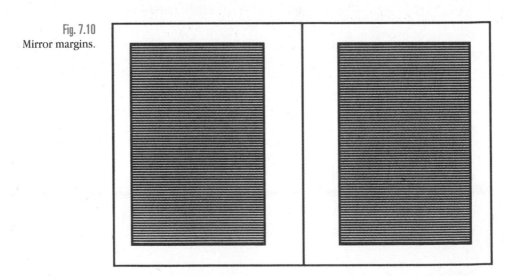

Fig. 7.10
Mirror margins.

Part I

Getting Started

For documents printed on both sides of the page, gutters and mirror margins can produce the same effect (extra room for binding), but Gutters prevent anything from printing in the space that is set aside. With gutters you cannot use indents to outdent text past the left margin. If you're using outdented headings and you want to make sure that none of them extend into the binding area, choose gutters instead of "faking" gutters with Mirror Margins and an extra-wide left margin.

Controlling Page Breaks

fter you fill a page with text, Word automatically starts a new page by inserting a *soft page break*. If you later add or delete text above the page break, Word adjusts the soft page break's location.

You can force Word to start a new page even before you fill a page with text. You may want to start a new page, for example, if you are starting a new chapter of a book or dissertation. When you force Word to start a new page, you choose a command (Page Break on the Insert menu) that inserts a *hard page break*. A hard page break forces the program to start a new page at the hard page break's location. Even if you add or delete text above the hard page break, Word still breaks the page at the hard page break's location.

Hard page breaks are not the only way to determine how and where Word breaks pages. Section breaks provide many useful options for breaking pages, especially if you plan to duplicate your document on both sides of the paper.

Hard page breaks and section breaks are justifiably used in many situations, but Word gives you additional ways to control page breaks, including the Paragraph dialog box's Keep Lines Together and Keep with Next options. You also can choose an option that suppresses *widows* (the last line of a paragraph left alone at the top of a page) and *orphans* (the first line of a paragraph left alone at the bottom of a page).

If you add hidden text to your document, be sure to turn the display of hidden text off before deciding whether your page breaks are accurate. When displayed, hidden text throws off your page breaks. To turn off the display of hidden text, choose Preferences from the Tools menu, and choose the View button. Turn off the Hidden Text option in the Show area, and then click the Close box to confirm your choice.

Repaginating Your Document

By default, Word updates soft page breaks while you create and edit your text. This active updating is called *background repagination*. If your Mac is slow (like an SE or Plus), you may want to turn background repagination off by choosing Tools from the Preferences menu and deactivating the Background Repagination option. Word waits until you print your document to paginate it.

If you turn background repagination off, the page breaks in your document may not be accurate while you are editing, but you can force pagination at any time by choosing Repaginate Now from the Tools menu.

Inserting Hard Page Breaks

Word gives you more than one way to insert a hard page break. You can use the Page Break option in the Insert menu, its keyboard shortcut, or Print Preview.

To insert a hard page break with the Page Break option, follow these steps:

1. Position the insertion point where you want the hard page break to occur.

2. Choose Page Break from the Insert menu, or press Shift-Enter.

   Word enters a row of little dots across the screen.

Word will not print your document if you inadvertently format the page break as hidden text. If you are using hidden text extensively in your document, select the page break and choose Character from the Format menu. If the hidden text option is activated, turn it off.

To insert a hard page break with Print Preview, follow these steps:

1. Position the insertion point in the page where you want the page break to occur.

2. Choose Print Preview from the File menu, or press ⌘-Option-I.

3. Move the mouse pointer to the soft page break (the dotted horizontal line just above the bottom margin shown in figure 7.11). The pointer changes to a cross hair.

Fig. 7.11
A dotted line just above the
bottom margin indicates a
soft page break.

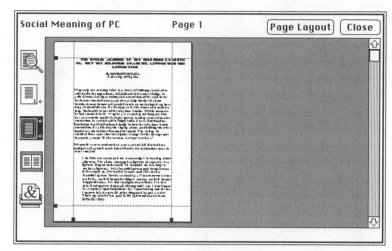

Fig. 7.11
A dotted line just above the
bottom margin indicates a
soft page break.

4. Move the page break up. When you do, keep your eye on the page number area, which shows the pointer's current location.

5. When the page break is where you want it, release the mouse button. Word repaginates your document.

6. Choose the Close button to return to your document, or choose the printer icon to print your document.

You should use hard page breaks as your last recourse to control page breaks. Suppose that you added headings to your document, and in previewing your document before printing, you discover that one of the headings is widowed at the bottom of the page (the text beneath it has been moved to the next page). You insert a hard page break just above the heading. If you add or delete some text above the heading, however, the hard page break is still in your document and forces a page break in an inappropriate location.

Removing Hard Page Breaks

Because a hard page break may outlive its usefulness, you may need to delete it. To delete a hard page break in Print Preview, drag the page break off the page. To delete a hard page break in Normal or Page Layout view, follow these steps:

TIP

Because hard page breaks can cause page break problems if you edit your text after inserting them, use them only to start new parts of your document, such as a new chapter. Prevent other page break problems by using the Paragraph dialog box's Keep With Next and Keep Lines Together options.

1. Select the hard page break by moving the mouse pointer to the selection bar next to the hard page break. When the arrow changes direction, click the mouse button.

2. Press Backspace or Delete.

Searching for Hard Page Breaks

If you want to remove hard page breaks from your document, use Word to find them.

To search for hard page breaks, follow these steps:

1. Choose Find from the Edit menu to see the Find dialog box.

2. From the Special list, choose Page Break.

   Word enters the ^d code in the Find What box (see fig. 7.12). You can type this code or choose it from the Special list.

3. Choose Find Next to find the next hard page break.

Fig. 7.12

Searching for hard page breaks (Find dialog box).

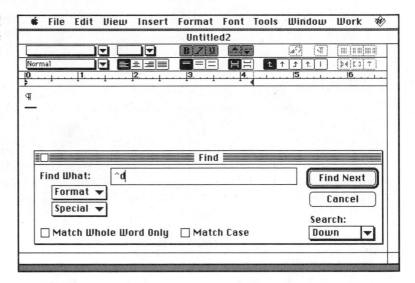

Using Section Breaks

The Section dialog box provides page-break options not available elsewhere. (Sections and section breaks are discussed thoroughly in Chapter 16.) You can insert a section break anywhere in your document by choosing Section Break from the Insert menu, or by pressing ⌘-Enter. Normally, you insert a section break to restart headers, footers, footnote numbers, or page numbers, as you might when you start a new chapter or an appendix in a lengthy document. See Chapter 16 for a discussion of these section applications.

Another rationale for inserting a section break is so that you can choose from page break options not available when you insert a hard page break. For example, you can choose to break the page so that the next page starts on an odd-numbered page. If necessary, Word can leave an entire page blank so that the next text appears on an odd-numbered page.

If you plan to duplicate your document using both sides of the page, you always should start a new chapter or section of your document on an odd-numbered page because odd-numbered pages appear right of the binding. For such documents, you always should use the Section Break command to start a new chapter or section of your document.

Insert a page break that starts the next page on an odd-numbered page by using the following steps:

SPEED KEY

1. Place the insertion point where you want the break to occur.

2. Choose Section Break from the Insert menu or press ⌘-Enter. Word inserts a double row of dots (called the *section mark*) across the screen, and positions the insertion point just beneath the section mark.

3. Choose Section from the Format menu. The Section dialog box appears.

4. Choose Odd Page from the Start list box.

5. Choose OK.

Printing a Paragraph at the Top of a Page

Another way to control page breaks is to choose a paragraph-formatting option that automatically inserts a page break before the paragraph. If you add this format to chapter titles, for example, Word will break the page before each new chapter.

To force Word to break a page before a paragraph, follow these steps:

1. Position the insertion point in the paragraph you want to format.

2. Choose Paragraph from the Format menu, or press ⌘-M.

3. Activate the Page Break Before option.

4. Choose OK.

SPEED KEY

Keeping Lines Together

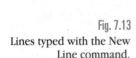

TIP

You can create heading styles for the headings in your document (see Chapter 8). If you want Word to break a page before a major heading, such as a chapter title, you can add this format to the heading.

You should use hard page breaks only to start a new chapter or section. You can control page breaks in better ways, such as with the Keep Lines Together option in the Paragraph dialog box. You can choose this option to prevent Word from breaking up the lines of any single paragraph. This option keeps all the lines of a paragraph together. If enough room isn't on the page, Word moves the whole paragraph to the top of the next page, keeping all the lines of the paragraph together.

To keep all the lines of a table, list, or poem together, you must type it so that Word considers the text to be all one paragraph. You can use the New Line command (Shift-Enter), as shown in figure 7.13.

Fig. 7.13
Lines typed with the New
Line command.

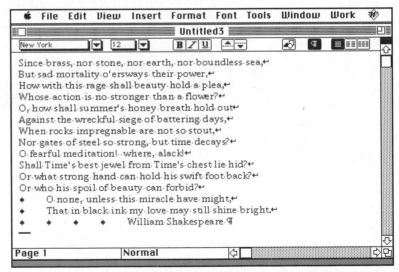

To create text that Word will keep together, follow these steps:

1. Type the text using the New Line command (Shift-Return) instead of pressing Return. The text should not exceed one page in length.

2. Position the insertion point in the newly created paragraph.

3. Choose Paragraph from the Format menu, or press ⌘-M.

4. Activate the Keep Lines Together option in the Pagination area.

5. Choose OK.

After you format a paragraph with the Keep Lines together option, Word inserts a black square next to the paragraph in the selection bar (see fig. 7.14). (To see the black square, choose Show ¶ from the View menu or choose the ¶ mark on the ribbon.) The black square indicates that you chose a *hidden* format—Keep Lines Together, in this case. When you see a black square next to a paragraph, you can double-click the square to display the dialog box containing the format you entered so that you can remember it, change it, or delete it.

Fig. 7.14
Hidden format indicator (after choosing Keep Lines Together).

Hidden format indicator

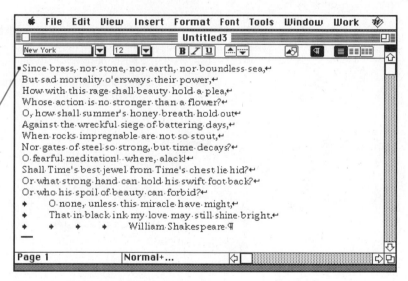

Preventing Page Breaks between Paragraphs

Some of your document's headings may be orphaned at the bottom of the page, with a page break dividing them from the body text beneath them. When you are in a rush to get your document out the door, you

Chapter 7
Formatting Pages

may forget to check for this common formatting problem before printing. The best policy is to prevent orphaned headings from occurring. You can format a heading so that Word automatically keeps the heading paragraph with the next paragraph. If the heading would print at the bottom of the page with no text under it, Word automatically moves the heading to the top of the next page. Word moves the heading only when needed.

To prevent Word from inserting a page break after a paragraph, follow these steps:

1. Position the insertion point in the paragraph you want to format.

2. Choose Paragraph from the Format menu, or press ⌘-M.

3. Activate the Keep With Next option.

4. Choose OK.

Turning off Widow and Orphan Control

By default, Word suppresses widows and orphans by preventing the first or last lines of a paragraph to be printed by themselves at the bottom or top of a page. To print the same number of lines on each page, turn off widow and orphan control and follow these steps:

1. Choose Document from the Format menu, or press ⌘-F14, to reach the Document dialog box.

2. Turn off the Widow Control option.

3. Choose OK.

> **TIP**
>
> Like the Keep Lines Together option, the Keep With Next option creates a hidden format, indicated by a small black square in the selection bar next to the paragraph. Double-click the square to bring up the dialog box that contains the format; you then can delete or change it.

Choosing Paper Sizes and Page Orientations

Your Apple Macintosh computer is designed for an international market, and Word easily can accommodate paper sizes other than the standard U.S. letter size (8 1/2- by 11-inch). Table 7.1 lists the paper size settings you can choose with Word. You can choose any of the default paper sizes as the standard paper size for formatting and printing, or you can define a custom paper size. You also can choose between portrait and landscape printing orientations. The following sections detail these procedures.

Table 7.1	
Standard Paper Sizes	

Name	Size (width by height)
US Letter	8.5 by 11 inches
US Legal	8.5 by 14 inches
A4 Letter	8.5 by 11.67 inches
LaserWriter II B5	7.2 inches by 10.1 inches
Tabloid	11 inches by 17 inches
International Fanfold	8.25 inches by 12 inches
Computer paper	14 inches by 11 inches

Choosing a Predefined Paper Size

Your printer must be specially equipped to handle paper size options other than U.S. Letter. Many printers can be adjusted to accommodate a variety of paper sizes. If you are not sure of your printer's specifications, check its manual.

To choose one of Word's predefined paper sizes, follow these steps:

1. Choose Page Setup from the File menu. The Page Setup dialog box appears (see fig. 7.15).

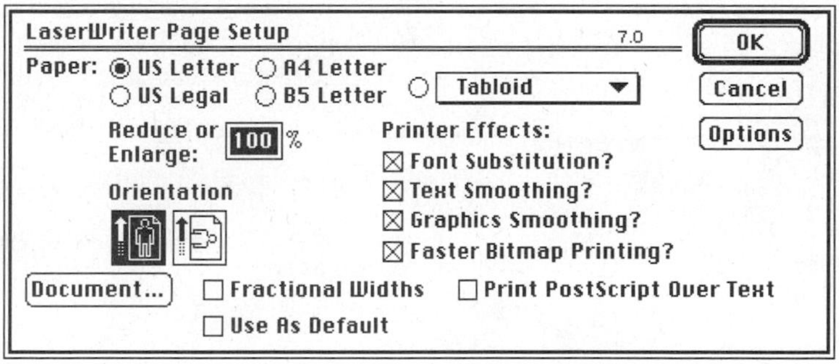

Fig. 7.15
The Page Setup dialog box.

2. Choose one of the paper size options. If the one you want is not visible, pull down the list box to see more options.

3. If you want to make this paper size the default for all documents, activate the Use as default option.

4. Choose OK.

Defining a Custom Paper Size

Some printers can print custom paper sizes, and Word is flexible enough to accommodate virtually any size of paper you can get into a printer. Use the following procedure to define and use a custom paper size.

To define a custom paper size, follow these steps:

1. Choose Preferences from the Tools menu.

2. Type the width and height of the paper in the Custom Paper Size area.

3. Click the Close box to confirm your choice.

4. Choose Page Setup from the Print menu.

5. Choose Custom from the list box.

6. To make your choice the new default for all documents, activate the Use as Default option.

7. Choose OK.

NOTE

Custom paper sizes aren't available with some printers, such as the LaserWriter NT. If the Custom Paper Size boxes are dimmed, you cannot choose a custom paper size for your printer.

Changing the Page Orientation

Normally, you print your document with the normal orientation, called *portrait orientation*. In portrait orientation, lines of text run across the shorter dimension of the page. You also can choose *landscape orientation* to position the lines of text across the longer dimension of the page (see fig. 7.16). You may want to use landscape orientation to print a wide table or figure that doesn't fit on the page with portrait orientation.

To choose a page orientation, follow these steps:

1. Choose Page Setup from the File menu.

2. Choose the portrait or landscape orientation button in the Orientation area.

3. Choose OK.

NOTE

The Page Setup Orientation you choose applies to the active document only.

Quick Review

This section concisely summarizes the most useful information in this chapter. Check "Productivity Tips" for a review of high-productivity tips and tricks, and review "Techniques" when you forget how to perform a specific procedure.

Part I

Getting Started

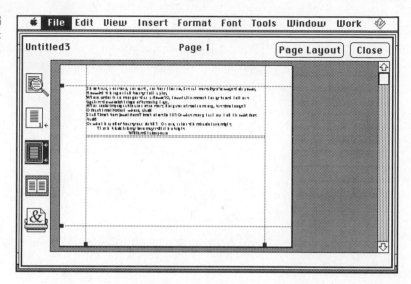

Fig. 7.16
Print Preview of document
with landscape orientation.

Productivity Tips

■ Use Print Preview to turn on page numbers, unless you want to
suppress page numbers on the first page. In Print Preview, double-
click the Page Number icon to place page numbers in the default
location (upper right corner).

■ To change margins quickly, adjust them in Print Preview. Alternatively, choose the margins button on the ruler, and drag the
margin brackets.

■ Do not use a hard page break unless absolutely necessary (like
when starting a new chapter in a lengthy document). If you plan to
duplicate your document using both sides of the page, use a
section break instead and format the new section so that it begins
on an odd-numbered page.

■ Use the Keep Lines Together and Keep With Next options (Paragraph dialog box) extensively to prevent undesirable page breaks.
Always format headings with the Keep With Next option, and be
sure to add blank space beneath the headings with the blank
spacing options rather than Return.

Techniques

This section provides concise, quick-reference summaries of all the procedures introduced in this chapter.

Adding Binding Gutters

To add a binding gutter to a document duplicated using one side of the page:

1. Choose Document from the Format menu.

2. Add space (try 0.5") to the measurement in the Left box.

3. Choose OK.

To add a binding gutter to a document duplicated using both sides of the page:

1. Choose Document from the Format menu.

2. Choose one of the following options:

   Type a measurement in the Gutter box (try 0.5").

   or

   Add space to the measurement in the Left box (try 0.5", and activate the Mirror Margins option.

Breaking Pages

To insert a hard page break with the Page Break option:

1. Position the insertion point where you want the hard page break to occur.

2. Choose Page Break from the Insert menu, or press Shift-Enter.

To insert a hard page break with Print Preview:

1. Position the insertion point within the page where you want the page break to occur.

2. Choose Print Preview from the File menu, or press ⌘-Option-I.

3. Move the mouse pointer to the soft page break.

4. Move the page break up.

5. When the page break is where you want it, release the mouse button.

6. Choose the Close button to return to your document, or choose the printer icon to print your document.

To delete a hard page break in Normal or Page Layout view:

1. Select the hard page break.

2. Press Backspace or Delete.

To delete a hard page break in Print Preview:

Drag the page break off the page.

To force Word to break a page before a paragraph:

1. Position the insertion point in the paragraph you want to format.

2. Choose Paragraph from the Format menu, or press ⌘-M.

3. Activate the Page Break Before option.

4. Choose OK.

To insert a section break that starts the next text on an odd-numbered page:

1. Place the insertion point where you want the break to occur.

2. Choose Section Break from the Insert menu or press ⌘-Enter.

3. Choose Section from the Format menu.

4. Choose Odd Page from the Start list box.

5. Choose OK.

Keeping Lines Together

To create text that Word will keep together:

1. Type the text using the new line command (Shift-Return) instead of pressing Return.

2. Position the insertion point within the newly created paragraph.

3. Choose Paragraph from the Format menu, or press ⌘-M.

4. Activate the Keep Lines Together option in the Pagination area.

5. Choose OK.

Keep Text With the Next Paragraph

To prevent Word from inserting a page break after a paragraph:

1. Position the insertion point in the paragraph you want to format.

2. Choose Paragraph from the Format menu, or press ⌘-M.

3. Activate the Keep With Next option.

4. Choose OK.

Changing Margins

To change margins in Print Preview:

1. Choose Print Preview form the Print menu, or press ⌘-Option-I.

2. If you don't see the boundary markers, activate the boundary marker button.

3. Move the pointer to one of the black squares until the pointer changes to a cross hair.

4. Drag the handle.

5. When the margin is where you want it, release the mouse button.

6. Choose Close to exit Print Preview, or choose the Print button to print your document.

To change the left or right margin with the ruler:

1. Activate the margin button.

2. To change the left margin, drag the left bracket. To change the right margin, drag the right bracket.

3. When the bracket is where you want it, release the mouse button.

4. Choose the Indent button to restore the indent markers on the ruler.

To set margins with the Document dialog box:

1. Choose Document from the Format menu.

2. Type measurements in the Top, Bottom, Left, and Right boxes.

3. To stop Word from adjusting the top or bottom margins to make room for lengthy headers or footers, choose Exactly in the list box next to the Top or Bottom boxes.

4. Choose OK.

Repaginating your Document

To turn off background repagination:

1. Choose Preferences from the Tools menu.

2. Turn off the Background Repagination option.

3. Choose OK.

To repaginate your document after turning off background repagination:

Choose Repaginate Now from the Tools menu.

Adding Page Numbers

To add page numbers with Print Preview:

1. Choose Print Preview from the File menu or press ⌘-Option-I.

2. Add the page numbers using the Page Number icon.

   To add page numbers quickly in the upper right corner of the page, double-click the Page Number icon. To position page numbers elsewhere, choose the Page Number icon and hold down the mouse button. Move the page number to the position where you want page numbers to print. Release the mouse button to confirm adding page numbers to your document.

3. Choose Close to return to your document, or choose the Printer icon to print your document.

To add page numbers with the Section dialog box:

1. Choose Section from the Format menu.

2. Activate the Margin Page Numbers option to turn page numbers on.

3. If you want to change the page number position, type the new position in the From Top and From Right boxes.

4. Choose OK to confirm your page number choices.

To suppress page numbering on the first page and number the second page *Page 2*:

1. Choose Section from the Format menu.

2. Activate the Margin Page Numbers option to turn page numbers on.

3. If you want to change the page number position, type the new position in the From Top and From Right boxes.

4. Activate the Different First Page option. This option suppresses the printing of page numbers on the first page of your document.

5. Choose OK to confirm your page number choices.

To suppress page numbering on the first page and number the second page *Page 1*:

1. Position the insertion point at the beginning of the second page.

2. Choose Section Break from the Format menu, or press ⌘-Enter.

3. Choose Section from the Format menu.

4. Activate the Margin Page Numbers option to turn page numbers on.

5. If you want to change the page number position, type the new position in the From Top and From Right boxes.

6. Activate the Restart at 1 option.

7. Choose OK to confirm your page number choices.

To reposition or remove page numbers with Print Preview:

1. Choose Print Preview from the File menu or press ⌘-Option-I.

2. Place the pointer on the page number in your document. When the pointer is positioned over the page number, it changes to a cross hair.

3. To reposition the page number, drag it to its new location. To remove the page number, drag it off the page.

4. Choose Close to return to your document.

To reposition page numbers with the Section dialog box:

1. Choose Section from the Format menu.

2. Type the new position in the From Top and From Right boxes.

3. Choose OK to confirm your page number choices.

To remove page numbers with the Section dialog box:

1. Choose Section from the Format menu.

2. Deactivate the Margin Page Numbers option.

3. Choose OK to confirm your page number choices.

To change the page number format:

1. Choose Section from the Format menu.

2. Activate the Margin Page Numbers option to turn page numbers on.

3. If you want to change the page number position, type the new position in the From Top and From Right boxes.

4. Open the Format list box by choosing the drop-down arrow.

5. Choose the page number format you want from the list.

6. Choose OK to confirm your page number choices.

Choosing Paper Size

To choose one of Word's predefined paper sizes:

1. Choose Page Setup from the File menu.

2. Choose one of the paper size options. If the one you want is not visible, pull down the list box to see more options.

3. If you want to make this paper size the default for all documents, activate the Use as Default option.

4. Choose OK.

To define a custom paper size:

1. Choose Preferences from the Tools menu.

2. Type the width and height of the paper in the Custom Paper Size area.

3. Click the Close box to confirm your choice.

4. Choose Page Setup from the Print menu.

5. Choose Custom from the list box.

6. To make the choice the new default for all documents, activate the Use as Default option.

7. Choose OK.

Choosing Page Orientation

To choose a page orientation:

1. Choose Page Setup from the File menu.

2. Choose the portrait or landscape orientation button in the Orientation area.

3. Choose OK.

Controlling Widows and Orphans

To turn off widow and orphan control:

1. Choose Document from the Format menu.

2. Turn off the Widow Control option.

3. Choose OK.

Formatting with Styles

Styles are simple, but perhaps unfamiliar tools for Word users. In brief, a style is a named and stored collection of formats that you can apply to one or more paragraphs in your document. When you create a style, you can include emphases (such as bold or italic), fonts, font sizes, indents, alignment options, blank space, tabs, and more.

Creating styles is easy and based on manual formatting skills you already know. (*Manual formatting* refers to these formatting techniques: the ribbon, ruler, dialog box, and keyboard shortcut techniques that format a paragraph directly.) When you apply a style, Word formats the selected paragraph with all the formats in the style definition. With styles as your building blocks, you can quickly create a beautifully formatted document.

Here's an example of styles in action. You create a style called Heading, which includes centered alignment, bold, 14-point Helvetica, 24 points of blank space before, 24 points of blank space after, and the Keep with Next option to prevent Word from inserting a page break under the heading. You also create a style called Body Text with a 1/2-inch first line indentation, the Times Roman font in 10-point type, and justified alignment.

With these two styles, you can quickly create your document (see fig. 8.1). Choose the Heading style to type a heading, and Word instantly enters all the formats you've chosen—centered alignment, bold, 14-point Helvetica, 24 points of blank space after, and the Keep with Next option. Then you choose Body Text to type your document's body text paragraph, and Word instantly enters all the Body Text formats.

Fig. 8.1
A document formatted
with Heading and
Body Text styles.

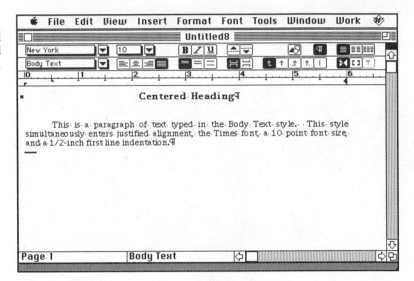

When you switch to the Heading style again, Word enters all the formats simultaneously (see fig. 8.2). No copying, no repetitive formatting commands—just fast, productive writing.

After you grow adept with styles, style formatting will become your basic formatting approach, and you will reserve manual formatting for adjusting text previously formatted with styles.

The following are some of the advantages of using styles:

- *You can quickly enter several formats*. Suppose that you create a style for a hanging indentation which combines Palatino 12, justified alignment, a 3/10-inch hanging indent, and the Keep Lines Together option. You plan to use this format to create bulleted lists. If you define this style as *Bulleted List*, Word enters all these formats instantly whenever you apply the Bulleted List style to a paragraph.

- *You can reformat your document quickly*. Suppose that you create a body text style which calls for Times Roman 12, right justification, auto line spacing, and 12 points of blank space before the paragraph. At the last moment, you decide to use the Garamond typeface instead of Times Roman. Does this mean you must reformat every body text paragraph manually? Not with styles. Change the style, and Word instantly updates all the paragraphs to which you applied the style.

- *You can redefine many of Word's default format settings*. These formats include headers, footers, the footnote reference mark, footnote text, page numbers, line numbers, headings, and more. After you redefine automatic styles, the formats you choose apply automatically to all new documents.

Fig. 8.2
Formatting another heading by choosing a style.

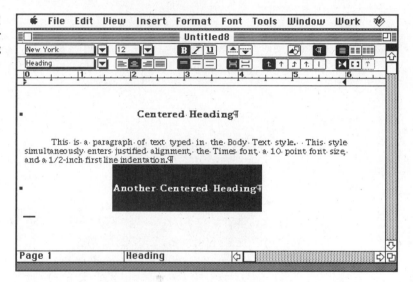

Style skills are fundamental to your knowledge of Word, so they are discussed in Part I of this text. This chapter is designed to get you up and running with styles and covers the following topics:

- *Creating Styles*. You learn how to record styles from text you already formatted and how to define styles with the Style command (Format menu). In addition, you learn how to create a *master style*, on which all the other styles in your style sheet are based.

Chapter 8
Formatting with Styles

■ *Applying Styles*. Like other Word formats, styles can be applied before or after you type. You can choose from three different techniques for applying styles.

■ *Revising and Managing Styles*. You can edit, rename, and delete styles after you create them, and even copy them to another document.

■ *Using Styles with Manual Formatting*. In this section, you learn how to combine styles with manually applied formats.

■ *Using Standard Styles*. In addition to the styles you create, Word provides many standard styles that cover formats such as page numbers, headers and footers, headings, footnote reference marks, footnote text, and more. By modifying these styles, you can change Word's defaults for these formats.

■ *Searching for Styles and Replacing Styles*. New to Word 5 are important new capabilities of the Search and Replace commands. You can search for styles, and you also can replace one style with another throughout your document.

Understanding Style Sheets

F ar too few Word users employ style sheets, perhaps because the word *style* is misleading; most people associate the word with character emphasis. Getting past such a minor terminology block, however, is definitely worth the potential gains in productivity. This section introduces the fundamental concepts of style sheet formatting. You learn what styles are, and you learn where they are stored.

Users of previous versions of Word will find only minor changes in Word's style commands. The most obvious change lies in the Format menu, where one style option (Style) replaces the Define Styles and Define All Styles commands. Another change lies in terminology: The new term for *automatic styles* is *standard styles*. Word 5 can use all the styles you created with earlier versions of the program. Word 5's new Stationery feature is not specifically Style-related, but you can use this feature to manage your style sheets (see Chapter 11).

What Styles Do

In Word, a *style* is a named and stored collection of formats—the same ones you now apply manually. When you apply the style to text in your document, the text takes on that style. As with any other Word format, you can format with styles before or after you type. Figure 8.3 introduces styles graphically. Three styles have been applied to this document—Body Text (justified, Palatino, 12 pt blank space after), Heading 1 (centered, bold, Helvetica, 24 pt blank space after), and Quotation (left indent 0.5", right indent 0.5", justified, Palatino, 12 pt blank space after).

Fig. 8.3
A document with three sample styles.

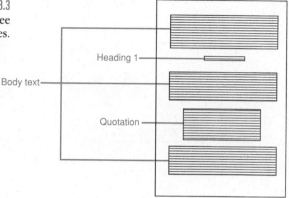

With styles, you can easily reconsider your formatting decisions. Suppose that after formatting this document, you decide you don't like the Palatino font you chose for the Body Text style, and you want to use Times Roman instead. Instead of reformatting all the paragraphs one-by-one, you simply make the change to the Body Text style. Word automatically modifies all the paragraphs to which you applied Body Text—the reformatting is nearly instantaneous.

Where Styles Are Stored

When you create a style, you can store it in the default style sheet or the document style sheet. A *document style sheet* is a storage area, attached to a document but invisible on-screen, in which your styles are stored. The default style sheet contains styles that are automatically available in all documents. You learn how to create and store your styles elsewhere in this chapter. For now, all you need to learn is the distinction between the default style sheet and the document style sheet.

If you store your style in the default style sheet, it becomes available to all new documents you create. Suppose that you create a style called Body Text. Every time you open a new document, you see this style as an option in the ruler's style selection list box (see fig. 8.4).

Chapter 8
Formatting with Styles

Fig. 8.4
Cropping down the Style
selection box.

```
┌─────────────────────────── Untitled2 ════════════════════┐
│ □  Palatino        ▼  14  ▼     B I U  ▲ ▼      ▣  ¶   ▤ │
│    Normal          ▼   ≡ ≡ ≡ ≡   ▬ ▬ ▬  ⊟ ⊟  ↳ ↑ ↥ ↑ |  ▣ │
│      Body Text        │12  │18  │24  │30  │36            │
│    ✓Normal                                               │
│   |                                                      │
│   ──                                                     │
│                                                          │
│ Page 1              Normal        ◁ □                ▷  │
└──────────────────────────────────────────────────────────┘
```

Style
selection
box

If you store your style in the document style sheet, it is available for the current document only. You see the style in the style selection list for the current document, but will not see it if you open or create another document. (Later in this chapter, you learn how to copy a document style sheet from one document to another.)

What the Normal Style Is

All the time you have been using Word, you have been using the default style sheet. You probably noticed the word *Normal* in the ruler's style selection box. When you open a new Word document and start typing, Word applies the default style sheet's Normal style to the text you type. The Normal style formats this text with the default font and font size you chose when you installed Word. In addition, this style uses plain text (no emphasis), auto line spacing (single space), flush left paragraph alignment, no blank space before or after, and Word's default tabs.

Think twice before adding a lot of styles to your default style sheet. If you add too many styles (more than 10 or 15), working with styles becomes cumbersome. For now, while you are learning to use styles, just add styles to your document style sheets.

Creating Styles

ou can create up to 221 styles in a document, although in practice you will find that 10 or 15 usually are sufficient. You can create styles by recording them or by using the Style command.

By far, the easiest way to create styles is to record them from text already formatted. You begin by choosing formats manually. Then you record and name the style. This technique is easy, but has important limitations. When you create styles this way, you can save them only to the document style sheet, not the default style sheet.

You also can create styles using the Style dialog box, which gives you more options. With the Style dialog box (shown later in fig. 8.7), you can save styles to the default style sheet as well as to the document style sheet. Moreover, the full range of Style options, including the Based On and Next Style options, is available when you use this command.

Rather than creating your own heading styles, you may want to use (and redefine, if you want) Word's standard heading styles (such as Heading 1, Heading 2). Word's standard heading styles are automatically linked to outline heading levels, and if you use these styles for your document headings, you get a handsome payoff when you switch to Outline view: your document headings become outline headings, and you can restructure your whole document just by moving the headings around. For more information on standard styles, see "Using Standard Styles," later in this chapter. For more information on heading styles and outlining, see Chapter 12.

TIP

If you just want to create a style quickly and store it in the document style sheet, use the recording technique. To save a style to the default style sheet, use the Style command in the Format menu.

Recording a Style

To record a style you have already created, follow these steps:

1. Format the paragraph using manual formatting techniques.

   You may choose any of the following formats: font, font size, emphasis, alignment, indentation, blank space settings, page break control (page break before, keep lines together, keep with next), tabs, borders, or Frame positions.

   All the formats you choose become part of the style definition. Moreover, when you apply the style, Word formats all of the selected text with these formats. For this reason, be sparing in your selection of character emphasis such as bold or italic. You should include bold, for example, only when you're creating a style in which all the text should be bold (like headings, headers, and footers).

TIP

If even one word or one character of the selection has a character emphasis such as bold or italic, Word includes this format in the style definition. To make sure Word doesn't include any character emphasis in your style definition, highlight the whole paragraph and press ⌘-Shift-Z before defining the style.

Chapter 8
Formatting with Styles

2. If the ruler isn't displayed, choose Ruler from the Format menu or press ⌘-R.

3. Click the style selection box, and Word highlights the box.

4. Type a name for the style.

   You can type up to 254 characters, including spaces. However, because the Style dialog box and the style selection box display only 16 characters, keep your style names short. Any character is permissible except a comma.

5. Press Return. A message box appears asking whether you want to define the style (see fig. 8.5).

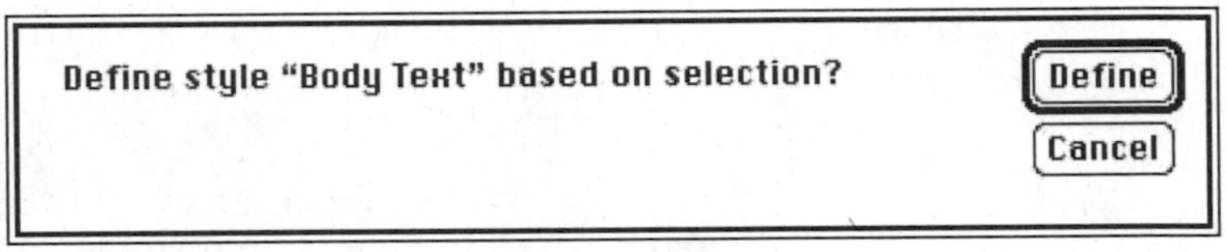

Fig. 8.5
The Defining a style
message box.

> **Define style "Body Text" based on selection?**   [Define]
>   [Cancel]

6. When the message box appears, click Define.

After you record the style, you see its name in the style selection box. The style becomes part of the document style sheet, and you can then use it within the current document. However, the style will not be available in other documents. To use this style in other documents, you must copy the entire style sheet to another document, following a procedure detailed elsewhere in this chapter.

Using the Style Command

Creating a style with the Style dialog box isn't as straightforward as recording styles, but it has two advantages: you can save the style to the default style sheet, and you can make use of the Based On and Next Style options, which are helpful adjuncts to a systematic style formatting approach. The Based On and Next Style options are discussed in subsequent sections. Here, you learn how to define a style with the Style dialog box.

Users of previous versions of Word will note some simplifications in the Style commands. The Style command combines the Define Styles and Define All Styles commands used in previous versions.

Before proceeding, note that the style name area at the bottom of the screen shows the current style name, as shown in figure 8.6.

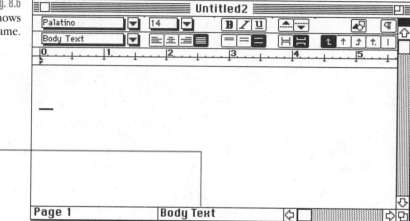

Fig. 8.6
The style name area shows current style name.

Current style name

To display the Style dialog box, choose Style from the Format menu (or use the ⌘-T keyboard shortcut, or double-click the style name in the status line). The Style dialog box appears with the current document's name in the title bar. This title indicates that you are looking at the document style sheet (see fig. 8.7). You see the following items in the Style dialog box:

SPEED KEY

Style List. In the list box, you see the styles that currently are available in your document. By selecting New Style, you can define a new style that will appear in this list.

Document Styles and All Styles Option Buttons. By default, Word displays the document styles—the default Normal style and the styles you defined for this document (if any). If you click All Styles, you see all of Word's standard styles.

Style Box. When you select a style, this box shows the name of the currently selected style (see fig. 8.8). The larger box shows the current style's definition. In figure 8.8, for instance, the larger box shows the formats stored with the style Body Text. You do not type in this box directly; instead, you choose formatting commands, and Word builds the definition for you.

Chapter 8
Formatting with Styles

Fig. 8.7
The Style dialog box.

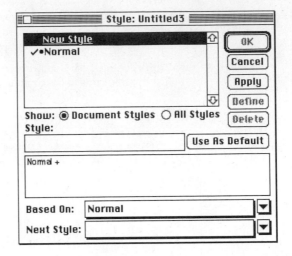

Based On. Every style can be based on another, which means that the style definition starts with the other style's formats. By default, most styles are based on the Normal style, which has an important implication: If you change Normal, all the styles based on Normal change too.

Next Style. In this box, you specify which style Word will enter after you finish typing a paragraph in the current style and press Return. For example, you can define a heading style so that Word returns to a body text style after you type the heading and press Return.

Command Buttons. After you finish choosing formats for a new style, you click Define to save the style. Alternatively, you can click the Use as Default button to save the style to the default style sheet. Choose the Apply button to see how the style looks without closing the Style dialog box. If you want to delete a style, you can highlight the style and click Delete.

To create a document style with the Style dialog box, follow these steps:

1. Choose Style from the Format menu or press ⌘-T. The Style dialog box appears, with New Style highlighted.

SPEED KEY

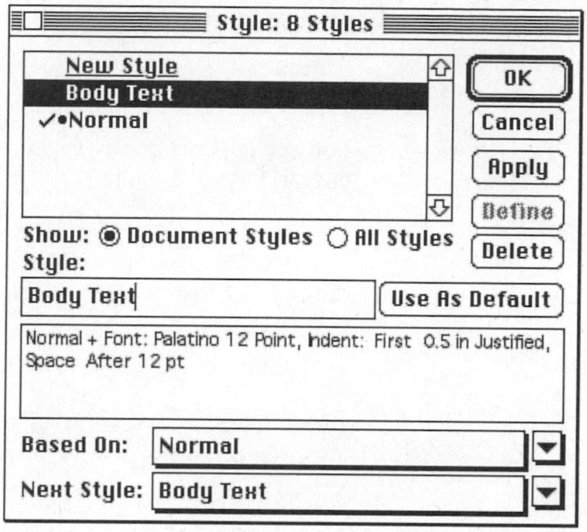
Style: 8 Styles
New Style
Body Text
✓•Normal
OK
Cancel
Apply
Define
Show: Document Styles All Styles
Delete
Style:
Body Text
Use As Default
Normal + Font: Palatino 12 Point, Indent: First 0.5 in Justified, Space After 12 pt
Based On: Normal
Next Style: Body Text

Fig. 8.8
The Style box shows the current style.

> **TIP**
> Note that Word displays the formats for the paragraph in which the insertion point is currently positioned. If you don't want to use these formats, be sure to change them using any manual formatting technique.

2. Type a style name in the Style box. You can use up to 254 characters; using fewer than 16 characters guarantees the name can fit in the style selection box.
3. Choose formats for the style, using any manual formatting technique, including using the pull-down menus and dialog boxes, making changes to the ribbon or ruler, or using keyboard commands.
4. If you want to see what the style looks like in your document without leaving the Style dialog box, choose Apply.
5. Choose OK to define the style and apply the style to the selected paragraph(s). Alternatively, click Define to define the style, and then click Close to exit the dialog box without applying the style you've created.

If you drop down the style selection box on the ruler, you see the style you just defined. This style is available in the current document only.

To create a default style with the Style dialog box, follow these steps:

1. Choose Style from the Format menu or press ⌘-T. The Style dialog box appears, with New Style highlighted.
2. Type a style name in the Style box.

3. Choose formats for the style.

4. **Important**: Choose Use as Default (not Define). This option ensures that the style is recorded in the default style sheet.

   You see an alert box with the message, `OK to record style in default style sheet?`

5. Choose OK to define the style and apply the style to the selected paragraph(s). Alternatively, click Define to define the style, and then click Close to exit the dialog box without applying the style you created.

   The style you created is now available in all your Word documents.

After you define a style, you can change its definition or delete it. For more information, see the section titled "Revising and Managing Styles," later in this chapter.

If you have used a previous version of Word, you will be glad to know that Microsoft has repaired an irritating shortcoming of previous Style dialog boxes. After naming a style and choosing formats for the style in Version 4, you had to click Define before choosing OK—and if you forgot to click Define, you lost all your choices! In Version 5, you click OK to define the style and close the dialog box.

Basing One Style on Another

As you see from the Style dialog box, you can base one style on another. By default, Word bases new styles on the Normal style. The Normal style, one of Word's standard styles, is defined by default to include your default font and font size choice, as well as auto line spacing, flush-left alignment, and tabs every 1/5-inch across the screen. If you want, you can base a new style on any other style you see in the list of styles.

When you base a new style on an existing one, the style you create will include the formats of the existing style. If you choose new formats that contradict the existing ones, however, Word uses your new choices instead of the formats of the base style. If you base a new style on the default Normal format and then choose justified alignment, for example, the new format will have justified alignment, not flush-left alignment. The new style will have any Normal formats, however, that are not specifically contradicted by your formatting choices. If you do not choose a new font, for instance, the new style will have the default font and font size character formatting, which are part of the Normal style.

Always define the default font for a document by redefining the Normal style with the font and size you want. Then base all new styles on Normal. If you create your styles this way, you can change the font of every style just by changing Normal. Suppose that you define Normal to include Geneva 12. When you create several new styles based on Normal, each is formatted with Geneva 12. Then you decide that the document would look better in Helvetica 12. To reformat your whole document with Helvetica 12, you simply redefine Normal so that it specifies Helvetica 12 instead of Geneva 12. For instructions on modifying existing styles, see "Revising Styles," in this chapter.

Defining the Next Style

After you create a style and apply it, you find that Word returns to Normal formatting when you press Return (instead of copying the format to the next paragraph). In other words, Word applies the Normal style automatically when you press Return. If you like, you can control the style Word applies when you press Return.

Controlling the next style is useful when you know that one style is always followed by another. For example, many corporate style guidelines instruct writers to type their department name just below the document title. In this setting, you can create a Document Title style that is followed by a Department Name style. Every time you apply the Document Title style, type some text, and press Return, Word applies the Department Name style to the next paragraph automatically.

To define the next style while you are creating a style, just type the next style's name in the Next Style box of the Style dialog box. You can change the Next Style setting after you create the style; just choose Style, type the style name in the Next Style box, and choose OK.

Overriding the Next Style

When you apply a style and type, Word always enters the Next Style when you press Return. For example, if you type *Text Paragraph* in the Next Style box when you define the Heading 1 style, Word enters the Text Paragraph format when you press Return after typing with Heading 1. However, you can override the Next Style setting in two ways:

If you press Shift-Return to start a new line without starting a new paragraph, Word continues using the current style without starting a new paragraph. If you want to start a new paragraph in the same style, press ⌘-Return.

Applying Styles

After you create or redefine a style, you can apply it. When you apply a style, Word formats the selected paragraph or paragraphs using the formats stored in the style's definition. Note that these formats apply uniformly to the whole paragraph. If the style definition includes bold or italic, for example, the whole paragraph receives this character emphasis.

To apply the styles to selected paragraphs in your document, you can use the style selection box, the Style command, or a keyboard command.

Undo and Repeat are useful after you apply styles. If you apply a style to the wrong paragraph, choose Undo immediately from the Edit menu (or use the ⌘-Z shortcut). To apply the style again, select another paragraph and choose Repeat from the Edit menu (or use the ⌘-Y shortcut). Remember: You can repeat a command only if you haven't chosen another command or typed any additional text since you chose the command.

Using the Style Selection Box

By far, the easiest way to apply a style is to use the style selection box in the ruler. To apply a style by using the style selection box, follow these steps:

1. Select the paragraph or paragraphs to which you want to apply the style, or press Return to start a new paragraph.

   If you are selecting just one paragraph, don't bother highlighting the whole paragraph. Just place the insertion point anywhere within the paragraph.

   If the ruler isn't displayed, choose Ruler from the View menu.

2. Point to the arrow next to the style selection box, and hold down the mouse button. Word drops down the style selection list (shown earlier in fig. 8.4).

3. Drag the highlight down the list until it reaches the style you want to apply.

4. When you have highlighted the style you want to apply, release the mouse button.

Word applies the style to the paragraph(s) and displays the current style name in the style box (on the bottom window border) as well as in the style selection box (on the ruler).

Using the Style Dialog Box

The Style dialog box is useful mainly for creating, editing, and deleting styles, but you can use it to apply styles. This technique would be of interest mainly to users of small Classic screens, who may work with the ruler hidden so that they can see more text in the document window.

To apply a style with the Style dialog box, follow these steps:

1. Select the paragraph or paragraphs to which you want to apply the style, or press Return to start a new paragraph.

   If you are selecting just one paragraph, don't bother highlighting the whole paragraph. Just place the insertion point anywhere within the paragraph.

2. Choose Style from the Format menu or press ⌘-T. Word displays the Style dialog box.

3. Highlight the style name in the style list box, and choose OK. Alternatively, just double-click the style name.

   Word applies the style to the paragraph(s) and displays the current style name in the style box (on the bottom window border). If you are displaying the ruler, you also see the style name in the style selection box (on the ruler).

Applying Styles with the Keyboard

The third way to apply a style is to choose the ⌘-Shift-S keyboard shortcut. This technique is fast, but has one drawback: You don't see a list of style names, so you must memorize the name of the style you want to apply.

To apply a style with the keyboard, follow these steps:

1. Select the paragraph or paragraphs to which you want to apply the style, or press Return to start a new paragraph.

2. Press ⌘-Shift-S. The word *Style* appears highlighted in the status line.

Chapter 8
Formatting with Styles

TIP

Chapter 27 contains important suggestions for customizing Word's menus and keyboard. Among them are two important Style tips: You can add style names to a special, custom menu (called Work), and you can also assign styles to keyboard commands.

3. Type the style name.

You need not type the whole name—just enough of it so that Word can distinguish the style you want from other styles with similar names. If you have given two names to the style separated by a comma (such as Bulleted List,BL), you can just type the shorter name.

4. Press Return.

Word applies the style to the paragraph(s), and displays the current style name in the style box (on the bottom window border). You also see the style name in the style selection box (on the ruler).

Applying Styles to Manually Formatted Text

If you are applying styles to paragraphs you previously formatted using manual techniques, bear these points in mind. Both points emphasize that, if you're planning to apply styles to the paragraphs in your document after you type, you shouldn't bother choosing manual formats before you type.

The style's paragraph formats completely overwrite your manual formatting choices. Suppose that you manually choose tabs, blank space options, indents, and New York 10. Then you apply a style. You lose all your manual formatting choices.

If a style includes emphasis such as bold, italic, underlining, or small caps, you may get unwanted effects when you apply the style to the paragraph. Emphasis formats act like toggles: The first time you apply the emphasis, Word turns the format on. The second time you apply the emphasis, Word turns the format off. Now suppose that you have formatted a few words in a paragraph with bold, and you apply a style that has bold as part of its definition. Word formats the whole paragraph with bold, except the words you manually formatted with bold! For those words, applying the style is like turning the format off. To avoid this unwanted effect, apply character emphasis after you apply styles, not before.

Revising and Managing Styles

 ou can edit, rename, or delete a style after you create it. When you edit a style, the redefined style applies automatically to all the paragraphs in the current document to which you applied the style.

Part I
Getting Started

If you revise a default style, the change affects all the Word documents to which you applied the style. After you change a default style, Word updates the affected documents automatically when you open them.

Revising Styles

If you are not happy with a style's appearance, you can change the style definition. As usual, you can do so in more than one way. By far, the easiest way is to use manual techniques, and then use the style selection box. You may also use the Style dialog box to edit the style.

To change a style definition using the style selection box, follow these steps:

1. Use manual formatting techniques to reformat a paragraph to which the style has been applied.

2. Click the style selection box so that the style name is highlighted.

3. Press Return. The alert box shown in figure 8.9 appears.

Fig. 8.9
The Style alert box.

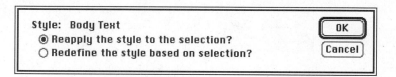

4. Choose Redefine the Style Based on Selection.

5. Choose OK.

To change a style using the Style dialog box, follow these steps:

1. Choose Style from the Format menu to see the Style dialog box.

2. From the list box, choose the style you want to edit.

3. Use any manual formatting technique to change the existing formats. You may also add new ones.

4. Choose OK to define the style and apply the style to the selected paragraph(s). Alternatively, click Define to define the style, and then click Close to exit the dialog box without applying the style you've created.

Renaming Styles

You can rename a style if the new name is not already in use for another style by following these steps:

1. Choose Style from the Format menu.

2. From the Style list box, select the style you want to rename.

3. Retype the name in the Style box.

4. Click OK.

Deleting a Style

You can delete any style you have added to a style sheet, whether it is stored in the document or the default style sheet. However, you cannot delete any of Word's standard styles. (See "Using Standard Styles" later in this chapter.) If you try to delete a standard style (one of the styles indicated with a dot next to its name), Word takes no action.

New to Word 5 is the Delete button in the Style dialog box. Previously, you had to choose Cut from the Edit menu if you wanted to delete a style.

To delete styles, use the following procedure:

1. Choose Style from the Format menu.

2. Choose the style name from the list box. If you want to delete a default style and you don't see the name in the list box, choose All Styles to display the style name.

3. Click the Delete button. An alert box asks if you really want to delete the style.

4. Confirm the deletion by clicking OK.

If you formatted any text with the deleted style, the text takes the Normal style after you delete the style. If the style also is part of the default style sheet, you are asked to confirm the deletion from that style sheet as well.

Copying a Document Style Sheet to a New Document

After you create a useful document style sheet, you may want to copy it to a new document. When you do, all the styles on that style sheet are available for the new document.

When you copy document styles, bear in mind what happens when the target document (the document to which you're copying the styles) has one or more styles with the same name: Word merges the two style sheets, and where two styles have the same name, the program *overwrites* the target document's styles. Suppose Document 2 has a style called Body Text. Into this document, you are copying Document 1's style. Document 1 also has a style called Body Text. When Word copies Document 1's styles into Document 2, the program overwrites Document 2's Body Text style.

Note, too, that style names are case-sensitive. As far as Word is concerned, *body text* and *Body Text* are two different styles, and the one will not overwrite the other.

To copy a document style sheet, use the following procedure:

1. In the new document, choose Style from the Format menu.

2. When the Style dialog box appears, choose Open from the File menu.

3. In the Open dialog box, choose the document that has the styles you want to copy.

4. Click the Open button.

   Word combines the new document's style sheet with the one you have just opened. If a style name in the new document conflicts, Word uses the incoming style's name and formats.

5. Choose Close to return to your document.

You can use stationery documents to simplify the management of document style sheets. Rather than copying styles from one document to another, create a stationery document to store the styles for a specific kind of document, such as a letter or proposal. When you want to start writing a new document, open the stationery document; Word creates a new, Untitled document that has the styles you saved to the stationery document. For more information on this splendid new Word 5 capability, see Chapter 11.

Using Styles with Manual Formatting

After you apply a style to a paragraph (or paragraphs), you can add additional character or paragraph formats. You should keep a few points in mind, however, when you apply additional formats manually to a paragraph formatted with a style.

The formats you add affect only the selected paragraph(s); the added formats do not change the style definition, and they do not apply to other paragraphs with the same style. (If you like the change, use the procedures for revising styles.)

If a format you add manually conflicts with the style definition, the added manual format overrides the style format. But Word leaves the other style formats intact. For example, suppose that you format a paragraph with the Body Text style, and this style includes Palatino 12 and justified alignment. Then you highlight the paragraph and choose Times Roman 10. Word changes the font and font size, but leaves the alignment alone.

After you format manually, you can restore the style formats in two ways: You can restore just the style's character formats, or you can restore all the style's formats.

To restore the style's character formats and remove any character formats you added manually, choose Revert to Style from the Format menu, or use the ⌘-Shift-space bar keyboard shortcut.

To restore all the style's formats and remove all the styles you added manually, reapply the style, and when the alert box appears, choose Reapply style to the selection, and click OK.

If you would like to remove the style from the paragraph completely, choose another style, or press ⌘-Shift-P. This command reapplies the Normal style to the selection.

Using Standard Styles

Word's standard styles are applied automatically by certain commands. For example, *footnote reference* and *footnote text* are two of Word's standard styles. Both are applied automatically when you create a footnote using the Footnote command (Insert menu). These styles are part of the default style sheet, and all of them are automatically copied to every document's style sheet, too. To see these styles in your document style sheet, choose the All Styles option in the Style dialog box. As shown in figure 8.10, dots designate the standard styles in the Style list box.

Because these styles are applied automatically, why bother learning about them? First, you can change any of the standard styles for the current document's style sheet. Suppose that you want to print footnote reference marks in 12-point characters, rather than using the default 9-point font size. By changing the footnote reference style, you change the size of footnote reference marks throughout your document. The changes affect only the current document.

Fig. 8.10
Dots designate standard
styles in the Style
dialog box.

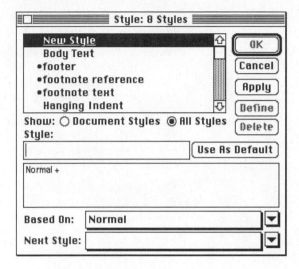

Second, you can change Word's defaults for any of the formats controlled by standard styles, and these changes apply automatically to all your documents. Suppose that you always want 12-point footnote reference marks. When you redefine the footnote reference style, you can choose the Use as Default option, which redefines the style in Word's default style sheet. All your footnotes will have 12-point footnote reference marks.

Reviewing Standard Styles

Table 8.1 lists all the Version 5 standard styles, together with their default definitions. Note that many of these styles are based on the Normal style. When you redefine Normal, all the styles based on Normal change too. You learn more about basing one style on another in the section titled "Basing One Style on Another," earlier in this chapter. For now, the following overview lists the kinds of styles you will find among the standard styles:

Header/Footer Styles. These styles control the character and paragraph formats of running heads and footers, which are positioned within the top and bottom margins of your document. For more information on headers and footers, see Chapter 16.

Heading Styles. These styles control the formatting of the heading levels that Word automatically inserts when you define heading levels in an outline (see Chapter 12).

Footnote Styles. The *footnote reference* style controls the formatting of footnote reference marks (the superscript number placed in your document to indicate a footnote or endnote). The *footnote text* style applies to the footnote or endnote text (see Chapter 16).

Index Styles. These styles control the formatting of the various levels of index entries created by Word's Index command (see Chapter 23).

Line Number. This style controls the format of the line numbers that Word can automatically insert in the margin of your document (see Chapter 19).

Normal. By far the most important style in Word, this style is the default style for all text-entry purposes. When you open a new document and start typing, you create text in the Normal style. Changing the Normal style has dramatic effects, because many other styles are based on Normal.

Page Number. This style automatically formats page numbers inserted with the Margin Page Numbers option of the Section dialog box or page numbers inserted with Print Preview. If you insert page numbers in a header or footer, you can control the formatting manually.

Table of Contents Styles. The *toc* styles control the formatting of the various levels of table of contents entries that Word automatically creates when you use the Table of Contents command (see Chapter 23).

Table 8.1
Default Format Definitions
of Automatic Styles

Format name	Format definition
footer	Normal + Tab stops: 3 inches centered, 6 inches flush right
footnote reference	Normal + Font: 9 point, superscript 3 point
footnote text	Normal + Font: 10 point

Format name	Format definition
header	Normal + Tab stops: 3 inches centered, 6 inches flush right
heading 1	Helvetica Bold Underline, 12 point, space before 12 point
heading 2	Helvetica Bold, 12 point, space before 6 point
heading 3	Normal + Bold, 12 point, indent left 0.25 inch
heading 4	Normal + Underline, 12 point, indent left 0.25 inch
heading 5	Normal + Bold, 10 point, indent left 0.5 inch
heading 6	Normal, 10 point, underline, indent left 0.5 inch
heading 7	Normal, 10 point, italic, indent left 0.5 inch
heading 8	Normal, 10 point, italic, indent left 0.5 inch
heading 9	Normal, 10 point, italic, indent left 0.5 inch
index 1	Normal
index 2	Normal + left indent 0.25 inch
index 3	Normal + left indent 0.5 inch
index 4	Normal + left indent 0.75 inch
index 5	Normal + left indent 1.0 inch
index 6	Normal + left indent 1.25 inch
index 7	Normal + left indent 1.5 inch
line number	Normal
normal	Default font and font size, flush left
PostScript	Normal + 10 point, hidden, bold
page number	Normal
toc 1	Normal + 0.5 inch right indent, Tab stops: 5.75 inches flush left with leader dots and 6 inches flush right
toc 2	Normal + left indent 0.5 inch, 0.5 inch right indent, Tab stops: 5.75 inches flush left with leader dots and 6 inches flush right
toc 3	Normal + left indent 1.0 inch, 0.5 inch right indent, Tab stops: 5.75 inches flush left with leader dots and 6 inches flush right

continues

Chapter 8
Formatting with Styles

Table 8.1 Continued	Format name	Format definition
	toc 4	Normal + left indent 1.5 inch, 0.5 inch right indent, Tab stops: 5.75 inches flush left with leader dots and 6 inches flush right
	toc 5	Normal + left indent 2.0 inch, 0.5 inch right indent, Tab stops: 5.75 inches flush left with leader dots and 6 inches flush right
	toc 6	Normal + left indent 2.5 inch, 0.5 inch right indent, Tab stops: 5.75 inches flush left with leader dots and 6 inches flush right
	toc 7	Normal + left indent 3.0 inch, 0.5 inch right indent, Tab stops: 5.75 inches flush left with leader dots and 6 inches flush right
	toc 8	Normal + left indent 3.5 inch, 0.5 inch right indent, Tab stops: 5.75 inches flush left with leader dots and 6 inches flush right
	toc 9	Normal + left indent 4.0 inch, 0.5 inch right indent, Tab stops: 5.75 inches flush left with leader dots and 6 inches flush right

Choosing Standard Styles Manually

Although most standard styles are applied automatically (when you add a footnote, for example), you may want to choose certain styles, such as the Heading styles, manually.

To apply a standard style with the style selection box, follow these steps:

1. Hold down the Shift key, and click and hold on the arrow next to the style selection box.

   Word lists all the standard styles in addition to your document styles.

2. Drag down the list to highlight the style you want.

3. Release the mouse button.

To choose a standard style with the Style dialog box, follow these steps:

1. Activate the All Styles button to display all the standard styles.

2. Highlight the style name you want.

3. Choose Apply.

Redefining a Standard Style

To redefine a standard style, follow these steps:

1. Choose Style from the Format menu to see the Style dialog box.

2. Choose the All Styles option. You see all the styles, including your document styles and the standard styles.

3. Highlight the name of the style you want to change.

   To change the style of *page number*, for instance, highlight this option. Word shows the current formats in the style definition box.

4. Use manual formatting techniques to change the style.

5. To redefine the style for the current document only, choose OK. To change the default style, click the Use as Default option, and when the alert box appears, choose OK.

Searching for Styles

New in Word 5 is an enhanced Find command, which can help you quickly locate styles you applied in your document. For example, suppose that you formatted one paragraph with a quotation format, and you want to preview its appearance.

You also can use styles to create a more focused search. Suppose that you want to find a paragraph that mentions *Civil War battle-grounds*. You know that you typed this text using the Bulleted List style. If you add the Bulleted List style to the search, Word searches only the paragraphs that have the Bulleted List style attached to them.

To search for a style, follow these steps:

1. Choose Find from the Edit menu or use the ⌘-F shortcut. The Find dialog box appears.

2. While the Find dialog box is on-screen, choose a style using the style selection box or the Style option in the Format list box. (You cannot use the Style dialog box or the style name area when the Find dialog box is on-screen.) You can choose only one style at a time.

After you choose the style, Word displays the style name under the Find What box, as shown in figure 8.11.

Fig. 8.11
Finding a style.

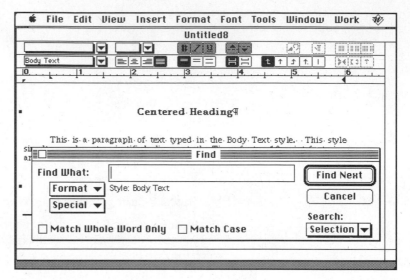

3. If you want to search for specific text that has the style you specified under the Find What text box, type the text in the Find What dialog box. To search for any text with this format or formats, just leave the Find What box blank.

4. If you want to change the direction of the search, use the Search dialog box.

5. Choose Find Next.

   If Word finds text with the style you specified, Word highlights the text. Choose Find Next to find the next occurrence of the style, or choose Cancel to return to your document.

   If Word cannot find any text with the style you specified, you see a dialog box asking whether you want to extend the search from the beginning of the document (or the end, if you are searching up). Choose Yes to extend the search, or No to cancel.

After you use the Find dialog box to search for a style, Word retains the style setting beneath the Find What text box, as well as any text you may have typed in the Find What text box, for the duration of the current operating session. If you choose Find again, you have to clear these settings to perform a different search. To clear the text from the Find What text box, you simply select the text and press Delete. To clear the format, pull-down the Format list box and choose Clear.

Replacing Styles

Using Word 5's enhanced Replace command, you can replace one style with another throughout your document. Suppose that you inadvertently formatted a few paragraphs with Lead Paragraph (no first-line indentation) when you should have used Text Paragraph (0.5" first-line indentation). You can use Replace to search for all the paragraphs that have the Lead Paragraph style, and if the format was wrongly applied, you can change it to Text Paragraph just by clicking Replace.

To replace one style with another throughout your document, follow these steps:

1. Choose Replace from the Edit menu, or press ⌘-F. The Replace dialog box appears.

2. With the insertion point in the Find What text box, use the style selection box to choose the style, or choose Style from the Format menu.

3. With the insertion point in the Replace With area, choose the style you want Word to insert in place of the style you just chose. Your choice is shown beneath the Replace With text box, as shown in figure 8.12. The settings in this box will find the paragraphs preceded by 12 points of blank space and will remove the blank space.

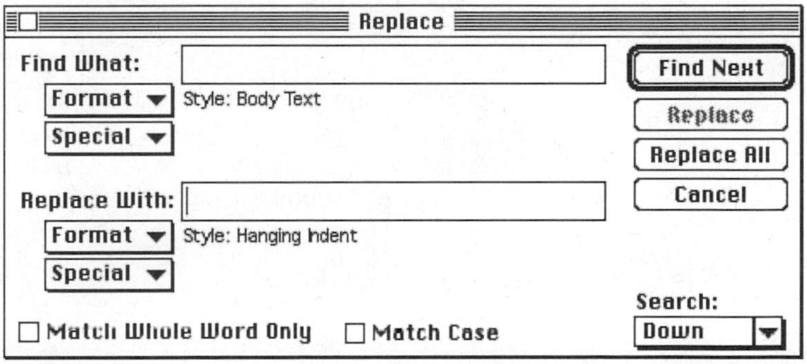

Fig. 8.12
Replacing one style with another.

Replace	
Find What:	**Find Next**
Format ▼ Style: Body Text	**Replace**
Special ▼	**Replace All**
Replace With:	**Cancel**
Format ▼ Style: Hanging Indent	
Special ▼	
☐ Match Whole Word Only ☐ Match Case	Search: Down ▼

4. If you want to search for specific text that has the style you specified beneath the Find What text box, type the text in the Find What text box. To search for any text with the formats you specified, leave the text box blank.

5. If you want to replace specific text that has the style you specified beneath the Replace With text box, type the text in the Replace With text box. To search for any text with the formats you specified, leave the text box blank.

6. If you want to change the direction of the search, use the Search dialog box.

7. Choose Find Next, or if you are sure you want to perform the replacement throughout your document, choose Replace All.

   Word highlights text with the style you specified. Choose Find Next to find the next occurrence of the format, or choose Cancel to return to your document.

   If Word cannot find any text with the style you specified, a dialog box appears, asking you whether you want to extend the search from the beginning of the document (or the end, if you are searching up). Choose Yes to extend the search, or No to cancel.

After you use the Replace dialog box to search for a style, Word retains the style setting beneath the Find What text box, as well as any text you may have typed in this text box, for the duration of the current operating session. Moreover, the format and text also appear in the Find dialog box. If you choose Replace or Find again, you have to clear these settings to perform a different search. To clear the text from the Find What text box, you simply select the text and press Delete. To clear the format, pull down the Format list box and choose Clear.

Quick Review

This section concisely summarizes the most useful information in this chapter. Check "Productivity Tips" for a review of high-productivity tips and tricks, and review "Techniques" when you forget how to perform a specific procedure.

Productivity Tips

- Apply styles before you type. If you use the Next Style option intelligently, Word can then enter the style that is most likely to follow a paragraph every time you press Return.

- Apply styles before you type because it saves you from having to apply styles paragraph-by-paragraph in your document.

- Avoid adding too many styles to your default style sheet. Instead, save styles to a document style sheet, and then save that document as a Stationery document (see Chapter 11). When you open the document, all the document styles are available in a new, Untitled document.

- Keep your style names short enough to be read in the style selection box. If you like to choose styles with the keyboard, don't forget to include the comma and abbreviation in the style name (such as Body Text,bt).

- If you want to use a font or font size other than the default as the base font for your document, redefine the Normal style. Your change will affect most of the standard styles and all new styles you create because Word uses the Normal style as the Based On style by default.

- Create styles with the Style dialog box instead of recording them because only the Style dialog box lets you choose the Next Style. Think carefully about which style is most likely to follow a paragraph to which you apply this style, and type its name in the Next Style box.

- If you prefer to apply styles after you type, avoid adding character emphases before applying styles.

- Always use Word's Heading styles for your document headings. (You'll probably want to redefine them.) Be sure to include the Keep With Next option, coupled with some blank space after, to keep Word from breaking a page beneath the heading. Define the display type for headings by modifying the Heading 1 style, and then use the Based On option to base all the other Heading styles on Heading 1.

Techniques

This section provides concise, quick-reference summaries of all the procedures introduced in this chapter.

Applying Styles

To apply a style using the style selection box:

1. Select the paragraph or paragraphs to which you want to apply the style, or press Return to start a new paragraph.

2. Point to the arrow next to the style selection box, and hold down the mouse button.

3. Drag the highlight down the list until it reaches the style you want to apply.

4. When you have highlighted the style you want to apply, release the mouse button.

To apply a style with the Style dialog box:

1. Select the paragraph or paragraphs to which you want to apply the style, or press Return to start a new paragraph.

2. Choose Style from the Format menu, or press ⌘-T.

3. Highlight the style name in the style list box, and choose OK. Alternatively, just double-click the style name.

To apply a style with the keyboard:

1. Select the paragraph or paragraphs to which you want to apply the style, or press Return to start a new paragraph.

2. Press ⌘-Shift-S.

3. Type the style name.

4. Press Return.

Cancelling a Style

To remove a style from text to which the style has been applied:

Press ⌘-Shift-P to reformat the paragraph in Normal style.

or

Apply another style.

To cancel character emphases you added to a paragraph after applying the style:

1. Highlight the paragraph or paragraphs that contain the unwanted emphasis.

2. Press ⌘-Shift-space bar, or choose Revert to Style from the Format menu.

To cancel all manual formatting that you added to a paragraph after applying the style:

1. Place the insertion point in the paragraph, or select more than one paragraph.

2. Click the style selection box and press Return.

3. When the alert box appears, choose Reapply the Style to the selection.

4. Choose OK.

Copying a Document Style Sheet

To copy a document style sheet:

1. In the new document, choose Style from the Format menu.

2. When the Style dialog box appears, choose Open from the File menu.

3. In the Open dialog box, choose the document that has the styles you want to copy.

4. Click the Open button.

5. Click the Close button.

Creating Styles

To record a style you have already created:

1. Format the paragraph using manual formatting techniques.

2. If the ruler isn't displayed, choose Ruler from the Format menu or press ⌘-R.

3. Click the style selection box.

4. Type a name for the style.

5. Press Return.

6. When the message box appears, click Define.

Chapter 8
Formatting with Styles

To create a document style with the Style dialog box:

1. Choose Style from the Format menu or press ⌘-T.

2. Type a style name in the Style box.

3. Choose formats for the style.

4. If you want to base the style on another style, type the base style's name in the Based On box.

5. If you want Word to enter another style automatically when you press Return after typing a paragraph with this style, type the style name in the Next Style box.

6. If you want to see what the style looks like in your document without leaving the Style dialog box, choose Apply.

7. Choose OK to define the style and apply the style to the selected paragraph(s). Alternatively, click Define to define the style, and then click Close to exit the dialog box without applying the style you've created.

To create a default style with the Style dialog box:

1. Choose Style from the Format menu, or press ⌘-T.

2. Type a style name in the Style box.

3. Choose formats for the style.

4. If you want to base the style on another style, type the base style's name in the Based On box.

5. If you want Word to enter another style automatically when you press Return after typing a paragraph with this style, type the style name in the Next Style box.

6. **Important**: Choose Use as Default (not Define).

7. Choose OK to define the style and apply the style to the selected paragraph(s). Alternatively, click Define to define the style, and then click Close to exit the dialog box without applying the style you've created.

Deleting Styles

To delete an existing style:

1. Choose Style from the Format menu.

2. Choose the style name from the list box.

3. If you want to delete a default style and you don't see the name in the list box, choose All Styles to display the style name.

4. Click the Delete button.

5. Confirm the deletion by clicking OK.

Finding Styles

To search for a style:

1. Choose Find from the Edit menu or press ⌘-F.

2. Choose the style from the style selection box. Alternatively, choose Style from the Format list box, choose the style name from the dialog box, and choose OK.

3. If you want to search for specific text that has the style you specified under the Find What text box, type the text in the Find What dialog box. To search for any text with this format or formats, just leave the Find What box blank.

4. If you want to change the direction of the search, use the Search dialog box.

5. Choose Find Next.

Renaming Styles

To rename a style:

1. Choose Style from the Format menu.

2. From the Style list box, select the style you want to rename.

3. Retype the name in the Style box.

4. Click OK.

Replacing Styles

To replace one style with another throughout your document:

1. Choose Replace from the Edit menu or press ⌘-F.

2. With the insertion point in the Find What text box, use the style selection box to choose the style. Alternatively, choose Style from the Format menu.

3. With the insertion point in the Replace With area, choose the style you want Word to insert in place of the style you just chose.

4. If you want to search for specific text that has the style you specified beneath the Find What text box, type the text in the Find What text box. To search for any text with the formats you specified, just leave the text box blank.

5. If you want to replace specific text that has the style you specified beneath the Replace With text box, type the text in the Replace With text box. To search for any text with the formats you specified, leave the text box blank.

6. If you want to change the direction of the search, use the Search dialog box.

7. Choose Find Next, or if you are sure you want to perform the replacement throughout your document, choose Replace All.

Revising Styles

To change a style definition using the style selection box:

1. Use manual formatting techniques to reformat a paragraph to which the style has been applied.

2. Click the style selection box so that the style name is highlighted.

3. Press Return.

4. Choose Redefine the style based on the selection.

5. Choose OK.

To change a style using the Style dialog box:

1. Choose Style from the Format menu.

2. If you want to revise a standard style, choose the All Styles option.

3. From the list box, choose the style you want to edit.

4. Use any manual formatting technique to change the existing formats. You may also add new ones, if you want.

5. Choose OK to define the style and apply the style to the selected paragraph(s). Alternatively, click Define to define the style, and then click Close to exit the dialog box without applying the style you created.

Checking Spelling and Grammar

Writing of professional quality needs to be free from errors in spelling, usage, style, and grammar. Even the most attractively printed document loses its authority when the reader encounters spelling errors or errors in style, usage, or grammar. Word cannot detect every writing error you make, but the program can detect many common errors—the errors that an unfriendly reader might use to justify an adverse opinion of you and your organization.

Word 5 is equipped with a spelling checker (called Spelling) and a new usage, style, and grammar checker (called Grammar). This important new addition to Word supports the program's status as the premier writing program for business and the professions.

This chapter details the use of Spelling and Grammar. The following is an overview of this chapter's contents:

- ■ *Checking Spelling*. In this section, you learn how to make Spelling work for you by customizing the way Word runs this utility. You learn how to choose among Spelling's many options and how to create custom dictionaries.

- ■ *Checking Grammar*. In this section, you learn how to use Word 5's new Grammar utility to help you write more strongly and clearly.

Keep in mind that running Spelling and Grammar will not save you from criticism if your document is poorly organized. Writing experts agree that the main determinants of writing quality are organization and coherence. A poorly organized brochure or proposal, or one that doesn't make sense, will not impress your clients and customers, even if the spelling is letter perfect. If you need help organizing your ideas, try using Word's Outline utility, discussed in Chapter 12.

Checking Spelling

Business and professional writing require perfect spelling. Many people consider spelling errors or typos to be signs of limited intelligence, lack of professionalism, or carelessness. You cannot afford to make a negative impression, and with Word's spell-checking feature, you can make sure that you don't. Run Word's spell-checking program on every document that will leave your computer.

Word 5's Spelling closely resembles its forebears, yet you will find some small (but welcome) changes. For example, you no longer need to choose the Start Spelling option after choosing Spelling; the utility goes right to work. You also can access the spelling options through the Preferences dialog box, which makes changing spelling options easier.

Spell-Checking Your Document

Like all computer spell-checking programs, Word doesn't really check spelling. Word compares the words in your document, one by one, with correctly spelled words stored in the program's dictionaries. When Word cannot find a match, the program indicates that the word is unknown.

Note that a word categorized as *unknown* may be spelled correctly. Many proper nouns—the names of people and places—aren't in the program's dictionaries. To prevent the program from flagging a frequently used proper noun, you can add the word to the dictionary. Be aware that Word's spell-checking program skips over a correctly spelled word used in the wrong context. Spell check your document, but remember that nothing can substitute for a final proofreading.

Word doesn't check the spelling of hidden text unless the text is displayed. To display hidden text, choose Show Hidden Text in the Preferences dialog box, which you access from the Tools menu.

You can check your entire document or a selected portion (a word,
sentence, paragraph, or block of text). If you don't select any text, Word
begins checking your document from the insertion point's location.
When Spelling reaches the end of the document, an alert box appears
and asks whether you want to continue checking from the beginning of
the document. If you choose OK, Word continues from the beginning
until reaching the insertion point again.

To check spelling, follow these steps:

1. To check the entire document, click the location at which you
   want the spell check to start. To check a selection, select the text.

2. Choose Spelling from the Tools menu or press ⌘-L.

   The Spelling window appears, and Word finds the first word
   that cannot be matched in the built-in spelling dictionaries
   (see fig. 9.1). The unknown word is displayed following
   Not in Dictionary.

   By default, the program displays a list of one or more potentially
   correct spellings in the Suggestions list box and places one of
   the suggestions in the Change To box, shown in fig. 9.1. If the
   program cannot suggest any words, (No Suggestions) is displayed in the Suggestions list box, as shown in figure 9.2, and the
   program echoes the unknown word in the Change To box.

Fig. 9.1
Suggestions shown in the
Spelling dialog box.

Spelling
Not in Dictionary: thier

Change To:	their		Ignore	Ignore All
Suggestions:	their		Change	Change All
	Thai		Add	Close
	there			
	thinner		Suggest	Options...
Add Words To:	Custom Dictionary ▼			

3. Take one of the following actions:

   Accept Word's suggestion. Choose Change to accept the suggestion
   that Word placed in the Change To text box. Choose Change All
   to make this change throughout your document without confirmation from you.

Chapter 9
Checking Spelling and Grammar

```
┌──────────────────────────────────────────────────────────┐
│ □    ▤▤▤▤▤▤▤▤▤▤        Spelling        ▤▤▤▤▤▤▤▤▤▤         │
│ Not in Dictionary: Albemarle                              │
│                                                           │
│ Change To:   │Albemarle         │   ┌─────────┐ ┌──────────┐│
│                                     │ Ignore  │ │Ignore All││
│ Suggestions: (No Suggestions)  ⇧    └─────────┘ └──────────┘│
│                                     ┌─────────┐ ┌──────────┐│
│                                     │ Change  │ │Change All││
│                                     └─────────┘ └──────────┘│
│                                     ┌─────────┐ ┌──────────┐│
│                                ⇩    │  Add    │ │  Close   ││
│                                     └─────────┘ └──────────┘│
│ Add Words To: │Custom Dictionary ▼│ ┌─────────┐ ┌──────────┐│
│                                     │ Suggest │ │Options...││
│                                     └─────────┘ └──────────┘│
└──────────────────────────────────────────────────────────┘
```

Choose another suggested word. If Word suggested the correct spelling but didn't place it in the Change To box, choose the correct spelling by highlighting it and choosing Change (or by double-clicking the word). Choose Change All if you want Word to make this change throughout the document without your confirmation for each change.

Make the change in the Change To box. If Spelling cannot make a suggestion for an incorrectly spelled word, edit the word in the Change To box. After you correct the spelling, choose Change. To make this change throughout the document without your confirmation, choose Change All.

Close the Spelling dialog box and make the change in your document. You may prefer this procedure if you see additional errors, such as a garbled sentence, that mandate rewriting as well as correcting the spelling error.

To return to Spelling, just choose Spelling again from the Tools menu, and choose the Start check box. Spell checking will resume from the insertion point's location.

Leave the word unchanged and continue. If the word is correctly spelled, but you will not use it in any other document, choose Ignore to skip the word once, or choose Ignore All to skip all instances of this word in your document.

Add the word to a custom dictionary. If the word is correctly spelled, and you plan to use it frequently, choose Add to add the word to the current dictionary. (By default, the current dictionary is the custom dictionary, as indicated in the Add Words To list box.)

Delete a repeated word. If Word finds a repeated word (such as *the the*), the message Repeated word appears, and the dialog box displays a Delete button (see fig. 9.3). To delete the repeated word, choose the Delete button.

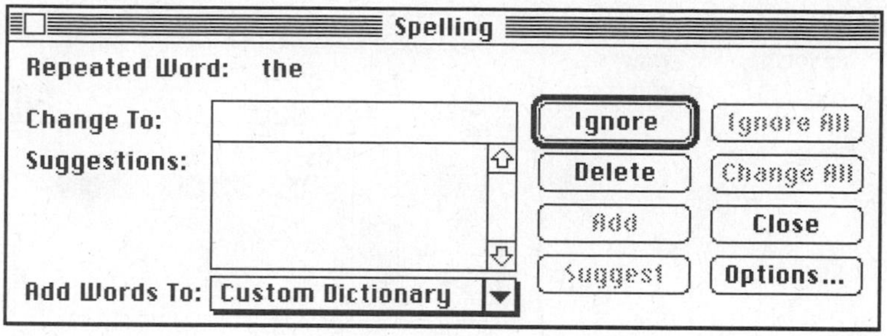

Fig. 9.3
Correcting a repeated
word.

Fig. 9.3
Correcting a repeated
word.

4. Repeat step 3 until Word informs you that the program has reached the end of the document or the selection.

   If Spelling reaches the end of the document without proofing all your text, a dialog box appears and asks whether you want to continue checking from the beginning. Choose OK to continue checking or choose Cancel to stop checking.

Choosing Spelling Options

> **TIP**
>
> On a slower Mac, you can speed Spelling's operation by turning off Suggestions. You still can request suggestions by choosing Suggest when you spell-check the document. You may want to disable Suggestions even if you're using a fast Mac; for correctly spelled proper nouns, the suggestions are useless.

By default, Word checks the spelling of all the text in your document, including words typed in all uppercase letters and words containing numbers. The program also suggests correct spellings by default. If you're typing a document that contains many acronyms or technical expressions, you may want to choose options that tell Spelling to skip such words. If you're using a Plus, Classic, or SE, you may want to disable suggestions so that Word checks spelling more quickly. You can change these defaults by using the Spelling options in the Preferences dialog box.

To choose spelling options, follow these steps:

1. Choose Preferences from the Tools menu. When the Preferences dialog box appears, choose the Spelling option. Alternatively, choose Options from the Spelling dialog box.

   The Spelling Preferences dialog box appears (see fig. 9.4).

2. To turn off automatic suggestions of correctly spelled words, deactivate the Always Suggest option.

3. To skip words in all uppercase letters, activate the Words in UPPERCASE option.

Chapter 9
Checking Spelling and Grammar

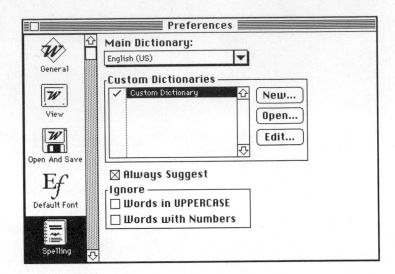

Fig. 9.4
The Spelling Preferences
dialog box.

4. To skip words that contain numbers, activate the Words with Numbers option.

5. Click the Close box.

Using Custom Dictionaries

As you learned in the preceding section, you can add correctly spelled words to Spelling's dictionary. You should add frequently used proper nouns, such as your name, street name, town name, company name, and the names of colleagues and coworkers. After you add these words, Spelling does not flag them as unknown, and spell-checking proceeds more quickly.

You cannot access the words in the main dictionary, which are stored in a special, compressed file format. When you add words to Spelling's dictionary, the program doesn't add them to the main dictionary—and for good reason. If you add an incorrectly spelled word to this dictionary, you cannot repair the error.

Rather than add words to the main dictionary, Spelling adds them to the default custom dictionary. A *custom dictionary* is a user-accessible dictionary that contains the words you add. You can remove a word you added to a custom dictionary by following the procedure detailed later in this section.

Using More Than One Custom Dictionary

By default, Spelling adds your words to a dictionary called Custom Dictionary. You can create more than one custom dictionary.

To get the best performance from Word, limit the size of your custom dictionaries to no more than 1,000 words. Unlike the main dictionary, a custom dictionary isn't stored in a special, compressed format designed to optimize the speed of word searches. Searching a custom dictionary takes longer. If you need to add more than 1,000 words to a custom dictionary, you might want to add words to two or more custom dictionaries, divided by subject. When you check spelling, open the custom dictionary relevant to the document you're proofing.

The following are some examples of custom dictionaries divided by subject:

> **General Correspondence.** Contains the names of friends and family members with whom you correspond frequently, and important proper nouns in your personal life (street names, city names, and so on).

> **Business Correspondence.** Contains the names of business associates, contacts, organizations, and companies; also contains important proper nouns in your business life (your boss's name, your boss's spouse's name, and your boss's club, for example).

> **Technical/Legal.** Contains terms, jargon, and proper nouns needed for spell checking technical or legal reports, proposals, and other documents.

Creating Custom Dictionaries

After you decide on a way to divide your user dictionaries, you can create new custom dictionaries as described in the following procedure:

1. Choose Preferences from the Tools menu.

   The Preferences dialog box appears.

2. Choose Spelling.

   The Spelling preferences are displayed.

3. Choose New.

   A Save As dialog box appears with the message `Save new custom dictionary as`.

Chapter 9

Checking Spelling and Grammar

4. Type a name for the new custom dictionary (no longer than 31 characters).

5. If necessary, open the Word Commands folder so that your new custom dictionary is placed in the same folder with Word's main dictionary.

6. Choose Save.

   Word creates the new custom dictionary and opens it. You can tell which dictionary is open by looking at the Custom Dictionaries list (shown in fig. 9.5). A check mark indicates that a custom dictionary is open.

Fig. 9.5
Open custom dictionaries.

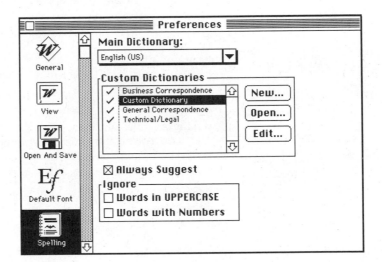

To add words to your new custom dictionary, you first must activate the dictionary by choosing it in the Add Words To list box (Spelling dialog box). When you choose the Add button in the Spelling dialog box, Word adds the word to the dictionary that currently is selected in the Add Words To list box.

When multiple custom dictionaries are open, Word consults all of them when it proofs your document. You can speed the spell-checking operation by closing custom dictionaries that aren't needed for the current document.

To close a custom dictionary, follow these steps:

1. Choose Preferences from the Tools menu.

   The Preferences dialog box appears.

2. Choose Spelling.

   The Spelling preferences are displayed.

3. Click the check mark next to the custom dictionary name to deactivate a custom dictionary.

   The check mark disappears.

4. Click the Close box.

After you close a custom dictionary, you can reopen it quickly.

To open a custom dictionary, follow these steps:

1. Choose Preferences from the Tools menu.

   The Preferences dialog box appears.

2. Choose Spelling.

   The Spelling preferences are displayed.

3. Click to the left of the custom dictionary name to open a custom dictionary.

   A check mark appears next to the name.

4. Click the Close box.

Deleting Words from a Custom Dictionary

If you accidentally add an incorrectly spelled word to a custom dictionary, don't be concerned; you can easily remove the word with the following procedure.

To remove a word from a custom dictionary, follow these steps:

1. Choose Preferences from the Tools menu.

   The Preferences dialog box appears.

2. Choose Spelling.

   The Spelling preferences are displayed.

3. In the Custom Dictionaries list box, highlight the name of the custom dictionary you want to edit.

4. Choose Edit.

The Edit Custom Dictionary dialog box appears (see fig. 9.6).

Fig. 9.6
Deleting Words from a
Custom dictionary.

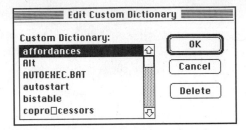

5. Highlight the word you want to delete.

6. Choose Delete.

7. Repeat steps 5 and 6 until you have removed all the words you want to delete.

8. Choose OK to close the dialog box. If you choose Cancel, Word disregards your deletion and closes the dialog box without making changes to the dictionary.

Checking Grammar

Computers cannot actually check grammar. To proofread a document for all possible grammatical errors, a program would have to understand the meaning of the words you typed. The technology needed to perform such a task lies decades into the future. Relying on the same pattern-matching technique that Spelling uses, Word 5's new Grammar command checks your document against a built-in dictionary of text patterns, each of which may indicate certain errors in style, usage, and grammar. When Grammar finishes proofing your document, the program displays a screen of document statistics that can help you assess the readability of your document.

In the sections that follow, you learn about Grammar's limitations and how Grammar can be worked into a fruitful revision strategy. You also learn how to use Grammar and how to choose Grammar options.

Understanding Grammar's Limitations

Like the Spelling feature, which cannot find spelling errors that occur when a correctly spelled word is used in the wrong context ("Their you go again!"), Grammar cannot ensure that your document is without error. The following is a list of Grammar's shortcomings, which you should understand clearly before using this utility:

- *Grammar flags only those errors in usage, style, and grammar that can be detected by pattern-matching*. Many errors, such as subject-verb agreement and the use of incorrect articles, cannot be detected easily by pattern matching.

- *Grammar questions many passages in which a word or phrase is used correctly*. Called false positives, these questionable passages may not need revision. For example, Grammar flags all instances of the passive voice. You may use the passive voice legitimately, however, when no need exists to state the sentence's subject. In contrast to Spelling, which requires relatively little judgment, you must consider virtually every word, phrase, or passage that Grammar questions, and in the end, only you can decide whether the utility truly has flagged an error.

- *Grammar stresses the themes of good business writing: positiveness, clarity, conciseness, freshness, and directness*. Grammar's suggestions may not apply to academic, legal, or professional documents. In particular, Grammar flags every instance of the passive voice. The passive voice is common, however, in formal reports and scientific papers. If you check such a document with Grammar, you may want to disable the passive voice rule and other rules. (For information on disabling specific rules, see the section "Choosing Grammar Options," later in this chapter.)

- *Grammar cannot detect organizational or logic problems*. Grammar looks for patterns on the surface, within sentences and phrases. Serious writing problems often lie deeper, at the level of the document's overall structure and logic. The program might place its stamp of approval on a completely incomprehensible document.

Grammar's shortcomings aren't unique; they're shared by all style, usage, and grammar checkers. Given these shortcomings, is running Grammar worthwhile? Unequivocally, the answer is yes, if you understand that Grammar cannot detect all possible errors in your document. Even with its shortcomings, however, Grammar might find an error that could cause you considerable embarrassment if the uncorrected document were released to the public. Don't let the use of Grammar lull you into thinking that *all* possible errors have been detected!

Chapter 9
Checking Spelling and Grammar

To use Grammar wisely, follow these steps before running Grammar:

1. Without paying attention to spelling or other surface errors, read your document and try to judge how well it is organized. Did you choose an organization that is right for the subject? Can you organize the material so that the document would be easier to understand?

2. Look for coherence flaws. Did you omit key facts or perspectives? Looking at what's on paper (and ignoring what *you* know to be true), does your document make sense? Think about your audience. Does your audience have enough knowledge to understand what you're trying to say? Did you define key terms? Did you use examples and analogies to explain unfamiliar material?

3. Are your paragraphs unified? Does each of them express and develop one idea?

You should run Grammar only *after* you scrutinize your document in this way. Think of Grammar as a final step in proofing your document: Grammar provides one last way to catch an error that might have escaped your revision. But Grammar cannot take the place of manual revision.

Using Grammar

TIP

If you don't want Grammar to check spelling when you check grammar, choose Grammar in the Rule Groups list box and deactivate the Spelling Errors option.

Like Spelling, Grammar searches your document sentence-by-sentence and looks for words or phrases that match the ones in its built-in dictionary. By default, Grammar checks spelling, too. If Grammar finds a spelling error, the Spelling dialog box appears.

To proof your document with Grammar, follow these steps:

1. Position the insertion point where you want Grammar to begin. (Grammar still checks your whole document, but begins at the insertion point's location.)

   Or select part of your document, and Grammar will check only the selection.

2. Choose Grammar from the Tools menu.

   The Grammar dialog box appears (see fig. 9.7) and shows the first error that Grammar detects. (If the Spelling dialog box appears, deal with the unknown word as you would when running Spelling. For more information, see "Checking Spelling" in this chapter.)

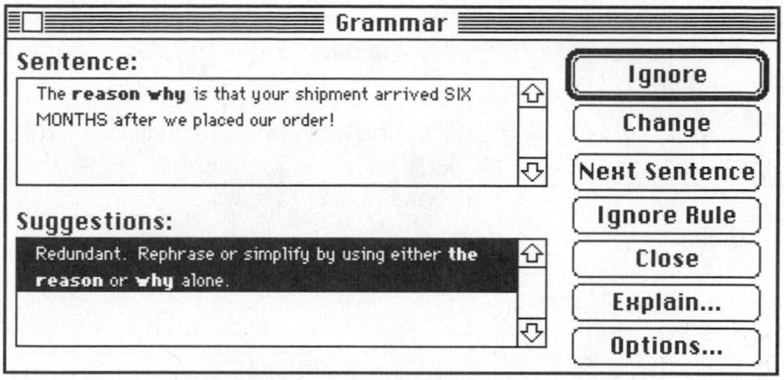

Fig. 9.7
The Grammar dialog box.

3. Choose an action from the following:

Choose Explain to view an explanation of the error and suggestions for its revision. When you choose Explain, the Grammar Explanation dialog box appears, such as the one shown in figure 9.8. Click the Close box to return to the Grammar dialog box.

Correct the error. Click in the document window to activate the document. Edit the sentence. To continue checking grammar, choose Grammar from the Tools menu. Grammar will check the new, revised sentences.

Choose Ignore to skip this occurrence of the error and continue. Grammar shows you any additional occurrences of this error in your document.

Choose Next Sentence to skip the rest of the errors in this sentence and go on to the next sentence.

Choose Ignore Rule to tell Grammar to quit flagging this kind of error in this and subsequent sessions. Choosing this option is the same as deactivating one of Grammar's rules in the Preferences dialog box, as explained later in this section.

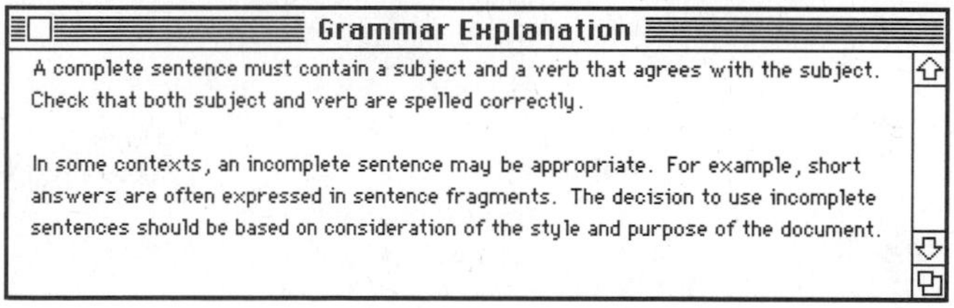

Fig. 9.8
Grammar explanation.

Chapter 9
Checking Spelling and Grammar

4. Repeat step 3 until Word informs you that the program has reached the end of the document or the selection.

If Grammar reaches the end of the document without proofing all your text, a dialog box appears and asks whether you want to continue checking from the beginning of the document. Choose OK to continue or choose Cancel to stop checking.

When Grammar finishes, the Document Statistics dialog box appears (see fig. 9.9).

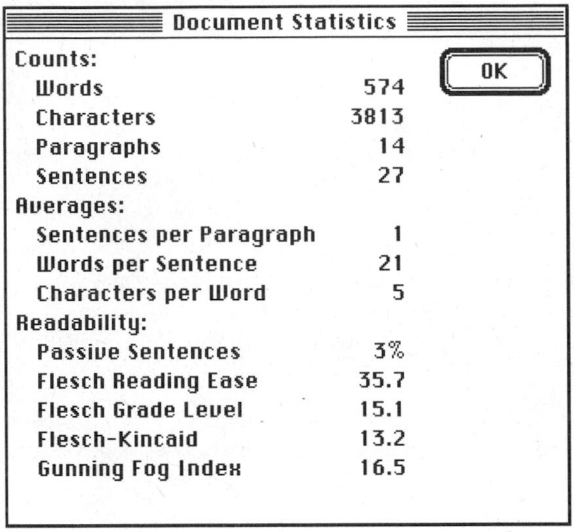

Fig. 9.9
The Document statistics dialog box.

```
═══════════ Document Statistics ═══════════
Counts:                                    ┌──────┐
    Words                      574         │  OK  │
    Characters                3813         └──────┘
    Paragraphs                  14
    Sentences                   27
Averages:
    Sentences per Paragraph      1
    Words per Sentence          21
    Characters per Word          5
Readability:
    Passive Sentences           3%
    Flesch Reading Ease       35.7
    Flesch Grade Level        15.1
    Flesch-Kincaid            13.2
    Gunning Fog Index         16.5
```

Understanding Document Statistics

The Document Statistics dialog box reports the results of several quantitative measures of your document's readability. The Flesch Grade Level, the Flesch-Kincaid score, and the Gunning Fog Index assess readability by using a grade level; the document measured in figure 9.9, for example, would require two to four years of college. These scores are only spuriously accurate (as suggested by the disagreement among them), so you should think of them in more general terms, as shown in table 9.1. This table also interprets the Flesch Index scores, which do not reflect grade levels.

	Reading Level	Grade Equivalent	Flesch Index
Table 9.1 Readability Levels	Very difficult	Postgraduate	0 to 30
	Difficult	College	30 to 50
	Somewhat difficult	High school	50 to 60
	Standard	Junior high school	60 to 70
	Fairly easy	Sixth grade	70 to 80
	Easy	Fifth grade	80 to 90
	Very easy	Fourth grade	90 to 100

Note that these readability scores use a crude numerical measurement of your text. The Gunning Fog Index, for example, is found by dividing the number of words by the number of sentences, and multiplying the result by an arbitrary constant. You could create an unreadable nonsense document that includes sentences such as Chomksy's famous "Colorless green ideas sleep furiously" and get an excellent readability score. In short, don't take these scores too seriously. Use them only as one index of your document's readability.

If you get a readability score higher than your readers' abilities, you can lower it by following these suggestions:

- Shorten sentences.

- Eliminate wordy expressions ("It will be seen that...").

- Eliminate grammatical expletives ("It is" and "There are").

- Rewrite passive voice sentences ("The ball was kicked by John") unless you disguised or omitted the sentence's subject for a good reason.

- Use simple, familiar words.

Choosing Grammar Options

When you choose the Options button in the Grammar dialog box, the Grammar options appear in the Preferences dialog box (Tools menu), as shown in figure 9.10. The following lists the options in the Grammar options section of the Preferences dialog box.

Fig. 9.10
Grammar options.

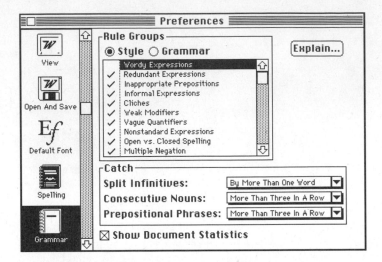

Rule Groups Area. Grammar enables you to activate or deactivate individual style or grammar rules. By default, all the rules are turned on. To disable a rule, click the check mark. To turn a rule back on, click in the check column next to the rule name.

Style and Grammar Buttons. Word displays in the Rule Groups list box only one rule group at a time. To see the Grammar rules, choose Grammar.

Explain Button. If you're not sure what a particular style or grammar rule does, highlight the rule and choose Explain. A brief explanation of the errors the rule detects is displayed.

Catch Area. In this area, you control how Grammar detects split infinitives ("To boldly go"), consecutive nouns ("failure detection feedback analysis procedure"), and repeated prepositional phrases ("In a box on a track on the way to town").

Split Infinitives. By default, Grammar doesn't flag split infinitives unless they're split by more than one word; you can choose By More Than Two Words or By More Than Three Words ("To boldly, bravely, and perhaps foolishly go"). You also can choose Always, to catch all split infinitives (this choice would catch "To boldly go"), and Never, to skip all split infinitives.

Consecutive Nouns. By default, Grammar flags consecutive nouns when more than three in a row occur; you also can choose More Than Two In A Row or More than Four In A Row. To disable flagging consecutive nouns, choose Never.

Prepositional Phrases. By default, Grammar flags more than three prepositional phrases in a row. You also can choose More Than Two In A Row, More Than Four In a Row, or Never.

Show Document Statistics. By default, Grammar displays document statistics. To skip document statistics, deactivate this check box.

Quick Review

This section concisely summarizes the most useful information in this chapter. Check "Productivity Tips" for a review of high-productivity tips and tricks, and review "Techniques" when you forget how to perform a specific procedure.

Productivity Tips

- Switch to Normal view before you choose Spelling.

- Add all the proper nouns you use—your name, your boss's and company's name, your street's name—to a custom dictionary so that the program doesn't flag these words in future spelling checks.

- Use Spelling Preferences to turn off suggestions.

- If you need to add more than 1,000 words to a custom dictionary, create more than one, apportioned according to the types of documents you create.

- Don't let Grammar take the place of a careful, hand proofreading of your document. Grammar cannot catch many of the serious errors in usage, style, and grammar.

- Disable irrelevant rules to speed Grammar's operation.

- Don't place too much emphasis on readability scores. Coherence and clarity matter more than these crude, quantitative scores. To lower your document's readability score, avoid the passive voice, shorten sentences, and use simple words.

Techniques

This section provides concise, quick-reference summaries of all the procedures introduced in this chapter.

Checking Grammar

To proof your document with Grammar:

1. Position the insertion point where you want Grammar to begin. You also can select part of your document, and Grammar will check only the selection.

2. Choose Grammar from the Tools menu.

3. When Grammar flags an error, perform one or more of the following actions:

   Choose Explain to view an explanation of the error and suggestions for its revision.

   Click in the document window to activate the document, and edit the sentence.

   Choose Ignore to skip this occurrence of the error and continue.

   Choose Next Sentence to skip the rest of the errors in this sentence and go on to the next sentence.

   Choose Ignore Rule to tell Grammar to quit flagging this kind of error in this and subsequent Grammar sessions.

4. Repeat step 3 until Word informs you that the program has reached the end of the document or the selection.

Choosing Grammar Options

To choose grammar options:

1. Choose Preferences from the Tools menu. When the Preferences dialog box appears, choose the Grammar option. You also can choose Options from the Grammar dialog box.

2. To disable Style or Grammar rules, deactivate the check mark next to the rule's name. Choose Explain to view an explanation of the highlighted rule. Disable Spelling in the Grammar rule list if you do not want Grammar to check your document's spelling.

3. Change the default settings for split infinitives, consecutive nouns, or prepositional phrases.

4. Deactivate the Show Document Statistics check box.

5. Click the Close box to save your choices and return to your document (or to the Grammar dialog box).

Checking Spelling

To check spelling, follow these steps:

1. To check a selection, select the text. To check your entire document, click the location at which you want the spell check to start.

2. Choose Spelling from the Tools menu or press ⌘-L.

3. When Spelling flags an error, take one of the following actions:

   Choose Change to accept the suggestion that Word placed in the Change To text box.

   Choose Change All to make this change throughout your document without any confirmation from you.

   Choose the correct spelling in the suggestions list by highlighting it and choosing Change (or double-click the word). Choose Change All to make this correction throughout the document.

   Manually correct the spelling in the Change To box, and then choose Change. Choose Change All to make this correction throughout the document.

   Close the Spelling dialog box and make the change in your document.

   Choose Ignore to skip the word once, or choose Ignore All to skip all instances of this word in your document.

   Choose Add to add the word to the current dictionary (by default, the current dictionary is Custom Dictionary, as indicated in the Add Words To list box).

   Choose the Delete button to correct a repeated word.

4. Repeat step 3 until Word informs you that the program has reached the end of the document (or the selection).

Choosing Spelling Options

To choose spelling options:

1. Choose Preferences from the Tools menu. When the Preferences dialog box appears, choose the Spelling option. You also can choose Options from the Spelling dialog box.

2. To turn off the automatic suggestion of correctly spelled words, deactivate the Always Suggest option.

3. To skip words in all uppercase letters, activate the Words in the UPPERCASE option.

4. To skip words that contain numbers, activate the Words with Numbers option.

5. Click the Close box to return to your document (or to the Grammar dialog box).

Using Custom Dictionaries

To create a custom dictionary:

1. Choose Preferences from the Tools menu.

2. Choose Spelling.

3. Choose New.

4. Type a name for the new custom dictionary (no longer than 31 characters).

5. If necessary, open the Word Commands folder so that your new custom dictionary is placed in the same folder with Word's main dictionary.

6. Choose Save.

To open a custom dictionary:

1. Choose Preferences from the Tools menu.

2. Choose Spelling.

3. Click to the left of the custom dictionary name.

4. Click the Close box.

To close a custom dictionary:

1. Choose Preferences from the Tools menu.

2. Choose Spelling.

3. Click the check mark next to the name of the custom dictionary you want to close.

4. Click the Close box.

To remove a word from a custom dictionary:

1. Choose Preferences from the Tools menu.

2. Choose Spelling.

3. In the Custom Dictionaries list box, highlight the name of the custom dictionary you want to edit.

4. Choose Edit.

5. Highlight the word you want to delete.

6. Choose Delete.

7. Repeat steps 5 and 6 until you have removed all the words you want to delete.

8. Choose OK to close the dialog box, or choose Cancel to close the dialog box without making changes to the dictionary.

10

Printing Documents

Compared with other computing environments, the Macintosh makes printing a breeze. After you hook up your printer and use the Chooser to tell your Mac which printer you're using, printing is a simple, straightforward process. You probably have printed successfully already.

This chapter reviews the basics of printing and shows you how to use Word's many print options. It covers the following topics:

- *Printing Your Document.* In this section you learn how to use the Print command to print your document—and what to do if something goes wrong.

- *Choosing Print Options.* This section surveys the many printing options from which you can choose. You learn, for example, how to print a selected range of pages and multiple copies of a document. You also learn how to use the printing options in the Page Setup dialog box.

- *Preparing a Document for Printing on Another System.* In this section you learn how to use the Chooser to change your printer to print your file on another Macintosh system that has a different printer. You also can use the Chooser to switch printers, if you have two printers or obtain a new one.

USING
WORD 5
FOR THE
MAC

Other chapters also cover subjects related to printing.

- To print mailing labels and envelopes with Word, see Chapter 25.
- To link documents together so that they print as if they were one document, with continuous pagination, see Chapter 26.
- To print one or more files that aren't open, see Chapter 11.
- To review Print Preview, see Chapter 2.

This chapter assumes that you installed and connected your printer, chose it with the Chooser desktop accessory (Apple menu), and successfully printed already. If you have not done so, see your printer's manual for installation instructions.

Printing Your Work

After you check spelling and preview document formats to your satisfaction, you are ready to print your document. Make sure that your printer is turned on, loaded with paper, and selected (on-line). Normally, printing is a simple process.

Before you start printing, make sure that you added page numbers. If you forgot to do so, you may waste a lot of paper before realizing the omission.

To print your document, follow these steps:

1. Choose Print from the File menu or press ⌘-P.
2. When the Print dialog box appears, click the OK button.
3. Cancel printing at any time by pressing ⌘-period or Esc.

You can choose from many print options in the Print dialog box and the Page Setup dialog box. The following sections examine these options.

Choosing Print Options with the Print Dialog Box

The Print dialog box contains options for controlling the number of copies, the range of pages to be printed, the type of paper to be used, and (for the ImageWriter) the print quality. With the exception of Page Range, Section Range, and Copies, all the options you choose in the Print dialog box are saved when you print your document. The options become the default for new documents.

The appearance of the Print dialog box changes depending on which printer you use. Figures 10.1 through 10.4 show the Print dialog boxes for current Apple printers.

Fig. 10.1
Print dialog box
(StyleWriter).

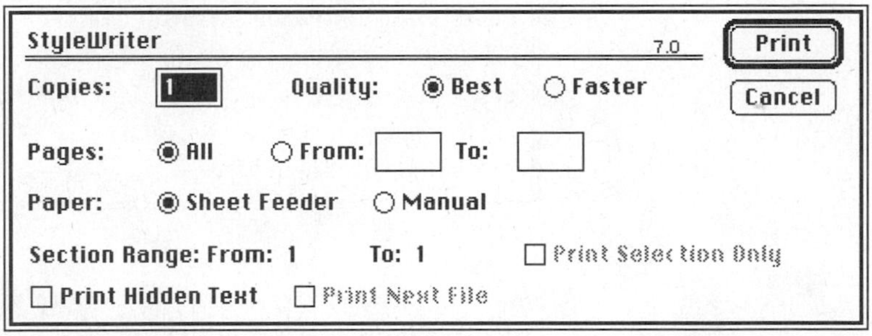

Fig. 10.2
Print dialog box (Personal
LaserWriter LS).

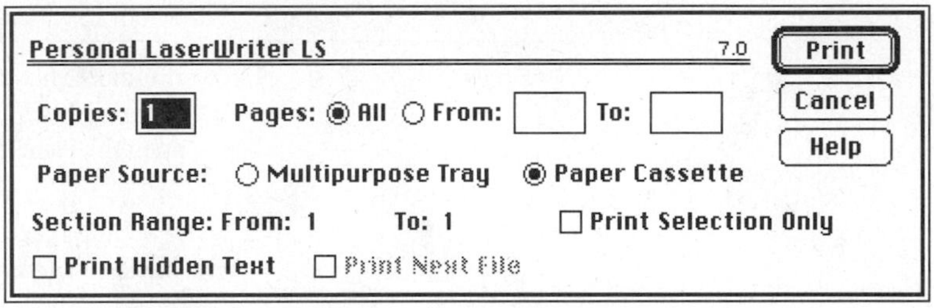

Fig. 10.3
Print dialog box (Personal
LaserWriter SC).

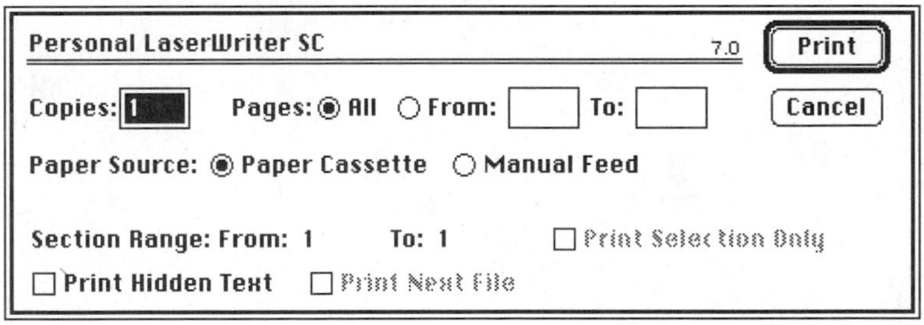

Chapter 10
Printing Documents

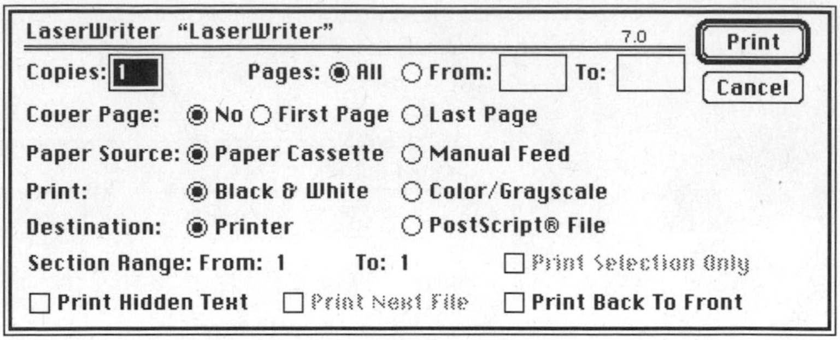

Fig. 10.4
Print dialog box
(LaserWriter).

```
┌─────────────────────────────────────────────────────────────────┐
│ LaserWriter  "LaserWriter"                    7.0    ┌─────────┐  │
│                                                      │  Print  │  │
│ Copies: [1]        Pages: ⦿ All ○ From: [    ] To: [    ]       │
│                                                      ┌─────────┐  │
│ Cover Page:    ⦿ No ○ First Page ○ Last Page        │ Cancel  │  │
│                                                                   │
│ Paper Source: ⦿ Paper Cassette  ○ Manual Feed                    │
│                                                                   │
│ Print:        ⦿ Black & White   ○ Color/Grayscale                │
│                                                                   │
│ Destination:  ⦿ Printer         ○ PostScript® File               │
│                                                                   │
│ Section Range: From: 1    To: 1         ☐ Print Selection Only    │
│                                                                   │
│ ☐ Print Hidden Text   ☐ Print Next File  ☐ Print Back To Front   │
└─────────────────────────────────────────────────────────────────┘
```

Some options vary, depending on your printer's capabilities. Table 10.1 lists the options available in all Print dialog boxes.

Table 10.1
Printing Options (Print dialog box)

Option	Function
Copies	To print more than one copy, type the number in the Copies box. The box is highlighted when you open the Print dialog box.
Pages	To print a range of pages, click From and type the beginning page number of the range. Then type the last page number in the To box. Leave the To box empty to print to the end of your document. To print one page, type the same number in the From and To boxes.
Section Range	To print a range of sections from a document that has more than one section, type the section range in the Section Range boxes.
Print Hidden Text	Click this option to print hidden text, even if this text is not displayed on-screen.
Print Next File	This check box is grayed unless you link files for printing by using the File Series button in the Document dialog box. For more information on this dialog box, see Chapter 26.
Print Selection Only	This check box is grayed unless you selected some text before choosing Print. Click this option to print only the text you selected.

Some printers offer additional options, as listed in table 10.2.

Table 10.2
Additional Printing Options

Option	Description
Cover Page (LaserWriter)	Prints a cover page that states the document title, the time of printing, and the user identification (for networked Macs). You can print the cover page before the document (First Page) or after the document (Last Page). When several Mac users are sharing one printer, the person operating the printer will find it easier to untangle the printed output.
Print (LaserWriter)	If you have a color or greyscale printer, you can choose the Color/Greyscale option to print the colors you selected in the Character dialog box.
Destination (LaserWriter II)	You can choose PostScript File to print your document to a file. You then can take the file to a printing service bureau and have your document printed on a high-resolution imagesetter.
Quality (ImageWriter, StyleWriter)	Choose Best to print each character twice (for the final printout); choose Faster to print each character once. With ImageWriters, choosing Draft omits character and paragraph formatting.

TIP

To print gray text on a black and white LaserWriter printer, use the Character dialog box to format the text with a color other than black and then choose Color/Greyscale in the Print dialog box.

Choosing Print Options with the Page Setup Dialog Box

With the Page Setup dialog box, you can choose additional print options, including the type of paper, paper orientation, and special printing effects. Like the Print dialog box, the Page Setup dialog box differs depending on which printer you choose (see figs. 10.5 through 10.7). The choices you make in the Page Setup dialog box remain in effect until you change them. To print with these options, choose them before you choose Print.

The following section explains the Page Setup options available with all or most printers. Sections devoted to the special printing capabilities of ImageWriter and LaserWriter printers follow.

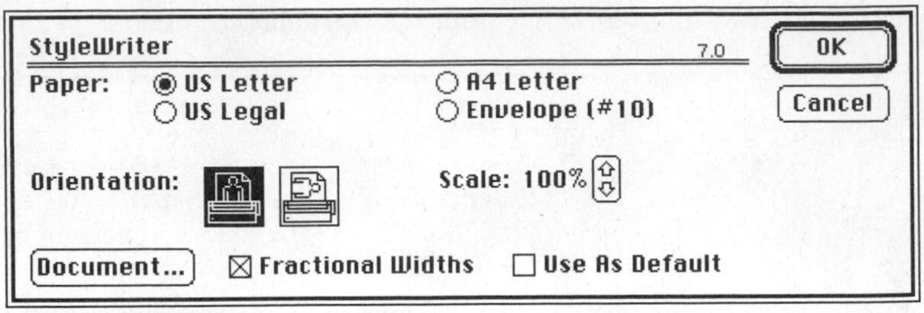

Fig. 10.5
StyleWriter Page Setup.

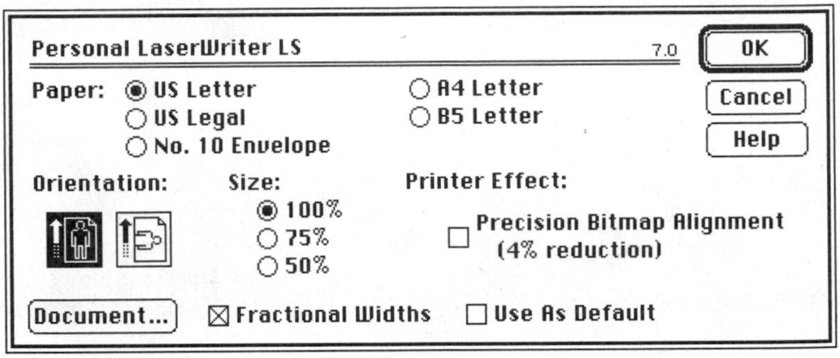

Fig. 10.6
Personal LaserWriter LS
Page Setup.

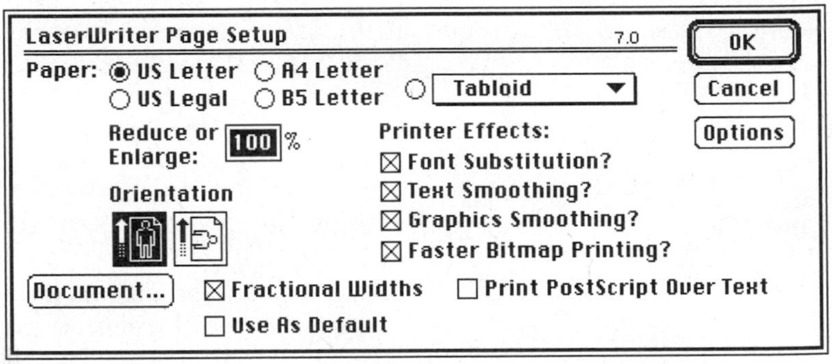

Fig. 10.7
LaserWriter Page Setup.

Understanding Page Setup Options

Table 10.3 explains the Page Setup options that you find in all or most of
the Page Setup dialog boxes.

	Option	Description
Table 10.3 Page Setup Printing Options	Paper	Choose from several standard paper sizes. For more information on choosing paper size, see Chapter 7.
	Orientation	Click the icon to print in Portrait mode (across the width of the page) or Landscape mode (across the length of the page).
	Size	Choose from a variety of reductions. 100% is full size; you also can choose 75% and 50%. If you can type or choose the scale, you can choose a reduction as low as 25% or as high as 400%. Word changes the right margin setting on-screen to show you how much text will fit on a printed line. The ruler measurements or font sizes, however, do not change in Normal or Page Layout views. To see how your document will look when printed, choose Print Preview.
	Fractional Widths	Tells Word to simulate on-screen the character spacing of proportionally spaced fonts (such as New Century Schoolbook, Times Roman, and Helvetica). Some fonts may be difficult to read with this option chosen (especially if you're using a small font size) because your Macintosh screen does not have sufficient resolution to perform this task accurately. If the text is difficult to read, try turning this option off. Be sure, however, to turn it back on before printing, or the line and page breaks that appear on-screen will not match the line and page breaks in your printed document. This option is on by default.
	Use As Default	Activate this check box to make your Page Setup choices the default for all documents. Your Page Setup options remain in effect, however, until you change them.
	Document Button	To set margins or make other page formatting choices, click this button and view the Document dialog box.

Understanding ImageWriter Page Setup Options

If you're using an ImageWriter printer, you see a Page Setup dialog box such as the one shown in figure 10.8. Table 10.4 lists the special printing options available with this printer.

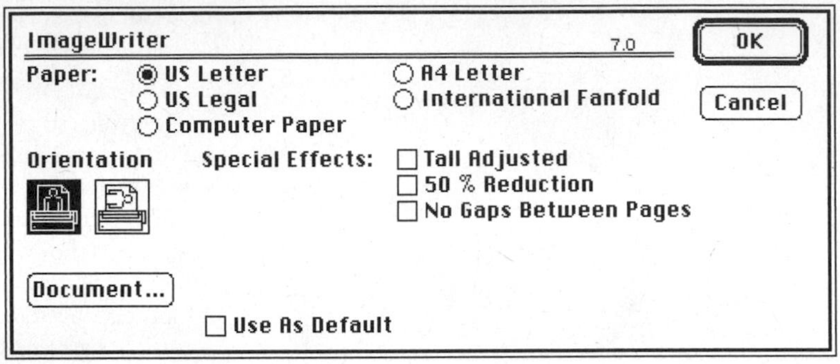

Fig. 10.8
Page Setup dialog box
(ImageWriter).

```
ImageWriter                                    7.0        ┌────────┐
                                                          │   OK   │
Paper:    ⦿ US Letter          ○ A4 Letter               └────────┘
          ○ US Legal           ○ International Fanfold    ┌────────┐
          ○ Computer Paper                                │ Cancel │
                                                          └────────┘
Orientation     Special Effects:    ☐ Tall Adjusted
                                    ☐ 50 % Reduction
 [🖨] [🖨]                           ☐ No Gaps Between Pages


┌──────────────┐
│ Document...  │         ☐ Use As Default
└──────────────┘
```

Fig. 10.8
Page Setup dialog box
(ImageWriter).

Table 10.4
ImageWriter Page Setup
Options

Option	Description
Tall Adjusted	Choose this option if the bit-mapped graphics you print look stretched horizontally (so that a circle prints like an oval).
50% Reduction	Prints the page half size. You can choose this option to produce high-resolution printouts: Before printing, choose a 24-point font size (which Word prints at 12 points). Word automatically doubles the margins.
No Gaps Between Pages	If you're using continuous mailing labels, you can choose this option to omit page breaks and vertical margins.

Understanding Laser Printer Page Setup Options

If you're using a laser printer, you have additional printing options. Table 10.5 lists the printing options available in the Page Setup dialog boxes of current Apple laser printers.

Option	Description
Precision Bitmap Alignment	Reduces bit-mapped (paint format) graphics so that they print more attractively. Sets aside large amounts of your printer's memory for graphics. Turn this option off to print if you're using downloadable fonts, or your document may fail to print.
Exact Bit Images	Reduces bit-mapped (paint format) graphics so that they print more attractively. (This option is the same as Precision Bitmap Alignment.)
Text Smoothing	Smooths the edges of bit-mapped fonts. This option is selected by default. If you're not using bit-mapped fonts, deactivate this option; it slows down your printer and can blur some fonts and graphics.
Font Substitution	Prints Geneva in Helvetica, New York in Times Roman, and Monaco in Courier. This option is selected by default. The word spacing will look irregular when the document is printed. It's best to choose Helvetica, Times Roman, and Courier in your document.
Graphics Smoothing	Smooths the edges and contours of graphics that appear jagged when printed. This option is selected by default. If you're not using bit-mapped graphics, deactivate this option; it slows down your printer and can blur some fonts and graphics.
Faster Bitmap Printing	Speeds the printing of bit-mapped fonts and graphics. This option is selected by default. Disable this option if the document doesn't print correctly.
Fractional Widths	Tells Word to simulate on-screen the character spacing of proportionally spaced fonts (such as New Century Schoolbook, Times Roman, and Helvetica). This option is selected by default. Your Macintosh screen does not have sufficient resolution to perform this task.

TIP

If you like the laser printer output generated by the TrueType versions of Geneva, New York, and Monaco (System 7), be sure to disable the Font Substitution option so that Word does not translate these fonts to Helvetica, Times Roman, or Courier. If you're not using bit-mapped fonts or bit-mapped graphics, turn off the Smoothing options.

If you're using a PostScript laser printer, you can choose the Options button to see additional printing options (fig. 10.9). Table 10.6 lists these options.

Fig. 10.9
LaserWriter Page Setup
Options.

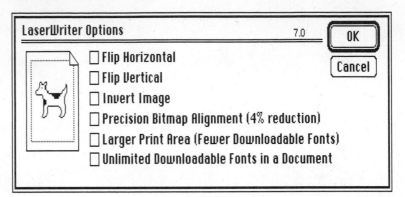

Table 10.6
LaserWriter Page Setup
Options

Option	Description
Flip Horizontal	Prints text and graphics backward—you need a mirror to read the document!
Flip Vertical	Reverses the page top to bottom. (The bottom of the page comes out of the printer first.)
Invert Image	Prints white text or graphics on a black background (like a photographic negative) for special effects.
Precision Bitmap Alignment	Improves printing of bit-mapped graphics.
Larger Print Area	Expands the print area by reducing the minimum margins. This option also reduces the number of downloadable fonts you can use.
Unlimited Downloadable Fonts in a Document	Removes the limitation on the number of downloadable fonts you can use with a given document. If you print a document with many fonts, printing may be slow.

TIP

Save toner by turning off the printing of that sample page each time your LaserWriter starts. Use the Finder to start the LaserWriter Font Utility, a utility provided with System 7. Choose Start Page Options from the Utilities menu. Click the Off button, and then choose OK.

Part I

Getting Started

Using Background Printing

If you're using a LaserWriter, you can use the PrintMonitor program—a utility provided with Apple's System software—to print in the background while you work with Word (or other applications). With System 6, you must activate MultiFinder before you can use PrintMonitor. With System 7, you can use PrintMonitor at any time.

Background printing with PrintMonitor is simple and convenient. You can print several documents at once. By bringing up the PrintMonitor dialog box while printing, you can monitor the status of each print job, cancel printing, change the order in which documents print, and set the time and date you want each document printed. You can continue to work with your Macintosh while your documents are printing.

If your printer runs out of paper or if PrintMonitor encounters a problem while printing, an alert box appears.

To turn on background printing, choose On in the Background Printing area of the Chooser dialog box. (To display this dialog box, choose Chooser from the Apple menu.) Background printing remains active until you turn it off by choosing the Off button in this dialog box.

When you print with PrintMonitor, Word quickly saves printing information to a temporary file and returns control of the keyboard to you. You can continue to work, but your Macintosh will pause frequently as it sends information to the printer.

While a document is printing, you can check the status of printing by displaying the PrintMonitor dialog box, shown in figure 10.10. To display the PrintMonitor dialog box with System 6, click the Multifinder icon (on the right side of the menu bar) until PrintMonitor is displayed. To display the PrintMonitor dialog box with System 7, choose Print-Monitor from the Applications menu (to pull down the Applications menu within Word, click the Word icon—the one with the italic *W*—on the right side of the menu bar).

In the PrintMonitor dialog box, the name of the document currently printing is displayed in the Printing window. In the Waiting window, a list of additional documents is displayed. These documents will be printed in the order they're listed. The following sections explain how to cancel printing a document and control the time and date a document prints.

Chapter 10
Printing Documents

Fig. 10.10
PrintMonitor dialog box.

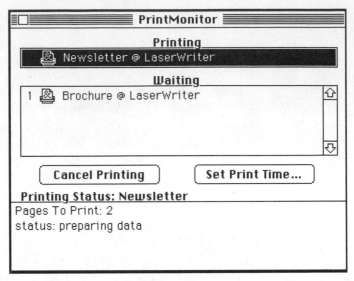

If you don't have a LaserWriter, consider purchasing a print spooler such as SuperLaserSpool to avoid tying up your Macintosh while a lengthy document is printing. (If you have a LaserWriter, you can choose the Background Printing option in the Page Setup dialog box.) A print spooler directs print output to your hard disk; after the output is stored on your hard disk, you can continue working with your Macintosh, and the spooler doles out the print output in the background without disturbing your work session.

Cancelling a Print Job

To cancel printing a document, follow these steps:

1. Click the MultiFinder icon until the PrintMonitor dialog box (System 6) appears, or choose PrintMonitor from the Applications menu (System 7).

2. Highlight the name of the document you don't want to print.

   If you're printing more than one document, this name could be in the Waiting window.

3. Choose Cancel.

4. Click the Close box to exit the PrintMonitor dialog box.

Postponing a Print Job

When you postpone printing a document, you tell PrintMonitor not to print the document until you are ready. To postpone printing a document, follow these steps:

1. Click the MultiFinder icon until you see PrintMonitor (System 6), or choose PrintMonitor from the Applications menu (System 7).

2. In the Waiting window, highlight the name of the document you want to print later.

3. Choose Set Print Time.

   The Set Print Time dialog box appears (see fig. 10.11).

Fig. 10.11
The Set Print Time
dialog box.

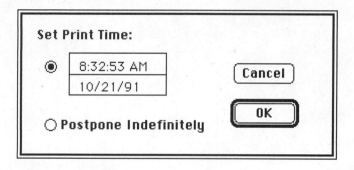

4. Take one of the following actions:

   Click the time area. When the arrows appear, change the time. You also can change the date this way.

   Click the Postpone Indefinitely option. If you choose this option, you must choose Set Print Time again and set a printing time for the document to print it.

5. Choose OK.

6. Click the close box.

Chapter 10
Printing Documents

Switching Printers

f you want to save your document to a floppy disk and print it on a different Macintosh system (one that has a printer other than the one you're using) you can use the Chooser to change printers temporarily. When Word formats your document, it uses settings specific to a particular printer. You therefore should use the Chooser to select the printer you intend to use to print your document, even if it's not the one connected to your system. After you save this document, remember to switch back to the printer that's connected to your system.

To change printers temporarily, follow these steps:

1. Choose Chooser from the Apple menu.

   The Chooser dialog box appears (see fig. 10.12). The available printers are displayed in the list box.

Fig. 10.12
The Chooser dialog box.

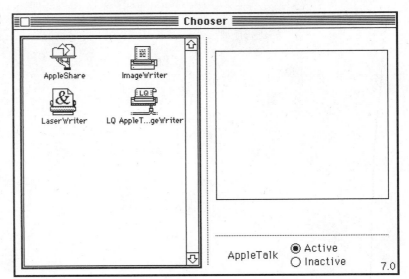

TIP

If you have connected two different printers to your system, you can use this procedure to choose one of them for a print job.

2. Choose one of the printers.

3. Choose port, AppleTalk, and background printing options.

Part I

Getting Started

4. Click the Close box.

5. If Word was running when you chose Chooser, choose Page Setup from the File menu (or use the Shift-F8 keyboard shortcut), and choose OK to confirm the new printer choice.

6. Format, save, and close your document.

7. Repeat Steps 1 through 5 to restore your system's printer.

Quick Review

Productivity Tips

- If you want your document to have page numbers, be sure to check whether you added them to your document before printing.

- If more than one person uses the printer, choose Cover Page in the Print dialog box.

- If you're using an ImageWriter or StyleWriter, choose the Faster option to print a quick draft of your document; use the Best option for the final copy only.

- Enable background printing so that you can continue to work with Word while documents print. If you're not using a LaserWriter, you can purchase a print-spooling program that enables background printing.

Techniques

This section provides concise, quick-reference summaries of all the procedures introduced in this chapter.

Background Printing with PrintMonitor and LaserWriters

To turn on background printing:

1. Choose Chooser from the Apple menu.

2. Choose the LaserWriter printer icon.

3. Choose a LaserWriter name from the list.

4. Choose On in the Background Printing area.

5. Choose OK.

To cancel printing a document:

1. Click the MultiFinder icon until you see PrintMonitor (System 6), or choose PrintMonitor from the Applications menu (System 7).

2. Highlight the name of the document you don't want to print.

3. Choose Cancel.

4. Click the Close box to exit the PrintMonitor dialog box.

To postpone printing a document:

1. Click the MultiFinder icon until you see PrintMonitor (System 6), or choose PrintMonitor from the Applications menu (System 7).

2. In the Waiting window, highlight the name of the document you want to print later.

3. Choose Set Print Time.

4. Take one of the following actions:

   Click the time area. When the arrows appear, change the time. You also can change the date this way.

   Click the Postpone Indefinitely option.

5. Choose OK.

6. Click the Close box.

Changing Printers Temporarily

To change printers temporarily:

1. Choose Chooser from the Apple menu.

2. Choose one of the printers.

3. Choose port, AppleTalk, and background printing options.

4. Click the Close box.

5. If Word was running when you chose Chooser, choose Page Setup from the File menu, and choose OK to confirm the new printer choice.

6. Format, save, and close your document.

7. Repeat Steps 1 through 5 to restore your system's printer.

Choosing Page Setup Print Options

To change printing orientation:

1. Choose Page Setup from the File menu.

2. Click the Landscape or Portrait icon.

3. Choose OK.

4. Print your document.

To change printing size:

1. Choose Page Setup from the File menu.

2. Type a size in the Reduce or Enlarge box, or click a size option.

3. Click OK.

4. Print your document.

Choosing Print Options

To print only the selected text:

1. Select the text you want to print.

2. Choose Print from the File menu or press ⌘-P.

3. Activate the Print Selection Only check box.

4. Choose OK.

5. To cancel printing at any time, press ⌘-period or Esc.

To print hidden text:

1. Select the text you want to print.

2. Choose Print from the File menu or press ⌘-P.

3. Activate the Print Hidden Text check box.

4. Choose OK.

5. To cancel printing at any time, press ⌘-period or Esc.

To print more than one copy:

1. Choose Print from the File menu or press ⌘-P.

2. In the Print dialog box, type the number of copies in the Copies box.

3. Choose OK.

4. To cancel printing at any time, press ⌘-period or Esc.

To print a range of pages:

1. Choose Print from the File menu or press ⌘-P.

2. In the Print dialog box, click From and type the beginning page number of the range.

3. In the To box, type the last page number in the range. To print to the end of your document, leave the To box empty. To print one page, type the same page number that you typed in the From box.

4. Choose OK.

5. To cancel printing at any time, press ⌘-period or Esc.

To print a section range:

1. Choose Print from the File menu or press ⌘-P.

2. In the Section Range From box, type the number of the first section you want to print.

3. In the Section Range To box, type the last section number in the range. To print to the end of your document, leave the To box empty. To print one section, type the same section number that you typed in the From box.

4. Choose OK.

5. To cancel printing at any time, press ⌘-period or Esc.

Printing Your Work

To print your document:

1. Choose Print from the File menu, or press ⌘-P.

2. When the Print dialog box appears, click the OK button.

3. To cancel printing at any time, press ⌘-period or Esc.

Managing Documents

T he Macintosh usually runs a 40M hard disk, but systems with disks of several hundred megabytes of storage space are increasingly common. After you fill any hard disk with dozens or hundreds of files, file management can become a burden. Stationery documents and Find File, Word's new file-management resources, provide useful new tools for coping with the multitude of files in a hard disk environment.

With Word's Open and Save dialog boxes, you can create and retrieve files easily enough. Even so, you will sooner or later encounter one of the following file-management problems:

- *Basing a new file on an existing one*. If you forget to choose the Save As command and save a file using a new name, you overwrite the existing, generic copy. You then must delete manually the text you added.

- *Getting document styles from an existing document*. You want to copy styles you have developed to a new document, but you already copied them several times. You need to know which document has the latest versions of your styles.

- *Finding an elusive file*. A file you desperately need is hidden somewhere in a nested folder. You open window after window with the Finder, but cannot locate the file.

USING
WORD 5
FOR THE
MAC

- *Managing groups of files*. You edit with two or three documents on-screen, and you print several files at a time, but you must repeat the Open and Print commands, one for each file.

This chapter shows how stationery documents and the Find File command can help you with these problems. The following is an overview of this chapter's contents:

- *Creating and Using Stationery Documents*. In this section, you learn how to create generic or template documents, which Word stores as read-only documents. When you open these documents, Word creates a new, untitled document that you can modify. You cannot overwrite the template. You also learn how stationery documents can help you manage styles more efficiently.

- *Finding and Managing File with Find File*. Word 5's new Find File command has impressive file-management capabilities. With this command, you can retrieve files quickly, regardless of where they're buried on your hard drive (or any other drive, including network drives). You can search for one file or a group of files according to criteria you specify (such as date of creation, document text, keywords, author, and so on). After you retrieve files, you can open, copy, print, or delete them.

Creating and Using Stationery Documents

As often as possible, develop new documents by opening and modifying generic versions of a template. A *template* is a "generic" version of a document (such as a letter that contains your return address and formats, but no text) that you save as a stationery document. The following is a list of template possibilities:

- *Letterhead*. Include your return address, a date code that enters the date at the time of printing, the complimentary close, and other needed information.

- *Memo*. Include the memo header (including To, From, Date, and Subject) but not the memo text.

- *Résumé*. Include all the information that belongs in every résumé. Open this template and add the specifics for a particular job.

- *Periodic Reports*. Include generic formats for tables, lists, and other information you must supply periodically. Also include titles, explanatory text, and other text that doesn't change from report to report.

- *Newsletters*. Include section formats, styles, borders, figure positions, and other layout information that doesn't change with each issue. Also include generic text, such as subscription information, editorial staff credits, and disclaimers.

- *Price Lists*. Include all the text that doesn't change (model names and numbers). Leave out the prices.

You can create templates with previous versions of Word. But these templates are ordinary Word files. If you open the template and add new text without saving your changes with Save As, Word overwrites the template, and you have to remove your changes manually.

When you open a stationery document, Word opens the document in a new, untitled file, ensuring that you cannot accidentally overwrite the original stationery document. In this section, you learn how to create, open, and revise stationery documents. In addition, you learn how to use stationery documents as storage places for document style sheets. This capability greatly enhances the convenience of Word's style capabilities, which were introduced in Chapter 7.

Creating a Stationery Document

TIP

Create a folder called Stationery documents to store your stationery files. If you're using System 6, you must create the folder with the Finder. If you're using System 7, you can create the folder with the Save As dialog box when you save your first stationery document.

Creating a stationery document is easy. When you save the document, you choose the Stationery option from the Save File as Type list box.

To create a stationery document, follow these steps:

1. Create a generic version of a document, like the one shown in figure 11.1.

   You can include graphics and formats of any kind, including styles.

2. Choose Save from the File menu.

   A Save As dialog box similar to the System 7 Save As dialog box shown in figure 11.2 appears. (If you're using System 6, the Desktop and New Folder buttons are not displayed.)

3. From the Save File as Type list box, choose the Stationery option.

   After you select this option, the Save File as Type box shows your selection (see fig. 11.3).

4. Type a name for the document in the Save Current Document As text box.

   Choose a name, such as *Letterhead Template*, that indicates that the document is a stationery document.

5. Choose Save.

Chapter 11

Managing Documents

Fig. 11.1
Generic version of a
letterhead.

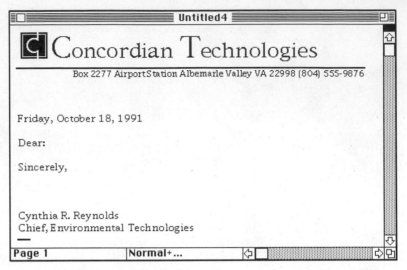

Fig. 11.2
Save As dialog box
(System 7).

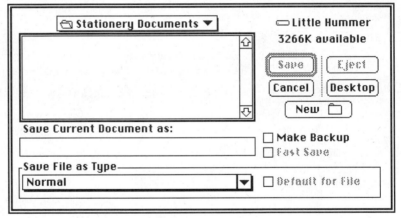

Opening a Stationery Document

After you create a stationery document, you can open it whenever you
need it. Word creates a new, Untitled document that you can change and
modify.

To open a stationery document, follow these steps:

1. Choose Open from the File menu, or press ⌘-O.

    The Open dialog box appears.

Part I

Getting Started

Fig. 11.3
Stationery file type
selected.

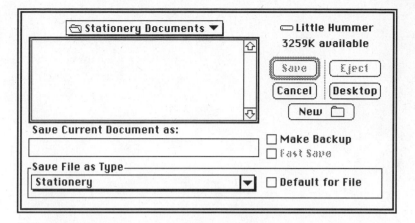

Fig. 11.3
Stationery file type
selected.

2. Choose the folder that contains your stationery document.

3. If this folder contains many files that are not stationery documents, choose Stationery in the List Files of Type list box. After choosing Stationery, Word displays only those files that were saved with the Stationery option.

4. Choose Open.

   Word opens the stationery document as a new, Untitled document. You can modify and save this document.

Revising a Stationery Document

Stationery documents are read-only documents; Word prevents you from overwriting the template. This section describes the procedure you follow to edit a template.

To revise a stationery document, follow these steps:

1. Choose Open from the File menu, or press ⌘-O.

2. Choose the folder that contains your stationery document.

3. If this folder contains many files that are not stationery documents, choose Stationery in the List Files of Type list box.

4. Choose Open.

   Word opens the document in an Untitled file.

5. Make the changes.

6. Choose Save As.

   The Save As dialog box appears.

7. In the Save File as Type list box, choose Stationery.

8. In the Save Current Document As box, type the name under which you previously saved the stationery document.

9. Choose Save.

   An alert box appears and asks you to confirm replacing the existing file.

10. Click Replace.

    Word overwrites the previous version of the template.

If you no longer need a stationery document, you can delete it as you would delete an ordinary Word document.

Using Stationery Documents To Store Frequently Used Styles

TIP

When you create useful document styles, save them to a stationery document. This document does not need to contain text. When you open the stationery document, Word creates a new, Untitled document, in which all these styles are available.

Word 5's stationery documents store generic versions of documents, such as letters or memos. Many Word 5 users may not realize, however, that stationery documents also can store document styles. When you open a stationery document, you get all the formats you saved with the template, including styles—even if the document contains no text. Word 5's Stationery capabilities provide an excellent resource for managing document styles.

Previous versions of Word provided no way to create an authoritative repository of your document styles. Suppose that you create several proposals in which you want to use the same styles. When you try to do so, however, you find a formatting error in one of the proposals. You make a change to one of the document styles but forget which document contains the update. To tell which proposal document contains the latest version of your styles, you must inspect each document's styles manually, which is tedious and time-consuming.

With Stationery, you can easily create an authoritative version of document styles. Consider this example, which a corporation or university scientist might use. You create a series of stationery documents (with or without template text) that contain document styles:

■ *Proposal Styles Template*. This stationery document contains the document styles you use for proposals.

- *Article Styles Template*. This stationery document contains the document styles you use for the articles you contribute to scientific research journals.

- *Correspondence Styles Template*. This stationery document contains the document styles you use for letters and memos.

When you create a new document, you open the appropriate template (such as correspondence styles), which contains all the document styles you want to use.

To correct an error in one of the styles, follow these steps:

1. Open the stationery document, and correct the style error in the stationery document. Don't make the correction in the document you're creating (the Untitled document).

2. To save the change, follow the procedure outlined in "Revising a Stationery Document," earlier in this chapter.

3. In the Untitled document, choose Styles.

   The Styles dialog box appears.

4. Choose Open from the File menu.

5. Open the stationery document that contains the document style you just changed.

   Word imports the styles from the stationery document, overwriting the styles of the same name in the current document.

This procedure ensures that the stationery document always contains the latest version of your styles.

Finding Files with Find File

Word 5's new Find File command (File menu) gives Macintosh users the file-management capabilities that have been standard in the DOS word processing world. Find File enables you to search an entire disk for documents based on search criteria you specify, including words you typed in the Summary Info dialog box. When Word finds a file that matches the criteria you specify, it displays the file name in the File List. If more than one file meets the criteria, more than one name is displayed in the list.

Chapter 11
Managing Documents

After a file is listed, you can sort the file list in a number of ways (including date and size), and you can view information about the file, including the document text. You also can perform group operations on the files in the file list: You can open, copy, print, or even delete all of them.

Improving Document Retrieval

You can retrieve documents more easily if you fill out the Summary Info dialog box when you save a new file (see Chapter 2). If you fill out Summary Info, you can ask Word the following questions:

- Show me all the files Suzy created between 11/3/91 and 11/8/91.

- Show me all the files on the subject "Smith Contract" that contain the text *Periodic payments*.

- Show me all the files whose File Name (the File Name typed in the Summary Info text box, not the Finder file name) contains the word *Proposal*.

If you didn't fill out Summary Info, Find File still can help you retrieve files in many ways. You can search for documents created on dates you specify and for documents that contain text you specify.

Find File also can search for information you typed in the Comments area of the Finder's Get Info dialog box. To use Get Info in the Finder, highlight the document's icon and choose Get Info (or press ⌘-I). The Get Info dialog box for the file you highlighted appears (see fig. 11.4). If you type comments about the file in the Comments area, Word can search for files based on the text you type in this area. To close the Get Info dialog box, click the Close box.

TIP

Find File searches aren't case-sensitive. In the File Name text box, you can retrieve all the Contracts files by typing *contracts* or *Contracts*. You also needn't type all the text: If you type *image* in the File Name box, Word retrieves Business Images, Images Stack, and Logo Image.

Specifying Search Criteria

To use Find File, you choose the command from the File menu. The Search dialog box appears (see fig. 11.5). As you will learn in subsequent sections, you locate files by typing text or choosing options in this dialog box. When you choose OK, Word uses your search criteria when it searches the entire drive. When the program finds files that match the criteria you specified, a new dialog box listing the files that match these criteria appears.

Part I

Getting Started

Fig. 11.4
Get Info dialog box for the
file Proofreader's List
(Finder).

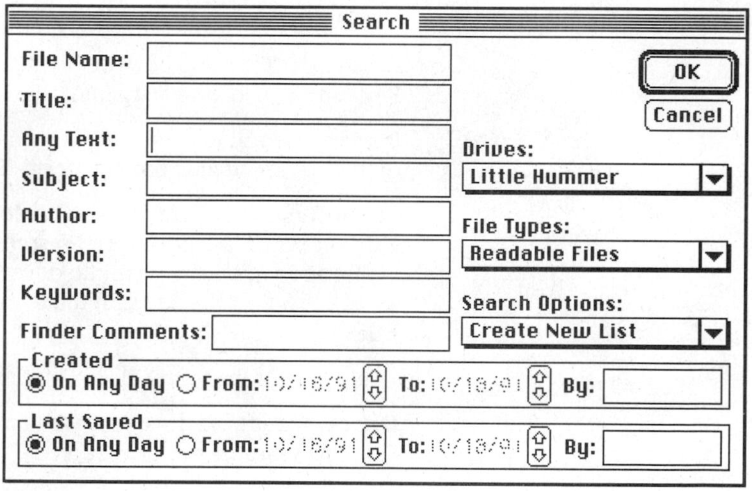

Fig. 11.5
The Search dialog box
(Find File).

You will learn more about the File List in the sections titled "Viewing File
Information" and "Sorting the File List." For now, look at the Search
dialog box to see what kinds of search criteria you can enter.

Chapter 11

Managing Documents

File Name. In this box, you type text (up to 255 characters) to match the file name you typed in the Save Current Document As box of the Save As dialog box. (This file name appears in the Finder.)

Title. Type text to match the file name you typed in the File Name box of Summary Info.

Any Text. Find File can search the full text of your document to match text you specify in this box. Type a word or phrase (up to 255 characters).

Subject. Type one or more of the describer words you typed in the Subject box of Summary Info.

Author. If more than one person uses the computer, you can search for documents by one of the authors by typing his or her name in this box. Type one of the names entered into the Author box of Summary Info. (By default, Word places the name currently listed in the Your Name box of the Preferences dialog box.)

Version. If you typed a version number in the Version box of Summary Info, you can search for the version by typing the number in this text box.

Keywords. Type one or more identifier words that you used in the Keywords box of Summary Info.

Finder Comments. Type text you entered in the Comments box of the Get Info dialog box (Finder).

Created and **Last Saved.** To search for a document by the date it was created or last saved, or to search for documents created within a range of dates, activate one of these areas and click the arrows to adjust the dates. In the By box, you can type the author's name.

On the right side of the Search dialog box, three list boxes are displayed:

Drives. Specify the drive you want Find File to search. By default, Find File searches the current drive. You can search only one drive at a time.

File Types. You specify what kinds of files you want Find File to search. By default, Find File searches Word Documents.

Search Options. You specify how you want Find File to build the file list. The first time you search, you use the default option, Create New List. After you perform one search, you can perform another. At that time, you can add new matches to the current list

(Add Matches to List), or you can tell Word to search only the list of files retrieved by the preceding search (Search Only in List).

In the following sections, you learn how to use these options.

Using Wild Cards and the OR Operator

When you type text in the Search dialog box's text areas, you can use wild cards and an OR operator (a comma). Both broaden a search so that you can retrieve more documents.

You can use a question mark to stand for any character. Suppose that you type *Essay ?* in the File Name text box. Word retrieves *Essay 1*, *Essay 2*, and *Essay 3*.

In a search, an OR operator tells the program to match records that contain *either* search term you type. If you type *contracts, proposals* in the Subject text box, Word retrieves all the documents that have the word *contracts* or the word *proposals* in the Subject area of Summary Info. (In contrast, if you type *contracts proposals*, Word retrieves only those documents that have both of these words in the Subject area.)

Finding the File

When you search for a file with Find File, you have one of two options:

- *Pinpointing a Specific File*. You can look for a file that is eluding you. You may want to see, for example, that letter in which you offered Mr. Jones a job.

- *Retrieving a Group of Files*. You can look for all the files that match one or more criteria you specify. You may want to see, for example, *all* the letters in which you discussed job offers.

In the following sections, you learn how to carry out searches in both situations. In subsequent sections, you learn what you can do with the files after you retrieve them and display them in the File List.

Searching for One File

To pinpoint a file you want to retrieve, you should type more than one criterion. You also should use criteria unique to this document. Ideally, File Find will retrieve the file you want.

To search for a file that meets your criteria, follow these steps:

1. Choose Find File from the File menu.

   The Search dialog box appears.

2. Type one or more criteria. Try to state criteria that no other file matches. The more criteria you type, the less likely it is that Word will retrieve files other than the one for which you're looking.

   If you know the exact file name, type the full file name in the File Name box. If you used identifiers, type one or more words that exclusively identify the document in the Keywords box. If you know that the document contains a word or phrase that's not in any other document, type this text in the Any Text box.

3. In the Drives list box, choose the drive you want to search.

4. In the File Types list box, choose the type of document you want Find File to search.

5. Choose OK.

The Find File dialog box appears. If Word cannot find any files that match your criteria, the Find File box contains the message, `No match-ing files found`, as shown in figure 11.6. If Word finds a file, the file name (or names) are displayed in the File List, as shown in figure 11.7. By default, Word displays the contents of the file.

> ## NOTE
>
> The folder indicator at the top of the Find File box lists the folder in which the highlighted document was found. In the scrollable window below the Contents list box, the current text of the highlighted document is displayed.

Fig. 11.6
No matching files found (Find Files dialog box).

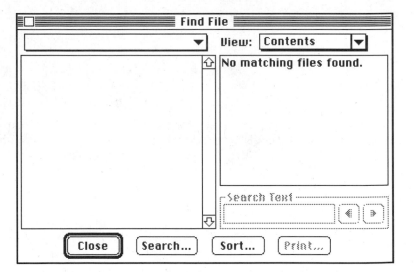

Fig. 11.7
File retrieved by pinpoint
search.

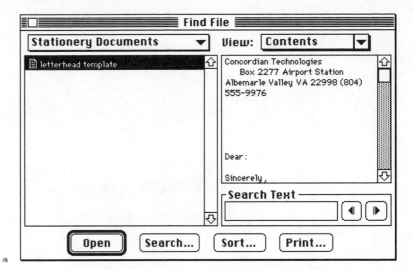

Searching for a Group of Files

To search for a group of files, you must type or choose criteria that all the files share. Avoid typing multiple criteria. The more criteria you type, the fewer files Find File is likely to retrieve.

To search for a group of files, follow these steps:

1. Choose Find File from the File menu.

2. Type a criterion that the file group shares.

   To retrieve all the documents with the word *Contracts* in the Subject box, type one criterion in the Subject box: *contracts*. If you type additional criteria, Find File probably will retrieve less files. To retrieve the Contracts files created between January and May 1992, for example, type *contracts* in the Subjects box and use the Created area to specify a From date of 1/1/92 and a To date of 3/30/92.

3. In the Drives list box, choose the drive you want to search.

4. In the File Types list box, choose the type of document you want Find File to search.

5. Choose OK.

Chapter 11
Managing Documents

The Find File dialog box appears. If Word didn't find any files that match your criteria, the Find File box contains the message, No matching files found. (refer to fig. 11.6). If Word finds a file group, the file names are displayed in the File List, as shown in figure 11.8. By default, Word displays the contents of the file.

Fig. 11.8
Group of files retrieved.

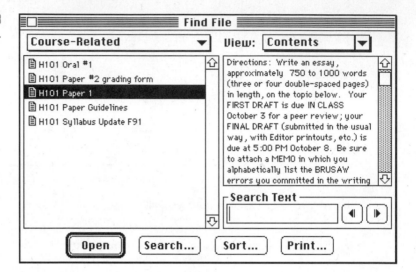

Viewing File Information

After you retrieve files, you have four options for viewing information about the files. If Word retrieved more than one file, information about the first file the program retrieved is displayed. You can view information about other files by selecting the file about which you want to see information.

The following is an overview of viewing options, which are listed in the View list box.

Contents. By default, Word shows the first 12 lines of text in the document highlighted in the File List. You can browse through the entire document. You can even search the text of this document. Type a search term or phrase (up to 255 characters) in the Search Text box, and use the forward or backward buttons to initiate the search. If you typed text in the Any Text box before starting the search, Find File echoes this text in the Search Text box, and instances of the text are highlighted in the file. Use the forward or backward buttons to display this text in context.

Statistics. Displays the author, version number, type of file, author, date of creation, date last saved, number of characters, and size (in K), as shown in figure 11.9.

Fig. 11.9
Statistics on retrieved file
(Find File).

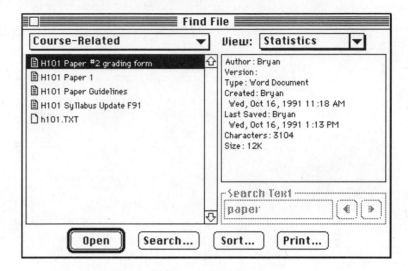

Comments. Displays the comments you typed in this document's Get Info dialog box in the Finder.

Summary Info. Displays the document's Summary Info, as you typed it when you saved the document for the first time.

Sorting the File List

If you retrieve a large group of files, you may want to sort the file list in a fashion other than the default sort (alphabetically, by file name). When you choose a sorting option, you can choose from two sort orders: Ascending and Descending. The following shows how your sort order choice affects your sorting options:

- *File Name.* Sorts in alphabetical order from A to Z (ascending) or Z to A (descending).

- *File Size.* Sorts in order of file size from smallest to largest (ascending) or largest to smallest (descending).

- *File Type.* Sorts in alphabetical order of file type from All Files to WordPerfect (ascending) or WordPerfect to All Files (descending).

Chapter 11
Managing Documents

- *Date Created*. Sorts in chronological order: oldest files first, by date of creation (ascending), or reverse chronological order, newest file first (descending).

- *Date Last Saved*. Sorts in chronological order: oldest-saved files first, by date of creation (ascending), or reverse chronological order, most recently saved file first (descending).

To sort the file list, follow these steps:

1. With more than one document displayed in the File List, choose Sort.

   The Sort dialog box appears (see fig. 11.10).

Fig. 11.10
The Sort dialog box.

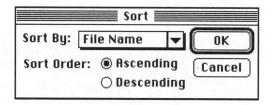

2. In the Sort By list box, choose a sorting option.

3. To sort in reverse chronological order, click Descending.

4. Choose OK to sort the File List.

Managing the Retrieved Files

After carrying out a search, you can perform the following tasks while the Search dialog box is on-screen:

- *Abandoning the Search*. Click the Close box to return to your document. (If you click the Close button after a search that fails to retrieve any documents, Word displays the Search dialog box again.)

- *Performing Another Search*. If the initial search criteria didn't work out, or if you want to change these criteria for any other reason, redo the search.

- *Opening One or More Files*. You can open the highlighted file, or you can open a group of files.

- *Printing One or More Files.* You can print the highlighted file, or you can print a group of files.

- *Copying One or More Files to Another Drive.* You can copy the highlighted file, or you can copy a group of files.

- *Deleting One or More Files.* If you install the Delete command, you can delete the highlighted file, or you can delete a group of files.

Performing Another Search

To perform another search, follow these steps:

1. Decide whether you want to reduce the current file list, add more files to the current file list, or create a completely new file list.

2. Perform one of the following actions:

   To reduce the size of the current file list without adding any new files, choose Search Only in List in the Search Options list box.

   To add more files to the current file list, choose Add Matches to List in the Search Options list box.

   To create a completely new file list, leave the Create New List option in the Search Options list box.

3. Change the search criteria or type additional search criteria.

   To broaden the search so that it retrieves more files, delete one or more of the search criteria you used, or use wild cards or the OR operator.

   To narrow the search so that it pinpoints the file you want, type search criteria that matches only that file.

4. Choose OK.

Opening One or More Files

When the File List displays one or more of the files you want, you probably should choose Open.

To open a file, highlight the file and choose Open or double-click the file name.

To open a group of files, follow these steps:

1. Select the first file you want to open.

Chapter 11
Managing Documents

2. Hold down the Shift key and click another file.

3. Repeat Step 2 until you have selected all the files you want to open.

4. Choose Open.

Printing One or More Files

With Find File, you can print files without having manually opened them, as in the following steps:

1. Use Find File to display one or more files.

2. Select the files you want to print.

3. Choose Print.

   Word opens the first file and displays the Print dialog box.

4. Choose printing options, and click OK.

5. Repeat Step 4 until you have printed all the documents.

   Word closes the documents after you print them.

Copying One or More Files

You can use the Find File command to make copies of documents, as in the following steps:

1. Use Find File to display one or more files.

2. Select the files you want to duplicate.

3. Choose Save As from the File menu.

   The Save As dialog box appears.

4. Choose a folder or drive other than the one in which you originally stored the document.

5. Choose Save.

6. To duplicate additional documents, repeat Steps 4 and 5.

   After Word duplicates the documents, it closes them.

Deleting One or More Files

If you install Word's Delete command, you can delete one or more files. (For information on installing the Delete command, see Chapter 27.)

To delete one or more files, follow these steps:

NOTE

This procedure works only for files that aren't currently opened and haven't been opened in the current operation session. Do not delete Word's temporary files while the program is running.

1. Use Find File to display one or more files.

2. Select the files you want to delete.

3. Choose Delete from the File menu.

   An alert box appears and asks whether you really want to delete the file.

4. Choose OK.

   If you selected more than one file, repeat Steps 3 and 4.

Quick Review

This section concisely summarizes the most useful information in this chapter. Check "Productivity Tips" for a review of high-productivity tips and tricks, and review "Techniques" when you forget how to perform a specific procedure.

Productivity Tips

■ Create templates for all your frequently used documents, such as letters, memos, periodic reports, newsletters, and résumés. Save these templates as stationery documents.

■ Use stationery documents to store authoritative versions of your document style sheets. If you need to modify a document's style, make the modification to the stationery document's style, and then copy the stationery document's style sheet into your current document.

■ Don't waste time hunting through folder after folder to find an elusive file. Use Find File.

■ Be sure to fill out Summary Info when you save new files. This information helps you retrieve files more efficiently with Find Files.

- To retrieve one file with Find File, type search criteria that matches only that document.

- To retrieve a group of files, type one search criterion (two at the most) that all the files are likely to share.

- To open more than one file in a working session, use Find File to group the files and then open all of them as a group.

- To print one or more files that aren't open, use Find File to display and print them.

- To copy or delete several files that aren't in the same folder, you may find Find File easier to use than the Finder.

Techniques

This section provides concise, quick-reference summaries of all the procedures introduced in this chapter.

Copying Files

To duplicate files, follow these steps:

1. Use Find File to display one or more files.

2. Select the files you want to duplicate.

3. Choose Save As from the File menu.

4. Choose a folder or drive other than the one in which you originally stored the document.

5. Choose Save.

6. To duplicate additional documents, repeat Steps 4 and 5.

Creating Stationery Documents

To create a stationery document:

1. Create a generic version of the document.

2. Choose Save from the File menu.

3. From the Save File as Type list box, choose the Stationery option.

4. Type a name for the document in the Save Current Document As text box.

5. Choose Save.

Finding a Specific File

To perform a pinpoint search for one file:

1. Choose Find File from the File menu.

2. Type two or more criteria. Try to state criteria that no other file matches.

3. In the Drives list box, choose the drive you want to search.

4. In the File Types list box, choose the type of document you want Find File to search.

5. Choose OK.

Finding a Group of Files

To find a group of files:

1. Choose Find File from the File menu.

2. Type a criterion that the file group shares. You can use wild cards or the OR operator (comma).

3. In the Drives list box, choose the drive you want to search.

4. In the File Types list box, choose the type of document you want Find File to search.

5. Choose OK.

To perform another search:

1. Perform one of the following actions:

   To reduce the size of the current file list without adding any new files, choose Search Only in List in the Search Options list box.

   To add more files to the current file list, choose Add Matches to List in the Search Options list box.

   To create a completely new file list, leave the Create New List option in the Search Options list box.

2. Change the search criteria, or type additional search criteria.

3. Choose OK.

Opening a Group of Files

To open a group of files:

1. Find the files with List Files and display the files in the file list.

2. Select the first file you want to open.

3. Hold down the Shift key and click another file.

4. Repeat Step 2 until you have selected all the files you want to open.

5. Choose Open.

Opening a Stationery Document

To open a stationery document:

1. Choose Open from the File menu, or press ⌘-O.

2. Choose the folder that contains your stationery document.

3. If this folder contains many files that are not stationery documents, choose Stationery in the List Files of Type list box.

4. Choose Open.

Printing a Group of Files

To print a group of files:

1. Find the files with List Files and display the files in the file list.

2. Select the first file you want to print.

3. Hold down the Shift key and click another file.

4. Repeat step 2 until you have selected all the files you want to print.

5. Choose Print from the File menu.

Revising a Stationery Document

To revise a stationery document:

1. Choose Open from the File menu, or press ⌘-O.

2. Choose the folder that contains your stationery document.

3. If this folder contains many files that are not stationery documents, choose Stationery in the List Files of Type list box.

4. Choose Open.

5. Make the changes.

6. Choose Save As.

7. In the Save File as Type list box, choose Stationery.

8. In the Save Current Document As box, type the name under which you previously saved the stationery document.

9. Choose Save.

10. Click Replace.

Sorting the File List

1. If more than one document is displayed in the File List, choose Sort.

2. In the Sort By list box, choose a sorting option.

3. To sort in reverse chronological order, click Descending.

4. Choose OK to sort the File List.

Creating More Complex Documents

Includes

USING
WORD 5
FOR THE
MAC

12

Outlining

A Word outline is simply another way of looking at your document. Changes you make to your outline change your document's structure. For this reason, Word's unique outlining feature provides wonderful tools for planning, creating, and revising your document.

This chapter discusses a few of the many ways you can use Word outlines. If you create an outline for your document, you can use the outline to see instantly what your document's overall structure looks like. For long documents, you can use outlining as an alternative to scrolling. For example, by switching to Outline view, you can quickly locate the beginning of a chapter, and by returning to Normal view, you can see the page on which the chapter begins.

In short, you can use Word's outlining capabilities not only for help with document planning, but also when you create long articles, business reports, books, or dissertations. If you create such documents, you can reap significant productivity gains by mastering Word's outlining features.

This chapter comprehensively covers outlining with Word 5 by discussing the following topics:

■ *Learning Outlining Concepts.* The chapter begins with an introduction to the concepts of computer outlining the Word way. You learn the meaning of key terms: outline levels, promoting and demoting headings, and collapsing and expanding headings.

- *Creating an Outline.* In this section, you learn all the major commands needed to create an outline. You learn how to understand the icons on the Outline icon bar, and then you follow a keystroke-by-keystroke tutorial to create and edit your first Word outline.

- *Restructuring the Outline.* This section introduces the commands you use to restructure your outline. You learn that when you move outline headings, Word also moves the body text under these headings. You can use this capability to restructure a long document quickly and easily by rearranging headings in the outline.

- *Using Additional Outlining Techniques.* In this section, you learn more about managing long documents with outlining, outlining a document you already have typed, automatically numbering the headings in an outline, and printing the outline (without the body text).

TIP

Does using outlining in every document you create make sense? No. Using outlining for short memos or letters is overkill. In general, you should begin with outlining only when you plan to use internal subheadings in a document.

Learning Outlining Concepts

Understanding a few key concepts and terms can help you grasp Word's outlining capabilities.

The standard arrangement for outlines is to indent headings and subheadings. Word's outlines are arranged in the same way. The first-level headings, called Level 1, are not indented; second-level headings, called Level 2, are indented once; and so on, as shown here:

Level 1 heading
Level 1 heading
  Level 2 heading
  Level 2 heading
    Level 3 heading
    Level 3 heading
  Level 2 heading
Level 1 heading

In a Word outline, you can change the position of an outline heading in the hierarchy of levels. You can *promote* an outline heading (move the heading up one logical level, such as from Level 2 to Level 1), or you can *demote* an outline heading (move the heading down one logical level, such as from Level 2 to Level 3).

You also can *collapse* (hide) the subheadings under a heading so that you can see the structure of your outline more clearly. For example, you see the subheadings in the following outline:

Part II

Creating More Complex Documents

I. Varietal wines of California
   A. Chardonnay
   B. Sauvignon Blanc
   C. Cabernet Sauvignon
   D. Merlot
II. Varietal wines of Australia
   A. Chardonnay
   B. Sauvignon Blanc
   C. Cabernet Sauvignon
   D. Merlot

If you collapse the subheadings, you have the following outline:

I. Varietal wines of California
II. Varietal wines of Australia

After you have collapsed the headings, you must *expand* them to see the subheadings again.

After you add text to your document, the document has *body text* (text paragraphs rather than headings) as well as outline headings. As you add text, you need to collapse the body text so that only the headings are visible in the outline.

If you have used a computer outlining program before, these features are not new to you. What makes Word's outlining feature stand out, however, is its seamless integration with your document. As you make changes in your outline, the changes are reflected in your document, and as you make changes in your document's headings and subheadings, the changes are reflected automatically in your outline. You can switch at any time to Outline view for a quick view of your document's overall structure. As writing experts know, having a solid overall structure is one of the best ways to ensure high quality in reports, articles, and other long documents you create.

Creating an Outline

SPEED KEY

The first step in creating an outline is to switch to the Outline view. To do so, choose Outline from the View menu, or use the ⌘-Option-O shortcut. The Outline icon bar appears, with icons that perform special functions in the Outline view (see fig. 12.1). In this view, you can enter headings and subheadings, demoting and promoting them to the levels you prefer.

Chapter 12
Outlining

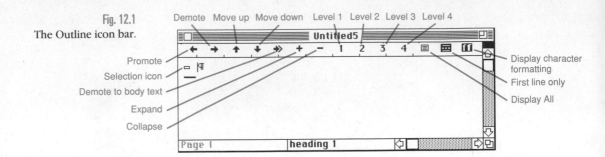

Fig. 12.1
The Outline icon bar.

This section gives you a brief overview of the icons on the Outline icon bar. You learn more about what these icons do in the following sections. For now, just note what these icons do and that most of them have keyboard shortcuts.

Users of previous versions of Word should note the many changes in Outlining keyboard shortcuts. Note that the arrow keys no longer move headings; you first must press Option.

Promote (Option-left arrow). Choose the Promote icon to move a heading up one logical level.

Demote (Option-right arrow). Choose the Demote icon to move a heading down one logical level.

Move Up (Option-up arrow). Choose the Move Up icon to restructure the outline by moving a heading up.

Move Down (Option-down arrow). Choose the Move Down icon to restructure the outline by moving a heading down.

Demote to Body Text (⌘-right arrow). Choose the Body Text icon to transform a heading into ordinary body text.

Expand (Keypad-plus). Choose the Expand icon to show any subheadings that have been collapsed under the current heading.

Collapse (Keypad-minus) Choose the Collapse icon to hide the subheadings under the current heading.

Level 1. Show only the Level 1 headings; collapse all others.

Level 2. Show the Level 1 and Level 2 headings; collapse all others.

Level 3. Show the Level 1, 2, and 3 headings; collapse all others.

Level 4. Show the Level 1, 2, 3, and 4 headings; collapse all others.

Display All (Keypad-*). The Display All icon works like a toggle command. On the first click, Display All collapses all the body text under all headings. (A dotted underline indicates that body text has been hidden under the headings.) On the second click, Display All expands the body text.

Display First Line Only (Keypad-equals) The Display First Line Only icon, which is highlighted by default, also works like a toggle. Word automatically displays all the body text under a heading. When you choose the Display First Line Only icon to turn off the highlight, Word shows only the first line of body text under a heading.

Display Character Formatting (Keypad-/). The Display Character Formatting icon, which is highlighted by default, displays the outline headings with the formatting Word automatically applies, or with whatever formatting you have chosen.

Level Marks. The small vertical marks along the bottom of the Outline icon bar are level marks, showing where Word aligns the headings by level.

The Outline icon bar is useful, but keep in mind that you can duplicate most of its functions by using mouse procedures that are unique to Outline view. For example, you can demote or promote a heading simply by dragging the Selection icon (the outlined dash or plus sign next to each heading or subheading) to the right or left. In the tutorial that begins in the next section, you learn how to use this and other mouse techniques in Outline view.

Creating a Sample Outline

T o explore outlining, start by opening an outline in a new document. (Start with a new document so that you don't have to deal with body text. You learn about outlining an existing document later in this chapter.) Follow these steps:

1. Start Word and display a new document or choose New from the File menu.

2. Choose Outline from the View menu, or press ⌘-Option-O. If you have an extended keyboard, you can press Shift-F13.

This tutorial continues in the following sections.

Creating Headings and Subheadings

When you type in Outline view, Word enters the lines you type as outline headings, not as body text. The following steps give you a quick guide to creating an outline for document planning purposes:

1. Begin typing your outline by entering the title (*Fall Quarter Report*) on the first line. Before you type anything under this heading, the first line is preceded by an outlined dash. This icon indicates that the line contains an outline heading, but no sub-headings.

2. After you type the Level 1 heading, press Return. Word moves the insertion point to the next line, and another outline heading icon appears.

3. Demote the current heading (the second line in the window), using one of the following procedures:

   Drag the Selection icon right. As you drag the icon, the mouse pointer changes shape to an arrow pointing both ways, indicating that you can demote or promote the heading. A dotted vertical line appears to help you align the heading with the level marks on the Outline icon bar. Drag the Selection icon right until you have aligned the vertical line with the Level 2 mark, and release the mouse button.

   Choose the Demote icon on the Outline icon bar.

   Press Option-right arrow.

Fig. 12.2
Starting the outline.

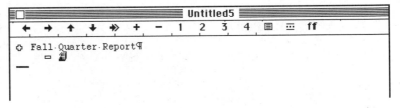

4. Type the Level 2 heading: *Introduction*.

5. Continue by typing additional Level 2 headings, as follows:

   Review of Summer Quarter Performance
   Fall Quarter Performance Data
       Sales
               Corporate
               Direct

Part II

Creating More Complex Documents

6. Choose Save from the File menu. When the Save As dialog box appears, type *Fall Quarter Report* in the Save Current Document As text box. Then choose Save.

Your outline should look like the one in figure 12.3.

Fig. 12.3
An outline with second-, third-, and fourth-level headings.

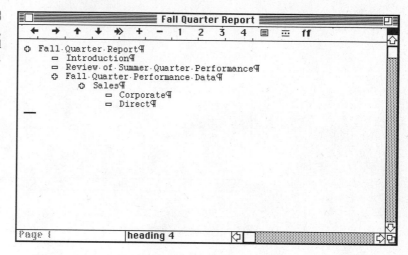

7. Press Return to start a new heading, and promote the heading one level, using one of the following methods:

Drag the Selection icon left until the icon aligns with the Level 2 mark.

Choose the Promote icon on the Outline icon bar.

Press Option-left arrow.

8. With the insertion point positioned in a blank Level 3 heading, continue typing the outline as follows:

> Inventory
> Shipping
> Quality Control
> Customer Service
>> Technical Assistance
>> Returns and Refunds
> Accounting
Analysis of Performance Data
Recommendations

Chapter 12

Outlining

Figure 12.4 shows the outline you have created.

Fig. 12.4
The finished draft of
the outline.

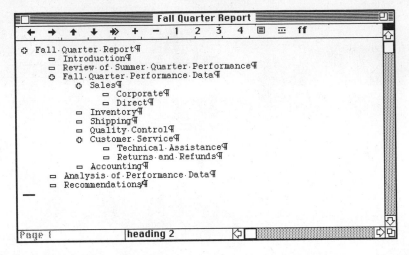

Returning to Normal View

After you have roughed out the overall plan for your document, you can return to Normal view to see how your headings look with the default heading styles that Word assigns to your headings when you choose outline levels. To return to Normal view, choose Normal from the View menu or press ⌘-Option-N.

If you aren't satisfied with the predefined styles for heading levels, you may want to redefine them.

Redefining the Heading Styles

You learn more about redefining Word's default styles in Chapter 8. So rather than explain everything about redefining styles, this section gives you a basic, step-by-step tutorial on how to redefine outline heading styles.

To redefine the heading styles, follow these steps:

1. If necessary, display the ruler (⌘-R) and the ribbon (⌘-Option-R).

2. Highlight the first heading, *Fall Quarter Report*.

3. Format the heading as follows: choose the Centered Alignment button in the ruler, choose the Underline button in the ribbon to turn off underlining, and then pull down the font size list box in the ribbon and choose 18. Your heading is now centered and boldfaced in 18-point Helvetica, and the underlining is removed.

4. Choose the style name in the style list box on the ruler, so that the style name in the box (Heading 1) is highlighted.

5. Press Return.

   You see the Style dialog box, as shown in figure 12.5.

Fig. 12.5
Redefining the
Heading 1 style.

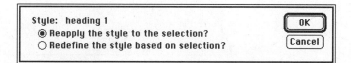

6. Activate the second option to redefine the style, based on the selected text.

7. Choose OK. Word redefines the Heading 1 style for this document only.

8. Place the insertion point within the first Level 2 heading (*Introduction*) and choose the Centered Alignment button in the ruler.

9. Repeat Steps 4 through 7 to redefine the Heading 2 style.

   The other Level 2 heads take on the same style, as shown in figure 12.6.

10. Place the insertion point within the first Level 3 heading (*Sales*). On the ruler, point to the lower of the two Left Indent buttons and drag left to align the left indent with the 0 mark on the ruler.

11. Repeat Steps 4 through 7 to redefine the Heading 3 style.

12. Select the first Level 4 heading (*Corporate*) and choose the Underline button on the ribbon to turn off underlining. Then choose the Italic button on the ribbon to turn on italic. On the ruler, point to the lower of the two Left Indent buttons and drag left to align the left indent with the 0 mark on the ruler.

Chapter 12
Outlining

Fig. 12.6
Redefined Level 1 and
Level 2 heading styles.

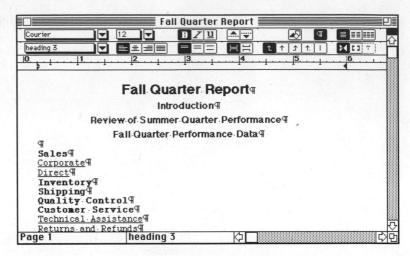

Fig. 12.6
Redefined Level 1 and
Level 2 heading styles.

13. Repeat Steps 4 through 7 to redefine the Heading 4 style.

Your headings should now look like those in figure 12.7.

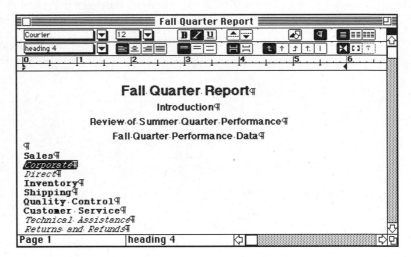

Fig. 12.7
The document after you
redefine the headings.

Don't worry about losing the outline's pattern of indentations when you redefine the styles. Even after you center the Heading 1 format and remove the indentations from the other heading styles, the indentation logic is preserved when you choose Outline view again (see fig. 12.8).

Part II

Creating More Complex Documents

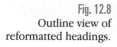
Fig. 12.8
Outline view of
reformatted headings.

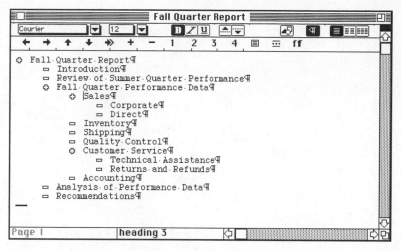

Adding Body Text

After you create and format the pattern of headings and subheadings for your document, you're ready to add body text. In the following tutorial, you add body text by typing some text and copying it elsewhere on your outline. (You wouldn't do so if you were creating a real document, but this tutorial gives you a way to explore this feature.)

To add body text to the Fall Quarter Report, follow these steps:

1. Choose Show ¶ from the Edit menu, if necessary, so you can see the paragraph marks.

2. If your document is still in Outline view, choose Normal from the View menu.

3. Place the cursor at the end of the first Level 2 heading (*Introduction*) but before the paragraph mark, and press Return.

4. Type the following text (or make up your own):

   This is a paragraph of body text. It serves no purpose other than to illustrate what text looks like when you put body text into a document that contains an outline.

5. Select the whole paragraph of text you just entered (but not the paragraph mark at the end of it).

Chapter 12
Outlining

6. Choose Copy from the Edit menu or press ⌘-C. You have copied the paragraph to the Clipboard.

7. Place the insertion point at the end of the next heading (but before the paragraph mark) and press Return to start a new line of body text.

8. Choose Paste from the Edit menu or press ⌘-V.

9. Repeat Steps 7 and 8 for each heading and subheading in your document to which you want to add body text. (Remember that Level 1, which is the document's title, does not need body text.)

10. Drag the scroll box to the top of the vertical scroll bar to display the beginning of the document. The paragraphs of body text are jammed up against the headings.

11. To add blank space between the body text and the headings, position the insertion point within the first paragraph of body text and choose the Blank Line Spacing button on the ruler. (The Blank Line Spacing button is positioned between the Line Spacing and Tab buttons and looks like a letter H with the top and the bottom parts of the letter pried apart.)

12. Redefine the Normal style by highlighting the style list box, pressing Return, and choosing the second option, Redefine the Style Based on Selection. You have added one blank line before each paragraph of body text.

13. Choose Save to save the document.

Your document should look like the one in figure 12.9.

Fig. 12.9
The document with body text added beneath each heading.

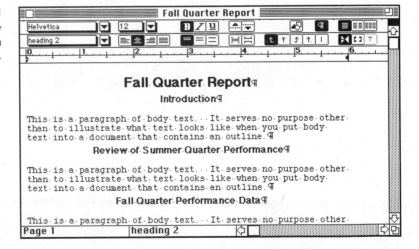

Part II

Creating More Complex Documents

Collapsing Body Text

After you add body text, you can see the body text when you return to the Outline view. In this part of the tutorial, you learn how to hide the body text.

To hide the body text you added to Fall Quarter Report, follow these steps:

1. To return to the Outline view, choose Outline from the View menu or press ⌘-Option-O. You see the outline with the first line of body text visible (see fig. 12.10)

Fig. 12.10
The outline with first line
of body text visible.

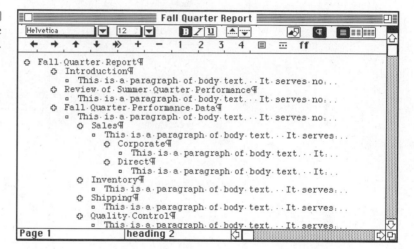

2. Choose the Display First Line icon on the Outline icon bar or press Keypad-equals until you see all the body text (see fig. 12.11).

3. To collapse all the body text, choose the Display All icon or press Keypad-*. After you hide (collapse) the body text, the headings with hidden body text are displayed with fuzzy gray underlining.

Adding and Deleting Headings

Adding and deleting headings is easy with Version 5 of Word. To add a heading, follow these steps:

Chapter 12
Outlining

Fig. 12.11
The outline with all body
text visible.

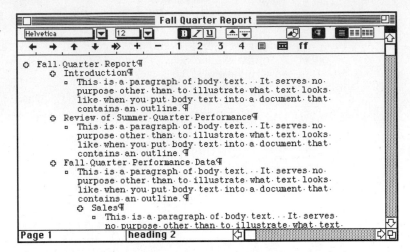

1. Position the insertion point after the subheading *Direct* (but before the paragraph mark), and press Return. Word creates a new Level 3 heading. (Note that the new headings you create this way always take on the level of the following heading.)

2. Press Return again to enter another new heading.

To delete a heading, follow these steps:

1. Move the mouse pointer over the Selection icon until the pointer shape changes to a symbol with arrows pointing four ways.

2. Click the mouse button to select the heading you want to delete.

3. Press Delete or Backspace to delete the heading.

4. Position the insertion point on the one new heading that remains, and type *Manufacturing*.

Your outline now should look like the one in figure 12.12. Note that because the new heading has no body text, no fuzzy gray underlining appears below the heading.

Collapsing and Expanding Headings

An outline with many levels of subheadings can become so long that it no longer gives you a quick way to view the overall structure of the document. You can avoid this problem by collapsing (hiding) subheadings. You can collapse all the subheadings under a specific heading or you can collapse all the subheadings in your outline down to a level you specify. After you collapse subheadings, you can expand them again when you need to view the subheadings.

NOTE

Whether you use the mouse or the keyboard, editing your outline in Word 5 is easy. The arrow keys work just like they do in a document. (In previous versions of Word, the arrow keys moved the headings; now you press Option before using the arrow keys to move headings.)

Part II

Creating More Complex Documents

Fig. 12.12
The outline with an
added heading.

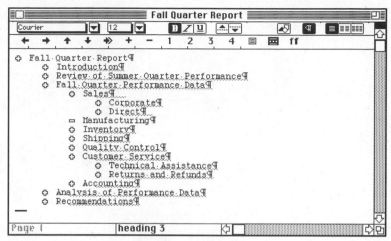

To collapse headings in the Fall Quarter Report document, follow these steps:

1. Place the insertion point on the heading titled *Fall Quarter Performance Data*.

2. Choose the Collapse icon (the minus icon on the Outline icon bar) or press Keypad-minus. Word collapses the Level 4 subheadings, leaving the list of Level 3 subheadings under the *Fall Quarter Performance Data* heading, as shown in figure 12.13.

Fig. 12.13
The outline with Level 4
subheadings collapsed.

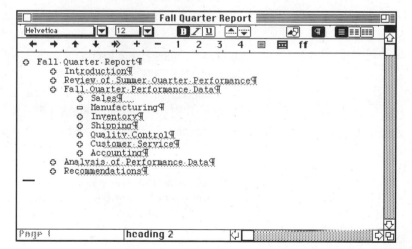

Chapter 12

Outlining

3. Choose the Collapse icon again or press Keypad-minus again. Word collapses the Level 3 subheadings this time, leaving only the Level 1 and 2 subheadings on-screen (see fig 12.14).

Fig. 12.14
The outline collapsed to
show only Level 1 and
Level 2 headings.

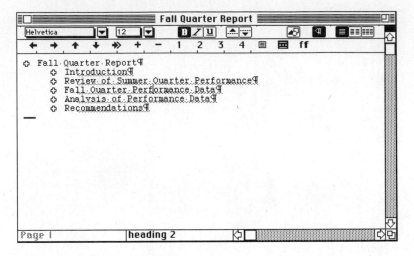

To expand headings in the Fall Quarter Report document, follow these steps:

1. Choose the Expand icon (the plus sign on the Outline icon bar,) or press Keypad-plus. Word expands the headings to show the Level 3 heads.

2. Choose the Expand icon again or press Keypad-plus again. Now you see the Level 4 heads, too.

3. Choose the Expand icon or press Keypad-plus a third time. Now you see the body text.

4. Choose the Collapse icon or press Keypad-minus twice so that only the Level 3 subheadings are displayed.

5. Place the insertion point within the *Customer Service* heading and choose the Expand icon or press Keypad-plus. Word expands only the subheadings directly under the Customer Service heading.

6. Choose the Collapse icon or press Keypad-minus so that only the Level 3 subheadings are displayed.

Part II

Creating More Complex Documents

Collapsing Headings to a Level You Specify

The Collapse and Expand icons (or Keypad-minus and Keypad-plus) affect only the current heading—the heading in which the insertion point is positioned. By using the Level icons on the Outline icon bar (the numbers 1 through 4), however, you can display the entire outline to a level you specify.

To display the outline to a level you specify, follow these steps:

1. Choose the Level 1 icon on the Outline icon bar. Only one heading, the Level 1 heading, appears on-screen.

2. Choose the Level 2 icon. Only the Level 1 and Level 2 headings appear on-screen.

3. Choose the Level 3 icon. Now, in addition to Levels 1 and 2, the Level 3 headings appear on-screen.

Restructuring the Outline

 hen you restructure an outline by moving headings, Word moves the body text, too. You also can sort headings. With these tools, you can restructure a huge document in seconds.

Moving Headings

TIP

Another way you can restructure your outline is to promote or demote headings. By demoting *Review of Summer Quarter Performance*, you can make the heading part of the Introduction. You also can promote or demote headings after you move them. For example, position *Review of Summer Quarter Performance* under *Recommendations*, then demote the *Review* heading so that it becomes part of *Recommendations*.

In the following steps, you learn how to move a heading up and down in the outline.

To restructure the Fall Quarter Report outline, follow these steps:

1. Place the insertion point in the *Accounting* subheading.

2. Choose the Move Heading Up icon in the Outline icon bar (the up arrow) or press Option-up arrow. Word moves up in the outline the *Accounting* heading—and all the body text under the heading.

3. Keep choosing Move Heading Up or pressing Option-up arrow to see what happens. Move the heading above the *Fall Quarter Performance* Data heading. Word keeps the heading at Level 3, no matter where you place the heading.

4. To move the Accounting heading down, choose the Move Heading Down icon in the Outline icon bar (the down arrow) or press Option-down arrow. Position the heading at the beginning of the headings under *Fall Quarter Performance Data*.

Chapter 12
Outlining

Sorting Headings

The Level 3 headings in this outline should be in alphabetical order. You can arrange them yourself, as you did when you moved the Accounting heading to the top of the Level 3 headings, or you can have Word do this tedious job for you.

To sort the Level 3 headings, follow these steps:

1. Choose the Level 3 icon in the Outline icon bar so that the Level 4 headings are hidden.

2. Select the Level 3 headings under *Fall Quarter Performance Data*, as shown in figure 12.15.

3. Choose Sort from the Tools menu. Word sorts the headings (see fig. 12.16).

Fig. 12.15
Selected Level 3 headings.

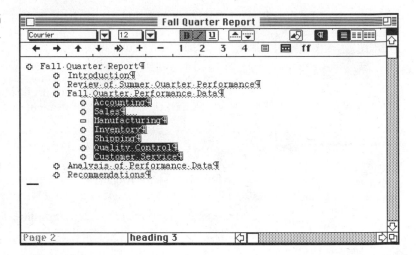

Using Additional Outlining Techniques

Now that you have learned how to type body text, automatically number the headings in an outline, and print the outline without the body text, you are ready to learn more about outlining in Word 5. In this section, you learn about managing long documents with outlining, outlining a document you already have typed, numbering the headings in an outline, and printing your document's outline without the body text.

Fig. 12.16
Sorted Level 3 headings.

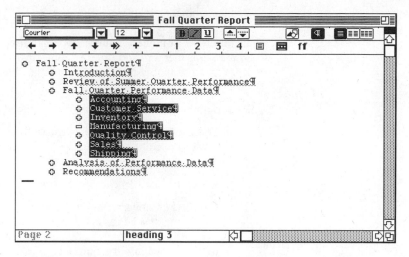

Fall Quarter Report

```
⌖ Fall·Quarter·Report¶
    ⌖ Introduction¶
        ⌖ Review·of·Summer·Quarter·Performance¶
        ⌖ Fall·Quarter·Performance·Data¶
            ⌖ Accounting¶
            ⌖ Customer·Service¶
            ⌖ Inventory¶
            ▱ Manufacturing¶
            ⌖ Quality·Control¶
            ⌖ Sales¶
            ⌖ Shipping¶
        ⌖ Analysis·of·Performance·Data¶
        ⌖ Recommendations¶
```

Page 2   heading 3

Managing a Long Document with Outlining

TIP

When you sort outline headings, you not only sort the headings, you also sort the whole document, including the body text under the headings. If you sort outline headings, you can restructure your document much more quickly than if you use ordinary cut-and-paste techniques.

When you create a long document, keep in mind the advantages of switching to Outline view to get a quick view of your document's structure. You can hide body text and collapse subheadings quickly by choosing one of the Level icons.

To use the Outline view to move quickly through a document rather than scroll page by page, follow these steps:

1. Choose Outline from the View menu.

2. Position the heading to which you want to scroll at the top of the outline window.

3. Choose Normal or Page Layout from the View menu.

Outlining an Existing Document

To take full advantage of outlining, you can add headings to an existing document. The key to adding headings is to format the headings with Word's built-in heading styles, such as Heading 1, Heading 2. In Chapter 8, you learn how to apply Word's built-in styles to headings. After you format your headings this way, they appear as outline headings when you switch to Outline view.

Numbering Outline Headings

If you prefer a numbered outline, you can use the Renumber command in the Tools menu to add numbers quickly. In the following tutorial, you learn how to number the Level 3 headings under *Fall Quarter Performance Data*.

To add numbers to selected headings, follow these steps:

1. Because Word numbers only the outline headings that are visible on-screen, collapse the Level 4 headings, if necessary, by choosing the Level 3 icon.

2. Select the Level 3 headings, as you did when you sorted them.

3. Choose Renumber from the Tools menu. The Renumber dialog box appears (see fig. 12.17). The default settings are fine. The numbering will start at 1 and all selected headings will be formatted. Word will use the number series 1, 2, 3, and so on, rather than the legal numbering series.

Fig. 12.17
The Renumber dialog box.

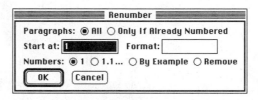

4. Choose OK. Word numbers the Level 3 headings.

You learn more about the other options in the Renumber dialog box in Chapter 19.

Printing Your Outline

Keeping a printout of your outline on-hand gives you another way of keeping your document's structure in mind. The procedure for printing an outline is simple. To print your outline, follow these steps:

1. Collapse headings and body text to a specific level by choosing one of the Show Level Numbers icons. Word prints only what is displayed, no matter how much body text or other material is collapsed.

TIP

Word does not change these numbers if you insert or delete a heading within the numbered list. When you insert or delete a heading, select the headings again, and then choose the Renumber command again.

2. Choose Print from the File menu or press ⌘-P.

3. Choose OK to print your document.

Quick Review

This section concisely summarizes the most useful information in this chapter. Check "Productivity Tips" for a review of high-productivity tips and tricks, and review "Techniques" when you forget how to perform a specific procedure.

Productivity Tips

■ Learn outlining techniques if you plan to write documents (such as articles or proposals) that will have internal subheadings. Word's Outline helps you get organized and provides powerful document-restructuring tools.

■ The icons on the Outline icon bar are useful, but most of the icons have powerful analogs in more direct mouse techniques. For example, you can promote or demote a heading just by dragging the Selection icon left or right.

■ If you do not like Word's default heading styles, you should redefine them before creating your document.

■ Let Word alphabetize or number the headings in your document. Switch to Outline view, display and select the headings, and then choose Sort or Renumber from the Tools menu.

■ If you're working with a long document that has headings and subheadings, you can find your way around the document by switching to Outline view. Use the Outline view to find a section rather than scroll page after page on-screen.

Techniques

This section provides concise, quick-reference summaries of all the procedures introduced in this chapter.

Collapsing Headings

To collapse the subheadings under a heading:

1. Place the insertion point within the heading.
2. Choose the Collapse icon or use the Keypad-minus shortcut.

To collapse headings to a level you specify:

Choose one of the Level icons on the Outline icon bar.

Demoting Headings

To demote a heading:

Drag the Selection icon right.

or

Choose the Demote icon on the Outline icon bar.

or

Press Option-right arrow.

Displaying Body Text

To toggle between full display and first-line display of body text:

Choose the Display First Line icon on the Outline icon bar or press ⌘-Shift-Down.

To hide body text:

Choose the Display All icon or press ⌘-Shift-Left.

To demote a heading to body text:

Choose the Demote to Body Text icon or press ⌘-right arrow.

Displaying Character Formatting

To toggle the display of character formatting on and off:

Choose the Display Character Formatting icon or use the Option-Shift-Up arrow or Keypad-/ keyboard shortcut.

Editing the Outline

To delete a heading:

1. Move the pointer over the heading's Selection icon until the pointer changes shape, and then click the mouse button to select the heading.

2. Press Delete or Backspace.

To move a heading up in the outline:

Choose the Move Heading Up icon or press Option-up arrow.

To move a heading down in the outline:

Choose the Move Heading Down icon or press Option-down-arrow.

Expanding Headings

To expand the headings under a heading:

1. Place the insertion point within the heading.

2. Choose the Expand icon or press Keypad-plus.

Numbering Headings

To number headings in an outline:

1. Collapse the subheadings under the headings you want to alphabetize.

2. Select the headings

3. Choose Renumber from the Tools menu.

4. Choose OK.

Printing an Outline

To print your outline:

1. Display the headings you want to print. Collapse body text, if you want to.

2. Choose Print from the File menu.

Promoting Headings

To promote a heading:

Drag the Selection icon left.

or

Choose the Promote icon on the Outline icon bar.

or

Press Option-left arrow.

Sorting Headings

To alphabetize headings:

1. Collapse the subheadings under the headings you want to alphabetize.

2. Select the headings.

3. Choose Sort from the Tools menu.

Using Glossaries

I f you have to say the same thing over and over, and if saying the right thing is important, Word's glossaries are for you. Using Word's glossaries, you can store carefully worded passages of text, ranging from a few words to dozens of pages. You can access these glossaries quickly and easily.

Using glossaries makes possible a range of high-productivity writing applications, as shown by the following examples:

- An attorney can store and retrieve standardized passages for documents, such as wills or contracts.

- A small-business owner can create and retrieve paragraphs that respond to typical questions people ask in letters of inquiry, so that answering a letter takes only a matter of seconds.

- Because glossaries can handle graphics as well as text, a graphics designer can store frequently used graphics such as logos or product illustrations and retrieve them from the glossary with a keystroke.

In short, glossaries are another of Word's many features for high-productivity writing. If you're not using glossaries, you're missing ways to save time and money.

This chapter covers the following subjects:

- *Learning about Glossaries.* In this section, you learn what glossaries are and how to create, store, and use them.

USING
WORD 5
FOR THE
MAC

■ *Creating and Managing Glossary Entries.* This section covers the procedures you use to create glossary entries, insert glossaries into your document, and manage glossary entries (editing, renaming, and deleting).

■ *Managing Glossary Files.* Most Word users find the Standard Glossary file fully adequate for their needs. Some users may want to create specialized glossary files for certain applications (such as keeping a storehouse of graphics for a newsletter). If you need to create specialized glossary files, this section explains how to create and use glossary files.

Compared to previous versions of Word, not much is new in Word 5's glossaries, except an expanded list of standard glossaries (also called supplied glossaries). In addition, you can use two new check boxes in the Glossary dialog box—Standard Entries and User Entries—to control the display of glossary entries. Both are activated by default. To hide all Word's predefined standard entries so that you see only glossary entries you have created (such as Author), deactivate Standard Entries. To hide your own entries, deactivate the User Entries check box, leaving only the standard entries displayed.

Learning About Glossaries

The term *glossary* isn't very descriptive. The term dates to the days when this feature really was used to store a glossary of words, terms, and phrases. Back in the days of limited computer memory (64K was considered wildly luxurious), you could store only limited amounts of text in a glossary entry. Writers used glossaries to store only single words or short phrases. If you had to type *autochthonous processes of spontaneous generation* over and over, for instance, you could store the phrase as a glossary item and retrieve it by typing *apsg* and entering a keyboard command.

The glossary feature is far more useful now than in the early days of personal computing. You still can use Word's glossaries to store terms and phrases, but now that storage space is limited only by the size of your disk, you can store long passages of text—or even graphics—in glossaries. Furthermore, Word's glossaries retain the formats you have applied to the text you store in them. With such increased versatility, glossaries could be called "cubbyholes" for frequently accessed units of fully formatted text, such as a return address complete with a corporate logo.

Each glossary item you create and store becomes a glossary entry in a glossary file. A *glossary entry* is a named unit of text or graphics. You can place hundreds of glossary entries in each glossary file. The only limit is the size of your disk. After creating the entry, you quickly and easily can insert the entry in your document, using a menu technique or a keyboard shortcut.

You can create more than one *glossary file*. By default, Word uses a glossary file called the Standard Glossary. If you plan to create only a few (one or two dozen) glossary entries, you can use the Standard Glossary to store all your entries. You can add hundreds of glossary entries to the Standard Glossary, but the list of entries would become too long to scroll through conveniently. For this reason, you can create additional, custom glossary files, in which you can place infrequently used or specialized glossary entries.

The Standard Glossary contains *standard glossary entries*, which all have special uses (see table 13.1). These standard glossaries are available in any glossary, even the ones you create. Note that most of these glossary entries fall into one of the following three categories:

- *Date and Time entries.* Glossary entries such as Date or Print Date can enter the current date or time directly into your document or add the date or time at the time of printing.

- *Summary Info entries.* Summary Info glossary entries enter text you type in the corresponding boxes of the current document's Summary Info dialog box. These boxes include Title, Subject, Author, Version, and Keywords. If you do not fill out Summary Info, Word does not enter anything when you choose the corresponding glossary entry (except Author, which uses the name you typed when you installed Word). This fact suggests yet another rationale for filling out those summary info sheets, which are advantageous for file management purposes. If you fill out the Title box, for instance, you can enter the document's title quickly just by choosing the Title glossary.

- *File Name entries.* These glossary entries place the name of the current file into your document.

Table 13.1
Standard Glossary Entries

Entry	Description
author	Enters the name of the author, as defined in the Summary Info dialog box
date abbreviated	Enters the current date in abbreviated form (*Sat, Apr 1, 1992*)
date long	Enters the current date in long form (*Saturday, April 1, 1992*)
date short	Enters the current date in short form (*4/1/92*)

Table 13.1 Continued	Entry	Description
	day abbreviated	Enters the current day of the week in short form (*Sat.*)
	day long	Enters the current day of the week (*Saturday*)
	day of the month	Enters the current day of the month (*15*)
	file name only	Enters the name of the current file (*Fall Quarter Report 1992*)
	file name with path	Enters the name of the current document including volume, folder, and filename (*HD80:Periodic Reports:Spring Quarter Report 1992*)
	keywords	Enters the current document's keywords, as currently defined in the Summary Info dialog box
	month abbreviated	Enters the current month in abbreviated form (*Oct*)
	month long	Enters the current month in long form (*December*)
	page number	Enters a page number at the insertion point's location. The number will print in this location on all pages of the current section
	print date abbreviated	Prints the date at the time of printing, in abbreviated form (*Sat, Apr 1, 1992*)
	print date long	Prints the date at the time of printing, in long form (*Friday, April 1, 1992*)
	print date short	Prints the date at the time of printing, in short form (*4/1/92*) index. Enters the proper index code as hidden text
	print day abbreviated	Prints the day at the time of printing, in long form (*Friday*)
	print day of the month	Prints the day of the month (*15*) at time of printing
	print merge	Inserts the special symbols used to create Print Merge instructions

Part II

Creating More Complex Documents

Entry	Description
print month abbreviated	Prints the current month in abbreviated form at the time of printing (*Apr*)
print month long	Prints the current month in long form at the time of printing (*April*)
print time	Prints the time (*10:51 AM*) at the time of printing.
print time with seconds	Prints the time with seconds (*10:51:46 AM*) at the time of printing
print year long	Prints the year at the time of printing (*1992*)
print year short	Prints the year in short form (*92*) at the time of printing
section	Enters the current section number
subject	Enters the text you placed in the Subject box of the current document's Summary Info
time	Inserts the current time (*10:51 AM*)
time with seconds	Inserts the current time with seconds (*10:51:46 AM*)
version	Enters the version number you placed in the Version box of the current document's Summary Info
year long	Enters the current year (*1992*)
year short	Enters the current year in short form (*92*)

TIP

If you create stationery documents as described in Chapter 11, use the Print entries to enter the date at the time of printing. Your letters and reports will always have the correct date.

These standard glossary entries are always available, even if you create your own glossary files. When you create a new glossary file, Word copies all default glossary entries to the new file. Glossary files always contain the standard glossary entries, and you cannot delete these entries. To help you distinguish the default glossary entries from the ones you create, a bullet precedes the names of the default entries in the Glossary dialog box (see fig. 13.1).

Chapter 13
Using Glossaries

Fig. 13.1
Bullets precede Standard
Glossary entries in the
Glossary dialog box.

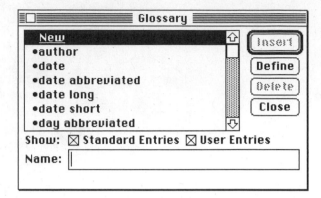

Creating and Managing Glossary Entries

To create a glossary entry, select the text or graphic and choose Glossary from the Edit menu. After creating a glossary entry, you can insert, edit, rename, or delete the entry. This section discusses these tasks.

Creating Glossary Entries

You can copy any amount of text to a glossary. You also can copy a graphic or text mixed with graphics. When you create the glossary entry, Word does not copy the formatting unless you include a paragraph mark(s) in the selection.

To create a glossary entry, follow these steps:

1. Select the text or graphic you want to store in a glossary. To include paragraph formats in the glossary, be sure to include the trailing paragraph mark in the selection.

2. Choose Glossary from the Edit menu. New is selected in the list box in the Glossary window (again see fig. 13.1).

3. Type a glossary entry name in the Name box. You can use up to 32 characters (including spaces) to name glossary entries. Keep the name as short and as easy to remember as possible.

4. Choose the Define button. Word defines the glossary entry and adds the name of the new entry to the glossary list.

5. Choose Close.

TIP

To include formatting in your glossary entries, choose Show ¶ from the View menu, press ⌘-J or choose the ¶ button on the ribbon. Include the paragraph mark in the selection before you choose the Glossary command.

Inserting Glossary Entries

After you create a glossary entry, you can use the menus or the keyboard to insert the entry into your text. If you use the menus to insert the entry, you don't need to know the exact name of the entry (you choose the entry you want from the list box). To insert the entry with the keyboard, you must know the exact name.

To use the Glossary dialog box to insert a glossary entry, follow these steps:

TIP

Defining a glossary entry isn't the same as saving the entry. Although you cannot quit the program without Word prompting you to save the changes you have made to your glossary, Word doesn't save your glossary entries when you save your document. Saving a glossary requires a separate procedure, described later in "Managing Glossary Files."

1. Place the insertion point where you want the glossary entry to appear.

2. Choose Glossary from the Edit menu or press ⌘-K.

3. From the Glossary window's list box, choose the entry you want.

   When you select an item in the list box, Word displays the entry's first line at the bottom of the dialog box (see fig. 13.2). To reduce the number of entries displayed, you can deactivate the Standard Entries or User Entries check boxes.

Fig. 13.2
Glossary contents shown at bottom of the Glossary dialog box.

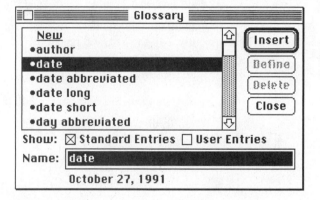

4. Choose Insert. Word inserts the glossary entry at the insertion point.

To insert a glossary entry with the keyboard, follow these steps:

1. Position the insertion point where you want the glossary entry to appear.

2. Press ⌘-Delete or press ⌘-Backspace.

TIP

If you forget to place the insertion point where you want the glossary entry to appear, choose Copy from the Edit menu to copy the entry to the clipboard. Then choose Cancel.

Chapter 13
Using Glossaries

TIP

If you frequently choose a certain glossary entry, add that entry to the Work menu. For information, see Chapter 27.

3. When the lower left corner of the status line displays the message Name, type the name of the glossary entry and press Return. You don't have to type the full name—just enough of it so that Word can differentiate the entry from others. For example, to insert the Author glossary, you can just type *au*, provided that no other entry begins with those letters. Word inserts the glossary entry at the insertion point.

To cancel without inserting a glossary, press Esc or ⌘-period.

Undoing or Repeating a Glossary Entry

After you insert a glossary entry, you can cancel the insertion by choosing Undo immediately or by pressing ⌘-Z. (If you perform other actions after inserting the glossary entry, you need to use normal deletion techniques to remove the glossary entry from your document. You also can use the Repeat command from the Edit menu to insert the same entry elsewhere before you perform another action.)

Editing Glossary Entries

Editing the text you have stored in a glossary entry is easy. You insert the entry, edit the text, and repeat the procedure you used to define the glossary entry.

To edit a glossary entry, follow these steps:

SPEED KEY

1. Choose Glossary from the Edit menu or press ⌘-K.

2. In the list box, choose the glossary entry you want to edit and then choose Insert.

3. Edit and format the entry as you would edit any document text.

4. Select the entry.

5. Choose Glossary from the Edit menu or press ⌘-K.

6. In the list box, choose the glossary entry's name and then choose Define.

7. Choose Close to close the Glossary window.

Renaming a Glossary Entry

To rename a glossary entry you already have created, follow these steps:

1. Choose Glossary from the Edit menu or press ⌘-K.

2. When the Glossary window appears, select the glossary name from the list box.

3. Select the name in the Name box and edit the name.

4. Choose Define.

Deleting Glossary Entries

Eventually some glossary entries you create lose their usefulness. You may have created the glossary entry for a special one-time purpose or perhaps you have found an easier way to do the same task. Whatever the reason, deleting unneeded entries in the Glossary list box makes using your glossaries easier.

To delete glossary entries, follow these steps:

1. Choose Glossary from the Edit menu or press ⌘-K.

2. In the list box, choose the glossary entry you want to delete.

3. Choose the Delete button. An alert box appears, asking you to confirm the deletion.

4. Choose Yes to delete the glossary entry.

Word doesn't automatically save the changes you make to a glossary file: the chapters are made in memory only. To make the changes permanent, you must save the glossary file, as described in the following section.

Managing Glossary Files

When you start Word, the program opens the Standard Glossary file stored in the Word folder. Don't delete or move this file. If you do, Word cannot open the Standard Glossary when you start the program.

You can save your changes to the Standard Glossary or to a custom glossary. Because Word opens the Standard Glossary when you start the program, the entries you place in the Standard Glossary are available by default. The Standard Glossary is the best place to save glossary entries that you frequently use.

You may want to save to a custom glossary entries that you use only for a certain type of document, such as a technical, medical, or legal document. These entries are not available in the Standard Glossary. To use custom entries, you must open the custom glossary.

Saving Glossary Files

Unlike styles, which are saved automatically when you save a document, glossary entries must be saved by choice. If you quit Word without saving changes, you lose them. You can save your glossary changes when you quit Word or before you quit Word.

To save your glossary changes when you quit Word, follow these steps:

1. Choose Quit from the File menu or press ⌘-Q. Word closes your document, and the alert box shown in figure 13.3 appears.

Fig. 13.3
A Save changes alert box.

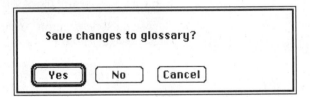

2. Choose Yes to save your glossary entries. A Save As dialog box appears, such as the one shown in figure 13.4. Word suggests saving your glossary changes to the Standard Glossary. Normally, that's the best place to store your changes.

3. To save changes to the Standard Glossary, choose Save. To save changes to a custom glossary, choose the name of the custom glossary and choose Save. To create a new custom glossary, type the new glossary name and choose Save. If the glossary file already exists, an alert box appears, such as the one shown in figure 13.5.

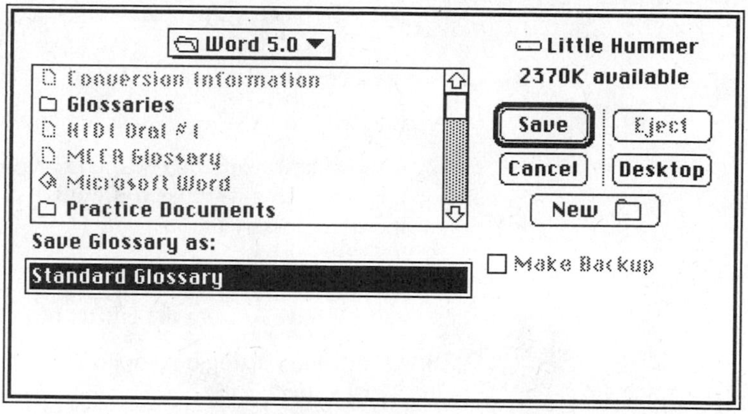

Fig. 13.4
A Save As dialog box.

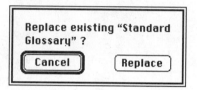

Fig. 13.5
A glossary name alert box.

4. If you see the alert box shown in figure 13.5, and if you're sure that you want to overwrite the preceding version of the glossary, choose Replace.

To save your glossary changes without quitting Word, follow these steps:

1. Choose Glossary from the Edit menu or press ⌘-K.

2. Choose Save from the File menu or press ⌘-S. Word displays a Save As dialog box (refer to fig. 13.4). The program suggests saving your changes to the Standard Glossary.

3. To save your changes to the Standard Glossary, choose Save. To save your changes to a custom glossary, choose the name of the custom glossary and then choose Save. To create a new custom glossary, type the new glossary name and choose Save. If the glossary file already exists, you see an alert box like the one shown in figure 13.5.

Creating a Custom Glossary

To create a custom glossary file, follow these steps:

1. Choose Glossary from the Edit menu or press ⌘-K.

2. Choose New from the File menu or press ⌘-N. An alert box appears asking whether you want to clear all the old entries from the new glossary file.

3. Choose Yes to clear all the old entries from the new glossary file.

4. Choose Save As from the File menu.

5. In the Open dialog box, open the Glossaries folder within the Word folder.

6. Type a name for the glossary in the Save Glossary As box.

7. Choose Save.

Opening a Custom Glossary

As you already know, Word automatically opens the Standard Glossary when you start the program. To open a custom glossary that you have created, follow the procedure described in this section.

When you open a glossary, Word merges the glossary's entries with the ones currently in memory. To prevent Word from mixing the incoming entries with the ones stored in the current glossary, you must clear Word's glossary before opening the custom one. (When you clear the glossary, you clear only the entries in memory. Nothing happens to the entries stored on disk.)

To open a custom glossary, follow these steps:

1. Choose Glossary from the Edit menu or press ⌘-K.

2. Choose New from the File menu. You see an alert box asking whether you want to clear all nonstandard glossary entries.

3. Choose Yes, unless you really want to merge all the current glossary entries into the custom glossary you are opening. When you choose Yes, you do not erase the glossary entries or the glossary file on disk—you remove them from Word's memory so that the program does not merge the current entries with those you are opening.

4. Choose Open from the File menu. Word displays a list of glossary files in the Open list box, as shown in figure 13.6.

Note that Word automatically switches to the folder, where Word's glossaries are stored. If you don't see the glossary you want to open, you can switch to another folder or you can choose Find File to search for all the glossaries on the current drive.

Fig. 13.6
Selecting a glossary.

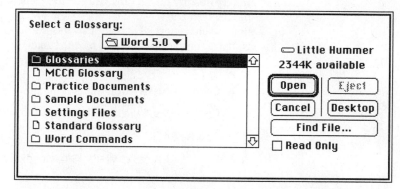

5. Choose the glossary you want to use and then choose Open.

   If you don't see the glossary you want to use, choose Find File. Word selects the Glossaries option from the File Type list box (see fig. 13.7) and quickly lists all the glossaries on the current drive.

Fig. 13.7
The Find File dialog box, with Glossaries automatically selected.

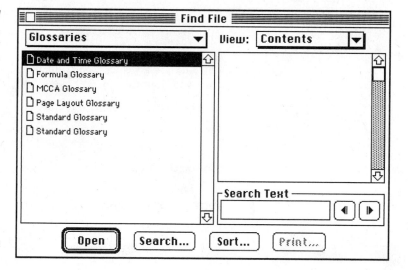

Printing a Glossary

If you use glossaries frequently, you may want to keep a printout of the contents of your glossary file for easy reference.

In the Glossary dialog box, you see the contents (but not the graphics) of the selected entry. Word uses a system font to display the entry. Only the first few characters of text appear on-screen, but the printout shows the complete entry, alphabetized by entry names.

To print a glossary, follow these steps:

1. Choose Glossary from the Edit menu or press ⌘-K.

2. Choose Print from the File menu. The Print dialog box appears.

3. Choose Print.

4. Choose Close to close the Glossary dialog box.

Copying a Glossary Entry

After you have created two or more glossary files, you may want to copy an entry from one glossary file to another. Suppose that you create a letterhead glossary and store the information in a glossary file called Correspondence Glossary. You like the format so much that you want to copy the letterhead glossary into your Standard Glossary.

To copy a glossary entry from one glossary to another, follow these steps:

1. Choose Glossary from the Edit menu or press ⌘-K. Then select the entry you want to copy.

2. Choose Copy from the Edit menu.

3. Choose New from the File menu or press ⌘-N to clear all the nonstandard glossary entries from Word's memory.

4. Choose Open from the File menu.

5. Select the name of the glossary file to which you want to copy the entry and then choose Open.

6. Choose Paste.

7. Choose the Close button.

Quick Review

T his section concisely summarizes the most useful information in this chapter. Check "Productivity Tips" for a review of high-productivity tips and tricks, and review "Techniques" when you forget how to perform a specific procedure.

Productivity Tips

■ Use a glossary entry to store and insert frequently used graphics, such as a logo.

■ Explore the Standard Glossary entries. Many entries can save you time by automatically entering the date, time, and details about the current document (such as author, subject, title, and keywords).

■ Create stationery documents that include the Print Date glossary. Word then prints the current date when you print a new document in which you are using a Stationery template.

■ If you want your glossary entries to include formatting, make sure that you include the trailing paragraph mark in the selection when you define an entry.

■ Save frequently used glossary entries to the Standard Glossary, which Word opens every time you start the program.

■ If you develop many glossary entries for a type of document you create infrequently, save these entries to a custom glossary.

■ To avoid merging glossaries, always clear Word's glossary memory (by choosing New from the File menu with the Glossary dialog box displayed) before you open a custom glossary or switch back to the Standard Glossary.

Techniques

This section provides concise, quick-reference summaries of all the procedures introduced in this chapter.

Clearing a Glossary File

To clear a glossary file of all user entries:

1. Choose Glossary from the edit menu or press ⌘-K.

2. Choose New from the File menu or press ⌘-N.

3. Choose Yes to remove all nonstandard glossary entries.

Copying a Glossary Entry from One Glossary File to Another

To copy a glossary entry:

1. Choose Glossary from the Edit menu (or press ⌘-K) and select the entry you want to copy.

2. Choose Copy from the Edit menu.

3. Choose New from the File menu (or press ⌘-N) to clear all nonstandard glossary entries from Word's memory.

4. Choose Open from the File menu.

5. Select the name of the glossary file to which you want to copy the entry and then choose Open.

6. Choose Paste.

7. Choose the Close button.

Defining a Glossary Entry

To create a glossary entry:

1. Select the text or graphic you want to store in a glossary.

2. Choose Glossary from the Edit menu or press ⌘-K.

3. Type a glossary entry name in the Name box.

4. Choose the Define button.

5. Choose Close.

Deleting a Glossary Entry

To delete a glossary entry:

1. Choose Glossary from the Edit menu, or press ⌘-K.

2. In the list box, choose the glossary entry you want to delete.

3. Choose the Delete button.

4. Choose Yes to confirm the deletion.

Editing a Glossary Entry

To edit a glossary entry:

1. Choose Glossary from the Edit menu or press ⌘-K.

2. In the list box, choose the glossary entry you want to edit and then choose Insert.

3. Edit and format the entry as you would edit any document text.

4. Select the entry.

5. Choose Glossary from the Edit menu or press ⌘-K.

6. In the list box, choose the glossary entry's name and then choose Define.

7. Choose Close to close the Glossary window.

Inserting a Glossary Entry

To insert a glossary entry with the Glossary dialog box:

1. Place the insertion point where you want the glossary entry to appear.

2. Choose Glossary from the Edit menu or press ⌘-K.

3. You may want to deactivate the Standard Entries or User Entries check boxes to reduce the number of entries displayed.

4. From the Glossary window's list box, choose the entry you want.

5. Choose Insert. Word inserts the glossary entry at the insertion point's location.

To insert a glossary entry with the keyboard:

1. Position the insertion point where you want the glossary entry to appear.

2. Press ⌘-Delete or press ⌘-Backspace.

Chapter 13
Using Glossaries

3. When the lower left corner of the page number area displays the message Name, type the full name of the glossary entry and press Return.

To cancel without inserting a glossary, press Esc or ⌘-Backspace.

To undo a glossary entry after inserting the entry (but before you perform another action), choose Undo from the Edit menu, or press ⌘-Z.

To repeat a glossary entry insertion before you perform another action, move the insertion point to the place where you want the entry to appear and choose Repeat from the Edit menu, or press ⌘-Y.

Opening a Custom Glossary

To open a custom glossary:

1. Choose Glossary from the Edit menu or press ⌘-K.

2. Choose New from the File menu or press ⌘-N.

3. Choose Yes to delete all the nonstandard entries (so that Word doesn't merge these entries with the glossary you're opening).

4. Choose Open from the File menu or press ⌘-O.

5. Choose the glossary you want to use and then choose Open.

Printing a Glossary File

To print a glossary file:

1. Choose Glossary from the Edit menu or press ⌘-K.

2. Choose Print from the File menu or press ⌘-P.

3. Choose Print.

4. Choose Close to close the Glossary dialog box.

Renaming a Glossary Entry

To rename a glossary entry:

1. Choose Glossary from the Edit menu or press ⌘-K.

2. When the Glossary window appears, select the glossary name in the list box.

3. Select the name in the Name box and edit the name.

4. Choose Define.

Saving Glossary Files

To save your glossary changes when you quit Word:

1. Choose Quit from the File menu or press ⌘-Q.

2. Choose Yes to save your glossary entries.

3. To save your changes to the Standard Glossary, choose Save. To save your changes to a custom glossary, choose the name of the custom glossary and choose Save. To create a new custom glossary, type the new glossary name and choose Save.

4. To resave an existing glossary, choose Replace when the alert box appears.

To save your glossary changes without quitting Word:

1. Choose Glossary from the Edit menu or press ⌘-K.

2. Choose Save from the File menu or press ⌘-S.

3. To save changes to the Standard Glossary, choose Save. To save changes to a custom glossary, choose the name of the custom glossary and choose Save. To create a new custom glossary, type the new glossary name and choose Save.

4. If you're resaving an existing glossary, choose Replace when the alert box appears.

Linking Data Dynamically

Imagine this scenario. You're writing a major report that includes several important tables of financial data you pasted into your Word document from Excel spreadsheets. You start Excel and check the figures because the bottom line on one of the tables looks curious. You find an error in one of the formulas and make the change. An old friend shows up unexpectedly, and you're distracted. After reminiscing for a while, you print the report and hand it to your boss.

The accuracy of the bottom-line figure in the affected table depends on whether you're using System 6 or System 7. Under System 6, you must update the link between the source document and the destination document manually. (In the preceding example, the document would have an incorrect figure.) Under System 7, the changes you make in the Source document are automatically reflected in the destination document. This chapter—more so than any other chapter in this book—reveals the impressive technical advantages of Apple's System 7 software.

This chapter comprehensively surveys the three ways you can link data dynamically using System 7. (If you're using System 6, read on because you still can use one of these techniques.) The following topics are covered:

■ *Understanding Dynamic Linking and Embedding*. In this section, you learn how to differentiate among dynamic linking, object linking and embedding, and Publish/Subscribe. You also learn the strengths and weaknesses of each approach.

USING
WORD 5
FOR THE
MAC

- *Using Dynamic Links*. This section introduces the first of the three dynamic data linking techniques (inserting data with Paste Link and Paste Special). System 6 users can use both commands but must update the linked data manually.

- *Embedding Objects in a Word Document*. This section covers a new System 7-enabled Word feature that enables you to treat other applications as if they were an extension of Word.

- *Publishing and Subscribing*. This section explains how to use Publish and Subscribe, System 7's new way of making data from your documents available for use by other documents, other applications, other users, and even other Macintoshes (if your Mac is linked to a network).

Understanding Dynamic Linking and Embedding

This section explains dynamic linking and embedding under System 7. An explanation of document linking under System 6 is at the end of this section. Beginning with an explanation of the clipboard's limitations for data exchange, this section introduces the concept of dynamic data exchange, contrasts the various data linking methods, and indicates when you should choose one method over the others.

Understanding the Limitations of the Clipboard

When the Macintosh was new, you could transfer data from one application to another only by using the clipboard. In the source application (the one from which you're copying), you select the data and copy it to the clipboard. In the destination application (the one to which you're copying), you choose Paste to import the data at the insertion point's location.

The clipboard is extremely handy, but it has two limitations:

- You lose the original data's formatting. In the destination document, the data appears as text and takes on the formatting of the destination document.

- After you paste the data into the destination document, the data has no link to the source document. The destination application cannot tell where the data came from. If you need the source application to fix an error in the data, you must remember which document contains the source data. You must switch to the source application, open the source document, and make the changes. You also must redo the transfer manually. Suppose that you make a change to the data in the source application. You must remember all the documents into which you pasted this data, because each now contains erroneous data. You must update all of them manually.

Looking at the Advantages of Dynamic Linking

The clipboard still is available and useful for many applications. Better techniques are available, however, for creating *dynamic* links between documents. In a dynamic link, the changes you make to the source document are updated *automatically* to all copies of the source information.

A dynamic link has two advantages over clipboard copying and pasting: the data you import retains some or all of the formatting you gave it in the source application, and the source document retains information about where the data came from. If you make a change to the source document, this information is used to update the data. Moreover, the change is made to *all copies* of the source information. You don't have to remember all the destination documents into which you pasted the data.

Understanding the Two Dynamic Linking Techniques

With System 7 and Word, you can link two documents dynamically with the Paste Link and Paste Special commands, or you can use System 7's new Publish and Subscribe commands. Linking creates a dynamic link between two documents. Publish/Subscribe creates a dynamic link between one source document and an unlimited number of destination documents. A quick overview of the difference between these two techniques follows.

Linking Two Documents Dynamically

Linking two documents dynamically is like copying with the clipboard, but you choose Paste Link or Paste Special instead of Paste. Word records information about the source document. If you make changes to the source document, these changes are reflected in the destination document. Word preserves the source document's formatting. With the

Update Link command, you can start the source application from within the destination application and easily edit the source document.

You can even use these commands to create dynamic links between Word documents. This technique is the best choice to link one source document and one destination document, but the applications must support dynamic data exchange (DDE).

Using Publish and Subscribe

Using the Publish and Subscribe dynamic linking technique bypasses the clipboard. To transfer data to other applications that support Publish/ Subscribe, you create a *publisher* by selecting some or all of your document and then choosing Create Publisher from the Edit menu. You save this information in a special document called an *edition.* After the edition is created, an unlimited number of documents can *subscribe* to the edition.

When you change the publisher, your Macintosh updates the edition and all the subscribers. To link one source document (the publisher) with many destination documents (subscribers), this technique is the best choice—especially if you're using a Macintosh connected to a network. (Publish and Subscribe are designed to work well on networks.) Subscribers cannot change the source document.

Understanding Object Linking and Embedding (OLE)

Object linking and embedding (OLE) isn't a dynamic data exchange technique; OLE is a way of *embedding* a source document within a *single* destination document so that you can edit the source document more easily. The embedded object is stored in Word as a picture. You embed objects by using the Object command in the Insert menu.

What's the difference between linking with Paste Link and OLE? As explained in the preceding section, Paste Link creates an active link to the source document. If you need to edit the document, you can use the Update Link to start the source application. With linking and OLE, you can edit the source document from Word.

With linking, you can create a dynamic link between one source document and many destination documents. With OLE, you can embed a source document in *one* destination document. To understand OLE, think of the procedure this way: you're not importing a copy of a chart, spreadsheet, or some other document; you're putting the document into your Word file in its native application's format. With OLE, you easily can edit the embedded object. When you double-click the object, or choose Edit Object from the Edit menu, Word starts the application and loads the document into it. You can edit the document with the source application's tools. The source application is like a Word dialog box with all kinds of powerful capabilities.

Keep in mind that you cannot use OLE unless you have enough memory to run both applications simultaneously—a great deal of memory under System 7. To run Word and Excel, for example, you are cutting it close with 4M of RAM.

System 7 users with plenty of disk space and 68030 processors should enable virtual memory to extend the amount of RAM available for running programs. Virtual memory tricks programs into thinking that you have much more RAM than you actually have. 1M of disk space is required, however, for every 1M of *total* memory. To configure your machine so that programs think they can use 8M of RAM, even though you only have 4M of RAM actually installed, you need 8M of disk space. Note that virtual memory is slower than "real" memory. If you're short on memory, however, virtual memory is much better than the notorious Low on memory message that requires you to save your work and exit applications.

Choosing the Right Method for Data Exchange

Now that you have been introduced to the three data exchange methods you can use with Word 5, the following section provides a quick guide to choosing the correct method.

To create a dynamic link between two documents, link the documents with Paste Link or Paste Special. If you use this technique to import an Excel spreadsheet into your Word document, the imported spreadsheet reflects the changes you make to the source document. You even can edit the source spreadsheet without leaving Word. To create such a link, both applications must support Microsoft's DDE standards. (Microsoft applications support these standards, but many other applications don't support them.)

To create a dynamic link between one source document and unlimited numbers of subscriber documents, use Publish and Subscribe. This option is the best choice if you're using a network and want to make a document available to people using other Macintoshes. Many System 7-compatible applications support Publish and Subscribe.

To include another application's document in your Word document, use embedding. Because the document is part of your Word file, you don't need dynamic updating—you have only one document. This technique is the best choice when you want to keep only one copy of the source data. To embed objects, the source application must be compatible with Microsoft's Object Linking and Embedding standards. (Microsoft's applications are compatible with these standards, but many others aren't compatible.)

Linking Documents with System 6

If you're running System 6, the picture is considerably simplified: You cannot use Publish/Subscribe or OLE. You can use the Paste Link command, however, to create a link that you can manually update by choosing the Update Link command. You cannot link two Word documents as you can with System 7. You must link a Word document with one created by another application that supports Microsoft's Dynamic Data Exchange (DDE) standards.

Using Dynamic Links

ith Paste Link, you can create dynamic links between a source document (created by Word or any other application that supports DDE) and a destination document (a Word document). You must store the two documents on the same machine. By default, changes in the source document are automatically reflected in the destination document. After you create the link, you can specify the frequency of updates, cancel the link, change the format of the link, or open and edit the source document. The sections that follow introduce the procedures you use to create and edit dynamic links.

If you're using System 6, you can create links between source documents created by other applications and Word documents. (You cannot create links between Word documents under System 6.) Changes in the source document, however, are not automatically reflected in the destination document: You must update the link manually.

After you create links between a source document and a destination document, do not move the source document. The destination application may not be able to find the source document. If you move the source document to another folder, you must edit the link by using the Edit Link option in the Link Options dialog box, as described later in this section.

Part II

Creating More Complex Documents

Creating a Dynamic Link with Paste Link

In this section, you learn how to create a link between another application's source document and a Word document by using the Paste Link command. This command creates a link using the best possible format. The process is virtually automatic.

To create a link with Paste Link, follow these steps:

1. Open the application that contains the data you want to use.

    Make sure that you formatted the data the way you want. After you import the data into your Word document, you cannot format individual characters in the unit of imported data.

2. Select the data you want to use.

    In figure 14.1, all the data in an Excel spreadsheet is selected.

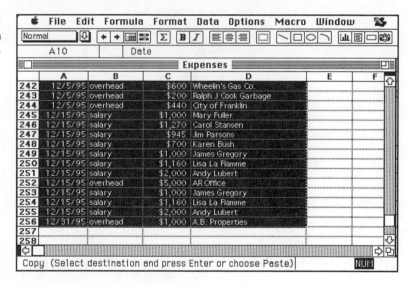

Fig. 14.1
Selected data in an
Excel spreadsheet.

3. Choose Copy from the Edit menu or press ⌘-C.

4. Switch to Word.

5. Open the destination document.

6. Position the insertion point where you want the data to appear.

Chapter 14
Linking Data Dynamically

7. Hold down the Shift key and choose Paste Link from the Edit menu or press Option-F4.

Word pastes a copy of the selected portion of the source document into your Word document, as shown in figure 14.2. If you're copying data from an Excel spreadsheet, as in this example, Word places the data in a table. (For more information on tables, see Chapter 17.) The linked information is surrounded by brackets, which are displayed only if you chose Show ¶ from the Edit menu. In figure 14.2, the leading bracket is displayed before Date on the first line of the table.

Fig. 14.2
Data pasted into Word with Paste Link.

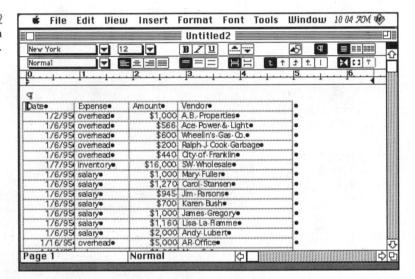

Creating a Link with Paste Special

When you link a document with Paste Link, Word automatically uses the best possible method of importing the data so that formatting is retained. You may want to choose the format manually, however. You can import the data as unformatted text, for example, or as a picture. If you want to choose the format Word uses in creating the link, use the Paste Special command instead of Paste Link.

To create a link with Paste Special, follow these steps:

1. Open the application that contains the data you want to use.

2. Select the data.

3. Choose Copy from the Edit menu or press ⌘-C.

Part II

Creating More Complex Documents

4. Switch to Word.

5. Open the destination document.

6. Position the insertion point where you want the data to appear.

7. Choose Paste Special from the Edit menu.

The Paste Special dialog box appears (see fig. 14.3). This dialog box indicates the name of the application and the file from which you are importing the data. In the Paste list box, a list of formats you can use is displayed. Which formats are displayed depends on which application you used to create the imported data.

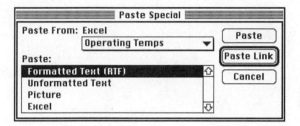

The following is a quick explanation of the formatting options you see in the Paste Special dialog box:

Formatted Text (RTF). This option is the default formatting option for Paste Link. Paste Special highlights this option by default.

Unformatted Text. Choose this option to create an active link without retaining formatting.

Picture. Choosing this option imports a PICT-format picture of the imported data. The data is displayed as it appears in its native application. Figure 14.4 shows an Excel spreadsheet imported in two ways. The spreadsheet on the left was imported as a picture. Word left the data alone. The one on the right was imported with the RTF option. Word placed the data in a table.

Native Application Format. When you choose this option, Word imports the data as an embedded object. This option does not create a dynamic link between the source document and the destination, however. Do not choose this option if you want to use dynamic links. This option works only if the application supports Microsoft's object linking and embedding (OLE) standards.

Chapter 14
Linking Data Dynamically

Fig. 14.4
A Spreadsheet imported
with PICT picture
format (left) and RTF
format (right).

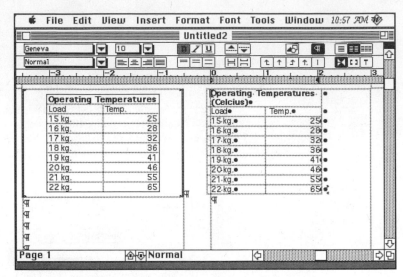

8. Choose a formatting option.

9. Choose Paste to import the picture without creating a link, or choose Paste Link to import the data and create a dynamic link with the source document.

Updating the Link

After you create a dynamic link, you can use the Link Options command to specify when links are updated, change the format of the link, edit the link, and cancel the link.

Under System 7, updates occur when you make a change to the source document. You quickly will discover, however, that your Macintosh runs sluggishly when you edit the source document with the destination document open. You may want to switch to manual updating so that you can edit the source document more easily. If you do, you must use this command to update the link by choosing the Update Now button.

To update the link, follow these steps:

1. Position the insertion point in the imported data.

2. Choose Link Options from the Edit menu.

The Link Options dialog box appears (see fig. 14.5). In the Link To area, Word indicates the portion of the document that was linked (in this example, a range of an Excel spreadsheet). Word also indicates the name of the source document and the source application.

Fig. 14.5
The Link Options
dialog box.

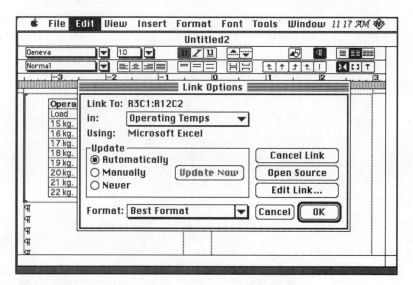

3. Perform one of the following actions:

   Choose Manually to switch to manual updating.

   Choose Update Now to update a manual link.

   Choose Never to retain the link but prevent further updates.

   Choose a different format in the Format list box. Which formats are available depend on the application used to create the source document.

   Choose Cancel Link to break the link to the source document.

   Choose Open Source to start the source application and edit the document.

   Choose Edit Link to change the path for the source document if you moved it to a new location on your disk.

4. Choose OK.

Chapter 14
Linking Data Dynamically

If you choose Open Source to edit the link, keep in mind that changes you make *outside* the originally selected area are not reflected in the destination document. If you're editing a spreadsheet, for example, the only changes reflected in the destination document are those changes that fall within the originally selected range. If you add a row or column of new data, you must redo the link if you want the new data to be reflected in the destination documents.

Embedding Objects in a Word Document

If your computer has lots of RAM (at least 4M) and you install other applications that support Microsoft's object linking and embedding standard, you can embed objects in your Word document. An embedded object is a picture, as far as Word is concerned, but one with some very special properties. If you double-click this object, Word starts the application that created it, and displays the object in the native application's window. You then can edit the object.

When you choose Update from the native application's File menu, the application closes, Word appears again, and the embedded object shows your changes. When you embed an object, it's as if you also are embedding other applications into Word. If you have a document into which you embedded an Excel chart, a PowerPoint graphic, and an Equation Editor equation, all the power of these applications is available at a double-click of the mouse.

You can embed objects in Word documents in two ways:

- *Import an existing document as an object.* If the object you want to embed already exists, you can copy it into Word with the clipboard. In your Word document, use the Paste Object command to embed the object.

- *Create the object within Word.* If you're creating a document and find that you need a chart, spreadsheet, equation, or illustration, you can start any OLE-compatible application by using the Object command (from the Insert menu). All the application's tools become available to you. After you create the document, choose Update to return to Word, and Word enters the document you created as an embedded object.

The following sections discuss both techniques. You also learn how to edit an object you embedded either way.

TIP

Packaged with Word is Equation Editor, a stand-alone OLE-compatible application. Even if you don't have Excel or some other OLE-compatible application, you can use Equation Editor to learn how OLE works. Turn to Chapter 18 for information on running OLE as an embedded application within Word.

Part II

Creating More Complex Documents

Importing an Existing Document as an Object

If the object you want to embed already exists in a document created with another application, follow these instructions to embed the document (or part of it) into your Word document. Keep in mind that doing so does not create a dynamic link, as does Paste Link or Paste Special. If you make changes to the source document, these changes will not be automatically reflected in the object you've embedded into your Word document.

To embed an existing document into Word, follow these steps:

1. Start the application you used to create the document.

2. Select the portion of the document you want to embed in your Word document.

3. Choose Copy from the Edit menu or press ⌘-C.

4. Switch to Word.

5. Hold down the Shift key and choose Paste Object from the Edit menu or press ⌘-F4.

   Word embeds the object as a picture in your document.

Creating the Object within Word

In the following instructions, you learn how to extend Word's capabilities by running another OLE-compatible application from Word.

To create the object without leaving Word, follow these steps:

1. Place the insertion point where you want the object to appear.

2. Choose Object from the Insert menu.

   The Insert Object dialog box appears (see fig. 14.6) and lists all the applications on your Macintosh that support OLE. Even if an application is OLE-compatible, it doesn't appear on this list if you never have run it before.

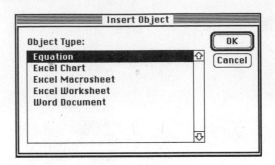

Fig. 14.6
Available OLE applications.

3. Choose the type of object you want to insert.

    Word starts the application and displays a blank application window, titled Word Object.

4. Use the application's tools to create the object.

SPEED KEY

5. Choose Update from the File menu or press ⌘-Q.

    Word returns to the screen, and you see the object you created.

Editing the Embedded Object

Editing an embedded object is easy—the best argument for preferring OLE over linking.

To edit an embedded object, follow these steps:

1. Position the insertion point on the object you want to edit.

2. Choose Edit Object from the Edit menu or double-click the object.

    Word starts the source application and displays the object in a Word Object window.

3. Use the native application's tools to edit the object.

4. Choose Update from the File menu to return to Word and update the object in your Word document or press ⌘-Q.

Publishing and Subscribing

 o create a Publish/Subscribe application, you select the publisher and create the edition. You then can choose publishing intervals. To use the edition, you subscribe. You can choose options that affect the subscription. All the relevant procedures are described in the sections that follow.

Defining the Publisher and Creating the Edition

To create a Publish/Subscribe application, you create the data you want to publish. You can create this data in any application, including Word, that supports Publish/Subscribe. The data can consist of text, graphics, or a combination of text and graphics.

To define the publisher and create the edition, follow these steps:

1. Select the information you want to publish.

    In figure 14.7, for example, a paragraph of boilerplate text has been selected.

Fig. 14.7
Boilerplate text selected.

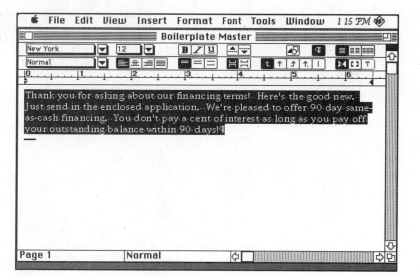

2. Choose Create Publisher from the Edit menu.

    The dialog box shown in figure 14.8 appears. On the left, you see a preview of your edition.

Chapter 14
Linking Data Dynamically

Fig. 14.8
Creating the edition.

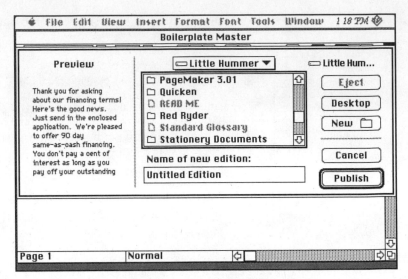

3. Choose the Editions folder or create one. Type a name for your edition in the Name of New Edition box.

4. Choose Publish.

   The application creates the edition. If you chose Show ¶, gray brackets showing the text that was published are displayed (see fig. 14.9).

Fig. 14.9
Gray brackets demarcate
published text.

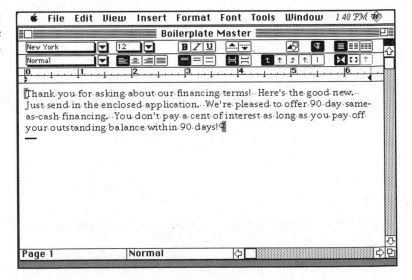

Part II

Creating More Complex Documents

Updating the Publisher

After you create an edition, you can change the update interval. By default, Word updates the edition every time you save changes to the publisher. With the Update Publisher command, you can choose an option that sends a new edition every time you edit the document. You also can choose manual updating, which sends the edition only when you choose the Send Edition Now option. If you want, you can cancel publication. The following procedures explain the steps you take to accomplish these operations.

To update the publisher, follow these steps:

1. In the document that contains the publisher, position the insertion point in the publication brackets.

2. Choose Update Publisher.

   The dialog box shown in figure 14.10 appears.

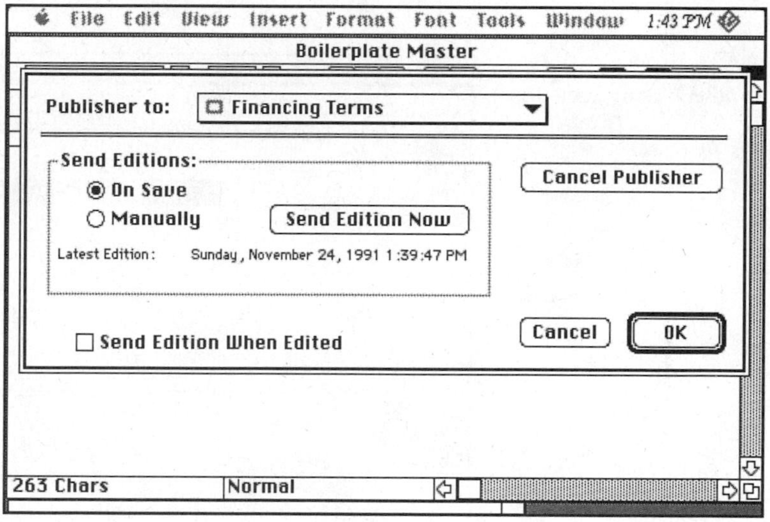

Fig. 14.10
Changing the
update interval.

3. Perform one of the following actions:

   Choose Manually to update the publication only when you choose the Send Edition now button.

Choose Send Edition Now to update an edition.

Choose Send Edition When Edited to send updates immediately.

Choose Cancel Publisher to stop publication.

4. Choose OK.

Subscribing to an Edition

After you create an edition, subscribing is easy. To subscribe, follow these steps:

1. Open the document in which you want to paste a copy of the edition.

2. Position the insertion point where you want the edition to appear.

3. Choose Subscribe To from the Edit menu.

   The dialog box shown in figure 14.11 appears.

Fig. 14.11
Subscribing to an edition.

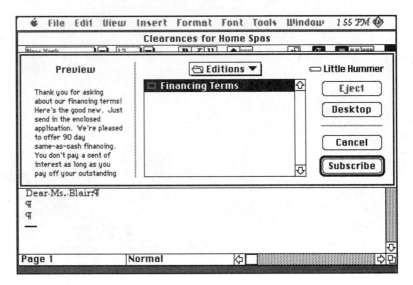

4. Highlight the edition you want to add.

   A preview of the edition's contents, shown in figure 14.11, is displayed on the left side of the dialog box.

5. Choose Subscribe.

Word inserts the edition into your document, surrounded by gray brackets. This inserted edition is called a *subscriber*. Word treats all this text as one character—you must select all the text as a unit, and you must format all the text as a unit.

Updating a Subscription

After you subscribe to an edition, you can specify the frequency of updates. By default, your Macintosh updates the subscriber when the edition changes. You can choose manual updating or specify a specific time for updating.

To update a subscription, follow these steps:

1. Place the insertion point within the subscriber.

2. Choose Subscriber Options.

   The dialog box shown in figure 14.12 appears.

Fig. 14.12
Subscriber options.

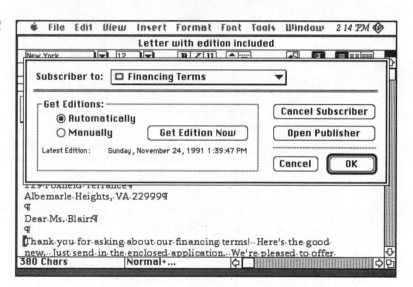

3. Perform one of the following actions:

   Choose Manually to prevent updates until you choose the Get Edition Now button.

Choose Get Edition Now to update the edition.

Choose Cancel Publisher to sever the link between the edition and the subscriber.

Choose Open Publisher to open the application that created the publisher and display the document in which the publisher is contained. You then can edit the publisher.

4. Choose OK.

Quick Review

This section concisely summarizes the most useful information in this chapter. Check "Productivity Tips" for a review of high-productivity tips and tricks, and review "Techniques" when you forget how to perform a specific procedure.

Productivity Tips

■ To create a dynamic link, use Paste Link or Publish/Subscribe. Publish/Subscribe is the best option if the data you're importing can be used in many documents and by other applications.

■ If you don't want to create a dynamic link but want ease of updating/editing from within Word, use embedding.

■ If you are using a 68030-based system, such as Mac Classic IIs and most of the newer Mac IIs, you can increase apparent RAM by using System 7's virtual memory capabilities, but you will sacrifice a great deal of disk space.

■ When you create the document that you're going to link or publish, be sure to add all the formatting you want. You cannot format the copy of the document that is inserted into the destination document.

■ If you move a linked or published source document, the dependent applications may not be able to find the source document or the publisher.

■ If you edit the source document, remember that changes you make outside the originally selected area will not be reflected in the linked documents. The gray brackets show you where the published part of the document is contained.

■ If you're using System 6, you can use Paste Link, but remember that you must update the link manually.

Techniques

This section provides concise, quick-reference summaries of all the procedures introduced in this chapter.

Creating a Dynamic Link with Paste Link

To create a link with Paste Link:

1. Open the application that contains the data you want to use.

2. Select the data.

3. Choose Copy from the Edit menu or press ⌘-C.

4. Switch to Word.

5. Open the destination document.

6. Position the insertion point where you want the data to appear.

7. Hold down the Shift key and choose Paste Link from the Edit menu or press Option-F4.

Creating a Dynamic Link with Paste Special

To create a link with Paste Special:

1. Open the application that contains the data you want to use.

2. Select the data.

3. Choose Copy from the Edit menu or press ⌘-C.

4. Switch to Word.

5. Open the destination document.

6. Position the insertion point where you want the data to appear.

7. Choose Paste Special from the Edit menu.

8. Choose a formatting option.

9. Choose Paste to import the picture without creating a link, or choose Paste Link to import the data and create a dynamic link with the source document.

To update the link:

1. Position the insertion point in the imported data.

2. Choose Link Options from the Edit menu.

3. Perform one of the following actions:

   Choose Manually to switch to manual updating.

   Choose Update Now to update a manual link.

   Choose Never to retain the link but prevent further updates.

   Choose a different format in the Format list box.

   Choose Cancel Link to break the link to the source document.

   Choose Open Source to start the source application and edit the document.

   Choose Edit Link to change the path for the source document if you have moved it to a new location on your disk.

4. Choose OK.

Embedding Objects in Word Documents

To embed an existing document into Word:

1. Start the application you used to create the document.

2. Select the portion of the document that you want to embed in your Word document.

3. Choose Copy from the Edit menu or press ⌘-C.

4. Switch to Word.

5. Hold down the Shift key and choose Paste Object from the Edit menu or press ⌘-F4.

To create the object without leaving Word:

1. Place the insertion point where you want the object to appear.

2. Choose Object from the Insert menu.

3. Choose the type of object you want to insert.

4. Use the application's tools to create the object.

5. Choose Update from the File menu or press ⌘-Q.

To edit an embedded object:

1. Position the insertion point on the object you want to edit.

2. Choose Edit Object from the Edit menu or double-click the object.

3. Use the native application's tools to edit the object.

4. Choose Update from the File menu to return to Word and update the object in your Word document, or press ⌘-Q.

Publishing a Document

To define the publisher and create the edition:

1. Select the information you want to publish.

2. Choose Create Publisher from the Edit menu.

3. Choose a destination folder for your edition.

4. Type a name for your edition in the Name of new edition box.

5. Choose Publish.

To update the publisher:

1. In the document that contains the publisher, position the insertion point within the publication brackets.

2. Choose Update Publisher.

3. Perform one of the following actions:

   Choose Manually to update the publication only when you choose the Send Edition now button.

   Choose Send Edition Now to update an edition manually.

   Choose Send Edition When Edited to send updates immediately.

   Choose Cancel Publisher to stop publication.

4. Choose OK.

Subscribing to a Published Edition

To subscribe to an edition:

1. Open the document into which you want to paste a copy of the edition.

2. Position the insertion point where you want the edition to appear.

3. Choose Subscribe To from the Edit menu.

4. Highlight the edition you want to add.

5. Choose Subscribe.

Adding Headers, Footers, and Footnotes

15

f you're creating reports, proposals, or even lengthier documents, chances are you want to add headers or footers. A *header* is text—often a short version of the document's or chapter's title—positioned within the top margin. A *footer* is text positioned within the bottom margin. With Word, creating headers or footers is easy. They can include automatically inserted page numbers, the date, and the author's name. You type the header or footer text just once, and Word inserts the text on each page.

You also may want to add footnotes or endnotes. A *footnote* is a reference note that prints at the bottom of the page, while an *endnote* prints at the end of a document or section. Adding footnotes is easy with Word. The program automatically numbers the notes—and renumbers them if you insert or delete footnotes while editing. Word also automatically positions the footnotes, reserving as much space as necessary at the bottom of the page. Endnotes are automatically grouped at the end of a document or section. Footnotes and endnotes can be more than one paragraph long, and you can format the notes—and the reference marks—as you please.

With both features—headers/footers and footnotes—Word's keynote is flexibility. Although the program's defaults for the placement of headers, footers, and footnotes are appropriate for many documents, you can position these elements virtually anywhere you want. You also have

complete control over how headers, footers, and footnotes are formatted, and you can include within them borders and graphics.

The following topics are covered in this chapter.

- *Using Headers and Footers.* In this section, you learn how to add headers and footers to your document and how to take advantage of the elements Word can automatically include in a header or footer—such as page numbers, the date, and the author's name. You learn how to view, edit, format, position, and delete headers and footers. You also learn how to set up different headers and footers for odd and even pages when preparing documents that will be duplicated using both sides of the page.

- *Creating and Editing Footnotes and Endnotes.* In this section, you learn how to add reference notes that Word automatically numbers. You also learn how to view, edit, move, format, and delete notes and how to customize the *footnote separator*—the line that separates the notes from the document's text. In addition, you learn how to control the position and numbering of footnotes.

If you're creating a lengthy document with more than one section, be sure to read Chapter 16. That chapter contains additional information about headers, footers, and footnotes in multiple-section documents.

Users of previous Word versions find little differences in headers, footers, and footnotes in Word 5, with one exception: the commands' locations on the pull-down menus. With Word 5, the View menu contains the Header and Footer commands (once located on the now-defunct Document menu). The Footnotes command—to display the footnote window—is part of the View menu; the Footnote command—to insert a footnote or endnote at the insertion point's location—is found on the Insert menu.

Using Headers and Footers

eaders and footers—text repeated at the top or bottom of each page—add valuable information and remind the reader of the document's title or topic. They also add security by helping the reader identify and reassemble a document that wasn't securely bound and became scrambled on a cluttered desktop.

Word gives you many header and footer options:

- You can quickly add page numbers, the current date, or the current time to your header or footer simply by clicking an icon in the Header or Footer dialog box. While you're creating a header or footer, you can add any item from Word's glossaries, including such Summary Info items as Author, Title, and Subject. For more information on glossaries, see Chapter 13.

- Headers and footers are preset with a special tab format—a centered tab stop in the middle of the page and a flush-right tab stop at the right margin. This feature simplifies and speeds formatting.

- You can create a header or footer with more than one line or paragraph, if you want. Word automatically adjusts the top or bottom margin to accommodate the header or footer.

- By default, Word aligns headers or footers with the right and left margins you have chosen for your document. (The default is 1.25 inches left and right.) You can extend the header or footer into the left and right margins by outdenting the header or footer paragraph.

- You can format header and footer text any way you want. By default, Word uses the Normal font and font size for header and footer text. You can change the formatting using manual formatting techniques or style formatting. If you change the Normal style for the current document, the header and footer text uses the font and font size you have chosen for the new Normal style. You also can use manual formatting techniques to modify the header and footer styles. For more information on styles, see Chapter 8.

- You can create different headers and footers for odd and even pages. If your document will be duplicated on both sides of the page for binding, you can create a visually pleasing pattern with page numbers always printed on the outside margin.

- You can suppress the printing of headers or footers on the first page of a document. You also can create a special header or footer to be printed on just the first page.

- If you haven't divided your document into sections, the header or footer you create applies to the whole document and prints on every page (except when you have suppressed headers or footers on the first page). If you want to print one header or footer in one part of your document and then change the header or footer in another part, you can divide your document into sections. For more information, see Chapter 16.

Headers and footers improve the appearance of any document more than two or three pages long. The procedures detailed in this section

Chapter 15

Adding Headers, Footers, and Footnotes

teach you how to add page numbers and headers or footers at the same time.

The procedure for adding headers or footers varies depending on which view you're using: Normal view or Page Layout view.

- *Normal view*. You add the header or footer in a Header or Footer dialog box. Just by clicking icons, you can easily add the time, date, and page number. You don't see the header or footer on-screen, however.

- *Page Layout view*. Word moves the insertion point to the header or footer location. You can add the time, date, and page number, but you must do so by choosing options from menus. However, you can see the header or footer on-screen.

In the sections to follow, you learn how to create and edit headers or footers using both techniques. You also learn how to suppress the printing of headers or footers on the first page of your document and how to create special first-page headers or footers. These techniques are useful for any document that contains a title or letterhead that might conflict with a header.

In addition, you learn how to change the vertical position at which headers and footers print. This technique is useful if you change the document's top or bottom margins. You also learn how to set up different headers and footers for odd and even pages. This technique is useful when you're duplicating a document using both sides of the page.

Adding a Header or Footer in Normal View

You add a header or footer by typing and formatting text in the Header or Footer window. To display these windows, choose Header or Footer in the View menu, and you see the Header or Footer dialog box (see fig. 15.1). The Footer dialog box is exactly the same as the Header dialog box shown in figure 15.1, except for its name.

Header and Footer dialog boxes have the following features:

Page Number Icon. Click this icon to insert a page number at the insertion point's location. Word will print page numbers at the location you specify.

Date Icon. Click this icon to insert the current date at the insertion point's location. The date becomes part of the header or footer.

Fig. 15.1
The Header dialog box.

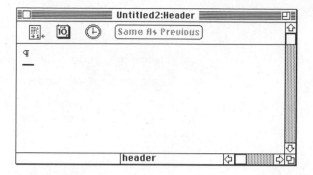

Time Icon. Click this icon to insert the current time at the insertion point's location. The time becomes part of the header or footer.

Same as Previous. This button becomes available only when you divide your document into sections. Its use is explained in Chapter 16.

When you open the Header or Footer dialog box, Word automatically applies the Header or Footer styles to the text you type. This style is based on the Normal style—the style automatically has the font and font size assigned to the Normal style for your document. In addition, this style includes tab stops at 3 inches (centered) and 6 inches (flush right). Using these preset tabs, you easily can add text, a date, and the page number to your header or footer, as shown in figure 15.2.

Fig. 15.2
Using the preset Header
style tabs.

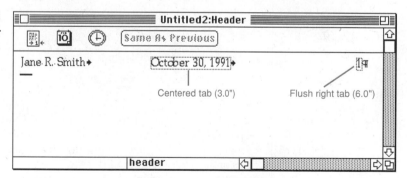

To add a header or footer to your document (Normal view), follow these steps:

1. Choose Header or Footer from the View menu.

Chapter 15

Adding Headers, Footers, and Footnotes

You see the Header or Footer window (refer to fig. 15.1).

2. Type the header or footer text in the window.

   This text will appear on all the pages of your document.

3. Format the header or footer as you choose.

   The Header and Footer windows have preset tabs at 3 inches (centered) and 6 inches (right). You can change these tabs (or add new ones) by choosing the Show Ruler option from the Format menu.

   You can choose other formatting options—character emphases, fonts, alignments, or indentations—by using any of the usual character or paragraph formatting techniques.

   To position header or footer text beyond the margins, drag the indent marks on the ruler or type negative numbers in the Left and Right indent boxes of the Paragraph dialog box.

4. To add page numbers, the current time, or the current date, click the insertion point where you want the number, the time, or the date to appear. Use the preset tabs to align the page number, date, or time. Then click the icon on the header or footer title bar. To delete the page number, time, or date, just select it and press Delete or Backspace.

5. Click the Close box to close the header or footer window.

To edit or delete a header or footer you have already added, use the following steps:

1. Choose Header or Footer from the View menu.

2. When the Header or Footer window appears, edit the text or delete it to cancel the header or footer.

3. Click the Close box to close the Header or Footer dialog box.

You usually don't want a header to print on the first page of a document, where it might conflict with the document's title. A Section dialog box option, Different First Page, suppresses the printing of headers and footers on the first page of your document or section. When you choose this option, the View menu displays two new commands, First Header and First Footer, which enable you to create headers or footers that print on only the first page. For more information, see "Managing First-Page Headers and Footers" later in this section.

TIP

If you have filled out Summary Info for the current document, you can quickly enter the document's title, author, subject, or other information into your header or footer. Just open the header or footer and choose Glossary from the Edit menu (or press ⌘-K). Choose one or more of the Summary Info glossaries (such as Author, Title, or Subject). Word inserts the glossary directly into the header or footer.

Adding a Header or Footer in Page Layout View

When you add a header or footer in Page Layout view, you do not see the Header or Footer window. Instead, the insertion point moves immediately to the first header or footer area in your document (see fig. 15.3). The ruler measures the header or footer with the zero set at the left margin. You type the header or footer directly, within the top or bottom margin.

Fig. 15.3
Header displayed in
Page Layout view.

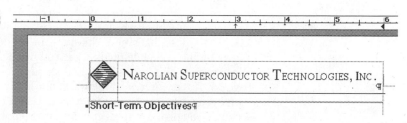

To create a header or footer in Page Layout view, follow these steps:

1. In Page Layout view, choose Header or Footer from the View menu.

   Word opens the header or footer area and scrolls the screen, if necessary, to display the header or footer.

2. Type the header or footer text, and if you want, format the text.

   Word automatically applies the Header or Footer styles to this text. By default, this style calls for the Normal font and font size, a centered tab at 3 inches, and a flush right tab at 6 inches.

   You can use any manual formatting technique to format the header or footer text. If you redefine the Header or Footer style, the changes you have made automatically apply to the text you're entering.

3. To enter the date, choose Date from the Insert menu. Alternatively, choose Glossary from the Edit menu (or press ⌘-K) and choose one of the Date glossaries. For more information on glossaries, see Chapter 13.

4. To enter the time, choose Glossary from the Edit menu (or press ⌘-K) and choose one of the Time glossaries.

5. When you finish creating the header or footer, just click the cursor outside the header or footer and continue working on your document.

After you have created a header or footer, you can edit the text easily. Just scroll up or down to bring the header or footer into view and edit the text using the usual techniques. To display the header or footer text quickly, choose Header or Footer from the View menu.

After you add a header or footer, the text you have placed within it appears on all the pages of your document. If you want to change this text, it doesn't matter which page is displayed when you make the change. Suppose that you're viewing your document in Page Layout view and you want to change the header. You make the change on page 14. The change applies to your whole document, even on the pages before page 14. This may seem a little weird, but just remember: The header or footer you create always applies to your whole document (or the whole section if you divide your document into sections).

If you change Word's default margins, text aligned with the preset header and footer tab stops may not look correct on-screen. Suppose that you redefine the default margins so that they're set at 1.0 inch left and right, producing a 6.5-inch line length. You may then want to redefine the preset header and footer tab stops—3.0 inches centered and 6.0 inches left—to 3.25 inches centered and 6.5 inches flush right. To learn how to redefine the Header and Footer styles, see Chapter 8.

Managing First-Page Headers and Footers

By default, Word prints the headers or footers you create on every page of your document. If you use the header shown in figure 15.4 on the first page of a two-page letter, for example, the header would conflict with your organization's letterhead and logo. For this document—and other documents where this setting also would prove unsatisfactory—you can suppress the printing of the header on the first page. Simply choose the Different First Page option in the Section dialog box, as explained in this section. If you want, you can make this option the default for all documents.

When you choose the Different First Page option in the Section dialog box, the View menu gains two new commands: First Header and First Footer (see fig. 15.5). Choose these commands to add special headers that print only on the first page of your document, following the procedures detailed in this section.

Fig. 15.4
The header for a
two-page letter.

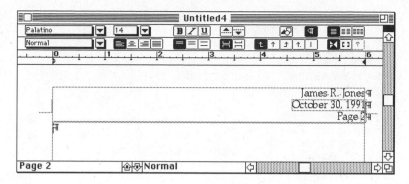

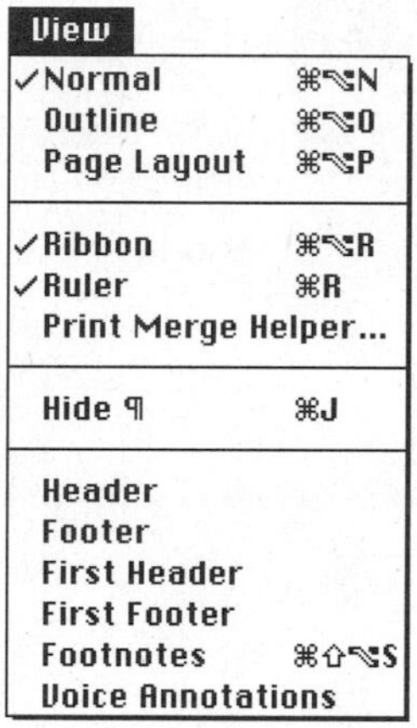

Fig. 15.5
The First Header and First
Footer commands on
the View menu.

The Different First Page option, which you choose in the Section dialog box, applies to the current section. If you haven't divided your document into sections, the whole document has just one section. If you create section breaks, as explained in the next chapter, the first-page choices you make in this dialog box apply only to the current section. If you want to suppress the printing of headers or footers throughout your document, choose Select All from the Edit menu (or press ⌘-A) before choosing the Section command from the Format menu.

To suppress the printing of headers or footers on the first page of your document or section, follow these steps:

Chapter 15

Adding Headers, Footers, and Footnotes

1. Choose Section from the Format menu.

2. Activate the Different First Page option.

3. To make this choice the default for all documents, choose Use as Default.

4. Choose OK.

Word activates the Different First Page option for the current section. The program does not print a header or footer on the first page; the header or footer begins on page 2.

After you have activated the Different First Page option in the Section dialog box, you can create a header or footer that prints only on the first page. To print special first page headers or footers in Normal view, follow these steps:

1. If necessary, activate the Different First Page option in the Section dialog box.

2. Choose First Header or First Footer from the View menu.

   You see a First Header or First Footer dialog box, which looks exactly like the Header or Footer dialog boxes you used previously.

3. Create the header or footer for the first page.

4. Click the Close box to confirm the header.

Adjusting the Vertical Positions of Headers and Footers

By default, Word prints headers or footers 0.5 inch from the top or bottom margin. If you choose margins wider or narrower than Word's default margins (1.0 inch top or bottom), you may want to change the vertical location of headers or footers so that they print in the middle of the margin. If you choose a 1.25-inch top margin, for instance, you would position the headers at 0.675 inch.

To change the vertical position of headers or footers, follow these steps:

1. Choose Section from the Format menu.

   You see the Section dialog box (see fig. 15.6).

2. In the Header/Footer area, type a measurement in the From Top box to change the vertical position of headers.

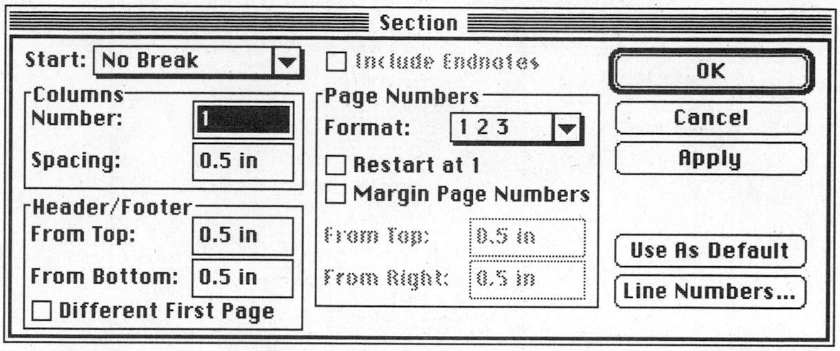

Fig. 15.6
The Section dialog box.

3. Type a measurement in the From Bottom box to change the vertical position of footers.

4. Choose OK.

Creating Different Headers or Footers for Facing Pages

If you're planning to duplicate your document on both sides of the page, take advantage of the Word feature that enables you to define different headers and footers for odd and even pages. The odd-page headers or footers appear to the right of the binding, and the even-page headers appear to the left of the binding. In the two-page Print Preview shown in figure 15.7, note how the corporate logo appears on the outside of both pages, creating an attractive look for a document duplicated on both sides of the page.

To create different headers for odd and even pages in Normal view, follow these steps:

1. Choose Document from the Format menu.

   You see the Document dialog box, as shown in figure 15.8.

2. Activate the Even/Odd Headers check box.

3. Choose OK.

4. Pull down the View menu.

   You see four new options on the View menu: Even Header, Even Footer, Odd Header, and Odd Footer (see fig. 15.9).

Chapter 15

Adding Headers, Footers, and Footnotes

Fig. 15.7
Different headers for
facing pages.

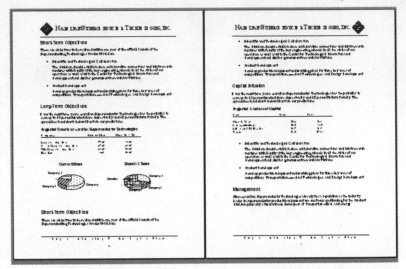

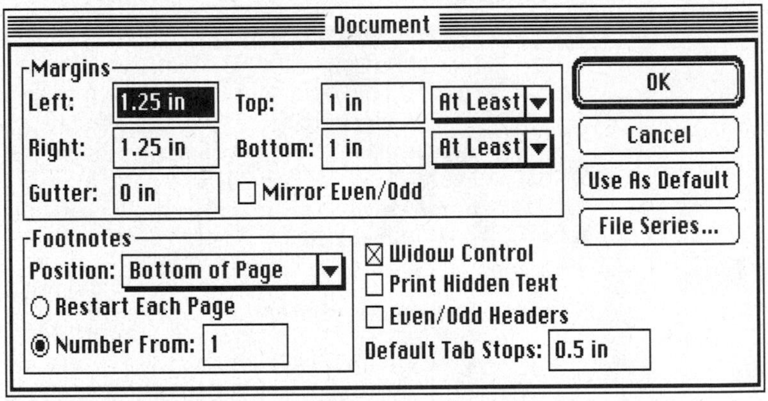

Fig. 15.8
Document dialog box.

5. Choose one of these options and create the header or footer.

6. Repeat step 5 until you have created all the headers or footers you want.

To create a pleasing effect, position the page numbers flush-right on odd pages and flush-left on even pages. Add lines below the headers and above the footers to frame the text on the page.

Part II

Creating More Complex Documents

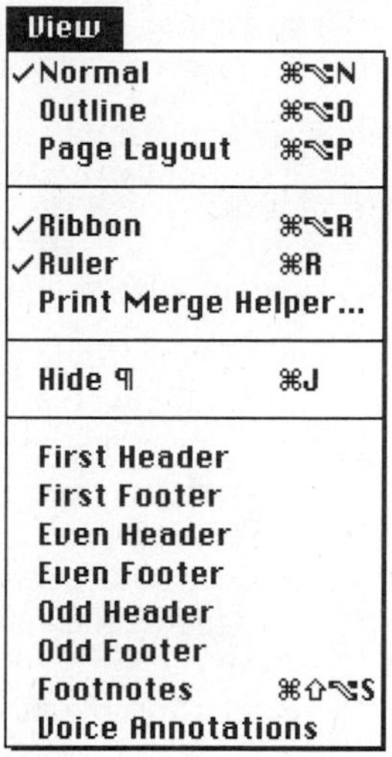

Fig. 15.9
The View menu with Odd
and Even header and
footer options.

```
┌─────────────────────────────┐
│ View                        │
├─────────────────────────────┤
│ ✓Normal            ⌘⌥N      │
│  Outline           ⌘⌥O      │
│  Page Layout       ⌘⌥P      │
├─────────────────────────────┤
│ ✓Ribbon            ⌘⌥R      │
│ ✓Ruler             ⌘R       │
│  Print Merge Helper...      │
├─────────────────────────────┤
│  Hide ¶            ⌘J       │
├─────────────────────────────┤
│  First Header               │
│  First Footer               │
│  Even Header                │
│  Even Footer                │
│  Odd Header                 │
│  Odd Footer                 │
│  Footnotes         ⌘⇧⌥S     │
│  Voice Annotations          │
└─────────────────────────────┘
```

If you're working in Page Layout view, the Odd and Even Header and Footer options aren't available on the View menu. To create an odd or even header or footer, activate the Even/Odd Headers in the Document dialog box, scroll to an odd or even page, and choose Header or Footer from the View menu. If you're displaying an odd-numbered page, Word creates the header or footer on odd-numbered pages only. If you're displaying an even-numbered page, Word creates the header or footer on even-numbered pages only.

Creating and Editing Footnotes and Endnotes

Many business and professional writers, not just scholars, must back up their claims by citing other experts. A simple way to refer to other works is to include within the text a bibliographic reference enclosed by parentheses. A reference list is then attached at the end of the document. In many cases, however, writers use footnotes or endnotes referenced in the text by a number (usually superscripted).

Word's footnote capabilities are superb. By default, Word numbers footnotes automatically and places them at the bottom of the page. A two-inch line is used to separate the notes from the body text. You also can customize Word's footnote capabilities in many ways, including the following examples:

- The program can automatically number your footnotes—and renumber them if you insert or delete any.

- If you want, you can create footnotes with reference marks other than numbers, such as an asterisk.

- When you create a footnote, Word automatically applies its standard Footnote Reference and Footnote Text styles to the footnote reference mark and footnote text. These styles call for footnote reference marks to be superscripted, boldfaced, and formatted with the Normal font in a 9-point font size. Footnote text would be printed in a 10-point version of the Normal font. By changing the Footnote Reference and Footnote Text styles, you can change the format for footnote reference marks and footnote text throughout your document.

- After you create a footnote in Normal view, Word opens a "smart" footnote window, which displays the text of the note referenced in the document window above. As you scroll through your document, the footnote window scrolls too, so that the relevant notes are always visible.

- Word automatically prints a two-inch separator line between the body text and the footnotes. If you want, you can delete the separator or create your own separator.

- If the footnote text is too long to fit on one page, Word floats the rest of the footnote text to the next page and prints a *continuation separator* above the notes. A line spanning the page, the continuation separator is longer than the usual separator. This greater length alerts the reader that the first note is a continuation of a note begun on the previous page.

- The program also can print a *continuation notice* telling the reader that the rest of the footnote's text can be found on the next page.

- If you prefer endnotes, you can print the notes at the ends of sections or at the end of the document.

Creating a Footnote

You add footnotes and endnotes to your document with the same procedure. The following steps detail this procedure. You learn how to choose endnotes instead of footnotes later in the section "Specifying Where Notes Will Print."

To create a footnote, follow these steps:

1. Position the insertion point in your text at the point where you want the footnote reference mark to appear.

2. Choose Footnote from the Insert window or press ⌘-E.

3. When the Footnote dialog box appears (see fig. 15.10), choose OK to have Word number the note automatically. Word inserts a 9-point, superscripted number after you choose OK.

SPEED KEY

Fig. 15.10
Footnote dialog box.

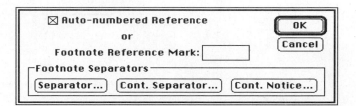

To insert a footnote reference mark other than a number (such as an asterisk), type the mark in the Footnote Reference Mark box before you choose OK. Word will not number the note. If you have added other notes using automatic numbering, an unnumbered reference mark does not affect the number sequence; Word simply skips that note as it numbers and renumbers the notes.

If you're viewing your document in Normal view, Word splits the screen after you choose OK. The footnote window appears below the document window (see fig. 15.11). Word echoes the footnote reference mark in the footnote window and positions the insertion point so that you can type the note.

If you're viewing your document in Page Layout view, Word moves the insertion point to the page's footnote area, as shown in figure 15.12.

4. Type the text of the note.

By default, Word formats the footnote text with 10-point characters.

Fig. 15.11
The Footnote window in
Normal view.

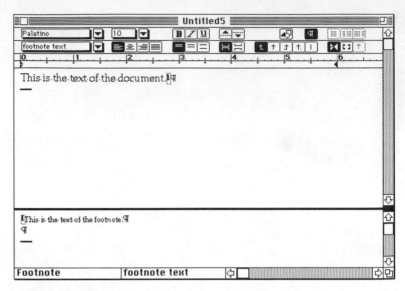

Fig. 15.12
The Footnote in
Page Layout view.

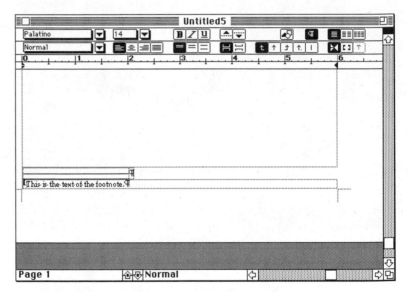

Part II

Creating More Complex Documents

5. When you finish typing the note, close the footnote window by double-clicking the split bar in Normal view or by pressing ⌘-Shift-Z (Go Back) in Page Layout view.

You can change the default formats for the footnote reference mark (superscript, 9-point characters) and footnote text (single-spaced, flush-left lines with 10-point characters). For details, see Chapter 8.

The footnote reference mark in your document isn't an ordinary number; it's a special character that links the reference mark to the footnote text. If you delete the footnote reference mark, you delete all the footnote text too! (If you accidentally delete the reference mark, immediately choose Undo from the Edit menu.)

Editing, Deleting, and Moving Footnotes and Endnotes

After you have created a footnote or endnote, you can add other notes, edit existing footnote text, delete the note, or move it to another location in your document.

To add footnotes, just place the insertion point where you want the footnote reference mark to appear and choose Footnotes from the Insert menu. Create the note in the usual way. Word adds the note, renumbering the existing ones automatically.

To edit the footnote text, do the following:

1. If you're working in Page Layout view, scroll down to view the footnotes. If you're working in Normal view, you can open the footnote window three different ways:

   Double-click a footnote reference mark.

   Choose Footnotes from the View menu.

   Hold down the Shift key and drag the split bar down from the top of the screen.

2. Edit the note.

To delete a footnote, follow these steps:

1. Select the footnote reference mark—*not* the footnote text.

2. Press Backspace or Delete, or choose Cut from the Edit menu.

TIP

If you see the message Can't delete paragraph mark in footnote window, you tried to delete the paragraph mark included with the footnote text. You cannot delete this mark. If you want to remove the footnote completely, including the mark, you need to delete the footnote reference mark.

To move a footnote, follow these steps:

1. Select the footnote reference mark. You don't have to select the footnote text—just the mark.

2. Choose Cut or press ⌘-X.

3. Position the insertion point at the footnote reference mark's new location.

4. Choose Paste from the Edit menu or press ⌘-V.

Word moves the footnote reference mark *and* the footnote text, though you selected only the mark.

Unless you have a full-page display, which can show the whole page (including footnotes), switch to Normal view when you're editing your document. Then choose Footnotes from the View menu to open the footnote window. As you scroll through your document, Word automatically displays the notes whose reference marks are visible in the document window.

If you're writing for a typographically conservative journal that requires you to use a short version of a citation after the initial reference (such as "Jones, *Challenge of Technological Innovation*," instead of the whole citation), create a new glossary and add to it the short version of the citation. Then enter later citations using the glossary. Be sure to type the citation the same way every time.

Modifying the Separators

By default, Word enters a two-inch separator between the footnotes and the body text. The program enters a longer line when a lengthy footnote is continued to the next page, but does not print a continuation notice. You can change any of these separator options.

The separator lines are graphics, not characters. This means that you cannot shorten or lengthen the separators by deleting or adding characters; you must delete the whole line and enter a new one. To add a new line, create it first using Word 5's new Draw capabilities, discussed in Chapter 20. Then select the graphic you have created and copy it to the clipboard before proceeding.

To change the separator, follow these steps:

1. From anywhere in your document, choose Footnotes from the Insert menu or press ⌘-E.

Part II

Creating More Complex Documents

You see the Reference Mark dialog box. Note that this is the procedure you usually use to add a footnote. However, Word does not enter a footnote reference mark after this operation.

2. Choose Separator, Cont. Separator, or Cont. Notice.

   Depending on which option you choose, you see the Footnote Separator dialog box (see fig. 15.13), the Footnote Cont. Separator dialog box (see fig. 15.14), or the Footnote Cont. Notice dialog box (see fig. 15.15).

Fig. 15.13
The Footnote Separator dialog box.

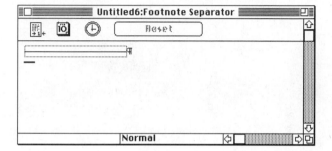

Fig. 15.14
The Footnote Cont. Separator dialog box.

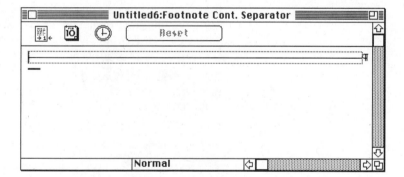

3. To delete the separator, select it and press Backspace or Delete. If you copied a shorter or longer line to the clipboard before choosing this command, select the existing line and choose Paste from the Edit menu to replace it. If you're adding a continuation notice, just type the text.

4. Click the Close box to return to your document without adding a footnote.

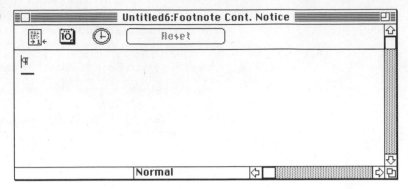

Fig. 15.15
The Footnote Cont. Notice
dialog box.

Specifying Where Footnotes Will Print

To see your options of where to print footnotes, choose Document from the Format menu and choose the Position drop-down list box.

Bottom of Page. Choose this option to place footnotes at the bottom of the page, even if the last page isn't completely filled with text.

Beneath Text. Choose this option to place footnotes at the bottom of the page, except on the last page or any other page where the text does not fill the page. Word then positions the notes on these pages just after the last line of text.

End of Section. Choose this option if you have created a multisection document and want the notes for each section to be collected and printed as endnotes at the end of each section.

End of Document. Choose this option to print all endnotes at the end of your document—even if you have divided it into sections.

After you choose the option you want, choose OK. The choice you make affects the entire document.

You can use the End of Section option to collect and print all the endnotes for each section at the end of that section, such as a chapter. As you learn in Chapter 16, sometimes you must create a section break for reasons other than starting a new chapter. For example, you must create a section break to change from single- to multiple-column formatting. You can stop Word from collecting and printing the endnotes for such a section. Just place the insertion point in the section and choose Section from the Format menu. Deactivate the Include Endnotes box. Word does not print the endnotes until the end of the next section.

Controlling Footnote Numbering

You can control footnote numbering in two ways:

■ *Resetting the Starting Number.* Many writers like to break very large documents, such as books or dissertations, into separate files. To print these files with the footnotes numbered consecutively, you must manually reset the starting number for each file so that it begins where the preceding file ended. Otherwise each file starts with 1. Suppose that Chapter 2 is contained in the file THESIS—CHAPTER 2. Because the last footnote in Chapter 1 was 119, you want to start Chapter 2's footnotes with 120.

■ *Restarting the Sequence at Page or Section Breaks.* If you have chosen footnotes (Bottom of Page option), the Document dialog box displays an option called Restart Each Page. If you choose this option, Word restarts the numbering sequence at 1 at the beginning of each page. If you have chosen endnotes grouped at the end of sections, you see an option called Restart Each Section. With this option, Word restarts the numbering sequence at the beginning of each section.

The following procedures detail the steps you take to control footnote numbering both ways.

To reset the starting number, follow these steps:

1. Choose Document from the Format menu or press ⌘-F14.

   You see the Document dialog box.

2. Type the starting number in the Number From text box.

3. Choose OK.

To restart the sequence at page or section breaks, follow these steps:

1. Choose Document from the Format menu or press ⌘-F14.

   You see the Document dialog box.

2. From the Position box, choose one of the Page options (Bottom of Page or Beneath Text) or the End of Section option.

3. Choose Restart Each Page or Restart Each Section.

4. Choose OK.

Quick Review

his section concisely summarizes the most useful information in this chapter. Check "Productivity Tips" for a review of high-productivity tips and tricks, and review "Techniques" when you forget how to perform a specific procedure.

Productivity Tips

■ Quickly add page numbers to your document by switching to Normal view, choosing Header or Footer, and clicking the page number icon. Add the time and date, if you want.

■ Use the Summary Info glossaries to add your name, your document's title, and other information to headers or footers.

■ By default, Word uses the Normal style's font and font size for headers and footers. If you want to change the font and/or font size for body text in your document, make the change to the Normal style, not directly to the text. That way, your change affects the Header and Footer styles too, because they're based on Normal. (For an explanation of styles and basing one style on another, see Chapter 8.

■ You probably very seldom want headers to print on the first page of your document. If so, choose Different First Page in the Section dialog box. To make this choice the default for all your documents, choose the Use as Default button.

■ If you have chosen margins other than 1.25" left and right, redefine the Header and Footer styles to position header and footer tab stops at the center of the page and at the right margin. If you're using 1-inch margins left and right, for instance, set the centered tab at 3.25 inches and the flush right tab at 6.5 inches.

Techniques

This section provides concise, quick-reference summaries of all the procedures introduced in this chapter.

Part II

Creating More Complex Documents

Adding a Footnote to Your Document

To create a footnote:

1. Position the insertion point in your text at the point where you want the footnote reference mark to appear.

2. Choose Footnote from the Insert window or press ⌘-E.

3. When the Footnote dialog box appears, choose OK to have Word automatically number the note.

4. Type the text of the note.

5. When you finish typing the note, close the footnote window by double-clicking the split bar in Normal view or by pressing ⌘-Shift-Z (Go Back) in Page Layout view.

Adding a Header or Footer

To add a header or footer to your document in Normal view:

1. Choose Header or Open from the View menu.

2. Type the header or footer text in the window.

3. Format the header or footer as you choose.

4. To add page numbers, the current time, or the current date, click the insertion point where you want the number, the time, or the date to appear. Use the preset tabs to align the page number, date, or time. Then click the icon on the header or footer title bar.

5. Click the Close box to close the header or footer window.

To add a header or footer to your document in Page Layout view:

1. Choose Header or Footer from the View menu.

2. Type the header or footer text, and if you want, format the text.

3. To enter the date, choose Date from the Insert menu. Alternatively, choose Glossary from the Edit menu (or press ⌘-K) and choose one of the Date glossaries.

4. To enter the time, choose Glossary from the Edit menu (or press ⌘-K) and choose one of the Time glossaries.

5. When you finish creating the header or footer, just click the cursor outside the header or footer and continue working on your document.

To add special first-page headers or footers in Normal view:

1. If necessary, activate the Different First Page option in the Section dialog box.

2. Choose First Header or First Footer from the View menu.

3. Create the header or footer for the first page.

4. Click the Close box to confirm the header.

To add special first-page headers or footers in Page Layout view:

1. If necessary, activate the Different First Page option in the Section dialog box.

2. Scroll to the first page of your document.

3. Choose Header or Footer from the View menu.

4. Create the header or footer for the first page.

Changing the Vertical Position of Headers or Footers

To change the vertical position of headers or footers:

1. Choose Section from the Format menu.

2. In the Header/Footer area, type a measurement in the From Top box to change the vertical position of headers.

3. In the From Bottom box, type a measurement to change the vertical position of footers.

4. Choose OK.

Creating Different Headers or Footers for Facing Pages

To create different headers for odd and even pages in Normal view:

1. Choose Document from the Format menu.

2. Activate the Even/Odd Headers check box.

3. Choose OK.

4. Pull down the View menu.

5. Choose one of header or footer options and, when the Header or Footer dialog box appears, create the header or footer.

6. Repeat step 5 until you have created all the headers or footers you want.

To create different headers for odd and even pages in Page Layout view:

1. Choose Document from the Format menu.

2. Activate the Even/Odd Headers check box.

3. Choose OK.

4. Scroll to an odd-numbered page.

5. Choose Header or Footer from the View menu.

6. Create the header or footer.

7. Scroll to an even-numbered page.

8. Create the header or footer.

Deleting a Footnote

To delete a footnote:

1. Select the footnote reference mark—*not* the footnote text.

2. Press Backspace or Delete, or choose Cut from the Edit menu.

Deleting a Header or Footer

To delete a header or footer in Normal view:

1. Choose Header or Footer from the View menu.

2. When the Header or Footer window appears, delete all the text.

3. Click the Close box to close the Header or Footer dialog box.

To delete a header or footer in Page Layout view:

1. Scroll the screen to display the header or footer.

2. Delete all the header or footer text.

Editing a Footnote

To edit a footnote:

1. If you're working in Page Layout view, scroll down to view the footnotes. If you're working in Normal view, you can open the footnote window three different ways:

   Double-click a footnote reference mark.

   Choose Footnotes from the View menu.

   Hold down the Shift key and drag the split bar down from the top of the screen.

2. Edit the note.

Editing a Header or Footer

To edit a header or footer in Normal view:

1. Choose Header or Footer from the View menu.

2. When the Header or Footer window appears, edit the text.

3. Click the Close box to close the Header or Footer dialog box.

To edit a header or footer in Page Layout view:

1. Scroll the screen to display the header or footer.

2. Edit the header or footer text.

Modifying Footnote Separators

To modify footnote separators:

1. From anywhere in your document, choose Footnotes from the Insert menu or press ⌘-E.

2. Choose Separator, Cont. Separator, or Cont. Notice.

3. To delete the separator, select it and press Backspace or Delete. If you copied a shorter or longer line to the clipboard before choosing this command, select the existing line and choose Paste from the Edit menu to replace it. If you're adding a continuation notice, just type the text.

4. Click the Close box to return to your document without adding a footnote.

Moving a Footnote

To move a footnote:

1. Select the footnote reference mark. You don't have to select the footnote text—just the mark.

2. Choose Cut or press ⌘-X.

3. Position the insertion point at the footnote reference mark's new location.

4. Choose Paste from the Edit menu or press ⌘-V.

Resetting the Starting Footnote Number

To reset the number with which Word starts numbering the footnotes in a document:

1. Choose Document from the Format menu or press Shift-F14.

2. Type the starting number in the Number From text box.

3. Choose OK.

To restart the sequence at page or section breaks:

1. Choose Document from the Format menu or press Shift-F14.

2. From the Position box, choose one of the Page options (Bottom of Page or Beneath Text) or the End of Section option.

3. Choose Restart Each Page or Restart Each Section.

4. Choose OK.

Suppressing First Page Headers or Footers

To suppress the printing of headers or footers on the first page of your document or section:

1. Choose Section from the Format menu.

2. Activate the Different First Page option.

3. Choose Use as Default to make this choice the default for all documents.

4. Choose OK.

Dividing a Document into Sections

16

When you start a new document, the whole document is one section. Any section formats you choose apply to the whole document. In this chapter, you learn how and when to enter *section breaks* to divide your document into two or more sections. You also explore additional features of the Section dialog box, including creating multiple columns (newspaper columns) and controlling page breaks, headers and footers, and footnotes.

A section break divides any Word document into two or more parts, or sections. When you press ⌘ Enter, Word enters a section break into your document. The section break looks like a double row of little dots across the screen. Word defines a *section* as a portion of a document that has been demarcated by a section break. In your documents, a section might correspond to chapters in a book or dissertation.

Most Word users employ section breaks for two purposes:

- *Dividing a Document into Chapters*. If you use section breaks to divide a report, proposal, or other lengthy document into chapters, you can give each chapter distinctive headers and footers, footnote numbering sequence, page number sequence, and starting page format. (Headers and footers are short versions of a chapter's title printed at the top or bottom of the page.) You can format chapters with continuous Arabic numbers located at the upper right, for example, but use lowercase alphabetical page numbers centered at the bottom of the page for appendixes.

USING
WORD 5
FOR THE
MAC

■ *Changing Column Formats*. As you learn in this chapter, Word easily can create multiple columns (also called newspaper columns). You can create a document with two, three, or more columns. You also can switch column formats as many times as you want, even in one page. You can create a newsletter, for example, with a page-wide (single-column) banner across the top and three columns of text below the banner. To change column formats, you must enter a section break.

This chapter is organized into two sections that parallel these two applications. You find additional information on section formatting in Chapters 15 and 19.

Dividing a Document into Chapters

Many of the documents commonly used in business and professional writing (such as proposals, technical reports, and business reports) are organized into chapters. Word's Section dialog box, shown in figure 16.1, helps you with chapter formatting in many ways.

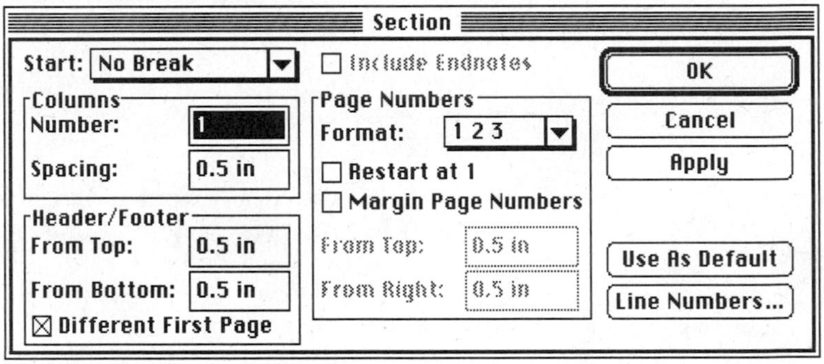

Fig. 16.1
The Section dialog box.

Page Breaks. With the Section dialog box, you can control how the chapter starts. By choosing an option in the Start list box, you instruct Word to start a section on a new page, on the next odd-numbered page, or the next even-numbered page. You should start documents that you plan to duplicate using both sides of the page on an odd-numbered page. If you don't want page breaks when a new chapter starts, you can choose the No Break option.

Page Numbers. You already have learned how to add page numbers to your document. When you break a section, you can choose to restart page numbering at 1 or to have continuous page numbers. You also can change the page number location and numbering format (Roman, Arabic, etc.).

Headers and Footers. When you break a section, Word continues the current header and footer—unless you add a new header or footer on the section's first page. You can create a document that has different headers or footers for each section. You also can change the header and footer positions.

Different First Page. If the first page of your chapter has a title, you don't want headers or page numbers to print on this page. By choosing Different First Page, you can suppress the printing of headers and page numbers on the first page of a section.

Endnotes. As you learned in the preceding chapter, you can choose to have footnotes printed at the end of each section. Each chapter can close with its own endnotes.

In the sections to follow, you learn how to control chapter titles, headers, footers, and other formats in a multisection document. First, however, you learn how to enter—and remove—section breaks.

Dividing a document into sections is an excellent idea for projects that rarely exceed 100 pages. For a very long document, however, Word's performance becomes sluggish, especially if you're using one of the slower Macs. You may want to break your document's chapters into separate Word documents. You still can print the document with continuous pagination and footnote numbering.

You can compile a table of contents and an index for all these documents. If you want continuous footnote numbering, however, you have to type the beginning footnote number at the beginning of each document. Each document prints with its own headers and footers as if it were a distinct section. For more information, see Chapter 26.

Creating and Removing Section Breaks

When you create a new Word document, the document has only one section. To enter a section break, follow these steps:

1. Place the insertion point where you want the section break to occur.

2. Choose Section Break from the Insert menu, or press ⌘-Enter.

   Word places the insertion point below the section break so that the insertion point is in the new section. Word copies the section formats currently in effect to the new section.

3. To format the new section with Section dialog box formats, choose Section from the Format menu.

After you enter a section break, the document has two sections. The page number area changes to show the page number and the section number (using the abbreviations *P* and *S*, as in P2 S2). The section break is visible as a double row of dots across the screen (see fig. 16.2).

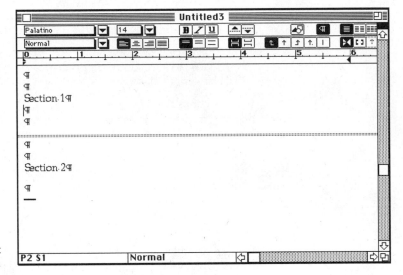

TIP

When you enter a section break, Word uses the current section formats for the new section. If you want the new section to have a different section format, choose Section from the Format menu and Options from the Section dialog box. Assuming that you want to format the new section, Word places the insertion point below the section break.

Fig. 16.2
Section break in document with two sections.

To remove a section break, follow these steps:

1. Choose the section mark by clicking in the selection bar (to the left of the section mark).

2. Press Backspace or Delete.

Understanding the Default Section Formats

When you insert a section break, Word copies the section formats currently in effect to the new section you created. Unless you chose section formats for the preceding section, these formats are the default section formats. To understand what happens when you create a section break, you should know what these default formats are. Table 16.1 lists Word's default section formats.

Table 16.1
Default Section Formats

Format	Default setting
Start	No Break
Columns	1
Spacing	0.5 inch
Header/Footer from Top	0.5 inch
Header/Footer from Bottom	0.5 inch
Different First Page	Deactivated (page numbers, if any, print on first page)
Include Endnotes	Activated (endnotes, if any, grouped and printed at end of section)
Margin Page Numbers	Deactivated (no page numbers, unless entered using Headers/footers or Print Preview)
Format	Arabic (1, 2, 3)
Restart at 1	Deactivated (page numbers printed continuously across section break)
Page Numbers from Top	0.5 inch
Page Numbers from Bottom	0.5 inch

TIP

Like paragraph marks, section marks store section formats. If you delete a section break, Word uses the *next* section's formats. If you copy a section break and insert it elsewhere, Word creates a new section that has the section formats you chose.

Because Word copies the current section formats to a newly created section, you should begin your document by choosing the section formats you want to apply to the whole document. Suppose that you want to begin each chapter on an odd page with page numbers printed at the center of the top margin. You also want to suppress the printing of page numbers on the first page of each chapter. When you begin your document, choose Section from the Format menu and choose these options from the Section dialog box. When you insert section breaks to divide your document into chapters, Word copies these formats to the newly created sections.

Selecting Sections for Formatting

When you create a section break, Word uses the section formats currently in effect. You can change section formats in two ways:

- *Formatting One Section.* To format one section, place the insertion point anywhere in the section you want to format and choose Section from the Format menu. The Section dialog box shows the formats currently in effect.
- *Formatting More Than One Section.* If you select two or more sections, you still can choose section formats. The formats you choose affect all the selected sections.

  When you choose Section from the Format menu, you see the Section dialog box with all the options blank (see fig. 16.3). Word applies only the formats you choose; it does not interfere with any other section formats in the selected sections.

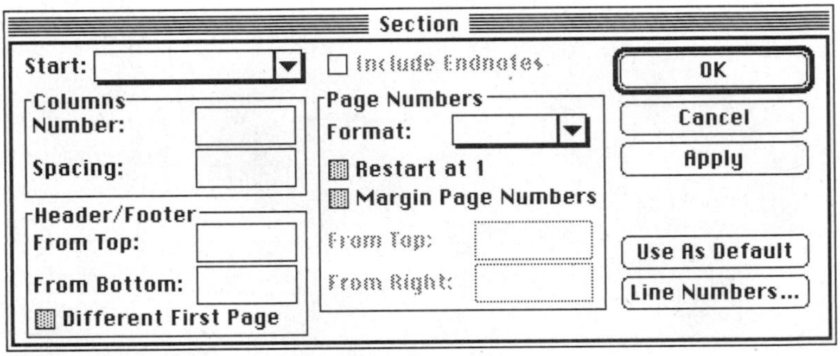

Fig. 16.3
Section dialog box after selecting two or more sections.

Controlling Page Breaks

By default, Word does not enter a page break when you start a new section. If you place the insertion point in the new section and choose Section from the Format menu, however, you can take advantage of several options for breaking pages at the start of a new section. You choose these options in the Start box:

No Break. The default option, No Break, tells Word not to break a page at the section mark. If you create a document with multiple columns, Word balances the columns above the section mark, as shown in figure 16.4.

New Page. Word starts a new page at the section mark.

New Column. In a document with multiple columns (newspaper columns), Word leaves the rest of the column blank and places the next text at the top of the next column.

NOTE

If the preceding section includes footnotes, Word starts the new section on a new page even if you choose No Break.

Fig. 16.4
Section break (No Break)
option in multiple-column
document.

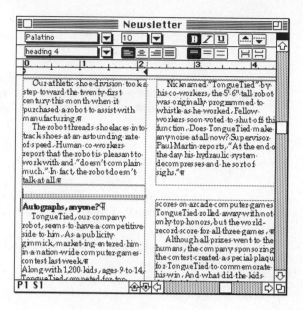

Odd Page. Word starts the next section on the next odd-numbered page. This option is the usual choice for documents to be duplicated on both sides of the page. If necessary, Word leaves a page blank—headers/footers and page numbers will be printed on this page.

Even Page. Word starts the next section on the next even-numbered page. If necessary, Word leaves a page blank—except for headers/footers and page numbers.

To control page breaks after entering a section break, follow these steps:

1. Place the insertion point in the section you want to format. Alternatively, choose two or more sections or choose Select All from the Edit menu (or press ⌘-A) to select the entire document.

2. Choose Section from the Format menu or press Option-F14.

   The Section dialog box appears.

3. Drop down the Start list box and choose a page start option.

4. Choose OK. Alternatively, choose Apply to see how the format will affect your document and then choose OK or Cancel.

Chapter 16
Dividing a Document into Sections

Controlling Page Numbers

As you already have learned, you can turn on page numbers in three different ways. In Chapter 7, you learned how to turn on page numbers with the Section dialog box's Margin Page Numbers option and how to add page numbers with Print Preview. In this section, you learn how section breaks affect page numbers.

Remember this rule: When you break a section, Word continues the current page number options you chose unless you deliberately change these options after that section break.

To illustrate, suppose that you place the insertion point in Section 1 of your document and choose Margin Page Numbers in the Section dialog box. Although you chose this option only in Section 1, Word prints page numbers throughout all sections.

Now suppose that you place the insertion point in Section 3 of the same document and deactivate Margin Page Numbers. Word stops printing page numbers after the Section 3 break, and subsequent sections don't have page numbers.

This same rule applies to page numbers added in headers and footers (see Chapter 15). If you add page numbers using a header or footer in Section 1, Word continues printing the header/footer and page numbers throughout your document—unless you change the header/footer in a subsequent section and leave page numbers out.

To add page numbers throughout a multisection document, follow these steps:

1. Position the insertion point within Section 1.

2. Choose Section from the Format menu or press Option-F14.

   The Section dialog box appears.

3. To suppress the printing of page numbers on the first page of a section throughout your document, activate the Different First Page option.

4. To turn on page numbers, activate Margin Page Numbers.

5. To change the page number position, type new measurements in the From Top and From Right boxes.

6. To begin each section's page numbers with the number 1, activate the Restart at 1 option.

TIP

Page numbers added with Print Preview work the same way as Margin Page Numbers. To add page numbers throughout a multisection document, position the insertion point in the first section and choose Print Preview. Double-click the Page Number button to place page numbers in the default position (upper right corner) or drag the page number to the position selected.

SPEED KEY

7. To use a page number format other than Arabic numbers (1, 2, 3), choose the format in the Format list box.

8. Choose OK.

Controlling Headers and Footers

Headers and footers, introduced in Chapter 15, work the same way as page numbers: the headers or footers you insert affect all subsequent sections until you change them. When you start a new section, Word continues using the headers or footers you chose. When you change the header or footer in the new section. Word applies the change to that section. Subsequent sections have the changed header or footer—unless you change it in a subsequent section.

Suppose, for example, that you insert the header *Chapter 1* in section 1. All the subsequent sections will have the header, *Chapter 1*. If you want your document to have different headers or footers for each section, you must change them after each section break.

To start a new header or footer after a section break, follow these steps:

1. Place the insertion point in the section you want to format.

2. Use the Header or Footer commands in the View menu to add the header or footer, following the procedures you learned in the preceding chapter.

If you change a header or footer and then decide the change was a bad idea, the Same As Previous button tells Word to use the preceding header or footer (see fig. 16.5). This button becomes available in the Header or Footer dialog boxes only when you have created a document with multiple sections and the preceding section's header or footer differs from the one entered.

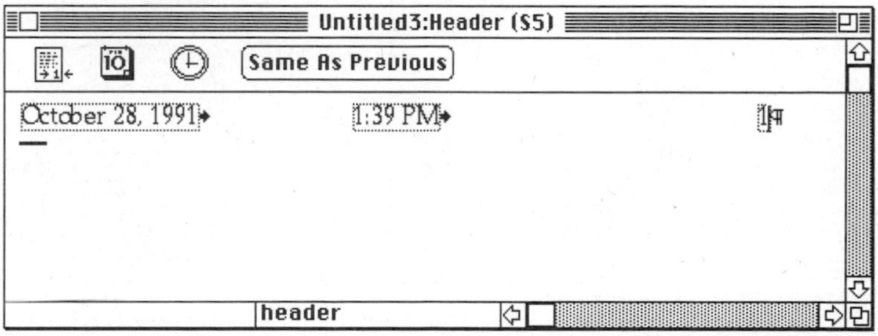

Fig. 16.5
Same As Previous button activates when header or footer changes after a section break.

```
Untitled3:Header (S5)

[icons]  [Same As Previous]

October 28, 1991    1:39 PM

header
```

Chapter 16
Dividing a Document into Sections

Creating Newspaper Columns

Among the many formats you can vary from section to section are columns. Word can format your text so that it appears in multiple columns (like the columns you see in newspapers or magazines). These columns are called *snaking columns* because the text, when it reaches the bottom of a column, *snakes* to the top of the next one. Word can create up to 100 columns, but for most applications you only need two or three columns.

If you add newspaper columns to your document, you probably will want to print some of your document with a one-column layout and the rest in a two-column or three-column layout, like the newsletter shown in figure 16.6. The newsletter's title is across the top of the page, and the text is printed in a three-column format.

Fig. 16.6
Print Preview of newsletter.

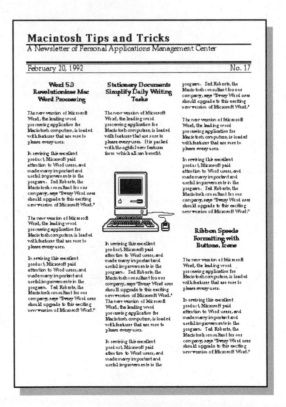

To switch from one column format to another, divide your document into sections and format each section with a different column layout. In short, column layouts are section formats. If you divide your document into sections, you can change section formats—or column formats—as often as you want.

In this section, you learn how to choose multiple column formats, using section breaks to change from one column format to another, and how to change column formats after you have created them. You also learn how to start new columns and how to use the keyboard to move the cursor from one column to the next.

Viewing Multiple Columns

Before you create multiple columns, you should learn how they're displayed on-screen. In Normal view, Word displays one column, and the ruler shows the column width (measured from the left margin of the column), as shown in figure 16.7. In Page Layout view, Word displays the columns as they will appear when printed (see fig. 16.8). Note that the ruler always positions the zero mark at the left margin of the column in which the insertion point is currently positioned.

Fig. 16.7
Normal view of multiple-column document.

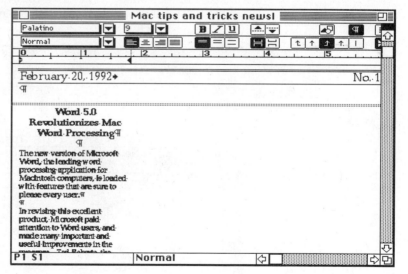

Fig. 16.8
Page Layout view
of multiple-column
document.

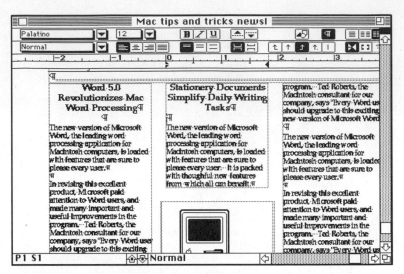

If you click the Margin button on the ruler so that Word displays the margin brackets rather than the indents, the ruler measures the page with the zero mark positioned at the left edge. With the Margin button activated, the ruler works this way in Normal view and Page Layout view. (See fig. 16.9 for an illustration of this display in Page Layout view.)

Fig. 16.9
Page Layout view of
multiple-column document
(Margin button activated
on ruler).

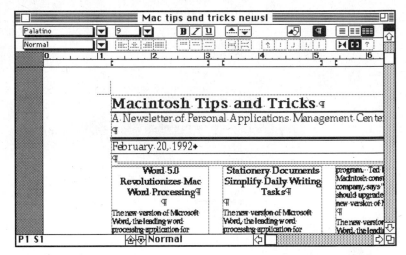

Adding Columns

You need to enter the section break just before the place where multiple columns begin. If you don't divide your document into sections, your whole document prints with the multiple-column format you chose.

You can add multiple columns in two ways:

- *Ribbon*. Choose this option to add two- or three-column formats to your document quickly. Word uses the default column spacing (0.5").

- *Section Dialog Box*. Choose this option to add more than three columns or to use a column spacing other than 0.5 inch.

To add a two- or three-column format to your document by using the Ribbon, follow these steps:

1. Place the insertion point in the section you want to format with multiple columns.

2. On the ribbon, choose one of the multiple-column buttons (see fig. 16.10).

   You can choose a two-column or three-column format.

Fig. 16.10
Multiple Column buttons on ribbon.

To add a multiple-column format by using the Section dialog box, follow these steps:

1. Choose Section from the Format menu or press Option-F14.

   The Section dialog box appears.

2. In the Number box, type the number of columns you want to create.

   You can create up to 100 columns, but doing so doesn't make much sense unless you want columns with only one or two characters each. For most common applications, such as newsletters or price lists, use two or three columns.

3. In the Spacing box, type a measurement to indicate how much white space you want between the columns.

Chapter 16
Dividing a Document into Sections

By default, Word inserts 0.5 inch of white space between the columns. If you're using a three-column layout, try using 0.25-inch spacing.

4. Choose OK.

Word creates the section format you have chosen.

Changing Column Formats

n the old days of word processing, programs could create multiple-column formats, but you could only use one column option per page. With Word, you can change column formats as many times as you want. In this section, you learn how to change column formats.

To change column formats without starting a new page, follow these steps:

1. Position the insertion point where you want the new column format to begin.

2. Press ⌘-Enter to create a section break.

3. With the insertion point positioned below the section break, choose Section from the Format menu.

4. In the Columns box, type the number of columns you want.

5. To change the default column spacing (0.5 inch), type a measurement in the Spacing box.

6. In the Start list box, choose No Break.

7. Choose OK.

Word creates the section break and starts the new column format.

Controlling Column Breaks

When you're typing a multiple-column document, you may want to start a new column before reaching the bottom margin. You do so by inserting a manual column break.

To start a new column before reaching the bottom margin, follow these steps:

1. Place the insertion point where you want to break the column.

2. Choose Page Break from the Insert menu.

   In a multiple-column section, this command breaks a column, not a page.

As you just learned, the Page Break command breaks a column, not a page, when the insertion point is positioned in a multiple-column section. To break a page in a multiple-section document, follow these steps:

1. Position the insertion point where you want to break the page.

2. Press ⌘-Enter to enter a section break.

   Word moves the insertion point beneath the section break.

3. Choose Section from the Format menu.

   The Section dialog box appears.

4. In the Start box, choose a page break option.

   You can choose from New Page, Odd Page (starts the new page on the next odd-numbered page), or Even Page (starts the new page on the next even-numbered page).

5. Choose OK.

TIP

To prevent unwanted column breaks, format paragraphs with the Keep with Next option. Word does not insert a page break after a paragraph formatted with this option.

Changing Column Width

When you create a multiple-column format, Word calculates the width of each column, based on the margins and the column spacing you have chosen (0.5 inch is the default). You can change the column spacing in two ways:

- *Changing the Column Spacing Setting*. By default, Word leaves 0.5 inch blank between the columns. Change this measurement to get broader or narrower columns.

- *Dragging the Margin Brackets on the Ruler*. Clicking the Margin Brackets button on the ruler displays the ruler scale. The left and right boundaries of each column are shown as brackets on the ruler. Dragging these brackets changes the width of the columns by increasing or decreasing the amount of blank space between them.

Note

You cannot create columns with unequal widths by using the Section dialog box. You can achieve this end, however, by inserting a table, as discussed in Chapter 17.

Balancing the Text on the Page

If you create a multiple-column section that doesn't completely fill up the page, the page may look unbalanced, as shown in figure 16.11. In this section, you learn how to balance the text on the page (see fig. 16.12).

Fig. 16.11

Multiple-section document that needs balancing.

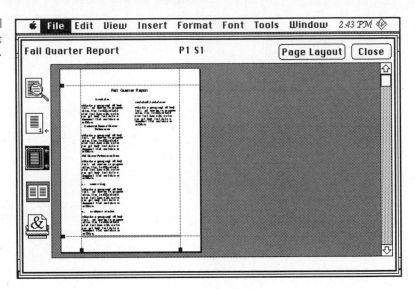

To balance the text on the page as shown in figure 16.12, insert a section break after the last text by following these steps:

1. Place the insertion point at the end of the text.

2. Press ⌘-Enter to create a section break.

3. With the insertion point positioned in the new section, choose Section.

   The Section dialog box appears.

4. In the Start list box, choose No Break.

Fig. 16.12
Multiple-section document after balancing the text on the page.

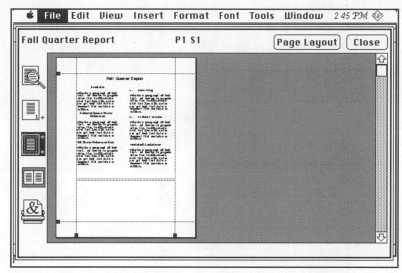

Quick Review

This section summarizes the most useful information in this chapter. Check "Productivity Tips" for a review of high-productivity tips and tricks, and review "Techniques" when you forget how to perform a specific procedure.

Productivity Tips

■ You can use section breaks to divide your document into chapters or to change column formats in your document. If you haven't divided your document by pressing ⌘-Enter or choosing Section Break from the Insert menu, your document has one section.

■ If you're creating a fairly brief multichapter document, such as a business report or a master's thesis, you can break the document into sections and keep the whole document in one file. For a long novel or book, however, you probably should consider keeping each chapter in its own separate file. See Chapter 26 for tips on printing these files with continuous pagination, a unified table of contents, and a unified index.

Chapter 16

Dividing a Document into Sections

- To create a two- or three-column format quickly, click the Multiple Column buttons on the ribbon.

- Bear in mind that after you enter a section break, Word places the insertion point *after* the break. If you choose Section, your choices in the Section dialog box affect the section below the section break.

- You can delete a section break just as you can delete a paragraph mark. If you delete a section break, the section above the deleted break takes on the following section's formats.

- To use more than one multiple-column format on a page, create a section break and then format the new section using the No Break option in the Section dialog box.

Techniques

This section provides concise, quick-reference summaries of all the procedures introduced in this chapter.

Changing Column Formats

To change column formats without starting a new page:

1. Position the insertion point where you want the new column format to begin.

2. Press ⌘-Enter to create a section break.

3. With the insertion point positioned below the section break, choose Section from the Format menu.

4. In the Columns box, type the number of columns you want.

5. If you want, change the default column spacing (0.5 inch) by typing a measurement in the Spacing box.

6. In the Start list box, choose No Break.

7. Choose OK.

Changing Column Width

To widen or narrow the columns with the ruler:

1. With the ruler displayed, click the Margin Brackets button.

2. Drag one of the margin brackets left or right.

To widen or narrow the columns with the Section dialog box:

1. Choose Section from the Format menu or press Option-F14.

2. Increase the measurement in the Spacing box to narrow the columns or decrease the measurement to widen them.

3. Choose OK.

Changing Headers or Footers

To change the header or footer text within your document:

1. Place the insertion point where you want the new header or footer text to begin printing.

2. To create a section break, choose Section Break from the Insert menu or press ⌘-Enter.

3. Choose Section from the Format menu and choose a page break option in the Start list box.

4. Choose OK.

5. Choose Header or Footer from the View menu and type the new header or footer text.

6. Choose OK.

Changing Spacing Between Columns

To change the default spacing between columns:

1. Place the insertion point in the section you want to format.

2. Choose Section from the Format menu or press Option-F14.

3. In the Spacing Box, type a measurement.

4. Choose OK.

Controlling Page Breaks

To control page breaks after entering a section break:

1. Place the insertion point in the section you want to format. Alternatively, select two or more sections or choose Select All from the Edit menu (or press ⌘-A) to select the entire document.

2. Choose Section from the Format menu or press Option-F14.

3. Drop down the Start list box and choose a page start option.

4. Choose OK. Alternatively, choose Apply to see how the format change will affect your document and then choose OK or Cancel.

Creating Newspaper Columns

To add a two- or three-column format to your document using the Ribbon:

1. Place the insertion point in the section you want to format with multiple columns.

2. On the ribbon, click one of the Multiple Column buttons.

To add a multiple-column format using the Section dialog box:

1. Choose Section from the Format menu or press Option-F14.

2. In the Number box, type the number of columns you want to create.

3. In the Spacing box, type a measurement indicating how much white space you want between the columns.

4. Choose OK.

Entering a Section Break

To enter a section break:

1. Place the insertion point where you want the section break to occur.

2. Choose Section Break from the Insert menu or press ⌘-Enter.

Removing a Section Break

To remove a section break:

1. Choose the section mark by clicking in the selection bar (to the left of the section mark).

2. Press Backspace or Delete.

Part II

Creating More Complex Documents

Starting a New Column

To start a new column before reaching the bottom margin:

1. Place the insertion point where you want to break the column.

2. Choose Page Break from the Insert menu.

Starting a New Page in a Multi-Column Section

To break a page in a multiple-section document:

1. Position the insertion point where you want to break the page.

2. Press ⌘-Enter to enter a section break.

3. Choose Section from the Format menu.

4. In the Start box, choose a page break option.

5. Choose OK.

Creating Tables

I f you frequently have to type tables, you know how tedious this task can be. Word includes some features that make creating tables much easier. Chief among these features is the Table command (Insert menu).

Word's Table command inserts a matrix of rows and columns, which—at least on first inspection—resembles an electronic spreadsheet. In a Word table, however, each cell (each intersection of a row and column) is an *expandable* text entry area. In figure 17.1, for example, the Capacity/ Specs column includes entries that occupy five or six lines. To create these entries, all you have to do is type—Word keeps the text within the cell and expands the whole row automatically.

The benefits of the Table command become obvious when you compare the table in figure 17.1 to a table created with tabs. To create a table like this with tabs, you must indent the second and subsequent lines by pressing the Tab key. Then you must use the new line command (Shift-Enter) to start a new line each time you reach the right edge of the column. Creating a table in this manner is easy enough, but what happens if you need to make changes? Adding or deleting a word can throw off the whole column.

With the Table command, Word keeps the text within cells, where you can make all the changes you want. Moreover, you cannot delete the table matrix accidentally, the way you can delete tabs or paragraph marks. You can edit without worrying about making a mess out of the table.

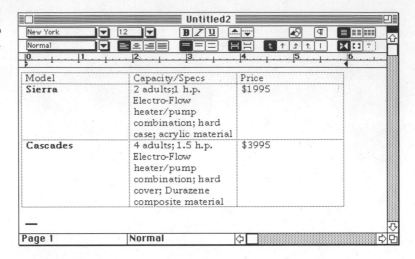

Fig. 17.1

Table cells expand to accommodate text.

Word's Table command provides wonderful tools for creating tables of all kinds, including such documents as price lists and brochures as well as the numerical tables found in academic articles or business reports. This chapter fully explores the various ways you can create tables with Word 5's Table command. In particular, the chapter covers the following topics:

- *Learning about Word's Tables.* You explore Word's Table command, learning how you can use this command not only to create tables of figures, but also to create side-by-side paragraphs and even to place text next to graphics.

- *Creating a Table.* In this section, you learn how to create a table in any Word document and how to create a table from existing tabbed text.

- *Moving the Insertion Point and Selecting Text.* When you create a table, special procedures become available for moving the cursor and selecting text. These procedures are covered in this section.

- *Editing the Table Matrix.* A table's layout of rows and columns, including Tab and Enter keystrokes, aren't like ordinary text—you cannot delete them the way you can delete characters. In the section on editing, you learn how to insert or delete rows, columns, or individual cells.

- *Formatting a Table.* After you insert a table, you can change the table's layout easily by adjusting column widths and changing row alignment. The procedures are covered in the section on formatting.

Word 5's Table commands have some notable improvements over Word 4. The former Insert Table command is now called Table, and the command is located in the new Insert menu. Word 5 also has two new commands in the Format menu: Table Cells and Table Layout. These commands are grayed until you create a table and place the insertion point within the table. These two commands bring together in a neat, logical way the various commands and procedures formerly needed to format and edit table cells and the table layout. If you created tables with Word 4, you can understand and appreciate the new commands within a few minutes.

Learning about Word's Tables

his section introduces tables. Specifics about creating, editing, and formatting tables are discussed later. For now, you need to know a few terms so that you can work effectively with tables.

When you create a table with the Table command, you specify first how many columns and rows you want. Word calculates column width so that each column has the same width. (You learn later in this chapter how to adjust the column widths.) In figure 17.2, for example, Word created a table with 5 columns and 15 rows. Each column is 1.2 inches wide. (The matrix of row and column lines do not print.)

Fig. 17.2
A table of 5 columns and 15 rows.

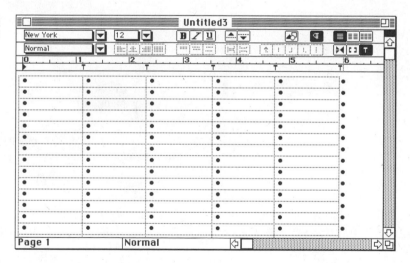

Chapter 17
Creating Tables

When you choose Show ¶ in the View menu, you see the end-of-column markers (the black dots in figure 17.2). Comparable to paragraph marks, these markers move right and down when you enter text.

When you choose Show Ruler in the View menu, and when the insertion point is positioned in a table, the ruler uses the letter T to show the column boundary positions (see fig. 17.2). As you learn elsewhere in this chapter, you can change column widths just by dragging the table boundary marks.

TIP

If you worked with side-by-side paragraphs in earlier versions of Word, you will be delighted at how much more easily you can create side-by-side paragraphs (paragraphs formatted so that they will always print next to each other) with the Table command.

With this overview of tables in mind, think of tables in terms of the following procedures:

- *Creating Tables*. To create a table, choose the Insert Table command in the Document menu, and Word inserts the matrix of rows and columns.
- *Editing Tables*. As you add text to the table, you may need to add rows or columns or to move columns. To insert or delete rows, columns, and cells, use the Table command in the Edit menu. To move and copy rows, columns, and cells, use the Cut, Copy, and Paste commands in the Edit menu.
- *Formatting Tables*. Changing the appearance of a table is easy. You can change column width, row height, and text alignment within columns or you can add borders so that the cell boundaries will print.

Creating a Table

To create a table, choose the Table command from the Insert menu. The Insert Table dialog box provides text boxes in which you specify how many columns and rows the table should have (see fig. 17.3).

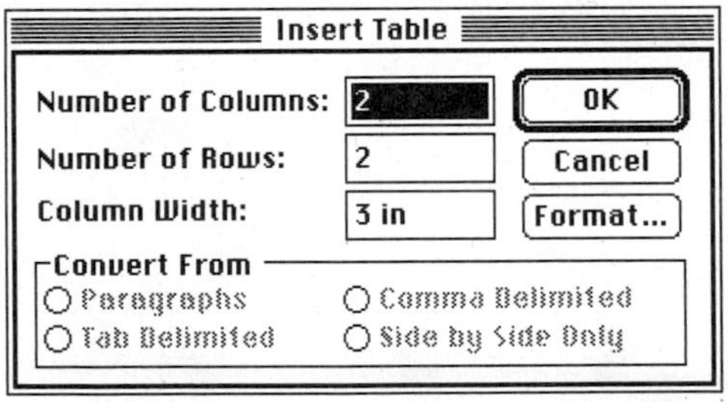
Insert Table
Number of Columns:
2
OK
Number of Rows:
2
Cancel
Column Width:
3 in
Format...
Convert From
Paragraphs
Comma Delimited
Tab Delimited
Side by Side Only

Fig. 17.3
The Insert Table dialog box.

The Table command inserts a two-column-by-two-row table by default. You may want to change these dimensions.

You can start a new table from scratch by setting tabs on the ruler to create a blank matrix of rows and columns, as explained in the next section. (A subsequent section explains how to convert a table you created by setting tabs.)

Before creating your table, decide whether you want to display the grid lines—the lines that mark cell boundaries, rows, and columns. Grid lines don't print unless you choose to print them, though by default they are visible on-screen. Grid lines are a handy way to visualize your table's overall form. To control the grid lines, use the Table Grid Lines check box in the View Preferences dialog box (Tools menu). To turn off gridlines on-screen, choose Preferences from the Tools menu, choose the View option, and then deactivate the Table Grid Lines box.

You also should decide whether you want to see the end-of-cell markers, the bullet characters that Word places in each cell. When the markers are displayed, you can easily see the alignment options you have chosen. If you have formatted a column with centered alignment, for instance, all the bullets are centered. To display these markers, choose Show ¶ in the View menu. (Alternatively, press ⌘-J or choose the Paragraph Mark button on the ribbon.)

Creating a New Table

To create a table, follow these steps:

1. Position the insertion point where you want the table to appear.

2. Choose Table from the Insert menu.

3. When the Insert Table dialog box appears, type in the Columns box the number of columns you want. Then type in the Rows box the number of rows you want.

   If you're not sure how many rows or columns you need, don't worry—you can add or delete rows and columns later.

   After you type the number of rows and columns you want, Word automatically calculates the column width, assuming that each column is the same width. You can adjust column widths later. To specify a column width (and override the automatic column-width calculation), type a number in the Column Width box.

4. Choose OK. Word creates the table and enters the grid pattern in your document.

Chapter 17
Creating Tables

Creating a Table from Existing Text

You can convert text that you created using tabs or other methods to a table format. To convert existing text to a table, select the text and choose Table. When you see the Insert Table dialog box, you can choose from the following options in the Convert From area:

Tab Delimited. Choose the Tab Delimited option to convert a table you created with tabs. Word transforms each line into a table row, even if the line ends in a soft return or a new line character. The program counts the number of tab characters in each line and uses this figure for the number of columns.

Comma Delimited. Choose the Comma Delimited option to make a table out of comma-delimited text imported from a database management program. Word transforms each line into a table row, even if the line ends in a soft return or a new line character. The program counts the number of commas in each line and uses this figure for the number of columns.

Paragraphs. Choose the Paragraph option to transform a series of vertical paragraphs into table cells. When you choose this option, Word proposes one column by default. You can choose more than one column. Suppose that you select six paragraphs and choose a three-column format. Word places paragraphs 1, 2, and 3 in Row 1, and paragraphs 4, 5, and 6 in Row 2.

Side-by-Side. Choose this option only to convert paragraphs formatted with Version 3.0's side-by-side paragraph format.

To convert an existing tab-formatted table to a Word table, follow these steps:

1. Select all text that you want to include in the table. Don't forget the paragraph marks.

2. Choose Table from the Insert menu. When the Insert Table dialog box appears, you see that Word proposes to base the conversion on the tabs and suggests a column width. You can adjust the column-width setting, if you want.

3. In the Convert From area, choose the option that describes how the existing text has been delimited (commas, tabs, paragraphs, or side-by-side paragraphs).

4. Choose OK. Word displays the table in the new cellular format.

Moving the Insertion Point and Selecting Text

After you create the table and place the insertion point in the table, the function of the Return and Tab keys changes, so take some time now to learn how to navigate within the table. You also need to learn a few additional selection techniques.

Using the Keyboard

Note that the following keys have unique functions within a table:

- Return does not start a new row. On the contrary, the Return key starts a new paragraph within the cell. Do not press Return unless you want to start a new paragraph inside the selected cell.

- Tab advances the insertion point to the next cell. If the insertion point is at the end of a row, pressing Tab advances the insertion point to the first cell in the next row down.

- Shift-Tab moves the insertion point back to the preceding cell. If the insertion point is at the beginning of a row, pressing Shift-Tab moves the insertion point to the last cell of the next row up.

- Option-Tab advances the insertion point to the next tab stop in a cell. You can set tabs in a cell, although this step is unnecessary in most cases. If you do set tabs, remember that pressing Tab advances the insertion point to the next cell, so you need to use Option-Tab to advance the insertion point to the next tab stop within a cell.

Selecting Rows and Columns

All the normal Word selection procedures operate within the Tables environment. In addition, each column has its own selection bar, which runs down the column just to the left of the left border of the column. Table 17.1 summarizes the methods of using the mouse to select text in a table.

To select	Mouse action
A cell's entire contents	Click the cell selection bar.
A row of a table	Double-click the cell's selection bar next to the row you want to select.
A column of a table	Click and drag within the column's selection bar, or hold down the Option key and click any cell in the column.
An entire table	Hold down the Option key and double-click anywhere in the table.

To type ordinary text in the middle of a table, position the insertion point below where you want the text to appear, and press ⌘-Option-space bar. Word breaks the table into two parts and inserts a normal paragraph between them.

Editing Table Text

One of the major advantages of creating a table using the Table command is that, after you create a table and add text, you can use any of Word's normal text editing commands to insert, copy, move, or delete text within the table. Your actions do not affect the table matrix, as they would in a tab-delimited table. (You use special commands to edit the table matrix by inserting or deleting rows, columns, or cells. These commands are discussed in the section titled "Editing the Table Matrix," later in this chapter.)

Copying, moving, and deleting, however, work slightly differently in tables. When you copy or move cells, exactly what Word copies or moves depends on whether you select the end of cell marker (the black dot, which you can see when you have chosen Show ¶ from the View menu).

If you copy or move without selecting the end-of-cell marker, Word copies or moves the cell contents, but not the cell itself. Use this technique to copy or move text into an existing cell or outside the table matrix entirely.

If you include the end-of-cell marker, Word copies or moves the cell contents *and* the cell. Use this technique to add cells as you copy or move. You also can use this technique to copy or move an entire table from one location to another. Note, though, that when you choose Cut to move the table, Word doesn't delete the table matrix. To remove the

TIP

To store a frequently used table matrix as a glossary entry, select the entire table, including the end of cell markers. Then choose Glossary from the Edit menu or press ⌘-K, and define the glossary entry following the usual procedures. For more information on glossaries, see Chapter 13.

table matrix from your document, you have to select the table and use the Table Layout's Delete command. The Table Layout command is covered in a subsequent section of this chapter.

When you select text in more than one cell, pressing Backspace or Delete cuts only the text in the first cell you selected. To delete the text in all the selected cells (but without removing the cells themselves), select the cells and choose Cut from the Edit menu, or press ⌘-X.

If you select one character outside of the table matrix, choosing Cut deletes the table matrix of the selected cells as well as the text within it. Normally, Cut doesn't delete the table matrix, just the cell contents. So be careful how you select text when you want to leave the cells intact. You can, however, turn this peculiarity into an advantage: To cut the entire table, text and matrix included, select the whole table and just one character, such as a paragraph mark, positioned outside the table, then choose Cut.

You can rearrange the rows in your table quickly and easily by using the Outline view.

To move a row up or down in your table, follow these steps:

1. Choose Outline from the View menu.

2. Select the row you want to move.

3. To move the row, press the up- or down-arrow keys or drag the black square that precedes the row.

4. Choose Normal or Page Layout to return to your document.

To move a column, you must insert a new, blank column, following the instructions given in the section "Editing the Cell Matrix." After moving the contents of the column to the newly inserted column, you can delete the blank column or use the column for additional data.

Formatting Your Table

You can format the table cells in many ways. For example, you can choose alignment options for the text within cells. By default, Word aligns text within cells flush left; however, you can align text flush right, justified, or centered. In figure 17.4, for example, note that the first column uses flush-right alignment, while the second column uses centered alignment. As far as Word is concerned, each cell is an independent paragraph, so you can format the cell contents with any alignment or indentation option you choose.

Fig. 17.4
Text aligned within cells.

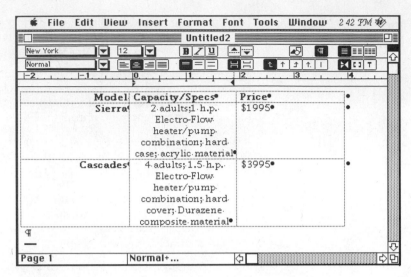

Understanding Table Formatting Options

The following is an overview of the formats you can control within table cells. Detailed instructions are given later in this section.

Character formats. Choose fonts, font sizes, and emphasis styles in the usual ways.

Paragraph formats. You can format text in each cell independently. You can choose from the normal alignment, blank line, line spacing, and indentation options. You can even apply styles.

Row alignment. You can align text within cells, as just explained. You also can align the entire row of cells. Your options are flush left (by default), centered, and flush right.

Column width. After you have created the table, you can change individual columns widths, or you can specify a new width to apply to all the columns.

Row Height. By default, Word uses the Auto line-spacing option to control row height. You can specify a row height in points, however.

Space Between Columns. By default, Word inserts 0.11 inch between columns. You can change this setting.

Indent. To indent text in every cell, you can specify an indentation. (By default, Word uses no indentation).

Part II

Creating More Complex Documents

You can format the text in tables using any of the normal Word formatting techniques such as keyboard shortcuts, pull-down menus, and the ribbon. When you position the insertion point within a table, the ruler changes and a grayed menu option, Table Cells (Format menu), becomes available.

When you position the insertion point in a table, the ruler changes so that the zero mark is located at the beginning of the active column (the one in which the insertion point is positioned). In figure 17.5, for example, the insertion point is in the third column. Note that Word has inserted the default 0.11-inch spacing between columns, so the zero mark isn't aligned exactly with the left-column boundary.

If you choose the Table Column Mark button (the T button on the ruler), the ruler scale changes (see fig. 17.6). The ruler scale now measures the page with the zero mark set at the left margin, and the T marks show where column boundaries have been inserted. You can change the width of the columns by dragging the markers.

Fig. 17.5
The ruler scale with the insertion point positioned within table.

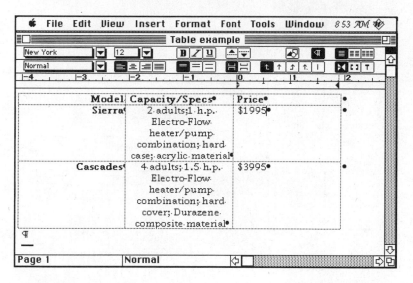

When you position the insertion point within a table, the Table Cells option becomes available in the Format menu. When you choose Table Cells, the Table Cells dialog box appears (see fig. 17.7). You can choose this command to change column width, row height, the space between columns, automatic indentation within each cell, and row alignment. You also can choose this option to apply borders to your table, as explained later in this chapter.

Chapter 17
Creating Tables

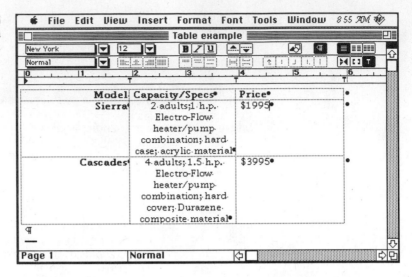

Fig. 17.6
The ruler with T marks on
the ruler.

When you use the Table Cells command, you can choose options that apply the format you have chosen to the selection (the default option in the Apply To list box) or to any of the following: each cell in the table, the entire column(s) selected, or the entire row(s) selected.

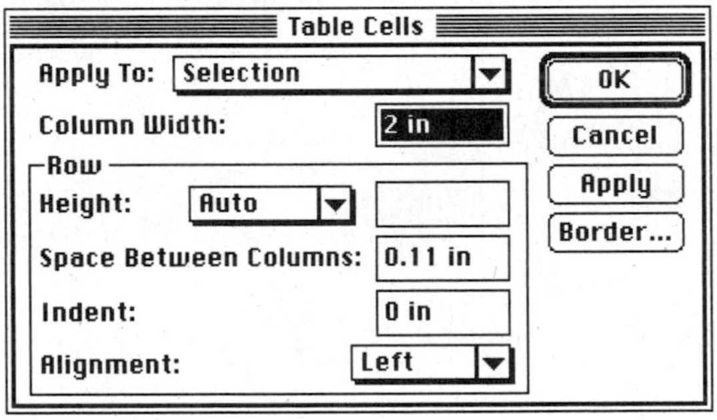

Fig. 17.7
Table Cells dialog box.

TIP

To adjust individual column widths quickly, choose the Table Mark button (the T button on the ruler) and drag one of the T marks. If you don't see the ruler, choose Ruler from the View menu or press ⌘-R.

In addition to these options, you can apply styles to the text in tables. If you frequently create tables that contain numbers, create a style (which you can call Table Numbers) that sets up a format with a decimal tab. When you apply this style to numbers in a cell, Word aligns the numbers by their decimal points.

Part II

Creating More Complex Documents

Editing the Table Matrix

To enter data into your table, use ordinary Word techniques to insert, modify, or delete text and numbers in the cells. To edit the matrix of rows and columns, however, you need special techniques. These techniques include commands for inserting and deleting rows and columns and for copying or moving cells.

Inserting Rows or Columns

You can easily add a new row or column in your table. When you add a new row, Word pushes existing rows down to make room. When you add a new column, Word pushes existing columns right to make room. To insert a row or column, follow these steps:

1. Position the insertion point in the row below where you want to place the new row. (If you're inserting a column, position the insertion point in the column to the left of the new column's location). To insert more than one row or column, select two or more rows or columns.

2. Choose Table Layout from the Format menu. The Table Layout dialog box appears (see fig. 17.8). By default, Word activates the Selection option. This option tells Word to apply your choice only to what you have selected.

Fig. 17.8
The Table Layout dialog box.

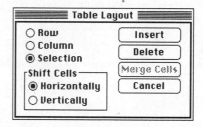

Fig. 17.8
The Table Layout dialog box.

3. Choose Row or Column. When you choose Row or Column, the options in the Shift Cells group are grayed.

4. Choose Insert.

To add rows to a table, do the following:

1. Position the insertion point just before the last end-of-cell marker in the table.

2. Press Tab. Word appends a new row to the end of the table.

To add a column at the right edge of your table, follow these steps:

1. Position the insertion point just beyond the right edge of the last cell in the first row, but just before the end of the cell mark at the end of the row.

2. Choose Table Layout from the Format menu.

3. Activate the Column option.

4. Choose Insert.

5. To insert additional rows, choose Repeat from the Edit menu or press ⌘-Y.

Deleting Rows and Columns

To prevent you from accidentally deleting rows or columns as you edit, you cannot delete cells by pressing Delete or by choosing Cut after you select the cells. Using Delete or Cut deletes only the cells' contents. You must use the Table Layout command in the Format menu to delete rows or columns.

To delete a row or column, follow these steps:

1. Place the insertion point in the row or column to be deleted. (To delete more than one row or column, select two or more rows or columns.)

2. Choose Table Layout from the Format menu. The Table Layout dialog box appears.

3. Choose Row or Column, depending on what you have selected.

4. Choose Delete.

Inserting and Deleting Individual Cells

In the preceding section, you learned how to insert or delete rows or columns from a table. You also can insert or delete individual cells. In figure 17.9, for example, a single cell has been added within the second row of the table.

Fig. 17.9
A single cell inserted within
the second row of a table.

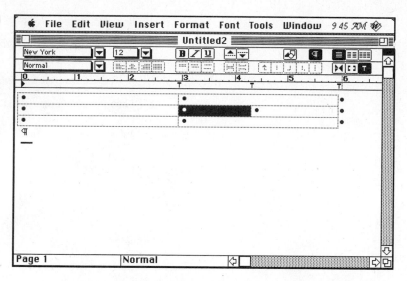

In addition to adding a cell to a row, you can push the cells of a column
down (without affecting adjacent columns) by inserting cells within a
column. Figure 17.10, for instance, shows the effect of inserting a cell in
the second column of the third row.

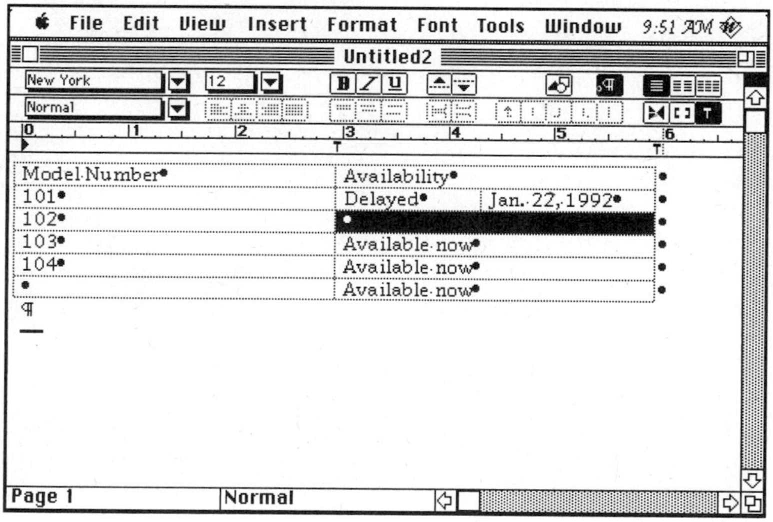

Fig. 17.10
A table after inserting an
individual cell and shifting
cells vertically.

To insert individual cells, follow these steps:

1. Select the cell or cells below or to the right of where you want to insert new cells.

2. Choose Table Layout from the Format menu.

3. When the Table Layout dialog box appears, choose the Selection button. Word activates the Shift Cells area. Decide whether to shift the cells horizontally (right) or vertically (down).

4. To shift the selected cells down, activate the Vertically button. To shift the selected cells right, activate the Horizontally button.

5. Choose Insert.

Merging and Splitting Cells

Sometimes you need to merge two cells into one. For example, in a complex table, a *decked head* is useful for organizing data (see fig. 17.11). The decked head spans the column headings (also called *box heads*) and clarifies the table's content. To create a decked head, you merge two or more cells so that they become one larger cell.

Fig. 17.11

Three cells merged into one to create a decked head (banner).

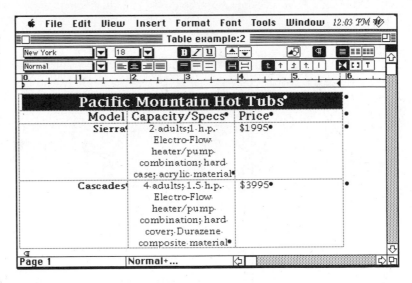

If you find the effects displeasing, you can split the cells you have merged.

To merge cells, follow these steps:

1. Select the cells to merge. You can select two or more cells.

2. Choose Table Layout from the Format menu.

3. Choose the Merge Cells button.

You cannot split a cell you have not previously merged. To split a merged cell, follow these steps:

1. Select the merged cell you want to split.

2. Choose Table Layout from the Format menu. The dialog box now displays a Split Cell button.

3. Choose the Split Cell button.

Converting a Table to Text

f you want to abandon the table matrix and work only with the text you have entered, you can delete the matrix and convert the table to text. Word will insert tabs to delimit the columns.

To remove the table matrix, follow these steps:

1. Select the entire table.

2. Choose Table to Text from the Insert menu.

Learning More Table Techniques

mportant techniques for expanding the usefulness of Word's Table command are discussed elsewhere in this book. This section gives you a quick overview of information about tables in other chapters.

Chapter 14 explains how to import spreadsheet data and convert the data into a Word table.

Chapter 18 discusses the use of Word's on-screen math capabilities to sum a column or row of figures quickly.

Chapter 19 includes instructions on adding numbers automatically to items in tables and lists, as well as using Word's automatic sorting capabilities to place the items in numerical or alphabetical order.

Chapter 20 shows how you can use a table format to place explanatory text next to a graphic—a useful technique for illustrating your document.

Chapter 22 explains how you can quickly add lines and borders to your table. Figure 17.12 shows a Word table to which graphics and borders have been added. Note that the banner line has two cells.

As figure 17.12 suggests, tables provide handy tools for placing text next to graphics. To position text next to graphics in your document, you may want to create a single-row table. For more information, see Chapter 20.

Fig. 17.12
A table with borders and graphics.

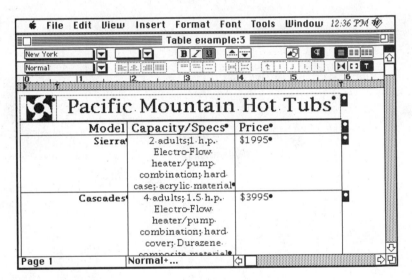

Quick Review

This section concisely summarizes the most useful information in this chapter. Check "Productivity Tips" for a review of high-productivity tips and tricks, and review "Techniques" when you forget how to perform a specific procedure.

Part II
Creating More Complex Documents

Productivity Tips

- Use the Table command rather than tabs to create tables in your document. The Table matrix enables you to move text in and out of your table without accidentally deleting your formatting.

- To edit tables easily, learn the mouse commands for selecting cells, rows, and columns.

- Switching to Outline view and dragging rows up or down is the quickest way to rearrange rows in your table.

- Remember that you must choose Table Cells to align the table rows horizontally on the page (flush left, centered, or flush right). Standard paragraph alignment commands affect the text within the cells, not the table rows.

- Merge cells to create headings that span two or more columns.

- Learn how the ruler works when the insertion point is in a table. Choose the three scale buttons, one by one, to see what they do.

- Read the chapters that discuss ways you can enhance your table by adding features such as lines, borders, numbers, and graphics.

- In tandem with Word's on-screen math (discussed in the next chapter), use a table to create a mini-spreadsheet within your Word document.

- Aligning text with a graphic element is much easier if you create for the text a two-cell, one-row table next to a graphic.

Techniques

This section provides concise, quick-reference summaries of all the procedures introduced in this chapter.

Aligning Tables

To align text within a cell:

1. Select the cell or cells.

2. Use any alignment technique, such as the Paragraph dialog box, the keyboard shortcuts, or the ruler buttons.

Chapter 17

Creating Tables

To align rows within the margins:

1. Select the row or rows you want to align.

2. Choose Table Cells from the Format menu.

3. Choose Selection in the Apply To list box to format only the rows you selected or choose All Cells in the Table menu to format all rows.

4. Choose an alignment option in the Alignment list box.

5. Choose OK.

Changing Column Width

To change the width of a single column:

1. Place the insertion point within the table.

2. Activate the table markers by choosing the T button on the ruler.

3. On the ruler, drag the T mark.

To change the width of all the columns:

1. Place the insertion point within the table.

2. Choose Table Cells from the Format menu.

3. Type a measurement in the Column Width box.

4. Choose OK.

Changing the Row Height

To change the row height:

1. Select one or more rows.

2. Choose Table Cells from the Format menu.

3. Type a row height in the Height box.

4. Choose At Least or Exactly in the Height list box.

5. Choose Selection in the Apply To box to change the row height for the selection only; choose Entire Rows Selected to change the row height for all the cells in the rows containing a selection, even if you didn't select all the cells in the row; or choose All Cells in Table to change the row height for the whole table.

6. Choose OK.

Part II

Creating More Complex Documents

Changing the Space between Columns

To change the space that Word automatically inserts between columns:

1. Place the insertion point within the table or select the column or columns you want to format.

2. Choose Table Cells from the Format menu.

3. Type a measurement in the Space Between Columns text box.

4. Choose Selection in the Apply To box to change the column spacing for the selection only; choose Entire Columns Selected to change the column spacing for the whole column, even if you didn't select all the cells; or choose All Cells in Table to change the column spacing for the whole table.

5. Choose OK.

Converting a Table to Text

To convert a table to ordinary text:

1. Select the table.

2. Choose Table to Text from the Insert menu.

Converting Existing Text into a Table

To convert text in your document into a table:

1. Select the text.

2. Choose Table from the Insert menu.

3. Choose a Convert From option (comma delimited, tab delimited, paragraphs, or side-by-side).

4. Choose OK.

Copying and Moving Cell Contents and Cells

To copy or move the cell contents (without affecting the cell):

1. Select the text, but not the end-of-cell mark.

Chapter 17
Creating Tables

2. Choose Copy or Cut from the Edit menu or use the keyboard shortcuts.

3. Move the insertion point to where you want the text to appear.

4. Choose Paste from the Edit menu.

To copy or move the cell contents and the cells:

1. Select the text, being sure to include the end-of-cell marker.

2. Choose Copy or Cut from the Edit menu or use the keyboard shortcuts.

3. Move the insertion point to where you want the text to appear.

4. Choose Paste Cells from the Edit menu.

Deleting Columns

To delete one or more columns, including the cell matrix and cell contents:

1. Select the column or columns.

2. Choose Table Layout from the Format menu.

3. Activate the Column option.

4. Choose Delete.

Deleting Rows

To delete one or more rows, including the cell matrix and cell contents:

1. Select the row or rows.

2. Choose Table Layout from the Format menu.

3. Activate the Row option.

4. Choose Delete.

Deleting Text in a Table

To delete the contents of a single cell:

1. Select the cell.

2. Use any deletion command, such as Backspace, Delete, or Cut (Edit menu).

To delete the contents of two or more cells (but without removing the cell matrix):

1. Select the cells.

2. Choose Cut from the Edit menu or press ⌘-X.

Deleting a Table

To remove the entire table, including the text and matrix:

1. Select the entire table by placing the insertion point anywhere in the table and then holding down the Option key and double-clicking the mouse button.

2. Choose Table Layout from the Format menu.

3. Choose Delete to delete all the rows of the table.

To remove the table matrix without removing the text:

1. Select the entire table by placing the insertion point anywhere in the table and then holding down the Option key and double-clicking the mouse button.

2. Choose Table to Text from the Insert menu.

Displaying Table Gridlines and End of Cell Marks

To display table gridlines and end of cell marks:

Choose Show ¶ from the View menu; or press ⌘-J; or click the paragraph button on the ribbon.

Indenting Text in Cells

To use the ruler to indent text within the cells:

1. Select the cell(s) you want to format.

2. If necessary, choose the Indent button on the ruler so that you see the indent marks.

3. Drag the indent marks.

To add an indent using a precise measurement:

1. Select the cells you want to format.

2. Choose Table Cells from the Format menu.

3. In the Indent box, type a measurement.

4. Choose OK.

Inserting a New Table

To insert a new table:

1. Place the insertion point where you want the table to appear.

2. Choose Table from the Insert menu.

3. In the Number of Columns box, type the number of columns you want.

4. In the Number of Rows box, type the number of rows you want.

5. To choose a column width other than the one Word chooses automatically, type a measurement in the Column Width box.

6. Choose OK.

Inserting Rows, Columns, or Cells

To insert a row or rows into your table:

1. Beginning just below where you want the new rows to appear, select the number of rows you want to insert.

2. Choose Table Layout from the Format menu.

3. Activate the Row button.

4. Choose Insert.

To insert a column or columns into your table:

1. Beginning to the right of where you want the new column or columns to appear, select the number of columns you want to insert.

2. Choose Table Layout from the Format menu.

3. Activate the Column button.

    4. Choose Insert.

To add a column at the right edge of your table:

1. Position the insertion point just beyond the right edge of the last cell in the first row, but just before the end of cell mark at the end of the row.

2. Choose Table Layout from the Format menu.

3. Activate the Column option.

4. Choose Insert.

5. To insert additional rows, choose Repeat from the Edit menu or press ⌘-Y.

To insert a cell into your table:

1. Beginning to the right of or directly below where you want the new cell or cells to appear, select the number of cells you want to insert.

2. Choose Table Layout from the Format menu.

3. Activate the Selection button.

4. In the Shift Cells area, choose Horizontally or Vertically.

5. Choose Insert.

Merging Cells

To merge two or more cells into one:

1. Select the cells.

2. Choose Table Layout from the Format menu.

3. Choose Merge Cells.

Moving a Column

To move a column:

1. Insert a new, blank column.

2. Select the column you want to move.

3. Choose Cut from the Edit menu or press ⌘-X.

4. Select the cells where you want the column to appear.

5. Choose Paste Cells from the Edit menu.

6. If you want, delete the blank column.

Splitting Cells

To split a cell that you have previously merged:

1. Select the cell.

2. Choose Table Layout from the Format menu.

3. Choose Split Cell.

Using Math and Typing Equations

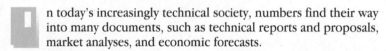

I n today's increasingly technical society, numbers find their way into many documents, such as technical reports and proposals, market analyses, and economic forecasts.

In keeping with the increasing use of numbers in business and professional writing, Microsoft Word offers two useful features, both of which are explored in this chapter:

- *On-Screen Math.* With Word's Calculate command (Tools menu), you can quickly add rows or columns of figures, multiply or divide numbers, and determine percentages. Word shows the result of a calculation in the page number area in the lower left corner of the document window. The program also copies the result to the clipboard, from which you can insert the result in your document. In tandem with Word's Table command (see Chapter 17), you can create a minispreadsheet within your Word documents.

- *Equation Editor.* A new external Word command, Equation Editor, greatly simplifies typing mathematical equations. If you have ever tried to type an equation by fussing with the Mac's Symbol font and mathematical typesetting techniques, you are sure to find that Equation Editor represents a major improvement. To build an equation, you choose symbols and templates from on-screen palettes. After you insert a template (such as an integral), you see *slots*, or areas in which you can type numbers or insert additional

USING
WORD 5
FOR THE
MAC

symbols or templates. As you build your equation, Equation Editor automatically sizes and formats the equation so that the printed symbols look good and conform to standard mathematical practice.

Using Math

Word is no spreadsheet program, but you still can perform useful calculations (such as adding a column or row of numbers in a table). For more extensive computations, create and analyze the data with a spreadsheet program, such as Excel, and transfer the data to Word by using the techniques discussed in Chapter 14.

Calculating On-Screen

You can perform calculations at any time by typing an arithmetic expression anywhere in your document, selecting the expression, and using the Calculate command (Utilities menu). The result appears in the page-number area (lower left corner of the screen). Word also places the result in the clipboard, from which you can insert the result by choosing Paste.

Word 5 observes parentheses in deciding the order of evaluation. In Version 4, expressions were evaluated left to right, and you could not override the default order of evaluation.

Table 18.1 lists the arithmetic operators you can use with the Calculate command.

Table 18.1
Arithmetic Operators

Operator	Operation	Example	Result
+	Addition	10+5	15
space	Addition	10 5	15
–	Subtraction	10-5	5
(x)	Subtraction	10 (5)	5
*	Multiplication	10*5	50
/	Division	10/5	2
%	Percentage	10*5%	.5

Keep the following points in mind as you create expressions:

■ Unless you include one of the arithmetic operators shown in table 18.1, Word sums the numbers you select.

■ Word calculates from left to right. If you select more than one line, the program evaluates each line left to right, moving down to the next line at the end of each line. In older spreadsheet programs, this calculation technique is called *row-wise calculation*.

■ If you group numbers and operator signs within parentheses, Word evaluates the group before proceeding with the rest of the calculations. If you type *8+(2 * 50)*, for example, Word displays 108 in the page number area. If you type *8 + 2 * 50*, Word displays 500. A single number enclosed in parentheses, however, indicates a negative number. For example, the expression 10 * (10) produces a result of –100.

■ If you include commas (as in 12,319) in any of the numbers in the expression, Word will include the commas in the result.

■ Word calculates the result to the largest number of decimal places you used in the numbers you typed. For example, when you type *10.1/4,* you get 2.5. If you type *10.100/4,* you get 2.525.

To calculate on-screen, follow these steps:

1. Type the expression. (You can use numbers, commas, decimal points, parentheses, and operators. If you include any letters or other punctuation marks, Word ignores them.)

2. Select the expression.

3. Choose Calculate from the Tools menu, or press ⌘-equals. Word displays the result in the page-number-area in the lower left corner of the screen (see fig. 18.1).

4. To insert the result in your document, position the insertion point where you want the result to appear, and choose Paste from the Edit menu, or press ⌘-V.

Chapter 18
Using Math and Typing Equations

Fig. 18.1
Result of a calculation
displayed in the page
number area.

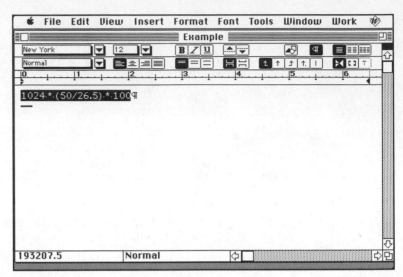

Fig. 18.1
Result of a calculation
displayed in the page
number area.

Calculating the Sum of Columns and Rows in a Tabbed Table

If you used tabs to create a table of numbers, you can quickly add these numbers by using column selection. Follow these steps:

1. Use decimal tabs to type columns of numbers, like the ones shown in figure 18.2.

2. Hold down the option key, and position the insertion point on the lower right or upper right corner of the column of numbers.

   If the column contains numbers that occupy varying numbers of places, you might not be able to select the longest numbers if you start selecting in the left corner. If you start selecting in the upper left corner, you leave out one of the numbers—as shown in figure 18.3—and your result will be incorrect.

3. Choose Calculate from the Tools menu, or press ⌘-equals.

4. Position the insertion point where you want the result to appear, and choose Paste from the Edit menu (or press ⌘-V).

   Word displays the total (see fig. 18.4).

TIP

To replace your
expression with the
result, just select the
expression and choose
Paste from the Edit
menu (or press ⌘-V).

Part II

Creating More Complex Documents

Fig. 18.2
Tabbed column correctly
selected beginning with
right corner.

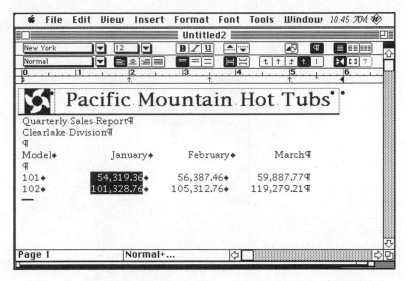

Fig. 18.3
Tabbed column incorrectly
selected, with selection
beginning from upper
left corner.

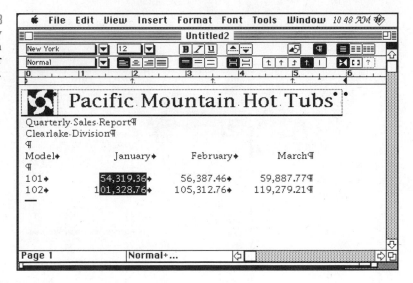

Fig. 18.4
Inserting the total.

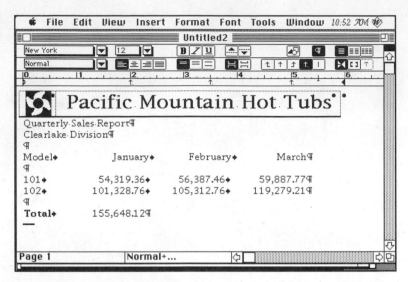

Summing rows is easy: You simply select the row using ordinary selection techniques, as shown in figure 18.5, and choose Calculate.

Fig. 18.5
Selecting a row
for calculation.

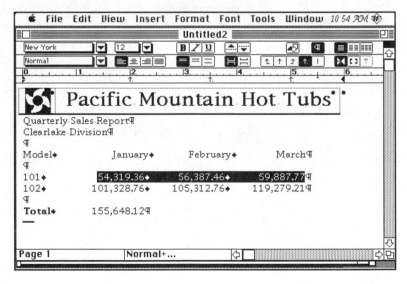

In calculating a row or column, you're restricted to addition. But keep in mind that you can include negative numbers by surrounding them with parentheses (a standard accounting practice). In figure 18.6, for example, the new model 102XL shows a loss during the January quarter, so Word subtracts 1,254.48 from the January total.

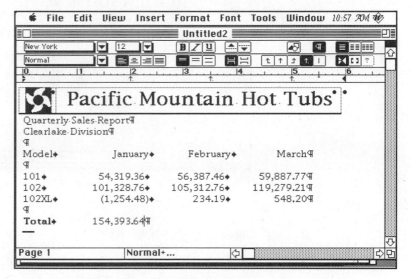

Calculating the Sum of Columns and Rows in a Table

In Chapter 17, you learned how to create, edit, and format a table using Word's Table command. The Table command creates a spreadsheet-like matrix of rows and columns. As you have already learned, creating tables using the Table command rather than typing a table with tabs has many advantages. Another advantage is using Calculate, which makes summing columns of numbers simple. In a tabbed table, you can inadvertently leave out a digit if you don't start the column selection in the right place (as explained in the previous section). When you select a column of numbers in a table, however, you don't have to worry about including every digit. You simply select the cells, and Word takes care of the rest.

To select a column, hold down the Option key and click anywhere in the column (see fig. 18.7). Word ignores cells that include text, even if they are included in your selection.

Fig. 18.7
Selecting a column in
a table.

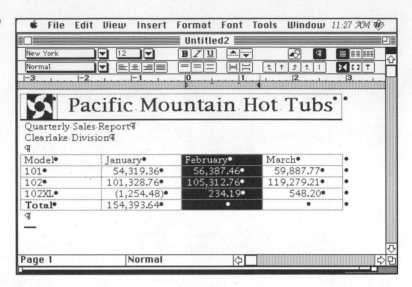

Word's Table command isn't really a spreadsheet, because you cannot
embed formulas into cells. However, Word's ability to sum columns and
rows accurately and quickly is adequate for many of the tables that find
their way into business reports and proposals. With Word's Calculate
and Table commands, you can build and calculate a table without
leaving Word.

Typing Equations with Equation Editor

quation Editor, an external command supplied with Word 5, helps
you build complex equations and insert them in your Word
documents. Simply by pointing at symbols and templates on an
on-screen palette and clicking, you can quickly and easily create equations that would be extremely tedious to construct using the mathematical typesetting techniques of earlier versions of Word. Equation Editor is
so easy to use that reading about this exceptional utility takes more
effort than using it. All you need is to know a few basic concepts and
techniques.

Equation Editor, which comes with Word 5 for the Macintosh, is an
extraordinary value. A stand-alone program that's capable of precision
typesetting for professional publications, Equation Editor includes
advanced features that cannot be fully discussed in this section. Enough

information is given here, however, so that you can get started with Equation Editor and create handsome-looking equations. From this starting point, you have a firm foundation from which to explore the program more fully.

Accessing Equation Editor

You can access Equation Editor in two ways: as a stand-alone program, and by using object embedding.

Equation Editor is a stand-alone program in your Word Commands folder. To start the program, double-click the Equation Editor icon. After you create your equation, copy the equation to your Word document, using clipboard techniques. Access Equation Editor as a stand-alone program if you're running System 6, or if your system has limited memory.

Equation Editor also fully supports the Object Linking and Embedding (OLE) scheme that was introduced in Chapter 14. If you're running Word under System 7, and have sufficient memory to run the Word and Equation Editor applications simultaneously, you can access Equation by choosing the Object command (Insert menu). When you choose Equation from the Object menu, Equation Editor starts. After you create your equation and quit Equation Editor, the formula you have created is embedded into your Word document as an *embedded object*.

With object embedding, you can produce high-quality equations no matter which way you access Equation Editor, and you can edit the equation more easily. You simply select the equation and choose Edit Object from the Edit menu. Word starts Equation Editor and displays the equation in Equation Editor's workspace.

To start Equation Editor using the Object command (System 7 only), follow these steps:

1. Place the insertion point where you want your equation to appear.

2. Choose Object from the Insert menu.You see the Insert Object dialog box (see fig. 18.8).

   If the Equation option does not appear in the list box, you have never run Equation Editor. Choose Cancel, switch to the Finder, locate Equation Editor in the Word Commands folder, and start Equation Editor. Then quit Equation Editor, switch back to Word, and try again.

NOTE

If you're planning to use Equation Editor, don't delete the MT Extra font that Word installed in your System file when you ran Word's setup program. To display symbols and templates on-screen, Equation Editor needs MT Extra.

TIP

To access Equation Editor using the Insert Object command, you first must run Equation Editor as a stand-alone program, so that you can see the Equation option in the Insert Object dialog box. To run Equation Editor as a stand-alone program, double-click the Equation Editor icon in the Word Commands folder. When Equation Editor appears, choose Quit from the File menu. (You need to perform this procedure only one time.)

Chapter 18
Using Math and Typing Equations

Fig. 18.8
The Insert Object
dialog box.

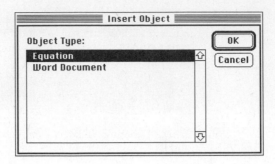

3. Choose Equation from the Object Type list box. You see the Equation Editor in the Word Object mode, as shown in figure 18.9.

Fig. 18.9
Equation Editor window.

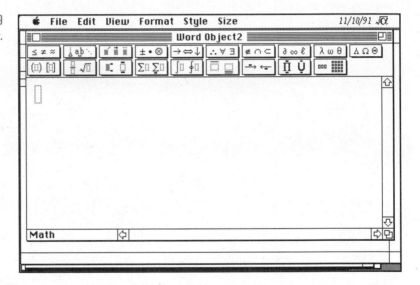

Understanding the Equation Editor Window

As a separate program, Equation Editor has its own menu bar options and window features. You already know how to use many of these features, such as the scroll bars and arrows, the Close, Zoom, and Size boxes, and the pull-down menus. In this section, you learn how to use the Equation Editor features you haven't seen before.

The following is a quick overview of the features you see in the Equation Editor window:

Menu Bar. You are already familiar with most of Word's commands. Many of the new commands are needed only if you want to override Equation Editor's default formats, styles, and sizes.

Symbol Palette. Positioned just below the menu bar, the Symbol Palette is the first row of options at the top of the document workspace. This palette enables you to choose from a wide variety of mathematical symbols. Simply click one of the palette buttons to drop down the full palette, from which you can choose a symbol (see fig. 18.10).

Fig. 18.10
Dropped-down
symbol palette.

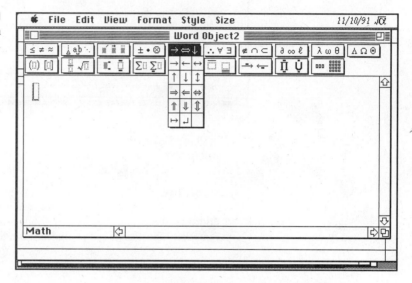

Template Palette. Below the Symbol Palette is the Template Palette, with dozens of *templates* for standard mathematical relationships. A template includes areas called *empty slots*, where you can plug in numbers, symbols, or additional templates. To access the templates, you drop down the palette, as shown in figure 18.11, and choose one of the options.

Empty Slot. Equation Editor uses an *empty slot* (a rectangular, dotted box) to show where you can insert symbols, numbers, text, or templates. Many templates enter additional empty slots, in which you can plug in additional templates, text, symbols, or numbers.

Chapter 18
Using Math and Typing Equations

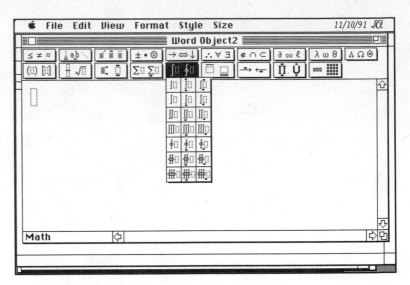

L-Shaped Insertion Point. A special insertion point shows you where text, symbols, or templates will be inserted. The horizontal bar along the bottom edge indicates which slot is selected.

Status Bar. The lower left corner of the screen indicates which mode Equation Editor is currently using. By default, Equation Editor uses the Math mode. The other modes are used to override Equation Editor's default formatting treatments of the text you enter, and for advance manual typesetting.

Building an Equation

The best way to understand the use of Equation Editor is to create an equation. In the following tutorial, you produce the equation shown in figure 18.12.

To create an equation with Equation Editor, follow these steps:

1. Start Equation Editor.

2. Without pressing the space bar, type $x=$ in the Equation Editor window. (Pressing the space bar has no effect in the Math mode, because Equation Editor handles spacing automatically.)

   Equation Editor enters and formats the characters you have typed, using general mathematical practices (see figure 18.13). By default,

NOTE

For clarity, this equation is shown in 400% view (four times normal size). The equation doesn't look this large in your document.

Equation Editor displays the equation using a 200% view, twice the normal size. The equation looks smaller in your Word document. If you want, you can choose 100% (normal size) or 400% (quadruple size) options in the View menu.

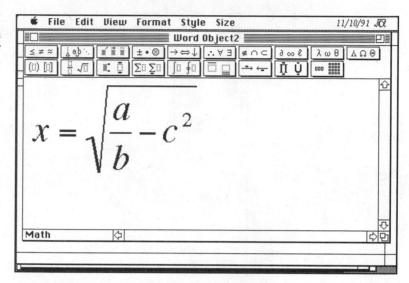

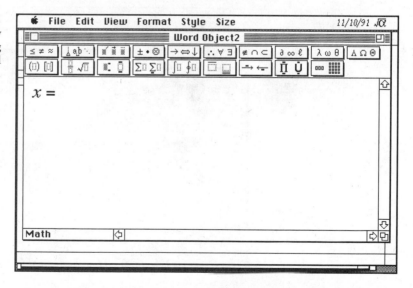

Chapter 18

Using Math and Typing Equations

3. Drop down the Fraction/Radicals template (the second template from the left), and choose the square root template (as indicated in figure 18.14). Equation Editor places the square root template in your document, as shown in figure 18.15.

Fig. 18.14
Choosing the square root template from the Fraction/ Radicals palette.

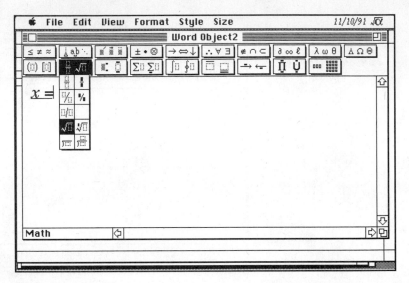

Fig. 18.15
Square Root Template entered in document.

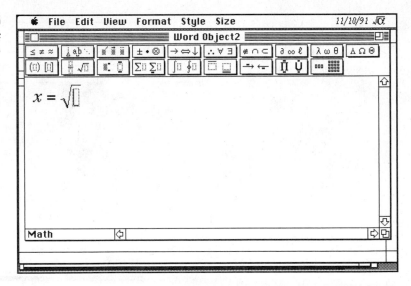

Part II

Creating More Complex Documents

Note that the square root template enters the empty slot in which the L-shaped insertion point is now positioned.

4. From the Fraction/Radicals palette, choose the fraction template, as shown in figure 18.16.

   The other vertical fraction template (the template with solid black squares above and below) enters a fraction template using a reduced size. Word inserts the fraction template into your equation, as shown in figure 18.17. Note that the fraction template brings two empty slots. Also note how the square-root template is adjusted automatically to make room for the fraction template.

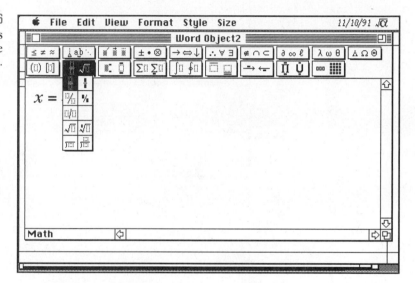

5. In the top slot of the fraction template, type the numerator a, and in the bottom slot, type the denominator b.

   To move to the denominator slot, you can click the slot, press Tab, or press the down-arrow key. Equation Editor enters these variables and formats them according to standard mathematical practice.

6. To move the insertion point out of the denominator slot, press Tab.

7. Type -c (using a hyphen for a minus sign). Your equation now should look like the one in figure 18.18.

Chapter 18

Using Math and Typing Equations

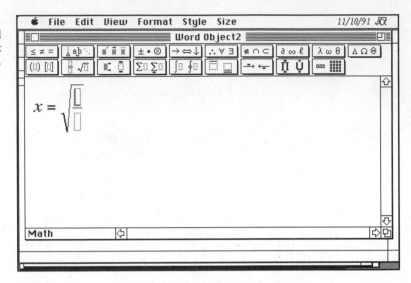

Fig. 18.17
Fraction template inserted within square-root template.

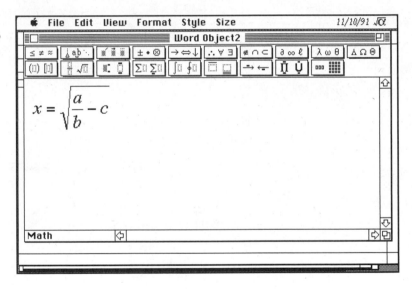

Fig. 18.18
Adding more terms to the equation.

8. To add a superscript, choose the superscript template from the Superscript/Subscript palette, as shown in figure 18.19.

   This palette has two kinds of templates. The first kind, indicated by a grayed rectangle, is chosen after you have already entered the symbol or variable. If you choose the second kind of template, indicated by the empty slots, Equation Editor enters two empty slots—one for the variable or symbol, and another for the superscript or subscript. Because you have already typed the variable, choose the grayed kind. (Note the many available options. The little black dots show where superscript and subscript slots will appear.)

Fig. 18.19
Choosing a superscript
template from the
Superscript/Subscript
Palette.

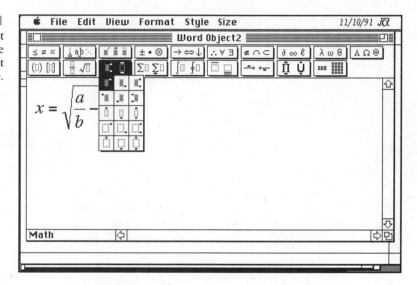

9. Type *2* to complete the equation.

10. To add the equation to your document, follow one of these steps:

If you started Equation Editor using the Object command, click the Close box to embed the equation in your Word document.

If you started Equation Editor as a stand-alone application, choose Select All from the Edit menu, or press ⌘-A. Then choose Cut from the Edit menu, or press ⌘-X. Start Word, display your document, and choose Paste (⌘-X) to insert the equation into your document.

Figure 18.20 shows how the equation appears in a Word document.

Chapter 18
Using Math and Typing Equations

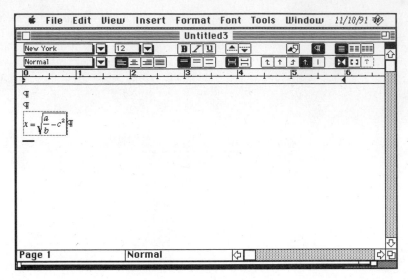

Fig. 18.20
Equation embedded in
Word document.

Editing an Equation

Whether you insert your equation using object embedding or the clipboard method, Word treats the equation like a picture: while the equation is a single character that you can move, copy or delete, you can't directly edit the equation. You may edit the equation in two ways.

If you embedded the equation using object embedding, you can edit the equation quickly by selecting the equation and choosing Edit Object from the Edit menu. Word starts Equation Editor and displays your equation in the application workspace. Make the changes you want, then click the Close box to place the edited equation in your Word document.

If you inserted the equation using the clipboard, you must use the clipboard to cut the equation back to Equation Editor for editing. To do so, select the equation and choose Cut from the Edit menu. Then quit Word, start Equation Editor, and choose Paste from the Edit menu. If you have enough memory to run both applications simultaneously, you can switch between the two programs (System 6 users must run MultiFinder to take advantage of this technique).

When you redisplay your equation in the Equation Editor window, you can use any of the standard Macintosh techniques to edit the equation (such as pressing Backspace or Delete to erase the selection). You also can add additional symbols, templates, or text.

Part II

Creating More Complex Documents

Looking at Additional Equation Editor Features

Because Equation Editor is an application in its own right, the program has far more features than this chapter can cover. The following are some additional features you may want to explore:

Getting Help. Choose Equation Editor Help from the Help menu, or press ⌘-? to see extensive on-screen help for a variety of Equation Editor subjects. In System 7, Equation Editor also supports Balloon Help.

Creating and Aligning a Pile of Equations. You can create more than one equation at a time in the Equation Editor window. When you finish an equation, press Return to insert a blank slot below the equation. A series of lines created in this way is called a *pile*. Align commands in the Format menu enable you to choose how you want the lines placed (flush left, centered, flush right, aligned at equals sign, or aligned at decimal point). To rejoin lines, place the insertion point at the beginning of the line and press Backspace or Delete.

Adding Embellishments. In mathematics, variables and symbols often have diacriticals, primes, overbars, or other embellishments. The Embellishment Palette offers a variety of embellishments you can add to a symbol or variable (see fig. 18.21).

Fig. 18.21
Embellishment palette.

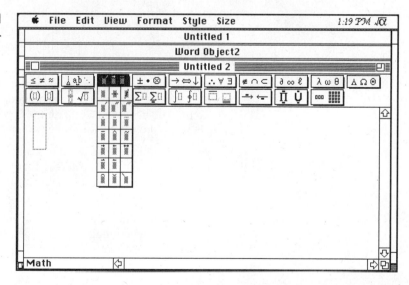

Chapter 18

Using Math and Typing Equations

Selecting Items in an Equation with the Option Key. You can use normal selecting techniques when editing an equation, but Equation Editor uses a special technique you should learn. To select within a template an object—such as a *fence*—that you cannot select using ordinary techniques, hold down the Option key and click the object.

Using Keyboard Shortcuts. Equation Editor includes many useful keyboard shortcuts for commonly accessed symbols and templates. For example, you can press ⌘-SR to insert a square root sign. To view a complete list of Equation Editor keyboard shortcuts on-screen, choose Equation Editor Help, then choose the Keyboard shortcuts option.

Choosing Fonts. By default, Equation Editor uses the standard Times and Symbol fonts to format your equations. You can, however, change the font assignments, using the Define option in the Style menu.

Quick Review

This section concisely summarizes the most useful information in this chapter. Check "Productivity Tips" for a review of high-productivity tips and tricks, and review "Techniques" when you forget how to perform a specific procedure.

Productivity Tips

■ Don't go hunting for a pocket calculator. You can calculate on-screen with Word by typing an expression and choosing Calculate from the Tools menu. To replace the expression with the result, again select the expression you typed and choose Paste.

■ If you're planning to use Word to sum up values in a table, create the table using the Table command rather than tabs. It's all to easy to make a mistake in a tabbed table by inadvertently leaving a digit out of the column selection.

■ Using Equation Editor, you can create equations without any mathematical typesetting. To build the equation, you choose options from on-screen palettes, then type constants and variables.

■ To speed up equation editing with System 7, use Word's object-embedding capabilities. Simply start Equation Editor by choosing Object from the Insert menu, rather than starting the program from the Finder, as a stand-alone program.

Techniques

This section provides concise, quick-reference summaries of all the procedures introduced in this chapter.

Creating a Formula with Equation Editor

To create a formula as an embedded object:

1. Position the insertion point where you want the equation to appear.

2. Start Equation Editor by choosing Object from the Insert menu.

3. In the Equation Editor window, type constants and variables, and choose symbols and templates from the palettes.

4. When you finish creating your equation, click the Close box to insert the equation into your Word document.

To create a formula using Equation Editor as a stand-alone program:

1. Double-click the Equation Editor icon in the Word Commands folder.

2. In the Equation Editor window, type the constants and variables, and choose from the palettes the symbols and templates you need.

3. When you finish creating your equation, choose Select All from the Edit menu, or press ⌘-A.

4. Choose Cut from the Edit menu, or press ⌘-X.

5. Choose Quit from the File menu to quit Equation Editor.

6. Start Word, display your document, and position the insertion point where you want your equation to appear.

7. Choose Paste from the Edit menu, or press ⌘-V.

Editing an Equation

To edit an equation you have inserted as an embedded object:

1. Double-click the equation.

2. In the Equation Editor window, edit the equation.

3. Click the Close box to embed the corrected equation in your Word document.

To edit an equation you inserted via the clipboard:

1. Select the equation.

2. Choose Cut from the Edit menu, or press ⌘-X.

3. Quit Word.

4. Start Equation Editor.

5. Choose Paste from the Edit menu, or press ⌘-V.

6. Edit the equation.

7. Choose Select All from the Edit menu, or press ⌘-A.

8. Choose Cut from the Edit menu, or press ⌘-X.

9. Quit Equation Editor.

10. Start Word, display your document, then position the insertion point where you want the corrected equation to appear.

11. Choose Paste from the Edit menu, or press ⌘-V.

Starting Equation Editor

To start Equation Editor from Word and create the formula as an embedded object (System 7 only):

1. Place the insertion point where you want your equation to appear.

2. Choose Object from the Insert menu.

3. Choose Equation.

To start Equation Editor from the Finder:

1. Open the Word Commands folder.

2. Double-click the Equation Editor icon.

Summing a Column in a Tabbed Table

To sum a column of numbers in a tabbed table:

1. Use decimal or flush-right tabs to type the columns of numbers.

2. Hold down the option key, and position the insertion point on the lower right or upper right corner of the column of numbers.

3. Choose Calculate from the Tools menu, or press ⌘-equals.

4. Position the insertion point where you want the result to appear, then choose Paste from the Edit menu (or press ⌘-V).

Using On-Screen Math

To calculate on-screen, follow these steps:

1. Type the expression, using operators (+, -, *, /, or %), if you want to. Use parentheses to override the default order of evaluation (left-to-right, line-by-line).

2. Select the expression.

3. Choose Calculate from the Tools menu, or press ⌘-equals.

4. To insert the result in your document, position the insertion point where you want the result to appear, then choose Paste from the Edit menu (or press ⌘-V).

Numbering and Sorting Lines and Paragraphs

A hallmark of fine word-processing technology is *task automation*. With task automation, the jobs you once had to perform manually are done for you at computer speeds. With Word, you can add numbers at the beginning of lines or paragraphs. You also can sort lines or paragraphs in alphabetical or numerical order, using a simple command. For legal documents, scripts, and critical editions of literary works, you can add line numbers to the left of the text column.

This chapter comprehensively covers all aspects of numbering and sorting with Word. The following list gives you an overview of this chapter's contents:

■ *Numbering lines.* You learn how to add line numbers to the left of the text column in your document, how to choose line numbering options, and how to change the line number increment (for example, you can choose to number every fifth line). You also learn how to turn off line numbering for selected paragraphs in your document.

■ *Numbering paragraphs.* You learn how to choose options when you number paragraphs, how to number paragraphs of different levels, how to number headings in outline view, and how to number only selected paragraphs.

- *Sorting paragraphs and tables.* You learn how to sort paragraphs and tables in alphabetical or numerical order, and how Word sorts text, paragraphs, and tables. You also learn how to undo a sort.

Numbering Lines

 ine numbers often are used for legal documents or for critical editions of a poem, story, or script to provide readers with reference points for a careful study of the text. Adding line numbers to a document is a good idea when you are preparing the document for staff or committee discussion. Figure 19.1 shows a draft of an employee handbook.

Fig. 19.1
A draft of an employee handbook.

Pacific Mountain Hot Tubs

Handbook for New Employees

Welcome

1 Welcome to Pacific Mountain Hot Tubs. This training notebook is
2 designed to introduce you to the company. You will find that it
3 answers most of your questions. Don't hesitate to ask if you have
4 others.

Orientation

5 Your departmental representative will enroll you in an employee
6 orientation session on the first Monday after you begin work.

7 At orientation, you'll learn some of the general policies of Pacific
8 Mountain Hot Tubs. You'll complete some forms for the Benefits and
9 Insurance office. And you'll meet your guide for the day—most
10 often a member of your department.

Checklist for the First Day

11 During your first day, you will meet the people you'll be working
12 with, and become acquainted with the Pacific Mountain Hot Tub
13 facilities--including your Employee Spa, naturally!--and
14 procedures. Your guide will help you complete the checklist
15 below.

Meeting Your Group Manager

16 During your first day at work, you'll get to meet your group
17 manager. He or she is the person who keeps things moving
18 smoothly, coordinating projects and people assigned to your
19 group.

Tour

20 Pacific Mountain Hot Tubs' production site, situated in the
21 historic Nevada City region of California's Sierra Nevada
22 mountains, includes the company's production and
23 administrative buildings. During the tour, you'll see just how
24 Pacific Mountain Hot Tubs are made--and why we believe they're
25 the finest hot tobs available today.

Use the Section dialog box to add line numbers to your document. The Section dialog box gives you several line numbering options. You can control how Word counts lines (by page, by section, or continuously) and you can specify how far you want to position the line numbers from the text. (By default, Word positions line numbers 0.25 inch from single-column text and 0.13 inch from multiple columns.)

By default, line numbers are not visible on-screen in Normal or Page Layout views. To preview line numbers, use Print Preview (File menu).

Numbering every line doesn't always make sense. In figure 19.1, for example, the headings aren't numbered. In the section "Numbering Lines Selectively," you learn how to suppress line numbering for headings or for other selected text.

If you want to number the lines of your document, don't add blank lines by pressing Return; add them by adding blank spacing to paragraphs. If you add blank lines by pressing Return, Word numbers the blank line. In figure 19.2, note the paragraph mark before the heading *Checklist for the First Day*. In figure 19.3, note that Word has numbered this line. To keep Word from numbering blank lines, always add blank space by using the Before and After boxes in the Spacing area of the Paragraph dialog box. Alternatively, choose the Blank Line Spacing button on the ruler to add 12 points of blank space before a paragraph. Word does not number blank space added this way.

Fig. 19.2
A blank line added by pressing Return.

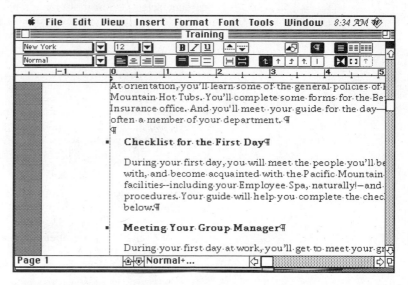

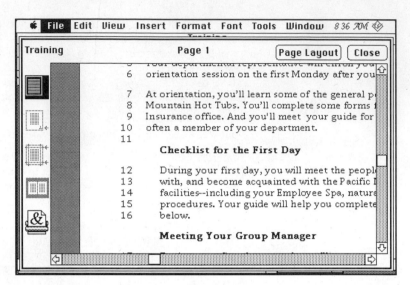

Fig. 19.3
A line numbering problem
caused by adding a blank
line with Return.

Adding Line Numbering

To add line numbers to your document, follow these steps:

1. To add line numbers to only some of the paragraphs in your document, select one or more paragraphs. If you don't select anything, Word adds line numbers to your whole document (or the current section, if you have divided your document into sections).

2. Choose Section from the Format menu. The Section dialog box appears.

3. Choose Line Numbers. The Line Numbers dialog box appears (see fig. 19.4). By default, the Off option is selected, and the line numbering options are grayed. When you choose a line numbering option in the Line Numbers list box, the other options become available.

4. Choose an option in the Line Numbers list box. You can choose By Page (starts numbering lines with 1 at the beginning of each page), By Section (starts numbering lines with 1 at the beginning of each section), or Continuous (numbers lines sequentially throughout the document).

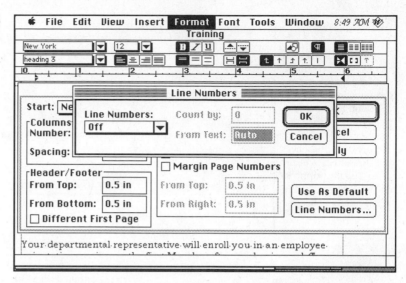

Fig. 19.4
The Line Numbers dialog
box.

TIP

If you have divided your document into sections, the line numbering options you choose affect only the section in which the insertion point is positioned. To add line numbers to your whole document, choose Select All from the Edit menu or press ⌘-A before choosing Section from the Format menu and adding line numbers.

5. In the Count by box, type the line number increment you want to use. By default, Word numbers every line. You can change this increment. For example, if you type 5 in the Count By box, Word numbers every fifth line.

6. In the From Text box, you can specify a distance from the end of the line number to the beginning of the text. The Auto setting places numbers 0.25 inch from the text in a single-column document and 0.13 inch from the text in a multiple-column document.

7. Choose OK.

To preview line numbers, choose Print Preview from the File menu.

Numbering Lines Selectively

In figure 19.1, the headings are unnumbered. In this section, you learn how to suppress line numbers for any paragraph. To suppress the printing of line numbers for selected paragraphs, follow these steps:

1. If you haven't done so already, add line numbers to your document.

2. Select the paragraph or paragraphs for which you don't want line numbers to print.

Chapter 19
Numbering and Sorting Lines and Paragraphs

TIP

If you format with styles, you can choose the Suppress Line Numbers option for any style you have defined. In figure 19.1, for example, you can suppress line numbers for all headings by adding the Suppress Line Numbers option to the Heading styles. For more information on styles, see Chapter 8.

3. Choose Paragraph from the Format menu or press ⌘-M. The Paragraph dialog box appears (see fig. 19.5). The Suppress Line Numbers option, which is ordinarily grayed, is now available.
4. Activate the Suppress Line Numbers check box.
5. Choose OK.
6. To suppress line numbers for another paragraph, move the insertion point to that paragraph and choose Repeat from the Edit menu or press ⌘-Y.

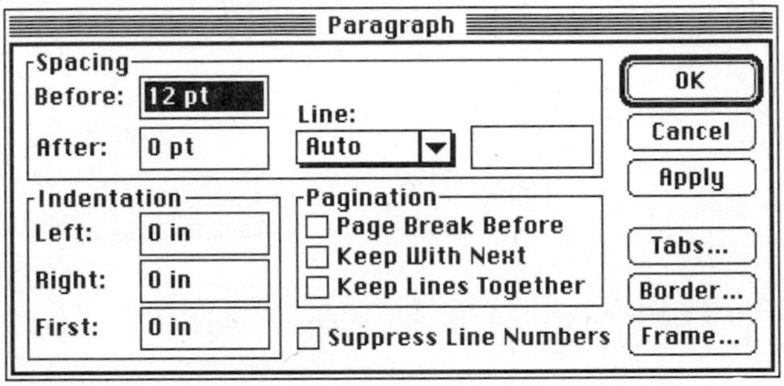

Fig. 19.5
The Suppress Line Numbers option in the Paragraph dialog box.

Numbering Paragraphs

With Word's Renumber command (Tools menu), you can add numbers automatically to the beginning of paragraphs; you can choose the format of the numbers (Arabic, Roman, or alphabetical letters); and you can choose any character to follow the number that Word inserts (normally a period). You also can number paragraphs differently by level and choose which paragraphs you want numbered.

NOTE

For information on numbering headings in an outline, see Chapter 12.

If you want to number paragraphs in your document, be sure to plan the paragraphing carefully. Use the New Line command (Shift-Enter) to group together all the lines you want to have numbered together. Figure 19.6 shows an instruction that should have two steps (the paragraphs beginning with *Before opening the door...* and *Close the door securely...*). The explanation, however, (*Feel the door...*) has been typed in a separate paragraph. In figure 19.7, notice that Word gives each paragraph a number, creating three steps, not two. Figure 19.8 shows how the New Line command can be used to make sure that Word numbers the paragraphs correctly.

Fig. 19.6
Poor paragraphing for
paragraph numbering.

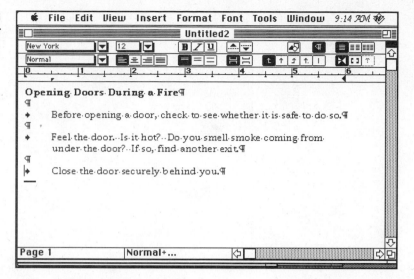

Fig. 19.7
Results of poor
paragraphing (incorrect
paragraph numbering).

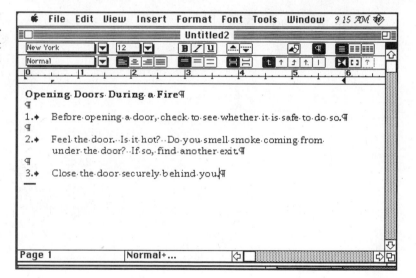

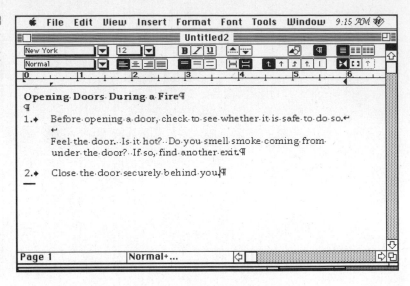

Fig. 19.8
Correct paragraphing for
paragraph numbering
(note arrows entered by
New Line command).

Adding Paragraph Numbers

To add paragraph numbers to your document, follow these steps:

1. Select the paragraph(s) you want to number. If you don't select any paragraphs, Word numbers all the paragraphs in your document.

2. Choose Renumber from the Tools menu or press ⌘-F15. The Renumber dialog box appears (see fig. 19.9).

Fig. 19.9
The Renumber dialog box.

TIP

If renumbering produces unwanted results, immediately choose Undo Renumber from the Edit menu or press ⌘-Z. If you perform some other action after using the Renumber command so that you can't use Undo to remove the numbers, see the section called "Updating and Removing Paragraph Numbers," later in this chapter.

3. To start numbering with a number other than 1, type the number in the Start At box. Type an Arabic number to control numbering even if you plan to use a number format other than Arabic, as explained in the following step. For example, suppose you choose uppercase alphabetical numbering (A, B, C). To start numbering with C, type *3* in the Start At box.

4. To use a number format other than Arabic (1, 2, 3), type the number format and the separator character you want to use in the Format box. See tables 19.1 and 19.2 for a list of the number format and separator character codes you can use. Type the codes the way you want the numbers to appear. Some examples of valid codes follow:

   -1-
   (1)
   {1}
   A),
   I)

5. Choose OK.

Table 19.1
Number Format Codes (Renumber Dialog Box)

Code	Number format
1	Arabic numbers (1, 2, 3)
I	Uppercase Roman numerals (I, II, III)
i	Lowercase Roman numerals (i, ii, iii)
A	Uppercase letters (A, B, C)
a	Lowercase letters (a, b, c)

Table 19.2
Separator Characters (Renumber Dialog box)

Character	Effect
None	1. (period added by default)
, (comma)	1,
- (hyphen)	1-
/ (slash)	1/
; (semicolon)	1;
: (colon)	1:
) (right parenthesis)	1)

continues

Chapter 19
Numbering and Sorting Lines and Paragraphs

Character	Effect
() (double parentheses)	(1)
[ ] (double brackets)	[1]
{ } (double braces)	{1}
^t (tab code)	1. followed by tab

Table 19.2
Continued

Numbering Paragraphs of Different Levels

With Word, you can use paragraph indentation to indicate logical relations among ideas in a document. In figure 19.1, for example, the indentations show that three of the topics—Checklist for the First Day, Meeting Your Group Manager, and Tour—are part of the Orientation section. If you have indented paragraphs in this way, you can choose a numbering option that shows the logical subordination of indented paragraphs. When you choose this option (the 1.1 button in the Line Numbers dialog box), Word uses a numbering scheme that indicates subordination. Figure 19.10 shows how the employee handbook looks after numbering the document this way.

Word recognizes different levels of paragraphs no matter which way you indent the paragraphs. You can change the indents on the ruler, type indents in the Paragraph dialog box, or use the Shift-⌘-N and Shift-⌘-M keyboard shortcuts. Figure 19.11 shows the effect of using two levels of indents beyond the normal, flush left paragraphs; Word can number up to seven levels of indents.

The Shift-⌘-N (indent one tab stop) and Shift-⌘-M (move indent back one tab stop) keyboard shortcuts are useful in a document you want to number by indent levels. Both commands are additive. If you press Shift-⌘-N three times, for instance, Word indents the paragraph three default tab stops (1.5 inches), producing a Level 4 indentation. To bring the indent back one level, press Shift-⌘-M.

To number paragraphs of different levels, follow these steps:

1. Select the paragraphs you want to number. If you don't select paragraphs, Word numbers all the paragraphs in your document.

2. Choose Renumber from the Tools menu or press ⌘-F15. The Renumber dialog box appears.

Fig. 19.10
An employee handbook
numbered to show logical
relationships among
paragraphs.

 Pacific Mountain Hot Tubs

Handbook for New Employees

1. Welcome

Welcome to Pacific Mountain Hot Tubs. This training notebook is
designed to introduce you to the company. You will find that it
answers most of your questions. Don't hesitate to ask if you have
others.

2. Orientation

Your departmental representative will enroll you in an employee
orientation session on the first Monday after you begin work.

At orientation, you'll learn some of the general policies of Pacific
Mountain Hot Tubs. You'll complete some forms for the Benefits and
Insurance office. And you'll meet your guide for the day—most
often a member of your department.

2.1. Checklist for the First Day

During your first day, you will meet the people you'll be working
with, and become acquainted with the Pacific Mountain Hot Tub
facilities--including your Employee Spa, naturally!--and
procedures. Your guide will help you complete the checklist
below.

2.2. Meeting Your Group Manager

During your first day at work, you'll get to meet your group
manager. He or she is the person who keeps things moving
smoothly, coordinating projects and people assigned to your
group.

2.3. Tour

Pacific Mountain Hot Tubs' production site, situated in the
historic Nevada City region of California's Sierra Nevada
mountains, includes the company's production and
administrative buildings. During the tour, you'll see just how

3. To start numbering with a number other than 1, type the number
   in the Start At box.

4. To use a number format other than Arabic (1, 2, 3), type in the
   Format box the number format and the separator character you
   want to use.

(See tables 19.1 and 19.2 for a list of the number format and separator character codes you can use.) Word indicates subordinate levels with Arabic numbers (II.1, II.2, II.2.1) and drops the right bracket, brace, or parenthesis for Level 2 and subsequent numbers. Therefore, don't enclose numbers for subordinate levels in brackets, braces, or parentheses.

5. Choose the 1.1 option to turn on subordinate level numbering.

6. Choose OK.

Fig. 19.11
Two subordinate levels of indentation.

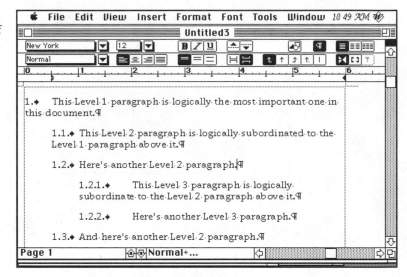

Numbering Paragraphs Selectively

If you do not want to number all the paragraphs in a document, you can use the New Line command (Shift-Enter) to define two or more paragraphs as a single paragraph. Word then attaches only one number to each paragraph you select. Rather than perform this procedure many times, however, you can add a number at the beginning of any paragraph you want numbered by typing *1.* at the beginning of the paragraph. When you choose Renumber, select an option that numbers only those paragraphs that you have indicated.

To number paragraphs selectively, follow these steps:

1. Type a number followed by a period (such as *1.*) and a tab at the beginning of every paragraph you want numbered. (You can type any number in a paragraph. Word replaces the number you have typed with the correct number.) To repeat the number you have

typed, move the insertion point to the beginning of the next paragraph you want Word to number and choose Repeat from the Edit menu, or press ⌘-Y.

2. Choose Renumber from the Tools menu or press ⌘-F15. The Renumber dialog box appears.

3. To start numbering with a number other than 1, type that number in the Start At box.

4. To use a number format other than Arabic (1, 2, 3), type in the Format box the number format and the separator character you want to use.

5. Choose Only If Already Numbered. This is important. If you forget to choose this option, Word numbers all the paragraphs in your document.

6. Choose OK. If the numbering does not work correctly, immediately choose Undo from the Edit menu.

Updating and Removing Paragraph Numbers

When you insert or delete paragraphs, Word doesn't automatically update the numbers inserted with the Renumber command. Word treats these numbers as ordinary characters, just like all the others in your document. If you add or delete paragraphs, Word doesn't automatically renumber (as some programs do). You must select the paragraphs and choose the Renumber command to number the paragraphs correctly. You also can use the Renumber command to remove numbers.

To update numbers, follow these steps:

1. If you add paragraphs that need numbers, type a number followed by a period (*1.*) and a tab at the beginning of every newly inserted paragraph you want Word to number.

2. Choose Renumber from the Tools menu or press ⌘-F15.

3. Choose Only If Already Numbered. This is important. If you don't choose this option, Word numbers all the paragraphs in your document.

4. To change the starting number and/or the number format, you can choose subordinate numbering (the 1.1 option), even if you didn't choose this option the first time you inserted the numbers.

5. Choose OK.

To remove paragraph numbers from your document, follow these steps:

1. Choose Renumber from the Tools menu or press ⌘-F15.

2. Choose Remove.

3. Choose OK.

Sorting Paragraphs and Tables

Alphabetizing can be a tedious job. Don't alphabetize paragraphs by moving paragraphs around. Let Word do the job. Word's Sort command (Tools menu) can sort paragraphs or table rows, and in ascending (a, b, c or 1, 2, 3) or descending (c, b, a or 3, 2, 1) order.

To sort paragraphs, plan your document with sorting in mind. Use the New Line command (Shift-Enter) to group lines together so that they aren't separated during a sort. In figure 19.12, the New Line command keeps the program from separating the parts of each bibliographic citation.

Fig. 19.12
The New Line command keeps bibliographic items together during a sort.

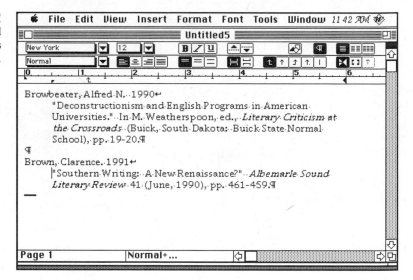

Understanding How Word Sorts Text

To use Word's sorting capabilities effectively, you need to know that the program sorts text in ASCII order: text that begins with punctuation marks comes first, followed by text beginning with numbers. Then Word sorts text beginning with uppercase characters, followed by text beginning with lowercase characters. The program ignores diacritical marks such as accents or umlauts.

Because Word sorts in ASCII order, a sort may not conform to your expectations. For example, notice that the last two items on the price list in figure 19.13 are out of order because uppercase and lowercase are used inconsistently. To avoid this problem, use case consistently at the beginning of the paragraphs you want to sort.

Fig. 19.13
Incorrect sort due to inconsistent use of upper- and lowercase letters.

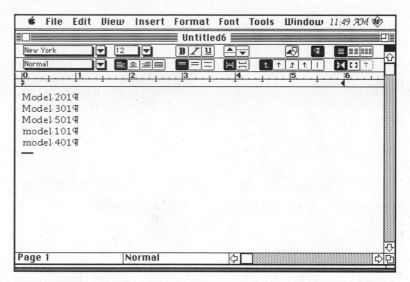

Sorting Paragraphs

Word sorts by using the first character of each paragraph you select. If the first character is a letter, Word sorts alphabetically. If the first character is a number, Word sorts numerically. If two paragraphs begin with the same character, the program uses additional characters—letters or numbers—to place the paragraphs in order. You can choose between an ascending sort (the default sort order) or a descending sort (3, 2, 1).

To sort paragraphs, follow these steps:

1. Be sure to save your document before you begin to sort.

2. Select the paragraphs you want to sort. If you don't select any paragraphs, the Sort option is grayed. To select the whole document, choose Select All from the Edit menu or press ⌘-A.

Chapter 19

Numbering and Sorting Lines and Paragraphs

3. For an ascending sort, simply choose Sort from the Tools menu. For a descending sort, hold down the Shift key and choose Sort Descending from the Tools menu. Word performs the sort.

4. If you don't like the results of the sort, immediately choose Undo Sort from the Edit menu or press ⌘-Z.

Sorting Tables

As you learned in Chapter 17, you can create tables by using tabs or by using Word's Table command. No matter which way you created the tables, you can sort the table using the Sort command.

When you sort a table, you can use column selection to show Word which column you want to use as a guide for the sort. In figure 19.14, for example, four cells in the Quantity column are selected. Selecting these cells tells Word to sort these four rows, but use this column as a guide for the sort. Figure 19.15 shows the results of the sort. Word has placed the rows in ascending numerical order by Quantity (Cascades Spa without Case is first, because its quantity—25—is the lowest.) Note that Word has kept the row items together without scrambling them.

Fig. 19.14
A column selected for sort.

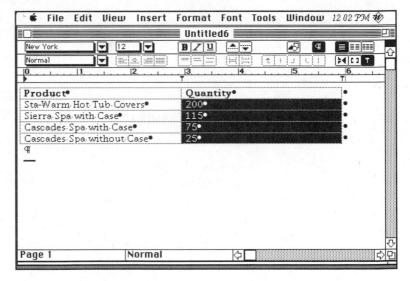

TIP

When you create a tabbed table that you plan to sort, think ahead. End each line with a Return key-stroke, rather than a New Line command, so that you can sort each line independently.

To sort a table, follow these steps:

1. Select the rows you want to sort or select one of the columns. (Don't include the table headings in the selection; if you do, Word sorts them too. If you leave the table headings out of the selection, the headings stay in place, as in figures 19.14 and 19.15.) Word uses the column you select as the guide for the sort. To select a column in a tabbed table that uses flush-right or decimal-aligned numbers, hold down the Option key and begin the selection at the lower right or upper right corner of the column.

2. To sort in ascending order, choose Sort from the Tools menu. To sort in descending order, hold down the Shift key and choose Sort Descending from the tools menu.

Fig. 19.15
Results of a sort with column selected.

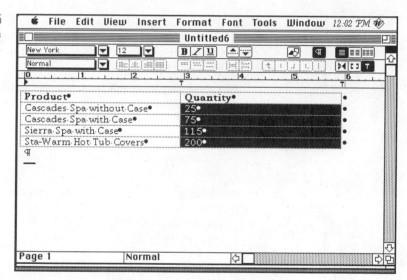

3. If the sort does not work correctly, immediately choose Undo Sort from the Edit menu.

TIP

For information on sorting headings in an outline, see Chapter 12.

Chapter 19

Numbering and Sorting Lines and Paragraphs

Quick Review

This section concisely summarizes the most useful information in this chapter. Check "Productivity Tips" for a review of high-productivity tips and tricks, and review "Techniques" when you forget how to perform a specific procedure.

Productivity Tips

■ Save your work before renumbering or sorting. If you perform another action and then decide that you don't like the results of the sort, you can abandon the changes by reloading the saved version of your document.

■ If you want to add line numbers to a technical or legal document, plan ahead. Add blank lines by using the Spacing options in the Paragraph dialog box or the Blank Line Spacing button on the ruler, not by pressing Return.

■ To keep Word from numbering lines that contain headings, format your heading styles with the Suppress Line Numbers option and apply these styles to your headings.

■ If you plan to number paragraphs in your document, use the New Line command (Shift-Enter) to keep together, in one paragraph, all the text you want numbered with only one number.

■ If numbering or sorting doesn't work out as you anticipated, remember that you can choose Undo to retrieve your document in presort condition. You must choose Undo immediately, however, before you perform another action (such as typing text or choosing a command).

■ To add paragraph numbers only to those paragraphs you want numbered, add a number, a period, and a tab to the beginning of each paragraph you want numbered. Then choose the Renumber command. Remember to choose the Only If Already Numbered option.

■ If you want to sort text, plan ahead. Group all the lines you want to keep together in the sort by typing them with the New Line command. Use case consistently.

■ When you sort a table, remember that you don't have to sort the table by the text or values in the first column. If you select a column other than the first one, Word uses the selected column as a guide for the sort.

Part II

Creating More Complex Documents

Techniques

This section provides concise, quick-reference summaries of all the procedures introduced in this chapter.

Numbering Lines

To add line numbers:

1. Select the paragraphs to which you want to add line numbers. If you don't select any text, Word adds line numbers to the whole document (or to the current section, if your document is divided into sections).

2. Choose Section from the Format menu.

3. Choose Line Numbers.

4. Choose By Page (numbers lines starting with 1 at the beginning of each page), By Section (numbers lines starting with 1 at the beginning of each section), or Continuous (numbers lines sequentially throughout document).

5. In the Count By box, type the line number increment you want to use.

6. In the From Text box, specify a distance from the end of the line number to the beginning of the text.

7. Choose OK.

Numbering Paragraphs

To add paragraph numbers to your document:

1. Select the paragraphs you want to number. If you don't select any paragraphs, Word numbers all the paragraphs in your document.

2. Choose Renumber from the Tools menu or press ⌘-F15.

3. To start numbering with a number other than 1, type the number in the Start At box.

4. To use a number format other than Arabic (1, 2, 3), type the number format and the separator character you want to use in the Format box.

5. Choose OK. If the numbering is not correct, immediately choose Undo from the Edit menu.

To number paragraphs of different levels:

1. Select the paragraphs you want to number. If you don't select paragraphs, Word numbers all the paragraphs in your document.

2. Choose Renumber from the Tools menu or press ⌘-F15.

3. To start numbering with a number other than 1, type the number in the Start At box.

4. To use a number format other than Arabic (1, 2, 3), type the number format and the separator character you want to use in the Format box.

5. Choose the 1.1 option to turn on subordinate level numbering.

6. Choose OK. If you don't like the way the numbering worked, immediately choose Undo from the Edit menu.

To number paragraphs selectively:

1. Type a number followed by a period (*1.*) and a tab at the beginning of every paragraph you want numbered.

2. Choose Renumber from the Tools menu or press ⌘-F15.

3. To start numbering with a number other than 1, type the number in the Start At box.

4. To use a number format other than Arabic (1, 2, 3), type the number format and the separator character you want to use in the Format box.

5. Important: Choose Only If Already Numbered.

6. Choose OK. If the numbering does not work correctly, immediately choose Undo from the Edit menu.

Removing Paragraph Numbers

To remove paragraph numbers from your document:

1. Choose Renumber from the Tools menu or press ⌘-F15.

2. Choose Remove.

3. Choose OK.

Part II

Creating More Complex Documents

Sorting Paragraphs

To sort paragraphs:

1. Important: Save your document.

2. Select the paragraphs you want to sort. If you don't select any paragraphs, the Sort option is grayed.

3. To perform an ascending sort, choose Sort from the Tools menu. To perform a descending sort, hold down the Shift key and choose Sort Descending from the Tools menu.

4. Important: If you don't like the results of the sort, immediately choose Undo Sort from the Edit menu or press ⌘-Z.

Sorting a Table

To sort a table:

1. Select the rows you want to sort or select a single column.

2. To sort in ascending order, choose Sort from the Tools menu. To sort in descending order, hold down the Shift key and choose Sort Descending from the Tools menu.

3. If the results of the sort are not what you want, immediately choose Undo Sort from the Edit menu.

Suppressing Line Numbers for Selected Paragraphs

To suppress line numbers for the selected paragraph or paragraphs:

1. If you haven't already done so, add line numbers to your document.

2. Select the paragraph or paragraphs for which you don't want line numbers to print.

3. Choose Paragraph from the Format menu or press ⌘-M.

4. Activate the Suppress Line Numbers check box.

5. Choose OK.

6. To suppress line numbers for another paragraph, move the insertion point to the paragraph and choose Repeat from the Edit menu (or press ⌘-Y).

Updating Paragraph Numbers

To update numbers:

1. When you add paragraphs that need numbers, type a number followed by a period (such as *1.*) and a tab at the beginning of every newly inserted paragraph you want numbered.

2. Choose Renumber from the Tools menu or press ⌘-F15.

3. Important: Choose Only If Already Numbered.

4. You can change the starting number and the number format. You can also choose subordinate numbering (the 1.1 option), even if you didn't choose this option the first time you inserted the numbers.

5. Choose OK.

20

Creating and Importing Graphics

T he Picture window, a new feature in Word 5, gives you many of the capabilities of drawing programs like MacDraw. Using the Picture window, you can create simple illustrations for your document, such as maps, simple technical diagrams, flow charts, organizational charts, or interior design sketches. Even when several elements are combined, each element of a drawing (a rectangle or line, for instance) is individually selectable and sizeable.

Although the Picture window does not have all the tools offered by stand-alone drawing applications, the option has sufficient tools to create and modify simple illustrations.

Word also can read most graphics files directly, including the bit-mapped graphics files created by paint programs such as MacPaint, the PICT files created by applications such as MacDraw and SuperPaint, and even the Encapsulated PostScript (EPS) graphics created by applications such as Aldus Freehand and Adobe Illustrator.

After you create or import a graphic, you can crop it or scale it. Cropping shows only part of the original graphic, while scaling resizes the graphic horizontally, vertically, or both. (As you quickly discover, you cannot resize bit-mapped graphics without introducing ugly distortions, but you can resize Picture's graphics, PICT files, and EPS graphics.)

This chapter covers the following aspects of Word's graphics capabilities:

- *Creating Illustrations with the Picture Window.* You learn how to create a simple illustration with Word's Picture command.

- *Editing Your Illustrations.* You learn how to move, resize, and delete elements within your illustration.

- *Importing Graphics.* You learn how to read many graphics files directly and how to import such files into your Word documents.

- *Cropping and Scaling Graphics.* You learn how to reduce the portion of the graph that is visible within the graphics frame, how to resize the graphic, and how to decide whether the result is acceptable.

Other chapters of this book contain information pertinent to graphics. In Chapter 14, you learn how to create active links between graphic applications and Word, as long as these applications support System 7's Dynamic Data Exchange (DDE) standards. In Chapter 21, you learn how to anchor graphics at an absolute position on the page (1.5 inches from the top margin and centered horizontally, for example) so that text flows around and past the graphic.

Creating Illustrations with the Picture Window

Word's Picture command is available in any Word document. When you choose Picture (Insert menu), the Insert Picture window appears (see fig. 20.1). In this window, you create and edit your illustration, using the tools in the tool bar. As you work, the status bar on the bottom border shows you the size of the selected object or the degree of rotation. When your illustration is finished, you click the Close box, and Word inserts the picture into your document within a graphics frame (see fig. 20.2).

Note the dotted lines that indicate the picture's boundary. These lines appear when you choose Show ¶ from the View menu.

Opening and Closing the Picture Window

You can open the Picture window in the following three ways:

Choose Picture from the Insert menu. An Open dialog box appears, asking you to choose the graphics file you want to open. Choose the New Picture button.

Choose the Picture button on the ribbon.

If you have already inserted a picture into your document, open the Picture dialog box (and display the picture for editing) by double-clicking the picture. When you open the Picture window this way, `Edit Picture` is displayed on the title bar.

Fig. 20.1
The Insert Picture window.

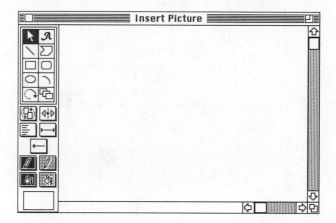

Fig. 20.2
An illustration inserted into
a Word document.

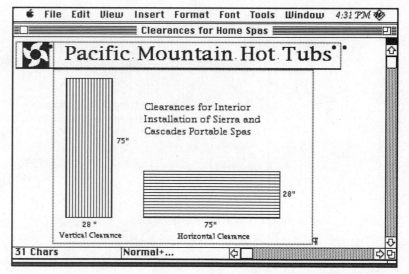

To close the Picture window, choose one of these techniques:

> Click the Close box.
>
> Choose Close from the File menu.
>
> Press ⌘-W.

SPEED KEY

After you close the Picture window, Word inserts the illustration into your document as a picture (see fig. 20.3).

Fig. 20.3
A picture inserted in
a document.

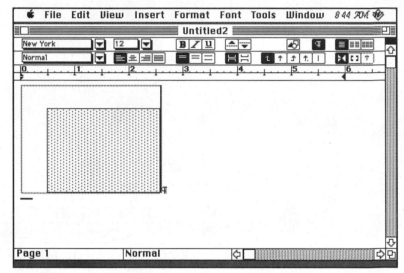

Word treats the picture as a single character. To delete the picture, select the picture so that you see the sizing and cropping *handles* (little black squares), and press Backspace or Delete. You can copy or move the picture just as you can any other character. You also can include a picture in a glossary entry (see Chapter 13 for more information on glossary entries).

Understanding the Tools

The Insert Picture window's tool bar provides many graphics tools for your use in creating illustrations (see fig. 20.4). Table 20.1 is an overview of these tools and their uses.

Fig. 20.4
Insert Picture dialog box
with graphics tool bar.

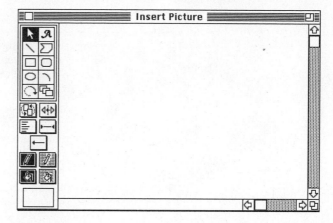

Table 20.1
Graphics Tools (Insert
Picture Window)

Tool	Function
	The Selection tool selects one element of your illustration, such as a line, arc, or rectangle.
	The Text tool creates a space for your text that reaches to the right edge of the window. To create a text box with dimensions you specify, drag the mouse. Watch the status area as you drag to see the changing dimensions of the box you're creating.
	The Text Alignment tool has a pop-up menu that offers the following choices: Align Left, Align Center, and Align Right. Choose one of these options to align the text within the box.
	Use the Line tool to draw a line. Hold down the Shift key to draw a perfectly horizontal or vertical line.
	The Line Width tool opens a palette of line width options. By default, Word uses a single-width line. To see the current line width, look at the box at the bottom of the tool bar. To close the palette, click the icon again.
	The Line Color Pallette opens a palette of line color options. By default, Word uses a black line. If you use a color monitor, you can see the current line color by looking at the box at the bottom of the tool bar. To close the palette, click the icon again.

continues

Chapter 20
Creating and Importing Graphics

Table 20.1 Continued	Tool	Function
		The Line Pattern Pallette opens a palette of line pattern options. By default, Word uses a solid pattern. To see the current line pattern, look at the box at the bottom of the tool bar. To close the palette, click the icon again.
		The Arrowhead tool opens a palette of arrowhead options. By default, Word does not add an arrowhead to lines. You can add arrowheads at the beginning of the line, the end of the line, or at both ends. To close the palette, click the icon again.
		The Arc tool draws arcs. Hold down the Shift key to create an arc that conforms to a portion of a circle.
		The Rectangle tool draws rectangles. Hold down the Shift key to create a square.
		Use the Rounded-Rectangle tool to draw rectangles with rounded corners. Hold down the Shift key to create a square with rounded edges.
		The Polygon tool draws irregular shapes.
		The Ellipse tool draws ellipses. Hold down the Shift key to draw a perfect circle.
		The Fill Color Palette offers a palette of fill colors. If you're using a color monitor, you see the current fill color in the box at the bottom of the tool bar.
		The Fill Pattern Palette offers a palette of fill patterns. You see the current fill pattern in the box at the bottom of the tool bar.
		The Rotation tool rotates the selected element to the position you want.
		The Duplication tool copies the selected element.
		The Stack Order tool sends the selected element to the background or brings the selected element to the foreground.
		The Flip tool flips the selected element horizontally or vertically.

Part II

Creating More Complex Documents

Drawing in the Picture Window

The Picture window is designed to help you develop simple illustrations. You can create the following elements: rectangles, squares, ellipses, circles, lines, arcs, arrows, and polygons. You can choose line widths, line colors, and line patterns, and you can choose fill colors and fill patterns.

To draw in Picture window, choose a tool, click where you want the element to begin, and drag. As you drag, Word creates the element you have chosen, such as a line or arc. The status bar shows you the length (or width and height) of the element. When you release the mouse, the element is selected. As explained later in this chapter, you use handles to resize and rotate elements (see fig. 20.5). The handles are not visible after you close the Picture window, and the program does not print them.

Fig. 20.5
Handles visible in
selected element.

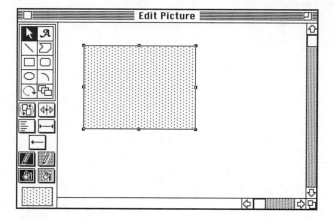

Each element you enter is independent. When you select an element by clicking, you manipulate the element independently of other elements. The capability to select elements independently makes Picture illustrations much easier to edit than graphics created with paint programs.

A Picture window drawing has two levels, the foreground and the background, so that you can superimpose one element on another. When you enter an element on top of an existing element, the existing one goes to the background, as shown in figure 20.6. Using the Stack Order tool, you can bring the background element to the foreground, as shown in figure 20.7.

Drawing a Rectangle or Ellipse

To draw a rectangle or an ellipse, follow these steps:

1. Choose the Rectangle, Rounded-Rectangle, or Ellipse tool.

2. If you want, choose one or more of the following:

   A line width from the line width palette

   A fill color from the line color palette

   A fill pattern from the line pattern palette

3. Click and drag to create the rectangle or ellipse. As you do, the status bar shows the width and height of the rectangle or ellipse.

Fig. 20.6
An ellipse in the fore-ground and a rectangle in the background.

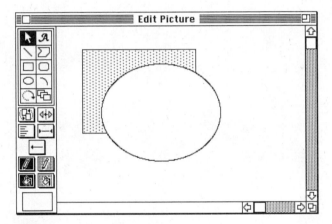

Fig. 20.7
A rectangle in the foreground and an ellipse in the background.

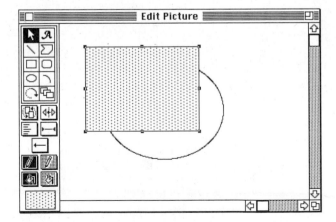

Part II

Creating More Complex Documents

Drawing a Line or Arc

To draw a line or arc, follow these steps:

1. Choose the Line tool or Arc tool.

2. If you want, choose one or more of the following:

   A line width from Line Width palette

   An arrowhead from Arrowhead palette

   A line color from Line Color palette

   A line pattern from Line Pattern palette

3. Click and drag to draw the line or arc. As you do, the status bar shows the length of the line you're drawing or the width and height of the rectangle that describes the arc you're drawing.

Drawing a Polygon

To create a polygon, follow these steps:

1. Choose the Polygon tool.

2. If you want, choose one or more of the following:

   A line width from Line Width palette

   A line color from Line Color palette

   A line pattern from Line Pattern palette

   A fill color from Fill Color palette

   A fill pattern from Fill Pattern palette

3. Click and drag to draw the first leg of the polygon.

4. Click to show the ends of additional legs of the polygon.

5. After you draw the polygon, double-click or choose another tool. Word adds a line connecting the last point with the first one and fills the shape with any color or pattern you have chosen.

Adding Text

You can add text such as a caption or explanatory text to your graphic. Like other elements in the illustration, the text is contained within an independently selectable box (see fig. 20.8). Note that the size of the box controls the text's indentation; within one box, Word wraps text

Chapter 20

Creating and Importing Graphics

automatically to keep the text in the box even if you insert or delete text, or resize the box. You can change the size of this box, and you can move the box independently of other elements in the illustration.

Fig. 20.8
Text within a selectable
box.

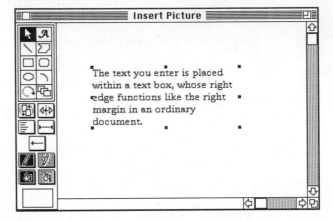

You cannot use the ribbon or ruler while the Picture window is on-screen. You can choose fonts, type styles such as bold or italic, and font sizes from the Font menu, however. In addition, you can use keyboard shortcuts and choose alignments with the Text Alignment tool.

To add text to your illustration, follow these steps:

1. Select the Text tool.

2. Do one of the following:

   Click within the Picture window to create a text box that extends all the way to the right edge of the window.

   Click and drag in the Picture window to create a text box that doesn't extend all the way to the right edge.

3. If you want, choose one of the following:

   A font and font size from the Font menu

   A type style or emphasis from the Font menu

   An alignment, using the Text Alignment tool

4. Type the text. At the right edge of the text box, Word extends the box and wraps the text down to the next line. The right edge of

the text box functions like the right margin in an ordinary document. To change the "right margin," click the Selection tool and drag the center handle on the right edge of the box.

5. Choose another tool to finish typing.

You can assign only one font, font size, emphasis, or alignment to each text box. For example, if you try to apply an emphasis such as boldface to part of the text in the box, the emphasis will apply to all the text in the box. If you want to use more than one font, font size, emphasis, or alignment, you must create two or more text boxes and format each separately.

Editing Text

After you create text in a text box, you can edit the text by following these steps:

1. Choose the Text tool.

2. Click the text box that contains the text you want to edit.

3. Edit the text as you would edit a document. You can use the keyboard shortcuts (⌘-V, ⌘-C, and ⌘-X), Backspace, Delete, and the editing commands on the Edit menu.

To create unusual effects, you can duplicate, flip, or rotate text in a text box. (See the rotated text shown in fig. 20.9.)

Fig. 20.9
Text rotated in
Picture window.

Converting Text to a Graphic

Because the Picture window limits you to the text formatting options you can choose with keyboard shortcuts and the Font menu, you may find the following trick useful:

1. Create the text in your document.

2. Cut the text to the clipboard.

3. Paste the text into the Picture window.

With this technique, you can use all the formats available in the Format Character dialog box, including large font sizes (see fig. 20.10).

Fig. 20.10
Text copied from
document.

To retain formatting when you copy text from your document to the Picture window, follow these steps:

1. Select the text.

2. Press ⌘-Option-D.

3. Open the Picture window. (To insert the text into an existing graphic, simply double-click the graphic to open the Edit Picture window.)

4. Place the insertion point where you want the text to appear.

5. Choose Paste from the Edit menu or press ⌘-V.

Editing Your Illustration

You can edit your illustration before or after you close the Picture window. To edit an illustration you already added to your document, simply double-click the graphic. You see the Edit Picture window, which is identical to the Insert Picture window except that Edit Picture displays an illustration you previously created.

Because each element you entered is independently selectable, you can alter your illustration easily by moving, resizing, scaling, flipping, rotating, duplicating, or switching the order of the stacked elements. The following sections detail each of these procedures.

Selecting Graphic Elements

To show Word which element you want to edit, begin by selecting the element. To select an element, follow these steps:

1. Choose the Selection tool.

2. Click the element.

To select more than one element, hold down the Shift key and select each element, or drag a selection box around the elements you want to select.

Moving Graphics Elements

To move a graphics element, follow these steps:

1. Select the element.

2. Click within the element and drag the element to its new location.

Resizing Graphics Elements

When you select a graphics element, such as a rectangle or line, you see *handles* (little black boxes). A line has two handles, one at each end. Rectangles and ellipses have eight boxes (see fig. 20.11). To resize a graphics element, drag one of the handles. What happens when you drag depends on which handle you drag. Figure 20.11 shows the direction a rectangle is resized when you drag one of the handles.

To resize a graphics element, follow these steps:

1. Select the element.

NOTE

To preserve formatting when you copy text from your document, you must use a special command (⌘-Option-D), not the usual Copy or Cut commands. If you use the usual commands to copy or cut text to the clipboard, you lose the formatting when you paste the text into the Picture window.

Chapter 20
Creating and Importing Graphics

2. Drag one of the handles. As you do, watch the status bar to see the size change as you drag.

Fig. 20.11
Handles on a rectangle.

Fig. 20.11
Handles on a rectangle.

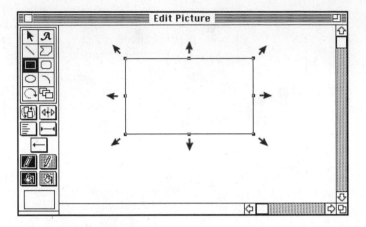

Flipping Graphics Elements

You can flip a graphic element vertically or horizontally. Figure 20.12 shows some of the effects possible when you duplicate graphics elements and flip them; you can create symmetrical, "mirror-image" elements this way. (To duplicate an element, select the element and choose the Duplicate tool.)

Fig. 20.12
Horizontal and
vertical flips.

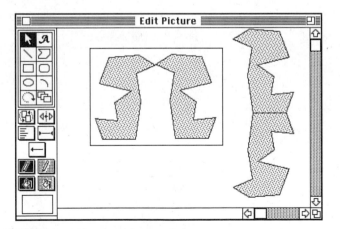

To flip a graphics element, follow these steps:

1. Select the element.

2. Choose the Flip tool. A pop-up menu appears with three options: Flip Horizontal, Flip Vertical, and Undo all Flips and Rotations.

3. Choose Flip Horizontal or Flip Vertical.

   To undo the flip, choose Undo from the Edit menu. If you have performed another action since the rotation, select the element, choose the Flip tool, and then choose Undo all Flips and Rotations.

Rotating Graphics Elements

You can rotate any selected element to any of 360 degrees of rotation. Figure 20.13 shows the effect of rotating by 90 degrees one of the symmetrical elements shown in figure 20.12.

Fig. 20.13
Rotated elements.

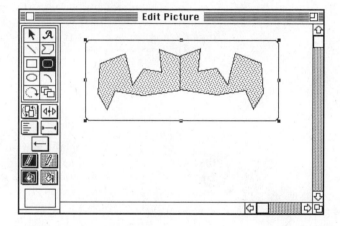

To rotate a graphics element, follow these steps:

1. Select the element.

2. Click the Rotation tool. The pointer changes to a circle, indicating that you can rotate the element.

3. Drag one of the handles. As you do, watch the status bar to see the degree of rotation.

4. Release the mouse button when you finish rotating the element.

Chapter 20

Creating and Importing Graphics

Switching the Order of Graphics Elements

When you superimpose elements, they stack up in the order they were drawn: the first element in the background and the most recently drawn element in the foreground.

To change the order, follow these steps:

1. Select the element you want to move.

2. Click the Stack Order tool and hold until the pop-up menu appears.

3. Choose Send to Back or Bring to Front.

Duplicating a Selected Element

The Duplication tool quickly makes a copy of one or more selected elements and places the copy next to the original. From there you can drag the copy to a new location.

Importing Graphics

SYSTEM 7

n addition to creating your own pictures, you have many options for importing graphics. You can import graphics from another application by copying the graphic to the clipboard and pasting the graphic into Word. If your System 7 graphics application supports Dynamic Data Interchange, you can create a dynamic link between the graphics application and your Word document. With a dynamic link, changes you make with your graphic application automatically are reflected in the graphic you pasted into your Word document. (For information on dynamic linking, see Chapter 14.)

Perhaps the most convenient way to import graphics from another application, however, is to use the Picture command (Insert menu) to open a graphics file directly. Word can read PICT, PICT2, TIFF, bit-mapped (paint), and Encapsulated PostScript (EPS) files directly, using built-in graphics file converters. When you open a graphic file, Word converts the graphic to Word's graphics format and places the graphic at the insertion point.

To open a PICT, PICT2, TIFF, paint, or EPS file directly, follow these steps:

TIP

Some graphics programs can save graphics to more than one file format. If your graphics application has this capability, save your file using a format that Word can read directly.

1. Position the insertion point where you want the graphic to appear.

2. Choose Picture from the Insert menu. The dialog box shown in figure 20.14 appears. (System 6 has a Drive button rather than the Desktop button.)

3. Choose the graphics file you want to open. Choose Find File to search your disk, if you cannot find the file right away.

4. Choose Open.

TIP

If you have a PostScript laser printer, EPS graphics will give you the best resolution. (EPS graphics always use the printer's maximum resolution. A PICT version of the file appears on-screen to show you what the printed file will look like.) The next best option is to use PICT graphics, which rely on the Mac's built-in QuickDraw routines to produce sharp graphic images with non-PostScript printers.

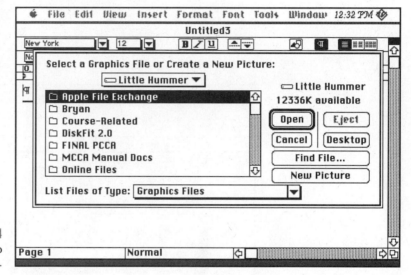

Fig. 20.14
Selecting a picture to open (System 7).

Cropping and Scaling Graphics

When you insert a graphic into your document, Word adds the graphic as a picture contained within a frame. If you have chosen Show ¶ from the Edit menu, you can see the frame on-screen. Selecting the frame reveals three handles, as shown in figure 20.15. You can use these handles to crop the graphic, so that part of the graphic doesn't show (see fig. 20.16). You also can scale (resize) the graphic (see fig. 20.17). Be aware, however, that many scaled graphics print with odd distortions. In general, scaled paint and TIFF graphics usually produce ugly results. You can resize some PICT graphics successfully, and you always can resize EPS graphics.

Chapter 20
Creating and Importing Graphics

Fig. 20.15
Handles on a
selected frame.

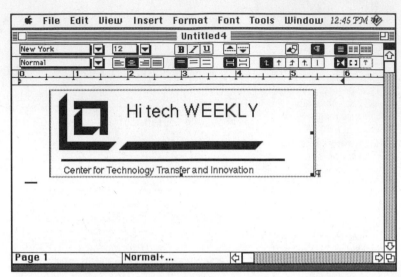

Fig. 20.16
A cropped graphic.

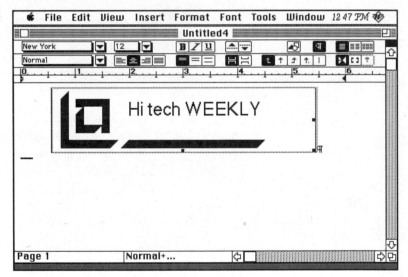

Part II

Creating More Complex Documents

Fig. 20.17
A scaled graphic.

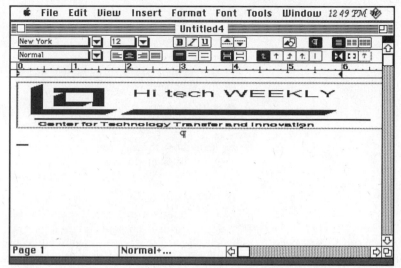

To crop a graphic, follow these steps:

1. Select the graphic so that you see the handles.

2. Drag one of the handles.

To scale a graphic, follow these steps:

1. Select the graphic so that you see the handles.

2. Holding down the Shift key, drag one of the handles. As you scale the graphic, you see the scale percentage in the page number area.

Quick Review

This section concisely summarizes the most useful information in this chapter. Check "Productivity Tips" for a review of high-productivity tips and tricks, and review "Techniques" when you forget how to perform a specific procedure.

Productivity Tips

■ You can create illustrations by using lines, rectangles, polygons, circles, arcs, patterns, and text by using the Picture command (Insert menu). For simple illustrations, you do not need to switch to a graphics application.

■ Take time to explore the tools on the Picture window's tool bar. Check out the palettes to see what useful options are available.

■ Remember the Shift-key drawing tricks: hold down the Shift key after choosing the appropriate tool to draw perfect circles, squares, horizontal lines, or vertical lines.

■ The Picture window gives you only limited text formatting capabilities. To format your text the way you want, create and format the text in your document and then use the ⌘-Option-D command to cut the text to the clipboard. When you paste the contents of the clipboard in the Picture window, Word transforms the text into a graphic and retains all the formats you have chosen.

■ Word can read PICT, PICT2, TIFF, paint, or EPS graphic files directly. To place one of these files into your Word document, use Word's Picture command (Insert menu) to open the graphics file.

■ Avoid scaling paint or TIFF graphics. You can scale some PICT graphics and you can scale all EPS graphics with excellent results.

Techniques

This section provides concise, quick-reference summaries of all the procedures introduced in this chapter.

Adding Text to Your Illustration

To add text to your illustration:

1. Select the Text tool.

2. Do one of the following:

   Click within the Picture window to create a text box that extends all the way to the right edge of the window.

   Click and drag in the Picture window to create a text box that doesn't extend all the way to the right edge.

Part II

3. Optionally, choose one of the following:

    A font and font size from the Font menu

    A type style or an emphasis from the Font menu

    An alignment, using the Text Alignment tool

4. Type the text.

5. Choose another tool to finish typing.

Converting Text to a Graphic

To retain formatting when you copy text from your document to the Picture window:

1. Select the text.

2. Press ⌘-Option-D.

3. Open the Picture window.

4. Place the insertion point where you want the text to appear.

5. Choose Paste from the Edit menu or press ⌘-V.

Cropping a Graphic within Your Word Document

To crop a graphic:

1. Select the graphic so that you see the handles.

2. Drag one of the handles.

Drawing a Line or Arc

To draw a line or arc:

1. Choose the Line tool or Arc tool.

2. If you want, choose one or more of the following:

    A line width from the Line Width palette

    An arrowhead from the Arrowhead palette

    A line color from the Line Color palette

    A line pattern from the Line Pattern palette

3. Click and drag to draw the line or arc.

Chapter 20
Creating and Importing Graphics

Drawing a Polygon

To create a polygon:

1. Choose the Polygon tool.

2. If you want, choose one or more of the following:

   A line width from the Line Width palette

   A line color from the Line Color palette

   A line pattern from the Line Pattern palette

   A fill color from the Fill Color palette

   A fill pattern from the Fill Pattern palette

3. Click and drag to draw the first leg of the polygon.

4. Click to show the ends of additional legs.

5. After you draw the polygon, double-click or choose another tool.

Drawing a Rectangle or Ellipse

To draw a rectangle or ellipse:

1. Select the Rectangle, Rounded-Rectangle, or Ellipse tool.

2. If you want, choose one or more of the following:

   A line width from the Line Width palette

   A fill color from the Line Color palette

   A fill pattern from the Line Pattern palette

3. Click and drag to create the rectangle or ellipse.

Duplicating Elements

To duplicate one or more elements:

1. Select the element or elements.

2. Choose the Duplicate icon.

3. Drag the copy to its new location.

Editing an Illustration

To open the Edit Picture window:

1. In your Word document, select the graphic.

2. Do one of the following:

   Choose Picture from the Insert menu.

   Choose the Picture button on the ribbon.

Editing Text in the Picture Window

To edit the text in a text box (Picture window):

1. Choose the Text tool.

2. Click the text box that contains the text you want to edit.

3. Edit the text as you would edit a document.

Flipping Graphics Elements

To flip a graphics element:

1. Select the element.

2. Choose the Flip tool.

3. Choose Flip Horizontal or Flip Vertical.

To unflip a graphics element:

1. Select the element.

2. Choose the Flip tool.

3. Choose Undo all Flips and Rotations.

Importing Graphics Files

To open a PICT, PICT2, TIFF, paint, or EPS file directly:

1. Position the insertion point where you want the graphic to appear.

2. Choose Picture from the Insert menu.

3. Select the graphics file you want to open.

4. Choose Open.

Chapter 20
Creating and Importing Graphics

Moving Graphics Elements

To move a graphics element:

1. Select the element.

2. Click within the element and drag the element to the new location.

Opening the Insert Picture Window

To open the Insert Picture window:

> Choose Picture from the Insert menu or choose the Picture button on the ribbon.

Resizing Graphics Elements

To resize a graphics element:

1. Select the element.

2. Drag one of the handles.

Rotating Graphics Elements

To rotate a graphics element:

1. Select the element.

2. Click the Rotation tool.

3. Drag one of the handles.

4. Release the mouse button after you finish rotating the element.

Scaling a Graphic within Your Word Document

To scale a graphic:

1. Select the graphic so that you see the handles.

2. Holding down the Shift key, drag one of the handles.

Selecting Graphics Elements

To select an element:

1. Choose the Selection tool.

2. Choose the element.

To select more than one element:

> Hold down the Shift key and select each element, or Drag a selection box around the elements you want to select.

Switching the Order of Graphics Elements

To change the order, follow these steps:

1. Select the element.

2. Click the Stack Order tool and hold so that the pop-up menu appears.

3. Choose Send To Back or Bring To Front.

Positioning Text and Graphics

ord 5 isn't a desktop publishing program, but you can quickly and easily create an attractive page design with Word. A page layout program (such as PageMaker) includes tools for creating a page design complete with areas into which you can "pour" text, just as you fill a graphic element with a color or pattern. Word does not have these capabilities, but you can fix paragraphs of text or graphics on the page at a fixed location—in the exact center of the page (see fig. 21.1), for example, or flush to the right margin at the top of the page. A paragraph, graphic, or table positioned in this way is called a *frame*.

With Word 5's Frame command, called the Position command in previous Word versions, you can fix the location of a paragraph (containing text or a graphic) on the page absolutely; no matter how much text you add or delete, the text or graphic you have formatted stays put. In Version 5, the Frame command is even easier to use because you can position the frame visually without leaving the Frame dialog box.

This chapter shows you how to use the Frame command to position paragraphs, graphics, and tables. The following is an overview of the chapter:

■ *Positioning a Frame on the Page*. In this section, you learn the three ways you can position text, graphics, or tables in an absolute position on the page.

TIP

As you consider how to position graphic elements on the page, keep in mind that a single-row table often provides the ideal solution to the problem of positioning a graphic next to explanatory text. For information on tables, refer to Chapter 17.

■ *Formatting Text in a Frame*. This section discusses text formatting within a frame and explains how the ruler measures frames in Page Layout view.

■ *Using Positions in Styles*. You learn how to add Frame position information to styles so that Word enters the frame information automatically when you apply the style.

■ *Position Formatting Examples*. You learn how to create drop caps, sidebars, and other page design elements with the Frame command.

Several other chapters contain information relevant to frames. Chapter 8 provides information on defining and applying styles. As you learn in this chapter, you can create styles that contain Frame position information so that when you apply the style, Word positions the text, graphic, or table using the Frame positions included in the style. Chapter 20 provides information on including graphics in your documents; with Frame, you can position the graphic so that it prints with text flowing around it on the page. Chapter 22 provides information on adding borders to frames.

Fig. 21.1
Graphic positioned in the center of the page.

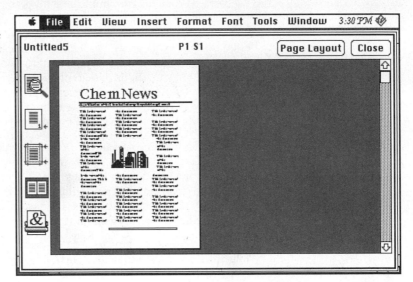

Part II

Creating More Complex Documents

Positioning a Frame on the Page

Frames provide the basis for many page design possibilities. Using Word's capability to rotate text that has been converted to a graphic (see Chapter 20) as well as the program's capability to position text and graphics absolutely on the page, you can create a huge variety of attractive page designs (see fig. 21.2). You specify just where on the page you want the frame to print—including beyond the margins, if you want, or spanning two or more columns in a multiple-column layout. You can control the width of the frame, and you can add borders and shading for even more attractive effects (see fig. 21.3). Text that normally prints where the positioned frame is located flows around the frame instead.

Fig. 21.2
Rotated text title positioned flush with left and top margins.

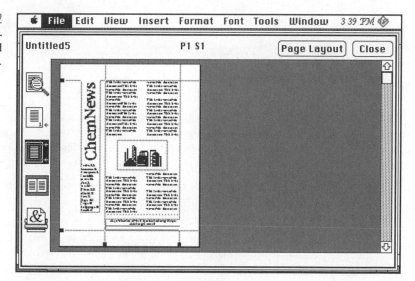

You can position one or more paragraphs, graphics, or tables in a frame. To position the frame, you select the element or elements (such as one or more paragraphs or graphics) and use the Frame command, which you access through the Format menu. Using the Position button in the Frame dialog box, you can visually choose a position for the frame by dragging the frame.

When you position a frame, you tell Word to disregard the position in which the selected elements appear in your text. Word removes the selected elements and places them in the position you specify.

Chapter 21
Positioning Text and Graphics

Fig. 21.3
Shading added to positioned title and graphic.

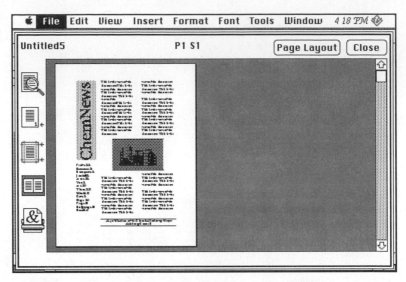

NOTE

The Frame command enables you to fix a frame's position on the page. If you want the frame to appear on a specific page, however, you must place the text, graphic, or table that you want to position within the text that prints on that page. If you want the frame to appear within a specific column in a multiple-column layout, you must position the element within the text that prints in that column.

Just what you see after positioning a frame depends on the view you are using. Normal view does not show the page layout; instead, you see the elements in line with surrounding text, as if you had not used the Frame command. Page Layout view shows the frame's position on-screen, but unless you are working with a fast Macintosh, you may find the Page Layout view too sluggish for writing and editing.

When you position a frame, you may do so in three ways:

■ *Position the frame visually.* When you choose the Position button in the Frame dialog box, Word shows you a Print Preview of your document. You drag the frame to its position. This technique is easy and fast, but it may not be the best choice if you want to center the frame or align it next to the page edge, margins, or column boundaries.

■ *Position the frame by choosing Position options.* This technique is best if you want to center a frame or align it next to the page edge, margins, or column boundaries. You choose these options from drop-down lists in the Frame dialog box.

■ *Position the frame by typing measurements.* This technique is best if you want to place the frame at an exact location on the page. You do so by typing measurements in the Frame dialog box.

Positioning the Frame Visually

You can position the frame visually using a Print Preview of the page on which you are working. To position a frame on the page using Print Preview, follow these steps:

1. Select the text, table, or graphic that you want to position.

   You can select more than one of these elements as long as they are *contiguous* (next to one another). To select a graphic, click the graphic to reveal the handles. To select an entire table, hold down the Option key and double-click anywhere in the table.

2. Choose Frame from the Format menu. The Frame dialog box appears (see fig. 21.4).

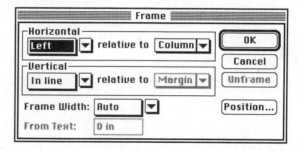

Fig. 21.4
The Frame dialog box.

3. If you are framing text, type a width for the text in the Frame Width list box.

   The default Auto setting chooses a text frame width equal to the width of the column in which the frame is situated. If you want text to flow around the frame, type a measurement narrower than the column width. If you have a single-column layout (6-inch line length), for example, you can type 3.5 in the Frame Width box to ensure that text flows around the frame.

   If you are framing a graphic, Word automatically determines the width of the graphic and uses this figure in the Frame Width box. If you want, you can change the default spacing from Text by typing a new measurement in the From Text box.

4. Choose Position. A Print Preview screen displays the page on which you are working (see fig. 21.5). When you move the pointer over the frame you are creating, the pointer changes to a cross hair.

Fig. 21.5
Preview of a frame
position.

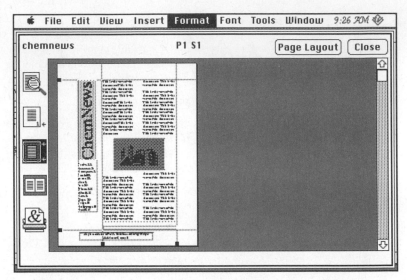

5. With the pointer on the frame, click and drag to position the frame anywhere on the page. As you drag, keep your eye on the page number area at the top of the Print Preview window; as you move the frame, this area shows the horizontal position of the left frame border (measured from the left of the page) and the vertical position of the top frame border (measured from the top of the page).

   If you position the frame over existing elements, Word reformats the page so that text flows around the frame (see fig. 21.6).

6. When you are satisfied with the frame's position, choose Page Layout to return to the Page Layout view of your document, or choose Close to return to the Normal view.

If you are using a laser printer, remember that most laser printers cannot print within 0.5 inch of the edge of the page. If part of the frame is cut off when the document prints, reposition the frame so that it isn't so close to the edge. (For information on repositioning a frame, see "Repositioning a Frame and Unframing" later in this chapter.)

Fig. 21.6
A repositioned frame.

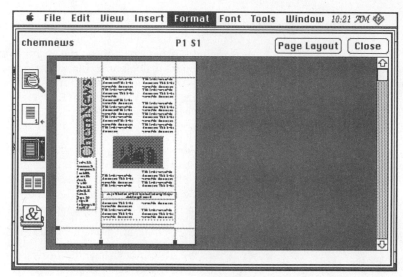

Choosing Position Options

This technique is best if you want to center a frame horizontally or vertically or position the frame flush to the page edge, margins, or column boundaries. When you position a frame, you specify the horizontal and vertical positions by choosing options from the Horizontal and Vertical list boxes of the Frame dialog box. For each option (such as Left or Center) that you choose, you also can choose an option from the Relative To list box. These options are Relative to Page and Relative to Margin for vertical positions; for horizontal positions, the list includes Relative to Column (used for multiple-column layouts). Using these options, you can position a frame centered horizontally relative to the left and right margins and positioned flush with the top margin.

The following options are available in the Horizontal list box in the Frame dialog box:

> **Left.** Aligns the left edge of the frame flush with the page, margin, or column.

> **Center.** Centers the frame horizontally relative to the page, margin, or column.

Chapter 21
Positioning Text and Graphics

Right. Aligns the right edge of the frame flush with the page, margin, or column.

Inside. If you have chosen the Mirror Even/Odd option in the Document dialog box so that you can produce your document using both sides of the page, this option appears in the Horizontal list box. It aligns the element flush right (relative to the page, margin, or column) on even-numbered pages and flush left (relative to the page, margin, or column) on odd-numbered pages.

Outside. If you have chosen the Mirror Even/Odd option, this option appears in the Horizontal list box. It aligns the element flush left (relative to the page, margin, or column) on even-numbered pages, and flush right (relative to the page, margin, or column) on odd-numbered pages.

The following options are available in the Vertical list box:

In Line. Does not change the vertical position of the frame as it occurs in the sequence of paragraphs in your document. If you add or delete text, the frame moves down or up. Text does not flow around the frame.

Top. Positions the top edge of the frame flush with the top of the page or the top margin.

Center. Centers the frame vertically on the page relative to the page or the margins.

Bottom. Positions the bottom edge of the frame flush with the bottom of the page or the bottom margin.

Figure 21.7 graphically shows some position options. Note the two-column layout and the large bottom margin. An element centered vertically relative to the page is lower than an element centered vertically relative to the margins. Note, too, the element centered horizontally relative to the column.

You may have been surprised to see the In Line option in the Vertical list box. After all, the purpose of the Frame command is to change the position of a text element so that it doesn't print in the same sequence with other paragraphs. Sometimes, however, you may want the positioned element to stay with the text above and below it. Figure 21.8, for example, shows two frames—a heading and a graphic—positioned in line with the surrounding text. They are framed horizontally so that they print within the document's wide left margin.

Fig. 21.7
Some position options.

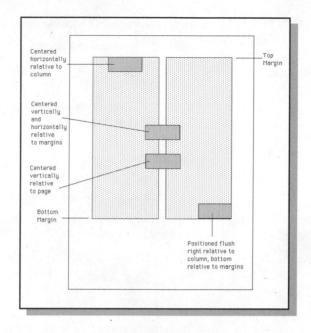

Fig. 21.8
Frames placed left relative
to the page and in line
vertically.

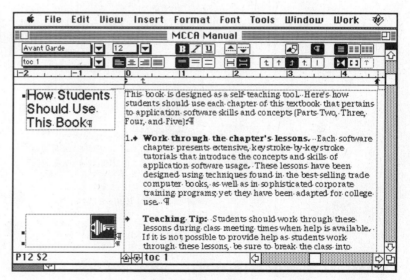

To position the frame by choosing position options, follow these steps:

1. Select the text, table, or graphic that you want to position.

2. Choose Frame from the Format menu. The Frame dialog box appears.

3. If you are framing text, type a width for the text in the Frame Width list box.

4. Choose an option in the Horizontal list box; in the Relative To list box, choose Column, Page, or Margin.

5. Choose an option in the Vertical list box; in the Relative To list box, choose In Line, Top, Center, or Bottom.

6. If you want, you can change the default spacing from text by typing a new measurement in the From Text box.

7. Choose OK to confirm the frame position.

Typing Measurements

In addition to the two position techniques just explained, you also can type measurements in the Vertical and Horizontal boxes of the Frame dialog box. No matter which default measurement you have chosen, you can type the distance in inches (" or in), points (pt), centimeters (cm), or picas (pi).

Repositioning a Frame and Unframing

I f you have positioned an object but are not happy with the results, you can change the frame's location, or you can unframe the elements to return them to their original, sequential location in your document.

To reposition a frame, follow these steps:

1. Choose Print Preview from the Print menu.

2. Position the pointer over the frame until the pointer changes to a cross hair.

3. Drag the frame to its new location.

4. Choose Page Layout to return to the Page Layout view or Close to return to the Normal view.

To cancel frame positioning, follow these steps:

1. Select all the elements within the frame.

2. Choose Frame from the Format menu.

3. Choose Unframe.

Formatting Text in a Frame

You can format text within a frame just as you format any text in a Word document. After you have created a frame and placed the insertion point within it in Page Layout view, the ruler changes to show the boundaries of the frame as shown in figure 21.9. The right boundary of the frame acts just like a right margin; when you are typing within the frame, text that reaches the margin wraps down to the next line.

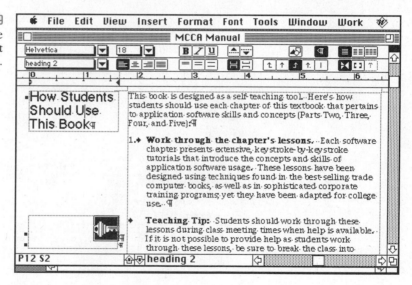

Fig. 21.9
Ruler measures frame boundaries (Page Layout view).

Within a frame, you can use paragraph indents just as within a normal text column. If you indent the text past the left or right frame boundaries, the text prints outside the frame (but Word cuts it off if it interferes with other text).

Chapter 21
Positioning Text and Graphics

Using Frame Positions in Styles

Because the choices you make in the Frame dialog box are paragraph formats as far as Word is concerned, you can include frame position information in styles (see Chapter 8). In figure 21.8, for example, the heading "Required Hardware and Software Installation" is a positioned version of the Heading 2 style. If you modify a style in this way, Word automatically enters the Frame position information when you apply the style.

To add position information to a style, simply create the style as usual. Apply the Frame command to the text and define the style by example. Alternatively, use the Style command to create the style and then use Frame to choose the position.

Position Formatting Examples

You have already learned how to position text elements, and you have seen many examples of the use of the Frame command in page design. This section presents additional examples that you may find useful.

Figure 21.10 shows a *sidebar*—text set aside for emphasis. This frame is positioned in line vertically and centered horizontally within the text column; the width is set manually at 3.0 inches. Thick borders have been added above and below the frame. (For information on borders, see Chapter 22.)

Fig. 21.10
A sidebar.

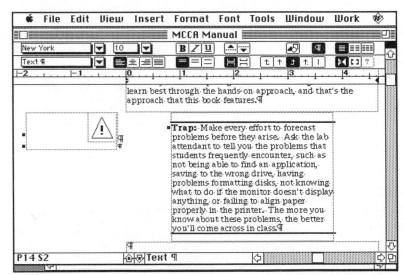

In figure 21.11, the 72-point initial uppercase letter was copied to the clipboard as a graphic using the ⌘-Option-D command (see "Converting Text to a Graphic" in Chapter 20). The graphic was created with the Picture command and reinserted into the document; the graphic then was positioned at the top of the page vertically and flush with the left margin horizontally.

Fig. 21.11
Initial letter formatted as a picture and framed.

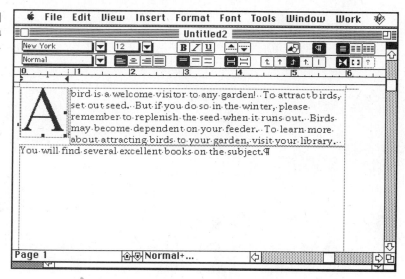

Quick Review

This section concisely summarizes the most useful information in this chapter. Check "Productivity Tips" for a review of high-productivity tips and tricks, and review "Techniques" when you forget how to perform a specific procedure.

Productivity Tips

■ Use the Frame command to position text, graphics, and tables in an absolute position on the page. Keep in mind that a single-row table may be the best solution if you are trying to position text next to a graphic.

■ Before you position an element, make sure it is positioned somewhere on the page or in the column where you want the element to appear.

■ To position a graphic element quickly, use the Position button in the Frame dialog box so that you can visually place the frame on the page. Use the Vertical and Horizontal drop-down boxes if you want to align the frame flush to the page, margins, or column boundaries or if you want to center the element horizontally or vertically.

■ You can quickly reposition an element by selecting it and choosing the Frame command (Format menu). Double-clicking the black square in the selection bar next to the frame to reveal the Frame dialog box is even faster.

Techniques

This section provides concise, quick-reference summaries of all the procedures introduced in this chapter.

Cancelling Frame Positioning

To cancel frame positioning:

1. Select all the elements within the frame.

2. Choose Frame from the Format menu.

3. Choose Unframe.

Positioning a Frame

To position a frame on the page using Print Preview:

1. Select the text, table, or graphic that you want to position.

2. Choose Frame from the Format menu.

3. If you are framing text, type a width for the text in the Frame Width list box.

4. Choose Position.

5. With the pointer on the frame, click and drag to position the frame anywhere on the page.

6. When you are satisfied with the frame's position, choose Page Layout to return to the Page Layout view of your document, or choose Close to return to the Normal view.

To position the frame by choosing position options or by typing measurements:

1. Select the text, table, or graphic that you want to position.

2. Choose Frame from the Format menu.

3. If you are framing text, type a width for the text in the Frame Width list box.

4. Choose an option in the Horizontal list box, or type a measurement.

5. Choose an option in the Relative To list box next to Horizontal.

6. Choose an option in the Vertical list box, or type a measurement.

7. Choose an option in the Relative To list box next to Vertical.

8. If you want, you can change the default spacing from Text by typing a new measurement in the From Text box.

9. Choose OK to confirm the frame position.

Repositioning a Frame

To reposition a frame:

1. Choose Print Preview from the Print menu.

2. Position the pointer over the frame until you see the pointer shape change to a cross hair.

3. Drag the frame to its new location.

4. Choose Page Layout to return to the Page Layout view or Close to return to the Normal view.

Using Borders and Shading

B *orders* (lines and boxes) and shading effects can transform an otherwise plain document into one that looks as though it has been professionally designed. Figure 22.1 shows a newsletter that takes full advantage of Word's border and shading capabilities. Note the single and double lines, called *rules,* below the newsletter's banner and the border around the graphic (centered on the page with Word's Frame command.)

Fig. 22.1
Print Preview of document with borders and shading.

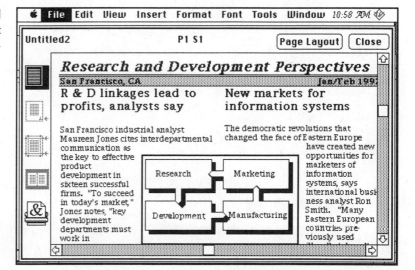

With Word, you can quickly add borders and shading to any of the following elements of your document:

- *Text.* You can add borders and shading to any amount of selected text (one or more paragraphs in length). In figure 22.1, a double rule appears beneath the newsletter's title; the paragraph beneath the title has 25 percent shading with a single rule below.

- *Table.* Word automatically treats a table as a unit as far as borders and shading are concerned. You can surround the entire table with a border and print a gray screen (a light gray shading) behind the table.

- *Cells.* Within a table, you can format the borders and shading patterns independently for each cell. Thus, you can easily and quickly create lines that make a table look less like a spreadsheet and more like a formal table (with lines only where you want them). In addition, you can choose options that quickly add borders and shading to rows, columns, or all the cells in a table.

- *Graphics.* Word treats each picture as a unit for borders and shading purposes. You can quickly add a box around a graphic.

This chapter surveys Word's border and shading capabilities. The following is a quick overview:

- *Understanding the Border Dialog Box.* This section explains the border and shading options.

- *Adding Borders and Shading.* In this section, you learn how to add lines, boxes, and shading to text, graphics, and tables.

- *Aligning Paragraph Borders.* This section explains how to use indents and tables to control text borders.

- *Changing and Removing Borders and Shading.* This section shows you how to alter or remove the border and shading options you have chosen.

> **TIP**
>
> With Word, borders and shading are paragraph formats. If you format a paragraph of text with borders and/or shading, Word repeats the format when you press Return. Chances are you do not want to repeat the format—after all, borders and shading should be used sparingly, for emphasis. For this reason, waiting to apply the shading until you have finished writing and editing your document is advisable.

Understanding the Border Dialog Box

 o add borders and shading, you use the Border command in the Format menu. This command reveals the Border dialog box (see fig. 22.2).

You also can bring up the Border dialog box by choosing the Border button in the Paragraph, Table Cells, or Picture dialog boxes.

Fig. 22.2
The Border dialog box with
text selected.

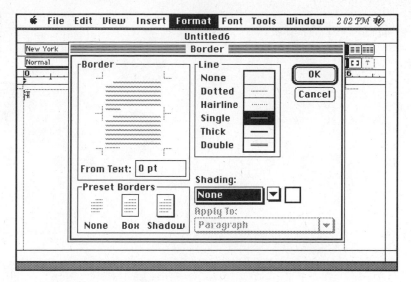

The following is an overview of the Border dialog box:

Line Area (Default: Single). In this area, you choose the line width you want to use. You can choose from Dotted, Hairline, Single, Thick, and Double. The hairline option prints a hairline with laser printers only; if you are using another kind of printer, this option has the same result as Single.

Preset Borders Area (Default: None). This area presents icons you can click to select a box or shadow box quickly. If you click Box, you get a box using the line width currently in effect in the Line area. If you choose Shadow, you get a shadow box.

Border Area. This area represents the text on the page and enables you to add lines where you want them. If you click the top, for example, you get a line across the top, and if you click the left, you get a line on the left. If you click the middle, Word prints lines between paragraphs in the selection. Figure 22.3 shows the Border area with a graphic selected; Figure 22.4 shows the Border area with a table selected.

From Text Area (Default: 0 pt). In this box, you type the *additional* distance you want the lines to be separated from the text. By default, Word enters 2 points (even though the From Text box shows 0 pt). If you type a number from 1 to 31 in this box, Word increases the default 2-point distance by the number of points you type. (*Note:* 72 points equals 1 inch.)

Chapter 22
Using Borders and Shading

Fig. 22.3
The Border dialog box with
a graphic selected.

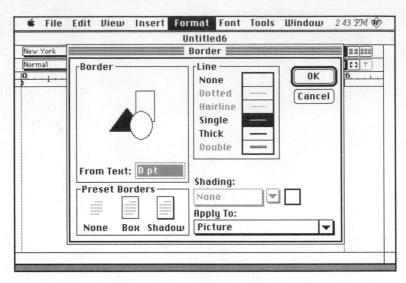

Fig. 22.3
The Border dialog box with
a graphic selected.

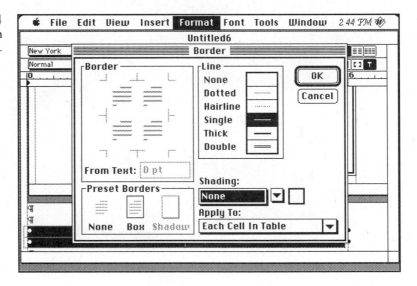

Fig. 22.4
The Border dialog box with
a table selected.

Apply To Area. This box becomes active when you need to indicate where you want the borders applied. When you select a graphic, for example, you can apply the border to the graphic only or to the paragraph in which the graphic is contained. When you select a table, you can apply the border to just the selected cell, all

Part II

Creating More Complex Documents

the cells in the table, the entire table (with no lines within), a selected column, or a selected row.

Shading List Box. When you click the Shading list box, you see the shading options shown in figure 22.5. If you are using an ImageWriter, choose shading options that are multiples of 12.5 percent for best results: 12.5, 25, 37.5, and so on. With laser printers or 300-dot-per-inch (dpi) ink-jet printers, you can choose any of the shading options.

Fig. 22.5
Shading options.

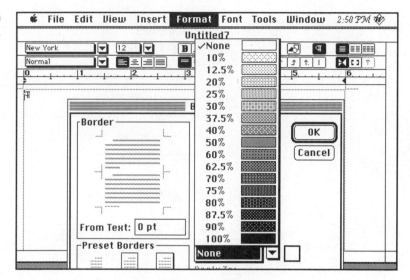

Adding Borders and Shading

he procedures you follow for adding borders and shading vary depending on whether you have selected text, a graphic, or a table. The following sections cover all three procedures.

Adding Borders and Shading to Text

You can format one or more paragraphs of text. If you select more than one paragraph, Word treats the selection as a block and places the borders around the entire selection.

When you add borders or shading to text, these elements become part of the paragraph format. As with all other paragraph formats, the border or

Chapter 22
Using Borders and Shading

shading options are "contained" in the paragraph mark. If you delete the mark, you delete the borders or shading along with all the other formats you have chosen for the paragraph.

To add borders and shading to text, follow these steps:

1. Select the text.

2. Choose Border from the Format menu. The Border dialog box appears.

3. To add borders, choose a line width.

4. Choose Box or Shadow in the Preset Borders area, or click in the Border area to choose the borders you want. If you click the middle border, Word places borders between paragraphs (if you have selected more than one paragraph).

5. If you want, increase the default distance from the text (2 pts) by typing a number from 1 to 31 in the From Text area.

6. To add shading, choose a shading percentage or type a percentage in the Shading box.

7. Choose OK.

Figure 22.6 shows thick borders above and below a paragraph of text.

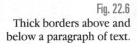

Fig. 22.6
Thick borders above and below a paragraph of text.

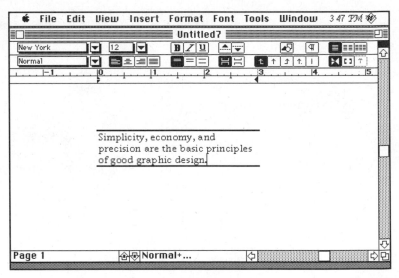

You can include borders and shadings in styles. If you frequently use borders or shadings for a text element, such as a title or heading, create a style that includes the border or shading formats. For more information on styles, see Chapter 8.

Adding Borders to a Graphic

The procedures you use to add borders to graphics are similar to those for adding borders or shading to text, with the following differences:

- You can add borders to only one graphic at a time. If you want to add borders to two or more graphics, format them one at a time.

- You cannot add shading to a graphic with the Border command; you must use the Edit Picture window to add shading.

- If the borders are too close to the graphic, you can enlarge the graphic frame by selecting it and dragging the handles.

To add borders to a graphic, follow these steps:

1. Select the graphic.

2. Choose Border from the Format menu. The Border dialog box appears with a graphic in the Border area.

3. To add borders, choose a line width.

4. Choose Box or Shadow in the Preset Borders area, or click in the Border area to choose the borders you want.

5. If you want to add shading, choose a shading percentage or type a percentage in the Shading box.

6. In the Apply To area, choose Paragraph if you want the border to surround the paragraph in which the graphic is situated. Choose Picture (the default) to place the border around the picture only.

7. Choose OK.

Figure 22.7 shows a graphic surrounded by a box that was added using the Picture option in the Apply To area. Because the Picture option was used, Word did not include the paragraph mark (the one that follows the graphic) within the selection.

Adding Borders and Shading to Tables

When you add borders and shading to tables, you begin by selecting the cells to which you want to add these features. If you want, you can add borders to all the cells; Word places the borders where the table gridlines are located, producing a spreadsheet-like appearance. Most tables look better, however, without all the possible borders. You can add borders just as you please: to just one or several rows or columns, to selected cells only, or to the entire table.

Fig. 22.7
Border surrounding a
graphic (but not the
paragraph).

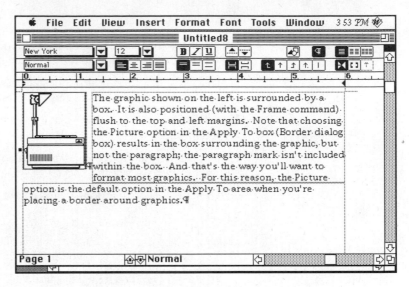

To add borders and shading to a table, follow these steps:

1. Select the table by placing the insertion point anywhere in the table and double-clicking. Alternatively, select one or more cells, one or more columns, or one or more rows.

2. Choose Border from the Format menu. The Border dialog box appears. What the Border area shows depends on what you have selected. If you have selected at least two rows and two columns, the Border area appears as a two-by-two table, as shown earlier in figure 22.4. If you have selected just one column, the Border area looks like the area shown in figure 22.8. If you have selected just one row, the Border area looks like the area shown in figure 22.9.

3. To add borders, choose a line width.

4. Choose Box or Shadow in the Preset Borders area, or click in the Border area to choose the borders you want.

   To place a box around the selected cells, double-click outside the border guides (see fig. 22.10). To add rules to the columns inside the table, click the vertical border guide (see fig. 22.11). To add rules to the rows inside the table, click the horizontal border guide (see fig. 22.12).

Fig. 22.8
One column selected.

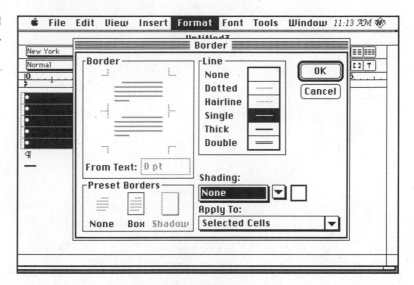

Fig. 22.9
One row selected.

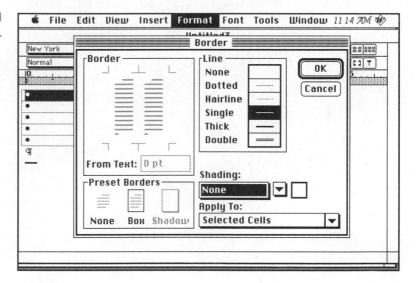

Chapter 22

Using Borders and Shading

Fig. 22.10
Box added around selected
cells.

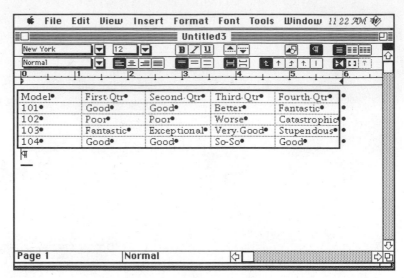

Fig. 22.11
Column rules added.

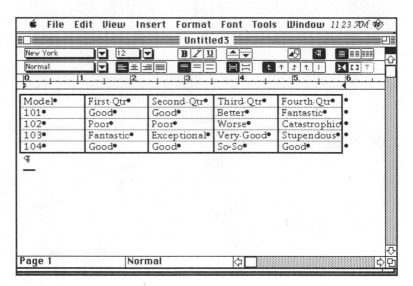

Part II

Creating More Complex Documents

Fig. 22.12
All borders added.

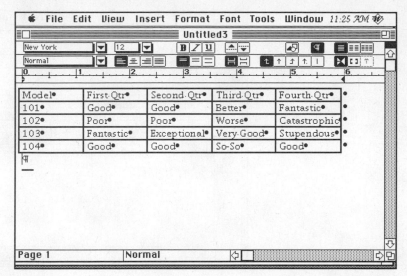

5. If you want to add shading, choose a shading percentage or type a percentage in the Shading box.

6. In the Apply To area, choose one of the following options:

    Selected Cells. Apply the borders only to selected cells, as a block.

    Entire Columns Selected. Apply the borders to all the cells in columns that contain a selected cell.

    Entire Rows Selected. Apply the borders to all the cells in rows that contain a selected cell.

    All Cells in Table. Apply the borders to all the cells in the table, whether or not you have selected them.

7. Choose OK.

Aligning Paragraph Borders

When you add vertical borders to text, Word places the borders just outside the left and right margins. In addition, the top and bottom borders extend the full width of the paragraph, from the left margin to the right. In figure 22.14, you see that the thick rule beneath the heading extends from the left to the right indents. As the bulleted list shows, however, indentations affect the placement of borders.

Chapter 22
Using Borders and Shading

Fig. 22.13
Combining line and
shading patterns.

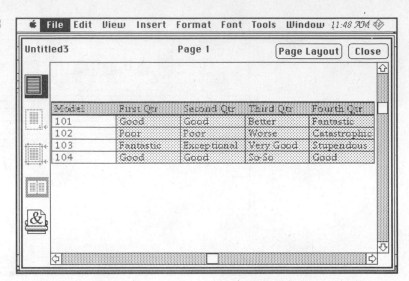

Fig. 22.14
Default alignment of
paragraph borders.

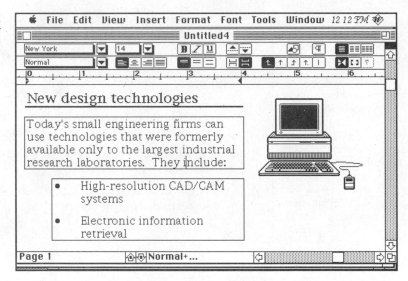

You can control the length of the top and bottom borders by indenting the text. In figure 22.15, the paragraph containing the heading has been indented from the right so that the thick rule under the heading doesn't extend to the right margin.

Fig. 22.15
Indenting the paragraph
from the right to shorten
the thick rule under the
heading.

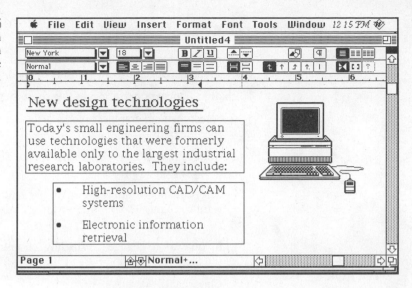

As you can see from figure 22.14 and 22.15, indentations can cause problems when you add borders. Suppose that you want the bulleted list to be enclosed in the same box with the text above it. To do so, you can convert all this text to a single-column table, and then enclose the table in a box, as shown in figure 22.16.

Fig. 22.16
Converting text to a table
in order to place a box
around all selected
paragraphs.

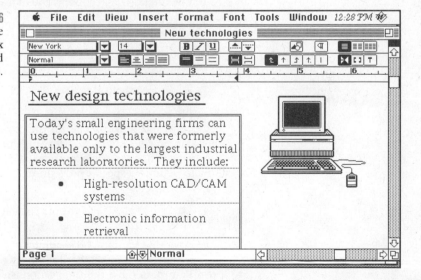

Changing and Removing Borders and Shading

After you have applied borders and shading to text, graphics, or tables, you can change or remove the borders or shading options.

To change a border or shading, follow these steps:

1. Select the text, graphic, or table cells that contain the border or shading option.

2. Choose Border from the Format menu. The Border area shows the borders previously chosen.

3. Select the line width you want to use, and click the borders you want to change. To remove unwanted borders, click the border you want to remove.

4. If you want to change the shading, choose a shading percentage in the Shading list box.

5. Choose OK.

To remove all borders and shading, follow these steps:

1. Select the text, graphic, or table cells that contain the border or shading.

2. Choose Border from the Format menu.

3. To remove all borders, choose None in the Preset Borders area.

4. To remove all shading, choose None in the Shading list box.

5. Choose OK.

Quick Review

This section concisely summarizes the most useful information in this chapter. Check "Productivity Tips" for a review of high-productivity tips and tricks, and review "Techniques" when you forget how to perform a specific procedure.

Productivity Tips

- Remember that borders and shading are paragraph formats; if you add them to a paragraph, Word duplicates the format when you press Return. Because this duplication isn't normally desirable with borders and shading, which should be used sparingly, wait to apply borders and shading until you have finished writing and editing your document.

■ You can add borders and shading to styles. If you frequently use a text element that includes borders or shading, include the border or shading choice in the style definition. When you apply the style, Word enters the border or shading automatically.

■ Create "generic" tables in two-, three-, and four-column versions, and add borders to conform to the style guidelines of your profession, organization, or educational institution. Select the tables and store them as glossary entries that you can enter and use when needed.

Techniques

This section provides concise, quick-reference summaries of all the procedures introduced in this chapter.

Adding Borders and Shading to Text

To add borders and shading to text:

1. Select the text.

2. Choose Border from the Format menu.

3. To add borders, choose a line width.

4. Choose Box or Shadow in the Preset Borders area, or click in the Border area to choose the borders you want. If you click the middle border, Word places borders between paragraphs (if you have selected more than one paragraph).

5. If you want, increase the default distance from the text (2 pts) by typing a number from 1 to 31 in the From Text area.

6. If you want to add shading, choose a shading percentage or type a percentage in the Shading box.

7. Choose OK.

Adding Borders to Graphics

To add borders to a graphic:

1. Select the graphic.

2. Choose Border from the Format menu.

3. To add borders, choose a line width.

4. Choose Box or Shadow in the Preset Borders area, or click in the Border area to choose the borders you want.

5. If you want to add shading, choose a shading percentage or type a percentage in the Shading box.

6. In the Apply To area, choose Paragraph if you want the border to surround the paragraph in which the graphic is situated. Choose Picture (the default) to place the border around the picture only.

7. Choose OK.

Adding Borders and Shading to Tables

To add borders and shading to a table:

1. Select the table or table cells.

2. Choose Border from the Format menu.

3. To add borders, choose a line width.

4. Choose Box or Shadow in the Preset Borders area, or click in the Border area to choose the borders you want.

5. If you want to add shading, choose a shading percentage or type a percentage in the Shading box.

6. In the Apply To area, choose one of the following options:

    Selected Cells. Apply the borders only to selected cells, as a block.

    Entire Columns Selected. Apply the borders to all the cells in columns that contain a selected cell.

    Entire Rows Selected. Apply the borders to all the cells in rows that contain a selected cell.

    All Cells in Table. Apply the borders to all the cells in the table, whether or not you have selected them.

7. Choose OK.

Part II

Creating More Complex Documents

Changing Borders and Shading

To change a border or shading:

1. Select the text, graphic, or table cells that contain the border or shading option.

2. Choose Border from the Format menu.

3. Select the line width you want to use, and click the borders you want to change. To remove unwanted borders, click the border you want to remove.

4. If you want to change the shading, choose a shading percentage in the Shading list box.

5. Choose OK.

Removing Borders or Shading

To remove all borders and shading:

1. Select the text, graphic, or table cells that contain the border or shading.

2. Choose Border from the Format menu.

3. To remove all borders, choose None in the Preset Borders area.

4. To remove all shading, choose None in the Shading list box.

5. Choose OK.

Adding an Index and Table of Contents

f you prepare reports, dissertations, or proposals that require an index, a table of contents, and other tables (such as tables of illustrations), Word has the tools you need to make short work of these tasks. Word can compile an index and table of contents, insert correct page numbers, and print both tables for you automatically. If you make changes to your document, you can reprint these tables, and Word will make all the corrections with no intervention on your part. This feature alone is sure to save you much time as you struggle to meet deadlines.

This chapter is useful if your reports and proposals will be reproduced directly from Word printouts, because the index and table of contents refer to the pages Word creates. If you're preparing a document to be typeset, you must prepare the table of contents and index from the page proofs the printer gives you; Word isn't of much help in such circumstances.

This chapter covers the following features:

- *Creating an Index.* In this section, you learn how to mark index entries so that Word can compile them into an index.

- *Creating a Table of Contents.* This section shows you how you can easily create an accurate table of contents for your document—espccially if you have used Word's standard Heading styles for chapter and section titles.

USING
WORD 5
FOR THE
MAC

Creating an Index

When you create an index, a certain amount of tedious, manual work is involved. Word saves you huge amounts of time by automating the compilation of the index, but you must read through your document and mark the words to be included.

You learn more about how to mark your document in this section, but for now you should consider which words to mark. You should mark the main ideas in your document, the main subject in each section, variations of chapter and section titles, special terms or nomenclature, abbreviations and acronyms, and proper nouns (such as names and places). In addition, you should include synonyms of main terms (*modernization* as well as *industrialization*) and inverted versions of main terms (*development, economic* as well as *economic development*).

You can identify the words or phrases to be included in your index in two ways:

You can mark words or phrases in your document. This technique creates a *concordance entry*, a word in your document that you mark for indexing. As you learn in this section, you mark a word by selecting it and choosing Index Entry from the Insert menu. Word marks the word and prints the concordance entry in the index.

You can type the word or phrase. You use this technique to create *conceptual entries* and *subentries*. A conceptual entry is a word you embed in the text (formatted as hidden text so that it won't print) and mark for indexing. Word doesn't print the conceptual entry, but the entry appears in the index. You use conceptual entries when the words in your document aren't quite right for indexing. A subentry is a subordinate term positioned beneath a main entry in a multilevel index, as shown here:

> industrialization
> > defined 7
> > origins 9
> > work roles 12
> industry
> > Third World, 14-19

The following sections show you how to mark all three types of entries: concordance entries, conceptual entries, and subentries.

TIP

Before you begin experimenting with indexing, choose Preferences and choose the Show Hidden Text option. You need to see hidden text on-screen so that you can tell whether you have coded the index entries correctly.

Part II

Creating More Complex Documents

Marking Concordance Entries

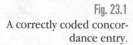

The Index Entry command (on the Insert menu) automatically formats a word or phrase as a *concordance entry* (an entry that is printed in the document and that appears in the index). The command inserts codes that Word needs in order to recognize the word as a word to be printed in the index. These codes are formatted as hidden text. A correctly coded concordance entry is shown in figure 23.1. Note the codes (the index code `.i.` before the word and the end-of-entry code, a semicolon, after the word) that are formatted as hidden text, as indicated by the dotted underline.

To mark a word as a concordance entry, follow these steps:

1. Select the word.

   To select the entire word quickly, just double-click from anywhere within the word.

2. Choose Index Entry from the Insert menu.

   Word marks the word automatically.

Fig. 23.1
A correctly coded concordance entry.

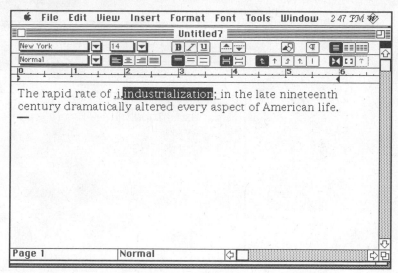

Marking Conceptual Entries

When you create a conceptual entry, the word or phrase you are indexing does not appear in the text—you are indexing a concept not

Chapter 23
Adding an Index and Table of Contents

actually mentioned in the text. To create a conceptual entry, you must type the entire entry, all of which is formatted as hidden text. Because the whole entry is formatted as hidden text, the conceptual entry isn't printed in the text; it appears only in the index.

To create a conceptual entry, follow these steps:

1. Position the insertion point where you want to type the entry.

   Place the entry on the page you want referenced in the index.

2. Choose Index Entry from the Insert menu.

   Word enters the index code (.i.) and the end-of-entry mark (the semicolon), and places the insertion point between them.

3. Type the conceptual entry.

   Word formats the entire entry as hidden text. This text will not be printed within your document, but the indexed term will appear in your index, after you use Word to compile the index.

Figure 23.2 shows a correctly formatted conceptual entry (industry) at the end of the sentence.

Fig. 23.2
A conceptual entry.

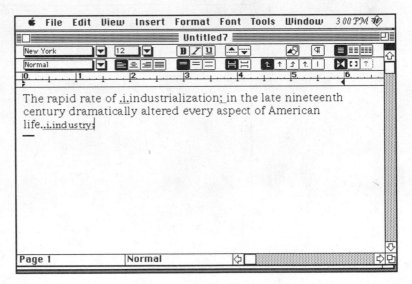

Marking Subentries

Subentries are preferred when an entry would be followed by a long list of page numbers. In this case, subentries, such as the following, help the reader locate the desired information:

Industrial ventures
aluminum cookware 60
graphite processing 32
luxury goods 59
matches 38
textiles 23

Subentries resemble conceptual entries in that the whole entry is formatted as hidden text—you don't want the subentry code to appear in your document.

To create subentries, follow these steps:

1. Place the insertion point within the discussion of the topic you want to index.

2. Choose Index Entry from the Insert menu.

   Word positions the insertion point between the index code (.i.) and the end-of-entry mark (the semicolon).

3. Type the main entry, a colon, and a subentry, as in this example:

   Industrial ventures:aluminum cookware

   Do not use spaces.

If you want, you can add as many as seven subordinate levels, although most style handbooks caution against using more than one or two levels. To add additional sublevels, just add additional subentries separated by colons, as in this example:

Industrial ventures:cookware:aluminum

Coding entries in this way produces an index that looks like this:

Industrial ventures
cookware
aluminum 18
pottery 29

Marking a Range of Pages

Often, you may want to index a topic that is discussed on more than one page, such as the following:

Industry 19-43

To create an entry that marks a range of pages, follow these steps:

1. At the beginning of the discussion of the topic, choose Index Entry from the Insert menu and type an entry using this coding scheme:

    .i(.subject;

    The only difference between this entry and an ordinary conceptual entry is the beginning parenthesis. Note that the parenthesis comes after the *i*, but before the second period.

    The word *subject* here refers to the topic you're indexing. If you're indexing the topic *industry*, the beginning code would look like this:

    .i(.industry;

2. At the end of the discussion of the topic, choose Insert Index Entry again and type an entry using a closing parenthesis:

    .i).subject;

    Note again that the parenthesis comes after the *i* but before the second period.

After Word compiles your index, the page range is indicated as follows:

Industry 19-43

Marking Cross References

You can direct Word to print text rather than a page number after the index entry. You can use this feature to create cross references, as in this example:

Industrial development. *See* industrialization.

To create a cross reference, follow these steps:

1. Select the term you want to cross reference.

2. Choose Index Entry from the Insert menu.

3. Type a number sign (#) followed by the text you want to print, as in this example:

    .i.Industrial development#. *See* industrialization;

Formatting Index Entries

When you code index entries, you can add special formatting codes that affect the appearance of the entries in the index. These formatting codes do not affect the appearance of the word within the text of your document.

To boldface the page number, type *b* between the *i* of the index code and the code's second period, as in this example:

.ib.industrialization;

To italicize the page number, type *i* between the *i* of the index code and the code's second period, as in the following example:

.ii.industrialization;

To boldface and italicize the page number, type *bi* between the *i* of the index code and the code's second period, as in this example:

.ibi.industrialization;

To add space between the index term and the page number, press the space bar at the end of the index entry, as in the following example:

.i.industrialization ;

To add a tab between the index term and the page number, press Tab at the end of the index entry.

To add a character (such as a comma) at the end of the index entry and before the page number, type the character after the index entry, as in this example:

.i.industrialization,;

Compiling an Index

When you are certain that your document is in its final form and you have marked all the index entries, decide how you want your index to appear. You can choose from the following two formatting options.

Nested subentries appear below the main entry and 1/4 inch to the right. Nested subentries can have distinct character styles. The following example shows a nested subentry:

Industrial ventures
Batteries, 29
    Fishing boats, 32
    Tires, 48

Chapter 23
Adding an Index and Table of Contents

Run-in subentries continue on the same line and cannot have distinct character styles. The following example shows a run-in subentry:

Industrial ventures: Batteries, 29; Fishing boats, 32, Tires, 48

To compile your index, do the following:

1. Choose Index from the Insert menu.

   You see the Index dialog box (see fig. 23.3).

2. Choose Nested or Run-in box.

3. If you want to create an index for only selected letters of the alphabet, type the range (such as *A* and *C*) in the From and To boxes.

4. Choose Start.

   Word compiles the index and places the completed index in its own section at the end of the document (see fig. 23.4).

If you find that terms are missing from your index or that the index contains errors, insert or correct the codes in your document. Then use Index again to recompile the index. On your confirmation, Word deletes the existing index when it compiles the new one.

Fig. 23.3
The Index dialog box.

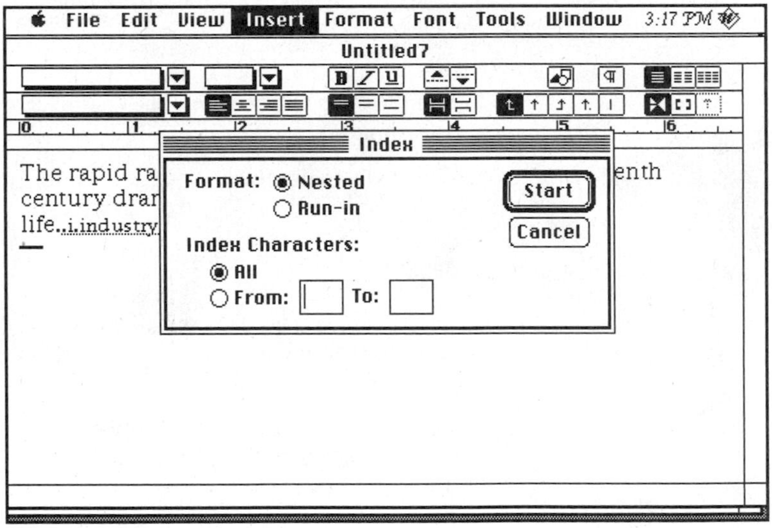

Part II

Creating More Complex Documents

Fig. 23.4
Index compiled from terms
coded in the document.

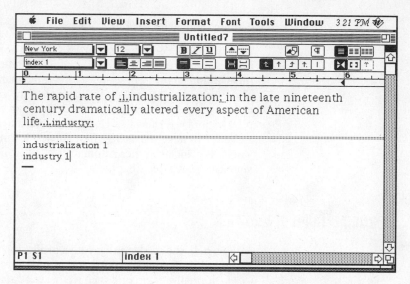

Updating an Index

If you make changes to your document that affect the page breaks, you should update your index. This section describes the procedure you can use to update your index quickly.

To update your index, follow these steps:

1. Choose Index from the Insert menu.

   Word detects the existing index and asks whether you want to replace it.

2. Choose Yes to replace the existing index, or if you prefer, choose No so that Word places the new index after the existing one.

Removing Index Codes

If you decide against including an index in your document, you can discard the index after your document prints. Should you prefer to remove the index codes, however, you can do so by choosing the Replace command. Leave the Find What box blank, but choose the hidden text format in this box. Leave the Replace with box blank. Word will delete all the hidden text in your document. For more information on removing formats with Replace, see Chapter 5.

Chapter 23
Adding an Index and Table of Contents

Understanding Index Styles

When you have compiled the index, you will notice that Word has formatted each entry by using the standard Index styles (such as Index 1, Index 2, and so on). These styles format the main entry with the normal character and paragraph styles. Subentries are indented 1/4 inch. You can change these styles if you want. You can define the Index 1 style to print in boldface Helvetica 12, for example, and print subentries in Helvetica 10 italic. To change index styles, just redefine them as you would redefine any other automatic style. For information on redefining automatic styles, see Chapter 8.

Creating a Table of Contents

T o help the reader and create a professional appearance, business and professional reports and proposals require a table of contents. Normally, compiling such a table is a chore. Word, however, can do the job almost automatically, especially if you have organized your document with outlining, as recommended in Chapter 12.

If you haven't outlined your document, you can mark the headings in your document so that Word can compile a table of contents from them. It's much easier, however, to outline your document than it is to code every heading. To do so, apply Word's standard Heading styles (Heading 1, Heading 2, Heading 3, and so on) to the titles and subtitles in your document. For more information on applying standard styles, see Chapter 8.

Creating a Table of Contents with the Outline Method

One of the advantages of outlining your documents is that you can almost automatically compile a table of contents from an outline that echoes the headings in your document (see Chapters 12 and 26 for more information on linking document headings and outline entries).

To create a table of contents from an outlined document, do the following:

1. Choose Outline from the View menu to switch to Outline view, or press ⌘-Option-O.

2. Choose Table of Contents from the Insert menu.

    You see the Table of Contents dialog box (see fig. 23.5).

3. Choose Outline.

4. In the Level area, type the levels of your outline that you want to appear in the outline.

   To print chapter titles and major headings, for example, type *1* in the From box and *2* in the To box.

5. Choose Start.

Fig. 23.5
The Table of Contents
dialog box.

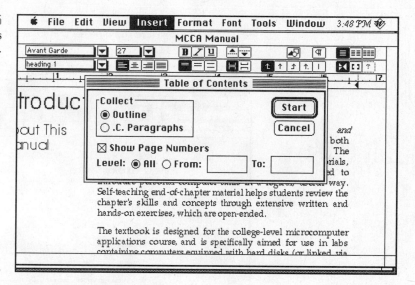

Word compiles the table of contents and places it at the beginning of your document, in its own, unpaginated section (see fig. 23.6). You can format the table of contents the way you want. Add character emphases, indentations, blank lines, and other formats to suit your tastes and style guidelines.

Creating a Table of Contents by Coding Entries

Marking headings for inclusion in a table of contents is much like creating concordance entries for an index. You must distinguish between three parts of each marked heading, as follows:

Table-of-contents code (.c.). This code, a lowercase *c* surrounded by periods, must be formatted as hidden text. The code tells Word that the text to follow should be treated as a table-of-contents entry. The number after the *c* code (see table 23.1) tells Word the level of the heading (you can distinguish as many as nine levels). If there is no number, Word assumes that the heading is a first-level heading.

The heading. So that the heading will print in your document, the heading should not be formatted as hidden text. If the heading contains a colon, semicolon, or quotation marks, enclose the heading in quotation marks formatted as hidden text.

End mark (;). This code, a semicolon formatted as hidden text, tells Word where the table-of-contents entry stops.

Fig. 23.6

Table of contents.

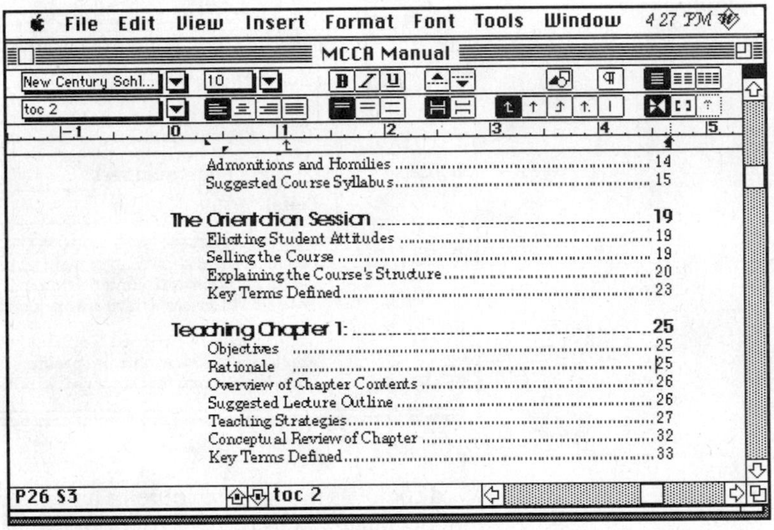
File Edit View Insert Format Font Tools Window
MCCA Manual
New Century Schl...
10
toc 2
Admonitions and Homilies 14
Suggested Course Syllabus 15
The Orientation Session 19
Eliciting Student Attitudes 19
Selling the Course 19
Explaining the Course's Structure 20
Key Terms Defined 23
Teaching Chapter 1: 25
Objectives 25
Rationale 25
Overview of Chapter Contents 26
Suggested Lecture Outline 26
Teaching Strategies 27
Conceptual Review of Chapter 32
Key Terms Defined 33
P26 S3
toc 2

Table 23.1

Table-of-Contents Codes

Level	*Code*
First level	.c. or .c1.
Second level	.c2.
Third level	.c3.
Fourth level	.c4.
Fifth level	.c5.
Sixth level	.c6.
Seventh level	.c7.
Eighth level	.c8.
Ninth level	.c9.

To create a table of contents by using the manual marking technique follow these steps:

1. Select the heading you want to appear in the table of contents.

2. Choose TOC Entry from the Insert menu.

   Word adds the .c. code and semicolon, and formats these codes as hidden text.

3. After the letter *c* in the table-of-contents code, type the number of the heading's level. For a second-level heading, for example, type .*c2*.

   Table 23.1 lists the heading-level codes.

4. If you want to suppress page numbers after the entry, type a colon before the semicolon, as in this example:

   .i.Chapter 3:;

   Make sure that the semicolon is formatted as hidden text.

5. Continue to code the headings, as explained in step 3.

6. When you finish coding all the headings, choose Table of Contents from the Insert menu.

7. When the Table of Contents dialog box appears, choose the .C. Paragraphs options under Collect.

8. Choose Start.

   Word compiles the table of contents and places it at the beginning of your document, in its own, unpaginated section. You can format the table of contents as you want. Add character emphases, indentations, blank lines, and other formats to suit your tastes and style guidelines.

> **TIP**
>
> If you edit your document after compiling the table of contents, you should recompile the table. To do so, just choose Table of Contents again from the Insert menu. When Word asks whether you want to replace the existing table of contents, choose Yes.

Understanding TOC Styles

Like entries in the indexes Word automatically creates, table-of-contents entries are formatted by automatic styles in Word's default style sheet, but you can modify these styles. By default, Word formats so that the headings are formatted with the normal character format and a flush-right tab stop (with dot leaders) at six inches. Subordinate headings are formatted with additional half-inch indentations. You can reposition tab stops, redefine a character style, or change the pattern of indentations. For information on redefining automatic styles, see Chapter 8.

Chapter 23
Adding an Index and Table of Contents

Quick Review

This section concisely summarizes the most useful information in this chapter. Check "Productivity Tips" for a review of high-productivity tips and tricks, and review "Techniques" when you forget how to perform a specific procedure.

Productivity Tips

- To create a good index for your document, try to anticipate what your readers will want to look up. Distinguish between *concordance entries* (words that appear in the text as well as in the index) and *conceptual entries* (words that don't appear in the text, but appear in the index). A good index has both concordance and conceptual entries.

- Resist the temptation to use too many levels of subentries; use two levels at the most.

- To create concordance entries, type the word you want to index, select it, and choose the Insert Index Entry command from the Document menu. To create conceptual entries, first choose the Insert Index Entry command. Then type the term.

- You can add page-range, major-entry, and text entries to your index. Use text entries to cross-reference other topics in your index.

- If your document needs a table of contents, format your document's headings and subheadings with Word's standard Heading styles, so that the headings are linked to outline levels. After formatting your document's headings and subheadings with these styles, you can compile a table of contents quickly and almost automatically.

Techniques

This section provides concise, quick-reference summaries of all the procedures introduced in this chapter.

Compiling the Index

To compile your index:

1. Choose Index from the Insert menu.

2. Choose Nested or Run-in box.

3. If you want to create an index for only selected letters of the alphabet, type the range (such as *A* and *C*) in the From and To boxes.

4. Choose Start.

Creating a Table of Contents by Marking TOC Entries

To create a table of contents by using the manual marking technique:

1. Select the heading you want to appear in the table of contents.

2. Choose TOC Entry from the Insert menu.

3. After the letter *c* in the table-of-contents code, type the number of the heading's level.

4. If you want to suppress page numbers after the entry, type a colon before the semicolon.

5. Continue to code the headings, as explained in step 3.

6. When you finish coding all the headings, choose Table of Contents from the Insert menu.

7. When the Table of Contents dialog box appears, choose the .C. Paragraphs options under Collect.

8. Choose Start.

Creating a Table of Contents from an Outlined Document

To create a table of contents from an outlined document:

1. Choose Outline from the View menu to switch to the Outline view, or press ⌘-Option-O.

2. Choose Table of Contents from the Insert menu.

3. Choose Outline.

4. In the Level area, type the levels of your outline that you want to appear in the outline.

5. Choose Start.

Creating Concordance Index Entries

To mark a word as a concordance entry:

1. Select the word.

2. Choose Index Entry from the Insert menu.

Creating Conceptual Index Entries

To create a conceptual entry:

1. Position the insertion point where you want to type the entry.

2. Choose Index Entry from the Insert menu.

3. Type the conceptual entry.

Creating Cross References

To create a cross reference (concordance entry):

1. Select the term you want to cross reference.

2. Choose Index Entry from the Insert menu.

3. Type a number sign (#) followed by the text you want to print.

Creating a Page-Range Index Entry

To create a page-range index entry: `

1. At the beginning of the discussion of the topic, choose Index Entry from the Insert menu and type an entry using this coding scheme:

    .i(.subject;

2. At the end of the discussion of the topic, choose Insert Index Entry again, and type an entry using a closing parenthesis:

    .i).subject;

Creating Index Subentries

To create subentries:

1. Place the insertion point within the discussion of the topic you want to index.

2. Choose Index Entry from the Insert menu.

3. Type the main entry, a colon, and a subentry.

Updating an Index

To update your index:

1. Choose Index from the Insert menu.

2. Choose Yes to replace the existing index, or if you prefer, choose No so that Word places the new index after the existing one.

24

Creating Form Letters

Form letters can be a help or a nuisance. At some time you probably have received a personalized form letter—a letter sent to many people, but personalized by a computer so that it appears as though it were sent to only you:

> Dear Mr. or Ms. So-and-So, here's great news for you and the So-and-So family. You have definitely won at least one of the following fantastic prizes: a Lincoln Continental Towne Car, a six-month trip to the South Seas, $30,000 in cash, or a cheap digital wristwatch. To claim your prize, all you have to do is visit our fine, new recreational center, the Happy Acres Landfill and Hazardous Waste Repository, and listen to six hours of grueling cross-examination by our sadistic sales staff!

More than likely, your name is printed slightly out of register, betraying the fact that everyone in your neighborhood is receiving the same letter.

Letters of this sort are irritating, but personalized form letters have many legitimate uses in business. Whenever you find yourself wanting to send the same message to many people but with a personal touch, think of sending a personalized form letter. When you do, remember that Word offers one of the most powerful form-letter features in any word processing package. The Print Merge feature "merges" information drawn from a data document with the text in a letter or some other document. This chapter introduces you to Word's Print Merge capabilities.

In previous versions of Word, the Print Merge feature was among the most challenging to use. Before Version 5, getting a form-letter application working correctly with Word wasn't easy. But Version 5's new Print Merge Helper (on the View menu) walks you through all three phases of a print-merge application: building a data document, creating a main document (the letter that contains the text you send to everyone), and printing form letters. With Print Merge Helper, you quickly and easily can create a form-letter application.

This chapter covers creating form-letter applications with Print Merge Helper. If you already have learned the techniques for creating form-letter applications manually with previous versions of Word, you still can use these techniques. Print Merge Helper is so much easier to use and more convenient, however, that it becomes the technique of choice for anyone learning form-letter applications with Word.

In this chapter, you learn about Print Merge applications and how a form-letter application works. You learn how to distinguish between the data document (the document that contains names and addresses) and the main document (the document that contains the text you send to everyone). You learn how to set up a data document to store names, addresses, and other information about your clients, customers, and contacts. You discover how to set up the main document, the document that contains the text you want to send to everyone.

You also learn how to print form letters using Print Merge, and how to print only the names and addresses that meet criteria you specify, such as a ZIP code. This chapter explains how to use Word's Print Merge keywords, such as IF, to print selected records. In addition, you learn how to print additional text when Word encounters a name and address that meets conditions you specify.

This chapter also explains Word's advanced form-letter capabilities. You learn how to prompt the user for information to be added to letters just before they're printed, such as an up-to-the-minute interest-rate quote.

Word 5's new Print Merge Helper creates a table to store your mailing-list data. For this reason, you should read Chapter 17 before proceeding with this chapter. You should know how to manipulate tables to use Print Merge Helper effectively. In addition, read Chapter 19 for information on sorting tables.

Understanding Print Merge Applications

When a Print Merge application is applied to form letters, it uses information from a mailing list and, one by one, creates copies of a letter personalized with each person's name, address, city, state, ZIP code, and other information. This type of application requires two Word documents: the *data document* and the *main document*.

You can use Print Merge for applications other than form letters, such as printing mailing labels. For information on printing mailing labels, see Chapter 25.

Understanding the Data Document

The data document contains the personalized information you want Word to insert automatically into each copy of the letter. Each line contains a *data record*—a basic unit of information, such as a person's complete name and address. Each data record contains *data fields*. Each field is a place for a particular kind of information, such as a street address, city, state, or last name.

To create a successful form-letter application, you should break down the data into as many fields as possible. Doing so enables you to sort and organize your data. Suppose that you store names like this: Mr. Clarence Jones, Ms. Roberta Garcia, Dr. Hiro Himekami, and so on. You can't alphabetize this list. If you break down the names into three fields (Last Name, First Name, and Salutation), you can alphabetize them easily.

This list shows a good plan for a name-and-address data document:

Last Name	Stevenson
First Name	Edwin
Salutation	Dr.
Address 1	Department of Radiology
Address 2	Albemarle University
City	Charlottesville
State	VA
Zip	22999-4567

Note that the list has two Address fields. Two fields are necessary if you are addressing people who work in organizations. If you are creating a mailing list for residences only, you may not need both Address fields.

In the "Creating the Data Document" section later in this chapter, you learn how to create a data document with two address fields.

Chapter 24

Creating Form Letters

Formatting in the data document has no effect on the way the main document prints, so don't bother with formatting when you create the data document. To format this information, you format the field codes in the main document, as explained in the following section.

Understanding the Main Document

The main document contains the text you want to send to everyone—the text of the letter. You write this document just as you would an ordinary Word document, except that you don't fill in the particulars about the person who will receive the letter. Rather, you use Print Merge Helper to insert field names. When Word prints the letter, the program substitutes the data for the field names. The data takes on the formatting that's applied to the field codes. For example, if you format your main document (including the field codes) in Palatino 12, Word uses that font to print the letter and the information merged into the letter.

After you create the data document and the main document, you use the Print Merge command (on the File menu) to print the main document. Word makes one copy of the main document for each record in the data document. For each copy, when Word encounters a field name, it retrieves from the data document the text you have placed in the data record.

In figure 24.1, for example, the data document contains three records (for Ed, Mary, and Sue), and each record contains two fields (Name and State). Two field names, Name and State, are in the main document. When you print the main document using Print Merge, you get three letters—one each to Ed, Mary, and Sue.

The basic concept is simple, and with Print Merge Helper, creating a successful form-letter application is easy. Word automatically inserts all the necessary codes.

Creating the Data Document

First, you create the data document, which is the Word file that contains the information you want Word to insert automatically into your form letter. In this section, you learn how to create a data document with Print Merge Helper.

To create the data document, follow these steps:

1. Choose Print Merge Helper from the View menu. Word displays the Open dialog box.

2. Choose New. The Data Document Builder dialog box is displayed (see fig. 24.2)

Fig. 24.1
An overview of mail merging.

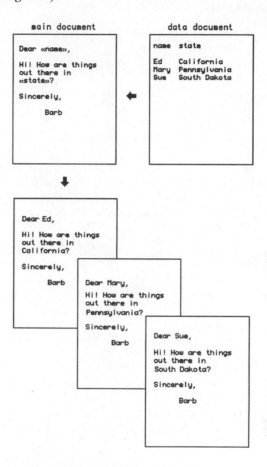

3. Type the first field name in the Field Name text box.

   Field names can have as many as 253 characters, although you should keep them shorter. If you use no more than 6 or 8 characters, you can fit more columns on-screen.

   Don't use the words *and*, *not*, or *or* as separate words in field names. These words have special meaning to Print Merge. If you must use them, enclose them in underline characters so that Word doesn't recognize them as separate words (Department_and_Building).

Chapter 24

Creating Form Letters

Fig. 24.2
The Data Document
Builder dialog box (Print
Merge Helper).

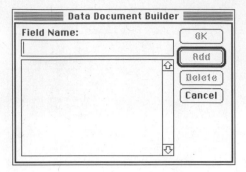

If you are creating a name-and-address database, begin by typing *last name*, as shown in figure 24.3. Whether you use uppercase or lowercase doesn't matter; Word converts the field name to all lowercase letters after you choose Add.

Fig. 24.3
Typing the first field name.

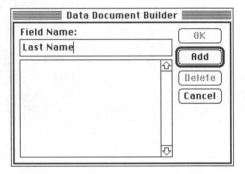

4. Choose Add.

    Word adds the field name to the Field Name list, as shown in figure 24.4.

Fig. 24.4
The field name added to
the field name list.

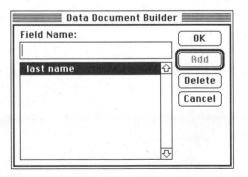

Part II

Creating More Complex Documents

5. Repeat Steps 3 and 4 to add all the rest of the fields to your data document.

   You can define as many as 127 fields for each form-letter application. If you are using a table to hold your data, however, you cannot exceed the maximum number of columns (22). Don't name a field using any of the words reserved for Print Merge applications, such as IF, NEXT, ELSE, INCLUDE, or DATA.

   When you are finished entering fields, you should see a complete field name list (see fig. 24.5).

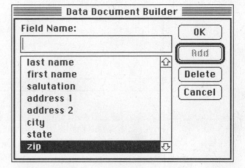

Fig. 24.5
A complete field name list.

> **TIP**
>
> If you misspell a field name or add the same field twice, you can delete it. Just select the field and choose Delete.

6. When you're sure that the field name list is complete and correct, choose OK. A Save As dialog box appears and prompts you to name the new data document.

7. Type a name for your new data document and choose Save. Word creates the data document and places the field names in the first row of a two-row table (see fig. 24.6). Word also opens a new, Untitled document, and places a DATA instruction at the beginning of the document. This document serves as the nucleus for your main document. For now, use the Window command to redisplay the data document.

   As you can see, Word has created a table. (If you haven't read Chapter 17, do so now; you should understand Word's tables before you can use Print Merge Helper effectively.) In the first row, you see the field names you created in the Data Document Builder window. The second row is blank—it is the first data record. In this row, you type a complete name and address. To type additional names and addresses, you extend the table.

> **TIP**
>
> As you can see in figure 24.6, the table Word created doesn't leave much room for typing names and other information. You can widen the columns, but don't make your table wider than 10 inches. You can print a 10-inch table by choosing the landscape-orientation option in the Page Setup dialog box.

Fig. 24.6
A data document created
by Print Merge Helper.

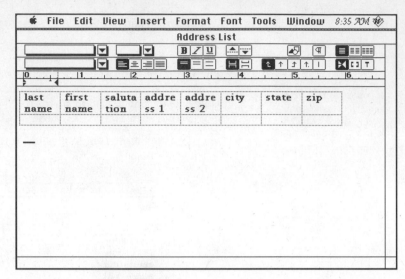

8. Click the table-boundaries button (the T button on the ruler) and widen the columns, as shown in figure 24.7.

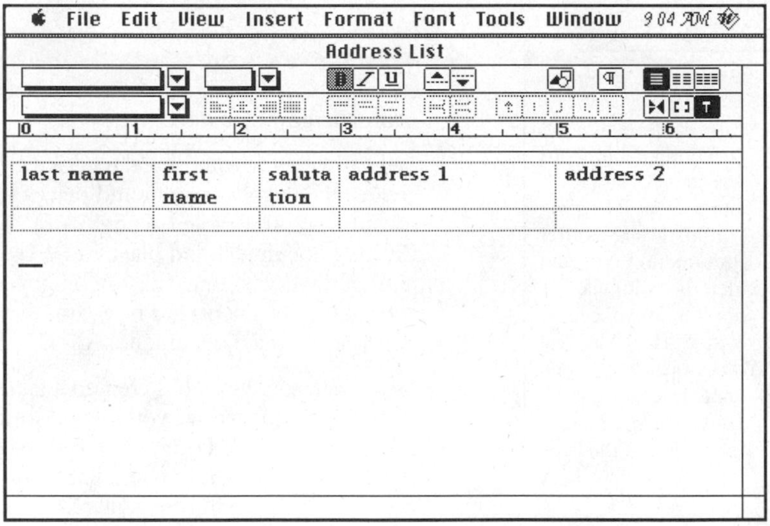

Fig. 24.7
Widening the columns.

As you widen the columns, remember that you don't have to widen them to accommodate the longest possible entry in the

Part II

Creating More Complex Documents

field. If you type an entry that's longer than the field width, Word wraps the text to the next line. The entry still prints on one line in your main document, however, if there's enough room.

In figure 24.8, you can see that Department of Radiology doesn't fit within the space allotted for the Address 1 field; Word wrapped Radiology to the next line in the table cell. If you were sending a letter to Dr. Stevenson, however, Word would print the address in the form letter as follows:

Dr. Edwin Stevenson
Department of Radiology
Albemarle University
Charlottesville, VA 22999-4567

You should widen the columns to allow for convenient data entry, but not so much that the rows are longer than 10 inches. (After all, you probably want to print your data document.) Note, though, that you still can print your data even if you create a table longer than 10 inches. You must use Print Merge techniques, however, rather than print the data document directly.

Fig. 24.8
The data record has been
added.

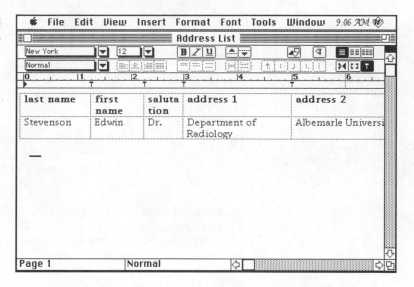

last name	first name	salutation	address 1	address 2
Stevenson	Edwin	Dr.	Department of Radiology	Albemarle Universi

9. Type the rest of the mailing-list data. To create a new row, press Tab at the end of the last row. Don't worry about putting the data in alphabetical order. You can sort the data easily, as explained in the following steps. Your completed data document should resemble the one in figure 24.9.

Chapter 24

Creating Form Letters

Fig. 24.9

A data document with data added.

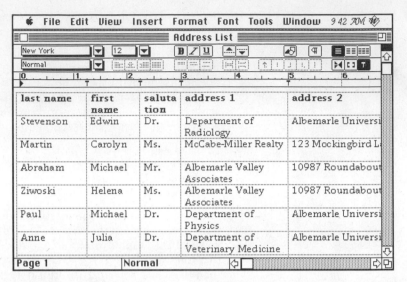

TIP

If you accidentally include the field-name cell in your sort selection, choose Undo from the Edit menu to undo the sort, and try again.

10. Select the column you want to use as the key for the sort (don't include the first row in the selection).

   To sort by last name, select the first column. To sort by ZIP code, select the ZIP code column.

11. Choose Sort from the Tools menu. Word sorts the data, using the column you selected as the key (see fig. 24.10).

12. Save the data document.

13. To print a copy of the data document, choose Page Setup from the Print menu, and choose the landscape icon in the Orientation Area. Choose OK, and then choose Print from the File menu to print the data document.

   Word has given you a head start on the main document: the program automatically creates an Untitled document and adds the DATA instruction that references the data document. If you don't want to create the main document in this session, be sure to save this document before quitting Word.

After you create a data document, you can easily insert a new field, such as Phone. Place the insertion point on the end-of-row mark after the last cell in the first row and choose Table Layout from the Format menu. Click the Column option and choose Insert. Type the new field name and add the data.

Part II

Creating More Complex Documents

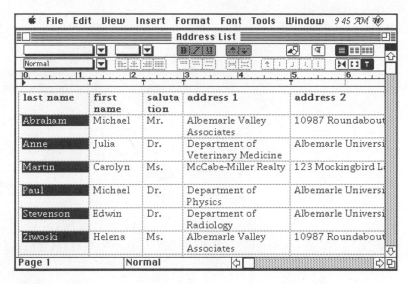

Creating the Main Document

In this section, you learn how to create the main document. This document is like any other letter you write with Word except that you leave out the specifics (name, address, city, and so on). With Print Merge Helper, adding the codes needed to fill in the specifics automatically is easy. First, you create the main document and add the codes. Then, you check your work. The following sections cover both procedures.

Adding Field Codes to the Main Document

With Print Merge Helper, you can easily create a workable form-letter application on the first try. To create the main document and add field codes, follow these steps:

1. Switch to the Untitled document that Word created when you saved your data document. This document has a DATA command on its first line. This command tells Word where to find the data for the mail merge operation.

2. **Important:** Position the insertion point after the DATA instruction. This instruction must come first.

Chapter 24

Creating Form Letters

3. Create or insert a letterhead, as shown in figure 24.11. Make sure that the DATA instruction comes first.

   Print Merge Helper adds to the beginning of your main document an instruction that identifies the data document (see fig. 24.11). The DATA instruction must appear at the beginning of your document, with no spaces or characters preceding it.

Fig. 24.11
Main document with letterhead and DATA instruction added automatically by Print Merge Helper.

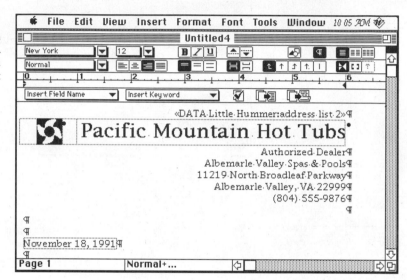

NOTE

If Print Merge Helper isn't displayed, choose Print Merge Helper from the View Menu.

Note that Print Merge Helper adds a bar just beneath the ruler. When you drop down the Insert Field Name list box (see fig. 24.12), you see the field names you created in your data document.

In the Insert Field name menu, you see the field names you defined in your data document. In addition, you see these fields:

SequenceNumber. This field, created automatically by Word, inserts a number into your document. This number shows the sequence of the documents that Word successfully prints. For example, the first document successfully printed is 1, the second is 2, and so on. Documents that don't print (usually because of errors in the data document) aren't numbered.

RecordNumber. This field, created automatically by Word, also inserts a number into your document. This number shows the row number of the data record in your data document.

Fig. 24.12
The Insert Field Name
menu.

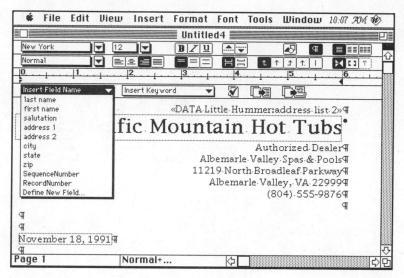

Define New Field. This option is used for special ASK and SET Print Merge applications, discussed later in this chapter.

The Print Merge Helper bar has other features, too. The following list is a quick overview:

Insert Keyword. You learn more about keywords later in this chapter.

Check Icon. You click this icon to have Word check your Merge application for errors.

Print to File Icon. You click this icon to print the form letters to new Word documents, which you then can customize and print later.

Print Icon. You click this icon to print your form letters directly, without creating intermediary files.

Before using any of these icons, however, you have to add field names to your document.

For simple Merge applications, you do not use the Insert Keyword list box.

8. With the insertion point positioned just below the date, choose first name from the Insert Field Name list box.

Chapter 24

Creating Form Letters

Word adds the field and surrounds the field name with chevrons (see fig. 24.13). Don't delete the chevrons—without them, Word cannot tell that the text within the chevrons is a field name.

Fig. 24.13
A field name added to the main document.

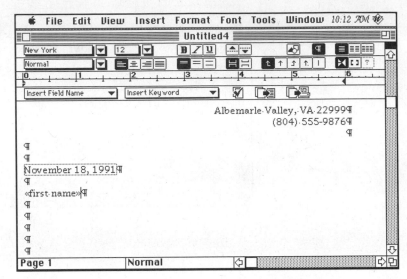

9. Use the Insert Field Name list box to add the rest of the field names, and add spaces, punctuation, and hard returns as necessary.

   Examine figure 24.14 carefully to see how to enter the field names correctly. Note that you can use the same field name more than once (*last name* appears twice).

10. Add text to your letter.

    Be careful not to erase any chevrons or disturb the field name codes in any way. Figure 24.15 shows an example of text you could send to everyone on your mailing list.

11. Save the data document.

After you create and save a main document, don't move your data document to a different folder. In the DATA instruction, Word saved information that shows where the data document is located. If you move this document to a different folder, Word will not be able to find the data document. (If this happens, all is not lost: Word asks you to help locate the document, and the merge operation proceeds.)

Part II

Creating More Complex Documents

Fig. 24.14
Field names entered
correctly.

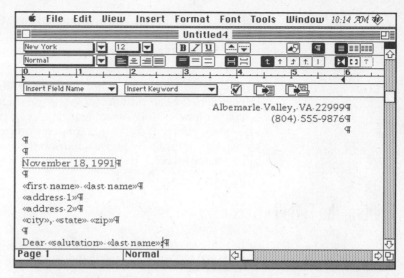

Fig. 24.15
Text added to the main
document.

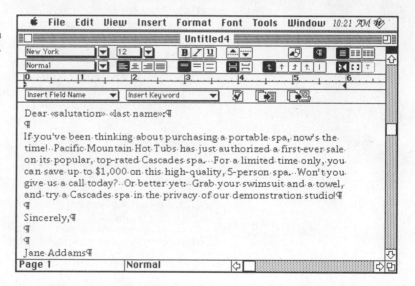

Checking Your Work

To check your work quickly, click the Check icon on the Print Merge
Helper bar. If you followed carefully the instructions in the previous
section, Word creates a temporary Merge document, and the message No

`errors found` appears. If Word finds an error, the program inserts an explanation at the place where the error was detected. In either case, close the temporary Merge document and return to your main document.

The most likely cause of errors in using Print Merge Helper is accidental deletion of the chevrons. If you see the message `Unknown Field Name` in the temporary Merge document, chances are that you have deleted one of the chevrons and Word cannot recognize the field name. Delete what's left of the field name and reinsert the entire field, using the Insert Field Name list box.

Printing the Form Letters

After you correctly set up a Print Merge application, printing your form letters is easy. You can do so in two ways:

- *Printing to a New Document.* If you choose this option, Word prints the letters to a new document, with each letter separated by a hard page break. You can scroll through this document and add personalized messages to letters. When you are ready to print, choose Print from the File menu.

- *Printing Directly.* When you choose this option, Word prints the form letters directly, without creating an intermediary document. Choose this method if you don't need to add any text to the letters.

To print your form letters to a new document, follow these steps:

1. With your main document and Print Merge Helper on-screen, choose the Print to New Document button.

   If you don't see Print Merge Helper, choose Print Merge Helper from the View menu.

   Word creates a Merge file containing the form letters.

2. Add text to the letters, if you want.

3. Choose Print from the File menu to print the letters.

To print your form letters directly, follow these steps:

1. With your main document and Print Merge Helper on-screen, choose the Print Directly icon.

   If you don't see Print Merge Helper, choose Print Merge Helper from the View menu.

TIP

When you print your form letters, make two copies so that you have one for your files.

The Print dialog box appears.

2. Choose Print.

Figure 24.16 shows a completed letter generated by Print Merge.

Fig. 24.16
A completed letter
generated by Print Merge.

Pacific Mountain Hot Tubs

Authorized Dealer
Albemarle Valley Spas & Pools
11219 North Broadleaf Parkway
Albemarle Valley, VA 22999
(804) 555-9876

November 18, 1991

Michael Paul
Department of Physics
Albemarle University
Charlottesville, VA 22999-9987

Dear Dr. Paul:

If you've been thinking about purchasing a portable spa, now's the time! Pacific Mountain Hot Tubs has just authorized a first-ever sale on its popular, top-rated Cascades spa. For a limited time only, you can save up to $1,000 on this high-quality, 5-person spa. Won't you give us a call today? Or better yet: Grab your swimsuit and a towel, and try a Cascades spa in the privacy of our demonstration studio!

Sincerely,

Jane Addams
President, Albemarle Valley Spas and Pools

Printing Selected Records

ometimes you don't want to send letters to everyone in your mailing list. In this section, you learn how to print only some of the records in your mailing list.

This technique should be used only when you have a convenient and obvious way to sort your data document so that all the records you want to print can be grouped together. Even if such a sort is possible, you still may want to use an alternative technique, described in the section "Conditional Merging" later in this chapter.

To print selected records, follow these steps:

1. In your data document, sort the data so that the records you want to print are grouped together.

   Suppose that you want to send letters to everyone with a 22999 ZIP code, but not to anyone else. Sort your data document by ZIP code so that all the 22999 addresses are grouped together. (To sort the table this way, select the ZIP code column—omit the first cell—and choose Sort from the Tools menu.)

2. In the main document, place the insertion point just after the letterhead, where you can see it without having to scroll down.

3. Choose RecordNumber from the Insert Field Name list box in Print Merge Helper.

4. Choose Print Merge from the File menu. The Print Merge dialog box appears (see fig. 24.17).

Fig. 24.17
The Print Merge dialog box.

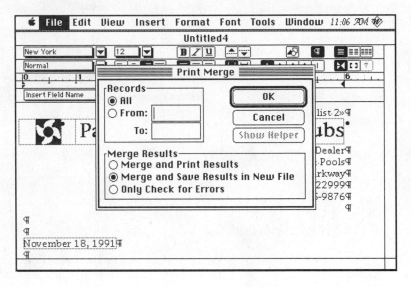

5. Choose Merge and Save Results in a New File, and choose OK to start merging.

   Word merges the data to a new MERGE document.

6. Scroll through the MERGE document and note the range of record numbers you want to print, such as 16 through 29.

7. Close the MERGE document without saving it, and switch back to the main document.

8. Choose Print Merge again from the File menu.

9. In the From box, type the number of the first data record you want to print.

10. In the To box, type the number of the last data record you want to print.

11. Choose one of the Merge Results options. Choose Merge and Print Results to print directly. Choose Merge and Save Results in New File to print to a new document. Choose Only Check for Errors to check your application for errors.

12. Choose OK.

Word merges only the documents that fall within the range you indicated.

Using Conditional Instructions

n Print Merge Helper, you probably noticed the Insert Keyword list box, in which you insert commands that perform a variety of advanced Print Merge operations. With Print Merge Helper's help, you can attempt one of these operations even if you're still a beginner in personal computing. One of these commands, IF, enables you to create a *conditional merge*. In a conditional merge, you instruct Word to print just certain records, the ones that meet criteria you specify.

There are two reasons to use conditional merge: You can specify the records you want to print without the hassle of sorting your data document, grouping the records you want to print, and using Print Merge to print a range of documents (procedures described in the preceding section). You can print, for example, all the records in which the field last name begins with A or B, and print all the records in which the field ZIP code contains *22999* or *22998*.

Using conditional merge, you can add text if a data record meets a criteria you specify. Suppose that you add to your data document a field called Bill Overdue? If this field contains *30 days*, you can set up an IF instruction so that Word will print additional text, such as Our records show that your bill is 30 days overdue. Won't you write us a check today?.

Chapter 24

Creating Form Letters

Thanks to Word 5's Print Merge Helper, conditional merging is much easier now. If you have tried conditional merging in previous versions of Word only to give up in frustration, try again!

Printing Records That Meet Criteria You Specify

Printing records that meet criteria you specify is the best technique to use when you want to print only some of the records in your data document. You can, for example, print just the records that contain the ZIP code 22999-9987 and skip all the others.

To print selected records, use the Insert Keyword menu to build a complex instruction, one that uses several keywords from the menu. If you ever have done a little computer programming, you understand what these keywords mean and what they do. If you haven't done any programming, read on: It's easy to understand. In essence, you create an instruction that tells Word, "If the current data record contains in a certain field the text I specify, print the record. If not, skip to the next one."

To print records that meet criteria you specify, follow these steps:

1. In the main document, place the insertion point above the correspondent's name and address.

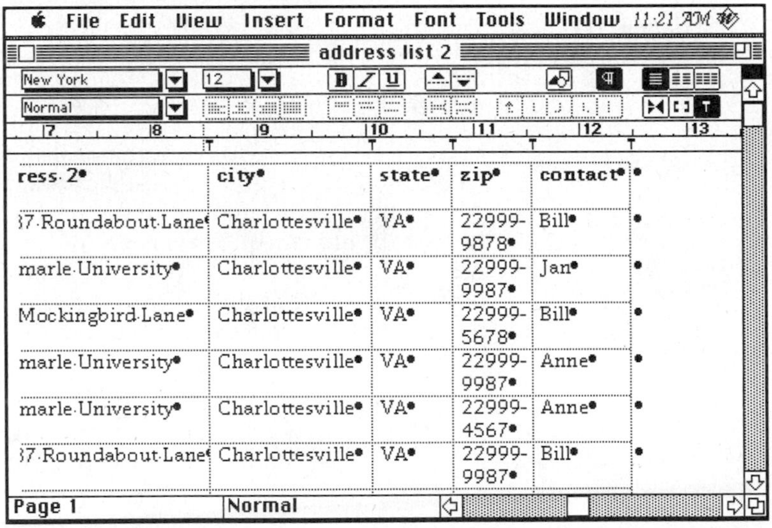

Fig. 24.18
The contact field added to the data document.

File Edit View Insert Format Font Tools Window 11:21 AM					
address list 2					
New York ▼ 12 ▼ **B** *I* U ▲ ▼					
Normal ▼					
7. 8. 9. 10. 11. 12. 13.					
ress·2•	city•	state•	zip•	contact•	•
37·Roundabout·Lane	Charlottesville•	VA•	22999-9878•	Bill•	•
marle·University•	Charlottesville•	VA•	22999-9987•	Jan•	•
Mockingbird·Lane•	Charlottesville•	VA•	22999-5678•	Bill•	•
marle·University•	Charlottesville•	VA•	22999-9987•	Anne•	•
marle·University•	Charlottesville•	VA•	22999-4567•	Anne•	•
37·Roundabout·Lane	Charlottesville•	VA•	22999-9987•	Bill•	•
Page 1	Normal				

2. On the Print Merge Helper bar, choose IF from the Insert Keyword list box.

   If you don't see Print Merge Helper, choose Print Merge Helper from the View menu.

   You see the Insert IF dialog box (see fig. 24.19).

Fig. 24.19
The Insert IF dialog box.

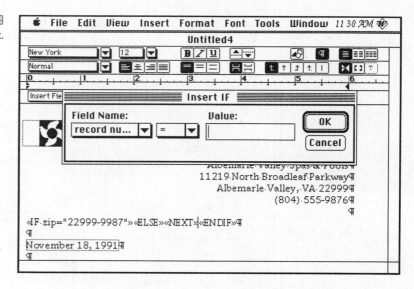

3. In the Field Name list box, choose the name of the field you want to use as the selection criterion.

   The Field Name list box contains the names of all the fields you created in your data document.

   If you want to select all records that contain 22999-9987 in the ZIP field, for example, choose *ZIP* in the Field Name list box.

4. In the Value text box, carefully type the value you want Word to match. See figure 24.20 for an example of correct choices in these boxes.

   Word inserts the IF instruction in your document, surrounded by chevrons (see fig. 24.21).

5. Without moving the insertion point, positioned at the end of the IF instruction, choose Else from the Insert Keyword list box.

Chapter 24
Creating Form Letters

Fig. 24.20
Filling out the Insert If
dialog box.

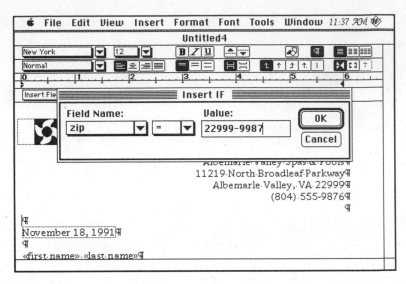

Fig. 24.21
An IF instruction added to
the main document.

Word inserts an ELSE instruction, surrounded by chevrons. This keyword starts an expression that tells Word what to do if it encounters a record in which the field doesn't contain the value you specified.

Part II

Creating More Complex Documents

6. Without moving the insertion point, choose Next from the Insert keyword list box.

   Word inserts a NEXT instruction, surrounded by chevrons. This instruction takes effect only when a data record's field doesn't contain the value you specified. This instruction tells Word to go on to the next record without printing anything.

7. Without moving the insertion point, choose ENDIF from the Insert keyword list box.

   The expression must end with an ENDIF instruction, or an error message appears when you try to print. Your instruction should look like the one in figure 24.22.

8. Choose Print Merge or click one of the printing icons to print your Merge application. Word prints only the records that meet the criteria you specify.

Adding Text That Prints Conditionally

In this section, you learn a different conditional-merging technique. You print all the data records; however, you include an instruction that tells Word to add to some of the data records additional text that doesn't show up in the rest of them.

Fig. 24.22
The completed
conditional-merging
expression.

In figure 24.18, shown earlier, you see in the data document a new field, called `contact`. The field contains the first name of the salesperson who originally contacted the customer; however, Bill Johnson—the Bill in the Contact column—has left your firm. You want to tell Bill's customers to contact Cindy Smith. For all the letters you send to customers who were contacted originally by Bill, you want to add this text:

> *Just give us a call, and ask for Cindy Smith. A pool and spa professional with years of experience, Cindy's waiting to help you enjoy your Pacific Mountain Spa!*

To add text that prints conditionally, follow these steps:

1. In the main document, position the insertion point where you want the text to print.

2. Choose IF from the Insert Keyword list box.

3. In the Field Name list box, choose the name of the field that contains the text you want to match.

4. In the Value text box, type the value you want to match.

5. Choose OK. Word inserts the IF instruction, such as the one shown in figure 24.23.

6. Type the text you want to print conditionally, and press Return when you reach the end of the text. You want to add the Return keystroke to your document only if this text prints.

Fig. 24.23
Adding an instruction to print text conditionally.

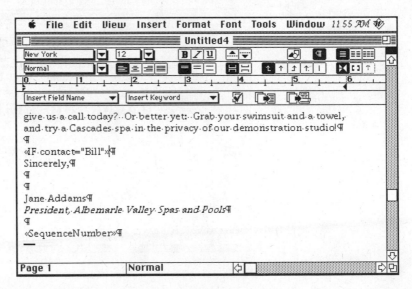

7. At the end of the text, choose ENDIF from the Insert Keyword list box. Your main document should look like the one in figure 24.24.

Fig. 24.24
Added text that prints
conditionally.

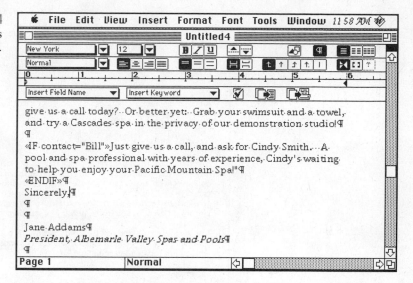

8. Print the merge application by choosing Print Merge or clicking one of the Print icons on the Print Merge Helper bar. For an example of a letter to which text was added conditionally, see figure 24.25.

As you develop your Print Merge application, think about the kinds of information you can collect and place in your data document that will help you take advantage of Word's conditional-instruction capabilities. Add new field names and columns to accommodate this information. If you're maintaining a membership mailing list, for example, you should record whether members have paid their dues for the current year. If the Duespaid field contains No, you can add in the next mailing an instruction that prints a request for payment.

Prompting the User to Supply Information

By now, you have learned how to use Word's Print Merge capabilities at an advanced level. This section describes one more advanced technique you're sure to find useful. Using the SET keyword, you can include in your main document an instruction to prompt the user—you, or anyone else using the application—to supply additional information at the time you print the letters.

Chapter 24
Creating Form Letters

Fig. 24.25
A letter printed with text
added conditionally.

 Pacific Mountain Hot Tubs

Authorized Dealer
Albemarle Valley Spas & Pools
11219 North Broadleaf Parkway
Albemarle Valley, VA 22999
(804) 555-9876

November 18, 1991

Helena Ziwoski
Albemarle Valley Associates
10987 Roundabout Lane
Charlottesville, VA 22999-9987

Dear Ms. Ziwoski:

If you've been thinking about purchasing a portable spa, now's the
time! Pacific Mountain Hot Tubs has just authorized a first-ever sale
on its popular, top-rated Cascades spa. For a limited time only, you
can save up to $1,000 on this high-quality, 5-person spa. Won't you
give us a call today? Or better yet: Grab your swimsuit and a towel,
and try a Cascades spa in the privacy of our demonstration studio!

Just give us a call, and ask for Cindy Smith. A pool and spa
professional with years of experience, Cindy's waiting to help you
enjoy your Pacific Mountain Spa!"

Sincerely,

Jane Addams
President, Albemarle Valley Spas and Pools

You use the SET instruction to define a variable not defined in the data
document. You also use SET to print the same information in each
version of the merged document. (A similar command, ASK, prints
different information for each version of the merged document.) In this
tutorial, you learn how to create a SET instruction that prompts you for
the value of the variable. You use Print Merge Helper to add an ASK
instruction, and then you change the Key word from ASK to SET. (You
could just enter the SET command by typing it manually, but it's easier
to let Print Merge Helper do the hard part for you.)

Suppose that your firm offers financing based on weekly fluctuations of
the prime rate. To avoid any misunderstanding, you want to make sure
that you quote the current rate when the letters are mailed. So, you add
to your main document some text that describes the financing, and you
include a SET instruction that prompts the user to supply the current
interest rate for loans. After you type the rate, Word inserts the correct
rate into the letters and prints them.

Part II

Creating More Complex Documents

To include an instruction that prompts the user to supply information, follow these steps:

1. Position the insertion point below the DATA instruction, on the second line of your document.

2. Choose ASK from the Insert Keywords list box. You will use the ASK dialog box to build the command, but you change the name of the command to SET in a later step.

   The Insert ASK dialog box appears (see fig. 24.26).

Fig. 24.26
The Insert ASK dialog box.

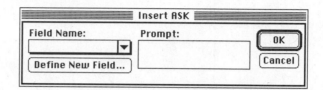

3. Choose Define New Field. You must choose this box because you are going to define a new field for the value you are asking the user to type. This new field is temporary and doesn't affect the data document. The Define New Field dialog box appears.

4. In the Field Name box, type the name of the temporary field and choose OK. The Insert ASK dialog box appears again.

5. In the Prompt area, type the message you want Word to display to the user. You can type as many as 253 characters; the text box scrolls to make room.

   When you're finished, the Insert ASK dialog box should look like the one in figure 24.27.

Fig. 24.27
The Insert ASK dialog box
with field name and
prompt.

6. Choose OK. Word inserts the ASK instruction in your document (see fig. 24.28).

Chapter 24

Creating Form Letters

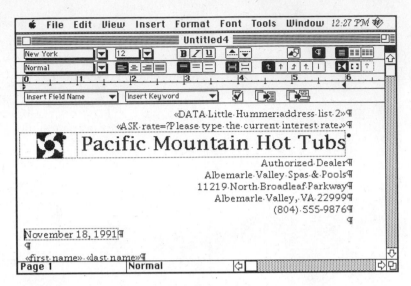

Fig. 24.28
The ASK instruction
included in main
document.

7. Highlight ASK, and press Delete or Backspace. Be careful not to erase the chevrons.

8. Type SET in place of ASK. Your command should appear as follows:

```
<<SET rate=?Please type the current interest rate.>>
```

9. Position the cursor where you want the user-typed value to appear in your document.

10. In the Insert Field list box, choose Define New Field. A dialog box prompts you to type the name of the new field.

11. Type the name of the field you just created. Be sure to type the name exactly the way you typed it in the Insert SET dialog box.

12. Choose OK. Word places the field in the document (see fig. 24.29).

13. Print the merge application by choosing Print Merge or clicking one of the Print buttons on the Print Merge Helper bar. A dialog box containing the prompt you wrote appears (see fig. 24.30).

14. Type the information you want Word to insert in your document.

15. Choose OK.

Fig. 24.29
Adding the new field to the
main document.

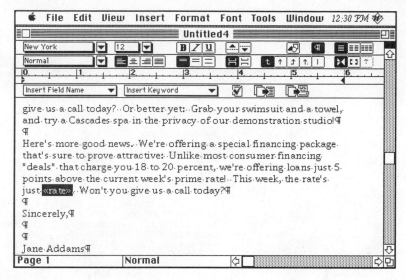

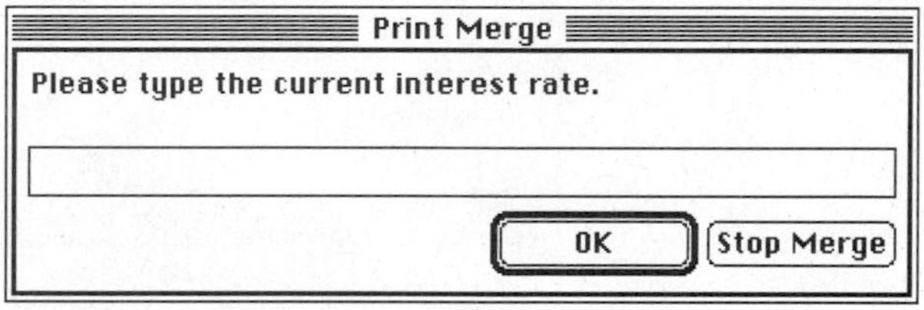

Fig. 24.30
The dialog box generated
by the SET instruction.

Figure 24.31 shows an example of a letter in which the interest rate was inserted automatically by the SET instruction.

Why substitute SET for ASK? ASK works, but with an unfortunate side effect: You would receive with each data record one request to type the interest rate! And, why can't you choose the SET option in the Insert Keyword list box? You can, but the SET option sets up the command in a different way.

You explore more uses of SET and ASK in Part III of this book, "Document Recipes."

Chapter 24
Creating Form Letters

Pacific Mountain Hot Tubs

Authorized Dealer
Albemarle Valley Spas & Pools
11219 North Broadleaf Parkway
Albemarle Valley, VA 22999
(804) 555-9876

November 18, 1991

Michael Abraham
Albemarle Valley Associates
10987 Roundabout Lane
Charlottesville, VA 22999-9878

Dear Mr. Abraham:

If you've been thinking about purchasing a portable spa, now's the
time! Pacific Mountain Hot Tubs has just authorized a first-ever sale
on its popular, top-rated Cascades spa. For a limited time only, you
can save up to $1,000 on this high-quality, 5-person spa. Won't you
give us a call today? Or better yet: Grab your swimsuit and a towel,
and try a Cascades spa in the privacy of our demonstration studio!

Here's more good news. We're offering a special financing package
that's sure to prove attractive: Unlike most consumer financing
"deals" that charge you 18 to 20 percent, we're offering loans just 5
points above the current week's prime rate! This week, the rate's
just 14.5 percent. Won't you give us a call today?

Sincerely,

Jane Addams
President, Albemarle Valley Spas and Pools

Quick Review

This section concisely summarizes the most useful information in
this chapter. Check "Productivity Tips" for a review of high-
productivity tips and tricks, and review "Techniques" when you
forget how to perform a specific procedure.

Productivity Tips

- Use Word 5's new Print Merge Helper to create quickly a data
  document and main document. Using Print Merge Helper, anyone
  can successfully create a form-letter application.

■ Before using Print Merge, learn all you can about tables (see Chapters 17 and 19). Because Print Merge Helper automatically creates a table to store your data, you will have more luck with Print Merge if you master tables first.

■ Plan your data document. In addition to names and addresses, what kinds of information would be helpful to collect and store in the data document? The best form-letter applications send letters tailored to a customer's situation.

■ In some cases you might find it useful to sort your data document and print a range of data records, but in general it's much better to learn how to use the IF instruction to select records conditionally. This chapter provides explicit instructions in the use of the IF, ELSE, NEXT, and ENDIF instructions to select records easily.

■ If you're mailing letters that could include up-to-the-minute information, use the SET command to prompt the user for information, as explained in this chapter.

Techniques

This section provides concise, quick-reference summaries of all the procedures introduced in this chapter.

Creating the Data Document

To create the data document:

1. Choose Print Merge Helper from the View menu.

2. Choose New.

3. Type the first field name.

4. Choose Add.

5. Repeat steps 3 and 4 to add all the rest of the fields to your data document.

6. When you're sure that the field name list is complete and correct, choose OK.

7. Type a name for your new data document and choose Save.

Creating the Main Document

To create the main document:

1. Position the insertion point at the beginning of the document.

2. Choose Print Merge Helper from the View menu.

3. Select the data document that contains your mailing list and choose Open.

4. Type the text that you want everyone on the list to see.

5. Position the insertion point where you want the first data field to appear, and drop down the Insert Field Name list box.

6. Use the Insert Field Name list box to add the rest of the field names, adding spaces, punctuation, and hard returns as necessary.

7. Save the data document.

Printing the Form Letters

To print your form letters to a new document:

1. With your main document and Print Merge Helper on-screen, choose the Print to New Document icon.

2. Add text to the letters, if you want.

3. Choose Print from the File menu to print the letters.

To print your form letters directly:

1. With your main document and Print Merge Helper on-screen, choose the Print Directly icon.

2. Choose Print.

Printing Records That Meet Criteria You Specify

To print records that meet criteria you specify:

1. In the main document, place the insertion point above the correspondent's name and address.

2. On the Print Merge Helper bar, choose IF from the Insert Keyword list box.

3. In the Field name list box, choose the name of the field you want to use as the selection criterion.

4. In the Value text box, carefully type the value you want Word to match.

5. Without moving the insertion point, positioned at the end of the IF instruction, choose ELSE from the Insert Keyword list box.

6. Without moving the insertion point, choose NEXT from the Insert keyword list box.

7. Without moving the insertion point, choose ENDIF from the Insert Keyword list box.

8. Choose Print Merge or click one of the printing icons to print your Merge application.

Adding Data to the Data Document and Sorting the Mailing List

1. If necessary, create the data document (see "Creating the Data Document" elsewhere in this section).

2. Click the table-boundaries button and widen the columns so that they accommodate the longest word you are likely to type in a cell.

3. Type the rest of the mailing-list data. To create a new row, press Tab at the end of the last row.

4. Select the column you want to use as the key for the sort. Remember: don't include the first row in the selection.

5. Choose Sort from the Tools menu.

6. Save the data document.

Adding Text That Prints Conditionally

To add text that prints conditionally:

1. In the main document, position the insertion point where you want the text to print.

2. Choose IF from the Insert Keyword list box.

3. In the Field Name list box, choose the name of the field that contains the text you want to match.

4. In the Value text box, type the value you want to match.

5. Choose OK.

6. Type the text you want to print conditionally, and press Return when you reach the end of the text.

7. At the end of the text, choose ENDIF from the Insert Keyword list box.

8. Print the merge application by choosing Print Merge or clicking one of the Print icons on the Print Merge Helper bar.

Printing Mailing Labels

Properly printed mailing labels provide the key for a variety of successful mailing applications, ranging from newsletters to collection notices. In this chapter, you learn how to generate mailing labels from your mailing-list data document (the one you created in Chapter 24). After printing the labels, you can apply them to newsletters, fliers, brochures, catalogs, and anything else you can mail to your clients and customers.

Although the procedures for creating a mailing-label application vary depending on the labels and printer you are using, the basic procedure is the same: You create a *main document* that includes field names. These field names draw data from your data document and print them on the label. That's the easy part. The tough part, as you will see in this chapter, is getting the printed names and addresses to align correctly on the labels. You probably will have to experiment with margin settings and other formatting options to get the labels to print correctly. Plan on wasting some labels!

Thanks to Word 5's new Print Merge Helper, printing mailing labels is easier than in previous versions of Word. You still have to fuss with column widths and margins before you can get the labels to print properly, however. Word isn't exactly a dedicated label-crunching program.

The following is an overview of this chapter's contents:

- *Printing One-Column Continuous Labels with an ImageWriter.* By far the easiest way to print mailing labels is discussed in this section. Hang on to that ImageWriter!

- *Printing Three-Column Continuous Labels with an ImageWriter.* This section teaches you how to use some fancy formatting tricks to print three-column continuous labels.

- *Printing Laser Labels with LaserWriter and StyleWriter Printers.* In this section, you learn how to finagle Word into printing 30 labels to a page of press-apply Avery labels. You can adapt the technique to the labels you are using.

You should have a mailing list in the form of a data document in order to try the applications discussed in this chapter. For information on creating a data document, see Chapter 24.

Buying Labels

 ou can buy mailing labels at any office-supply store. For Macintosh printers, mailing labels fall into two categories: *continuous* labels and *sheet* labels.

Continuous labels, designed for use on ImageWriter printers, come in one-column or three-column formats. The tops of the labels are exactly one inch apart. A paper backing includes the pinholes used to draw the labels through the printer, which makes it easier to get the single-column labels to print correctly.

Some sheet labels, designed for StyleWriter and LaserWriter printers, have 27 one-inch labels, in three columns, each with nine labels. These labels often are called *laser labels*, but you can use them with inkjet printers such as the DeskWriter and StyleWriter. Other labels come with 30 labels to a sheet.

Printing One-Column Continuous Labels with an ImageWriter

The ImageWriter printer has been supplanted by newer and snazzier models, but many of them are still out there—and they have their advantages: ImageWriters are much cheaper to operate than StyleWriters or LaserWriters and are well suited to mailing-label applications. In many offices, the ImageWriter that once bore major printing responsibilities has been relegated to a background role, cranking out drafts and printing labels as needed.

With single-column labels, you have to align only one dimension: the vertical. If you choose three-column labels, you must set up a three-column format and also gauge the horizontal dimension correctly. Altogether, it's a longer (and trickier) process.

To print labels in one column with an ImageWriter, you first set up the main document, then set up the page, and, finally, print the labels.

To set up the main document, follow these steps:

1. Open a new Word document.

2. Choose Print Merge Helper from the View menu.

   You see an Open dialog box, prompting you to choose the file that contains your data document.

3. Choose your data document.

   Word inserts a DATA instruction at the beginning of your new document, identifying the file from which the data will be drawn (see fig. 25.1).

Fig. 25.1
A DATA instruction inserted.

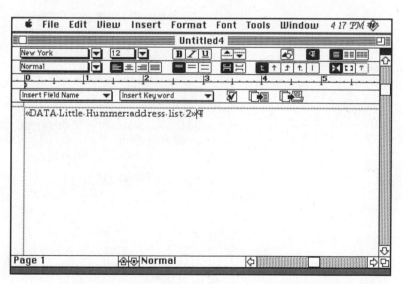

4. Without moving the insertion point, choose the first field you want to insert (the field containing your correspondent's first name) from the Insert Field Name list box.

Chapter 25

Printing Mailing Labels

5. Press the space bar to leave a space after the first name.

6. Choose the last name field from the Insert Field Name menu.

   Your main document should look like the one in figure 25.2.

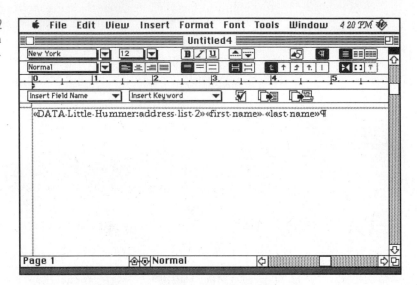

7. Press Return to start a new line.

8. Choose the first address field from the Insert Field Name list box.

9. Press Return to start a new line.

10. If your data document includes a second address field for organizational addresses, choose the name of this field from the Insert Field Name list box and press Return.

11. Choose the name of the city field from the Insert Field Name list box, type a comma, and press the space bar.

12. Choose the name of the state field from the Insert Field Name list box and press the space bar.

13. Choose the name of the ZIP-code field from the Insert Field Name list box.

    At this point, your main document should resemble the one in figure 25.3.

Fig. 25.3
All the field names added
to the main document.

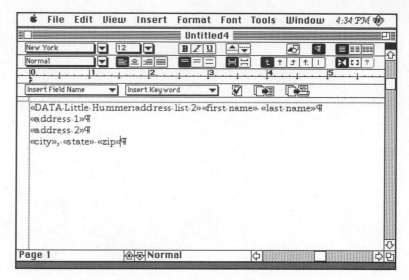

14. Save your main document.

To set up the page, follow these steps:

1. Choose Preferences from the Tools menu and, when the Preferences dialog box appears, enter the width of your label paper in the Custom Paper Size Width box.

2. Type *1* (the label height in inches) in the Custom Paper Size Height box.

   Your Preferences dialog box should look like the one in figure 25.4.

3. Choose OK to close the Preferences dialog box.

4. Choose Page Setup from the File menu.

   You see the Page Setup dialog box (see fig. 25.5). Note that the custom paper-size option you just defined is presented as an option.

5. Choose the Custom Paper size and No Gaps Between Pages options.

   The No Gaps Between Pages option ensures that Word moves to the next label without skipping any space.

Chapter 25
Printing Mailing Labels

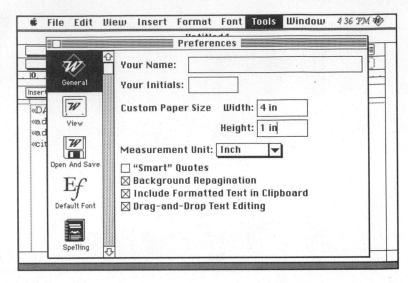

Fig. 25.4
Custom Paper Size settings
in the Preferences dialog
box.

Fig. 25.5
The Page Setup dialog box.

6. Choose Document.

   You see the Document dialog box.

7. Enter *0* in the Top, Bottom, and Right boxes, and enter *0.2* in the Left box.

   Your document dialog box should look like the one in figure 25.6.

8. Choose OK.

To print the labels, follow these steps:

1. Load the continuous-label paper so that the top of the first label is even with the print head. (Remember that there is no top margin.)

Fig. 25.6
The Document dialog box.

Document

Margins

Left:	0.2 in	Top:	0 in	At Least ▼
Right:	0 in	Bottom:	0 in	At Least ▼
Gutter:	0 in	☐ Mirror Even/Odd	

OK

Cancel

Use As Default

File Series...

Footnotes

Position: Bottom of Page ▼

○ Restart Each Page

◉ Number From: 1

☒ Widow Control
☐ Print Hidden Text
☐ Even/Odd Headers
Default Tab Stops: 0.5 in

2. Choose Print Merge from the File menu.

3. Choose the From button. Enter *1* in the From box and *1* in the To box.

4. Choose Print and inspect the alignment of the first label. If the printing is satisfactory, choose Print Merge again and choose the All button; if you are not satisfied with the printing, adjust the label paper. Choose Print Merge and then the From button, and try another test.

Printing Three-Column Continuous Labels with an ImageWriter

Printing three-column labels requires you to create a multiple-column main document. You enter three sets of address fields, one for each column. This procedure is more difficult than the single-column procedure described in the preceding section.

To print labels in three columns on continuous, tractor-fed label paper, set up your main document, set up the sections and page layout, and then print the labels:

1. Begin your main document by following steps 1 through 13 in the preceding section.

   You add a DATA instruction and one complete set of field names.

2. Press ⌘-Enter to enter a section mark.

3. Choose NEXT from the Insert Keyword list box.

4. Highlight the name and address field names, being careful to include the beginning and trailing chevrons as well as the section mark that comes after the <<zip>> field. See figure 25.7 for an example of a correct selection.

Fig. 25.7
Selecting field names and
section marks.

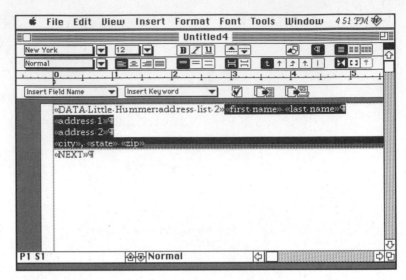

5. Choose Copy from the Edit menu or press ⌘-C.

6. Position the insertion point just after the NEXT command and choose Paste from the Edit menu. Alternatively, press ⌘-V.

7. Choose NEXT from the Insert Keyword list box.

8. Choose Paste again, or press ⌘-V.

    Your document should look like the one in figure 25.8.

9. Select the whole document and choose Section from the Format menu.

10. Enter *3* in the Number box and *0* in the Column Spacing box.

11. Choose New Column in the Start box, and choose OK.

12. Choose Preferences from the Edit menu and, when the Preferences dialog box appears, type the width of your label paper (usually 8.5 inches) in the Custom Paper Size Width box.

13. Enter *1* (the label height) in the Custom Paper Size Height box.

14. Choose OK, and then choose Page Setup from the File menu.

15. Choose the Custom Paper size and No Gaps Between Pages options.

16. Choose Document, and enter these margin settings: Left, *0.25* in; Right, Left, and Top, *0* in.

Part II

Creating More Complex Documents

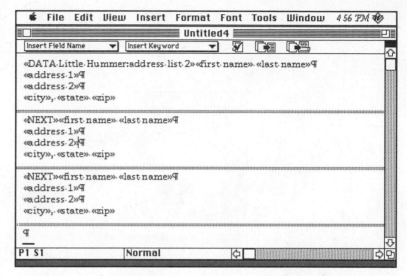

Fig. 25.8
Fields properly entered
for three-column,
continuous labels.

17. Choose OK and load the continuous-label paper so that the top of the first label is even with the print head (remember that there is no top margin.)

18. Choose Print Merge from the File menu.

19. Choose the From button, and enter *1* in the From box and *3* in the To box.

20. Choose Print, and inspect the alignment of the first label. If the printing is satisfactory, choose Print Merge again, and choose the All button; if you are not satisfied with the printing, adjust the label paper. Then choose Print Merge, and try another test.

If all goes well, the labels should print three across (see fig. 25.9).

> **TIP**
>
> If you have trouble getting an entire name and address to fit within the allotted space, try selecting the whole document and choosing a 10-point font size.

Printing Laser Labels with LaserWriter and StyleWriter Printers

To print laser-label sheets, you must create a main document with the same number of address field sets as there are labels on the sheet. One popular brand of laser labels offers 1-inch-by-3-inch labels, with 30 labels per sheet, allowing room for 1/2-inch top and bottom margins.

The following instructions work for printing four-line address labels on laser label stock. If you are using a LaserWriter, you may have to reduce the font size to nine points so that the left and right columns of labels can accommodate the half-inch margin needed for printing. Almost certainly, you will have to experiment to get this technique to work correctly.

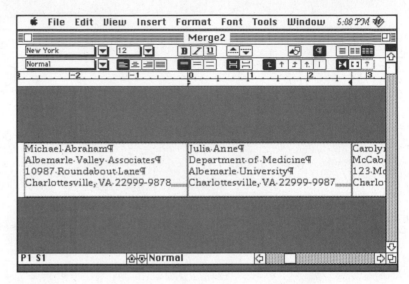

To print laser label sheets with a LaserWriter or StyleWriter printer, follow these steps:

1. Begin your main document by following steps 1 through 13 in the earlier section titled "Printing One-Column Continuous Labels with an ImageWriter."

2. Press Return.

3. Choose NEXT from the Insert Keyword list box.

4. Press Return twice.

5. Carefully select all the name and address field names, including the beginning and trailing chevrons. Include the NEXT instruction (*and* the trailing paragraph mark) in the selection, as shown in figure 25.10. Don't forget the first chevron!

6. Choose Copy from the Edit menu, or press ⌘-C.

7. Cancel the selection, and place the insertion point at the end of the document (before the last paragraph mark).

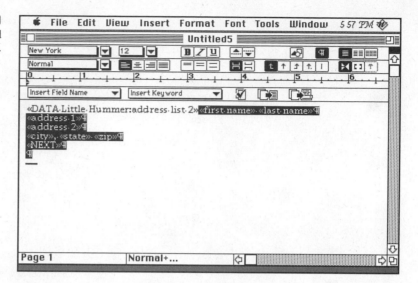

Fig. 25.10
Selecting name and
address field names.

8. Press Return.

9. Press ⌘-V 29 times.

    You've entered 29 copies of the name and address field names, making 30 in all.

10. Choose Section from the Format menu.

11. Enter *3* in the Number of Columns box.

12. Enter *0.25* in the Column Spacing box.

    Unlike three-column continuous labels, laser labels have 1/4-inch spacing between the three columns. Try this measurement initially to see whether it spaces the columns adequately.

13. Choose OK to confirm the section format.

14. Choose Select All from the Edit menu to select the entire document, or press ⌘-A.

15. Choose Paragraph from the Format menu.

    You see the Paragraph dialog box.

16. In the Line list box, choose Exactly, and type *12* in the text box.

    You have chosen a line spacing of exactly 12 points. This setting ensures that, even if you choose a smaller font, Word prints exactly six lines per inch.

Chapter 25

Printing Mailing Labels

17. Choose OK to confirm the paragraph formats.

18. With the entire document still selected, choose 9 from the font-size list box on the ribbon.

    You will have a tough time packing your addresses into the allotted four lines unless you use 9- or 10-point type.

19. Choose Document from the Format menu.

    You see the Document dialog box.

20. Try these margin settings:

    > Left: 0.75 in
    > Right: 0.75 in
    > Top: 0.5 in
    > Bottom: 0.5 in

21. After loading the laser label sheets in your printer, choose the icon on the Print Merge Helper bar that prints to a new document.

22. Try printing the first page of the merge document to see how the setting works. If necessary, make changes to the margins, column width, and font size until you have solved the remaining formatting problems.

23. Return to the main document, make the same changes you made to the merge document, and choose the icon that prints the records directly to the printer.

    Word prints the three-column layout in precise alignment with the labels, as shown in figure 25.11.

Printing Mailing Labels with Varying Numbers of Lines

This chapter has emphasized the printing of four-line mailing labels, such as those used in sending a mailing to individuals at their business addresses. In all likelihood, however, your mailing list consists of a mixture of three- and four-line addresses. A four-line label should look like the following:

> Dr. Ralph Johnson
> Department of Epidemiology
> Albemarle University
> Charlottesville, VA 22999

Fig. 25.11
A mailing list merged to
three-column laser labels.

Michael Abraham Albemarle Valley Associates 10987 Roundabout Lane Charlottesville, VA 22999-9878	Edwin Stevenson Department of Radiology Albemarle University Charlottesville, VA 22999-4567	Carolyn Martin McCabe-Miller Realty 123 Mockingbird Lane Charlottesville, VA 22999-5678
Julia Anne Department of Veterinary Medicine Albemarle University Charlottesville, VA 22999-9987	Helena Ziwoski Albemarle Valley Associates 10987 Roundabout Lane Charlottesville, VA 22999-9987	Michael Paul Department of Physics Albemarle University Charlottesville, VA 22999-9987
Carolyn Martin McCabe-Miller Realty 123 Mockingbird Lane Charlottesville, VA 22999-5678	Michael Abraham Albemarle Valley Associates 10987 Roundabout Lane Charlottesville, VA 22999-9878	Edwin Stevenson Department of Radiology Albemarle University Charlottesville, VA 22999-4567
Michael Paul Department of Physics Albemarle University Charlottesville, VA 22999-9987	Julia Anne Department of Veterinary Medicine Albemarle University Charlottesville, VA 22999-9987	Helena Ziwoski Albemarle Valley Associates 10987 Roundabout Lane Charlottesville, VA 22999-9987
Edwin Stevenson Department of Radiology Albemarle University Charlottesville, VA 22999-4567	Carolyn Martin McCabe-Miller Realty 123 Mockingbird Lane Charlottesville, VA 22999-5678	Michael Abraham Albemarle Valley Associates 10987 Roundabout Lane Charlottesville, VA 22999-9878
Helena Ziwoski Albemarle Valley Associates 10987 Roundabout Lane Charlottesville, VA 22999-9987	Michael Paul Department of Physics Albemarle University Charlottesville, VA 22999-9987	Julia Anne Department of Veterinary Medicine Albemarle University Charlottesville, VA 22999-9987
Michael Abraham Albemarle Valley Associates 10987 Roundabout Lane Charlottesville, VA 22999-9878	Edwin Stevenson Department of Radiology Albemarle University Charlottesville, VA 22999-4567	Carolyn Martin McCabe-Miller Realty 123 Mockingbird Lane Charlottesville, VA 22999-5678
Julia Anne Department of Veterinary Medicine Albemarle University Charlottesville, VA 22999-9987	Helena Ziwoski Albemarle Valley Associates 10987 Roundabout Lane Charlottesville, VA 22999-9987	Michael Paul Department of Physics Albemarle University Charlottesville, VA 22999-9987
Carolyn Martin McCabe-Miller Realty 123 Mockingbird Lane Charlottesville, VA 22999-5678	Michael Abraham Albemarle Valley Associates 10987 Roundabout Lane Charlottesville, VA 22999-9878	Edwin Stevenson Department of Radiology Albemarle University Charlottesville, VA 22999-4567
Michael Paul Department of Physics Albemarle University Charlottesville, VA 22999-9987	Julia Anne Department of Veterinary Medicine Albemarle University Charlottesville, VA 22999-9987	Helena Ziwoski Albemarle Valley Associates 10987 Roundabout Lane Charlottesville, VA 22999-9987

And, here's what a three-line label looks like:

Mr. Barnaby Smith
109 Birdwhistle Drive

Periwinkle, VA 22998

The appearance of the second label, with the blank line, is far from catastrophic: it's just an aesthetic problem, which you may or may not be willing to tolerate. The mailing labels still will print fine—every label will have the required six lines.

To keep Word from printing blank lines on your labels, you can use a special IF command that tells Word to print a line only if the field contains something. If the field is blank, Word will print the next line without leaving a blank one. The following instructions tell you how to type the field names and merge instructions so that Word doesn't print blank lines in addresses. You also must add a second IF instruction so that Word adds a blank line at the bottom of the label if a field is skipped; otherwise, the spacing between labels is thrown off.

To set up the fields and instructions so that Word will not leave blank lines in labels, follow these steps:

1. Position the insertion point where you want the field to print if it isn't blank.

   In figure 25.12, two fields were entered. The next field, called Company, might be blank if the address is a residential address.

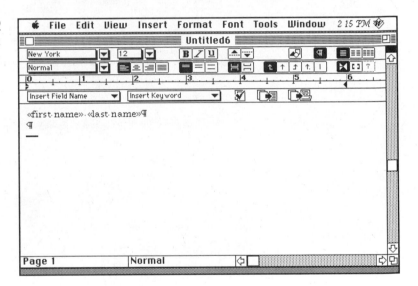

Fig. 25.12
Positioning the insertion point correctly.

2. Without pressing Return, choose IF...ENDIF from the Insert Keyword list box.

   The Insert IF dialog box appears (see fig. 25.13).

3. From the Field Name list box, choose the name of the field that might be empty.

Fig. 25.13
The Insert IF dialog box.

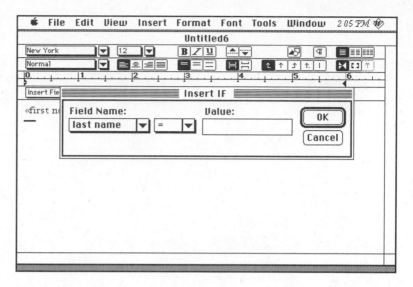

4. From the middle list box (the Operator list), choose the Field Not Empty option.

5. Choose OK.

Word enters the IF and ENDIF instruction in your main document (see fig. 25.14).

Fig. 25.14
IF and ENDIF instruction
added.

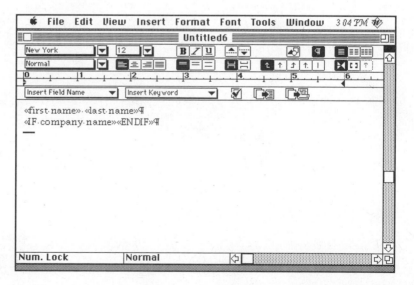

Chapter 25

Printing Mailing Labels

6. Without moving the insertion point, choose the same field again by using the Insert Field Name list box. Word adds the field name.

7. Without moving the insertion point, press Return.

   Your instruction should resemble the ones in figure 25.15.

8. Continue adding the fields, as shown in figure 25.16.

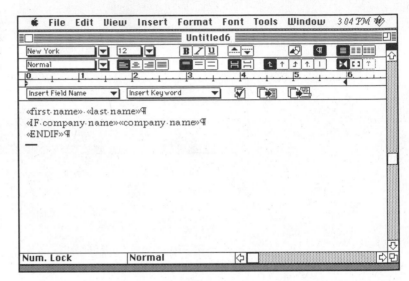

Fig. 25.15
Completed IF instruction that tells Word to skip a blank field.

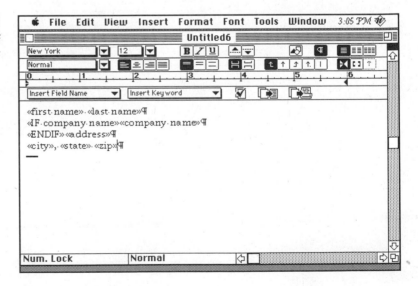

Fig. 25.16
Adding the rest of the fields.

9. Place the insertion point at the end of the Zip field, and repeat steps 3, 4, and 5. Words enters another IF...ENDIF instruction.

10. Press Return.

11. Choose Next from the Insert Keyword list box.

12. Place the insertion point before the ENDIF instruction, and press Return twice.

13. Place the insertion point after the NEXT instruction, and choose ELSE from the Insert Keyword list box.

Your main document should look like the one in figure 25.17.

Fig. 25.17
Completed IF...ENDIF
instruction.

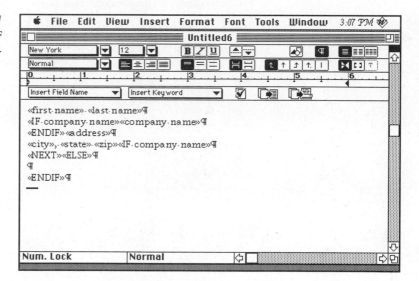

Quick Review

T his section concisely summarizes the most useful information in this chapter. Check "Productivity Tips" for a review of high-productivity tips and tricks, and review "Techniques" when you forget how to perform a specific procedure.

Chapter 25
Printing Mailing Labels

Productivity Tips

■ If you have invested the time and energy to set up a mailing-list data document with Word, by all means learn how to print mailing labels. You will have to adjust margins and column widths to get the labels to print properly, but after the application works correctly, you can print labels whenever you want with no further hassle.

■ By far the easiest way to print mailing labels with Word is to crank them out on an ImageWriter using single-column, tractor-fed continuous labels.

■ If you are working with a LaserWriter, look for laser labels that leave a half-inch margin at the top and bottom. That way, you can print on all 30 labels on the sheet. The instructions in this chapter show you how to print using 30-label, Avery laser label sheets, commonly available in business-supply stores.

■ Clever use of Word's Merge keywords can solve problems caused by mixing three- and four-line addresses.

Techniques

This section provides concise, quick-reference summaries of all the procedures introduced in this chapter.

Printing Laser Labels

To print laser label sheets with a LaserWriter or StyleWriter printer:

1. Begin your main document by following steps 1 through 13 in the section titled "Printing One-Column Continuous Labels with an ImageWriter."

2. Press Return.

3. Choose NEXT from the Insert Keyword list box.

4. Press Return twice.

5. Carefully select all the name and address field names, including the beginning and trailing chevrons. Include the NEXT instruction (*and* the trailing paragraph mark) in the selection.

6. Choose Copy from the Edit menu, or press ⌘-C.

7. Cancel the selection and place the insertion point at the end of the document (before the last paragraph mark).

8. Press Return.

9. Press ⌘-V 29 times.

10. Choose Section from the Format menu.

11. Enter *3* in the Number of Columns box.

12. Enter *0.25* in the Column Spacing box.

13. Choose OK to confirm the section format.

14. Choose Select All from the Edit menu to select the entire document, or press ⌘-A.

15. Choose Paragraph from the Format menu.

16. In the Line list box, choose Exactly, and type *12* in the text box.

17. Choose OK to confirm the paragraph formats.

18. With the entire document still selected, choose 9 from the font-size list box on the ribbon.

19. Choose Document from the Format menu.

20. Try these margin settings:

    Left: 0.75 in
    Right: 0.75 in
    Top: 0.5 in
    Bottom: 0.5 in

21. After loading the laser label sheets in your printer, choose the icon on the Print Merge Helper bar that prints to a new document.

22. Try printing the first page of the merge document to see how the settings work. If necessary, make changes to the margins, column width, and font size until you have solved the remaining formatting problems.

23. Return to the main document, make the same changes you made to the merge document, and choose the icon that prints the records directly to the printer.

Printing One-Column Continuous Labels with an ImageWriter

To print labels in one column with an ImageWriter:

1. Open a new Word document.

2. Choose Print Merge Helper from the View menu.

3. Choose your data document.

4. Without moving the insertion point, choose the first field you want to insert (the field containing your correspondent's first name) from the Insert Field Name list box.

5. Press the space bar to leave a space after the first name.

6. Choose the last name field from the Insert Field Name menu.

7. Press Return to start a new line.

8. Choose the first address field from the Insert Field Name list box.

9. Press Return to start a new line.

10. If your data document includes a second address field for organizational addresses, choose the name of this field from the Insert Field Name list box and press Return.

11. Choose the name of the city field from the Insert Field Name list box, type a comma, and press the space bar.

12. Choose the name of the state field from the Insert Field Name list box, and press the space bar.

13. Choose the name of the ZIP code field from the Insert Field Name list box.

14. Save your main document.

15. Choose Preferences from the Tools menu and, when the Preferences dialog box appears, enter the width of your label paper in the Custom Paper Size Width box.

16. Type *1* (the label height in inches) in the Custom Paper Size Height box.

17. Choose OK to close the Preferences dialog box.

18. Choose Page Setup from the File menu.

19. Choose the Custom Paper Size and No Gaps Between Pages options.

20. Choose Document.

21. Enter *0* in the Top, Bottom, and Right boxes, and enter *0.2* in the Left box.

22. Choose OK.

23. Load the continuous-label paper so that the top of the first label is even with the print head. (Remember that there is no top margin.)

24. Choose Print Merge from the File menu.

25. Choose the From button. Enter *1* in the From box and *1* in the To box.

26. Choose Print and inspect the alignment of the first label. If the printing is satisfactory, choose Print Merge again and choose the All button; if you are not satisfied with the printing, adjust the label paper. Then choose Print Merge and the From button, and try another test.

Printing Three-Column Continuous Labels on an ImageWriter

To print labels in three columns on continuous, tractor-fed labels:

1. Begin your main document by following steps 1 through 13 in the preceding section.

2. Press ⌘-Enter to enter a section mark.

3. Choose NEXT from the Insert Keyword list box.

4. Highlight the name and address field names, being careful to include the beginning and trailing chevrons, as well as the section mark that comes after the <<zip>> field.

5. Choose Copy from the Edit menu or press ⌘-C.

6. Position the insertion point just after the NEXT command, and choose Paste from the Edit menu. Alternatively, press ⌘-V.

7. Choose NEXT from the Insert Keyword list box.

8. Choose Paste again, or press ⌘-V.

9. Select the whole document and choose Section from the Format menu.

10. Enter *3* in the Number box and *0* in the Column Spacing box.

11. Choose New Column in the Start box, and choose OK.

12. Choose Preferences from the Edit menu, and, when the Preferences dialog box appears, type the width of your label paper (usually 8.5 inches) in the Custom Paper Size Width box.

13. Enter *1* (the label height) in the Custom Paper Size Height box.

14. Choose OK, and choose Page Setup from the File menu.

15. Choose the Custom Paper Size and No Gaps Between Pages options.

16. Choose Document, and try these margin settings:

    Left: 0.25 in
    Right: 0 in
    Top: 0 in
    Bottom: 0 in

17. Choose OK, and load the continuous-label paper so that the top of the first label is even with the print head (remember that there is no top margin.)

18. Choose Print Merge from the File menu.

19. Choose the From button, and enter *1* in the From box and *3* in the To box.

20. Choose Print, and inspect the alignment of the first label. If the printing is satisfactory, choose Print Merge again and choose the All button; if you are not satisfied with the printing, adjust the label paper. Then choose Print Merge, and try another test.

Working with Long Documents

More than a few doctoral dissertations, 1,000-page novels, textbooks, and trade books are composed on Macintoshes running Word 5—and the book you're reading is an example! Taking up several megabytes of disk space, the text of a lengthy book such as this one could make one heck of a big file—and could easily cause problems proportional to its size, such as sluggish performance, low memory messages, and all-your-eggs-in-one-basket disasters, if the file became corrupt for some reason. Prudent Word users keep sections of a document in a series of separate files.

What happens, however, when you want to print a document with continuous pagination, as well as an accurate table of contents and index? New features in Word 5, including the File Series option in the Document dialog box, enable you to chain documents for printing in a series without having to type complicated Print Merge commands, as users of previous versions of Word were obliged to do.

This chapter presents a complete strategy for tackling a huge writing project with Word. The following is an overview of this chapter's contents:

- *Creating a Template Document.* You begin by creating a stationery document that contains the styles and formatting choices you want to apply to every section of the document.

- *Linking the Files in a File Series.* After you have completed the files and are ready to print, you link the files in a file series by following the instructions in this section.

- *Numbering Pages, Lines, and Footnotes Consecutively.* In this section, you learn how to make sure that pages, lines, and footnotes are numbered consecutively and correctly throughout your lengthy document.

- *Creating an Index and Table of Contents.* This section discusses creating a unified index and table of contents when you have linked files in a file series.

- *Assembling a Document Using the Include Command.* You can use this Print Merge command to include one lengthy file within another, as this section explains.

Creating a Template Document

f you are creating a document you plan to assemble from a series of linked files, all the files *must* have exactly the same formats and styles. Otherwise, you could see formatting inconsistencies when you print your document. By far the best way to prevent such inconsistencies is to begin the project by creating a stationery document that serves as a template for all the sections in the document. You add to this document all the styles you want to use throughout your document, and you also choose formats and add text, such as chapter titles and headers. After creating the stationery document, you start each file by opening the stationery document.

To create the master template document, follow these steps:

1. In a new Word document, choose the section and document formats you want to apply to all the files.

   Choose margins, header and footer locations, footnote preferences (such as footnotes or endnotes printed at the end of sections), and page numbers (unless you want to add page numbers with headers).

   To suppress the printing of page numbers on the first page of a chapter, choose Different First Page in the Section dialog box.

   To make sure that Word starts each chapter or section on an odd-numbered page, choose Odd Page in the Break list box in the Section dialog box.

2. Create styles for your document, and redefine standard styles to suit your taste or style guidelines.

   To create the styles, you may want to experiment by creating dummy text, as shown in figure 26.1. See Table 26.1 for a list of the styles used to create this document.

3. Add headers and footers, and if you didn't choose Margin Page Numbers in the Section dialog box, add page numbers to the header or footer.

4. Choose Select All from the Edit menu to select all the dummy text.

5. Choose Cut to delete the text (but not the styles you have created).

6. Choose Save.

   You see the Save As dialog box.

7. In the Save File As Type list box, choose Stationery.

8. In the File Name box, type a name which indicates that the file is a template, such as Report Chapter Template or Thesis Chapter Template.

9. Choose Save.

   Word creates the template document and changes the name of the current document to Untitled. Now you can use this document to create the first chapter of your report or thesis!

Table 26.1
Styles for a Report or Dissertation

TIP

If you need to add styles later, be sure to add the style to the template document. Then copy the style from the template document to all the other files. For more information on using a template document to store styles, see Chapter 8.

Style name	Use and formats
Heading 2*	Used for chapter titles; Helvetica 24 Bold, 48 points before, 18 points after; centered; keep with next paragraph
Heading 3*	Used for major subheadings; Helvetica 14 Bold, 18 points before, 6 points after; flush left; keep with next paragraph
Lead ¶	Used for lead paragraphs; New York 12, at least 24 points line spacing (double space); justified
Text ¶	Used for text paragraphs; New York 12, at least 24 points line spacing (double space); 1/2-inch first-line indentation; justified

continues

Chapter 26
Working with Long Documents

Table 26.1
Continued

Style name	Use and formats
Quotation	Used for extended quotations; New York 12, automatic line spacing (single space); 1/2-inch indentation left, 1/2-inch indentation right; justified
Footnote Text*	Used for footnote text; New York 12, automatic line spacing (single space); 1/2-inch first-line indentation; 12 points before; justified

*Redefined standard style.

Fig. 26.1
Design for the Marker
Template Document.
(page 1 of 2)

Chapter Heading

This is a lead paragraph, a paragraph of text that opens a section. Note that the paragraph does not have a first-line indentation. The lack of a first-line indentation produces a handsome block effect.[1]

This is a text paragraph. In contrast to the lead paragraph, the text paragraph format includes a first-line indentation.

Major Subheading

This is a lead paragraph, a paragraph of text that opens a section. Note that the paragraph does not have a first-line indentation. The lack of a first-line indentation produces a handsome block effect.

This is a text paragraph. In contrast to the lead paragraph, the text paragraph format includes a first-line indentation.

> This paragraph is used for an extended quotation. Single-spaced, it is indented from both margins. Most style guidelines call for this formatting when a quotation exceeds four lines of text.[2]

This is a text paragraph. In contrast to the lead paragraph, the text paragraph format includes a first-line indentation.

---

[1]This is a paragraph of footnote text. To leave room between the separator and the footnote, as well as between one footnote and the next, the footnote text is formatted with 12 points of blank space before the paragraph. In addition, the footnote text has a first-line indentation.

[2]This is a second paragraph of footnote text. To leave room between the separator and the footnote, as well as between one footnote and the next, the footnote text is formatted with 12 points of blank space before the paragraph. In addition, the footnote text has a first-line indentation.

Fig. 26.1
Design for the Marker
Template Document.
(page 2 of 2)

Chapter XX   2

Major Subheading

This is a lead paragraph, a paragraph of text that opens a section. Note that the paragraph does not have a first-line indentation. The lack of a first-line indentation produces a handsome block effect.

This is a text paragraph. In contrast to the lead paragraph, the text paragraph format includes a first-line indentation.

> This paragraph is used for an extended quotation. Single-spaced, it is indented from both margins. Most style guidelines call for this formatting when a quotation exceeds four lines of text.[3]

This is a text paragraph. In contrast to the lead paragraph, the text paragraph format includes a first-line indentation. This is a text paragraph. In contrast to the lead paragraph, the text paragraph format includes a first-line indentation. This is a text paragraph. In contrast to the lead paragraph, the text paragraph format includes a first-line indentation.

> This paragraph is used for an extended quotation. Single-spaced, it is indented from both margins. Most style guidelines call for this formatting when a quotation exceeds four lines of text.[4]

This is a text paragraph. In contrast to the lead paragraph, the text paragraph format includes a first-line indentation. This is a text

---

[3]This is a third paragraph of footnote text. To leave room between the separator and the footnote, as well as between one footnote and the next, the footnote text is formatted with 12 points of blank space before the paragraph. In addition, the footnote text has a first-line indentation.

[4]This is a fourth paragraph of footnote text. To leave room between the separator and the footnote, as well as between one footnote and the next, the footnote text is formatted with 12 points of blank space before the paragraph. In addition, the footnote text has a first-line indentation.

Linking the Files in a File Series

After you have created all the files that make up your lengthy project, you use the Document command (on the Format menu) to link the files in a series. When you have done so, Word numbers the pages consecutively and accurately, and you can compile an index and table of contents, as though the files were part of one, long document. This section describes the procedure you use to link the files in a series.

To link files in a series, follow these steps:

1. Open the first document.

2. Choose Document from the Format menu.

3. Choose File Series.

   You see the File Series dialog box (see fig. 26.2).

Fig. 26.2
The File Series dialog box.

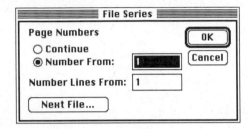

4. Choose Next File.

   You see an Open dialog box.

5. Choose the next file in the series.

   Word shows the name of the next file at the bottom of the File Series dialog box, and the Next file button changes to Reset Next File.

6. Choose OK.

7. Save and close the first document.

8. Open the next document, and repeat steps 2 through 7. In step 6, choose Continue before closing the File Series dialog box so that Word will number the pages consecutively.

9. Repeat step 8 until you have linked all the files, except the last one.

When you link files by using the File Series dialog box, Word automatically prints the next file—and the file linked to the next file, and so on, until all the documents are printed.

To print the linked files with continuous pagination, follow these steps:

1. Open the first document.

2. Choose Print from the File menu.

If you want to print a draft of just the current file, without printing all the rest of the files, deactivate the Print Next File check box in the Print dialog box before printing the document.

Numbering Footnotes Consecutively

n many style guidelines, footnote renumbering restarts at 1 at the beginning of every major section or chapter. Word renumbers exactly this way when you place chapters in separate files and link them for printing. However, you may prefer to number footnotes consecutively. To do so, you must specify the starting footnote number for each file in the series.

To number footnotes consecutively, follow these steps:

1. Open the first document.

2. Choose Footnotes from the View menu to open the footnote window.

3. Scroll to the end of the document, and note the number of the last footnote.

4. Close the document.

5. Open the next document.

6. Choose Document.

   You see the Document dialog box, as shown in figure 26.3.

Fig. 26.3
The Document dialog box.

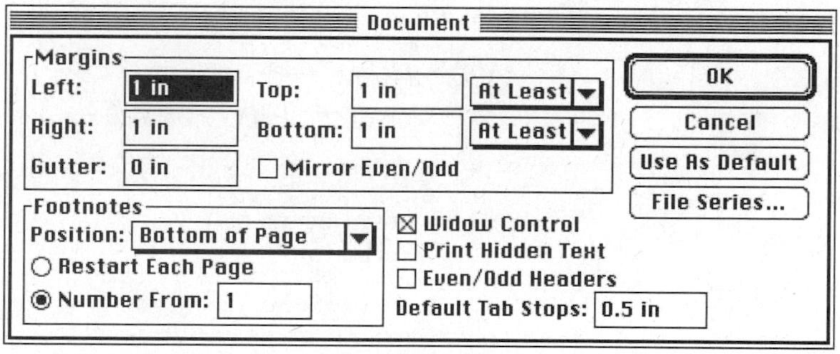

7. In the Number From text box, type the number Word should use to start consecutively numbering the footnote. (To get this number, just add 1 to the number of the last footnote in the previous document.)

Chapter 26
Working with Long Documents

8. Choose OK.

9. Choose Footnote from the View menu.

10. Scroll to the end of the document, and note the last footnote number.

11. Save the document.

12. Close the document.

13. Repeat steps 5 through 12 for all the rest of the documents in the series.

Numbering Lines Consecutively

f you're creating a lengthy legal document that requires continuous line numbering throughout, you must manually set the beginning line number for each of the linked documents in the file series.

To number lines consecutively in a file series, follow these steps:

1. In the first document, choose Section from the Format menu.

2. Choose Line Numbers.

   The Line Numbers dialog box appears.

3. Choose Continuous in the Line Numbers list box.

4. Choose OK.

5. Choose Print Preview.

6. Scroll to the last page.

7. Using the Magnifier icon, determine the last page numbers.

8. Open the next document in the series.

9. Choose Document from the Format menu, and choose the File Series button.

10. In the File Series dialog box, type the starting line number in the Number Lines From box.

11. In the same document, choose Section from the Format menu, and choose the Line Numbers button.

12. Choose Consecutive from the Line Numbers list box, and choose OK.

13. Repeat steps 5 through 12 for each additional document.

Creating an Index and Table of Contents

To add an index and table of contents to a series of files you linked in this way, mark the index entries in all the documents, as explained in Chapter 23. Then open the first document, and compile the index and table of contents just as you would with any other document. Word automatically opens the rest of the documents in the series and extracts the table of contents and index entries. The index and table of contents that Word builds includes correct page numbers.

Assembling a Document Using the Include Command

In previous versions of Word, you used the INCLUDE command, one of Word's Print Merge keywords, to link documents for printing with continuous pagination. In Word 5, the File Series dialog box provides a much easier way to chain files for printing. You still can use the Include command, however—and it even has one advantage: By using INCLUDE, you can *insert* a file *within* another one when you print. (You can't insert a file within another one with File Series, which always starts the next file at the end of the current one.) Because the INCLUDE command is just a placeholder, your document doesn't grow in size beyond a few additional characters. The text is inserted only when it is printed.

A good argument, though, is that you shouldn't use INCLUDE in this way unless the file you are inserting is truly enormous in size. If you are inserting a short or medium-size file (as long as 20 or 30 pages), it may be better to insert the text by using the File or Object commands on the Insert menu. For more information on inserting one file within another with these options, see Chapter 14.

To include one file within another when you print, with continuous pagination, follow these steps:

1. Place the insertion point where you want the file to appear when the document is printed.

2. Choose Print Merge Helper from the View menu.

   You see an Open dialog box.

3. Choose None to open Print Merge Helper without assigning a data document.

4. Choose INCLUDE from the Insert Keyword list box.

   You see an Open dialog box, with a message requesting you to choose the file you want to include.

5. Choose the file you want to include and choose Open.

   Word inserts the INCLUDE command in your document, as shown in figure 26.4.

6. To insert additional documents when you print, repeat steps 3 through 5.

7. Save your document.

Fig. 26.4

The INCLUDE instruction included in a document.

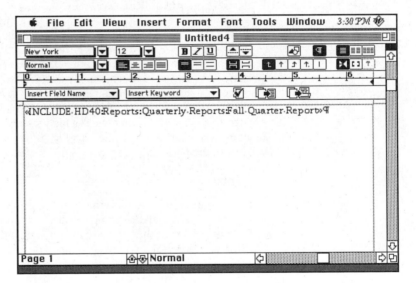

To print the document that contains the INCLUDE instructions, follow these steps:

1. Choose Print Merge from the File menu.

   You see the Print Merge dialog box.

Part II

Creating More Complex Documents

2. Choose an option in the Merge Results area.

   You can choose Merge and Print Results to New File or Merge and Print Results.

3. Choose OK.

Word prints the linked documents with continuous pagination. The included documents take on the formatting from the document in which you placed the INCLUDE commands.

Quick Review

This section concisely summarizes the most useful information in this chapter. Check "Productivity Tips" for a review of high-productivity tips and tricks, and review "Techniques" when you forget how to perform a specific procedure.

Productivity Tips

- If you are creating a lengthy document, break up its chapters or sections into separate files and link them with File Series. Word will run faster, and you eliminate the possibility of losing all your work if even one file becomes corrupted.

- Before starting to write a lengthy document, create a template to store the formats and styles you want each section to have. Save the file as a Stationery document, and retrieve this file to start each chapter or section.

Techniques

This section provides concise, quick-reference summaries of all the procedures introduced in this chapter.

Adding an Index to a File Series Document

To add an index to a File Series document:

1. In each document, mark the terms you want indexed.

2. Open the first document.

..

3. Choose Index from the Insert menu.

4. Choose Start to begin compiling the index for all the linked documents.

Adding a Table of Contents to a File Series Document

To add a table of contents to a File Series document:

1. Format chapter titles, headings, and subheadings using Word's standard Heading styles.

2. Open the first document.

3. Choose Table of Contents from the Insert menu.

4. Choose Outline.

5. In the From and To boxes, indicate the outline levels you want to appear in the table of contents.

6. Choose Start to begin compiling the table of contents.

Creating the Master Template Document for a File Series

To create the master template document:

1. In a new Word document, choose the section and document formats you want to apply to all the files.

2. Create styles for your document, and redefine standard styles to suit your taste or style guidelines.

3. Add headers and footers, and if you didn't choose Margin Page Numbers in the Section dialog box, add page numbers to the header or footer.

4. Choose Select All from the Edit menu to select all the dummy text.

5. Choose Cut to delete the text (but not the styles you have created).

6. Choose Save.

7. In the Save File As Type list box, choose Stationery.

8. In the File Name box, type a name which indicates that the file is a template, such as Report Chapter Template or Thesis Chapter Template.

9. Choose Save.

Linking the Files in a Series

To link files in a series:

1. Open the first document.

2. Choose Document from the Format menu.

3. Choose File Series.

4. Choose Next File.

5. Choose the next file in the series.

6. Choose OK.

7. Save and close the first document.

8. Open the next document, and repeat steps 2 through 7. In step 6, choose Continue before closing the File Series dialog box so that Word will number the pages consecutively.

9. Repeat step 8 until you have linked all the files except the last one.

Numbering Footnotes Consecutively in the File Series

To number footnotes consecutively:

1. Open the first document.

2. Choose Footnotes from the View menu to open the footnote window.

3. Scroll to the end of the document, and note the number of the last footnote.

4. Close the document.

5. Open the next document.

6. Choose Document.

7. In the Number From text box, type the number Word should use to start the footnote numbering consecutively. (To get this number, just add 1 to the number of the last footnote in the previous document.)

8. Choose OK.

9. Choose Footnote from the View menu.

10. Scroll to the end of the document, and note the last footnote number.

Chapter 26
Working with Long Documents

11. Save the document.

12. Close the document.

13. Repeat steps 5 through 12 for all the remaining documents in the series.

Printing Files Linked in a Series

To print the linked files with continuous pagination:

1. Open the first document.

2. Choose Print from the File menu.

Printing Only the Current Document

To print the current document without printing the rest of the files in the file series:

1. Open the document.

2. Choose Print from the File menu.

3. Deactivate the Print Next File check box.

4. Choose Print.

Customizing Word 5

B y now, you have mastered the Word interface—including its menus, keyboard shortcuts, and dialog box defaults—and you may have ideas about how you can improve the interface. In this chapter, you learn how to customize this interface so that Word works exactly the way you want.

The following overview shows you how you can customize this amazing program:

■ You can choose Section, Document, and Page Setup defaults for all your documents. When you choose these options, Word applies them to all the new documents you create.

■ You can choose the operating defaults you want in the Preferences dialog box. You can tell Word to open all documents in Page Layout view, for example.

■ You can add or remove commands from menus. Many Word commands—such as Move to Next Window—aren't listed on menus. If you want, you can add this command, and many more, to an appropriate menu.

■ You also can set up the keyboard the way you want by assigning a keyboard shortcut to any Word command, including many dialog box options.

■ You can create a new menu (called Work) that contains frequently accessed dialog box items, including glossaries. If you often find yourself wading through dialog boxes to choose an option, you can save significant amounts of time by adding such an option to the Work menu.

After you make changes to Word's interface, you save these changes to a customized settings file. Such a file lists all your Preferences dialog box options, keyboard shortcut assignments, menu additions or removals, and Work menu assignments.

You can even create more than one settings file so that you can choose the one that's right for a particular application. You can create a settings file called Letters, for example, which contains keyboard shortcuts, menu items, and Work menu assignments that are appropriate for writing letters. Or you can create another settings file, called Reports, which contains the proper settings for creating business reports with graphics.

The customization procedures may sound complicated, but they're not. They're as easy as the other Word operations you have learned. You also cannot ruin Word by making ill-advised customization choices. With one easy command, you can remove all your customization choices and restore Word to its pristine, default state, just as it was when you first started the program after installation.

This chapter surveys the many techniques you can use to customize Word. The following is an overview of this chapter's sections:

■ *Redefining the Default Style Sheet*. By redefining styles and saving them to the default style sheet, you can change Word's default formats in many ways.

■ *Choosing Page Formatting Defaults*. This section illustrates many ways you can change defaults for page numbers, margins, and other page formatting choices.

■ *Choosing Preferences*. This section surveys the options you can choose in the Preferences dialog box (accessed from the Tools menu).

■ *Understanding Word's Commands*. This section introduces a unique feature of Word, which gives you complete control over just which command names appear on menus.

■ *Customizing Word's Menus*. In this section, you learn how to add commands to menus—and how to remove menus commands you don't use.

- *Customizing Word's Keyboard*. This section surveys the techniques you can use to assign commands to keyboard shortcuts (and how to remove keyboard shortcuts you don't use).

- *Creating a Work Menu*. In this section, you learn how to assign dialog box options to a special Work menu, which Word creates and places right of the Window option on the menu bar.

- *Managing Settings Files*. This section shows you how to save your configuration choices. You also learn how to create two or more alternative settings files, to which you can switch in order to use a different set of configuration choices.

Redefining the Default Style Sheet

A s you learn in Chapter 8, you can save often-used styles to the default style sheet so that you have these styles available for every new document you create. You also can use this technique to redefine many of Word's formatting defaults, which are encoded in the program's standard styles. Word formats footnote text using the Normal font, for example, but uses a 10-point font size. If you find yourself redefining this style every time you open a new document, you should redefine and save the style to the default style sheet.

This section summarizes the procedure you use to redefine styles in the default style sheet. For more information on choosing formats for styles, see Chapter 8.

To redefine a default style, follow these steps:

1. Choose Style from the Format menu or press ⌘-T.

   The Style dialog box appears.

2. Highlight the name of the style you want to change. If necessary, activate the All Styles option.

3. Choose the formats you want.

4. Choose Use as Default.

   You see an alert box with the message OK to record style in default style sheet?

5. Choose OK.

6. Choose Close.

Other styles you may want to redefine include Word's standard heading styles. If you redefine those styles, be sure to choose the Keep with Next option in the Paragraph dialog box so that Word doesn't insert a page break after the heading.

Besides redefining existing styles, you can save newly created styles to the default style sheet. You can create a Text ¶ style with the following formats, for example: Normal font, 12 points, 0.5" first line indentation, one blank line before, double line spacing. If you save this style to the default style sheet, the style appears in the document style sheets of all new documents.

Choosing Page Formatting Defaults

TIP

Reflect on your usage of Word to determine which defaults you should change. What do you do when you open a new Word document? Do you frequently find yourself changing margins, turning on page numbers, or choosing endnotes? If so, reset the defaults so that you don't have to perform such operations every time you create a new document with Word.

SPEED KEY

B y redefining standard styles, you can change the default formats that Word uses when the program inserts elements such as headers, footers, page numbers, and footnotes. However, you cannot redefine page or section formats, such as margins, columns, or page size, by redefining the default style sheet. In this section, you learn how to redefine Word's default section and page formats.

Changing Section Formatting Defaults

The Section dialog box includes many defaults you may want to change (see fig. 27.1). Suppose that you always want your documents to include page numbers printed and centered at the bottom of the page but never want page numbers to appear on the first page. For more information on section formats, see Chapter 16.

To change these Section defaults, follow these steps:

1. Choose Section from the Format menu or press Option-F14.

   The Section dialog box appears.

2. Choose the formats you want Word to apply to the current document and to all the new documents you create.

3. Choose Use as Default.

4. Choose OK.

Your choices apply to the current document and all the subsequent documents you create.

Part II

Creating More Complex Documents

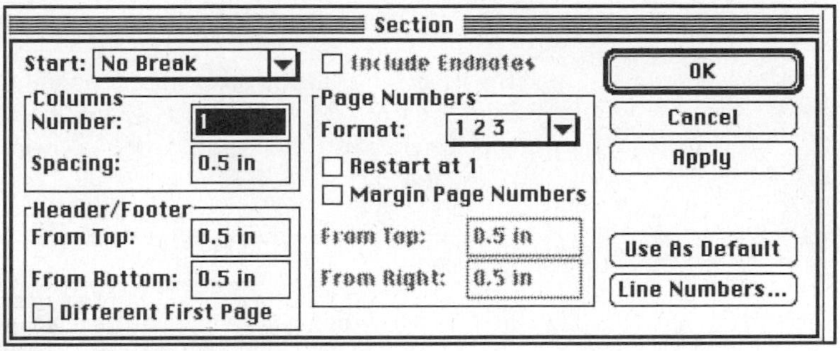

Fig. 27.1
The Section dialog box.

```
┌──────────────────── Section ────────────────────┐
│ Start: [No Break      ▼]  ☐ Include Endnotes    ┌──────────────┐ │
│ ┌Columns──────────┐  ┌Page Numbers────────┐     │      OK      │ │
│ │ Number:  [  1  ] │  │ Format:  [ 1 2 3 ▼]│     └──────────────┘ │
│ │                  │  │                    │     ┌──────────────┐ │
│ │ Spacing: [0.5 in]│  │ ☐ Restart at 1     │     │    Cancel    │ │
│ └──────────────────┘  │ ☐ Margin Page Numbers    └──────────────┘ │
│ ┌Header/Footer────┐   └────────────────────┘     │    Apply     │ │
│ │ From Top: [0.5 in]  From Top:  [0.5 in]   └──────────────┘ │
│ │ From Bottom:[0.5 in] From Right: [0.5 in]  ┌──────────────┐ │
│ │ ☐ Different First Page                      │Use As Default│ │
│ └──────────────────┘                         │ Line Numbers…│ │
└──────────────────────────────────────────────────────────────┘
```

Changing Document Formatting Defaults

To change Word's default document formats, such as margins, use the
Document dialog box's Use as Default button (see fig. 27.2). For more
information on document formats, see Chapter 7.

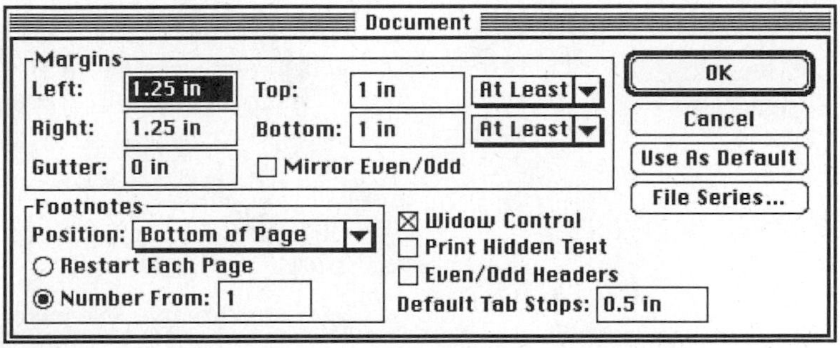

Fig. 27.2
The Document dialog box.

```
┌──────────────────── Document ────────────────────┐
│ ┌Margins─────────────────────────────┐  ┌──────────────┐ │
│ │ Left:  [1.25 in]  Top:   [1 in]  [At Least▼]  │     OK     │ │
│ │ Right: [1.25 in]  Bottom:[1 in]  [At Least▼]  └──────────┘ │
│ │ Gutter:[0 in]  ☐ Mirror Even/Odd  ┌──────────────┐ │
│ └─────────────────────────────────┘  │   Cancel     │ │
│ ┌Footnotes──────────────────────┐    │Use As Default│ │
│ │ Position:[Bottom of Page    ▼] │    │ File Series… │ │
│ │ ○ Restart Each Page    ⊠ Widow Control  └──────┘ │
│ │ ◉ Number From: [1]     ☐ Print Hidden Text │
│ │                        ☐ Even/Odd Headers  │
│ │             Default Tab Stops: [0.5 in]    │
│ └────────────────────────────────────────┘ │
└──────────────────────────────────────────────┘
```

Suppose that you always want Word to open new documents with 1 inch
margins all around, and you prefer to position footnotes at the end of
the document (endnotes). To change these document formatting
defaults, follow these steps:

1. Choose Document from the Format menu.

   You see the Document dialog box.

2. Choose the document formatting options you want Word to apply
   to the current document and to all the new documents you create.

3. Choose Use As Default.

4. Choose OK.

Changing Page Setup Defaults

The Page Setup dialog box varies depending on which printer you're using. Figure 27.3, for instance, shows the Page Setup dialog box that appears after you choose the StyleWriter option in the Chooser desk accessory.

Fig. 27.3
The Page Setup dialog box.

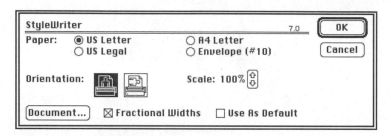

No matter which printer you choose, however, you can choose Page Setup defaults by using the Use as Default check box, which appears in every version of the Page Setup dialog box. You may want to change the Page Setup defaults if you're taking your Mac overseas or if you want to take advantage at all times of other Page Setup options, such as document reduction or enlargement.

To change Page Setup defaults, follow these steps:

1. If you haven't done so, choose your printer using the Chooser desk accessory (from the menu).

2. Choose Page Setup from the File menu or press Shift-F8.

   The Page Setup dialog box appears.

3. Activate the Use as Default option.

4. Choose OK.

Choosing Preferences

With the Preferences option in the Tools menu, you can change many of Word's operating defaults. This section comprehensively surveys these options, many of which have been mentioned or discussed in earlier chapters.

As figure 27.4 shows, the icon list running down the left side of the Preferences dialog box gives you a way of choosing different categories of options. When you choose Preferences, you see the General options (discussed in the next section). Additional options are View, Open And Save, Default Font, Spelling, Grammar, Thesaurus, and Hyphenation. When you choose one of these icons, you see a different set of options to the right of the icon list.

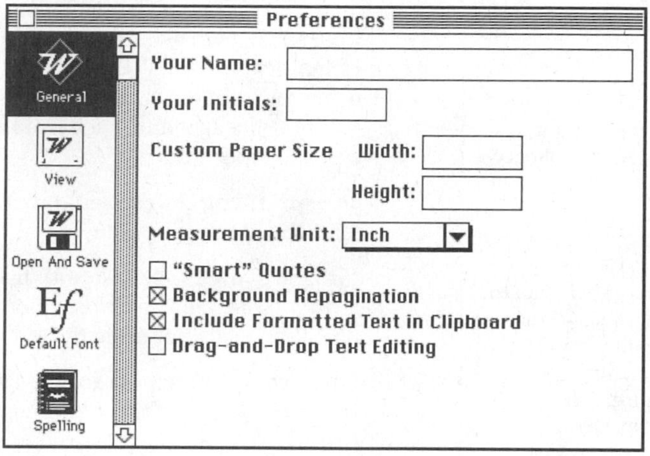

Fig. 27.4
General options in the Preferences dialog box.

The following sections discuss the General, View, and Open And Save options. See Chapter 5 for information on Default Font options. See Chapter 9 for information on the Spelling and Grammar options.

The Thesaurus and Hyphenation options are useful only if you buy optional thesaurus and hyphenation dictionaries other than the ones provided with Word. You can buy such dictionaries from Microsoft. You can use these options to choose these dictionaries so that Word uses them instead of the ones provided with Word. (If you're a North American preparing a document for publication in Britain, for example, you can buy and load the British versions of the thesaurus and hyphenation dictionaries.)

Choosing General Options

In the General list, you see fundamental options that affect the way Word works, including the name it assigns to the files you create, the default measurement unit, and other basic options. You can choose the following options in the General list:

Your Name (default: the name you type when you installed Word). Make sure that this dialog box contains your name so that Word can retrieve your documents.

Your Initials (default: blank). If you have Word 5's new Voice Annotation feature, type your initials here. Word adds your initials to the voice annotation icons you add to your document. (Voice Annotations is a feature available to user's of Macs equipped with full sound capabilities.)

Custom Paper Size (default: blank or dimmed). In the Width and Height text boxes, type the dimensions of special paper you're using for printing, such as mailing labels. This option is dimmed if you're using a printer, such as a LaserWriter, that cannot use custom paper sizes.

Measurement Unit (default: inch). You also can choose centimeters (cm), printer's points (pt), or picas (pi).

"Smart" Quotes (default: off). If you activate "Smart" Quotes, Word enters open and close quotation marks (" ")and apostrophes(' '), instead of using the same character.

Background Repagination (default: on). With this option activated, Word actively repaginates your document while you're writing. You see where page breaks occur. If you're using a sluggish Macintosh, you can deactivate this option to improve Word's performance.

Include Formatted Text in Clipboard (default: on). By default, Word retains character formatting when you copy or cut text via the Clipboard. (Paragraph formatting is retained only if you include the paragraph mark in the selection.) Including formatting requires more memory, however. If your Macintosh's memory is severely limited, you can deactivate this option to reduce the amount of memory required for editing operations.

Drag-and-Drop Text Editing (default: on). Activate this option to take advantage of Word 5's drag-and-drop editing capability, which enables you to move text by dragging the selection. For more information on drag-and-drop editing, see Chapter 4.

TIP

If you're creating a document you want to send to others via modem, be sure to keep the "Smart" Quotes option turned off. "Smart" Quotes enters special Macintosh characters for leading and trailing quotation marks and apostrophes, which come across as odd control characters when you transmit your document as an ASCII text file.

WORD 5

Choosing View Options

When you choose the View icon in the Preferences dialog box, you see the View options, as shown in figure 27.5. These options control what you see on-screen.

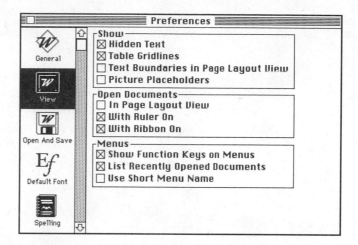

Fig. 27.5
View options in the
Preferences dialog box.

You can choose the following View options:

Show Hidden Text (default: on). When this option is activated, you can see hidden text on-screen. Moreover, Word takes the hidden text into account when computing page breaks. To see how your document is paginated without hidden text, turn this option off.

Show Table Grid lines (default: on). When activated, this option shows the table grid lines when you create a table. (The grid lines don't print.) If you prefer not seeing the grid lines, turn this option off.

Show Text Boundaries in Page Layout View (default: off). With this option active, Word uses gray lines to display the boundaries of columns and frames in Page Layout view. If you turn on text boundaries while working with multiple column text and frames, you have an easier time grasping where you can enter text in your document.

Show Picture Placeholders (default: off). If you have added graphics to your document, you probably have noticed how much the graphics slow down Word's scrolling speed. You can improve that speed dramatically by choosing this option, which substitutes a gray screen for your graphics. Although Word does not show them on-screen, your graphics are still in your document and still print.

Open Documents In Page Layout View (default: off). If you're using a Mac based on the Motorola 68030 processor (or a Quadra), you can choose this option to open documents in Page Layout view instead of the default Normal view. If you use a slower Macintosh, leave this option off so that Word opens documents in Normal view. You always can switch to the much slower Page Layout view to preview page formats before printing.

Open Documents With Ruler On (default: on). The ruler is handy for paragraph formatting, styles, and tabs, but you may want to hide the ruler by deactivating this check box if you use a Classic with a 9-inch screen. You still can toggle the ruler on and off with the Ruler command on the View menu.

Open Documents With Ribbon On (default: on). Like the ruler, one of Word 5's best new features, the ribbon, is handy for formatting (fonts, font sizes, character emphases, and multiple-column formats). You may want to hide the ribbon by deactivating this check box, however, if you use a Classic with a 9-inch screen. You still can toggle the ribbon on and off with the Ribbon command on the View menu.

Show Function Keys on Menus (default: off). If you're using a Macintosh with an extended keyboard including function keys (F1 through F12), choose this option to see function key shortcuts next to menu names.

List Recently Opened Documents (default: on). This useful feature places the names of the four last documents you opened on the File menu. To open one of these documents again quickly, you just choose its name from the File menu.

If you're using Disk Doubler or some other file-compression program to save space on your hard disk, turn off the List Recently Opened Documents option and don't try to open documents this way. When you open a compressed document with the Open dialog box, your file compression program detects the use of this command and decompresses the file. If you open a document with the File menu option, however, the file compression program does not decompress the file.

Use Short Menu Name (default: off). If you choose On, Word shortens the names on the menu bar to give more room (Format becomes Fmt, Window becomes Wnd, and so on). You may want to choose this option if you're running additional programs, such as SuperClock, that require room on the menu bar to display menu names or other information.

Choosing Open and Save Options

When you choose the Open And Save icon in the Preferences dialog box, you see the Open And Save options (see fig. 27.6), which include many important options that can help you to avoid lost work. You can choose the following options:

Fig. 27.6
The Open And Save
options in the Preferences
dialog box.

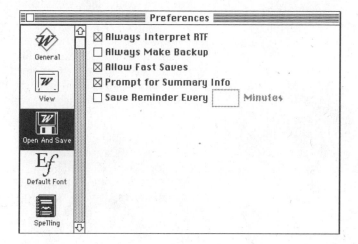

Always Interpret RTF. By default, Word correctly decodes formatting instructions when you import RTF documents. An RTF document has been saved with Microsoft's Rich Text Formatting codes, which enable users of different programs to exchange documents without losing formatting. Because RTF uses only standard ASCII characters, RTF enables you to exchange documents via electronic mail and other telecommunications links without losing formatting. You can save memory, though, by turning this option off.

Always Make Backup. As explained in Chapter 3, this option really doesn't make a backup of your document. If you turn on the option, Word preserves the previous saved version of your file. The default setting, Off, tells Word to overwrite the previous version of a file.

You may want to activate this option if you're the kind of writer who likes to save all preliminary drafts of a work. Turning this option on eats up disk space very quickly, however.

Allow Fast Saves (default: on). This option enables a rapid file-saving technique when you resave a file. Rather than rewrite the whole file, Word saves your changes.

The Fast Save method is as safe as the normal file-saving technique, but requires more memory. If your Mac has limited memory, turn this option off. Note, though, that much more time is needed to save files with the normal technique—as much as several minutes for a file that's a megabyte or more in size.

Prompt for Summary Info (default: on). As explained in Chapter 3, many good reasons exist to fill out Word 5's new Summary Info dialog boxes when you save a document for the first time. If you don't want to do so, deactivate this option so that the Summary Info dialog box doesn't appear when you save a new file.

Save Reminder (default: off). By all means, activate this option and type a reminder interval (such as **10** or **15** minutes) in the text box. Word displays a dialog box, reminding you to save your work. This new Word 5 feature helps you avoid one dangerous aspect of work with the computer—significant work losses due to crashes or power failures.

Customizing Word's Menus

This section discloses a remarkable feature about Word: the program's pull-down menus can be completely customized, showing just the commands you want. And as you will learn, many command options are available that don't currently appear on the menus, such as Assign to Key (a command that enables you to assign a menu option to a key), Copy Formats (available only via a keyboard command by default), and many more.

Word achieves its menu flexibility by separating its commands from the command names that appear in the pull-down menus.

In most programs, all or most of the commands are listed on the menus, and you cannot add or remove any of them. Word, however, draws a complete distinction between its built-in list of commands and the menu command names. You have complete control over which commands appear on menus.

By default, each command is linked to a certain menu. The Set Ruler Scale to Page command, for example—which tells Word to measure the page from the left page edge rather than the left boundary of the text area—is linked to the View menu. If you choose this command and tell Word to add it to the menus, Word adds this command to the View menu. You can override the default menu linkage and control where the item appears on the menu, however.

Many more commands exist than you see on the menus. Should you add each command to the menus, however, the menus become ridiculously long. Figure 27.7 shows a menu with all its commands added.

Fig. 27.7
A menu with all options added.

View	
Normal	⌘⌥N
Outline	⌘⌥O
✓Page Layout	⌘⌥P
Outline On/Off	
Page Layout On/Off	
✓Ribbon	⌘⌥R
✓Open Documents With Ribbon	
✓Ruler	⌘R
✓Open Documents With Ruler	
Show Styles on Ruler	
Set Ruler Scale Normal	
Set Ruler Scale Table	
Set Ruler Scale Page	
Print Merge Helper...	
Quick Record Voice Annotation	
Hide ¶	⌘J

Many Word commands are options available in dialog boxes and on the ribbon and ruler. Table 27.1 lists Word's many commands and their menu linkages. You can add any of these commands to the linked Word menu.

In practice, you can bring to the menus commands that normally are buried deep within dialog boxes. The TLBR Single Paragraph Border command, for example, is basically the Box option you see in the Borders dialog box. (*TLBR* stands for *Top, Left, Bottom, Right*.) If you want to add a single-line box to a paragraph quickly, you can add this command to the Format menu, with which it is linked. (An even better idea is to assign this command to a keyboard shortcut, as explained later in this chapter.)

Many of Word's commands have obvious functions, with which you're already familiar, such as Save (on the File menu). Others are new to you or cryptically named. To find out what a "mysterious" command does, choose Commands from the Tools menu and highlight the name of the command in the list box. You see a brief description of the command's function in the Description list box (see fig. 27.8).

Customize as much as you want, but bear in mind that your changes may make your version of Word look unfamiliar to another Word user. You also may find someone else's version of Word unfamiliar.

Fig. 27.8
The Commands dialog box.

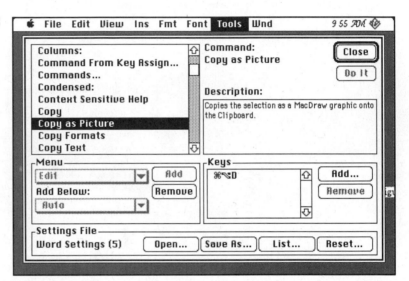

Table 27.1
Commands and Menus
Linkages

Command name	Menu linkage
1-1/2 Line Spaced	Format
9 Point	Font
10 Point	Font
12 Point	Font
14 Point	Font
18 Point	Font
24 Point	Font
About Microsoft Word	(None)
Activate Keyboard Menus	Edit

Part II

Creating More Complex Documents

Command name	Menu linkage
Add to Menu	Tools
All Caps	Format
Alphabetic Page Numbers	Format
Always Interpret RTF	Tools
Always Make Backup Files	Tools
Arabic Page Numbers	Format
Assign to Key	Tools
Athens	Font
Auto Page Numbering	Format
Avant Garde	Font
Background Repagination	Tools
Backspace	(None)
Black	Format
Blue	Format
Bold	Format
Bookman	Font
Border	Format
Cairo	Font
Calculate	Tools
Cancel	(None)
Cell Borders	Format
Centered	Format
Change Case	Format
Change Font	Edit
Change Style	Edit
Character	Format
Chicago	Font
Clear	Edit
Close	File
Close Spacing	Format

continues

Chapter 27
Customizing Word 5

Table 27.1 Continued	Command name	Menu linkage
	Collapse Selection	View
	Collapse Subtext	View
	Columns 1	Format
	Columns 2	Format
	Columns 3	Format
	Command From Key Assignment	Tools
	Commands	Tools
	Condensed 1.5 pt	Format
	Context Sensitive Help	(None)
	Copy	Edit
	Copy as Picture	Edit
	Copy Formats	Edit
	Copy Text	Edit
	Courier	Font
	Create Publisher	Edit
	Cut	Edit
	Cyan	Format
	Date	Insert
	Delete	File
	Default Font	Font
	Default: Cms	Tools
	Default: Inches	Tools
	Default: Picas	Tools
	Default: Points	Tools
	Delete	File
	Delete Cells, Shift Left	Format
	Delete Cells, Shift Up	Format
	Delete Columns	Format
	Delete Forward	Edit
	Delete Next Word	Edit
	Delete Previous Word	Edit

Part II

Creating More Complex Documents

Command name	Menu linkage
Delete Rows	Format
Demote Heading	Edit
Document	Format
Dotted Underline	Format
Double Space	Format
Double Underline	Format
Down	Font
Drag-and-Drop Text Editing	Tools
Edit Link (QuickSwitch)	Edit
Edit Object	Edit
Even Footer	View
Even Header	View
Expand Subtext	View
Expanded 3 pt	Format
Extend to Character	Tools
Fast Save Enabled	Tools
File	Insert
Find Again	Edit
Find File	File
Find Formats	Edit
Find	Edit
First Footer	View
First Header	View
First Line Indent	Format
First Page Special	Format
Flush Left	Format
Flush Right	Format
Footer	View
Footnote Cont. Notice	View
Footnote Cont. Separator	View

continues

Chapter 27
Customizing Word 5

	Command name	Menu linkage
Table 27.1 Continued		
	Footnote Separator	View
	Footnotes	View
	Footnote	Insert
	Fractional Widths	File
	Frame (Format)	Format
	Frame (Insert)	Insert
	Full Repaginate Now	Tools
	Geneva	Font
	Glossary	Edit
	Go Back	Edit
	Go To	Edit
	Grammar	Tools
	Green	Format
	Hanging Indent	Format
	Header	View
	Help	Window
	Helvetica	Font
	Hidden Text	Format
	Hyphenation	Tools
	Include Endnotes in Section	Format
	Include Formatted Text in Clipboard	Tools
	Index Entry	Insert
	Index	Insert
	Insert Cells Down	Format
	Insert Cells Right	Format
	Insert Columns	Format
	Insert Formula	Insert
	Insert Glossary Entry	Edit
	Insert Nonbreaking Hyphen	Insert
	Insert Nonbreaking Space	Insert

Command name	Menu linkage
Insert Optional Hyphen	Insert
Insert Rows	Format
Insert Tab	Insert
Insert ¶ Above Row	Insert
Italic	Format
Italic Cursor	Tools
Justified	Format
Keep Lines Together	Format
Keep with Next ¶	Format
L Thick Paragraph Border	Format
Larger Font Size	Font
Larger Font Size	Font
Line Break	Insert
Line Numbers By Page	Format
Line Numbers By Section	Format
Line Numbers Continuous	Format
Link Options	Edit
List All Fonts	Font
List Recently Opened Documents	Tools
London	Font
Los Angeles	Font
Lower Case	Format
Lowercase Alphabetic Page Numbers	Format
Lowercase Roman Page Numbers	Format
Magenta	Format
Make Backup Files	Tools
Make Body Text	Edit
Merge Cells	Format
Monaco	Font

continues

Chapter 27
Customizing Word 5

Command name	Menu linkage
More Keyboard Prefix	(None)
Move Down One Text Area	Tools
Move Heading Down	Edit
Move Heading Up	Edit
Move Left One Text Area	Tools
Move Right One Text Area	Tools
Move Text	Edit
Move to Bottom of Window	Tools
Move to End of Document	Tools
Move to End of Line	Tools
Move to First Text Area	Tools
Move to Last Text Area	Tools
Move to Next Cell	Tools
Move to Next Character	Tools
Move to Next Line	Tools
Move to Next Page	Tools
Move to Next Paragraph	Tools
Move to Next Sentence	Tools
Move to Next Text Area	Tools
Move to Next Window	Window
Move to Next Word	Tools
Move to Previous Cell	Tools
Move to Previous Character	Tools
Move to Previous Line	Tools
Move to Previous Page	Tools
Move to Previous Paragraph	Tools
Move to Previous Sentence	Tools
Move to Previous Text Area	Tools
Move to Previous Word	Tools
Move to Start of Document	Tools

Table 27.1 Continued

Command name	Menu linkage
Move to Start of Line	Tools
Move to Top of Window	Tools
Move Up One Text Area	Tools
MT Extra	Font
N Helvetica Narrow	Font
Nest Paragraph	Format
New	File
New Century Schlbk	Font
New Paragraph	Insert
New Picture	Insert
New Window	Window
New York	Font
New ¶ After Ins. Point	Insert
New ¶ with Same Style	Insert
No Line Numbers	Format
No Line Numbers in Paragraph	Format
No Paragraph Border	Format
Normal	View
Normal Paragraph	Format
Normal Position	Format
Normal Spacing	Format
Numeric Lock	Tools
Object	Insert
Odd Footer	View
Odd Header	View
Open Any File	File
Open Documents in Page View	View
Open Documents With Ribbon	View
Open Documents With Ruler	View
Open Mail	File

continues

Chapter 27
Customizing Word 5

Table 27.1 Continued	Command name	Menu linkage
	Open Spacing	Format
	Open	File
	Other	Font
	Outline (Format)	Format
	Outline (View)	View
	Outline Command Prefix	Edit
	Outline On/Off	View
	Page Break	Insert
	Page Break Before	Format
	Page Layout	View
	Page Layout On/Off	View
	Page Number	Insert
	Page Setup	File
	Palatino	Font
	Paragraph Borders	Format
	Paragraph	Format
	Paste	Edit
	Paste Cells	Edit
	Paste Link	Edit
	Paste Object	Edit
	Paste Special Character	Edit
	Paste Special	Edit
	Picture	Insert
	Plain Text	Format
	Preferences	Tools
	Print Merge Helper	View
	Print Merge	File
	Print Preview	File
	Print	File
	Promote Heading	Edit
	Prompt for Summary Info	Tools

Part II

Creating More Complex Documents

Command name	Menu linkage
Quick Record Voice Annotation	View
Quit	File
Red	Format
Redefine Style From Selection	Format
Remove From Menu	Tools
Renumber	Tools
Repaginate Now	Tools
Repeat	Edit
Replace	Edit
Reset Footnote Cont. Notice	View
Reset Footnote Cont. Separator	View
Reset Footnote Separator	View
Restart Page Numbering at 1	Format
Revert To Style	Format
Ribbon	View
Roman Page Numbers	Format
Ruler	View
Same As Previous	View
San Francisco	Font
Save	File
Save As	File
Save Copy As	File
Screen Test	Tools
Scroll Line Down	Tools
Scroll Line Up	Tools
Scroll Screen Down	Tools
Scroll Screen Up	Tools
Section Break	Insert

continues

Chapter 27
Customizing Word 5

Table 27.1 Continued	Command name	Menu linkage
	Section Starts on Even Page	Format
	Section Starts on New Column	Format
	Section Starts on New Page	Format
	Section Starts on Odd Page	Format
	Section Starts with No Break	Format
	Section	Format
	Select All	Edit
	Send Mail	File
	Sentence Case	Format
	Set Ruler Scale Normal	View
	Set Ruler Scale Page	View
	Set Ruler Scale Table	View
	Shadow	Format
	Shortened Menu Names	Tools
	Show All Headings	View
	Show Body Text	View
	Show Clipboard	Window
	Show Formatting	View
	Show Function Keys on Menus	Tools
	Show Heading 1	View
	Show Heading 2	View
	Show Heading 3	View
	Show Heading 4	View
	Show Heading 5	View
	Show Heading 6	View
	Show Heading 7	View
	Show Heading 8	View
	Show Heading 9	View
	Show Hidden Text	View
	Show Styles on Ruler	View
	Show Table Grid lines	View

Command name	Menu linkage
Show Text Boundaries	View
Show/Hide ¶	View
Side by Side	Format
Single Line Spaced	Format
Small Caps	Format
Smaller Font Size	Font
Smart Quotes	Tools
Sort	Tools
Sort Descending	Tools
Spelling	Tools
Split Cell	Format
Split Window	View
Strikethru	Format
Style	Format
Subscribe To	Edit
Subscript 2 pt	Format
Summary Info	File
Superscript 3 pt	Format
Symbol	Font
Symbol Font	(None)
Symbol	Insert
Table Cells	Format
Table Layout	Format
Table of Contents	Insert
Table to Text	Insert
Table	Insert
Tabs	Format
Text to Table	Insert
Thesaurus	Tools
Time	Insert

continues

Chapter 27
Customizing Word 5

Table 27.1 Continued	Command name	Menu linkage
	Times	Font
	Title Case	Format
	TLBR Single Paragraph Border	Format
	TLBR Single Shadow Paragraph Border	Format
	TOC Entry	Insert
	Toggle Case	Format
	Unassign Keystroke	Tools
	Underline	Format
	Undo	Edit
	Unnest Paragraph	Format
	Up	Font
	Update Link	Edit
	Upper Case	Format
	Use Picture Placeholders	View
	Venice	Font
	Voice Annotation	Insert
	Voice Annotations	View
	White	Format
	Word Count	Tools
	Word Underline	Format
	Yellow	Format
	Zapf Chancery	Font
	Zapf Dingbats	Font
	Zoom to Fill Screen	Window

Adding Commands to the Menus

As Table 27.1 suggests, a wealth of command resources lies within Word's Commands command. If you like to choose commands from the pull-down menus, you may want to add one or more commands.

You can customize Word's pull-down menus in two ways:

■ *Using the keyboard shortcut.* By far the easier of the two techniques, this one enables you to add or remove dialog box, ribbon, or ruler items to or from menus quickly. Word adds the item to the menu to which it is linked by default.

■ *Using the Commands dialog box.* You can use this dialog box to add commands to the menus to which they're linked—and if you want, you can override the default linkage. You even can specify where the command should appear on the menu. You also can remove commands from menus by using this dialog box.

Adding Menu Items with the Keyboard

You can use the keyboard to add an item buried within a submenu or dialog box so that the item is available on the top level of the pull-down menus. You can choose many options on Word's dialog boxes, including items in list boxes and many of the options you see in check boxes. You also can use this technique to add to the menus items you see on the ruler.

To add menu items with the keyboard, follow these steps:

1. Display the option you want to add.

2. Press ⌘-Option-plus sign (use the keyboard, not the numeric keypad).

   The pointer becomes a big plus sign. (To cancel, press Esc or ⌘-period.)

3. Choose the option you want to add.

Word adds the item to the appropriate menu. If you choose a glossary entry, style, or document name, Word creates a new menu called Work and places it to the right of the Window menu. (For more information on the Work menu, see "Creating a Work Menu" later in this chapter.)

Removing Menu Items with the Keyboard

To clean up the menus, you can delete items. If you don't plan to create documents with indexes or tables of contents, for example, you can delete the Index Entry and TOC Entry commands from the Insert menu.

Don't worry about adverse consequences of deleting menu items. If you delete an item from a menu, you haven't sent the item off to a computer version of Nowhere. You can retrieve the item by using the Commands dialog box or the keyboard technique.

To delete menu items with the keyboard, follow these steps:

SPEED KEY

1. Press ⌘-Option-hyphen.

   The pointer becomes a big minus sign. To cancel, press Esc or ⌘-period.

2. Choose the command you want to remove, as if you were choosing the command normally. Word deletes the command instead of carrying it out.

Adding Menu Items with the Commands Dialog Box

The Commands dialog box provides tools for adding items to Word's menus (refer to fig. 27.8). Using this dialog box has two major advantages over the keyboard technique: you can add items that aren't available now in dialog boxes, and you can choose the menu in which Word places the command. You even can determine where Word places the item in the menu.

The list box in the Commands dialog box includes every Word command, alphabetized by name. For a complete list, browse through table 27.1 to get an excellent idea of Word 5's power and versatility. Look more carefully, however, for commands not assigned to menus or keys that may prove useful to you in your work.

To add a command to Word's menus, follow these steps:

1. Choose Commands from the Tools menu.

   The Commands dialog box appears (refer to fig. 27.8).

2. In the list box, choose the item you want to add to a menu.

   The Description box briefly indicates what the command does.

If a colon follows the name of the item you have chosen, you must choose from a drop-down list box, which appears under the word Command in the center panel of the box. In figure 27.9, for example, the Columns: option produces the list box shown to the right of the command list. Choose the item you want from this drop-down list so that the correct option appears in the text box at the top of the list.

Fig. 27.9
A command drop-down
list box.

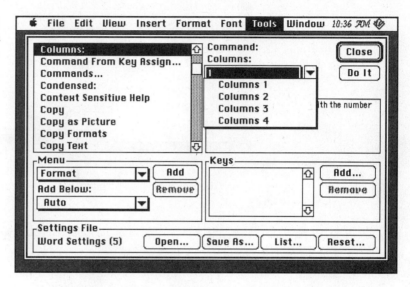

After you choose the command you want, the Menu section shows the name of the menu to which the command is linked. If the Menu area is grayed, the command already appears on a menu. If you want to move the command to another menu, remove the item by following the directions in the next section and then add the command to the new menu. Alternatively, choose another command to add or choose Close to return to your document.

3. If you want to change the default menu linkage, drop down the Menu list for a list of the menu names (see fig. 27.10). Choose the menu to which you want to add the command.

4. If you want to choose where the command appears on the menu you have chosen, drop down the Add Below list box and choose the name of the command below which you want the command name to appear.

5. Choose Add to add the item to the menu you have chosen.

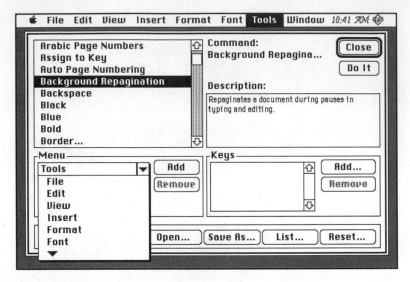

6. Choose Close to return to your document.

Removing Menu Items with the Commands Dialog Box

When you highlight in the Commands dialog box a command that's already on a menu, Word dims the Menu and Add Below list boxes. The program also enables the Remove button, which you can choose to remove the item from the menu.

To remove an item from a menu using the Commands dialog box, follow these steps:

1. Choose Commands from the Tools menu or press ⌘-Shift-Option-C.

   The Commands dialog box appears.

2. Highlight the name of the command you want to remove.

3. Choose Remove.

4. Choose Close.

Word saves your Commands dialog box choices when you exit the program. You lose your choices, however, if you cannot quit Word in the normal fashion (by choosing Quit from the File menu) due to a crash or power failure. To make sure that you save your Command changes,

Part II

Creating More Complex Documents

choose the Save As button and then choose Save to overwrite the existing settings file. For more information on settings files, see the section titled "Managing Settings Files" later in this chapter.

Customizing Word's Keyboard

If you're a good typist, you may want to assign some additional commands to keyboard shortcuts or change existing assignments. See Appendix B for a list of keyboard shortcuts. Table 27.2 lists the commands that now aren't assigned to keyboard shortcuts.

Table 27.2

Commands Not Assigned to Keyboard Shortcuts

1-1/2 Line Spaced	Context Sensitive Help	Geneva
9 Point	Copy	Green
10 Point	Courier	Header
12 Point	Create Publisher	Help
14 Point	Cut	Helvetica
18 Point	Cyan	Include Endnotes in Section
24 Point	Date	Include Formatted Text in
About Microsoft Word	Default Font	Clipboard
Alphabetic Page Numbers	Default: Cms	Index Entry
Always Interpret RTF	Default: Inches	Index
Always Make Backup Files	Default: Picas	Insert Cells Down
Arabic Page Numbers	Default: Points	Insert Cells Right
Athens	Delete Cells, Shift Left	Insert Columns
Auto Page Numbering	Delete Cells, Shift Up	Insert Tab
Avant Garde	Delete Columns	Italic
Background Repagination	Delete Forward	Italic Cursor
Backspace	Delete	Keep Lines Together
Black	Demote Heading	Keep with Next ¶
Blue	Drag-and-Drop Text Editing	Line Numbers By Page
Bold	Edit Object	Line Numbers By Section
Bookman	Even Footer	Line Numbers Continuous
Border	Even Header	Link Options
Business Report	Expand Subtext	List All Fonts
Cairo	Expanded 3 pt	List Recently Opened Documents
Calligraphic	Fast Save Enabled	London
Cancel	File	Los Angeles
Cell Borders	Find File	Lower Case
Change Case	Find Formats	Lowercase Alphabetic Page Numbers
Character	First Footer	Lowercase Roman Page Numbers
Chicago	First Header	Magenta
Clear	First Page Special	Make Backup Files
Close Spacing	Footer	Make Body Text
Collapse Selection	Footnote Cont. Notice	Merge Cells
Collapse Subtext	Footnote Cont. Separator	Monaco
Columns 1	Footnote Separator	Move Heading Down
Columns 2	Fractional Widths	Move Heading Up
Columns 3	Frame (Format)	Move to Bottom of Window
Command From Key Assignment	Frame (Insert)	Move to Next Cell
Condensed 1.5 pt	Full Repaginate Now	Move to Next Character

continues

Chapter 27

Customizing Word 5

Move to Next Line	Red	Show Styles on Ruler
Move to Previous Character	Redefine Style From Selection	Show Table Gridlines
Move to Previous Line	Repaginate Now	Show Text Boundaries
Move to Top of Window	Reset Footnote Cont. Notice	Side by Side
MT Extra	Reset Footnote Cont. Separator	Single Line Spaced
N Helvetica Narrow	Reset Footnote Separator	Smart Quotes
New	Restart Page Numbering at 1	Sort
New Century Schlbk	Revert To Style	Sort Descending
New Paragraph	Roman Page Numbers	Spelling
New Picture	Same As Previous	Split Cell
New York	San Francisco	Subscribe To
No Line Numbers	Save	Summary Info
No Line Numbers in Paragraph	Save Copy As	Symbol
Normal Position	Screen Test	Symbol
Normal Spacing	Scroll Screen Down	Table Cells
Numeric Lock	Scroll Screen Up	Table Layout
Object	Section Starts on Even Page	Table of Contents
Odd Footer	Section Starts on New Column	Table to Text
Odd Header	Section Starts on New Page	Table
Open Documents in Page View	Section Starts on Odd Page	Tabs
Open Documents With Ribbon	Section Starts with No Break	Text to Table
Open Documents With Ruler	Send Mail	Thesaurus
Open Mail	Sentence Case	Time
Open	Set Ruler Scale Normal	Times
Other	Set Ruler Scale Page	Title Case
Outline On/Off	Set Ruler Scale Table	TLBR Single Paragraph Border
Page Break Before	Shortened Menu Names	TLBR Single Shadow Paragraph Border
Page Layout	Show All Headings	
Page Layout On/Off	Show Body Text	TOC Entry
Page Number	Show Clipboard	Toggle Case
Palatino	Show Formatting	Underline
Paragraph Borders	Show Function Keys on Menus	Undo
Paste	Show Heading 1	Untitled1
Paste Cells	Show Heading 2	Upper Case
Paste Special	Show Heading 3	Use Picture Placeholders
Preferences	Show Heading 4	Venice
Print Merge Helper	Show Heading 5	Voice Annotation
Print Merge	Show Heading 6	Voice Annotations
Print	Show Heading 7	White
Promote Heading	Show Heading 8	Yellow
Prompt for Summary Info	Show Heading 9	Zapf Chancery
Quick Record Voice Annotation	Show Hidden Text	Zapf Dingbats
		Zoom to Fill Screen

You can assign commands to keyboard shortcuts in two ways:

- *Using the keyboard.* Press ⌘-Option-plus sign and, when the pointer changes to a big plus sign, choose an existing menu option, dialog box option, or button.

- *Using the Commands dialog box.* You can create keyboard shortcuts for commands that now aren't listed on the menus.

Part II

Creating More Complex Documents

As you plan keyboard shortcuts, remember that you must use certain key combinations, which table 27.3 lists. You can use no more than four keys in a keyboard shortcut. If you're assigning numeric keypad keys, make sure that Num Lock mode is off. If you have an extended keyboard, you can reassign the function keys. You cannot create keyboard shortcuts with the Escape, Tab, Enter, or Return keys, nor can you redefine ⌘-period.

Table 27.3
Available Key Combinations

⌘-*character*	Control-*character*
⌘-Control-*character*	Control-Shift-*character*
⌘-Option-*character*	Control-Shift-Option-*character*
⌘-Shift-*character*	Option-*keypad character*
⌘-Shift-Option-*character*	Shift-*keypad character*
⌘-Control-Option-*character*	Shift-Option-*keypad character*
⌘-Control-Shift-*character*	

Note, too, that certain ⌘ key combinations distinguish Word's default keyboard assignments, as follows:

⌘. Chooses a command, using (as far as possible) the standard Macintosh nomenclature (⌘-X for Cut, ⌘-S for Save, and so on)

⌘-Option. Chooses an editing command, such as scrolling the screen or deleting text

⌘-Shift. Chooses formatting commands, such as italic, boldface, or flush-right paragraphs

You can assign more than one keyboard shortcut to a single command—and, as you discover while you browse through the current keyboard assignments listed in Appendix B, Microsoft already has assigned some. (Many commands have two keyboard shortcuts—one of them being a function key shortcut for users of extended keyboards.)

Using the Keyboard Technique

To assign a keyboard shortcut with ⌘-Option-plus sign (from the keypad, not the keyboard), follow these steps:

TIP

Avoid reassigning any of the ⌘-*character* shortcuts that are part of Apple's standards for all Macintosh programs, such as ⌘-A (Select All), ⌘-S (Save), and ⌘-X (Cut). If you reassign these keys, you may become confused when using another program.

1. Press ⌘-Option-keypad plus sign. The pointer becomes a ⌘ symbol.

   If you see a big plus sign, you pressed ⌘-Option-keyboard plus sign. Press Esc or ⌘-period and try again.

2. Use the ⌘ pointer to choose the menu item you want.

3. When an alert box prompts you for the key combination you want to assign to the chosen command, press the desired keys.

   To assign the command to the key sequence ⌘-Control-B, for instance, press these keys as though you were giving the command at the keyboard.

4. If the key is assigned already, an alert box warns you that you will erase the existing key definition. To erase the existing assignments, choose OK.

Using the Commands Dialog Box

With the Commands dialog box, you can choose from many commands not on the menus. You also can delete existing keyboard assignments when you assign new ones.

To assign a command to Word's keyboard by using the Commands dialog box, follow these steps:

1. Choose Commands from the Tools menu.

2. Scroll the list box and choose the command you want to assign to a shortcut.

3. When you have selected the command you want to assign to a keyboard shortcut, look at the Keys list, which lists all keyboard shortcuts already assigned to the chosen command.

   Figure 27.11 shows the current key assignments, listed in the Keys list, for the Plain Text command.

4. Choose Add.

   A dialog box prompts you to press the key combination you want to use, as shown in figure 27.12.

5. Press the key combination you want to use as though you were giving the command.

   Press Control-space bar, for example, to assign the command to those keys.

Fig. 27.11
Current key assignments
for the Plain Text
command.

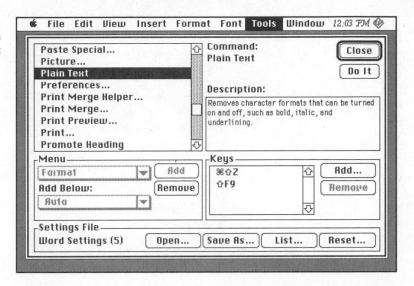

Fig. 27.12
Assigning a command to a
key combination.

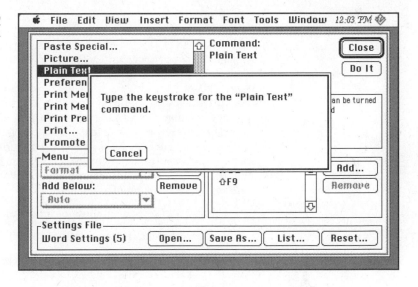

6. If you see an alert box warning you that the shortcut keys are assigned already, think twice about reassigning them. If you're sure that you want to redefine the shortcut keys, choose OK. Otherwise, choose Cancel.

7. Choose Close to close the Commands dialog box.

Chapter 27
Customizing Word 5

Deleting Keyboard Shortcuts

As mentioned earlier, try to avoid deleting existing keyboard shortcuts. You may want to delete, however, if you find yourself continually pressing a key by accident. ⌘-N (New), for example, is easy to press by accident when you're trying to press ⌘-B (Bold), and inadvertently reach too far. Pressing the former key combination by accident also causes a hassle: Word opens a new document, which you must close to return to your work.

To delete an unwanted keyboard shortcut, follow these steps:

1. Choose Commands from the Tools menu.

2. In the Commands dialog box, select the name of the command to which the keyboard shortcut is assigned.

   You see the keyboard assignment in the Keys area.

3. Select the key assignment you want to delete.

4. Choose Remove.

5. Choose Close to return to your document.

Assigning Styles to Keyboard Shortcuts

As you already have learned, you can save the styles you create to the default style sheet or to the document style sheet. (See Chapter 8 for more information on styles.) If you save a style to the default style sheet, the style is automatically available in all the documents you open or create. Assigning default styles to keyboard shortcuts makes good sense. You also can assign a document style to a keyboard shortcut, but keep in mind that the key will work only when you have placed the insertion point in the document containing that style.

To assign styles to keyboard shortcuts, follow these steps:

1. Choose Commands from the Tools menu or press ⌘-Shift-Option-C.

2. In the Commands dialog box, choose Apply Style Name from the list box.

   A drop-down list box lists the styles available in this document.

3. Choose the style.

   Word displays the name of the style you have chosen in the Apply Style Name list box.

4. Choose Add in the Keys area.

   A dialog box prompts you to press the key combination you want to use for this style.

5. Press the key combination you want to usc.

6. Choose Close to return to your document.

Assigning Glossary Entries to Keyboard Shortcuts

If you like to choose options with the keyboard, use this additional time-saving trick: You can assign glossary entries to keyboard shortcuts.

To assign a glossary entry to a keyboard shortcut, follow these steps:

1. Choose Commands from the Tools menu or press ⌘-Shift-Option-C.

   The Commands dialog box appears.

2. Choose Glossary Entry from the list box.

   A drop-down box lists the available glossary entries.

3. Choose the entry you want assigned to a key.

   Word displays the name of the style you have chosen in the Glossary Entry list box.

4. Choose Add in the Keys area.

   A dialog box prompts you to press the key combination you want to use for this style.

5. Press the key combination you want to use.

6. Choose Close to return to your document.

Creating a Work Menu

n this section, you learn a valuable customization technique—creating a new menu (called Work), which Word positions to the right of the Window menu and to which you can add often-accessed styles, glossary entries, and document names. Figure 27.13, for example, shows a Work menu with two frequently used glossary entries added. You can easily add these items to the Work menu. You press ⌘-Option-plus sign so that the insertion point changes to a big plus sign, and then choose the style, glossary, or document as if you were applying, inserting, or opening it. Instead of carrying out the action, Word adds the item to the Work menu. If the Work menu doesn't exist, Word creates it the first time you add an item.

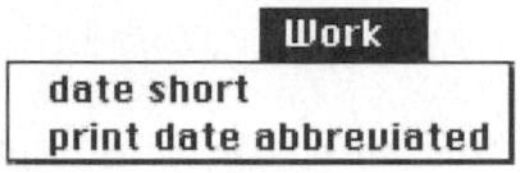

Fig. 27.13

A Work menu with two frequently used glossary entries.

Work
date short
print date abbreviated

To create a Work menu (if it doesn't already exist) and add an item to it, follow these steps:

1. Press ⌘-Option-plus sign (use the keyboard, not the numeric keypad).

   The pointer changes to a big plus sign.

TIP

If you have created stationery documents, as described in Chapter 11, add their names to the Work menu so that you can open them quickly.

2. Choose the name of the glossary entry, style, or document you want to add to the Work menu. Use the appropriate command and choose the option you want, as if you were carrying out the command. If you're adding a document to the menu, choose Open from the File menu and choose the document's name from the file list.

   Word adds the option to the Work menu instead of applying the style.

Word adds the glossary entry, style, or document to the Work menu.

Managing Settings Files

W hen you start Word for the first time, the program creates a file called Word Settings (5), which is stored in your Mac's System folder (System 6) or in the Preferences folder of the System folder (System 7). As you redefine the default style sheet, choose preferences, customize the menus, and create new keyboard shortcuts, Word stores your choices in this file.

If you know how to save and open settings files, you can create two or more versions of Word, each configured in a different way. By changing settings files, you can change the way Word functions.

Knowing how to change settings files also gives you access to five alternative settings files, which you can choose to make Word resemble another program. The Settings Files folder, which was created in the Word folder when you installed the program, contains settings files for MacWrite II, Word 4.0, Word for Windows (Version 2), and Short menus (a simplified version of Word 5). Note that these settings files cannot change the way Word saves files, handles formatting, or deals with document elements such as headers, footnotes, or page numbers. They just rearrange the menus to make Word resemble another program.

If you're switching to Word 5 from Word 4 or MacWrite II, you can choose one of these settings files to ease the transition, but doing so isn't recommended. Word 5's menus give you access to Word 5's features; the other options disguise these features. Because you bought Word 5 for its advanced features, you probably will want to learn Word 5's menus.

The exception to this suggestion is the Word for Windows (Version 2) option. If you use Word for Windows on another machine, such as a 386 system at your office, you may want to choose the Word for Windows settings file for Word 5. You then can move effortlessly between your Mac system and the Windows system. Word for Windows (Version 2) closely resembles Word 5, so you don't lose functionality by choosing the Word for Windows settings file.

Saving Your Settings File

Before experimenting with different settings files, be sure to save your current settings file. When you save your configuration choices, you can save these choices to the default configuration file or give the settings a new name, preserving the original settings file intact.

Unless you want to create different settings files for different purposes—such as a settings file for letters and another for reports—you probably should save your settings choices to the Word Settings (5) default configuration file. Don't worry about messing up Microsoft's defaults. Later, in "Restoring the Defaults," you learn how to remove your changes and restore the settings file to the original defaults.

To save your settings file, follow these steps:

1. Choose Commands from the Tools menu or press ⌘-Shift-Option-C.

2. In the Commands dialog box, choose Save As.

   The Save As dialog box appears. Word proposes the name of the default settings file.

3. Choose Save to overwrite the default settings file. Alternatively, type a new name and then choose Save.

   The Commands dialog box reappears. Word displays the name of the current settings file in the Settings area.

4. Choose Close to return to your document.

Switching Settings Files

To switch to a new settings file, follow these steps:

1. Choose Commands from the Tools menu.

2. In the Commands dialog box, choose Save As to save the current settings file.

   The Commands dialog box reappears.

3. Choose Open.

   The Open dialog box appears.

4. Locate the settings file you want to open.

   You find several sample settings files in the Settings Files folder, located within Word's folder.

5. Choose Open.

   Word displays the name of the current settings file in the Settings area.

6. Choose Close to close the Commands dialog box.

Restoring the Defaults

If you're unhappy with the changes you have made to Word, you can undo those changes quickly by reverting to the last saved version of the configuration file or by restoring Microsoft's defaults.

Part II

Creating More Complex Documents

To undo your configuration choices, follow these steps:

1. Choose Commands from the Tools menu or press ⌘-Shift-Option-C.

2. Choose Reset.

    The dialog box shown in figure 27.14 appears.

Fig. 27.14
Choosing reset options.

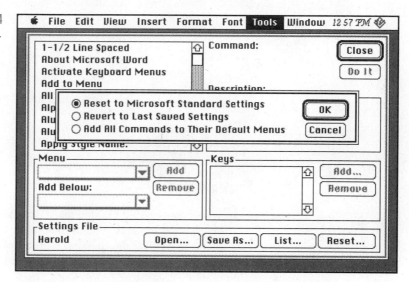

3. Choose one of the options.

    You can choose to reset to Microsoft's standard settings, to revert to the last saved settings, or to add all commands to their default menus. (The last option isn't recommended unless you thrive on information overload.)

4. Choose OK.

Listing Key Assignments

As you customize Word's menus and keyboards, you find that creating a list of key assignments is handy. Word generates an up-to-date list that also shows current menu assignments.

To create a list of key assignments, do the following:

1. Choose Commands from the Tools menu or press ⌘-Shift-Option-C.

2. Choose List.

Word creates a table of all Word commands and their key assignments, and puts the table in a new, untitled document. You can print the document and save it, if you want.

Quick Review

This section concisely summarizes the most useful information in this chapter. Check "Productivity Tips" for a review of high-productivity tips and tricks, and review "Techniques" when you forget how to perform a specific procedure.

Productivity Tips

- You can customize Word in many ways. If you often find yourself changing margins or other formats after you create a new document or plowing through dialog boxes to locate frequently accessed commands, you probably can save much time by customizing Word's defaults.

- You can redefine Word's standard styles so that they enter the formats you want. Add to the default style sheet any custom styles that you use in all or most documents.

- You can redefine Section, Document, and Page Setup options by choosing the Use As Default option in these dialog boxes. With this technique, you can make such changes as turning on page numbers for all new documents, resetting the margins, and choosing a different page size.

- If you're using a slow Macintosh, choose Preferences. Turn off Background Repagination and make sure that the Open Documents in Page View option is deactivated. Activate the Use Picture Placeholders option.

- If your Macintosh is low on memory, choose Preferences and turn off the Include Formatted Text in Clipboard, Always Interpret RTF, and Allow Fast Saves options.

- Add frequently accessed dialog box options to the menus. Remove from the menus commands you don't use.

- If you like to use the keyboard to choose commands, assign frequently accessed dialog box options, styles, and glossary entries to keyboard shortcuts.

- Create a Work menu that contains the names of frequently accessed glossary entries, styles, and stationery (and other) documents.

Techniques

This section provides concise, quick-reference summaries of all the procedures introduced in this chapter.

Adding Commands to Menus

To add a dialog box or ruler option to the menus using the keyboard technique:

1. Display the option you want to add.

2. Press ⌘-Option-plus sign (use the keyboard, not the numeric keypad).

3. Choose the option you want to add.

To add a command to Word's menus with the Commands dialog box:

1. Choose Commands from the Tools menu or press ⌘-Shift-Option-C.

2. In the list box on the Commands dialog box, choose the item you want to add to a menu.

3. If a colon follows the name of the item you have chosen, you must choose from a drop-down list box. Choose the item you want from the list so that the correct option appears in the text box at the top of the list.

4. If you want to change the default menu linkage, drop down the Menu list. Choose the menu to which you want to add the command.

5. If you want to choose where the command appears on the menu you have chosen, drop down the Add Below list box and choose the name of the command below which you want the command name to appear.

6. Choose Add to add the item to the menu you have chosen.

7. Choose Close to return to your document.

Adding Styles, Glossary Entries, and Document Names to the Work Menu

To add glossary entries, styles, or document names to the Work menu (and create the menu, if it doesn't exist):

1. Press ⌘-Option-plus sign (use the keyboard, not the numeric keypad).

2. Choose the name of the glossary entry, style, or document you want to add to the Work menu. If you're adding a document to the menu, choose Open.

Assigning Commands to Keyboard Shortcuts

To assign a keyboard shortcut with ⌘-Option-keypad plus sign:

1. Press ⌘-Option-keypad plus sign. To cancel, press Esc or ⌘-period.

2. Use the plus sign-shaped pointer to choose the menu item you want.

3. When an alert box appears, prompting you to press the key combination you want to assign to the chosen command, press the desired keys.

4. If the key is already assigned, an alert box warns you that you will erase the existing key definition. To erase the existing assignments, choose OK.

To assign a command to Word's keyboard by using the Commands dialog box:

1. Choose Commands from the Tools menu or press ⌘-Shift-Option-C.

2. Scroll the list box to choose the command you want to assign to a shortcut.

3. After you select the command you want to assign to a keyboard shortcut, look at the Keys list, which lists all keyboard shortcuts already assigned to the chosen command.

4. Choose Add.

5. Press the key combination you want to use as though you were giving the command.

6. If you see an alert box warning you that the shortcut keys already are assigned, think twice about reassigning them. If you're sure that you want to redefine the shortcut keys, choose OK.

7. Choose Close to close the Commands dialog box.

Assigning Glossary Entries to Keyboard Shortcuts

To assign a glossary entry to a keyboard shortcut:

1. Choose Commands from the Tools menu or press ⌘-Shift-Option-C.

2. Choose Glossary Entry from the list box.

3. Choose the entry you want assigned to a key.

4. Choose Add in the Keys area.

5. Press the key combination you want to use.

6. Choose Close to return to your document.

Assigning Styles to Keyboard Shortcuts

To assign a style to a keyboard shortcut:

1. Choose Commands from the Tools menu or press ⌘-Shift-Option-C.

2. Choose Apply Style Name from the list box.

3. Choose the style.

4. Choose Add in the Keys area.

5. Press the key combination you want to use.

6. Choose Close to return to your document.

Changing Document Formatting Defaults

To change document formatting defaults:

1. Choose Document from the Format menu.

2. Choose the document formatting options you want Word to apply to the current document and to all the new documents you create.

3. Choose Use As Default.

4. Choose OK.

Changing Page Setup Defaults

To change Page Setup defaults:

1. If you haven't done so, choose your printer using the Chooser desk accessory (on the ★ menu).

2. Choose Page Setup from the File menu or press Shift-F8.

3. Activate Use as Default.

4. Choose OK.

Changing Section Formatting Defaults

To change Section defaults:

1. Choose Section from the Format menu or press Option-14.

2. Choose the Section formats you want Word to apply to the current document and to all the new documents you create.

3. Choose Use as Default.

4. Choose OK.

Choosing Preferences

To choose preferences:

1. Choose Preferences from the Tools menu.

2. To access preferences other than the General preferences, click an icon.

3. Choose the option you want.

4. Click the Close box.

Deleting Keyboard Shortcuts

To delete an unwanted keyboard shortcut:

1. Choose Commands from the Tools menu.

2. Highlight the name of the command to which the keyboard shortcut is assigned.

3. Select the key assignment you want to delete.

4. Choose Remove.

5. Choose Close to return to your document.

Redefining Styles in the Default Style Sheet

To redefine a default style:

1. Choose Style from the Format menu or press ⌘-T.

2. Highlight the name of the style you want to change. If necessary, activate the All Styles option.

3. Choose the formats you want.

4. Choose Use as Default.

5. Choose OK.

6. Choose Close.

Removing a Command from the Menus

To remove menu items with the keyboard:

1. Press ⌘-Option-hyphen.

2. Choose the command you want to remove.

To remove a menu item using the Commands dialog box:

1. Choose Commands from the Tools menu or press ⌘-Shift-Option-C.

2. Select the name of the command you want to remove.

3. Choose Remove.

4. Choose Close.

Saving Your Settings File

To save your settings file:

1. Choose Commands from the Tools menu or press ⌘-Shift-Option-C.

2. Choose Save As.

3. Choose Save to overwrite the default settings file. Alternatively, type a new name and choose Save.

4. Choose Close to return to your document.

Switching Settings Files

To switch to a different settings file:

1. Choose Commands from the Tools menu.

2. In the Commands dialog box, choose Save As to save the current settings file.

3. Choose Open.

4. Locate the settings file you want to open.

5. Choose Open.

6. Choose Close to close the Commands dialog box.

Document Recipes

Includes

Designing Résumés

Tackling Business Correspondence

Creating Business Forms

Designing Résumés

I f you have read this far in *Using Microsoft Word 5 for the Mac,* Special Edition, you have learned a great deal about this magnificent word processing program. In Part III of this book, you will follow step-by-step tutorials that assist you in creating specific documents — which you will find useful. Even better, you will learn how to combine Word's high-productivity word processing features in ways that can pay off for you. This part of the book is fun because you see how to put together the various pieces of your knowledge—with impressive results!

In this chapter, you learn how to use Word's Frame and Style capabilities to your advantage as you design an important document: your résumé. You will learn why it's sometimes a neat idea to anchor a frame horizontally but not vertically, and you will learn how to use the Style dialog box's Next Style option to make the application of styles virtually automatic.

Planning Your Résumé

A good résumé is simple, straightforward, and easy-to-read. Most résumés merit little more than a glance. Does your résumé convey any information in the brief moment or two that your prospective employer's eyes pass over it? It is wise to put simplicity, clarity, and

grace on your side. Figure 28.1 shows a simple résumé that employs a graceful, standard format. In the steps that follow, you learn how to create a résumé like this one for your own use.

Fig. 28.1
Design for a résumé.

Paula Anne Smith
273 West Ninth Street
University Village, IN 74788
(913) 555-1212

Objectives   Junior Research Analyst in financial research department, leading to management position in corporate finance.

Education   M.B.A., Buick State University
   Major: Finance and Accounting
   Minor: Computer Science
   G.P.A.: 3.65 on a 4-point scale
   Honors: Dean's List, Senior Honor Society

Experience   University National Bank, Research Department
   Intern research assistant: Assisted manager of department in analysis of corporate and estate planning (Summer, 1991)

   Hoosier Memorial Trust, Analysis Division
   Intern research assistant: Assisted research analyst in compiling statistics on pension and trust funds managed by the firm (Summer, 1990)

Skills   Computer skills: Extensive experience in IBM and Macintosh systems, including Microsoft Word, Lotus 1-2-3, Excel, and PowerPoint

   President, Future Managers of America, Buick State University (1987-1989)
   Managed club of approximately 75 members, organized events and symposia, served as liaison to university administration

   Editor, *The Buick State Clarion*, student newspaper (1989-1990)
   Managed staff of approximately 25 reporters, typists, and advertising personnel; increased circulation by 32% and advertising revenues by 56%

References   Available on request from Office of Career Planning and Placement, Buick State University, Badplains, ND 78987

To create a résumé by following the steps in this chapter, choose Page Layout from the View menu. In addition, display the ruler and ribbon.

Starting Your Résumé

What's visually interesting about this document design is the wide left margin, in which headings are positioned. In this section, you learn how to position these headings by using the Frame command.

To start creating a résumé with the design shown in figure 28.1, follow these steps:

1. In a new Word document, choose Document from the Format menu.

   The Document dialog box appears.

2. In the Left box, type *3 in*.

   You are creating a large left margin with this choice. You position the headings, such as *Objectives*, within this margin by using the Frame command.

3. Choose OK.

   You have created a three-inch left margin, as shown in figure 28.2.

Fig. 28.2
A document with a three-inch left margin.

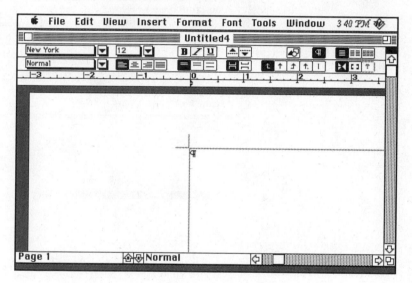

4. Choose the font and font size you want, and type your name and address.

5. Press Enter four times to leave some blank space.

6. Choose Frame from the Format menu.

   The Frame dialog box appears. Now you will position this paragraph within the left margin.

Chapter 28
Designing Résumés

7. In the Horizontal box, type *1.0*.

8. Choose Page in the Relative To list box, next to the Horizontal box.

9. In the Frame Width box, type *1.75*.

   Your Frame dialog box should look like the one in figure 28.3. Note that the Vertical position is left of the default In line setting. You want these headings to move up and down as you delete or add text to your document. Then, they will remain in alignment with the text to which they refer.

Fig. 28.3
Framing the heading.

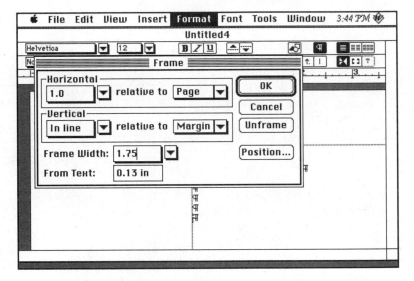

10. Choose OK.

    Word creates a frame that's positioned within the wide left margin, as shown in figure 28.4.

11. Type *Objectives*, and apply bold to the heading.

12. Press Return to start a new line.

    Word enters another paragraph within the left margin. You will use this paragraph to create the paragraph format that holds your résumé text. To do so, you first must unframe the paragraph because Word copied the Frame information when you pressed Return.

Fig. 28.4
A frame positioned within
the left margin.

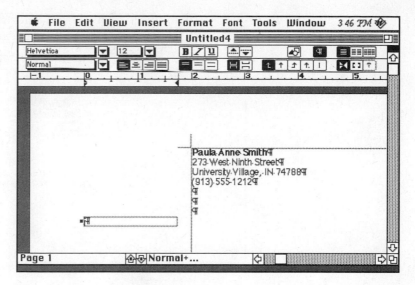

13. Choose Frame from the Format menu.

14. Choose Unframe.

15. Choose OK.

    Word unframes the paragraph and places it to the right of the
    Objectives heading.

16. Drag the indent marks to produce a 1/4-inch hanging indentation.

    Hold down the Shift key so that you can manipulate the bottom
    indent mark independently. As you drag it to the right, keep your
    eye on the page-number area. When you see 0.25, release the
    mouse button.

17. Choose Paragraph from the Format menu.

    You are going to add some blank space after the paragraph. You
    can't add it before the paragraph; if you do, the text doesn't align
    with the headings.

18. Type *12 pt* in the After box.

19. Choose OK.

20. Choose the font and font size you want, and type a line or two of
    text.

Your document should resemble the one in figure 28.5.

Chapter 28

Designing Résumés

Fig. 28.5
Adding text to a document.

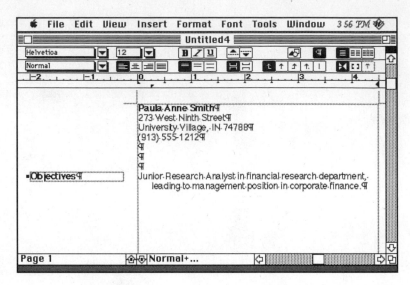

Creating the Styles

At this point, you are ready to create styles. This document uses just two styles, called Heading and Resume Text.

To create the styles, follow these steps:

1. To define the Heading style, place the insertion point in the heading text (the one that reads "Objectives").

2. Click the style name box on the ruler. When it turns black, type *Heading* and press Return.

   A dialog box asks whether you want to define the style.

3. Choose Define.

4. To define the Resume Text style, place the insertion point in the résumé text you just typed.

5. Click the style name box on the ruler. When it turns black, type *Resume Text* and press Return.

   A dialog box asks whether you want to define the style.

6. Choose Define.

You have created the two styles. Now you have one more task: You are going to tell Word to enter a Resume Text style after you type the Heading style and press Return.

To specify the style to follow the Heading style, follow these steps:

1. Choose Style from the Format menu, or press ⌘-T.

   The Style dialog box appears.

2. Highlight Heading in the style list.

   The text box below the Style text box shows the formats you chose for this style when you defined it by example.

3. In the Next Style box, choose Resume Text.

   Your Style dialog box should resemble the one shown in figure 28.6.

4. Choose Define.

Fig. 28.6
The Next Style setting for
Heading style.

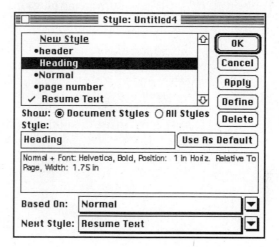

Typing the Rest of the Document

Now that you have created and defined the styles, it's a snap to type the rest of the document.

To complete the résumé, follow these steps:

1. With the insertion point positioned at the end of the first paragraph of résumé text, press Return.

    Word starts a new paragraph of résumé text.

2. Choose Header from the style list box.

    The insertion point jumps to the frame, which is positioned within the left margin.

3. Type the second heading.

4. Press Return.

    The insertion point jumps back into the résumé text area, and you see Resume Text in the style name box.

5. Continue typing the rest of the document. When you want to enter a heading, just press Return to start a new line, and choose the Heading style. You don't have to choose Resume Text: You just press Return after typing a heading.

6. Save your résumé.

This chapter has presented some techniques you will want to remember. To position headings to the left of the body text, define a wide left margin, and then use the Frame command to anchor the heading paragraph horizontally (but leave it in-line vertically). Think of ways you can automate style application by using the nifty Next Style command. It makes sense to use this option, of course, only when the next style is always or almost always the same—usually true after headings.

Tackling Business Correspondence

No matter what your line of business, your mailing list is one of your most valuable resources. Although you should update your mailing list regularly, entering names and addresses in a letter and in your mailing list can be tedious and time-consuming.

With Word's Print Merge feature, you use Print Merge instructions to move the name and address to the response letter you write. Word searches the data document, finds the name and address, places them in the letter, and prints the letter. Using this system, you type the name and address only once, and you always type it directly into your mailing list data document. With every contact letter you send, your mailing list grows by one customer's name and address—one more name and address for your next promotional mailing.

This chapter presents (by a guided tutorial) a comprehensive approach to the mailing list problem. Be sure to read Chapter 24 before proceeding because it discusses intermediate to advanced Print Merge applications.

Creating the Main Document

n Print Merge applications, you use two documents: a *data document* and a *main document*. This chapter assumes that you have created a mailing list data document such as the one discussed in Chapter 24. This chapter concentrates on the main document, which contains the Print Merge instructions that make the application work. In this section, you create the main document and add the necessary merge instructions.

To create the main document, follow these steps:

1. Create the letterhead and return address, such as the one shown in figure 29.1.

   To position a graphic next to text, as in figure 29.1, use a one-row table, but be sure to leave a blank line before the table so that you can insert the DATA instruction. Choose Date from the Insert menu to add the date.

2. Position the insertion point at the beginning of the document.

3. Choose Print Merge Helper from the View menu.

   A dialog box appears and prompts you to locate the data document.

Fig. 29.1
Creating the letterhead.

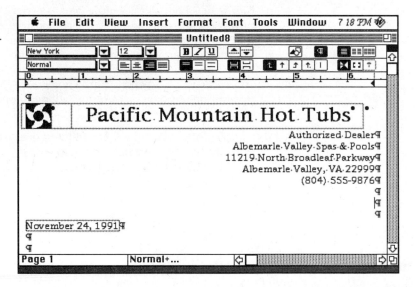

Part III

Document Recipes

4. Locate the data document and choose Open.

   Word places the DATA instruction at the beginning of the main document, as shown in figure 29.2. What you see on-screen varies depending on the name of your disk and the name and location of your data document.

Fig. 29.2
The DATA instruction
added.

5. Use the Insert Field Name list box to add beneath the date the field names from your data document, as shown in figure 29.3.

   In the next step, you add Print Merge instructions to the name and address field names that mix residential and organizational addresses. If you don't add these instructions, Word prints a blank line when the program encounters a residential address, which takes up only three lines. (For more information on this problem, see Chapter 25.) The instructions you enter say, in effect, "If the field address 2 has text in it, print the contents of this field on the next line. Otherwise, print the city, state, and ZIP."

6. Position the insertion point just after the <<address 1>> field name, and press Option-\ (backslash).

   You have entered a left chevron.

7. Type *IF address 2* followed by Shift-Option-\ (backslash).

Fig. 29.3
Adding field names.

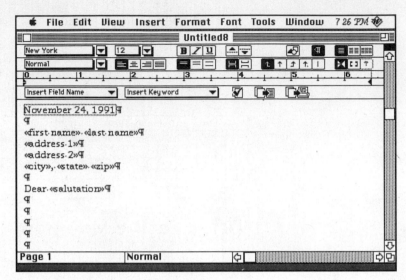

8. Position the insertion point just after <<address 2>>, and choose ENDIF from the Insert Keyword list box.

Your Print Merge instructions should look like the ones in figure 29.4.

Fig. 29.4
Print Merge instructions for three- and four-line addresses.

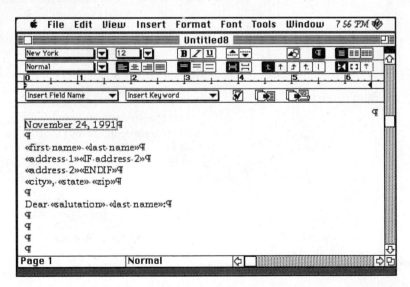

Now add more Print Merge instructions after the DATA instruction, as highlighted in figure 29.5. The best way to add these instructions is to type them directly (without using Print Merge Helper).

These instructions tell Word to do the following: When you choose Print Merge, the SET instruction presents you with a dialog box that asks you to type the last name of the person to whom you want to address the letter. Word accepts the name you type and assigns this name to the newly created field called *name*. The next instruction, the IF instruction, says: "If the last name is the same as the text that's stored in the *name* field, print all the text that follows (the letterhead and the rest of the letter)."

Fig. 29.5
Adding additional Print Merge instructions.

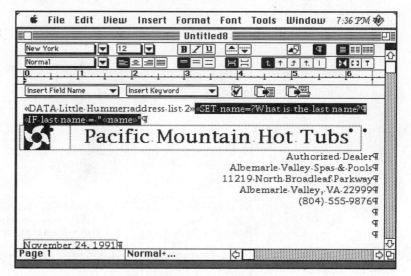

9. To type these instructions, place the insertion point just past the right chevron that closes the DATA instruction. Press Option-\ (backslash) to enter the left chevron, and type the following:

   SET name=?What is the last name?

   Press Return.

10. Press Option-\ (backslash) again to enter a left chevron, and type the following:

    IF last name ="

Chapter 29

Tackling Business Correspondence

11. Press Option-\ (backslash) to enter another left chevron, and type the following:

    name

12. Press Shift-Option-\ (backslash) to enter a closing right chevron, and then type a quotation mark.

    Carefully check your work to make sure that you typed these instructions exactly as they are shown in figure 29.5.

13. Type the text of the letter, such as the text shown in figure 29.6.

14. Add a line at the end of the document, and add ELSE, NEXT, and ENDIF instructions by using the Insert Keyword list box. Delete the right chevron at the end of the ENDIF instruction so that Word doesn't leave a blank line here when the program prints the letter.

    Your instructions should look like the ones in figure 29.7. These instructions tell Word what to do if a data record does not contain the last name for which you're looking. They tell Word to go on to the next record without printing a letter.

NOTE

If you check these instructions carefully, you might notice an apparent error: both lines lack a closing right chevron. Although this omission may look like an error, the omission tells Word not to leave a blank line when you print the letter with Print Merge.

Fig. 29.6
The text of the main document.

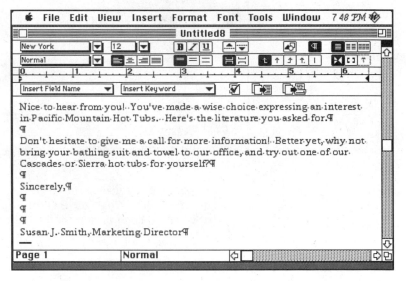

15. Check your work carefully, comparing it to the instructions and field names you see in figure 29.8.

16. Save your main document as a stationery document using a name like Routine Inquiry Letter.

Part III

Document Recipes

Fig. 29.7
Print Merge instructions
added at the end of the
main document.

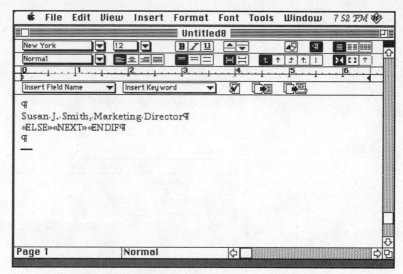

Fig. 29.8
The completed main
document with field
names and Print Merge
instructions.

Chapter 29
Tackling Business Correspondence

Printing a Letter

S uppose that you get a call from Bobbie MacKenzie, asking for more information about a Cascades hot tub. To prepare the reply letter, follow these steps:

1. Begin by typing the new customer's name and address in the data document, as shown in figure 29.9. Make sure that you type the last name and all the rest of the data correctly.

Fig. 29.9
The new customer's address in the data document.

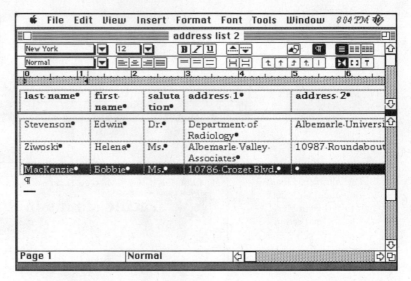

last name•	first name•	saluta tion•	address 1•	address 2•
Stevenson•	Edwin•	Dr.•	Department of Radiology•	Albemarle Universi
Ziwoski•	Helena•	Ms.•	Albemarle Valley Associates•	10987 Roundabout
MacKenzie•	Bobbie•	Ms.•	10786 Crozet Blvd.•	•

2. Open the main document and choose Print Merge Helper from the View menu.

3. Click the icon that prints the data to a file.

   Word opens a Merge document, and the Print Merge dialog box appears (see fig. 29.10).

Fig. 29.10
Supplying the correspondent's last name.

Print Merge

What is the last name?

[OK]   [Stop Merge]

Part III

Document Recipes

4. Type the correspondent's last name. Check your typing very carefully, and then choose OK.

If you type the last name incorrectly, Word cannot print the letter.

Word searches your data document to find a record that matches the text you type. When Word finds the match, the program creates one form letter (see fig. 29.11).

Fig. 29.11
A form letter generated by the main document.

Pacific Mountain Hot Tubs

Authorized Dealer
Albemarle Valley Spas & Pools
11219 North Broadleaf Parkway
Albemarle Valley, VA 22999
(804) 555-9876

November 24, 1991

Bobbie MacKenzie
10786 Crozet Blvd.
Charlottesville, VA 22999

Dear Ms. MacKenzie:

Nice to hear from you! You've made a wise choice expressing an interest in Pacific Mountain Hot Tubs. Here's the literature you asked for.

Don't hesitate to give me a call for more information! Better yet, why not bring your bathing suit and towel to our office, and try out one of our Cascades or Sierra hot tubs for yourself?

Sincerely,

Susan J. Smith, Marketing Director

As figure 29.11 shows, Word printed the three-line address correctly. The program also prints the four-line addresses correctly.

You can use this application even if you're not a high-powered business executive. Every time you write a letter, you add one more name and address to your mailing list. Think how useful this mailing list can be if you add some additional fields to the data document—fields that allow you to try some of the conditional merging techniques discussed in Chapter 24.

Creating Business Forms

Forms are essential tools for making sure that you get the information you need. Whether you're going through employment applications, quarterly reports, or time sheets, every form must contain all the information that your organization requires. A well-designed form—one that prompts you for all the required information—is a real asset in a business or professional setting.

You can create two kinds of forms with Word: forms you print and reproduce in quantity, and on-screen forms that you fill in as you sit at your Macintosh. The forms you print and reproduce, such as employment application forms or order forms, take the place of forms you otherwise would have to pay a print shop to design. With Word's desktop publishing capabilities, you no longer need to hand over substantial sums to layout artists. You easily can design a professional-looking form with Word and save your organization a tidy sum of money. If the form needs revision, you can make the necessary changes with Word in a matter of minutes and save the trouble and time of contacting the printer for another expensive go-around with the layout artist.

On-screen forms also have their place in your strategy to improve your business productivity. These forms are especially useful for invoices, period reports, or other applications. Continuing Part III's theme of integrating Word techniques, you learn in this chapter how you can use Print Merge instructions to set up a system that makes filling in such forms virtually automatic. You also will take advantage of new Word 5 instructions that enable you to compute subtotals and totals from information stored in data fields.

Creating your own business forms with Word is one of this book's biggest money- and time-saving applications. The key to creating business forms with Word is to use Word's Table commands, introduced in Chapter 17. To illustrate the use of these commands for creating business forms, this chapter presents an extended tutorial. Figure 30.1 shows the form you will create. To illustrate Word's many applications for the creation of on-screen forms, you also learn how to create a form that bills clients for the time you spend providing professional services.

This chapter assumes that you're familiar with the Table command (see Chapter 17) and borders (see Chapter 22). If you haven't done so, read these chapters before tackling this one.

Creating the Business Form

This tutorial teaches you how to create a business form you can print and duplicate; the form you create is designed to be filled in by hand. If you have your own business form design in mind, you can adapt the tutorial to your needs as you go along. Even if you don't have your own design in mind, following the tutorial quickly teaches you the techniques you need to produce professional-looking business forms.

The example shown in figure 30.2 shows the banner with a graphic placed next to the firm's name and address. To create such a banner, you use a one-row, two-column table to place the graphic adjacent to the text. The tutorial that follows shows you how to create the remainder of the form.

To start this tutorial, open a new Word document:

1. Type *SALES INVOICE* and press Return twice.

2. Choose Table from the Insert menu.

3. When the Insert Table dialog box appears, type *3* in the Number of Columns box and *4* in the Number of Rows box.

4. Click OK. Word enters the table, as shown in figure 30.3.

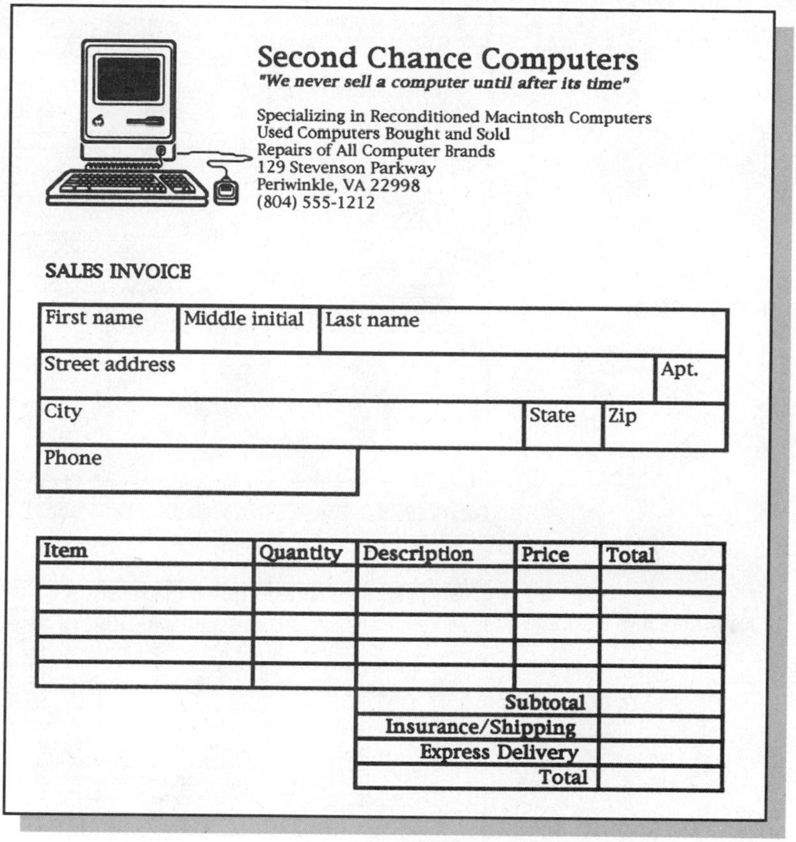
Second Chance Computers
"We never sell a computer until after its time"

Specializing in Reconditioned Macintosh Computers
Used Computers Bought and Sold
Repairs of All Computer Brands
129 Stevenson Parkway
Periwinkle, VA 22998
(804) 555-1212

SALES INVOICE

First name	Middle initial	Last name

Street address	Apt.

City	State	Zip

Phone

Item	Quantity	Description	Price	Total
		Subtotal		
		Insurance/Shipping		
		Express Delivery		
		Total		

Fig. 30.1
Business form created with Word 5.

5. Click the scale icon on the ruler to show the cell boundary markers.
6. Type the headings shown in figure 30.4. Press Return after typing each heading to double-space the cells as shown.

Removing Unwanted Cells

To delete unwanted cells in your form, follow these steps:

1. Select one of the empty, unwanted cells.
2. Choose Table Layout from the Format menu.
3. Choose the Selection button in the Table Layout dialog box.

Fig. 30.2
Heading for form.

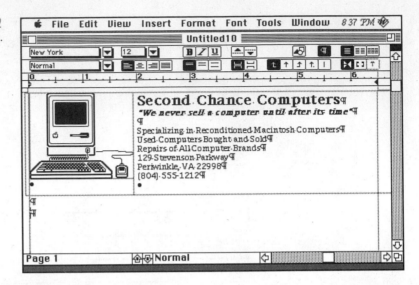

Fig. 30.3
Table added to the form.

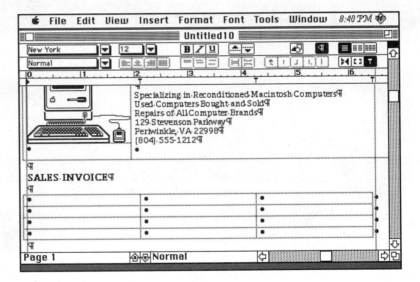

4. Choose the Delete button in the Table Layout dialog box. Word deletes the cell.

5. Select the next cell you want to delete. Choose Repeat from the Edit menu (or press ⌘-Y) to repeat the deletion.

Part III

Document Recipes

Fig. 30.4
Headings added to the
table.

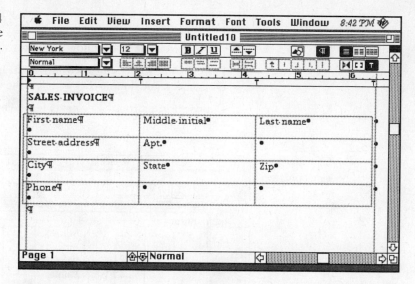

After you delete the unwanted cells, your table should look like
figure 30.5.

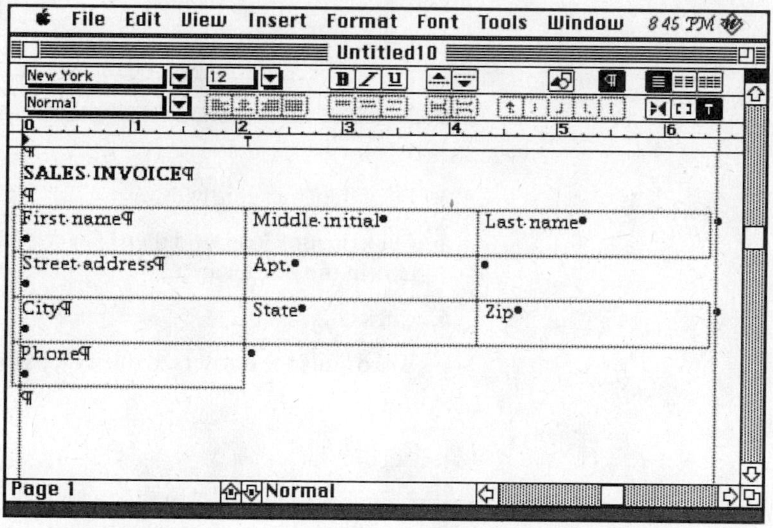

Fig. 30.5
Table with cells deleted.

Adding Borders

To add borders to your table, follow these steps:

1. Place the insertion point anywhere in the table, hold down the Option key, and double click to select the whole table.

2. Choose Border from the Format menu. The Border dialog box appears (see fig. 30.6).

Fig. 30.6
Choosing borders.

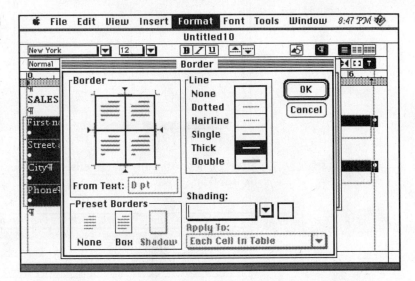

3. Click the Thick line width.

4. Click the Box icon, and then click the horizontal and vertical cross bars in the Border area.

5. Click OK.

Word adds the borders to the table, as shown in figure 30.7.

Adjusting Cell Width

To adjust the width of the cells, you need more room for Last name, less for Middle initial, and even less for State and Apt:

Fig. 30.7
Borders added to table
cells.

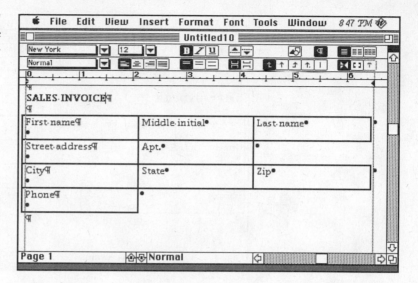

1. Place the insertion point in the first cell in the first row (First name).

   If the T marks are not displayed on the ruler, choose the Table Boundary button (the one with the T) on the ruler.

2. Drag the first T left until you have reduced the size of the first cell to about 1.3 inches. Watch the lower left corner of the status line as you drag the boundary markers; a measurement showing where you positioned the marker on the ruler is displayed.

3. Select the Middle initial cell and shrink the column to about 1.38 inches in width.

4. Expand the Last name scale to the right margin (the dotted line on the ruler) by dragging the T marker right.

5. Continue in this way to size all the cells, as shown in figure 30.8.

6. Save your form with a name such as *Sales Invoice*.

Creating the Order Information Section

In this section, you learn how to create the bottom half of the form shown in figure 30.1. You enter another table, and then delete some cells (and merge others) to create the form shown in the figure.

Chapter 30
Creating Business Forms

Fig. 30.8
Adjusting the cell widths.

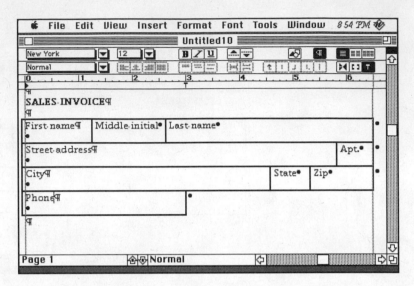

To create the spaces for order information, follow these steps:

1. Press Return twice and choose Table from the Insert menu.

2. Type *5* in the Number of Columns box and *10* in the Number of Rows box. Click OK. Word enters the table.

3. Place the insertion point in the first cell of the first row, hold down the Option key and click the mouse button to select the column.

4. Click the scale icon on the ruler, if necessary, to display the boundary markers, and drag the column marker to the 2-inch mark on the ruler.

5. Continue sizing the columns, as shown in figure 30.9. Type the headings shown in that figure.

   Now you delete cells from the last four rows.

6. In the last four rows, select the cells, as shown in figure 30.10.

7. Choose Table Layout from the Format menu.

8. Click the Delete button.

9. Select the last four rows of the first column and adjust their size and position, as shown in figure 30.11.

Fig. 30.9
Adding and sizing the
order grid.

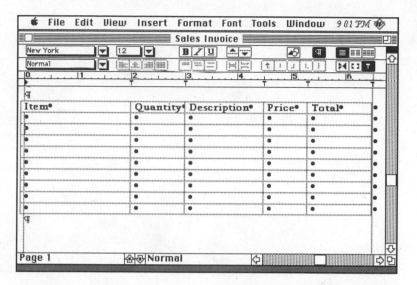

Fig. 30.10
Cells selected for deletion.

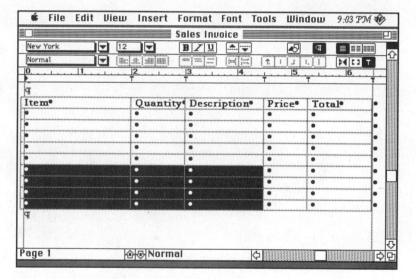

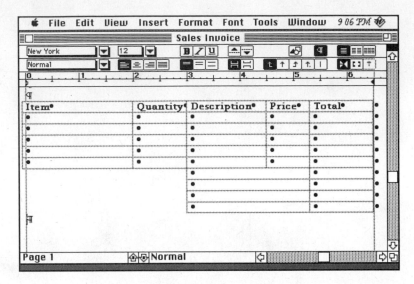

10. To add the headings to the last four rows, as shown in figure 13.12, drag down the first column in these rows. Choose the T button in the ruler until the paragraph alignment icons appear. Click the Right Alignment icon, and then type the headings.

11. Select the whole table by placing the insertion point anywhere within it, holding down the Option key, and double-clicking. Use the Borders command (on the Format menu) to add thick borders to all cells, as shown in figure 30.12.

You created in a matter of minutes a form that would have cost at least $100 to have professionally typeset. You can change the form in minutes without a time-consuming (and costly) trip to the printer.

Creating On-Screen Forms

The tutorial you have completed shows you how to create forms you can print and then reproduce in quantity. These forms are for other people to fill in—people such as your clients, customers, or employees. To save time with the forms you fill in yourself, you can use on-screen forms (forms you fill in as you sit at your Macintosh and then print in their completed version).

Fig. 30.12
The completed form.

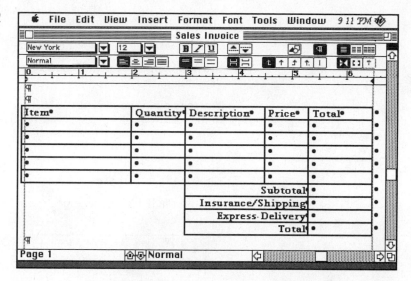

The application described in this section is of greatest value to you when you automate a form that you must complete periodically, such as a weekly time sheet, an invoice, or a quarterly report. Such forms aren't reproduced in quantity; at most, you make only two or three copies of them. To help you remember to fill in all the necessary information, this application uses the ASK instruction from Word's armada of Print Merge commands, which are normally employed for form letter applications (see Chapter 24 for more information on form letters). You also can use this Print Merge technique to produce one copy of a completed form.

You can use ASK instructions to display a series of dialog boxes, each of which prompts you to supply an item of information needed to fill in the form. Word completes the form from the information you supply. You can print the form right away, or Word will display the filled-in form in a new document in which you can perform calculations or add additional text.

With a little experimentation, you can see for yourself how the ASK instruction works. Try the following tutorial to learn how to use the ASK instruction.

If you tried to use ASK in previous versions of Word, you will be glad to know that Print Merge Helper makes this command much easier to use. A dialog box guides you through every step of building the form.

Chapter 30
Creating Business Forms

Using the ASK Instruction

To use the ASK instruction, follow these steps:

1. In a new Word document, choose Print Merge Helper from the View menu.

   You see a dialog box asking you to locate the data document. You don't need a data document, however, for an application that employs ASK.

2. Choose None.

3. Choose ASK from the Insert Keyword list box.

   The Insert ASK dialog box appears (see fig. 30.13).

Fig. 30.13
The Insert ASK dialog box.

4. Choose Define New Field.

   A dialog box asking you to type a field name appears.

5. Type *your name* (the two words, not your actual name), and choose OK.

6. In the Prompt text box, type *Hi! What's your name?*

   Your Insert ASK dialog box should look like the one in figure 30.14.

Fig. 30.14
Filled-out areas of the
Insert ASK dialog box.

Part III

Document Recipes

7. Choose OK.

   Print Merge Helper builds the ASK expression and inserts it into your document.

8. Press Return, and choose the new field name (*your name*) from the Insert Field Name list box.

9. On the Print Merge Helper bar, click the icon that merges to a new document.

   A dialog box like the one shown in figure 30.15 appears.

Fig. 30.15
Dialog box asking for
user input.

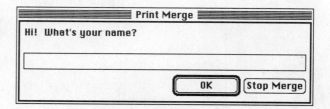

10. Type a response, and choose OK.

    Word creates a new Merge document, and adds the name to the document. Choose Stop Merge.

You can put this feature to work for you on a regular basis because creating an ASK application is easy. In the next section, you will learn how to create an application that uses many ASK instructions.

Setting Up a Client Billing System

Suppose that you run a part-time computer repair business. Most of your billing is a one-shot deal: you perform one service for your customer, and you need to create an accurate invoice quickly. Figure 30.16 shows a Print Merge application that prompts for all the needed information, computes the total, and prints the bill on a form. Because all the ASK instructions lack a trailing chevron, Word doesn't leave a blank line when it prints the document.

Fig. 30.16

Print Merge application for
billing clients.

```
«ASK first name=?What is the client's first name?
«ASK last name=?What is the client's last name?
«ASK address=?What is the client's street address?
«ASK city=?What is the client's city?
«ASK state=?What is the client's state?
«ASK zip=?What is the client's zip code?
«ASK repair=?What repair was performed?
«ASK date=?What was the date of the repair?
«ASK charge=?What was the charge for the repair?
«ASK parts=?What was the total cost for parts?
```

Albemarle Valley Computer Specialists
Repairing IBM and Macintosh Computers
221 University Terrace
Albemarle Valley, VA 22999

INVOICE FOR SERVICES RENDERED

«first name» «last name»
«address»
«city», «state» «zip»

Repair performed : «repair»
Date repair performed : «date»

Fee for «repair»		«charge»
	Parts	«parts»
	Total	«charge+parts»

The Print Merge instructions include many ASK instructions and some calculated fields (note the expression in the Total box). When you print this main document, you get a series of ASK dialog boxes that prompt you to supply all the needed information. Word prints the document by filling in the placeholders with the data you typed (see fig. 30.17).

This example closes Part III, which showed you some ways that you can combine your Word skills for high-productivity document processing. With the knowledge you now possess, you surely will discover many more ways you can put Word to work.

Fig. 30.17
Document generated from
ASK instructions.

Albemarle Valley Computer Specialists
Repairing IBM and Macintosh Computers
221 University Terrace
Albemarle Valley, VA 22999

INVOICE FOR SERVICES RENDERED

John Robertsen
125 Fifth St. Extended
Albemarle Valley, VA 22999

Repair performed: disk drive alignment
Date repair performed: May 21, 1992

Fee for disk drive alignment	75.00
Parts	0.00
Total	75.00

Chapter 30
Creating Business Forms

Installing Word 5

Word has achieved a milestone in its size and complexity. You no longer can run the program from an 800K floppy disk. Installing the program on a hard disk is easy, but you should keep in mind a few things before you install the program.

■ Before running Word's Installer program, disable any virus-detection programs running on your hard disk. Be especially sure to disable Gatekeeper, a public-domain, virus-detection utility that looks for "suspicious" activities on your disk. Although Installer's activities are entirely legitimate, some will look suspicious to many virus programs and may prevent Installer from running.

■ If you are using MultiFinder (System 6) or System 7, quit from any other application programs before you run Installer. You cannot install Word while other programs are running.

■ Make sure that you have enough disk space. To install the full version of Word, you need 5.5M of disk space. If you don't have enough room, you can install selected portions of Word. This step is not recommended, however, because it disables Word features that may prove useful. You should remove unused programs and archive unneeded data files to make room.

USING
WORD 5
FOR THE
MAC

Installing Word 5

To install Word 5, follow these steps:

1. Insert the Install disk in the floppy drive.

2. Double-click the Installer.

   A screen appears that encourages you to register.

3. Choose OK.

   The Easy Install screen appears (see fig. A.1). Easy Install installs the whole program.

```
┌────────────────────────────────────────────────────────────┐
│  Easy Install                                                │
│  ┌──────────────────────────────────────────────┐           │
│  │ Click "Install" to install                     │           │
│  │   • Microsoft Word Version 5.0                 │           │
│  │   • Plug-In Modules                │ ┌──────────┐          │
│  │   • File Converters                │ │ Install  │          │
│  │   • System Resources for Word 5.0  │ └──────────┘          │
│  │ on the hard disk named                         │           │
│  │  ⊂⊃ Little Hummer                              │           │
│  └──────────────────────────────────────────────┘           │
│                                        ┌────────────┐         │
│                                        │ Eject Disk │         │
│                                        └────────────┘         │
│                                        ┌────────────┐         │
│                                        │ Switch Disk│         │
│                                        └────────────┘         │
│                                        ┌────────────┐         │
│                                        │ Customize  │         │
│                                        └────────────┘         │
│          ┌──────────┐                  ┌────────────┐         │
│          │   Help   │                  │   Quit     │         │
│  3.3     └──────────┘                  └────────────┘         │
└────────────────────────────────────────────────────────────┘
```

4. To install all the Word files, choose Install. The Installer informs you when you should remove and insert disks. Alternatively, choose Customize to select the Word files you want to install.

   If you select Customize, the screen shown in figure A.2 appears. If you highlight one of the files in the list box, Word provides an explanation of what the file does and how much space it occupies (see fig. A.3). To choose selected files for installation, hold down the Shift key and choose all the files you want to install. Then choose Install.

   When Install has finished, the screen that appears asks you to choose the default font and font size. Word proposes

Appendix A
Installing Word 5

New York 12—a good choice if you're running System 7 with its TrueType fonts. If you're using System 6 with a LaserWriter, you may want to choose Times or some other font that this printer directly supports.

Fig. A.2
The Installer screen for custom installation.

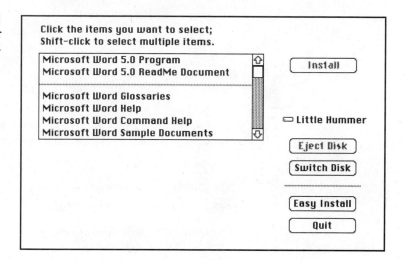

Fig. A.3
Getting information about a file.

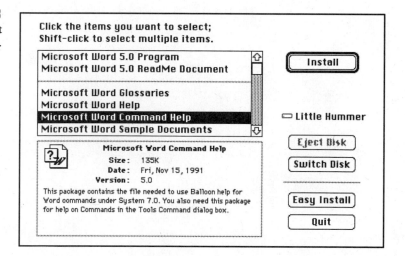

5. Choose any other font or font size that Word has detected on your system. Choose OK when you have chosen the font.

The Installer program completes the installation automatically.

Creating an Alias (System 7)

ystem 7 enables you to create *aliases*, icons that look like files but are just copies that "know" where the file is located. By double-clicking an alias, you start the "real" program, without having to wade through folder after folder to find it.

If you are running System 7, follow these steps so that you can start Word by choosing the Microsoft Word alias from the Apple menu:

1. Open Word's folders.

2. Highlight the Word program icon.

3. Choose Make Alias from the File menu.

4. Drag the Microsoft Word Alias icon to the Apple Menu folder, inside the System folder.

   The Microsoft Word Alias option appears on the Apple menu. To start Word, just choose this alias from the Apple menu.

Word 5 Keyboard Shortcuts

Keyboard Shortcuts (Alphabetized by Command)

Command	Key combination
Activate Keyboard Menus	⌘-Tab
Activate Keyboard Menus	Keypad .
Add to Menu	⌘-Option-=
Add to Menu	⌘-Shift-Option-=
All Caps	⌘-Shift-K
All Caps	Shift-F10
Assign to Key	⌘-Option-Keypad +
Assign to Key	⌘-Shift-Option-Left
Backspace	Delete
Bold	⌘-B
Bold	⌘-Shift-B
Bold	F10

USING
WORD 5
FOR THE
MAC

Command	Key combination
Calculate	Command-=
Cancel	Clear
Cancel	⌘-.
Centered	⌘-Shift-C
Change Font	⌘-Shift-E
Change Style	⌘-Shift-S
Character...	⌘-D
Character...	F14
Close	⌘-W
Commands...	⌘-Shift-Option-C
Context Sensitive Help	⌘-/
Context Sensitive Help	help
Copy	⌘-C
Copy	F3
Copy as Picture	⌘-Option-D
Copy Formats	⌘-Option-V
Copy Formats	Shift-F4
Copy Text	⌘-Option-C
Copy Text	Shift-F3
Cut	⌘-X
Cut	F2
Delete Forward	⌘-Option-F
Delete Forward	Del
Delete Forward	Keypad Clear
Delete Next Word	⌘-Option-G
Delete Previous Word	⌘-Option-Delete
Delete Rows	⌘-^X
Document...	⌘-F14

Appendix B
Word 5 Keyboard Shortcuts

Command	Key combination
Dotted Underline	⌘-Shift-\
Dotted Underlinc	Option-F12
Double Space	⌘-Shift-Y
Double Underline	⌘-Shift-[
Double Underline	Shift-F12
Down	⌘-Shift-Option-<
Down	⌘-[
Edit Link (QuickSwitch)	⌘-,
Edit Link (QuickSwitch)	Option-F2
Extend to Character	⌘-Option-H
Extend to Character	Keypad -
Find Again	⌘-Option-A
Find Again	Keypad =
Find...	⌘-F
First Line Indent	⌘-Shift-F
Flush Left	⌘-Shift-L
Flush Right	⌘-Shift-R
Footnotes	⌘-Shift-Option-S
Footnote...	⌘-E
Glossary...	⌘-K
Go Back	⌘-Option-Z
Go Back	Keypad 0
Go To...	⌘-G
Grammar...	⌘-Shift-G
Hanging Indent	⌘-Shift-T
Hidden Text	⌘-Shift-V
Hidden Text	⌘-Shift-X
Hidden Text	Option-F9

Appendix B
Word 5 Keyboard Shortcuts

Command	Key combination
Hyphenation...	Shift-F15
Insert Formula	⌘-Option-\
Insert Glossary Entry	⌘-Delete
Insert Nonbreaking Hyphen	⌘-`
Insert Nonbreaking Space	⌘-space bar
Insert Nonbreaking Space	Option-space bar
Insert Optional Hyphen	⌘--
Insert Rows	⌘-^V
Insert Tab	Option-Tab
Insert Tab	Tab
Insert ¶ Above Row	⌘-Option-space bar
Italic	⌘-I
Italic	⌘-Shift-I
Italic	F11
Justified	⌘-Shift-J
L Thick Paragraph Border	⌘-Option-2
Larger Font Size	⌘-Shift-.
Larger Font Size	⌘-Shift->
Line Break	Shift-Return
More Keyboard Prefix	⌘-Option-'
Move Down One Text Area	⌘-Option-Keypad 2
Move Left One Text Area	⌘-Option-Keypad 4
Move Right One Text Area	⌘-Option-Keypad 6
Move Text	⌘-Option-X
Move Text	Shift-F2
Move to Bottom of Window	end
Move to End of Document	⌘-end

Appendix B
Word 5 Keyboard Shortcuts

Command	Key combination
Move to End of Document	⌘-Keypad 3
Move to End of Line	Keypad 1
Move to First Text Area	⌘-Option-Keypad 7
Move to Last Text Area	⌘-Option-Keypad 1
Move to Next Character	⌘-Option-L
Move to Next Character	Keypad 6
Move to Next Character	Right
Move to Next Line	⌘-Option-,
Move to Next Line	Down
Move to Next Line	Keypad 2
Move to Next Page	⌘-page down
Move to Next Page	Keypad 3
Move to Next Paragraph	⌘-Down
Move to Next Paragraph	⌘-Keypad 2
Move to Next Paragraph	⌘-Option-B
Move to Next Sentence	⌘-Keypad 1
Move to Next Text Area	⌘-Option-Keypad 3
Move to Next Window	⌘-Option-W
Move to Next Word	⌘-Keypad 6
Move to Next Word	⌘-Option-;
Move to Next Word	⌘-Right
Move to Previous Cell	Shift-Tab
Move to Previous Character	⌘-Option-K
Move to Previous Character	Keypad 4
Move to Previous Character	Left
Move to Previous Line	Keypad 8
Move to Previous Line	Up

Appendix B
Word 5 Keyboard Shortcuts

Command	Key combination
Move to Previous Page	⌘-page up
Move to Previous Page	Keypad 9
Move to Previous Paragraph	⌘-Keypad 8
Move to Previous Paragraph	⌘-Option-Y
Move to Previous Paragraph	⌘-Up
Move to Previous Sentence	⌘-Keypad 7
Move to Previous Text Area	⌘-Option-Keypad 9
Move to Previous Word	⌘-Keypad 4
Move to Previous Word	⌘-Left
Move to Previous Word	⌘-Option-J
Move to Start of Document	⌘-home
Move to Start of Document	⌘-Keypad 9
Move to Start of Line	Keypad 7
Move to Top of Window	⌘-Keypad 5
Move to Top of Window	Home
Move Up One Text Area	⌘-Option-Keypad 8
Nest Paragraph	⌘-Shift-N
New	⌘-N
New	F5
New Paragraph	Enter
New Paragraph	Return
New Window	Shift-F5
New ¶ After Ins. Point	⌘-Option-Return
New ¶ with Same Style	⌘-Return
No Paragraph Border	⌘-Option-1
Normal	⌘-Option-N
Normal Paragraph	⌘-Shift-P

Appendix B
Word 5 Keyboard Shortcuts

Command	Key combination
Open Any File...	Shift-F6
Open Spacing	⌘-Shift-O
Open...	⌘-O
Open...	F6
Outline (Format)	⌘-Shift-D
Outline (Format)	Shift-F11
Outline (View)	⌘-Option-O
Outline (View)	Shift-F13
Outline Command Prefix	⌘-Option-T
Page Break	Shift-Enter
Page Layout	⌘-Option-P
Page Layout	F13
Page Setup...	Shift-F8
Paragraph...	⌘-M
Paragraph...	Shift-F14
Paste	⌘-V
Paste	F4
Paste Link	Option-F4
Paste Object	⌘-F4
Paste Special Character	⌘-Option-Q
Picture...	⌘-^ P
Plain Text	⌘-Shift-Z
Plain Text	Shift-F9
Print Preview...	⌘-Option-I
Print Preview...	Option-F13
Print...	⌘-P
Print...	F8

Appendix B
Word 5 Keyboard Shortcuts

Command	Key combination
Quit	⌘-Q
Remove From Menu	⌘-Option--
Renumber...	⌘-F15
Repeat	⌘-Y
Replace...	⌘-H
Revert To Style	⌘-Shift-space bar
Revert To Style	F9
Ribbon	⌘-Option-R
Ruler	⌘-R
Save As...	Shift-F7
Save	⌘-S
Save	F7
Scroll Line Down	⌘-Option-/
Scroll Line Down	Keypad +
Scroll Line Up	⌘-Option-[
Scroll Line Up	Keypad *
Scroll Screen Down	⌘-Option-.
Scroll Screen Down	page down
Scroll Screen Up	page up
Section Break	⌘-Enter
Section...	Option-F14
Select All	⌘-A
Select All	⌘-Option-M
Shadow	⌘-Shift-W
Shadow	Option-F11
Show/Hide ¶	⌘-J
Small Caps	⌘-Shift-H
Small Caps	Option-F10

Appendix B
Word 5 Keyboard Shortcuts

Command	*Key combination*
Smaller Font Size	⌘-Shift-,
Smaller Font Size	⌘-Shift-<
Spelling...	⌘-L
Spelling...	F15
Split Window	⌘-Option-S
Strikethru	⌘-Shift-/
Style...	⌘-T
Subscript 2 pt	⌘-Shift--
Superscript 3 pt	⌘-Shift-=
Symbol Font	⌘-Shift-Q
Unassign Keystroke	⌘-Option-Keypad -
Underline	⌘-Shift-U
Underline	⌘-U
Underline	F12
Undo	⌘-Z
Undo	F1
Unnest Paragraph	⌘-Shift-M
Up	⌘-Shift-Option-<
Up	⌘-]
Update Link	Option-F3
Word Count...	Option-F15
Word Underline	⌘-F12
Word Underline	⌘-Shift-]

Appendix B
Word 5 Keyboard Shortcuts

Keyboard Shortcuts (Alphabetized by Key)

Key combination	Command
Clear	Cancel
⌘-,	Edit Link (QuickSwitch)
⌘--	Insert Optional Hyphen
⌘-.	Cancel
⌘-/	Context Sensitive Help
⌘-=	Calculate
⌘-A	Select All
⌘-B	Bold
⌘-C	Copy
⌘-D	Character...
⌘-Delete	Insert Glossary Entry
⌘-Down	Move to Next Paragraph
⌘-E	Footnote...
⌘-End	Move to End of Document
⌘-Enter	Section Break
⌘-F	Find...
⌘-F12	Word Underline
⌘-F14	Document...
⌘-F15	Renumber...
⌘-F4	Paste Object
⌘-G	Go To...
⌘-H	Replace...
⌘-Home	Move to Start of Document
⌘-I	Italic
⌘-J	Show/Hide ¶
⌘-K	Glossary...

Appendix B
Word 5 Keyboard Shortcuts

Key combination	Command
⌘-Keypad 1	Move to Next Sentence
⌘-Keypad 2	Move to Next Paragraph
⌘-Keypad 3	Move to End of Document
⌘-Keypad 4	Move to Previous Word
⌘-Keypad 5	Move to Top of Window
⌘-Keypad 6	Move to Next Word
⌘-Keypad 7	Move to Previous Sentence
⌘-Keypad 8	Move to Previous Paragraph
⌘-Keypad 9	Move to Start of Document
⌘-L	Spelling...
⌘-Left	Move to Previous Word
⌘-M	Paragraph...
⌘-N	New
⌘-O	Open...
⌘-Option-'	More Keyboard Prefix
⌘-Option-,	Move to Next Line
⌘-Option--	Remove From Menu
⌘-Option-.	Scroll Screen Down
⌘-Option-/	Scroll Line Down
⌘-Option-1	No Paragraph Border
⌘-Option-2	L Thick Paragraph Border
⌘-Option-;	Move to Next Word
⌘-Option-=	Add to Menu
⌘-Option-A	Find Again
⌘-Option-B	Move to Next Paragraph
⌘-Option-C	Copy Text
⌘-Option-D	Copy as Picture

Appendix B
Word 5 Keyboard Shortcuts

Key combination	Command
⌘-Option-Delete	Delete Previous Word
⌘-Option-F	Delete Forward
⌘-Option-G	Delete Next Word
⌘-Option-H	Extend to Character
⌘-Option-I	Print Preview...
⌘-Option-J	Move to Previous Word
⌘-Option-K	Move to Previous Character
⌘-Option-Keypad +	Assign to Key
⌘-Option-Keypad--	Unassign Keystroke
⌘-Option-Keypad 1	Move to Last Text Area
⌘-Option-Keypad 2	Move Down One Text Area
⌘-Option-Keypad 3	Move to Next Text Area
⌘-Option-Keypad 4	Move Left One Text Area
⌘-Option-Keypad 6	Move Right One Text Area
⌘-Option-Keypad 7	Move to First Text Area
⌘-Option-Keypad 8	Move Up One Text Area
⌘-Option-Keypad 9	Move to Previous Text Area
⌘-Option-L	Move to Next Character
⌘-Option-M	Select All
⌘-Option-N	Normal
⌘-Option-O	Outline (View)
⌘-Option-P	Page Layout
⌘-Option-Q	Paste Special Character
⌘-Option-R	Ribbon
⌘-Option-Return	New ¶ After Ins. Point
⌘-Option-S	Split Window
⌘-Option-space bar	Insert ¶ Above Row

Appendix B
Word 5 Keyboard Shortcuts

Key combination	Command
⌘-Option-T	Outline Command Prefix
⌘-Option-V	Copy Formats
⌘-Option-W	Move to Next Window
⌘-Option-X	Move Text
⌘-Option-Y	Move to Previous Paragraph
⌘-Option-Z	Go Back
⌘-Option-[	Scroll Line Up
⌘-Option-\	Insert Formula
⌘-^P	Picture...
⌘-P	Print...
⌘-page down	Move to Next Page
⌘-page up	Move to Previous Page
⌘-Q	Quit
⌘-R	Ruler
⌘-Return	New ¶ with Same Style
⌘-Right	Move to Next Word
⌘-S	Save
⌘-Shift-,	Smaller Font Size
⌘-Shift--	Subscript 2 pt
⌘-Shift-.	Larger Font Size
⌘-Shift-/	Strikethru
⌘-Shift-<	Smaller Font Size
⌘-Shift-=	Superscript 3 pt
⌘-Shift->	Larger Font Size
⌘-Shift-B	Bold
⌘-Shift-C	Centered
⌘-Shift-D	Outline (Format)
⌘-Shift-E	Change Font

Appendix B
Word 5 Keyboard Shortcuts

Key combination	Command
⌘-Shift-F	First Line Indent
⌘-Shift-G	Grammar...
⌘-Shift-H	Small Caps
⌘-Shift-I	Italic
⌘-Shift-J	Justified
⌘-Shift-K	All Caps
⌘-Shift-L	Flush Left
⌘-Shift-M	Unnest Paragraph
⌘-Shift-N	Nest Paragraph
⌘-Shift-O	Open Spacing
⌘-Shift-Option-<	Down
⌘-Shift-Option-<	Up
⌘-Shift-Option-=	Add to Menu
⌘-Shift-Option-C	Commands...
⌘-Shift-Option-Left	Assign to Key
⌘-Shift-Option-S	Footnotes
⌘-Shift-P	Normal Paragraph
⌘-Shift-Q	Symbol Font
⌘-Shift-R	Flush Right
⌘-Shift-S	Change Style
⌘-Shift-space bar	Revert To Style
⌘-Shift-T	Hanging Indent
⌘-Shift-U	Underline
⌘-Shift-V	Hidden Text
⌘-Shift-W	Shadow
⌘-Shift-X	Hidden Text
⌘-Shift-Y	Double Space

Appendix B
Word 5 Keyboard Shortcuts

Key combination	Command
⌘-Shift-Z	Plain Text
⌘-Shift-[	Double Underline
⌘-Shift-\	Dotted Underline
⌘-Shift-]	Word Underline
⌘-space bar	Insert Nonbreaking Space
⌘-T	Style...
⌘-Tab	Activate Keyboard Menus
⌘-U	Underline
⌘-Up	Move to Previous Paragraph
⌘-^V	Insert Rows
⌘-V	Paste
⌘-W	Close
⌘-X	Cut
⌘-^X	Delete Rows
⌘-Y	Repeat
⌘-Z	Undo
⌘-[	Down
⌘-]	Up
⌘-`	Insert Nonbreaking Hyphen
Del	Delete Forward
Delete	Backspace
Down	Move to Next Line
end	Move to Bottom of Window
Enter	New Paragraph
F1	Undo
F10	Bold
F11	Italic
F12	Underline

Appendix B
Word 5 Keyboard Shortcuts

Key combination	Command
F13	Page Layout
F14	Character...
F15	Spelling...
F2	Cut
F3	Copy
F4	Paste
F5	New
F6	Open...
F7	Save
F8	Print...
F9	Revert To Style
help	Context Sensitive Help
home	Move to Top of Window
Keypad . (period)	Activate Keyboard Menus
Keypad *	Scroll Line Up
Keypad +	Scroll Line Down
Keypad -	Extend to Character
Keypad 0	Go Back
Keypad 1	Move to End of Line
Keypad 2	Move to Next Line
Keypad 3	Move to Next Page
Keypad 4	Move to Previous Character
Keypad 6	Move to Next Character
Keypad 7	Move to Start of Line
Keypad 8	Move to Previous Line
Keypad 9	Move to Previous Page
Keypad =	Find Again

Appendix B
Word 5 Keyboard Shortcuts

Key combination	Command
Keypad Clear	Delete Forward
Left	Move to Previous Character
Option-F10	Small Caps
Option-F11	Shadow
Option-F12	Dotted Underline
Option-F13	Print Preview...
Option-F14	Section...
Option-F15	Word Count...
Option-F2	Edit Link (QuickSwitch)
Option-F3	Update Link
Option-F4	Paste Link
Option-F9	Hidden Text
Option-space bar	Insert Nonbreaking Space
Option-Tab	Insert Tab
page down	Scroll Screen Down
page up	Scroll Screen Up
Return	New Paragraph
Right	Move to Next Character
Shift-Enter	Page Break
Shift-F10	All Caps
Shift-F11	Outline (Format)
Shift-F12	Double Underline
Shift-F13	Outline (View)
Shift-F14	Paragraph...
Shift-F15	Hyphenation...
Shift-F2	Move Text
Shift-F3	Copy Text

Appendix B
Word 5 Keyboard Shortcuts

Key combination	Command
Shift-F4	Copy Formats
Shift-F5	New Window
Shift-F6	Open Any File...
Shift-F7	Save As...
Shift-F8	Page Setup...
Shift-F9	Plain Text
Shift-Return	Line Break
Shift-Tab	Move to Previous Cell
Tab	Insert Tab
Up	Move to Previous Line

Appendix B
Word 5 Keyboard Shortcuts

Index

Index

Index

Index

G

Index

Index

Index

Index

W

X-Y-Z